FACTS
&
FALLACIES

READER'S DIGEST

FACTS & FALLACIES

The Reader's Digest Association, Inc.
Pleasantville, New York/Montreal

FACTS & FALLACIES

Edited and designed by Dorling Kindersley Ltd.

Project Editors *Simon Adams, Lesley Riley*
Art Editor *Alex Arthur*
Assistant Editors *Ann Kramer, Susan Mennell*
Picture Researcher *Frances Vargo*

Editorial Director *Jackie Douglas*
Art Director *Roger Bristow*

Contributors *Neil Ardley, Russell Ash, Peter Brookesmith, Christopher Cooper, Fern Fraser, Maurice Geller, Hildi Hawkins, Sarah Litvinoff, Caroline Richmond, Chris Riley, Theodore Rowland-Entwistle, Jeanne Ruzicka, Bernard Thompson, Simon Welfare, Liz Wilhide*

Researchers *Janet Abbott, Nicholas Booth, Kevin Dowd, Andrew Duncan, Martin Greenwood, Miren Lopategui, Ran Lorimer, Christine O'Neill, Gill Scott, Alan Seccombe, David Wood*

Reader's Digest staff

Editor *Charles L. Chesnut*
Associate Editor *Diana Marsh*

Reader's Digest General Books

Editor in Chief *John A. Pope, Jr*
Managing Editor *Jane Polley*
Art Director *David Trooper*
Group Editors *Norman B. Mack, Joel Musler* (Art), *Susan J. Wernert*

The credits and acknowledgments that appear on page 448 are hereby made a part of this copyright page.

Library of Congress Cataloging in Publication Data

Facts & fallacies.
    At head of title: Reader's digest.
    Includes index.
    1. Curiosities and wonders. 2. Handbooks,
vade mecums, etc. I. Reader's Digest Association.
II. Title: Facts and fallacies. III. Title: Reader's
digest facts & fallacies.
AG243.F3 1988   031'.02   87-20627
ISBN 0-89577-273-6

Printed in the United States of America
Second Printing, December 1988

INTRODUCTION

FOR NEARLY 25 YEARS one of the most popular sculptures in the Egyptian Wing of the Metropolitan Museum of Art in New York City was a bronze cat, believed to be 2,300 years old.

Despite its popularity, museum officials began to doubt the figure's authenticity. After X-raying the 15-inch-high statue and scanning a small piece of it with an electron microscope, the museum in 1987 announced that the sculpture is most likely a fake—"in all probability a modern forgery."

Even experts at eminent institutions are sometimes misled: what today appears to be fact may tomorrow become fallacy. A fresh piece of evidence, a new discovery, a theory put to the test, can turn fantasy into fact, truth into fiction, overnight—as many stories in this book make clear.

But whether or not a fact in this volume is someday proved fallacious—or what is thought to be false turns out to be true—your time will never have been wasted.

As you roam through these pages—from the United States to India, Great Britain to the Antarctic, Scandinavia to Tibet, and from the distant past into the future—consider each visit a current report, based on the most reliable information available.

Above all, we think you'll be reminded, repeatedly, that despite everything man has discovered, we actually still *know* surprisingly little about some of the miracles that are constantly taking place within our bodies, our minds, the world around us—and the universe beyond.

Dip into the book wherever you like. You'll be entertained, enlightened, and surprised. And you'll share with experts the experience of happening upon a startling new truth or disproving a long-standing misconception in the ever-changing, wondrous world we live in.

— **The Editors**

CONTENTS

PART 3

PART 4

PART 5

PART

1

WONDERS OF THE NATURAL WORLD

A JUNGLE BATTLE

Survival of the fittest

IN THE TROPICAL FORESTS of Central and South America a struggle for survival has been taking place—not between two mighty giants of the jungle, but between some brightly colored butterflies and a family of climbing plants.

Heliconius butterflies choose to lay eggs only on the leaves of passionflower vines. When the eggs hatch, the offspring feed hungrily on the leaves, threatening to eat the vines out of existence. But the vines have learned to fight back; they have evolved a series of defenses to limit the damage.

Plant cunning

Since heliconius butterflies rely mainly on their sight to find the vines, the vines vary the shapes of their leaves so that they look like other plants.

But not every butterfly is fooled. Some distinguish between the leaves of the passionflower vine and those of other plants by touch: they drum their legs on the surface of the leaf.

But far from giving up, the vines use yet another trick. Because the offspring of the heliconius butterfly have a tendency to eat one another, female butterflies are reluctant to lay their eggs on leaves with eggs that may contain potentially lethal larvae. So the vines produce fake eggs in the form of yellow spots. Experiments carried out by Lawrence Gilbert of the University of Texas indicate that butterflies often ignore leaves bearing mimic eggs.

Additional weapons the vines employ include tendrils that drop off soon after forming (any eggs laid on them will quickly perish on the ground); the secretion of nectar to attract predatory wasps and ants; and, on some species, spikes with chemicals that can paralyze the young caterpillars.

What benefits do the butterflies receive from this seemingly unequal struggle? Since the vine leaves are poisonous to all caterpillars except those of the genus *Heliconius* and a few other insects, competition for food is reduced. And because they absorb toxins from the leaves, the butterflies themselves are unpalatable to birds. Consequently, they live longer than many other species of butterfly—perhaps long enough to devise fresh ways to outwit the resourceful passionflower vines to which their life cycle is inextricably linked.

SURVIVAL GAME *Day after day the passionflower vine and the handsome heliconius butterfly engage each other in a dramatic fight for survival in the tropical forests of Central and South America. The outcome is still uncertain, but the battle rages on.*

THE MAGNIFICENT OPAL

A gem of ill omen?

THE OPAL is a gem of magical beauty; in its depths flash brilliant sparks of constantly changing colors that have entranced and fascinated people for centuries. Considered by many to be the most precious of stones, the opal is also the most fragile, and its sensitivity to light, atmosphere, and temperature has given it an air of unpredictability that has added to its appeal.

But despite its unique properties—or perhaps because of them—the opal, more than any other stone, has inspired bigotry and superstition. Over the centuries it has waxed and waned in public favor, being viewed alternately as a charm for good luck and as an object of fear and dread.

Opals come in many colors and varieties. Of these, the best known are the white, or light-colored; the black, or dark-colored; the harlequin, or multicolored opal; and the spectacular, reddish-tinged fire opal.

Although once mined exclusively in Hungary, today opals usually come from Australia and Mexico. They are found in the seams of volcanic rock, into which they originally flowed as part of a boiling silica-water solution; deposited in the rock crevices, the solution eventually cooled and "opalized," or hardened into stones.

The natural brittleness of opals means that they can be splintered or fractured during cutting. Some

NATURAL SPLENDOR
Today opals are mined almost exclusively in Australia and Mexico, where they are found as natural deposits in the lining of cracks in volcanic rock (at right). Throughout history the opal has been highly prized for its infinite range of colors. Below: Two examples of these magnificent hues.

The stories of ill omen began in the 11th century when Robert the Devil, the father of William the Conqueror, claimed that the opal gave him magical evil powers. Robert also maintained that he was the son of the devil, who had bought his mother's favors with an opal stone.

The idea that the opal was evil gained currency in the 14th century at the time that thousands were dying of the Black Death. The opal was a favorite with Italian jewelers, who used it in their work. In Venice, where the plague was particularly virulent, it was observed that the stones became more brilliant when their wearers contracted the disease, but dulled when the afflicted persons died.

From then on, opals were associated with death and came to be regarded with dread. In those days, of course, it was not known that the change in the opal was brought about by changes in body temperature, which inevitably affect the stone's brilliant luster.

Opals also had a poor reputation in the 17th-century court of the French king Louis XIV, where the royal coaches were named for gemstones. The driver of the "opal" was a drunk—therefore, that coach was considered unlucky.

believe that the misfortune bestowed on jewelers who damaged them may have been the basis of the prejudice against the precious stones.

Changing fortunes

At first the opal was considered to be a lucky gem with healing powers. As long ago as the sixth century B.C., ancient Greeks believed that it endowed its wearer with foresight and vision. For the Romans, on the other hand, the opal represented majesty and power. According to legend, in the first century B.C., a Roman senator, Nonius, chose to be exiled rather than hand over to Mark Antony a ring containing an opal.

The favorable reputation of the opal continued until well into medieval times, when it was regarded as a protection against ailments of the eyes and heart, and against diseases such as cholera.

The final blow

Perhaps the greatest damage to the opal's reputation occurred in 1829 with the publication of *Anne of Geierstein* by Sir Walter Scott. In the story, the baroness of Arnheim, mother of the heroine, wore an opal and would not cross her brow with holy water because she wanted no water to come near it. When rumors grew that it was God Himself that she feared, her husband flicked a few drops of holy water on her forehead as a test. Some of the water dropped on the opal, which "became the instant afterwards lightless and colourless as a common pebble." The baroness fainted and was carried to her room. Two hours later nothing was left of her but a pile of light gray ashes. Although this was pure fiction, it is said that the value of the stone decreased by as much as 50 percent after Scott's novel was published.

The fate of the 19th-century Spanish royal family further added to the opal's unpopularity. A former mistress gave Alfonso XII an opal ring when he married the princess Mercedes. Alfonso in turn gave the ring to his bride; she died a few months later. Thereafter, everyone who wore the ring also died, including Alfonso.

Those who blame the opal forget that at the time a cholera epidemic was raging in Spain; more than 100,000 people died of the disease during the summer and autumn of 1885, when the Spanish royal family suffered so many deaths.

The English royal family, however, did not share the Spanish doubts about the opal: Queen Victoria claimed that the opal was her favorite jewel. Its popularity was confirmed by another member of the English aristocracy, Lord Redesdale of Northumberland.

In 1874 the peer was persuaded to buy a black opal by a friend who assured him that it would bring him luck. When Redesdale made the purchase, his friend told him that he would receive a favorable letter within 10 days. Before the time was up Prime Minister Benjamin Disraeli sent Redesdale a letter asking him to join the government.

Today the opal is a popular gemstone, widely used in rings and other items of jewelry. Few people are aware of its turbulent history.

THE BARK OF BARKS

A long-kept secret cure

ACCORDING to legend, the first European to be cured of malaria was the countess of Chinchón, wife of the Spanish viceroy in Peru. As each wave of fever and chills brought her closer to death, the anguished count pleaded with the court physician to save her.

But in 1638 the doctor's sole recourse was bloodletting, which only weakened his patient further. As a last resort, he turned to the medicine of the local Indians, who treated fevers with a potion made from the bark of a tree that grew on the eastern slopes of the Andes Mountains.

The countess survived the malarial attack. According to legend, she took the miracle cure with her when she returned to Europe in the 1640's. Whether or not the story is true, the 18th-century Swedish naturalist Carolus Linnaeus certainly believed it; he named the fever-bark tree for the countess, calling it—in slightly misspelled form—cinchona.

It seems more likely, however, that Spanish Jesuits, not the countess, brought the cinchona to Europe. Jesuit missionaries learned of the fever cure from Peruvian Indians when they founded missions in Latin America in the 16th century. They sent a few samples to Europe and by 1650 were sending the bark there regularly.

For years people had sought to find the origin of the deadly fever. For malaria may have killed more people than any other disease in history. At one time it was generally thought to be carried in noxious vapors rising from marshes and swamps, and it is from this belief that the term malaria—literally, "bad air"—was derived. In 1880 a French scientist, Charles Laveran, discovered that the exhausting fever and chills that characterized the disease were caused by several species of dangerous parasites found throughout the world, and transmitted from person to person through the bite of the female anopheles mosquito.

An ungrateful mob

A remedy for such a killer disease should have been welcome. But this was not to be the case: instead of showing gratitude, most of 17th-century Protestant Europe rejected "Jesuits' bark" as a papist conspiracy. In London, rioters thronged the streets, spreading the rumor that the crushed bark was part of a Catholic plot to wipe out Protestantism. It was even claimed that the Jesuits themselves were trying to poison the king. Meanwhile, learned physicians scorned the cure as a folk remedy.

One example of the prejudice against the Jesuits was exhibited by the English Puritan ruler, Oliver Cromwell, who suffered recurring bouts of malaria all his life. He eventually died from it rather than take what he called the "devil's powder."

But only 20 years later, Charles II, England's "merry monarch," did not hesitate to call in a fashionable London charlatan, Robert Talbor, who had become well known among the wealthy for his malaria cures. While publicly mocking the Jesuits, the wily Talbor was secretly giving his patients a bitter-tasting concoction made from Jesuits' bark.

Not only did Talbor cure the king of malaria, but—to the dismay of the medical profession—he was knighted for his efforts and, on the king's orders, made a member of the prestigious Royal College of Physicians. Talbor's reputation spread abroad. In 1679 he was summoned to France by Louis XIV, whose son and heir had malaria. After curing him, Talbor was rewarded with a lifetime pension plus 3,000 gold crowns for the prescription—which Louis then promised to keep secret until after Talbor's death.

When Talbor died, in 1681, the French king revealed the formula: six drams of rose leaves, two ounces of lemon juice, and a strong infusion from the powdered Jesuits' bark—dispensed in wine. Wine was necessary since the alkaloids in the bark, not soluble in water, dissolve in alcohol.

With the prescription at last made public, the Jesuits' cure was finally accepted by the now-eager medical profession. Although it was certain that the cinchona bark produced the cure for malaria, it was not until 1820, more than 100 years later, that two French doctors, Joseph Pelletier and Joseph Caventou, isolated the alkaloid in the bark that was the curative agent. They called it quinine, after the Quechua word *quinquina,* "the bark of barks."

THE SARAWAK CHAMBER

Stumbling into the record books

LATE ONE DAY in January 1981, three Englishmen—among the most experienced cave explorers in the world—were coming to the end of an exhausting 12-hour survey of their latest discovery. Andy Eavis, Dave Checkley, and Tony White had just walked the length of an enormous underground passage, hidden deep under the dense, largely unpopulated Mulu jungle of Sarawak in northern Borneo.

The explorers were all very tired, but before returning to the surface they had to carry out one last survey, this time of the width of the passage. Little did the three men realize that they were on the verge of one of the most spectacular discoveries of the 20th century.

Uncharted territory

In 1977 Eavis had been invited by the Royal Geographical Society to join an expedition to Sarawak the following year. While looking at photographs and maps of the region in preparation for the trip, he noticed that the mountains were formed of limestone, a rock that is easily eroded by water. Eavis's extensive experience as a cave explorer led him to the conclusion that, over the centuries, the heavy tropical rains in the area must have dissolved the limestone and carved out a labyrinth of caves inside the mountains.

During that 1978 expedition, Eavis explored the region, discovering many previously unknown caves. Certain that many more lay undiscovered, he decided to mount a later expedition to find and map the entire system of caves in the area.

The next group arrived in Sarawak in late 1980 and, once inside the caves, began to map the dark, subterranean world. Eavis, Checkley, and White set off to survey the caves. They soon found themselves inching their way, in almost total darkness, along the walls of a passage. They knew that the passage was long: the measurements they recorded suggested more than 2,000 feet. But how wide was it? Their voices echoed for several seconds before the heavy silence returned. They guessed that it could be as wide as 300 feet. The only way to find out: locate the far wall.

No end in sight

Their compasses set, the three men began their journey into the unknown. Time and time again their path was impeded by huge, precariously balanced boulders—some as high as 80 feet. Slowly and deliberately they continued on in the darkness, but even with the strong beam of their headlamps, they still could see no sign of the other wall. And then, to their surprise, they emerged from the passage onto a flat, sandy plain.

They immediately realized that they were not in a passage at all, but in the middle of a gigantic subterranean chamber. They had walked about 500 feet and still no end was in sight.

For one of the explorers, having to acknowledge the cave's limitless boundaries was overwhelming. He was accustomed to squeezing his body down the narrowest of passages. He had explored vast caves all over the world. But this was something different. Never before had he experienced the sensation of agoraphobia, an acute aversion to open spaces, that now engulfed him. He was paralyzed with fear, and could not move for hours.

Record breaker

Although they did not yet know it, the three explorers had stumbled upon the largest known enclosed space in the world.

The Sarawak Chamber, as it was later named in honor of the Malaysian state of Sarawak, is three times the size of the Carlsbad Cavern in New Mexico, previously considered to be the largest underground cave in the world. Measuring 2,300 feet long, 1,300 feet wide, and at least 230 feet high, the Sarawak Chamber is a colossal black void that can hold as many as 38 football fields.

The discovery of the chamber proved that Eavis's original hunch had been right. Thanks to his educated guesswork, this spectacular natural feature is now situated firmly in the record books.

BLACK HOLE *Four members of the 1984 British-Malaysian Speleological Expedition to Sarawak, northern Borneo, survey the world's largest underground cave — the Sarawak Chamber — eerily illuminated by powerful headlamps. The chamber is so colossal that 10 jumbo jets would fit nose to tail inside it (inset).*

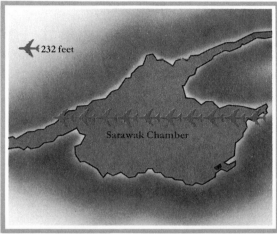

232 feet

Sarawak Chamber

SMELLING ROSY

The essential ingredient of costly perfumes

ON A WARM SPRING day in the palace gardens of the Mogul emperor, a wedding celebration was taking place. The bride, a Persian princess named Nur Jehan, was delighting in the stream of rose water that meandered through the garden in honor of the occasion. A shimmering golden film on the water caught her eye, and she ordered her servants to collect the perfumed, buttery substance. This was how, in the 17th century, the costly attar of roses was discovered.

The attar, sometimes called otto, is the precious, essential oil extracted from especially fragrant roses. Its use in the manufacture of perfumes helps to account for their extravagant price. Although rose water was known to the Romans in ancient times, no one before Princess Nur Jehan had learned the secret of extracting the attar. The discovery spread throughout Arabia, India, and Turkey and eventually to the Balkans. By the mid-18th century, the Valley of Roses in Bulgaria was producing most of the world's finest attars.

Harvesting a fortune

Even today, during the last week of May each year, a traditional festival is held in the Bulgarian valley to celebrate the harvesting of acres of beautiful crimson damask roses. Their fragrance sweetens the air for miles around. And no wonder: it takes 170 damask roses to produce one drop of the pale gold liquid. To yield a single ounce, some 250 pounds of rose petals must be distilled. In dry weather the flowers suffer from evaporation,

GLOWING MINERALS

At the end of the 18th century, when prospectors began mining near Franklin, New Jersey, they were looking for iron ore. But what they stumbled upon was more valuable: the most important source of rare minerals in the world. More than 300 different kinds of minerals have been identified to date. Even more impressive: 60 of them glow in the dark.

Electrons in their atoms absorb ultraviolet radiation, become agitated, and fluoresce, or emit radiation that we see as colored light. But most minerals do not do so in a pure state; impurities known as activators— manganese and zinc are the most common—must be present. The combination of the ore and the mineral gives the color: for example, zinc makes calcite fluoresce pink and willemite, green.

The results are spectacular. In 1968 the New Jersey legislature named Franklin the Fluorescent Mineral Capital of the World.

IN THE DARK *Seen in ordinary light, this piece of zinc ore appears to be black, brown, and white. Viewed under ultraviolet light, however, the minerals in the ore are revealed.*

The combination of the zinc and the minerals determines the color. Calcite appears pink; willemite, green; and zincite, blue. Franklinite, which does not fluoresce, remains black.

reducing even this meager yield. It is hardly surprising that dealers in essential oils keep their vials of attar in bank vaults.

The value of the crop is very much governed by the weather. Ideal conditions are a gentle rain with occasional sunshine.

The blooms are picked just before sunrise, when they are still dewy and not yet fully opened. The rose petals are placed in a still with water, which is heated to draw out the precious oil. The result of this first distillation is rose water. Next, the petals are removed and the rose water is further distilled to allow the lighter, oily attar to rise to the surface. The attar is then carefully removed and stored in glass flasks. The process is repeated several times.

Liquid gold

Bulgarian attar is considered the liquid gold of the perfume industry. It sells for about $450 an ounce. Attar produced in France and Morocco is only about half as costly. Unlike Bulgaria, these two countries rely mainly on the centifolia, or cabbage, rose, which is less fragrant than the damask rose and is often used in the production of rose water.

Rose water, which is delicately perfumed, is an ingredient in some liqueurs and in expensive candies and pastries. It is also used by the cosmetics industry in soap and beauty treatments. The attar, on the other hand, is usually reserved for only the costliest of perfumes.

However, the less expensive Moroccan attar is used in the practice of aromatherapy, the art of healing with the essential oils of plants. It is said to be useful as an antidepressant and in the treatment of liver and digestive complaints.

Since Roman times attar has been considered an aphrodisiac because of its legendary association with Venus, the goddess of love. In view of its exorbitant price, however, half a dozen oysters might be a less expensive alternative.

WHICH WAY IS NORTH?

A revolution is brewing deep in the earth

FOR MORE THAN 2,000 YEARS—ever since the Chinese first devised a compass by stroking a spoon with a lump of magnetic rock—the explorers of the world could plot their course. No matter how wild the territory, the traveler could always find his way because the magnetic needle of his compass always pointed north.

But 30,000 years ago the compass would have pointed south, and it may well do so again in the future. This dramatic shift in polarity takes place on a global scale, and its causes lie deep in the countless trillions of atoms that make up the earth.

Circular motion

Within an atom, electrons ceaselessly circle the atomic nucleus; the activity generates a minute electric current, which in turn creates a weak magnetic field. In some substances, such as iron and nickel, the combined effect of the electrons' magnetic fields is strong enough to make the entire atom magnetic. When magnetized atoms are packed together in large numbers, as they are in even the smallest fragment of iron, the electrons align in the same direction, creating an easily detected magnetic field.

The earth, too, is a magnet. Like the electrons in an atom, the planet is in constant motion, spinning on its axis in space. The electric charges in the atoms that make up the earth are moving as well, and the resulting current generates a large-scale magnetic field that runs from south to north.

Changing places

In the early part of the 20th century, however, geologists made the astonishing discovery that the earth's magnetic field can flip over. They studied volcanic lava—which, as it cools, picks up and retains the earth's magnetism—and found that in some places the direction of the magnetism was, instead, north to south. Further research revealed that rocks of the same age the world over shared the same pattern. The earth's magnetic field had changed direction as the lava solidified.

And this had happened more than once. Geographic north (the North Pole) and the direction of magnetic north have coincided for 700,000 years, with at least five brief reversals, one of which occurred about 30,000 years ago. But over the past 4.5 million years, the magnetic poles have changed places at least 20 times. The changes are irregular and unpredictable, but by geologic standards they happen rapidly, within a few centuries.

The clue to how and why these reversals occur lies in the molten mass of iron and nickel that surrounds the earth's solid core. The molten outer core is forever shifting, as currents of hotter alloy flow into areas where the core is comparatively cool. These movements help to create magnetic effects. But the currents are in permanent turmoil, which is why the magnetic north pole wanders around near the geographic North Pole.

At unpredictable times, when the hotter and cooler areas of the outer core approach a state of balance, the movements of molten metal will slow down, or become smaller. This lull reduces the strength of the earth's magnetic field.

Gradually, these huge subterranean tides gather impetus again, and the magnetic field regains its former strength. But if the new currents flow in a new direction, the field will reverse itself too.

On the surface of the planet, compass needles will swing south, not north. But there will be more dramatic changes as well. The earth's magnetic field acts as a shield against the constant shower of radioactive particles from space. It sweeps them toward the poles, where they spangle the skies in the form of auroras. At its lowest ebb, the earth's magnetic field will be too weak to stop this radiation, and not only humans but all living things will suffer the effects. Some will be destroyed, and others may be altered by genetic damage.

Disastrous as this seems, biologists believe that such influxes of radiation, which take place at intervals varying from 100,000 to 50 million years, also act as a spur to evolution. Man may have developed from a small, shrewlike creature that was the first recognizable animal to evolve after just such a shift in the earth's magnetic field.

UNDERSEA WEALTH

Secrets of the ocean depths

THE BOTTOMS OF THE OCEAN are the last unexplored areas of the planet. Although comprehensive mapping of the ocean floors started in the early 1900's, most of the detail has been added only within the past 20 years. Many remarkable discoveries have been made, but few as extraordinary as the hot springs deep under the sea.

From the springs a mile or more below the surface, water bubbles up at a temperature of about 660°F, warming the immediate waters to between 45°F and 62°F. (The temperature of the sea at this depth is normally about 36°F.) Such springs were unknown 20 years ago. Today scientists are wondering whether they could offer the world a new source of valuable mineral deposits.

Cracking the crust

The hot springs occur in the rifts where the earth's plates are moving apart, particularly under the Pacific and Atlantic oceans, where the earth's crust cracks into deep fissures. Cold seawater penetrates these cracks to a depth of four miles or more, reaching the hot magma. In the bowels of the earth the water becomes superheated, and gushes upward again to form a hot spring on the seabed.

As the pressurized water rushes up through the crust, it gives up magnesium and sulfate, which are absorbed into the crust, and picks up barium, calcium, copper, iron, lithium, manganese, zinc, and other minerals.

When this mineral-enriched water reaches the ocean floor, it interacts with the cold seawater and

"BLACK SMOKERS" *Plumes of blackened water billow out from vents on the seabed of the Pacific Ocean. Such vents could be a source of untapped mineral wealth.*

releases the minerals in mounds as large as 180 feet high and 600 feet wide. In some places the springs emerge through tall, thin chimneys built up over time from accretions of sulfide minerals. So dark and cloudy is the water flowing from the chimneys that they have been dubbed "black smokers."

Potential wealth

The mounds and chimneys are of great interest to scientists, who have identified similar ores on land in areas that once formed part of the ocean floor. In Cyprus, 90 different deposits of copper-iron-zinc sulfides occur in just one section of rock. If scientists can determine where and how mineral deposits occur underwater, they may be able to better predict their occurrence on land that was originally covered by the sea.

At one time it did not seem economically viable to scoop up these undersea deposits, but technological advances and the increasing scarcity of land-based mineral deposits are making deep-sea mines increasingly attractive.

The first undersea mining is likely to be in the Red Sea, where the seafloor is spreading as Saudi Arabia gradually moves away from the coast of the Sudan in Africa. Just northwest of Jidda, the principal port of Saudi Arabia, is the Atlantis II Deep, a 23-square-mile basin. The bottom of it is covered with a layer of mud as thick as 80 feet.

Sudan and Saudi Arabia have established a joint Red Sea Commission to investigate the possibility of mining the mud. It has been estimated that as much as 29 percent is iron; up to 5 percent, zinc; plus smaller amounts of copper, silver, and gold. Interest is also being expressed in deposits in areas under both the Atlantic and the Pacific oceans.

It has been estimated that hot springs may spew out as much water as the flow of the Amazon River every year, and that in the span of 10 million years the springs circulate every drop of ocean water through the earth's crust. As they do so, they continually create a renewable supply of rare minerals. If that supply can be exploited, the world may not run short of the minerals it needs.

DESERT SONG

At first sight a sandy beach on the rocky and desolate Isle of Eigg, off the west coast of Scotland, appears to be like any other. But nothing could be further from the truth. When these white sands are walked on or are touched, they produce a musical sound.

In fact, the sands sing—and not just on one note. When slowly sifted through the fingers, the sands emit musical tones that can range from high soprano to low bass.

The "singing sands"—their Gaelic name is *camas sgiotaig*—are a mystery that has frequently been investigated. Scientists believe that the music arises from the structure of the sands.

They are made up of tiny grains of the mineral quartz, which the sea has ground to a rounded shape. Each grain is surrounded by a minute pocket of air; the friction between the grain and the air sets off a vibration that creates the musical note.

The note varies according to the amount of moisture in the atmosphere and the amount of pressure being applied. No dust or foreign matter can be present, however; in experiments in the laboratory, even a minute pinch of flour halts the vibrations.

The mystery of why the sands sing seems to have been solved. But why the sands should be found on this remote Scottish island is a question to which there is still no satisfactory answer.

On this Scottish beach, the sands "sing" musical notes.

THE CROP THAT SAVED THE WHALE

A hero of the plant kingdom

AT ONE TIME the future of the sperm whale looked bleak. For decades it was hunted for its oil, a commodity much in demand by heavy industry for making lubricants.

After years of campaigning by conservationist groups, in 1970 the U.S. Congress passed the Endangered Species Conservation Act; it banned the importing of sperm whale products. Some other countries soon followed suit, and the sperm whale was saved from extinction.

But not all of the credit can be taken by the conservationists. The legislation might not have been passed so easily if scientists had not already found a substitute for sperm whale oil in the jojoba, a plant that had flourished in Mexico and Arizona for hundreds of years.

Potential realized

The jojoba is a gray-green or blue-green evergreen shrub that can grow six feet high. The foliage is handsome and luxuriant, but the plant is most highly prized for the oil contained in the nuts.

Many botanists believe that the jojoba may date back to prehistoric times, but the first record occurs in the 18th-century chronicles of Jesuits traveling through Mexico. They mention the plant's popularity with the local Indian tribes, who

INDISPENSABLE *Oil from the nuts of the jojoba plant has almost unlimited uses, in car waxes and wood polishes, in salad oils and shampoos.*

used it for both medicinal and cosmetic purposes. The ground nuts were said to cure a wide range of medical complaints, from dandruff and skin inflammations to problems during childbirth. The men used the oil to dress their hair and mustaches; the women put it on their braids.

The Jesuits' reports did not stir popular interest in Europe, however, and until the 20th century, jojoba continued to be valued chiefly by the Indians. Then, intrigued by the many historical references to its medicinal properties, researchers at the University of Arizona began to study the plant. But it was not until 1933 that they made their real breakthrough: the oil in the jojoba nut was composed not of fat but of liquid wax.

The implications of this discovery were enormous. The absence of fat meant that jojoba oil was much purer and needed less processing than other oils—an important factor, since it kept labor costs down. Further research revealed that the oil's potential was almost limitless. It could be used in food processing and preservation; to make lubricants, floor waxes, and car waxes of unsurpassed hardness and sheen; disinfectants, resins, and protective coatings; corrosion inhibitors; bases for creams, ointments, and shampoos; salad oils; and polishes for wood and leather.

The oil has also been found to have medicinal benefits for arthritis, rheumatism, and tuberculosis, and many medical researchers have used it as a vehicle for transporting the antibiotic penicillin through the body.

Future benefits

Great social and economic benefits may also be derived from the plant's ability to survive in arid lands. Instead of competing with existing crops for high-grade agricultural land, it can bring marginal and arid land into use. Consequently, pilot plantations have been established in the United States, Israel, India, Africa, and Australia, giving employment to millions while keeping the price of the raw material low. As if this were not enough, residue from the plant can be used to feed animals.

Therefore, the jojoba may be considered a true hero of the plant kingdom. Not only has it saved the sperm whale, it has also provided a number of practical benefits and promised increased prosperity for the inhabitants of some of the world's harshest regions. Given the jojoba's amazing versatility, how did we ever manage without it?

CURRENT CLASHES

Nature's own jacuzzis

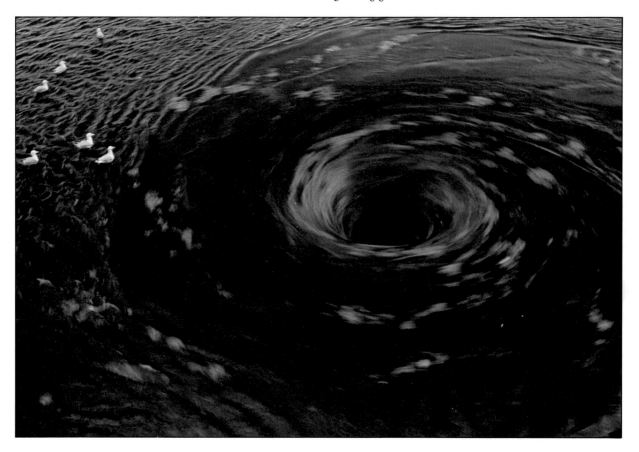

BEFORE THE WORD *whirlpool* became associated with the relaxing bath that Candido Jacuzzi invented, it struck terror into the hearts of many, especially seafarers. In the 19th century Edgar Allan Poe expressed the awe generated by ocean whirlpools in his description of the famed Maelstrom, off the coast of Norway:

> A smooth, shining and jet-black wall of water... speeding dizzily round and round with a swaying and sweltering motion, and sending forth to the winds an appalling voice, half shriek, half roar such as not even the mighty cataract of Niagara ever lifts up in its agony to Heaven.

This account by a writer whose trade was to make the flesh creep illustrates how whirlpools conjure up visions of ships being lost forever in a vortex. In olden times mariners understandably felt vulnerable, since their vessels were small and relatively unstable. Out of their fear grew legends about how whirlpools came into existence.

POWER OF NATURE *Whirlpools such as the one off the coast of St. Malo in Brittany, France, have been the source of many legends. However, all are natural phenomena.*

One of the first legends to be recorded was that of Charybdis, a whirlpool in the Strait of Messina between the Italian mainland and the island of Sicily. In Homer's *Odyssey*, written in the eighth century B.C., Charybdis is represented as a sea monster sucking and belching forth water as it preys on passing ships.

In Japan, local superstition connects whirlpools in the Naruto Strait, near the city of Osaka, with underwater devils, or *kappa*—evil goblins who derive pleasure from drowning humans.

There is even a myth about the Maelstrom itself. It is said to have been created by magical millstones that rotated in the sea and made a deep hole into which water flowed. This idea is reflected in recent folktales about whirlpools created by seawater rushing through holes in the center of the earth. But nothing of the kind actually happens: the action of whirlpools is caused by the head-on clash of tidal flows, coupled with the uneven surface of the ocean floor.

Major whirlpools are usually located in narrow channels between two larger expanses of sea. When tides fail to synchronize, differences in sea levels of as much as five feet can occur. Consequently, currents of seawater rush toward each other through the channels, much like rapids in a turbulent river. And as they come into contact with seabed obstructions, such as shelves of rock, the water surges upward, bubbling and seething on the surface. The turbulence becomes even more violent in stormy weather, particularly if the winds are blowing against the flow of the stream.

A navigational hazard

One of the most treacherous of whirlpools is Corryvreckan, located off the west coast of Scotland in a narrow channel between the islands of Jura and Scarba. The British Admiralty publication *West Coast of Scotland Pilot* offers a sharp warning:

"The navigation is at times most hazardous, and no stranger would under any circumstances be justified in attempting it."

Even sailors with local knowledge sometimes get into trouble here. In 1951 a Glasgow engineer and three companions had a harrowing experience while attempting to cross from Jura to the Scottish mainland. Some distance from the shore the engine of their motor cruiser, *Dewey Red,* had to be shut down when a water pump stopped. As the engineer worked to repair the damage, the vessel drifted into the swiftly flowing tidal race between Jura and Scarba. Everyone on board had to escape in a dinghy. Somehow they reached slack water.

But the *Dewey Red* was not so fortunate: she went to her doom into the whirlpool of Corryvreckan. Apart from one small cask bobbing in the water, no trace of her was ever seen again.

Despite all the knowledge that has been gained about whirlpools and how they work, no way of combating them has yet been discovered. Today it seems ironic to think that something so powerful could provide the basis for a relaxing bath.

THE BONE WARS

Fighting over the remains of the past

THE STRANGEST and longest battle of the American West was fought not between early settlers and Indians but between two collectors of fossils. The Bone Wars, as the bitter clash became known, raged in the shadow of remote cliffs, in desert encampments, in university laboratories, and on the pages of academic journals.

On one side was Othniel Charles Marsh, professor of paleontology at Yale University. A wealthy collector of fossils since childhood, he would stop at nothing to secure rare specimens for his collection. On the other side was Edward Drinker Cope, a naturalist from Philadelphia—also rich and determined. Although the West was littered with dinosaur bones, both men jealously guarded their own excavations and vied for the honor of being the first to describe a new species.

A battle of wits

No one knows exactly when the hostilities began— perhaps when Cope invaded what Marsh considered to be his territory in Kansas in 1871, or maybe when Marsh ridiculed Cope for assembling the skeleton of an aquatic lizard, *Elasmosaurus platyurus,* back-to-front.

By 1872, when the two met in the Bridger Basin of Wyoming, war had been declared between them. Marsh claimed that he had the exclusive right to dig at the site, but Cope ignored him, hired the only local guide not in his rival's pay, and set to work.

Marsh's men laid false trails for Cope and spent hours digging in spots where they knew there were no bones. One time, certain that Cope was watching them, the men planted a broken fragment of skull and a few teeth for him to find. Cope fell for the bait, and declared that the bone and teeth, which actually came from different creatures, were the remains of a hitherto undiscovered species.

Coded telegrams flew from west to east as the prehistoric graveyards yielded their riches. Academic papers announcing new discoveries were hurriedly written and rushed to the printer, only to have the date of each find routinely disputed. Guards were posted at important sites; spies lurked behind piles of recently unearthed spoils; and assistants were enticed from rival camps with irresistible offers of higher pay.

The results were not positive for the science of paleontology. One witness to the hostilities, pioneer paleontologist Joseph Leidy, gave up his research into fossil vertebrates in favor of less contentious fields of study. In addition, the speed with which the warring camps published their findings created confusion about the names some of the unearthed fossils had been given.

Eventually, the private feud became public knowledge. Cope charged Marsh with hoarding fossils owned by the government and with plagiarizing the work of his assistants by taking credit for their findings. Marsh replied with equal vehemence, accusing Cope of theft and ignorance.

The rivalry ends

Only with Cope's death in 1897 did the Bone Wars finally end. Marsh survived his enemy by less than two years. Both men died poor: Cope had lost his fortune in a mining fraud; Marsh had spent $200,000 in pursuit of fossils.

Yet despite the undignified rivalry that marred the reputation of each (prompting one of Marsh's assistants to refer to both rivals as "big men with little heads"), the achievements of the "bone warriors" are undisputed. Cope described more than 1,200 species or genera of fossil vertebrates from North America, and Marsh discovered more than 500. Many of the meticulously reconstructed dinosaur skeletons in museums throughout the world today are their legacy.

ARCH RIVALS *In the 1870's a long and bitter battle started between two fossil collectors, Cope and Marsh; the latter is fifth from right below. Although their rough-and-ready technique of fossil-hunting led to many finds (above), valuable specimens were often damaged in the process.*

ANCIENT WATERS RUN DEEP

The Ice Age answers a contemporary need

THE WORLD'S POPULATION, today more than 5 billion, may be double that number by the year 2010. By then, a very large number of people will probably be facing severe drought. Globally, there is enough fresh water for twice the estimated population. The problem: the water is not in the right places.

Facing the worst difficulties are people living in Africa and the Middle East, where the rainfall is meager and irregular. However, two of the countries most seriously affected, Egypt and Israel, are considering whether the last Ice Age can provide the water they need so desperately both to irrigate the arid land and to supplement the existing supplies of drinking water.

Underground riches

Deep under the Negev Desert and the Sinai Peninsula, shared by Egypt and Israel, lies a huge aquifer—a layer of porous rock that holds water. It contains an estimated 260 billion cubic yards of water; approximately 90 billion lie under the Negev Desert in Israeli territory.

The ideal conditions for an aquifer are those produced by a syncline. In this basin-shaped dip in the crust of the earth, porous rock that holds the water is sandwiched between two layers of rock that is more or less waterproof. Water collected in the aquifer is under high pressure. When it is tapped, either by a natural fault in the overlying rock or by drilling, water spurts to the surface.

The water from the Sinai aquifer has been known since ancient times, for it feeds springs and lakes all year round—in contrast to the seasonal springs dependent on the two to four inches of rain the desert receives each year. In the Book of Exodus the Bible records how Moses and the Israelites came to a place in the Sinai wilderness where the water was too bitter to drink. The Israelites called the place Marah, meaning bitter. It is known today as 'Ayun Musa, the Springs of Moses, and its waters are indeed full of bitter carbonates and sulfates.

Dating the water

Carbon-14 dating of the bicarbonate dissolved in the water at 'Ayun Musa indicates that the water is about 30,000 years old—the period of the last Ice Age. In that prehistoric era a giant ice cap covered northern Europe, and any clouds driven across the North Atlantic Ocean (which today drop rain on Europe) were deflected south to shed their water over the Sinai Peninsula and the Negev, among other areas. There, the rainwater percolated down through the rock and was trapped in the aquifer. A similar, even larger aquifer lies deep under the Sahara in northern Africa.

The arid Negev covers about half the total area of Israel. But its dry soil is fertile when irrigated, and with so little land, the Israelis are anxious to use every square mile. Already the Israelis draw 33 million cubic yards of water a year from the aquifer for irrigation and industry, and there are plans to draw 12 times that amount in the next century.

But although the reserves under the Sinai-Negev region are huge, the water, like coal and oil, is a finite resource. Its future use will have to be carefully planned.

WATER FROM THE ROCK *When a layer of porous rock lies between layers of impervious rock, rainwater that flows into the porous layer is under extreme pressure. The deeper the water underground, the greater the forces that push it upward through a fault or a borehole.*

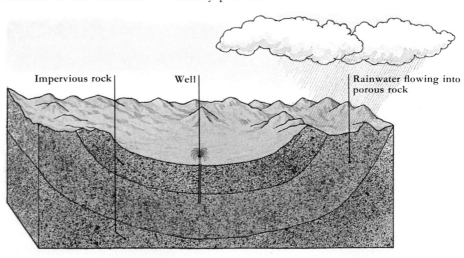

Impervious rock | Well | Rainwater flowing into porous rock

OF TABLECLOTHS AND FUNERAL SHROUDS

The fiery history of asbestos

MOST OF EUROPE was under the sway of the mighty emperor Charlemagne in the eighth century. Legend has it that when threatened by invasion, he invited the ambassadors of his enemy to a banquet. When the meal was finished, the ambassadors watched the emperor take the tablecloth and throw it on the fire. Several hours later he removed it from the embers; it was clean and completely undamaged. Convinced that Charlemagne was a magician, the ambassadors called off their plans for war.

Charlemagne's magic tablecloth was made of asbestos, a unique mineral composed of long, slender crystals that form threadlike fibers that can be woven into cloth.

In ancient Rome members of the nobility were cremated in asbestos shrouds so that their ashes could be kept separate from those of the funeral pyre and could be recovered, undefiled, to be placed in urns. Allegedly the Roman vestal virgins had asbestos lamp wicks that never burned out. The Arabs used asbestos to make armor for protection when they set fire to enemy towns. The emperor of Tartary, the Great Khan, protected his precious jewels from fire by wrapping them in asbestos cloth.

In ancient and medieval times very few people had ever seen the rare and costly "magic flax," but many considered it to be a mysterious, even sinister substance. Legends about it were numerous, and the most persistent concerned its origin. People thought that the fibers were spun from the wool, or skin, of the magical salamander, a small lizard commonly believed to be able to live in fire without harming itself.

In the 13th century Marco Polo, traveling across Siberia to China, discovered the true origin of "salamander wool" when the Great Khan showed him the quarries in the mountains where the mineral was dug out of the rock.

Invaluable fiber

Ancient people regarded asbestos as sinister because it resisted fire, and their instincts were right, although for a different reason. Today we know that asbestos fibers, if inhaled and ingested, can cause a range of crippling and fatal diseases.

But the mineral is still invaluable in industry. Mixed into cement, it is used to make pipes, to construct ductworks, and to provide fireproof coatings. Woven into fibers, it is used in brake linings, insulation, fireproof theater curtains, and conveyor belts for transporting hot materials. But asbestos is no longer used as it was in ancient China: in removable sleeves on clothing, because they could be cleaned by putting them into the fire.

THE GUAYMAS BASIN

A unique oil refinery

IN 1980 DR. PETER LONSDALE of the Scripps Institute of Oceanography, in San Diego, was on board the research vessel *Melville* searching for minerals raised to the seabed by volcanic activity in the Gulf of California. A dredge from the mile-deep Guaymas Basin brought up muddy sediments containing some of the minerals Lonsdale was seeking, but a distinctive smell alerted him to the presence of oil.

A further investigation of the same site in 1982 proved even more exciting. Using a deep-sea submersible named *Alvin,* the scientist and his colleagues watched plumes of gas bubbles and oil droplets rise from the seabed. They had discovered an extraordinary phenomenon: a natural oil refinery under the sea.

The Gulf of California is what geologists call a "young" ocean basin. Slowly, for the past 3 million years, the older, thicker North American continental plate has been moving apart from the younger, thinner Pacific oceanic plate. Volcanic eruptions usually occur under these circumstances, but the many rivers that flow into the Gulf of California carry an enormous amount of sediment that smothers the volcanic activity. Instead of erupting, the molten rock is forced to spread out and cool.

The sediments are rich in organic material carried by the rivers; the remains of dead plankton and other marine life add to it. Heat from the molten rocks below and pressure from the newer layers of sediments and the mile of water above act much like a huge pressure cooker that turns these sediments into deposits of "young" petroleum. The result: crude oil forms in thousands rather than in millions of years.

Such is the geography of the Guaymas Basin that these crude oil deposits are being refined where they lie. Because the movements of the great plates of the crust of the earth have created large fissures and cracks in the rocks beneath the Guaymas Basin, seawater percolates deep into the crust, where it is heated by the molten rocks below. This heat again forces the water upward. As it dissolves minerals from the rocks it passes through, it becomes a mineral-laden chemical solution. When this solution reaches the seabed, it meets cold seawater and rapidly cools, precipitating the minerals that Lonsdale was seeking in 1980.

Where the chemical solution flows through the young oil deposits, it heats the oil in much the same way as in an industrial refinery. The result: the hot oil rises toward the cooler regions next to the seabed. Here the oil cools and is condensed into tars, oils, and gases, in a remarkable copy of the way in which a refinery processes crude petroleum. The heavier oils and tars are forced out into the sediments on the seabed, together with the other minerals brought up from within the earth's crust; the lighter oils and gases float away in the sea.

Speedy oil

Although the oil discoveries in the Guaymas Basin are startling, they are not extensive enough to warrant commercial exploitation. Their great value is in demonstrating that oil can be formed more than 10 times faster than previously thought possible, and that nature can refine the oil itself.

Perhaps scientists will find a way to pressure-cook organic material to make oil the same way nature does in the Guaymas Basin. In the future the Guaymas Basin may hold a partial solution to some of the world's energy problems.

THE METAL OF URANUS

The neglected element that changed the world

WE LIVE IN A NUCLEAR AGE, and uranium is the metallic element that fuels the nuclear power plants of the world; indirectly, it also provides the materials for nuclear weapons. In the near future, countries with significant deposits of uranium may become as politically powerful as were the oil-producing countries in the recent past.

Yet uranium has not always been an important resource. The German chemist Martin Klaproth discovered it by accident in 1789. He had been analyzing a sample of the mineral ore pitchblende from a silver mine in what is today Czechoslovakia. The dark, heavy mineral had been mined in substantial quantities because it was thought to contain some silver. When no silver was found, the pitchblende was thrown away with the debris.

Sometimes known as black tin ore, pitchblende had variously been identified as a compound of iron, zinc, or tungsten. But after months of diligent experimentation and analysis, Klaproth found that it contained a metallic element completely unlike any other known metal. He named it after a recently discovered planet, Uranus.

Uranium is a relatively common metal—more common than silver, for example—and is found in granite and sandstone rocks in North America, southern Africa, and Australia, and in small traces in seawater. It is a dense, lustrous material that tarnishes rapidly when exposed to oxygen.

Yet initially only chemists and mineralogists showed any interest in uranium. Apart from small-scale applications, such as making yellow paint and coloring glass and china, no practical use was made of the new element. Of far more importance was the pitchblende ore in which it was first found.

Image making

In 1896 the French physicist Henri Becquerel noticed that pitchblende had one very unusual property: photographic plates exposed to a sample of pitchblende reacted as if they had been exposed to light. This property was called radioactivity, but at the time many scientists dismissed it as being of little importance. However, the investigation of what caused the radioactivity was to lead to one of the most significant discoveries in science, a discovery that laid the foundations for modern nuclear physics.

It was the husband and wife team of Pierre and Marie Curie who in 1898, after years of painstaking experiments, first isolated the element in pitchblende responsible for the radioactive effect. They named it radium, and obtained about one centigram of the pure element for every ton of pitchblende processed.

Radium exposes photographic plates because the nucleus of its atom is unstable and breaks down, releasing particles and electromagnetic radiation. Although uranium is also radioactive, it went almost unnoticed, since it is much less so than radium. In terms of the radioactivity each emits, the two could be compared to a searchlight and a candle.

All interest, therefore, focused on obtaining radium from the pitchblende ore. Uranium itself was considered an undesirable by-product. For example, every ton of ore processed at the Great Bear Lake refinery in Canada in the 1930's produced one gram of radium and about half a ton of uranium, for which few uses were found.

The breakthrough arrived in 1938 when it was proved that uranium atoms, when bombarded with neutron particles—found in the nucleus, or center, of all atoms—split into two. When they split, futhermore, the uranium atoms released neutrons of their own—which could in turn split other uranium atoms. Thus a chain reaction of fissioning uranium atoms could be started. It was this principle upon which development of both the nuclear reactor and the atom bomb would be based.

Fission

Only one form, or isotope, of uranium (uranium 235) readily undergoes the fission reaction. This isotope accounts for less than 1 percent of naturally occurring uranium. The rest is mainly the comparatively stable uranium 238, which explains why natural deposits of uranium do not spontaneously become nuclear reactors or nuclear bombs.

Scientific progress was rapid after the initial discovery of the fission reaction. From their understanding of nuclear processes, physicists knew that if they could make the fission reaction occur in uranium with a high percentage of 235 isotope, large amounts of energy would be released.

The first controlled fission reaction was carried out in December 1942. The first uncontrolled fission reaction—the first atom bomb—was exploded at Alamogordo, New Mexico, in July 1945. Three weeks later the Japanese city of Hiroshima became the first target of nuclear weapons in war. For better or worse, uranium had become an element of destiny in world affairs.

The nuclear age

The technological advance of the nuclear industry has been accompanied by an increasing unease about the safety of nuclear power. Opponents point to reactor failures, such as the threat at Three Mile Island in the United States and at Chernobyl in the U.S.S.R., which released harmful radioactivity into the environment. Nuclear power stations also produce radioactive wastes—wastes that will have to be safely stored for hundreds of years.

Today in some parts of the world the future of nuclear energy, and of uranium, hangs in the balance. Many countries are trying to develop safer, cleaner technologies, such as solar power. If such projects eventually replace nuclear energy, and the world lays its nuclear armory aside, uranium may once again become the neglected element it was a hundred years ago.

A DROP TO DRINK

Water, water, every where,
And all the boards did shrink;
Water, water, every where,
Nor any drop to drink.

So cried Samuel Taylor Coleridge's Ancient Mariner. But had he known where to look, he could have lowered a cask into the sea and hauled up fresh water.

The miracle of drinking water at sea is possible when rainwater falls on land and then seeps below the sea to supply springs on the ocean floor. The phenomenon occurs when the aquifer—the porous chalk or limestone sandwiched between two layers of waterproof rock—extends beneath the sea.

Fresh water filtering down through the aquifer to the seabed is under sufficient pressure to force its way through any cracks in the overlying clay and gush out into the sea. Since its higher temperature and lack of salinity give the fresh water a lighter density than salt water, it does not mix with the ocean water but floats up to the surface. There it forms pockets of drinking water.

The existence of freshwater springs at sea has been known for hundreds of years. One of the earliest written references to them was made by a 15th-century Arabian navigator who described such a spring off Bahrain, in the Persian Gulf. Other springs exist off the southeast coast of the United States and off the coasts of Britain and Ireland.

Had he been in the right spot, the Ancient Mariner would have had no problem whatsoever finding a drop of fresh water to drink.

LIGHT SHOWS IN THE SKY

MOST PEOPLE know the colors of the rainbow: red, orange, yellow, green, blue, indigo, violet. But few have been fortunate enough to see some of the rarer manifestations of this natural phenomenon. Some rainbows are all purple, all red, or even white. Some, instead of arching into the sky, lie flat or stand vertically in glowing pillars. And sometimes from an airplane, one can see a complete circle of multicolored light.

Rainbows may be visible whenever droplets of water catch the rays of the sun. The splashes from a ship plowing through the waves, the mist remaining after a shower on a sunny day, dew on a spider's fragile web, or the spray rising over a waterfall —each can put on a vibrant light show. To see the spectacular effects, one needs only to be in the right place at the right time.

White rainbows *can appear either in daylight or in moonlight, but for entirely different reasons. During the day, rays of sunlight may be reflected from very small droplets of moisture—so small that the emerging bands of color are close enough to overlap, creating white light. But a white rainbow seen by moonlight is not white at all. It only seems so because the eye cannot detect color in light as weak as what the moon is reflecting. However, a photograph of a lunar rainbow, taken at the correct exposure, will be in full color.*

Purple rainbows *are seen only before or at sunrise. A rare occurrence, they can be formed by high clouds that scatter the blue and violet light, which raindrops reflect back to the observer. At sunset, when the sun is low in the sky, a rainbow may be a dramatic red arc, because the shorter wavelengths (blue, green, and yellow) have been dispersed during their relatively long trip through the atmosphere.*

Why is a rainbow different colors, *unlike the uniform "white" light of the sun? Sunlight is a mixture of light of different wavelengths. Although we can see each as a separate color, combined they appear to be white. As a ray of sunlight enters a raindrop, its colored components are bent, or refracted, at different angles and then reflected off the raindrop's inner surface. Then, as it leaves the raindrop, the light is bent once again. Red, the longest wavelength, is reflected to the highest or outermost arc; violet, the shortest wavelength, to the lowest or innermost arc; yellow and green, to arcs between the two.*

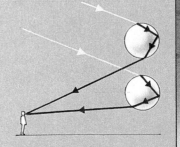

Standing like pillars at the ends of a curved rainbow, **straight rainbows** *are usually seen over a large expanse of water. Scientists suggest that reflections from the water create a number of rainbows, one above the other, but that only the ends of the rainbows are visible.*

A curious feature of **double rainbows** *is that the colors of the two bows are mirror images. This is because the light in the outer rainbow is reflected not once but twice inside the raindrops, and emerges at such an angle that the order of the colors is reversed.*

Rainbows that appear to be **horizontal** *are sometimes seen above dew-covered fields or water—often with a second, "conventional" rainbow behind them.*

Why you can never see the end of a rainbow *The reason is simple: it doesn't have one. Theoretically, the light continues to bend into a complete circle—a circle we can't see because it is cut off by the horizon.*

KEEPING THE WORLD TOGETHER

Can the force of gravity be changing?

PEOPLE WHO did not gain or lose a single ounce last year today weigh less than they did a year ago. Newton's apple took exactly one second to fall in 1665; today it would take longer. And friends on opposite sides of the world are moving farther apart every year. Although the differences in each case are minuscule—about 28-millionths of an ounce, about 20-billionths of a second, and one-fiftieth of an inch, respectively—they are real, and they are all related.

The story of how they are related begins in the 1930's when astronomers checked back on observations made over several centuries. They came up with the surprising discovery that earth's day had been growing steadily longer—by about a fifth of a second every century. Confirmation came from paleontologists, who study fossil life. They found that patterns of coral growth about 400 million years ago indicate that a year in that distant time was some 400 days long. The earth used to spin faster, making each day slightly shorter.

Mathematicians accounted for this phenomenon by factoring in the moon's gravitational pull on earth, which would slow down the earth's rotation. But their calculations could not explain all of the slowing down. Then, in 1938, the English physicist Paul Dirac pointed out that the laws of the universe led to some strange predictions concerning the behavior of gravity—specifically, that it would grow weaker as the universe aged.

Expanding the globe

Dirac's observation remained little more than an interesting footnote until the 1970's, when mounting geologic evidence suggested that the earth was originally only about 80 percent of its present size. Scientists were then led to an inescapable conclusion: Since it is gravity that holds the earth together, weakening gravity must be allowing the globe to expand. This expansion would slow down the rotation of the earth.

Further, it was suggested that at one time the continents as we know them today covered the entire surface of a smaller globe, and almost all of them were underwater. As the globe expanded, the surface cracked and the fragments began to separate. The water drained into ever-widening gaps and eventually formed today's oceans.

When similar calculations are applied to the entire universe, the predicted expansion rate turns

---

THE OLDEST LIVING THING

For many years a 4,600-year-old bristlecone pine in California, Methuselah, was thought to be the oldest living thing in North America. Today there is a challenger for the title.

The claimant is the box huckleberry (*Gaylussacia brachycera*), a low evergreen shrub that bears a mass of pink flowers in spring. A single specimen of this sprawling plant grows for more than a mile along a slope beside the Juniata River in Pennsylvania. The plant is estimated to be an incredible 13,000 years old. When it began growing, Asia and North America were connected by a land bridge and mammoths roamed the earth.

The plant was discovered in 1920. Botanists are certain it is just one plant because, although the box huckleberry produces abundant fruit, the plants cannot fertilize themselves. Seedlings

The box huckleberry in bloom

grow only when fertilization occurs between two different plants.

The shrub, the rarest of the huckleberries, spreads by means of runners that creep along under the ground at the rate of six inches a year. Knowing its rate of growth enables botanists to determine the age of the plant.

Another box huckleberry in Pennsylvania covers eight acres. Its age is estimated at a mere 1,200 years. Other colonies of the plant have been found in Delaware, Kentucky, Maryland, Virginia, and West Virginia.

But Methuselah does retain at least one title: the oldest living *tree* in North America.

out to be amazingly close to the expansion that has already been observed. Such a close correlation would have settled the argument—except for the awkward fact that when the same calculations are applied to our solar system, they indicate that during the first billion years in which life evolved, the earth would have had an average temperature of around 212°F. Such a temperature would have been too high to sustain any form of life.

However, as the British astronomer Sir Fred Hoyle has pointed out, during that billennium the only life-forms resembled modern bacteria, some of which can thrive at 212°F. Furthermore, falling temperatures over the next billennium saw the arrival of blue-green algae, which can tolerate temperatures as high as 160°F; and the *next* billennium ushered in fungi and other algae that can tolerate temperatures up to 140°F. The most recent billion years, with temperatures below 120°F, saw the growth of multicelled animals and plants that flourish in the lower temperatures.

As objections to the theory crumble, many scientists have concluded that everything in the universe is getting bigger and lighter—for no better reason than that it is also getting older, and gravity is growing weaker.

GREEN MEDICINE

A grass-roots approach to illness

DOCTORS AND SURGEONS were very baffled. The kidney transplant patient at Dulwich Hospital in London had developed an infection in the operation incision that would not clear up. Then a young doctor remembered a remedy he had seen native doctors, practicing traditional medicine, use successfully in South Africa. He laid strips of a papaya fruit across the infected wound. The wound healed.

This unorthodox medical success, achieved in 1977, was met with ridicule. Even the doctor himself admitted, "It's not awfully scientific." But although treatment by "green medicine"—the use of plant remedies—is often derided by the medical profession in Europe and North America, it is commonplace in many other parts of the world, especially in China.

A green movement

Influenced by European and American ideas, much of China adopted Western medical practices in the 1920's, and its traditional medicine, developed over thousands of years, was declared illegal. But in 1958 the Chinese Communist leader Mao Tse-tung lifted the ban because there were not enough doctors to treat China's millions, and few could afford sophisticated drugs from Western manufacturers.

Today many of the illnesses suffered by the Chinese are treated by so-called barefoot doctors—paramedics with minimal training who usually use the traditional green medicines. At the same time, China has a large number of what many in the Western world would consider orthodox medical practitioners. In China the two kinds of doctors work in tandem to heal the sick.

In addition the Chinese are applying modern research ideas to their traditional remedies. If a popular folk remedy seems to work, they test it to find its active ingredient and then use this ingredient on a large scale. Thus have Chinese doctors devised a number of important medicines, including a drug derived from a species of holly to reduce chest pains in patients with coronary disease. Another, concocted from a variety of sage, stimulates blood circulation. Yet another, derived from a fungus, is used to treat skin disorders.

Cost-effective

One major advantage of Chinese herbal remedies is that they are relatively inexpensive—certainly in comparison with the $28.5 billion that people in the United States recently spent on "drugs and sundries" in one year. It was the cost factor that in 1974 led the United Nations World Health Organization (WHO) to encourage all countries in the Third World to develop their own traditional systems of medicine. At the time, the move was criticized as "giving the green light to witch doctors," but its proponents called it a very necessary measure because of the urgent health problems of developing countries.

The Third World is populated with 3 billion people, 90 percent of whom must rely on their own traditional healers, since they do not have access to Western-trained doctors. The task facing WHO is to develop and reinforce the use of green medicine in as many of these countries as possible.

The director-general of WHO, Dr. Halfdan Mahler, has said: "An army of traditional healers and herbalists can help to make attainable a goal of health care for all by the year 2000." Already countries such as Burma, Nigeria, and Peru have established training courses in which traditional medicine men can learn modern techniques as well as pass on their own knowledge to orthodox doctors. The International Association of Folk Medicine was established in the 1980's.

Conquering disease

Green medicine may already have helped solve one of the most urgent medical problems of the Third World: schistosomiasis, formerly known as bilharzia. This debilitating disease, which causes dysentery and cirrhosis of the liver, can prove fatal if untreated. There are at least 300 million sufferers. Its cause is a parasitic worm that spends part of its life in water snails.

In the past, one way to curb the disease was to kill the snails. But the synthetic chemicals needed to do this are expensive, and the snails eventually become immune to them. Today, Egyptian scientists investigating the possibilities of green medicine have discovered that the leaves of a tiny plant related to the American ragweed contain a chemical that is fatal to the snails. Conveniently, this plant grows near the snails' breeding areas and will, it is hoped, curb or prevent schistosomiasis.

Other uses of green medicine include a tea brewed from stems of a shrub (called *mahuang* by the Chinese) to relieve asthma, colds, and coughs. Garlic is known for its antiseptic properties, and research shows that it may help to reduce blood pressure.

Despite the support of WHO, many Western doctors remain skeptical. Yet every day they are themselves prescribing drugs derived from herbal remedies: digitalis, from the foxglove, to treat heart conditions; ipecac, from the root of two Brazilian plants, to treat coughs; hydrocortisone, from wild yams, for conditions such as severe asthma; and belladonna, from the deadly nightshade, to treat a variety of conditions.

The ever-spiraling costs of modern synthetic drugs may force Western medicine to take another look at the plant remedies used by past generations and by Third World countries. In time, papaya may be a standard treatment for infected wounds.

FLOWERING TIME

The petal-powered clock

PEOPLE THE WORLD OVER enjoy growing flowers, but few realize that one can grow a garden that will tell the time of day.

This was the ingenious idea of Carolus Linnaeus, the 18th-century Swedish naturalist who is best known for setting down the principles for the naming and categorizing of plants and animals.

Opening time

On his many journeys throughout Sweden observing and collecting plants, Linnaeus had noticed that some plants open and shut their flowers at different times of the day. Modern scientists call this photoperiodism, a phenomenon that controls the flowering of plants according to the daylight.

One summer morning in 1749, Linnaeus rose early to study the habits of two species of wildflowers. He noticed that one of them, hawk's-beard, had opened its flowers by 6:30 A.M. But the other, hawkbit, did not display its blooms until 7 A.M.

Linnaeus then made a list of 41 different species with blooms that opened and closed at different times of the day and arranged them in a "floral clock." He believed it would enable him to "tell the time, even in cloudy weather, as accurately as by a watch." A friend joked that Linnaeus would make himself highly unpopular by putting all the watchmakers in Sweden out of business.

Linnaeus observed that the earliest riser in his garden at Uppsala was goatsbeard, which in the long days of the Swedish summer was in flower by 3 A.M. An hour later wild chicory was in bloom. During the balance of the morning other plants blossomed at various intervals. The last to display its blooms was the ice plant at about 11 A.M. The hours at which the plants closed their flowers also told the time. First to close was the rough hawkbit at 10 A.M.; last was the day lily at 8 P.M.

Although Linnaeus never actually planted his floral clock, in the 19th century several European botanical gardens attempted to do so. None was entirely successful: many of the plants Linnaeus listed did not flower in the same season or would not grow elsewhere in Europe, and in rainy weather some did not open their petals at all.

So clockmakers never became too alarmed at the prospect of floral clocks sprouting up as competitors. But Linnaeus's experiments did offer yet one more way in which a garden can surprise and further delight its owner.

MORNING GLORY

People living along the shores of the Gulf of Carpentaria in north-eastern Australia wake up to one of the most spectacular daybreaks on earth. As the heavens brighten at the end of a warm tropical night, a rotating ribbon of cloud advances across an otherwise cloudless sky like a giant rolling sea wave. Australians have a name for this beautiful phenomenon; they call it morning glory.

The long horizontal clouds occur at all times of the year but are most frequent during September, October, and November—spring in the Southern Hemisphere. The clouds form over nearby Cape York Peninsula and move across the gulf in a south-westerly direction. They bring with them sudden wind squalls but rarely any rain.

Viewed from the ground, the morning glory is shaped like a gently curving arch. Although only 100 to 200 yards thick, the clouds can stretch from horizon to horizon. The pilot in a small airplane once flew along the edge of one for more than 75 miles and did not reach the end.

Double morning glories have frequently been reported, and on occasion as many as seven have passed overhead within one hour. A fine mist sometimes accompanies the multiple waves.

Even after years of detailed research, the weathermen can only speculate about conditions that give rise to the development of these unique clouds, but the experts believe the answer may lie in conflicting airflows on Cape York Peninsula.

Strong sea breezes on the eastern coast often reach far inland and clash with weaker breezes blowing from the west. Currents also form on the mountains in the peninsula as air cools at night. The three airflows are believed to interact and produce disturbances that ultimately lead to a rotating surge of air moving west. As moisture is sucked in, the cloud becomes visible.

A complete explanation will not be forthcoming until further experiments are carried out on the Cape York Peninsula. But it is an extremely remote area, covered almost entirely by dense eucalyptus forest; only a single dirt road leads to the interior. For some time it is likely that morning glories will remain natural wonders not fully understood.

A spectacular morning glory, photographed from the air over Queensland

FROM FLINT AX TO PRECISION WATCH

The miracle mineral

IT MAY SEEM a far cry from a Stone Age hunter's flint ax to a precision watch with less variation than 0.1 second annually. But the prehistoric axmaker and the 20th-century watchmaker used the same basic mineral: quartz.

About one-eighth of the earth's crust consists of quartz, which makes it the most abundant mineral in the world. It is also one of the most versatile.

Quartz is a mixture of the two most common chemical elements in the earth's crust, oxygen and silicon, and is the basic ingredient of the group of silica minerals that includes sand, sandstone, and flint. Quartz consists of very hard crystals that come in all sizes, from that of a pinhead to a block weighing more than five tons.

In its pure state, quartz is colorless and is called rock crystal. But impurities such as copper or iron can color the quartz. Many of these colored quartzes, highly prized as gemstones, are used in jewelry. Colored quartzes include yellow citrine and cairngorm, pink rose-quartz, apple-green chrysoprase, red cornelian, violet-tinted amethyst—derived from the Greek word for "not drunken," because the ancient Greeks believed it to be a remedy for drunkenness—and the multi-colored agate, jasper, and onyx.

Crystal clear

Today it is the technological uses of quartz that are the most important. Because of its hardness, pure quartz is used extensively as an abrasive, most commonly in sandpaper and in sandblasting.

But it is the silica minerals, composed largely of quartz, that have the most varied uses. Sand is an essential ingredient of concrete and mortar, as well as a vital raw material for porcelain, and sandstone is an important building stone. Flint can be chipped to shape and, when freshly processed, has a very sharp cutting edge. When struck together, flint and steel produce sparks—for centuries the main way of igniting gunpowder. Today flint pebbles are used in industry to grind paint pigments.

Rock crystal has many uses. Perhaps the best known is as crystal balls for fortune-telling, but more often it is cut and polished to form prisms and lenses for microscopes and cameras, which require extra-hard-wearing qualities.

Since another useful property of quartz is its resistance to heat, it is used in electrical insulators and in molds for casting metals. When heated in a flame of oxygen and hydrogen, quartz becomes

COSMETIC QUARTZ *Silicone, a derivative of quartz, is the main ingredient in most cosmetics. In hair gel it is the substance that fixes the hair in place, achieving dramatic results—as in the style favored by singer Tina Turner.*

silica glass, and can withstand sudden changes of temperature much better than ordinary glass—another product of silicon derived from quartz. Silica glass is ideal for ovenproof dishes and laboratory test tubes; when drawn out into fine threads, it is used for highly sensitive weighing devices and in fiber optics.

Keeping time

The most amazing quality of quartz is its piezo-electricity. In common with many other crystals, quartz *produces* an electric charge when distorted by pressure; conversely, quartz crystals change shape when an electric charge is applied *to* them. When an alternating current is employed, the crystals vibrate imperceptibly at a constant rate of millions of vibrations per second.

The piezoelectric effect has brought quartz crystals into the forefront of modern technology: electrically charged vibrating quartz, cut into plates of precise dimensions, can control the movement of hands or digital numerals in clocks and watches. Because it resists temperature changes, quartz is unaffected by the weather. Vibrating quartz crystals are also used in radio transmitters and receivers, and in television transmitters.

When compressed with a force of 1,000 pounds, a half-inch cube of quartz crystal can generate a current of up to 25,000 volts. Lesser currents are used to ignite a flame in a gas stove, start a gasoline engine, or set off an explosive device.

As the world's supply of quartz diminishes, synthetic quartz crystals are used increasingly. But whatever its source, quartz will probably continue to be the most variedly useful of all minerals.

DO TREES TALK?

Some scientists think they do

"STONES HAVE BEEN KNOWN to move and trees to speak," said Shakespeare's Macbeth, voicing an old superstition. Today a team of scientists at the University of Washington in Seattle, led by Professor David F. Rhoades, claim to have evidence that proves that trees really do "talk." Humans cannot hear their conversations, but one tree can be understood by another.

Under the weather

The scientists gathered their evidence in the course of experiments on the effects of stress on trees. Plant stress can be caused by drought, frost, pollution, or lack of nutrients in the soil. Under such conditions they are more vulnerable to attacks by insects and other plant-eating creatures because their natural defenses are low. This vulnerability is much like people catching a cold when they have been soaked by rain: it is not the rain that causes the cold, but the fact that the soaking lowers the body's resistance to any cold viruses.

Stress in plants is accompanied by chemical changes, just as it is in humans. The scientists discovered that when under stress, plants produce more nutrients, such as amino acids, and smaller amounts of the chemicals that help to protect them against the ravages of insects.

The scientists then began a series of experiments with willows, placing hungry caterpillars on some trees but not on others. The latter were the controls. At first the caterpillars flourished. But before long it became apparent that they were doing surprisingly little damage to the trees. Analysis showed that after the initial attack the trees produced more defensive chemicals such as proanthocyanidin, a kind of natural insecticide.

Then came the surprise. After a few weeks the control trees were also producing more proanthocyanidin. They were defending themselves in advance of attack. It seemed that the affected trees were somehow signaling to the others: "There is danger around here!"

Professor Rhoades and his colleagues wondered if the trees were "communicating" through the roots and the soil. But experiments in and out of the laboratory proved conclusively that this was not so. In any case, the trees were apparently "talking" over a distance of more than 100 yards.

The scientists then proposed that airborne pheromones might hold the clue. These chemical substances given off by plants and animals act as signals between members of the same species. Although present in very small quantities, pheromones are amazingly powerful. For example, the pheromones emitted by female moths will attract males hundreds of yards away.

After further tests Professor Rhoades and his colleagues came to the conclusion that the pheromone hydrocarbon ethylene, emitted by trees through the leaves, was a likely carrier of the danger signals from one tree to another. Research along these lines is still continuing.

Vocal or dumb?

Not all scientists are convinced by this evidence, however. Two British biologists from York University, Dr. Simon V. Fowler and Professor John H. Lawton, maintain that the suppositions of the U.S. team can be explained equally well by the spread of infectious diseases carried by the caterpillars themselves. The two scientists conducted their own experiments with birch trees. Their finding: no evidence that trees "talk."

The story is still unfinished. Both sides are very cautious in their claims. But as Professor Rhoades points out, if trees really do "talk" to each other, we may have to reassess our view that trees are totally inanimate.

A REMEDY FOR ALL

More than a cure for vampires?

AS DEVOTEES of horror stories know, the way to keep a vampire at bay is to hang garlic around the doors and windows of the house. To make sure a corpse does not rise again after burial and become a vampire, its mouth should be filled with garlic.

Garlic has been used as a charm to ward off all kinds of evil spirits throughout the ages. But it has also been a popular remedy for more prosaic misfortunes, such as dog bites, constipation, asthma, pimples, and athlete's foot, to name a few.

One of the earliest cultivated plants, garlic, or *Allium sativum,* is a member of the lily family and a close relative of the onion. Its medicinal properties have been well documented—it is even mentioned in the Bible. As recently as 1900 garlic was recommended by some doctors as a cure for tuberculosis. During World War I, it was believed that it could fight dysentery; and World War II saw it being used on battle wounds to prevent septic poisoning and gangrene. Even the world-famous Albert Schweitzer used garlic to cure cholera and typhus. In the Soviet Union, garlic is so popular for fighting colds and flu that it is known as "Russian penicillin"; in China it has been used for centuries to treat high blood pressure.

Healing powers

Until recently, most members of the medical profession have viewed such practices with intense skepticism. But scientific evidence is beginning to support views that this pungent and commonplace plant does have remarkable curative powers—as an antibiotic, a fungicide, a laxative, a diuretic, and even as an anticoagulant.

As long ago as 1858 Louis Pasteur observed that garlic could destroy harmful bacteria; in 1985, tests in the United States showed it to be effective against influenza B and herpes simplex, the cold-sore virus. But the most important findings concern the way it acts in the blood.

Experiments in Japan and West Germany have proved that garlic lowers blood cholesterol, counteracting the effects of a fatty diet. And in Spain, Dr. David Greenstock at the English College in Valladolid has discovered that garlic increases the body's absorption of vitamin B. This benefits the nervous system and blood vessels, and stimulates the pituitary gland, which regulates the way fats and carbohydrates are digested. Other research demonstrates that garlic inhibits blood clotting; eaten raw, even half a clove a day has been found to prevent embolisms.

The precise explanation of garlic's medicinal properties is not understood. It is known, however, that in its raw, crushed state, garlic contains an amino acid rich in sulfur. The sulfur gives garlic its characteristic odor and is believed to provide protection against heart disease.

Ironically, in the light of all the current research, garlic's most famous role as a vampire repellent may turn out to be its most inappropriate. After all, who would want to take the risk of using an anticoagulant with a bloodthirsty vampire nearby?

AS STEADY AS A ROCK?

The moving stones of Death Valley

THE VAST Death Valley National Monument in California is a place of extremes. Snow-capped mountains dotted with pine trees and wildflowers tower over hundreds of square miles of desert that include salt and alkali flats as well as drifting dunes. Nearly 300 feet below sea level, the valley is the lowest, driest, hottest place in the United States.

Of all the many natural wonders in the valley, the most remarkable are the stones that move. These stones litter the cracked surface of the Racetrack, a three-mile-long playa, or dried-up lake.

Ranging in size from pebbles to boulders, the stones look ordinary enough. What is curious are the long, shallow furrows trailing behind each stone. Some of the tracks are dead straight; others zigzag or curve gently. The tracks are created as the stones move, apparently of their own accord, over the playa and often over considerable distances; some of the tracks are hundreds of feet long.

How do the stones move? Some people claim that a strange, unearthly force is responsible; some insist that there is a connection with UFO's; others believe there is a natural explanation.

Dr. Robert P. Sharp thinks he knows the secret. A professor of geology at the California Institute of Technology, Sharp made a seven-year study of the phenomenon. He selected 30 stones of different shapes and sizes, tagged and named them, and marked each one's position with a metal stake to see if any stone moved from its original site.

All but two obliged. In just under a year, one rock moved 860 feet in several moves, and a nine-ounce stone made the biggest single move: 690 feet.

Sharp studied the tracks the stones had made and checked the local weather conditions at the time of each movement. He concluded that the combined forces of wind and water were responsible, a conclusion supported by the fact that the course of the tracks corresponded to the direction of the prevailing winds. The average annual rainfall in the playa is rarely more than two inches, but even a light rainfall will form a sheet of moisture over the hard clay surface, making it slick. On such a surface, one powerful gust of wind, channeled in by the surrounding mountains, is all it takes to start a stone skidding across the slippery playa as fast as three feet per second.

The stones of the Racetrack have become a great tourist attraction. Knowing how the stones move is not enough to dispel the sense of mystery and wonder that such a phenomenon instills.

TRAIL OF A ROLLING STONE *In the arid landscape of Racetrack Playa, a dry lake bed in Death Valley, California, stones leave trails hundreds of feet long. Some run straight, some change direction, others loop back on themselves.*

TULIPOMANIA

The blooming boom of Holland

WHAT WOULD YOU expect to get in return for two loads of wheat plus four loads of rye plus four fat oxen, eight fat pigs, 12 fat sheep, two hogsheads of wine, four barrels of beer, two barrels of butter, 1,000 pounds of cheese, a bed, a new suit of clothes, and a silver beaker?

In fact this was the extraordinary price—worth 2,500 florins (about $1,000) at the time—that one man paid for a single tulip bulb in Holland in the 1630's. Even higher sums than that changed hands at the height of what has come to be known as "tulipomania"—a rage for trading in tulip bulbs that swept the nation between 1634 and 1637.

TULIP MADNESS *Flora, goddess of flowers, sits in a wheeled "ship of fools" in this 17th-century engraving satirizing the mania that led people to pay huge sums of money for the bulbs of rare tulips. In their eagerness to join the ship, people in the crowd trample their weaving looms underfoot and fail to notice, in the distance, the wreck of another "ship" that has capsized.*

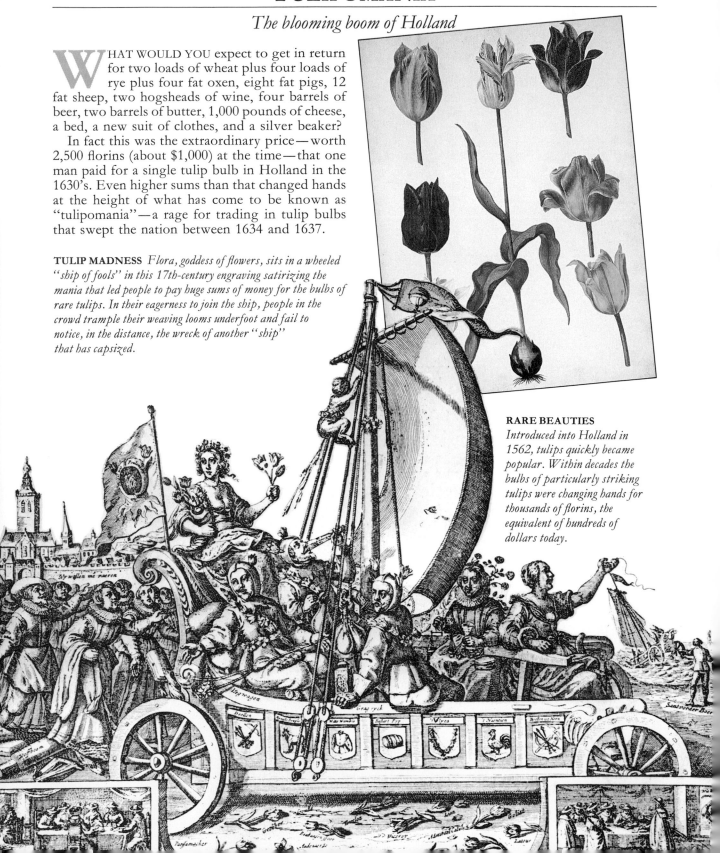

RARE BEAUTIES
Introduced into Holland in 1562, tulips quickly became popular. Within decades the bulbs of particularly striking tulips were changing hands for thousands of florins, the equivalent of hundreds of dollars today.

Hardly anyone escaped the fever: merchants, noblemen, farmers, chimney sweeps—all were caught up by the fact that it was suddenly possible to become very rich, very quickly, by owning even one of these humble bulbs.

How did such an extraordinary state of affairs come to be?

The "breaking" of a bulb

Tulips were still comparatively rare in 17th-century Holland, and as early as 1623 unusual ones were fetching high prices. But during the mania of the 1630's, prices reached astronomical levels because cultivated tulips were found to have an extraordinary property. Any tulip bulb that usually produces a flower of a single color will eventually "break" and produce a flower, sometimes stunningly beautiful, of two or more colors. Once this happens, the change is permanent: the bulb will continue to produce a multicolor flower.

The market in tulips during the mania was really based on a massive gamble, not unlike a risky speculation on the modern stock market. A buyer would invest money in a tulip bulb in the hope that —sooner, rather than later—it would break into an especially remarkable flower. If it did, huge profits could be made from selling bulbs grown from the one bearing this rare, possibly unique, new bloom.

Invisible assets

Anyone who could acquire a few bulbs had a chance to make a fortune. For instance, one bulb was sold for 4,600 florins (about $1,800 today) *plus* a fine new carriage and a pair of horses.

One of the bizarre aspects of tulipomania was that most of those who bought and sold tulips never saw the bulbs themselves: ownership was transferred from dealer to dealer while the bulb remained in the ground. Opportunities for fraud were rife. One contemporary writer said that more bulbs "were sold and purchased, bespoke and promised to be delivered, than in all probability were to be found in the gardens of Holland." In two separate years, the variety called Semper Augustus failed, and no bulbs were produced. Even so, a roaring trade in that tulip continued.

To own a few bulbs of *any* variety, some workingmen sold everything they had, even the tools on which their lives depended; some of them made fortunes and "gained in a few months," said

THE UNDERGROUND ORCHID

On a warm spring day in 1928, as a young Australian farmer named Jack Trott bent down to examine an odd crack in the ground, he noticed a sweet smell. After carefully scraping away a thin layer of soil, the farmer saw, to his astonishment, a tiny flower a mere half-inch across, growing underground.

What Trott had found was, in fact, a new species of orchid: *Rhizanthella gardneri*—an extraordinary plant that spends its entire life in total darkness.

The name *Rhizanthella* is derived from two Greek words: *rhiza,* meaning root, and *anthos,* meaning flower. And that is just what it looks like: a waxy white root, two inches long, with white petals enclosing a spiral of tiny purplish-red flowers.

How does this orchid of the underworld manage to survive? Unlike other plants, it cannot use sunlight to obtain energy. Instead it takes its food from another plant, living off the decaying stumps of the broom honey myrtle, a shrub. It is linked to the stumps by a fungus, *Rhizoctamia,* that botanists believe is essential for the orchid's survival.

The orchid flowers in May and June. The blooms never appear above the ground, which makes them difficult to find, but they do raise the soil slightly, creating little cracks in the surface. These telltale cracks, and the faint sweet smell of the flowers, are the only signs of the orchid's existence. Such is its rarity that fewer than 250 specimens have been identified, all in Western Australia.

The underground orchid exposed

one writer, "houses, coaches and horses, and figured away like the first characters in the land."

Not that riches always brought contentment. A cobbler at The Hague found that his investment had broken to produce a previously unheard-of black tulip. In due course he was approached by a group of florists from Haarlem who eventually persuaded the cobbler to part with his singular bulb for 1,500 florins ($600 today). He was appalled when his customers promptly stamped the precious bulb into the ground. One of the group silenced his cries of protest with: "We, too, have a black tulip. We would have paid 10,000 florins, if you had asked for it, to ruin your chances of competing with us." One version of the story says that the cobbler was so distressed at the thought of the riches he had so carelessly given away that he hanged himself.

Boom years

Of course not everyone was infected by the mania. One professor of botany became so enraged by the whole business that the mere sight of a tulip was enough to make him attack it ferociously with his stick. Nonetheless, the madness continued. In the three boom years of tulipomania, transactions worth more than $15 million in today's currency were made in Haarlem alone. To this day the city remains the center of the Dutch tulip industry.

Early in 1637, the bubble burst. Amateur traders grew bored—and the wiser ones realized how shaky were the foundations of a business fueled by such rabid speculation. There was a rush to sell out, and the market collapsed. Everyone wanted to sell, no one wanted to buy.

An enormous number of people found that their riches were merely paper fortunes, for they were owed huge sums of money by buyers who had been intending to pay only after they had, in turn, sold the bulbs and made their own vast profits. But all prospect of those profits had now vanished. In the end many sellers had to be content with as little as 10 percent of the price they had originally asked.

For Holland tulipomania brought in its wake a financial crisis as serious as the crash of the U.S. stock market in 1929, when many a paper fortune was resting on little more than wishful thinking. The year 1637 became renowned as one in which, as one observer put it, "one fool hatched another, and the people were rich without property and wise without understanding."

A HARD STICK TO BEAT

A strange life—and stranger uses

CENTURIES BEFORE the invention of air conditioning, the Japanese had found a way to sleep peacefully on sweltering summer nights. When others might have been tossing and turning because of the heat, they would put their arms around a "bamboo wife"—a long cylinder of bamboo basketwork. This simple device allowed air to pass around the sleeper's body, guaranteeing a good night's rest.

People have used, and still use, bamboo in thousands of surprising ways. Bamboo is one of the plant kingdom's most extraordinary members. It is a giant grass that grows almost everywhere in the world except in Europe. It can be found in all kinds of terrain, from lowland plains to mountain slopes. Some species grow only a few inches high; others tower 100 feet or more. And bamboo grows at an amazing speed. A Japanese scientist recorded one stalk that grew nearly four feet in 24 hours.

On the other hand, most bamboo puts out flowers only at extremely long intervals—between 20 and 120 years apart. But when a plant does burst into flower, every bamboo of that species, wherever it is in the world, flowers at the same time. How and why this happens is still one of nature's great unsolved mysteries.

There are more than 1,000 species of bamboo, and the woody stalks vary enormously in color, shape, and size. They may be golden, black, mottled, or have green stripes. The joints that give bamboo its strength may be knobby, spiked, smooth, or pitched at curious angles on the stalk. The diameter of the stalk can vary from a fraction of an inch to more than a foot.

Ubiquitous bamboo

Cheap and abundant, easily worked, and immensely strong for its light weight, bamboo has found a place in everything from bows for archery to musical instruments, from coffin making to shipbuilding, and from hats to cooking utensils.

Long before the Chinese invented paper in the second century A.D., they wrote on strips of green bamboo. They also used the moisture from black bamboo to treat kidney ailments. The great suspension bridge across the Min River in Szechuan,

China, is slung on bamboo cables almost seven inches thick; after more than 1,000 years, the bridge is still in use today.

The Chinese also still use bamboo as scaffolding, and virtually every part of a Japanese house that is not paper is made of bamboo: the ceiling, gutters, and supports. Japanese families use bamboo furniture, the children play with bamboo dolls, and crows are frightened by bamboo scarecrows.

In the United States, Thomas Edison had experimented with more than 6,000 different materials for the filament of the world's first electric light bulb before he decided, in 1880, to use charred fibers of bamboo. More recently, scientists have distilled a form of diesel fuel from bamboo. At least one early aircraft, the French *Demoiselle,* had a bamboo frame. And everywhere in the world, fishermen have used bamboo rods for generations.

Bamboo aid

The ubiquitous grass is also helping the economies of very poor countries. In Zambia, Japanese engineers have imported a traditional drilling method to help solve that African country's chronic water shortage cheaply and simply. The only equipment needed is a homegrown bamboo drill with an iron head and a bamboo-and-timber flywheel. The drill is driven into the ground; when the iron head strikes the water, the hollow bamboo acts as a ready-made pipe to bring water to the surface. Other bamboo pipes then carry the water away to irrigate fields at a fraction of the cost of metal plumbing.

Lighter, infinitely cheaper, and in some instances stronger than steel, bamboo would seem to have limitless potential in a world of dwindling mineral resources. We may yet see the day when bamboo finds a place in space technology—a natural enough adaptation for a plant that has played a part in so much of mankind's intriguing history.

WATER-LOGGING *In order to prepare newly cut bamboo for use, the stalks are submerged in water for up to two weeks—as on the reservoir in China at left— before being scrubbed clean with sand and left to dry for 10 days. Bamboo is so strong that it can be used as scaffolding, as seen above on a construction site in Hong Kong.*

ACID RAIN

One nation's fuel is another country's pollution

DEAD AND STUNTED trees, clear but lifeless water: the forests and lakes of western Europe are dying.

In 1984 it was estimated that in Germany alone one-third of the forests were dying and that thousands of Scandinavia's beautiful lakes were lifeless. North America, too, is suffering the same ecological mortality. In the Adirondack region of New York State, more than 200 ponds and lakes can no longer support fish life. Across the border in Ontario, Canada, some 1,200 lakes are already dead; an estimated 150,000 more are dying. And the same bleak pattern is being repeated in the rivers, streams, and forests of many other nations, including Switzerland, Britain, and Norway.

THE PRICE OF PROGRESS *Acid rain now afflicts large areas of the industrialized world, where it has resulted in poisoned waters, dying vegetation and wildlife, and damage to buildings. Although many complex factors are involved in the production of acid rain, scientists today believe that two major contributors are industrial pollution and fumes from automobile exhaust pipes.*

Nor is it only the natural world that is being destroyed. Ancient buildings, such as the Parthenon in Athens and the Colosseum in Rome, are suffering unprecedented corrosion.

The problem: pollution—acid rain in particular—caused by the burning of fossil fuels. British chemist Robert Angus Smith described the link between acid rain and pollution as early as 1872. But only recently have the effects become the subject of pressing international concern.

How acid is rain?

Because raindrops contain dissolved carbon dioxide, all rain is slightly acid. But acid rain is created when sulfur dioxide and nitrogen oxide discharged

into the air react with water vapor to form droplets of sulfuric and nitric acid. About a tenth of sulfur dioxide emissions are caused naturally by volcanic activity, forest fires, and the decay of organic matter. But the largest volume of sulfur dioxide released over North America and western Europe comes from the burning of coal, oil, gasoline, and natural gas in power stations, factories, offices, homes, and automobiles. The result: in parts of North America and western Europe rain is today as much as 100 times more acid than normal.

Acid rain may be wet or dry. Dry deposits occur when the gases, together with solid particles of sulfate and nitrate from the air, are blown by the wind and fall on the land. These pollutants stick to surfaces, attacking stonework and metals and damaging plants—especially when they combine with rain to become concentrated liquids. Wet deposits occur when the pollutants remain in the atmosphere for some days and react with water vapor to form acid rain, snow, mist, or dew. Both types are equally harmful. Prevailing winds may sometimes transport oxides thousands of miles.

Killing the planet

Although gaseous emissions from natural sources have been taking place for thousands of years, today industrialized society is literally poisoning the earth with acid rain. When it permeates the soil, plant nutrients are dissolved and washed away. As a result, trees, plants, and crops die and the soil becomes impoverished. Acid groundwater dissolves metals such as aluminum from the soil; this water then seeps into rivers and lakes. As the level of acidity rises, animal, insect, and plant life vanish. Ironically, acid lakes often look particularly beautiful; because the sterile water is barren of living organisms, it is completely clear.

Britain, the United States, the U.S.S.R., Germany, France, Czechoslovakia, Poland, and Canada produce the most acid rain, exporting much of it to their neighbors. Some estimate that the United States is responsible for 65 percent of Canada's total acid pollution, and acid rain that falls on Austria, Finland, Norway, Sweden, and Switzerland comes from beyond their borders.

Preventive measures

Various techniques have been employed to reduce emissions of toxic pollutants. The sulfur content of fuels can be reduced before burning, lower temperatures can cut down the amount of nitrogen oxides generated in furnaces, and filters can restrict pollution from power plant chimneys and automobile exhaust pipes. Individuals can also help by conserving energy in their homes.

In 1984, 20 European nations and Canada formed the 30 Percent Club. The club's aim is to reduce sulfur emissions by at least 30 percent by 1993. However, experts in some of the countries most responsible for air pollution claim that the formation of acid rain is only partly understood and that many other complex factors are involved in the destruction of lakes and forests. They therefore have asked for further research before agreeing to cost-effective plans.

The research and the concern continue. Unfortunately, so do the effects of acid rain.

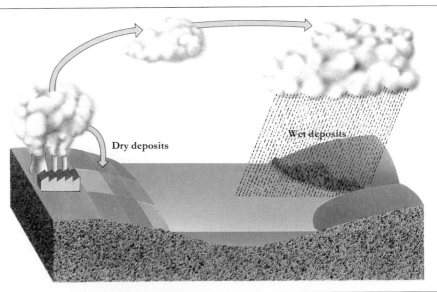

CAUSE AND EFFECT *Acid rain begins when toxic sulfur dioxide and nitric oxides emitted from industrial wastes are discharged into the air to become dry deposits or wet deposits. These then go on to poison soil and lakes, and erode building exteriors.*

Dry deposits

Wet deposits

THE YEARS THE WEATHER WENT MAD

The "child" that brought disaster

THERE WERE STRANGE OMENS everywhere. Nature itself seemed disturbed. Far from their native habitats, subtropical barracuda were swimming in the ocean off Portland, Oregon, and red crabs appeared on the beaches at San Diego, California. Areas of the Rocky Mountains had record snowfalls. Farther south, in Ecuador, unseasonal torrential rains destroyed 800 houses, ruined the rice and banana crops, and washed away roads and bridges. In Peru, fishermen sat idle, for the shoals of anchovy had vanished from the ocean. The sea had become unusually warm.

Even then, few people realized the extent of the devastation that was yet to come. But 12 months later the world took stock of the havoc.

Thousands were dead in Africa from drought and famine. In Australia the century's worst drought had cost farmers $2.5 billion in dead stock, and an entire township and 75 inhabitants had perished in bush fires. Freak hurricanes had devastated islands in the Pacific.

These were not scenes from a disaster movie, but statistics from 1982 and 1983, the years the weather went mad. The cause: *El Niño*, a complex interaction of wind and water that stretches the breadth of the South Pacific.

The face of the deep

El Niño, the Spanish term for the Christ Child, is the name given by fishermen to the mild warming up of the ocean that occurs off northern Peru and Ecuador every year around Christmastime. The change occurs as the cool, northward-flowing Peru Current is displaced by a warmer stream that flows southward. Its usual effect is to drive fish, especially tuna and anchovy, away from the coastal fishing grounds for a while, since the plankton on which the fish feed need cold water.

The shift in the ocean currents is related to two centers of atmospheric pressure located near Easter Island in the eastern South Pacific and over Indonesia and northern Australia in the west.

High atmospheric pressure maintains hot, dry weather in the east; low pressure creates wetter, cooler conditions in the west. Between the two zones, easterly winds blow warm water away from

EL NIÑO *In the normal weather pattern over the Pacific Ocean (top, right), a zone of low pressure in the west draws winds in from a high pressure zone in the east. Currents of warm water then flow west. But every few years this pattern changes (bottom, right) and the low pressure zone moves to the east, weakening the high. Currents of warm water then reverse their direction and flow east. Known as* El Niño, *the phenomenon can have potentially catastrophic effects on weather and on marine life worldwide.*

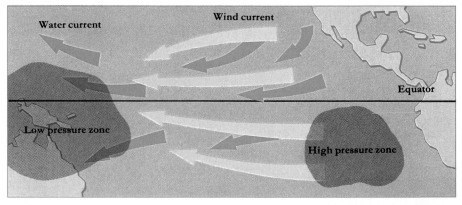

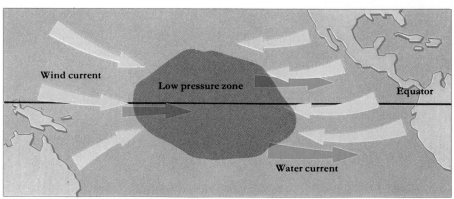

the coast of South America. When the trade winds intensify, the difference in pressure between the two areas evens out. Then the winds relax, and warm water—*El Niño*—begins to sweep back toward Peru. But occasionally, and unpredictably, *El Niño* takes place on a grand scale—with catastrophic consequences around the world.

No two alike

It happened in 1982 and 1983, and was made worse because there was no warning. *El Niño* did not wait for the trade winds to blow more intensely, and meteorologists could not predict the sudden evening-out of atmospheric pressure and the dramatic rise in ocean temperature that quickly followed in the east. The scale of the change threw weather systems all over the globe out of balance; it even affected the northern Atlantic, where the number of icebergs increased and threatened many of the deep-sea oil rigs off Newfoundland.

Although scientists formerly believed that *El Niño* was a consistent phenomenon with occasional surges in intensity that could be detected at an early stage, they have concluded, reluctantly, that its real cause remains unknown.

Today a 10-year research program is under way in an attempt to unravel the intriguing mystery of this disruptive force. But the complexity of the problem is immense, for both the atmosphere and the oceans are inherently unstable and changeable. As one leading oceanographer wryly observed: "Weather is always abnormal."

MYSTERIOUS IMAGES

Nature abounds with images that are reminiscent of something else. Known as simulacra, these visual coincidences are found in such natural phenomena as clouds and rock formations, and the images are often venerated. One of the best-known examples can be found in the outcrop known as Camel Rock, near Santa Fe, New Mexico (below). And a common simulacrum is that of Christ; the example at right was photographed in snow.

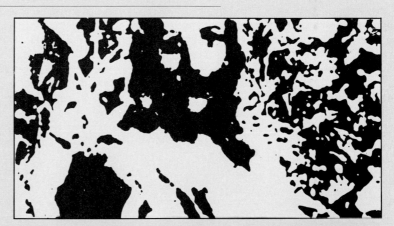

ROCK OF AGES

A missing link in a billion-year gap

IN 1983 A GROUP of geologists and geophysicists from the Australian National University in Canberra discovered what may be the oldest rocks in the world.

Using an ion microprobe—an instrument that can date a rock fragment by investigating changes in its radioactivity—the scientists analyzed ancient sandstone from the Mount Narryer region in Western Australia. They discovered tiny crystals of the mineral zircon dating back 4.2 billion years, 400 million years older than any previously discovered rocks. Further investigations on rocks in the same area confirmed their findings; some samples even indicated ages of 4.3 billion years—100 million years earlier.

The tiny fragments are so old that they may have been among the very first rocks to have been formed when a molten globe was cooling from the gas cloud that gave birth to our solar system.

Out of the clouds

Scientists believe that the earth—and the rest of the solar system too—emerged from a cosmic gas cloud 5 billion to 6 billion years ago. About a billion years elapsed before the gas cloud cooled and condensed enough to allow the first minerals to crystallize. These early rocks formed as a crust on the surface of the still hot and gaseous globe. Violent upheavals from deep within the earth melted and cracked the newly formed crust again and again, until enough heat had been released for the crust to solidify and form the land masses.

Until the discovery in Western Australia, evidence for the formation and appearance of the earliest rocks of earth has been incomplete: no rocks have been found that are old enough to provide proof of these early events. Therefore, scientists have had to look elsewhere for evidence of the age of the earth.

Synchronicity

It is known that the earth, moon, planets, and meteorites were formed at approximately the same time. By measuring the amount of radioactive decay in meteorite fragments found on earth, geologists have dated meteorites to about 4.6 billion years. This figure has been matched by moon rocks thought to be part of the moon's original crust—also dated as 4.6 billion years old. The amount of argon (a gas created by the radioactive decay of potassium) in the earth's atmosphere points to the same age for the earth as well.

Until 1983 the world's oldest known rock was a pebble of lava found at Isua, Greenland. Identified in 1971, it was dated at 3.8 billion years, indicating that by that time the earth already had a solid crust. But there remained a tantalizing gap of almost a billion years in the rock record.

Today that gap has been partly filled. The grains of 4.2-billion-year-old zircon in Western Australia provide tangible proof. Until any earlier rocks are found, the discovery presents scientists with a unique opportunity to study the history and evolution of the earth's crust.

WOODEN FIGURES

Reviving an ancient art

IN GILROY, CALIFORNIA, a specially constructed theme park features the life's work of farmer Alex Erlandson: 30 trees grow in the park, each of them unique.

The collection of trees Erlandson planted includes no normal specimens. Each grows in a bizarre and fantastic pattern. Some trees have branches that loop; others have double trunks that spiral around each other or cross in zigzags. One has a single trunk that grows into nine "legs"; another has multiple trunks that regularly part and rejoin in a lacelike pattern.

But Erlandson did not simply bend or train these trees into shapes. To achieve his spectacular effects he grafted branches and even entire trees together, making each design an intricate, living whole.

Grafting technique

Erlandson first became fascinated with the idea of shaping trees after noticing how the branches of certain species would graft onto each other as a result of prolonged contact. Taking advantage of this fact of nature to develop his living sculptures, he unwittingly recreated pleaching. This technique had been common in medieval Europe both as an ornamental device and as a practical means of making hedges tough, dense, and animalproof. The word *pleaching* means "braiding" or "weaving"— an apt description of Erlandson's singular designs.

When Erlandson reinvented the art in the 1940's, pleaching had long been forgotten, even in Europe. Working by trial and error, he stripped bark from the parts of branches that he wanted to graft together, exposing the layer of tissue from which both bark and wood develop. He then bent the branches into the desired shape and bound them together with cloth tape.

To train young trees into the shapes he wanted, Erlandson built frames of zigzags, spirals, and diamonds, and bent the trees to grow around them. Sometimes he would plant several trees at once, form a pattern from the young trunks, and then graft them together to form a single trunk above his design. Or he would divide a single trunk into a pattern of branches and then reunite them.

By 1963 Erlandson had created some 80 trees, and earned a modest living from visitors who paid to see his Tree Circus in Scott's Valley near Santa Cruz, California. But at the age of 79 he found the work too demanding, and decided to sell the Tree Circus and retire.

Memories of Erlandson's work faded until the late 1970's, when landscape gardener Joseph Cahill drew attention to the trees. Untended for years, they were threatened by plans to redevelop the site. In 1984 businessman Michael Donsante bought the 30 trees that had survived the years of neglect, shipped them in trucks to their present home in Gilroy, and replanted them. And so, a major portion of Erlandson's remarkable work lives on.

GRAFTING AWAY *In the 1940's Alex Erlandson resurrected the ancient craft of pleaching, a highly skilled grafting technique common in medieval Europe. By grafting the branches of different trees with the aid of a frame, he created a unique collection of extraordinary sculptures known as the Tree Circus. Needle and Thread, the specimen illustrated, is a fine example of Erlandson's distinctive style.*

TREASURES UNDER THE SEA

Some jewels of the ocean

THE SUN GLINTS on the blue ocean as the pearl fisher casts anchor. A flash of white. A human figure dives into the deep water. After 50 seconds or more, the *ama,* or Japanese pearl diver, reemerges, triumphantly bearing her prize: a netful of oysters.

All over the world divers risk their lives in the perilous business of retrieving pearls from the bottom of the sea. In Japan the *amas* are always women; they plunge as deep as 40 feet with nothing more to protect them from the sharks, sea eels, and jellyfish than the hook-nosed iron knife they use to dislodge the oysters.

Pearl-producing oysters are also found in the Persian Gulf, the Gulf of Manaar (the stretch of water that lies between India and Sri Lanka), and the Red Sea, as well as the Great Barrier Reef off Australia's eastern coast. In many of these places, notably Sri Lanka, pearl divers still use traditional methods; elsewhere, sophisticated equipment, such as scuba gear, has made their task easier.

Self-defense

From the outside, oysters give no hint of the treasure they may conceal. The shell—gray, gnarled, and frequently misshapen—contains a moist, fleshy, living oyster, surrounded by flaps of tissue called the mantle. Nature has devised a way of protecting the oyster's delicate body: the mantle secretes a substance called nacre that covers the inner shell surface in a smooth layer known as mother-of-pearl.

Pearls are formed from the same material. The oyster feeds by opening its shell slightly and sucking in plankton, the tiny organisms that drift through the ocean. Occasionally, however, it sucks in something less desirable—perhaps a grain of sand or a small piece of shell. To protect itself against such uninvited guests, the oyster simply covers the offending particle with layer upon layer of mother-of-pearl. Sometimes the oysters have been found with tiny fish perfectly rendered in mother-of-pearl.

Most pearls are white, ranging to delicate pink. But they come in many other colors, too, depending upon the pigments in the nacre: black, blue, and golden yellow pearls are greatly prized.

Real or imitation?

But by no means do all oysters produce pearls. On average, in a haul of three tons of oysters only three or four shells contain good pearls. But in Japan around the turn of the 20th century a reliable way of cultivating pearls was discovered. Today, with a little human intervention, almost all oysters can be made to yield.

Cultured pearls are produced by inserting a perfectly spherical artificial irritant into the oyster's body. The oysters are then carefully tended in special beds until the pearls are ready—usually three to six years later.

Essentially, cultured pearls are formed in the same way that natural pearls are, and it is almost impossible to tell the two apart. The only ways to distinguish between them are to dissect the pearl or X-ray it: the one with a completely round original center is cultivated.

PEARLY DEPTHS *A pearl diver with his catch, a* Pinctada maxima *oyster—one of the largest pearl-bearing types. Until recently divers worked with primitive equipment to retrieve the oysters from the ocean bed.*

Imitation pearls vary widely. Some are made from high-quality materials, such as mother-of-pearl, conch, and coral; others, simply from glass beads coated with a solution containing fish scales, known as *essence d'Orient*. These can make acceptable jewelry. But unlike genuine pearls, whether natural or cultured, imitation pearls do not have the same weight, their surface is smoother, and in time their luster will dim.

Neither do false pearls command the same price. But through genetic engineering techniques, now in their infancy, it may become possible to keep the mantle tissue alive in a test tube. If so, an amazing prospect may open up: the cost of cultured pearls may tumble to a lower level, and we may, at last, be able to purchase laboratory-grown pearls at a more affordable price.

ENDLESS STRING *The variations in shape, size, and color of pearls are almost infinite. The black pearl at right, center, is surrounded by three "blisters" (semispherical pearls) and freshwater pearls. Top: A worker at the Naga Pearl Farm in Thailand selects "blisters" according to size.*

THE SURPRISING ANIMAL KINGDOM

THE RAVENOUS MILLIONS

Death and destruction follow man's oldest enemy

ON JULY 28, 1962, radar operators at the Indian National Physical Laboratory in Delhi sounded the alarm. They had spotted a gigantic airborne invasion in progress, and the enemy was already only 60 miles south of the city.

Specialized emergency teams were instantly alerted. India and her traditionally hostile neighbor, Pakistan, joined forces: aircraft from both countries roared into action, flying only 65 feet above the ground in a skillful counterattack. The initial battle raged for a week; sporadic fighting continued until December, when the two countries declared themselves victorious. The enemy dead numbered more than 100 *billion*.

It had been no human invasion, but a far more fearsome and rapacious threat: locusts. Using chemicals sprayed from aircraft, humans wreaked havoc with these prodigiously destructive pests. But throughout most of history it has been people who have suffered most.

The earliest written record of a locust plague is probably in the Book of Exodus, which describes an attack that took place in Egypt about 3500 B.C.:

"They covered the face of the whole earth, so that the land was darkened . . . and there remained not any green thing in the trees, or in the herbs of the field, through all the land of Egypt." Another biblical account, in the Book of Joel, describes trees "made white" as locusts even stripped the bark from the branches.

A voracious appetite

Locusts have always spelled disaster. In 125 B.C. they destroyed the grain crop in northern Africa; 80,000 people died of starvation. In A.D. 591 a plague of locusts in Italy caused the deaths of more than a million people and animals. In 1613 disaster struck the French region of La Camargue when locusts ate enough grass in a single day to feed 4,000 cattle for a year. The Nile Valley suffered in 1889 when locusts so thoroughly destroyed crops that even the mice starved in their wake. Between 1949 and 1963 locust swarms in Africa caused an estimated $100 million worth of damage annually. In 1958 the Ethiopian cereal crop was laid waste, leaving a million people without food.

Until this century, locust plagues were as unpredictable as they were catastrophic. Swarms of locusts appeared as if from nowhere and vanished just as mysteriously. But in the 1920's scientists observed that wherever the locusts disappeared, bands of wingless grasshoppers took their place.

Careful observation showed that the two creatures were the same: the hoppers were in fact young locusts. Heavy rainfall provided an ideal climate for breeding and often resulted in a population explosion. The grasshoppers, feeding voraciously, soon underwent a transformation into the gregarious winged locusts that hunt in millions, flying with the prevailing winds in search of food.

Predicting the threat

Such studies made it possible to predict when and where the insects would swarm, and today the red-legged locust and the African migratory locust have been brought under control. A third species,

the desert locust, remains an international threat, with potential predation stretching across 60 countries, from the Atlantic to the Indian Ocean.

The scale of the problem becomes even more apparent in light of the desert locust's appetite. An individual locust weighs only about one-tenth of an ounce, but it will consume its own weight in food every 24 hours. The largest swarm ever recorded, more than 300 billion locusts in South Africa in 1784, covered an estimated 2,000 square miles. This seething mass was capable of devouring 600,000 tons of food a day. Fortunately, the locusts were blown out to sea and destroyed by a storm. The bodies washed up by the tide formed a bank along the shore 4 feet high and 50 miles long.

Even the smallest swarms of desert locusts rarely contain fewer than 100 million insects able to consume 200 tons of food a day. As long as the locust breeds, the food supply for hundreds of millions of people remains at risk.

Senegal Grasshopper
Desert Locust
Migratory Locust
Red Locust
Brown Locust

AERIAL INVASION *In 1986–87 Africa suffered the worst plague of locusts in 50 years. Five different species of locust and grasshopper were breeding, hatching, feeding, and swarming at the same time. Threatened with a famine as devastating as that created by the drought of 1985, authorities used aerial spraying and other measures to prevent the locusts from destroying all the crops. The most affected areas are highlighted on the map.*

THE UNGAINLY OSTRICH

A much misunderstood bird

AT MORE THAN eight feet tall and a weight of about 300 pounds, the ostrich is one of nature's oddities. The largest of all birds, it cannot fly. Its huge body is precariously balanced on two long legs, each supported by only two toes, one of them so small as to appear to be virtually useless. At the top of the ostrich's lengthy neck is a small, flattened head with a short beak, very large eyes, and conspicuous eyelashes. It is not surprising that many erroneous tales have grown up around such an ungainly creature.

Clever tactics

Although the ostrich's brain is smaller than one of its eyes, the bird is not stupid. Contrary to popular belief, it does not bury its head in the sand when faced with danger; rather, it sits down and stretches its neck out along the ground, a ploy it also uses while guarding the nest. To a predator, an ostrich in this position can look like just another grassy mound. The dull-brown-colored hen guards the nest during the day, when her feathers blend best into the surrounding terrain; the black male guards the nest at night.

On the go, however, an ostrich is not so clever. Although it can stride in 14-foot paces at more than 30 miles an hour, easily outdistancing most of its enemies, the ostrich sometimes prefers to run around in circles.

The bird's eating habits are almost legendary. Although it lives mainly on grass, leaves, and fruit, and swallows stones and pebbles as an aid to digestion, it will eat almost anything. It finds shiny objects particularly attractive, and happily gulps down watches, jewelry, and bits of glass and metal without visible ill effects.

Approach with caution

Today most ostriches are born in captivity and are farmed in their native Africa for their meat, feathers, and hide, which makes a good-quality leather. They can be domesticated, and some have even been trained for riding and for pulling carts.

But the ostrich is a far from perfect choice for these social chores, since it is a rather bad-tempered and aggressive bird. A single kick from one of its powerful legs can break a human leg or put a right-angle bend in an iron bar half an inch thick. Farmers approach an ostrich with caution, but they have found that putting a paper bag over its head has a calming effect, which lends some believability to the head-in-the-sand myth.

SHARKS BEWARE!

The strange powers of a fish

ACCORDING TO LEGEND, when Moses parted the waters of the Red Sea so that the Israelites could flee from the Egyptians, a small fish was caught in the middle and split in two; the halves became flatfish—and are known to this day as Moses soles.

But the truth about the Moses sole (*Pardachirus marmoratus*), which flourishes in the Gulf of Aqaba between the Sinai Peninsula and Saudi Arabia, is much stranger. In self-defense this little fish secretes a milky substance that is lethal to other sea creatures. The poison, pardaxin, is produced in glands along its rear fins.

Scientists have found that just one part of pardaxin in 5,000 parts of seawater is enough to kill mollusks, sea urchins, and small fish. When a group of researchers placed a Moses sole into a pool with two white-tip sharks, the sharks made a dive for the fish and then retreated, their jaws agape as if the sharks were unable to close them. Because it enters the shark's bloodstream and causes paralysis, pardaxin seems to be the ideal shark repellent.

Common power

In theory pardaxin could be used by divers as protection against sharks. But not only are there not enough soles to provide the poison in the required quantity, its chemistry is too complex to produce it artificially. However, researchers have found that pardaxin lowers the surface tension of water, just as household detergent does. Additional tests indicate that some common detergents scare off sharks as effectively as pardaxin.

If this theory proves reliable, possibly in the future divers in shark-infested waters will arm themselves with a bottle of dishwashing detergent.

A REGAL JOURNEY

The incredible migration of the monarch butterfly

WITH ITS LARGE WINGS distinctively marked in a brilliant pattern of orange and black, the North American monarch butterfly is a splendid sight. But the most remarkable feature of the monarch is its epic annual migration, a journey that can take it from as far north as states in New England or the shores of Lake Superior in the Midwest to the Sierra Madre in the heart of Mexico—distances as great as 2,000 miles.

More amazing still is that generation after generation of these butterflies find their way back to the same place on the other side of the continent year after year. How do they do it?

Mass exodus

The monarchs' migratory pattern is unusual. During spring and summer they lead solitary lives, but as fall approaches they band together in huge swarms and set out to the south to escape the killing frosts of winter.

COMMUNAL ROOST *Every year millions of monarch butterflies in the United States escape the rigors of winter by heading south to the wooded slopes of the Sierra Madre Mountains in Mexico. Literally thousands of butterflies come to rest on a single tree, where they cling, in a semidormant state, in clusters that resemble pale, dead leaves.*

With a strong, gliding flight, the butterflies complete their journey in just three to four weeks. Unlike most other species, monarchs do not really flutter; they flap their wings once or twice and then coast on the wind. In this way they can cross long, open stretches without rest, reaching speeds up to 30 miles an hour.

Monarchs seem to navigate by the sun and sometimes orient to a distant landmark or follow landscape features, such as mountains or rivers. To reach Mexico some groups fly the length of Florida and eventually reach the Yucatán Peninsula. But the majority follow an almost diagonal path, flying from northeast to southwest across the United

States through Texas. Finally, the butterflies converge on the wooded slopes of the Sierra Madre.

In this spectacular hideaway, millions of monarch butterflies congregate for the single winter of their brief lives, covering every inch of the stately oyamel fir trees. The conditions are ideal. At 9,000 feet above sea level, the cold temperatures enable the creatures to remain in an inactive, semidormant state so that they expend none of the energy reserves they will need for the return flight.

In January, as the sunlight increases, the monarchs begin to stir and spread their wings in readiness for the spring exodus. At the equinox, toward the end of March, they leave the communal roost one by one for the long, meandering journey north.

As the days lengthen, the butterflies start to mate. The females lay their eggs during their gradual northern migration. But since few of the adults survive long enough to complete the return trip, it is the offspring that continue the journey north: up to five new generations of monarchs will emerge during the summer months.

What instinct brings them together, and what is it that will guide those summer generations back to a remote mountain enclave as far as 2,000 miles away? So far, those mysteries remain impenetrable.

KING RAT

Will these rodents inherit the earth?

SOON AFTER World War II, the island of Engebi in the western Pacific was selected by the United States as a testing site for nuclear weapons. As a result, plants, animals, birds, and fish were completely destroyed or severely damaged by intensive radiation. When scientists ventured onto Engebi a few years later, they did not expect to find any normal, healthy life there.

They were mistaken. Rats emerged from their burrows, fit as ever and with an even longer life span than they had before.

Superrat

Fear of the "superrat" is a staple of many horror movies, and with good reason. Rats have a phenomenal capacity to adapt and survive. Many groups of rats have already become immune to warfarin, a poison that prevents their blood clotting so that they bleed to death internally. Rats have adapted by developing blood that clots despite the poison; today they actually *need* to eat warfarin regularly to keep it from clotting too much.

Rats are versatile and tough. They can squeeze through a hole the size of a quarter, climb almost any vertical surface, burrow through the earth, swim almost a mile even against a strong current, tread water for up to three days, jump as high as three feet, and drop from a height of 45 feet. Rats can kill quarry more than twice their own size, and they can chew through live electrical cable.

In addition, they seem to be intelligent, although it is more likely that they are just extremely wary. Legends about their shrewdness abound, but these are probably greatly exaggerated, the result of an age-old, and well-founded, fear.

In 1348, rats brought the plague to Europe. They traveled in the holds of ships sailing from ports on the Black Sea to Genoa and carried the bacterium on fleas that lived in their coats. It is difficult to imagine the vast scope and the horror of the Black Death. The epidemic raged for three years and killed 25 million people, a quarter of the population of Europe. Over the next few decades, that number more than doubled. It can be said that rats changed the history of the world.

Today rats continue to spread disease. They are responsible for typhus, trichinosis, Lassa fever, and salmonella. At the same time, they are valuable in testing new drugs in medical research. Docile when captive, rats require little space, reproduce very quickly, and will eat anything.

Public Enemy No. 1?

Rats also wreak enormous damage. In the United States, they gnaw through more than $1 billion worth of property a year. Countless buildings are destroyed by fire because the rodents have stripped electrical cables with their teeth.

In the country, rats feast on grain crops, chickens, ducks, geese, and even young lambs and pigs; in cities they gorge on garbage. In Asia rats pillage some 48 million tons of rice a year.

Rats may be man's worst enemy, but in some ways man is the rat's best friend. Humans provide the warmth, shelter, and food on which rats thrive. And rats' amazing capacity for reproduction always ensures that, no matter how many are eliminated, the next generation will quickly replace them. One male and one female can have as many as 15,000 descendants in a single year.

THE LIVING HELICOPTER

The tiny hummingbird of the Americas, with its jewellike iridescent coloring, has long been admired. Some of these exquisite blue-and-green birds are little more than two inches long, and milliners have been known to trim hats with them.

But the hummingbird, of which there are more than 320 different species, is remarkable for far more than its decorative qualities. Its flying abilities are unique: the man-made helicopter is the only other flying object that comes near to matching the bird's versatility.

Unlike most other birds, the hummingbird's wings have particularly long "hand" bones to which the flight feathers are attached. These unusual wings can move in many directions in much the same way as the human wrist. This flexibility allows the bird to keep its body perfectly still while hovering. Its wings move very fast—up to 78 beats a second—in a figure-eight shape; all that can be seen is a propellerlike blur that creates the characteristic hum for which the bird is named.

All directions

The action of its wings also enables the bird to fly backward, forward, and upside down; to accelerate to full speed at takeoff; and to stop abruptly when it arrives at its destination.

The hummingbird's extraordinary hovering ability enables it to obtain its staple food: nectar. The many species of the bird have evolved side by side with certain flowers; the shape of the bill of each type of hummingbird matches the shape of the particular flower it feeds on.

GIVE AND TAKE *When the hummingbird pushes its long bill inside a flower in order to extract nectar with its tubelike tongue, the top of its head is dusted with pollen. The bird then carries the pollen to another flower.*

While feeding, the hummingbird pollinates the flowers, and as the bird extracts the nectar with its long, extendable tongue, it collects traces of pollen that are transferred to the next flower it visits. Seemingly motionless and hanging in midair, the hummingbird inserts its bill deep inside the flower, extracts the nectar, and then gently withdraws by moving backward.

WHIRLYBIRD *The unique figure-eight motion of a hummingbird's wings enables it to hover up, down, backward, forward, and even upside down.*

THE NOT SO MIGHTY MONGOOSE

In *The Jungle Book,* Rudyard Kipling tells the story of Rikki-Tikki-Tavi, an Indian mongoose that becomes a household pet. Among Rikki's more memorable adventures is his fight with two cobras, Nag and Nagina, which he eventually kills. In telling the tale, Kipling was drawing on a popular belief that the mongoose and the cobra are sworn enemies, and that in any fight the mongoose always wins.

But the truth is somewhat different. Mongooses will kill and then eat almost anything—small rodents, birds, shellfish, eggs, fruit—but snakes are not a major part of their diet. Indeed, one Indian species of mongoose eats almost nothing but crabs, while an African species feasts on crocodile eggs.

So reluctant is the mongoose to engage the cobra in battle that Indian snake charmers sometimes stage fights between the two just to see what happens. The quick-footed mongoose is usually able to overpower the slower-witted cobra, and can use its sharp teeth to break the cobra's back. But when this tactic does not succeed, the mongoose is swiftly killed by the venomous bite of the cobra. Contrary to popular belief, it is not immune to snake venom.

It seems that Rikki-Tikki-Tavi had more than his share of luck.

IN AN EGGSHELL

Nature's complex life-support system

FROM SHAPE TO CONTENT, every feature of the chicken's egg is an example of perfect construction. Its shape is its strength, just as curving domes or arches in a building give it support. Despite the delicate thinness of the shell, a hen's egg is quite tough—too tough, it is said, to be broken by one hand squeezing the two ends.

The egg's five principal parts provide the entire life-support system for the developing bird. Made entirely of calcium carbonate, the shell provides firm support for the rest of the egg and supplies the chick with calcium.

Breath of life

But however tough and protective, the eggshell is still porous. Just as an animal needs to breathe, so does an egg. Consequently, the shell has hundreds of tiny pores that allow moisture to evaporate and oxygen to replace it. This maintains a perfect balance: as the chick matures and its oxygen needs increase, the water content recedes. In the 21 days it takes for an egg to incubate, it will absorb more than 8 pints of oxygen and release about 7 pints of carbon dioxide and $17\frac{1}{2}$ pints of water vapor.

The shell membranes line the inside of the shell. The two layers of membrane lie close to each other except at the larger end of the egg, where they separate and create an air pocket. A newly laid egg contains no air pocket; however, the longer an egg is kept, and the more water and gas that escape from it, the larger the pocket becomes.

It might seem that nothing could be less interesting than albumen, or egg white. It is, in fact, quite complex—as well as being vital to the developing embryo. Albumen contains many crucial proteins, stores water so that the yolk does not dry out, and offers insulation against any sudden changes in outside temperature.

Egg white is made up of four different layers, alternatively thick and thin. Twisted like rope at each end of the yolk, the last thick layer, the chalaza, helps anchor the yolk and keep it centered as the growing chick feeds off it. The yolk itself is a mixture of proteins, fats, and carbohydrates suspended in a watery yellow medium. Everything is held in a sac, known as the vitelline membrane; it keeps the yolk and white from mixing but at the same time allows water, salts, some sugars, and even necessary proteins to pass from white to yolk.

Finally comes the most important part, the germ. About the size of a pinhead, it is this tiny blob, sitting on top of the yolk, that eventually develops into a new chick.

Not one part of the egg is superfluous. Everything exists to protect and nourish the developing life within. It is not difficult to understand why, in so many cultures, the egg is a time-honored symbol of birth and renewal.

THE LANGUAGE OF DANCE

The bee-wildering world of the honeybee

ANYONE who has ever looked into a beehive must have asked himself how such a confusing mass of insects manages to work with such efficiency to produce honey. The answer: bees have abilities out of proportion to their size.

Bees are highly developed insects, with sophisticated systems of organization and communication. Even though the population of some colonies is as large as 60,000, each individual bee works as part of a team, knowing exactly what needs to be done—and when.

An efficient worker state

A typical colony consists of three types of bees: queen, drones, and workers. The majority are workers. The queen is the only fertile female, and her sole function is to lay eggs. All the drones are males; their main task is to fertilize the queen. The jobs of the workers, or remaining females, are much more complex. Each has several definite, specialized duties to perform. There are, for example, cleaning bees, brood nurses that care for the growing larvae, building bees, guard bees, and bees that collect pollen and nectar.

Each worker bee performs all these tasks in a sequence that is determined by age. Thus the young bee's first job is to clean the cells of the hive for about three days. As she gets older, she progresses in turn to nursing, building, storing, guarding, and foraging. This arrangement also allows for some flexibility. Each worker takes it upon herself to patrol and inspect the hive at regular intervals to see what has to be done. If, for example, there is more need for nursing or foraging at a particular time, the worker will adapt accordingly.

An essential factor in the efficiency of the bees is their ability to communicate with one another. Like other insects, they accomplish this primarily by transmitting their own chemical messages called pheromones—odors secreted from various glands in the body. Each odor tells its own story, and together they form a powerful language.

Food dancing

Honeybees have another, more unusual way of communicating: through food dances. When a foraging bee finds a food source, she must let the other bees know its location as soon as possible. If the source is nearby, she will perform the relatively simple but energetic round dance, involving a series of rapid circles. This will signal the other bees to search in the vicinity of the hive. If the source is farther away, more information is needed, and the more complicated waggle dance—consisting of a figure eight with the loops separated by a straight run—is employed. That honeybees manage to understand such a complicated code is amazing, yet scientists have devised experiment after experiment that proves that the bees do understand.

After the food has been gathered, it must be properly stored. Regardless of what the temperature is outside, inside the hive it must remain at a constant 95°F. Surprisingly, the bees are up to the challenge. If it is very warm, the insects spread tiny droplets of water over the food cells. As the water evaporates, it cools the air in the hive. On the other hand, if it is very cold, the workers cluster together to reduce heat loss.

Although scientists have long marveled at the honeybee, they are a long way from understanding it fully. How, for instance, do bees manage to construct the near-flawless hexagonal cells that make up the honeycombs? Such delicacy might challenge the ingenuity of many a human architect.

The more we discover about this extraordinary and intelligent insect, the more we realize how little we really know.

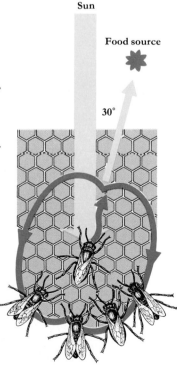

WAGGLE DANCE *When a forager bee wants to let her fellow workers know the location of a food source, she performs a waggle dance on the face of the honeycomb. The dance takes the form of the figure eight in which the two loops are separated by a straight run. The bee wags her body only on the straight run. Using the sun as a reference point, the forager uses the path of the run to indicate the location of the food. A straight run indicates that the food is in the direction of the sun; if she runs 30° to the right of the vertical, the food is 30° to the right of the sun. Once the direction is indicated, the other bees will immediately follow the forager bee to the food.*

Sun

Food source

30°

DEADLIER THAN THE MALE

Fireflies do not glow in the dark—they flash. Males flash to attract a mate, and females flash back a reassuring response.

A firefly's "lamp" at the end of its tail contains a concentration of luciferin, a chemical pigment that produces light after reacting with the enzyme luciferase and the oxygen breathed by the insect.

Each species of firefly has its own particular code for attracting a mate. The signals may be long or short, simple or complex; the time lapses in between are just as important as the number and length of the flashes themselves. Most firefly suitors will ignore the flashes sent out by fireflies of different species. But there is one deadly exception.

The female of the *Photuris* genus is known as the *femme fatale* of the firefly world. She habitually mimics the signals of *Photinus* females in order to lure their males. But when a male responds, his reception is far from an amorous one: the *Photuris* female promptly grasps her unsuspecting victim and eats him.

The behavior of this particular female firefly is doubly remarkable because adult fireflies rarely, if ever, eat anything. However, a number of these female cannibals have been found to be carrying eggs at the time they attack. It may be that they need extra protein at such a time—and have found an expedient and seemingly effective way to acquire it.

HOME IS WHERE THE HEART IS

How felines find their way

CATS MAY LIKE TO STAY out at night, but they almost always come home. In fact, some have taken their liking for familiar surroundings to extremes. Numerous stories tell of cats who move to a new house with their owners only to return to their old haunts a few days later. And some cats find their way back to their "real" home even after journeys of hundreds of miles. How do they do it?

Apparently, cats navigate by the sun. On home ground they register where the sun is positioned in the sky at certain times of the day. If a cat is lost or far from home, it works by trial and error until it finds the place where the position of the sun matches what is lodged in its memory. By then the cat has probably recognized the familiar landmarks and smells of its own territory as well.

A sixth sense?

But there is another class of cats with an ability that has no explanation. These cats do not find their way back to a familiar place, but are able to track down their owners when they have moved to completely new locations.

When a doctor and his family moved from Poughkeepsie, New York, to Livermore, California, in 1959, they left their cat, Sparky, behind. Nine months later Sparky turned up in Livermore. A crook in his tail, the unusual color of his eyes, and the pattern of his fur confirmed his identity.

Smoky, a three-year-old Persian cat, was traveling with his owners from Tulsa, Oklahoma, to their new home in Memphis. At a rest stop only 18 miles from Tulsa, Smoky wandered off and could not be found. A year later he appeared at the new house in Memphis. There was no doubt that it was Smoky: a distinctive tuft of dark red fur under his chin and a curious habit of joining the daughter of the family at the piano while she played convinced the owners that this was the same Smoky they had lost in the outskirts of Tulsa.

Sweet journey

The most celebrated traveling cat is probably Sugar, who belonged to the Woods family in Anderson, California. In 1951 the Woodses moved to a farm in Gage, Oklahoma, but had to leave Sugar behind because the cat refused to travel in the family car. A neighbor adopted the cat, but after three weeks Sugar vanished.

Thirteen months later Sugar announced his arrival in Gage by leaping onto Mrs. Woods's shoulder. At first she thought the cat was simply a look-alike, but the cream-colored Persian had a peculiar deformity of the hipbone, just as Sugar had. His 1,500-mile journey had not been in vain.

LIFE UNDERFOOT

A cast of billions

A HANDFUL OF soil may not look very exciting; it is unlikely that it will show any signs of life. However, in fact it is a stage on which is featured a cast of billions. One ounce of soil can contain as many as 70 billion bacteria.

Basically, soil is a mixture of finely ground rock particles and humus, the organic material that is in the process of decaying. The spaces between the particles are filled with air and water, which house microscopic plants and animals. The wealth of life in a tiny bit of soil is staggering.

The smallest organisms are the bacteria; they act as decomposers, gradually breaking down organic material to create humus.

Next in size are the protozoans. These simple one-celled animals are of three kinds: ciliates, amoebas, and flagellates. Protozoans live on the bacteria and are themselves eaten by larger animals. A one-ounce sample of soil yields some 560 ciliates, 42,000 amoebas, and 900,000 flagellates.

Star part

Worms in the soil include the nematodes, many of which can be seen only with a microscope. It has been estimated that an acre of good farm soil may contain several billion nematodes. At the other end of the scale are the familiar earthworms. Earthworms play a major role in churning up the soil; as they tunnel their burrows, they break down organic matter and introduce air. Some worms have even confused archeologists by raising buried artifacts from the layer of soil in which they were originally deposited to higher layers.

Insects, also, are found in the soil in large numbers, often in the immature or larval forms that will later fly. But some forms, such as the protura (which include primitive springtails and bristletails), are wingless. Of the larger insects, many species of termites and ants live in the soil. The population of their colonies can range from fewer than 50 to more than 700,000.

Some mites and spiders live within the soil too. But most are found on the surface, sometimes in great numbers. One field in southern England was found to have more than 2 million spiders per acre, feeding on the springtails and other insects. One naturalist calculated that the weight of the insects that the spiders of Britain eat every year is greater than the total weight of the human population—an amazing amount, considering that approximately 55 million people live in the British Isles.

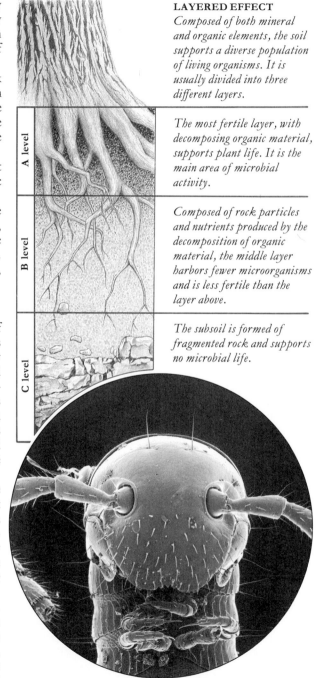

LAYERED EFFECT
Composed of both mineral and organic elements, the soil supports a diverse population of living organisms. It is usually divided into three different layers.

A level
The most fertile layer, with decomposing organic material, supports plant life. It is the main area of microbial activity.

B level
Composed of rock particles and nutrients produced by the decomposition of organic material, the middle layer harbors fewer microorganisms and is less fertile than the layer above.

C level
The subsoil is formed of fragmented rock and supports no microbial life.

SCIENCE FICTION MONSTER? *The majority of the creatures living in the soil are invisible to the naked eye. Above is the head of a typical soil organism, the millipede, magnified 130 times.*

THE LIFE-GIVING SNAKES

Snake venom is often dangerous, sometimes lethal. But it can also be lifesaving.

For many years the venom of the Russell's viper has been used to stop bleeding in hemophiliacs, whose blood lacks the ability to clot. But a chance discovery in 1960 of the effects of another snake venom is today helping to achieve the opposite result by dissolving blood clots, the cause of so many serious illnesses.

While working in Malaysia, a British doctor from the Liverpool School of Tropical Medicine was called upon to treat a patient who had been bitten by the deadly Malayan pit viper. He noticed that the victim's blood flow had undergone a very rapid change after the bite: the blood flowed more easily and the clotting process slowed down.

Little research was done at the time into the implications of this observation, but scientists in the United States and Britain are currently looking into ways that extract of Malayan pit viper venom may be of benefit.

The venom extract is already employed to prevent the clotting that sometimes occurs in the veins of the legs as a result of a hip operation, but research is focusing on using the venom to dissolve the blood clots that can cause coronary thrombosis and some kinds of stroke.

LIFESAVING VENOM *One of the deadliest snakes in the world, the Malayan pit viper may help to prevent heart attacks.*

While much work remains to be done, scientists are very hopeful that the lethal venom may one day benefit the health of mankind.

A CHARGED-UP MEAL

The dinner with a difference

THE DUCK-BILLED PLATYPUS of eastern Australia is one of nature's strangest creatures—so strange that when the first complete specimen of a platypus arrived in London in 1798, scientists at the British Museum thought that someone was playing a practical joke on them.

Never before had they seen a furry four-legged animal without "proper" ears, a tail like a beaver's, webbed feet, and a duck's bill. And it seemed that the extraordinary creature not only laid eggs but also suckled its young.

But for nearly two centuries the most remarkable feature of the platypus remained a secret. In 1986 Henning Scheich, a German scientist, and several Australian colleagues discovered that platypuses feel that ordinary flashlight batteries are good to eat. The scientists also discovered why.

A sensitive touch

Platypuses normally feed exclusively on live prey, such as shrimps, worms, frogs and tadpoles, snails, insect larvae, and small fish.

Although an aquatic hunter, the platypus is virtually deaf and blind underwater. When it dives, its eyes are shut and its "eyelids" cover its earholes. Scientists had concluded that the animal found its food through a sense of smell and a very acute sense of touch in the bill.

After a series of tests with platypuses, however, Scheich noticed that they were remarkably successful at finding shrimps hidden in hollow bricks. He also knew that when a shrimp flicked its tail there was a significant increase in the minute electrical charge that all living things emit. Could platypuses detect these charges?

To investigate the possibility, Scheich and his colleagues put a number of platypuses in a tank of water and, in a series of experiments, let them choose between a menu of a charged flashlight battery, a shrimp, and a dead battery.

Ignoring the dead battery, the platypuses attacked the live battery more often than they went for the shrimp. And when a weak electrical field was created around a hollow brick, the platypuses would investigate it more than twice as frequently as they did when the current was off.

Electrifying discovery

Scheich's experiments led to the discovery that sensors in their bills enable platypuses to detect electrical charges. The sensors are connected to a point directly behind an area of the animal's brain that is especially sensitive to electrical stimulation.

Thanks to Scheich and his colleagues, we now know why platypuses are so successful at finding their food underwater. It can be said with confidence that platypuses get a real charge when they go out to dine.

THE PETER PAN SYNDROME

An amphibious creature that rarely grows up

WHEN THE SCOTTISH playwright Sir James Barrie created the character of Peter Pan, the boy who refused to grow up, he probably did not realize that nature had beaten him to it. There are several creatures in the animal world that refuse to grow up. The most outstanding is the axolotl.

Aztec monster

The axolotl is an amphibian—one of a group of animals that spend their lives both on land and in water. In the wild, the axolotl is found only in Lake

Xochimilco near Mexico City. It takes its name from the Aztec word meaning "water monster."

For years people were baffled by the axolotl. It looked like an immature or larval form of salamander, yet it was sexually mature and able to breed. Then, in 1865, French scientists made an amazing discovery: the axolotl was in fact an immature salamander. Several young specimens in laboratory tanks were spontaneously changing into adult salamanders; they began to lose their feathery gills and develop longer tails.

A child at heart

The axolotl is one of a number of creatures, including some other salamanders and several species of newts, that retain their juvenile form in later life—a characteristic known as neoteny. However, the axolotl advances one stage further than this: it develops sexual organs so that it can reproduce. Scientists have labeled this phenomenon paedogenesis.

What is the reason for the Peter Pan behavior, and what makes the axolotl suddenly grow up? Laboratory experiments show that adulthood can be induced by adding iodine to the water in which the axolotl lives. It seems that neoteny results because the axolotl lacks a hormone called thyroxine, which is produced in the thyroid gland. Iodine helps to stimulate thyroxine production. Apparently, a physical jolt can have the same effect: some

PRECOCIOUS AMPHIBIAN *The axolotl becomes sexually mature while still in the larval stage.*

axolotls change into the adult form after a bumpy journey from one laboratory to another. At other times, the change can occur spontaneously, for no apparent reason.

In their Mexican lake home, axolotls exist in both forms, but the immature ones greatly outnumber their adult counterparts. It may be that something in the composition of the water of the lake causes the Peter Pan syndrome.

But there is another possible reason. Lake Xochimilco is surrounded by dry, bare land—a desolate habitat that provides little food for an adult salamander. By retaining its juvenile form, the axolotl can spend all its life within the safe confines of the water.

As the British naturalist Charles Darwin discovered, the most enduring animals are those that can adapt to their environment, however hostile.

THE BARRIER METHOD

Microscopic empire builders of the ocean

THE GREAT BARRIER REEF stretches nearly 1,300 miles along the northeastern coast of Australia. A brilliantly colored underwater kingdom, the reef is inhabited by many exotic plants and creatures. One of these creatures, the coral polyp, created that kingdom.

Not more than half an inch long, coral polyps are close relatives of jellyfish and sea anemones. They are cylindrical in shape, with a round disc on top. The simple opening in the center of the disc is the mouth; around the edge of the disc is a row of stinging tentacles. Any unwary prey that brushes against the tentacles will be paralyzed and then swiftly drawn into the polyp's mouth.

Although they are individual creatures, polyps may not appear to be. As a polyp matures it secretes limestone, which forms a protective casing, the corallum. The polyp then reproduces by splitting into two identical polyps. The new polyp remains in physical contact with its "parent" and soon grows a casing of its own; then it, too, reproduces. And so the cycle continues.

This asexual reproduction is rapid, and an extensive colony of thousands of united polyps, linked by their limestone casings, is soon formed. In time the older polyps die and are covered by the casings of their offspring.

Animated behavior

Over thousands of years the gradual accretion of limestone casings creates a spectacular reef covered with a colony of living coral. In daylight the polyps stay inside their casings and the reef appears to be a lifeless mass of limestone. But at night the polyps extend their bodies in order to feed, and the reef is transformed into a richly colored display of swaying tentacles.

Not all forms of coral create reefs. Building reefs is reserved for corals that live in warm, shallow

waters and maintain a symbiotic relationship with a type of algae called zooxanthellae. The microscopic single-celled plants that make up the algae live inside the coral; it is thought that they accelerate the process of waste disposal, providing their hosts with an additional source of oxygen. Clearly the algae have a dramatic effect on the growth rate of the polyps. Those with the "guest" algae develop 10 times faster than those without; they are thus stronger and better able to withstand the effects of the buffeting tide.

Blueprint for survival

Because the algae need sunlight in order to survive, the relationship between zooxanthellae and the reef-building corals confines the latter to shallow waters. The most flourishing reefs are between 15 and 90 feet deep; rarely is coral found below 180 feet. The highly oxygenated warm water that polyps themselves require further restricts their location. The Continental Shelf off Queensland, Australia, offers an ideal environment.

It is amazing that this unique partnership— between a tiny creature no more than half an inch long and a microscopic plant invisible to the human eye—has given rise to immense, impenetrable natural barriers that have withstood the pounding of the sea for thousands of years.

ALL FOR ONE, ONE FOR ALL *The individual coral polyp is similar in appearance to a sea anemone or even the underside of a jellyfish. It takes millions of these simple invertebrate organisms to make up the complex network of the coral garden.*

FRINGE BENEFITS *The scale of the Great Barrier Reef of Australia can be appreciated best from the air. Fairfax Island, left, is one of the hundreds of small coral islands in the reef. Sitting in warm, shallow waters, it offers the perfect home to living coral and to a multitude of other sea creatures.*

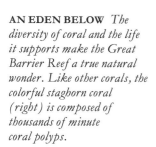

AN EDEN BELOW *The diversity of coral and the life it supports make the Great Barrier Reef a true natural wonder. Like other corals, the colorful staghorn coral (right) is composed of thousands of minute coral polyps.*

HOME TWEET HOME

Some ingenious building techniques

FOR EVERY CREATURE a home is an important factor. It provides protection from predators and affords shelter from the elements. Birds, in particular, devote considerable time to creating a suitable abode. The vast majority build their own nests, although there are some exceptions. For example, some owls use a hollow in a tree, and most falcons and nightjars dispense with a nest altogether and lay their eggs on bare earth.

Throughout the world one finds an extremely wide range of different types of nest, tailored to meet the specific needs of the birds in their local climates and to offer protection from the potential dangers of their environments.

BLACK TERN *Native to northern and arctic regions, the black tern builds a free-floating nest on freshwater marshes.*

Feathering the nest

Most bird's nests are built of twigs, grass, or leaves bound together with mud, saliva, or even threads taken from spiderwebs. Usually the nests are lined with soft, downy material from plants or with feathers from the parent bird. But birds will build nests from whatever materials they can find; in one North American osprey nest were three shirts, a bath towel, an arrow, and a garden rake.

Many birds have developed ingenious methods of making nests. Some weave scraps of grass or twigs like basketwork; the homes of penduline tits in Africa, which are closely related to titmice in the United States, are so strong that members of the Masai tribe use the nests as purses. The gregarious

weaverbirds of the Kalahari Desert weave communal nests that are the avian equivalent of apartment houses; one nest may have as many as 500 individual bird dwellings, each with its own entrance.

Tailorbirds, a familiar sight in India, have devised an unusual method. Using their beak as a needle, they can make a pocket for the nest by literally sewing two living leaves together without detaching the leaves from the tree.

GRAY FANTAIL *Snug within the confines of their cup-shaped nest, a brood of young fantails await the arrival of food.*

Safety in the home

Most people think of nests as being cup- or bowl-shaped, but that is not always the case. Birds are talented architects and use sophisticated structures to outwit predators or to keep their eggs at the correct temperature for incubation whatever the external conditions.

Ovenbirds, for instance, build almost spherical nests, comprising an antechamber and a brood chamber, with access from one small entrance. Their common name is derived from the resemblance of their nests to the clay ovens of the local inhabitants. Found in the tropics of Central and South America, ovenbirds build nests during the rainy season, when supplies of the soft mud they use are plentiful.

In Africa the hammerhead bird builds a nest that may be up to six feet wide; it houses three internal chambers, with the entrance at the bottom. Eggs are incubated in the top chamber, the safest from both predators and flooding. When the eggs are hatched and the chicks outgrow their nursery, they

OVENBIRD *Territorial by nature, the ovenbird often builds its nest in high places so that it can keep a watchful eye on intruders. The nest is made of plants, animal hair, and dung; mud is an effective binding agent.*

Cross section of nest

move down to the middle chamber. The lowest chamber serves as an entrance hall.

The African gray-capped social weaverbird has developed an even more sophisticated design. Its nest features an emergency escape route that occupants can use if a predator gains access through the main entrance.

But perhaps one of the most extraordinary nests is built in the arid regions of Australia by the mallee fowl, which has to contend with temperatures that range from below freezing to more than 100°F during its breeding season. The male buries the eggs under a huge mound of sand, into which it pushes leaves and twigs. The decaying vegetation generates heat that keeps the eggs warm.

The male mallee tends the eggs for the incubation period, which lasts several months. In warm weather he piles on sand to protect the eggs from the heat; when it is cold, he scrapes away some of the sand to expose the eggs to the sun. With its height of 3 feet and a width of as much as 15 feet, the nest of the mallee fowl is believed to be the largest in the world.

HOW DOES YOUR GARDEN GROW?

There's a fungus among us

I N BRAZIL, TRINIDAD, and areas of North and Central America, armies of ants can be seen on the march. Each individual ant seems to be shading itself from the sun with a tiny piece of leaf. Although they are commonly called parasol ants, the creatures are not using the leaves to keep off the sun. They do not eat them either. Parasol ants are farmers; they use the leaves as a compost on which to grow their food.

The ants spare no effort in gathering the leaves. Lines of worker ants in the thousands may forage 100 yards or more from the nest, along paths so well-trodden that the routes become etched into the ground. Each ant bites off a section of leaf, hoists it onto its back, and returns home.

Once inside the nest, the ant chews the piece of fresh leaf to a pulp, wets it with a drop of liquid deposited from the tip of its abdomen, and then adds the pulp to a pile of similarly treated leaves on which a fungus is growing. The ant plants tufts of the fungus on the new leaf and tends its growth.

Other ants join in the process. They walk over the heap, adding more liquid from their abdomens, licking the fungus and probing with their antennae to determine the condition of their crop.

For parasol ants, the fungus is the sole source of food; its cultivation is vital. The ants' gardens are often enormous, extending as deep as 12 feet underground in a labyrinth of chambers. Scientists have found one six-year-old nest in which 40 tons of earth had been shifted to create its 1,920 chambers. Some 44,000 ants occupied the space. The colony had stripped nearby trees of an estimated six tons of leaves.

A mutual advantage

Within the colony the fungus flourishes and keeps thousands of ants alive. Yet in the wild, without the ants to tend it, the fungus barely survives, since it is highly vulnerable to infection and to attack by other, harmful fungi.

At first researchers believed that the ants' bodily secretions might contain antibiotics that protected the fungus. But no such antibiotics were found. Instead, the scientists discovered that the drop of liquid the ants always add to the chewed leaf contains powerful fertilizers and nutrients that make the fungus so strong that it overcomes all competition and grows steadily—and ensures that the ants will survive with plenty of food.

A SHAGGY DOG STORY

To the rescue

IT IS LATE ONE NIGHT, and in the pasture the flock is restless. Somewhere out in the darkness a coyote lurks, scenting his prey, creeping closer for the kill. Suddenly the silence is shattered by wild barking. A huge dog with a shaggy coat bounds in the direction of the predator, who turns and runs. The sheep are safe from attack.

Their comical-looking savior is no ordinary sheepdog but a komondor. The breed is being employed by sheep farmers in the United States to tackle the economic threat posed by coyotes: the loss of 10 percent of a flock every year.

Guarding the flock

Coyotes used to be controlled by a poison called Compound 1080. But in 1972 the government banned the substance because it harmed other wildlife. Since then the coyote population has increased significantly, and alternative methods of control have proved ineffective, expensive, and time-consuming—until the arrival of the komondor. The dog's fierce territorial instincts make it ideal for protecting sheep.

An ancient working breed, native to Hungary, the komondor has a long white corded coat, stands about two feet high, and weighs approximately 100 pounds. It is powerful and fast on its feet. Because it is devoted to its master and intensely protective, it is used to guard flocks rather than herd them.

Since the late 1970's these qualities have proved invaluable to farmers. Part of a komondor's training is to introduce it to sheep while the dog is still young, so that it learns to treat the flock as its own.

Although expensive to purchase, komondors save farmers money in the long run—and help to save the environment too.

The most effective protector of sheep is the komondor.

DUMB BUT NOT STUPID

Intelligence in the animal kingdom

FOR EVERY ANIMAL LOVER who claims that a pet is "almost human," there is a cynic who considers pets "dumb animals." But according to the latest scientific experiments on animal intelligence, the animal lovers may be right.

Some of the most convincing evidence about animal intelligence has been collected by Alan and Beatrice Gardner at the University of Nevada. They have taught a female chimpanzee named Washoe to communicate with humans, using the sign language of the deaf.

Sign language

Almost from birth, only signs were used to communicate with Washoe, and she was encouraged to respond in the same way. During four years of training she acquired a vocabulary of 130 signs and used them to identify objects that she recognized. Sometimes she would even be clever enough to invent new signs, such as *water-bird* the first time she saw a swan.

The use of tools by mammals and birds has reinforced the belief that animals are capable of some reasoning. At the Miami Seaquarium in Florida, a green heron has become well-known for using fish-food pellets as bait to catch his dinner. The heron picks up stray pellets, drops them into the water and, if fish are not attracted quickly, retrieves the pellets in order to try again. One observer reported that in one 25-minute period, the bird baited and caught 24 fish, and that it failed on only two occasions.

Other bird species employ tools also. A group of ravens in Oregon hit on the novel idea of picking up stones to bombard people who stray too close to their nests. Darwin's finches, native to the Galapagos Islands, use cactus spines to probe crevices for insects. In Texas, green jays have been observed selecting twigs for poking under loose bark to dislodge insects.

Mammals are equally enterprising. Sea otters open shells by pounding them with stones. And— perhaps even more impressive—chimpanzees strip branches of side shoots and leaves, forming probes of just the right length to extract termites from deep holes in mounds.

Brain power

Recent research is also overturning a few long-cherished beliefs about which animal is the cleverest. For example, it seems that pigeons may be as intelligent as chimpanzees and dolphins, the animals commonly thought to be second only to humans in their brain power.

After one experiment researchers believed that chimpanzees were capable of thought because the animals actually decided to move a box to a spot where, by climbing onto it, they could eat bananas that hung out of reach. But when similar tests were carried out at Harvard University using pigeons that were specially trained to push boxes, the pigeons proved just as capable of solving a problem. And in tests that involved distinguishing red and green lights in order to obtain food, dolphins and pigeons performed equally well.

One of the leading authorities on animal intelligence, Professor Donald R. Griffin of Rockefeller University, New York, believes that all the evidence indicates that animals are capable of what he calls "conscious mental experience."

Not all of his colleagues agree with Professor Griffin. But most of them no longer insist that only instinctive, automatic behavior characterizes members of the animal kingdom.

LIFESAVING ENGINEERING

In Greek legends the chimera was a fire-breathing monster with the head of a lion, the body of a goat, and the tail of a serpent. Today, such weird hybrid creatures are no longer imaginary; for research purposes, scientists have created living animals that are part sheep and part goat.

A sheep-goat chimera has four parents: a male and a female sheep and a male and a female goat. One embryo is taken from a pregnant sheep and another from a pregnant goat. Then cells from both embryos are combined to form a sheep-goat embryo. This embryo is then returned to the sheep or goat, where it grows until birth.

By creating chimeras, scientists hope to find ways of enabling one animal to give birth to a different species of animal. The aim: to enable a sheep embryo, for example, to develop in a goat "host" mother but to be born as a sheep. If the offspring of a species could be successfully bred, the technique could save animals in danger of extinction.

SHEEP-GOAT CHIMERA *The product of a breeding experiment, this chimera may point to a new way to save endangered species.*

THE PLAINFIN MIDSHIPMAN

Strange noises disturb San Francisco residents

IN SEPTEMBER 1985, houseboat residents in the exclusive Richardson Bay area across from San Francisco began to suffer from a mysterious complaint. Many could not sleep at night; others developed chronic headaches. All complained about a persistent humming, a noise that occurred only at night.

"It's like 10 electric razors running at once," said one resident. "A powerful generator," confirmed another. Harbormaster Ted Rose stressed the seriousness of the problem. "Sometimes it gets so loud you have to talk above it. It can drown out conversations and wake people from a dead sleep."

A mystery is solved

Suggestions were plentiful as to the cause of the strange nocturnal noise: a diesel generator, sewer pumps, underground electrical power lines. But none of these theories made much sense, for the noise was coming not from the land but from *underwater*. Acoustical engineers from the University of California at Berkeley were called in and, with the help of instruments and a diver, finally located the source of the sound.

What was keeping the citizens of Richardson Bay awake was a *fish*—the singing toadfish, also known as the plainfin midshipman.

Many members of the toadfish family produce sounds of one kind or another, but the plainfin midshipman, or *Porichtys notatus,* is easily the most spectacular. An ugly-looking creature with a short, thickset body and a wide, flattened head, it produces its characteristic hum by vibrating the muscles of its air bladder.

Love songs

Why the toadfish makes this noise is not fully understood. But we do know that only the male "sings." The call, which it makes only between September and April, is believed to be part of the courtship ritual and may serve to warn off other males as well. When threatened or frightened, the fish also emits loud grunts or burping sounds.

The plainfin midshipman is not alone in these peculiar abilities. The male oyster toadfish produces a characteristic whistle; the electric catfish hisses; the horse mackerel grunts like a pig; the trunkfishes and puffers growl like dogs; and the family of fish known as drums creak, hum, purr, and whistle loudly enough to be heard from the deck of a ship directly above them.

These are all perfectly natural phenomena, however, and the residents of Richardson Bay just had to learn to live with the noise.

A KNIGHT IN SHINING ARMOR

The ancient armadillo fights a war against disease

FEW CREATURES are stranger in appearance than the curious nine-banded armadillo, one of the last remaining members of the ancient order Xenarthra, which flourished 55 million years ago. Until recently this engaging animal was best known for its "armor plating"—two leathery shields, one in front and the other at the back, connected by nine or more horny bands—that protects it from predators. But in recent years this survivor of prehistoric times has been helping scientists solve one of the world's most pernicious problems: leprosy.

Today leprosy is not as rare as is often thought. In many parts of the world it is still a major crippling disease and in its most severe form can lead to blindness, disfigurement, and deformity. In Africa and Southeast Asia, as many as 15 million

people are thought to be affected, and it is reported that approximately 5,000 people in the United States are afflicted with it.

Although drugs can be used to control the more severe forms of leprosy, no complete cure has ever been found and, until now, the possibility of a vaccine has been remote. Although Armauer Hansen, a Norwegian scientist, had identified the organism responsible for the disease (*Mycobacterium leprae*) in 1873, the bacillus refused to grow in the laboratory. Consequently, tests that might have led to a vaccine could not be carried out. Nor could the bacillus be grown or tested in animals, because scientists could not find any that were susceptible to leprosy.

New hope of eradicating leprosy worldwide came in 1972 when two American scientists,

Eleanor Storrs and Waldemar Kirchheimer, discovered the link between leprosy and armadillos.

Storrs, who had been studying armadillos for some time, believed that they might make suitable candidates for experiments on leprosy. First, armadillos had a lower body temperature than any other mammal, and it was known that leprosy attacks the cooler extremities of the body. Also, armadillos lived for up to 15 years—long enough to develop the disease, which has a protracted incubation period. Finally, their tendency to produce litters of identical quadruplets offered a perfect opportunity to test a long-held theory that susceptibility to leprosy might be inherited.

Long-awaited proof

In 1970 Storrs joined forces with Kirchheimer, who was with the U.S. Public Service Hospital at Carville, Louisiana, and began to carry out experiments on armadillos. In the beginning, unrelated animals captured in the wild were inoculated with the leprosy bacillus. Proof that armadillos were susceptible to the disease came when one of the animals developed it and died.

A few years later, the researchers inoculated 11 sets of quadruplet armadillos. Within six months one set of four had developed leprosy almost simultaneously. Since the odds of this happening by chance were extremely low, earlier theories of inherited susceptibility were supported.

The implications of the work of Storrs and Kirchheimer for human sufferers are considerable. Infected armadillo tissue provides a plentiful source of a substance known as lepromin; when injected into a leprosy patient, it indicates how likely he or she is to be affected by the disease. Therefore, extreme cases can be singled out at an early stage and the progress of the disease monitored. In 1974 the World Health Organization started a program to develop a vaccine based on armadillo-grown bacilli. Trials on human beings have already begun in Venezuela and in Malawi (formerly Nyasaland) in southeast Africa.

If the vaccine proves successful (the results of the trials should be known by 1996), the world may begin to eradicate this centuries-old affliction—thanks to nature's knight in shining armor, the nine-banded armadillo.

THE ULTIMATE DELICACY

Eat it at your peril

THE PUFFER FISH is probably the most poisonous creature in the sea. It contains a poison 275 times more deadly than cyanide. Yet, to the Japanese the raw flesh of the puffer, or *fugu* as they call it, is the ultimate delicacy.

Diners will pay $150 per person for a complete *fugu* meal. But for real gourmets, nothing can match the flavor of its liver. It is here that the poison is most concentrated. Although chefs are forbidden by law to serve it, they are sometimes begged, bribed, or bullied into doing so. The results are delicious—and often lethal.

It is a grim way to die. The toxin acts on the nervous system. The first symptoms are a tingling on the lips and mouth. Then the fingers go numb and paralysis starts to spread through the body.

"Even though you can think very clearly," says one Japanese restaurant owner, "your arms and legs become numb. It becomes impossible to sit up. You cannot speak, cannot move, and soon cannot breathe." Death may follow within minutes, or it may take six hours. There is no known antidote.

If properly prepared, the flesh is usually quite safe—but there is no way of telling until one has

ALL PUFFED UP *The puffer fish—long prized as a delicacy in Japanese cuisine—is named for its strange habit of puffing up when angry or agitated. As it furiously gulps air or water, it can swell up like a balloon to two or three times (above) its normal size (top).*

eaten it. Strict regulation of restaurants has lowered the death toll from *fugu* poisoning; even so, some 200 people have died from it in the past 10 years.

The puffer fish is not confined to Japanese waters. There are some 100 species around the world, many of them just as deadly.

The poison in its system may be the puffer's revenge for the hand it has been dealt by nature. It is a strange and very ugly fish. The name comes from its habit of puffing up to three times its size whenever it is attacked.

The puffer cannot swim like other fish. It has no ribs or pelvic bones and just drifts lazily through the water. It has huge goggle eyes, large nostrils, and buck teeth that may look comical but can tear open a clam shell or crab and have been known to bite through fishermen's hooks and lines.

But none of this deters the Japanese. They have made a cult of *fugukun*—dear little *fugu*. They pray to it, build statues of it, and above all, eat it. Ugly, vicious, and deadly as it is, the Japanese consume a staggering $50 million worth every year.

GENTLE GIANT

The tragedy of Lonesome George

IN A PEN on the Galapagos island of Santa Cruz in the Pacific Ocean is a large black tortoise, Lonesome George. He is the last known survivor of his species, the giant saddleback tortoises of neighboring Pinta Island.

When the Galapagos were discovered by Spanish explorers in 1535, hundreds of thousands of giant tortoises roamed the islands. (*Galapago* is the Spanish word for tortoise.) Survivors of prehistoric times when reptiles were of enormous size,

SAVED FROM EXTINCTION *The giant tortoises of the Galapagos Islands have benefited from the captive breeding program initiated at the Charles Darwin Research Station. The tortoises are released when large enough to defend themselves against predators.*

some of the tortoises grow to four feet in length and weigh as much as 500 pounds. They may live for more than a century.

Massacre of the innocents

In the 1700's and early 1800's, their numbers were drastically reduced by pirates and whalers who filled the holds of their ships with live tortoises to provide fresh meat for the long voyages; tortoises have an extraordinary ability to survive without food or water for a year or more.

Slaughter continued as late as the 1930's. Traders killed the tortoises for their meat and clean-tasting oil, and scientists killed or captured the animals in the name of research.

Even when the human persecution stopped, the tortoises were still not safe. Pigs, dogs, rats, and cats introduced into the islands destroyed tortoise nests and eggs and preyed upon the young.

Then, in 1965, scientists at the Charles Darwin Research Station based in the Galapagos set up an emergency program to save the giant tortoises from extinction. They found that three groups of tortoise were in particular danger: those on Pinzon, Hood, and Pinta islands.

The researchers discovered that the only tortoises on Pinzon Island were veterans. For at least 50 years, every egg and young tortoise had been eaten by black rats. To ensure the continued existence of the species, the scientists collected eggs and took them to Santa Cruz. Once the eggs had hatched and the young had grown too large for the rats to eat, the tortoises were taken back to Pinzon. So far, about 200 young have been reared and returned to the island.

On Hood Island large herds of goats had destroyed much of the island's vegetation on which the giant tortoises depend. Researchers found only 12 females and 2 males. No breeding had taken place for some time: the tortoises were so scattered that they simply could not find each other. The only solution was to take the tortoises back to the research station and establish a breeding colony. Around 130 youngsters have been produced, 80 of which have been returned to their home island.

Goats were also a problem on Pinta Island. Three were introduced in the 1950's; by the 1970's they had multiplied to a staggering 50,000. During the 1960's no tortoises were to be seen, and the Pinta Island tortoise was officially declared extinct. Then, in 1971, George appeared.

George was moved to Santa Cruz in the hope that a mate might be found for him. But the future appears bleak. Although the research station has offered a $10,000 reward for a female saddleback tortoise, a search of zoos throughout the world has failed: the reward is unclaimed.

There is one faint ray of hope. In 1981 tortoise droppings were seen on Pinta. But unless the tortoise itself is found, and proves to be female, George seems doomed to remain lonesome.

LEGS AS LUNGS

The tiny sand-bubbler crab of Australia is a cautious creature, scuttling back to its burrow in the beach at the slightest disturbance. Biologists have long believed that the sand-bubbler is successful at avoiding potential hazards because of a unique early-warning system: the large, membranous discs on each leg, believed to be a form of ear.

However, there is one puzzling thing about the sand-bubbler. Unlike other crabs that stay out of water for any length of time, the sand-bubbler has no lungs, only gills. Yet it spends half its life feeding while the tide is out. How does it breathe when it is out of the water?

In the mid-1980's Australian scientist David P. Maitland decided to find out. He measured the rate at which sand-bubblers consumed oxygen, and then how much they used when the leg membranes were painted over. Oxygen consumption in crabs with painted membranes fell drastically. Therefore, concluded Maitland, the membranes were not ears at all; they were noses —of a sort.

The membrane lets in air while keeping water and sand out. Lying immediately beneath the membrane are hundreds of tiny channels. The crab's blood runs through these and absorbs the oxygen taken in through the membrane.

The mystery of how sand-bubblers breathe on land has been solved. But at present, no one is quite sure how well they can hear.

WHY SAND-BUBBLER? *The name derives from the thousands of sand pellets the crab makes while feeding. After scooping sand into its mouth, the crab carefully extracts any food particles and then expels the waste sand in the form of pellets; it passes them through its legs and deposits them back on the beach.*

DIMINUTIVE CRAB
Since the sand-bubbler has no lungs, how does it breathe when it is on dry land? After years of doubt, at last scientists have found the answer.

CREATURES OF THE ABYSS

THE SEAS AND OCEANS of the world cover approximately 70 percent of the earth's surface; in places they are more than 36,000 feet deep. Water below 3,000 feet is known as the abyss—a dark, sunless area where temperatures are barely above freezing. No plants grow there, and the rocky seabed is covered with a muddy sediment and the skeletal remains of fish and other creatures that lived in the waters nearer the surface. However, a number of remarkable creatures do survive in this hostile environment.

To live in the abyss, these creatures have specially adapted to their environment. Because of the lack of food, most are small and frail, and all nonessential organs have atrophied. Some animals are totally blind. To compensate, many have developed organs highly sensitive to touch and to smell. The creatures also have specialized guts, with bacteria that break down the remains of dead matter on the seabed that these animals ingest.

Until the development of deep-sea submersible craft, the existence of these creatures was largely unknown. But today more than 4,000 species of fish and invertebrates have been discovered in the world more than 3,000 feet below the waves.

LIVING OFF THE SEABED *Most creatures in the abyss are highly efficient filter feeders, drawing in any substance that might contain even a trace of nourishment. Creatures that walk or crawl on the seabed itself, such as starfish, suck up its sediments and extract the nutrients. Anemones, sponges, and other life-forms that are anchored to the seabed live off microorganisms suspended in the water.*

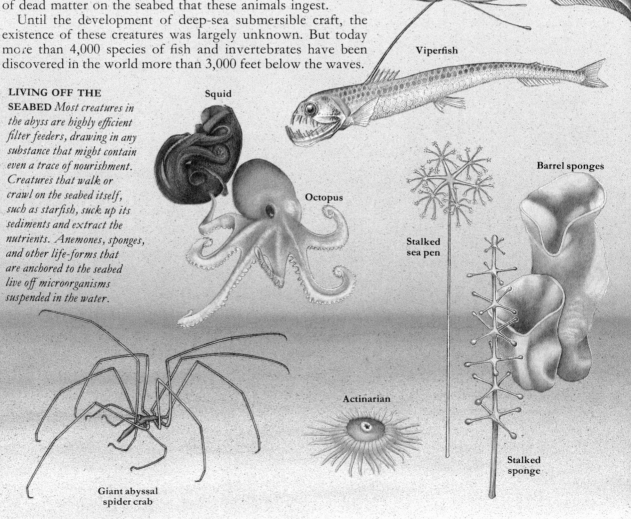

Lanternfish

Whalefish

Atelopus

Viperfish

Squid

Octopus

Barrel sponges

Stalked sea pen

Stalked sponge

Actinarian

Giant abyssal spider crab

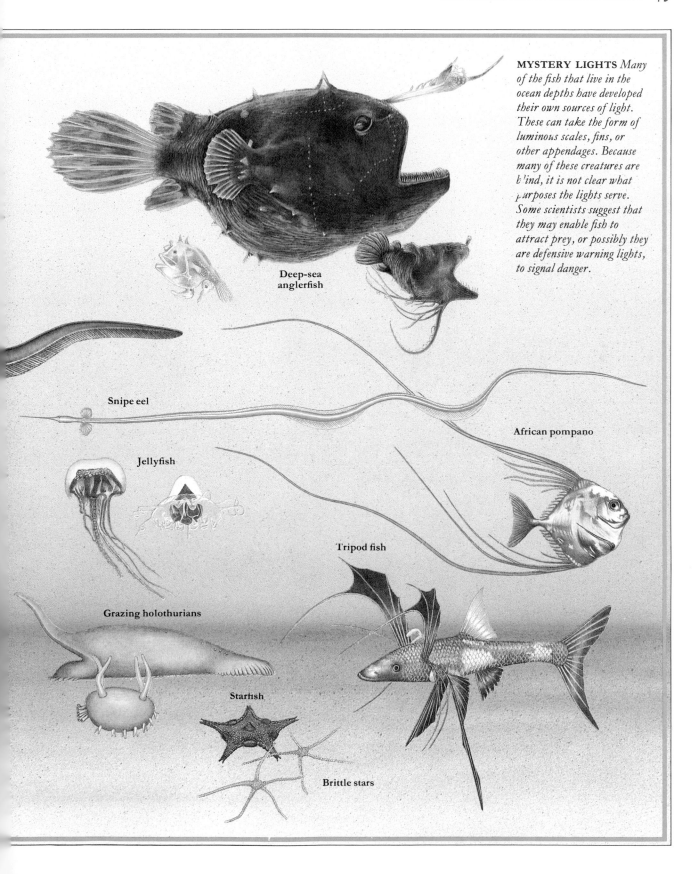

MYSTERY LIGHTS *Many of the fish that live in the ocean depths have developed their own sources of light. These can take the form of luminous scales, fins, or other appendages. Because many of these creatures are blind, it is not clear what purposes the lights serve. Some scientists suggest that they may enable fish to attract prey, or possibly they are defensive warning lights, to signal danger.*

Deep-sea anglerfish

Snipe eel

African pompano

Jellyfish

Tripod fish

Grazing holothurians

Starfish

Brittle stars

BEATING ITS BRAINS OUT?

Woodpeckers are very hungry birds. A black woodpecker, a native of North America, can eat 900 beetle larvae or 1,000 ants at a single sitting; a European green woodpecker will gobble up 2,000 ants in just one day.

To find its food, a woodpecker hammers wood at the rate of 15 or 16 times a second. Each peck takes one-thousandth of a second or less— a "rate of fire" nearly twice as fast as that of a submachine gun. Moreover, the woodpecker's head is traveling at 1,300 miles per hour—more than twice the speed of a bullet.

Impact

The suddenness with which the head is brought to a halt during each peck results in a stress equivalent to 1,000 times the force of gravity—more than 250 times the force to which an astronaut is subjected in a rocket during lift-off.

Nature's cushion

What prevents woodpeckers from beating out their brains?

For starters, the skull is greatly reinforced with bone, and the beak and the brain itself are cushioned against impact. But this is only part of the story. If the woodpecker's head were to twist even slightly while hammering the tree, the rotation of its head, combined with the force of pecking, would almost certainly tear away the bird's brain.

But the woodpecker's superbly coordinated neck muscles keep its head and beak in a perfectly straight line. Thus the bird can withstand the enormous shock it inflicts on itself year in, year out, as often as 12,000 times a day.

The woodpecker searches for food by boring into the tree.

THE BIG SLEEP

Making winter bearable

GOING WITHOUT FOOD for seven months is not a prospect most people would relish. But the black bear does it every year, disregarding its hunger pangs by going to sleep. More remarkably, female bears give birth while they are asleep.

Bears hibernate in winter in order to conserve energy at a time when there is little to eat or drink. They prepare for their long rest by consuming large quantities of food, adding some 100 pounds to their normal body weight.

Then they prepare a den, which may be in a cave, a burrow they dig out, or even a hollow tree. (Bears never use the same den twice.) Inside, they make beds from leaves, moss, grass, and strips of bark. During the fall bears spend increasingly more time sleeping in the den. When winter arrives and the temperatures drop below freezing, the animals doze off, often for several weeks at a time.

Maintenance plan

During their winter sleep, bears lose most of the weight that they added in fall. Their digestive system stops, and accumulated body fat provides their only nourishment. No one knows how they do it, but somehow bears break down their body wastes and convert them back into protein, which helps to maintain muscle tissue.

Somehow, too, their bodies cope with the large amounts of cholesterol that tend to build up during hibernation. In a human being these could cause hardening of the arteries or gallstones, but it seems that bears remain unaffected.

Also, according to the Indians of the Winnebago Bear Clan, bears survive hibernation by sucking their feet. After walking on berries all summer, crushing different kinds into their paws, in winter bears can gain sustenance from them.

The pace for life

Meanwhile, the bear's heartbeat slows from its normal rate of about 80 beats per minute to as few as 8. But thanks to the bear's thick fur, its body temperature drops just a few degrees below normal. Its sleep is relatively light: the slightest disturbance wakes it.

Females are little bothered by the birth of their cubs. Born in January and February, usually two or three to a litter, the cubs are little bigger than rats at first, weigh less than a pound, and have no fur. Nourished by their slumbering mother's milk, by spring the growing cubs may weigh as much as eight pounds.

How does a bear know when to prepare for hibernation? Part of the process involves the release of hormonelike substances that control the bear's bodily functions. But whether hibernation is triggered by the shortening of the days, the increasing scarcity of food, or changes in the weather still remains a tantalizing mystery.

MORE ROOM IN THE ARK?

A search that continues

JUST HOW MANY different kinds of living things exist in the world is a question people have been trying to answer for more than 2,000 years. One of the first to attempt an answer was the Greek philosopher Aristotle, who died in 322 B.C. He identified about 1,000 different species of plants and animals.

In 1758 the Swedish naturalist Carolus Linnaeus, who devised the system of classification still in use, identified about 12,000 plant and animal species. Today we have lists of some 265,000 different plant species and 1,700,000 animals.

Although the lists are far from complete, exactly how many new species are still to be discovered in the world and are therefore neither identified nor classified is something on which the experts do not see eye to eye.

Beetlemania

New animal species are being identified at the rate of some 5,200 a year, yet there is common agreement that only a small percentage of the world's plant and animal species have so far been discovered. As many as 30 million animal species may still be unidentified. Most of the unknowns will probably be invertebrates—tiny creatures with no skeletons. It seems likely that nearly 18 million will be insects, based on the knowledge that of the total animal species already known, more than half are insects. Chances are, $5\frac{1}{2}$ million of the insects will turn out to be beetles, since one-third of known insect species are beetles.

An unlikely pair

Although the likelihood that larger creatures will be found is very small, occasionally a discovery is made. One example is the okapi, the only relative of the giraffe. Standing only about five feet high at the shoulders and with a shorter neck than the giraffe, it was first sighted in the forests of the Belgian Congo (Zaire today) in 1901. In 1972 an 80-pound peccary, a type of pig, was discovered in the thorny scrublands of Paraguay's Chaco region. Although the peccary had long been known to the local Guarani Indian hunters, scientists were delighted with their find.

Most plant discoveries are less dramatic. Although the vast majority are small mosses and lichens, in 1986 botanists in Panama identified a new variety of tree. A member of the genus *Talauma,* a group common throughout Central America, the tree is more than 100 feet high and bears eight-inch-long green fruit.

However, despite such a wealth of new prospects, scientists are worried. Many of the world's animal and plant species are currently threatened by pollution and the decimation of the world's forests. It is estimated that 25,000 species of plants, about a tenth of those known, are under imminent threat of extinction. If the plants disappear, the animals and insects that depend on them will too—including some species that have not yet been discovered or classified. It is very possible that some species will remain unknown forever.

FISH OUT OF WATER

Mudskippers are goggle-eyed, four-inch-long fish that infest the swamps of Southeast Asia. So plentiful are they that a visiting scientist asked a villager why he did not catch them for food.

"True, it is a fish," the villager replied. "But it climbs trees. How can you eat a thing like that?"

The villager was telling no fishy tale. Mudskippers spend more than half their life on land, hauling themselves along with their forefins. The fins have suckers at the end; using these to grip the bark, a mudskipper has no problem shinnying up a tree.

Before climbing onto land, the fish fills its gill chambers with air and water. With its gills moist and aerated, the versatile mudskipper can spend hours out of water at a time.

Southeast Asia boasts two other species of fish that prefer dry land to life underwater. One is the climbing perch, a 10-inch-long freshwater fish with breathing organs that can take oxygen directly from the air. As its name

TREE CLIMBING *Using its fins, the mudskipper scales a mangrove shoot.*

indicates, the perch can also climb trees, although it rarely exercises this talent. However, the fish does spend most of its life walking on land, using its fins as crutches and its tail to propel.

Balancing act

The walking catfish, another native of Asia, invaded Florida in the 1960's when a number of specimens imported by a tropical-fish dealer literally walked away from captivity. This 20-inch catfish walks by slithering along the ground and thrashing its tail vigorously from side to side; long, stiff spines in its pectoral fins help a catfish maintain its balance. Behind the gills, organs resembling lungs enable the catfish to breathe on land. Even when swimming, it frequently comes to the surface of the water to breathe.

To date no one has reported seeing a catfish in a tree, but these fishy oddities have been known to disrupt traffic when they cross a highway by the hundreds.

TRUNK CALL

The unspoken language of elephants

ANIMAL RESEARCHERS have long been puzzled by certain aspects of elephant behavior. In particular they have wondered how apparently random groups of elephants, sometimes separated by miles, can manage to move in a cohesive, coordinated manner toward the same destination. Equally mysterious is how, without any discernible means of communication, male elephants are able to track down a female in heat even if she is many miles away.

Today researchers have discovered that the elephants *are* communicating—by using sounds at such a low frequency that the human ear is incapable of detecting them.

Talking heads

In 1985 Katherine Payne, a researcher at Cornell University in New York State, was observing a group of elephants at a zoo when she became aware of a spasmodic throbbing in the air "like the slight shock wave one can feel from far-off thunder." She then noticed that it coincided with a fluttering on an elephant's forehead, between the eyes, and concluded that these signs were evidence of a special means of communication.

Payne and her colleagues at Cornell started to investigate this discovery by using sophisticated

WITH ONE ACCORD *How large groups of elephants suddenly move off together, seemingly coordinated, is one of the great mysteries of animal behavior. Since no visible signal is given, how are the elephants communicating? Researchers believe that they may, at last, have the answer.*

ultrasonic recording equipment. In due course, recordings confirmed what Payne suspected: the throbbing she had previously experienced was created by sounds below the range of human hearing but capable of being captured on tape. Produced by the fluttering of an elephant's forehead, the sounds most often accompanied such activities as the arrival or departure of the keepers. But the observers also saw a female communicating with a male, even though a concrete wall separated the two animals.

Although the animals studied were in captivity, researchers concluded that these sounds would be of most practical use in the wild. Audible elephant noises—trumpeting, growling, and rumbling—would not carry far because they would soon be absorbed by grass, shrubs, and trees. But inaudible, low-frequency sound carries far greater distances than high frequencies.

Key factor

People who have worked with elephants have always known that they have a keen sense of hearing. When using elephants as mounts, hunters say that the animals can distinguish between 27 different verbal commands, and scientists have been impressed by the elephant's ability to recognize subtle musical variations.

But until recently no one realized that acute hearing was a key factor in the elephant's mysterious ability to synchronize scattered groups and in a male elephant's finding a female during the critical two days a month that she is in heat.

THE ASTONISHING HUMAN BODY

A NEW EYE ON THE WORLD

Alternative vision in sight?

ONE DAY IN 1945 a man named Kuda Bux climbed onto his bicycle and pedaled into New York City traffic. He rode blithely through busy Times Square and came to rest without mishap. To those watching him, it was an astonishing feat. Blindfolded throughout the trip, Bux had still been able to see where he was going.

This was perhaps the most dramatic demonstration of a talent that made Bux famous in the 1930's and 40's. But he was by no means the only person who was able to see without using his eyes.

The 17th-century Irish scientist Robert Boyle recounted the case of a man who could identify colors through touch. The first Europeans to reach Samoa in the 18th century reported that blind islanders were able to describe their appearance.

In 1893 doctors in Brooklyn, New York, described how blind Mollie Fancher read standard printed books with her fingertips. And in Italy at about the same time, a neurologist, Dr. Cesare Lombroso, treated a 14-year-old blind girl who could "see" with her left earlobe and the tip of her nose. When Lombroso attempted to prod her nose with a pencil, the girl jerked away and cried, "Are you trying to blind me?"

Cases such as these intrigued French scientist Jules Romains. After years of experimentation, in 1920 Romains published a long treatise on the phenomenon entitled *Eyeless Sight*. Romains noted that some subjects "saw" without any contact with the objects they described; others "saw" with their fingertips, cheeks—even their stomachs.

Visionary experiments

Although the book by Romains attracted little response from the medical profession, further instances of what he called "paroptic vision" occasionally made headlines. In 1960 fourteen-year-old Margaret Foos of Ellerson, Virginia, underwent elaborate tests conducted by experts. Securely blindfolded, Margaret read randomly selected passages of print, identified colors and objects, and even played a game of checkers.

Scientific attention focused on the phenomenon only after 1963, when Russian medical researchers reported on the case of Rosa Kuleshova. In several rigidly controlled experiments, during which she was blindfolded, Rosa had read newsprint and sheet music with her fingertips and her elbow.

The Kuleshova experiments awakened the interest of Dr. Richard P. Youtz, a psychologist at Columbia University in New York City, and he decided to pursue the subject. After several tests of his own, Youtz concluded that Kuleshova and others like her were abnormally sensitive to the amount of heat absorbed by different colors.

According to Dr. Youtz, sightless reading is possible because black print absorbs more heat and is warmer than the surrounding white page, which reflects heat very efficiently.

While this may account for people "seeing" with their fingertips or elbows, it does not explain how people such as Kuda Bux or Margaret Foos could see objects without coming in contact with them. This type of eyeless sight remains a fully documented—but so far inexplicable—mystery.

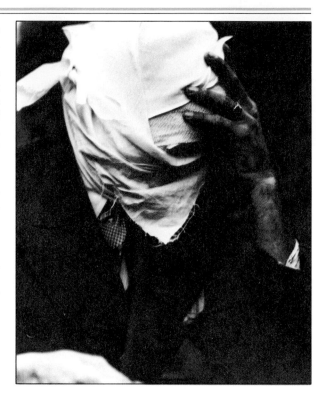

BLIND READING *One of the best-known examples of the phenomenon of eyeless sight occurred in the 1930's when Kuda Bux (right), heavily blindfolded, astounded people by being able to read faultlessly from books.*

THE STRANGE SLEEP

"I am a living candle"

WHILE WORKING in a hospital for incurables in New York City in 1966, English neurologist Oliver Sacks chanced upon the survivors of one of the strangest epidemics of modern times. "These wards," he wrote later, "were full of strange frozen figures, human statues as motionless as stone—a terrible . . . sight."

The patients were victims of *encephalitis lethargica,* or sleeping sickness. The disease had appeared in Europe quite suddenly in 1915, and by 1918 had spread throughout the world. The illness took so many forms that doctors were bewildered at first. Some believed that dozens of different diseases had broken out; others simply called it "an obscure disease with cerebral symptoms."

It affected 5 million people, but no two cases were the same. About a third soon died, some fell into a coma from which they never woke up, others suffered so many days and nights of sleeplessness that they, too, perished. Those who did survive often found their personalities cruelly altered. According to Sacks, children became "impulsive, provocative, destructive, audacious, salacious, and lewd." Other victims "neither conveyed nor felt the feeling of life; they were as insubstantial as ghosts and as passive as zombies."

By 1927 the epidemic was over; it had vanished as suddenly and mysteriously as it had arrived. More than 40 years later, at the hospital in New York, Sacks came upon some 80 survivors. The long-term effects of sleeping sickness, which had developed into a form of Parkinson's disease, had turned many of the patients into "living statues."

The great awakening

Soon after Sacks began working at the hospital, he learned of the successful trials of the experimental drug L-dopa, which was revolutionizing the treatment of Parkinson's disease. Could it be used to help these patients as well? In March 1969 Sacks began to prescribe L-dopa for them.

The effect was amazing. The living statues came to life. "Patients motionless and frozen, in some cases for almost five decades, were suddenly able, once again, to walk and talk, to feel and think, with perfect freedom." The once quiet wards hummed with activity and excitement. Some patients described the limbo in which they had lived: "I ceased to care about anything," said one. "Nothing *moved* me—not even the death of my parents. I forgot what it felt like to be unhappy. Was it good or bad? It was neither. It was nothing."

Although they became aware that almost half a century had passed since the onset of their illness, many patients behaved as if it were still the 1920's. For them, time had stopped. A man who had raced cars in his youth continually drew what were, by 1969, vintage vehicles. A woman afflicted in 1926 spoke of that era as if she were still living in it.

But the great awakening did not last. While some patients thrived on L-dopa, others underwent almost unbearable tribulation. As Sacks put it: "Joy became mania; mobility, frenzy. It seemed as if our patients could no longer be contained, as if

some essential moderator were missing. . . . There occurred a bursting-forth, not only of involuntary movements by chorea, but tics and mannerisms, bizarre motions and notions, of an increasingly complex, capricious, and compulsive kind—entire behaviors, entire repertoires, of a most primitive and even prehuman sort were seen."

A learning experience

Today all but a handful of the victims of this strange epidemic and its protracted aftermath have died. Yet they taught doctors much about the workings of the brain and the possible effect of drugs such as L-dopa.

The patients of Oliver Sacks asked him to tell their story. One wrote for all: "I am a living candle. I am consumed that you may learn. New things will be seen in the light of my suffering."

THESE FOOLISH THINGS

Does the past take us out of our minds?

MAGIC MOMENTS, images and scents from childhood, things we wish we could forget—there are all kinds of memories. We know our brains conjure them up, and so we have assumed that the memories themselves are stored in the brain. But this view may be mistaken, suggests a British biochemist, Dr. Rupert Sheldrake.

Many scientists believe that memories imprinted on the brain are held there by electrical activity in the synapses, the bridges between the brain's nerve cells. According to this theory, memories should be stored in particular places in the brain.

But if the theory is true, it ought to be possible to locate precisely where particular memories are registered. Yet many studies have indicated that all memory remains intact unless very large portions of the brain have been damaged. Memory, as one baffled scientist has put it, seems to be "everywhere and nowhere in particular."

Acid test for DNA

Sheldrake's answer to the paradox is that the brain is not a warehouse full of memories but a device for "tuning them in." He arrived at this conclusion while developing an explanation for the way that animal species inherit their unique characteristics—for instance, why a cat is always cat-shaped.

Conventional theory maintains that an animal's form is determined by the genetic code carried in the deoxyribonucleic acid (DNA) molecules of its

cells, although scientists have not yet established exactly how this transmission takes place. Because DNA cells are the same wherever they are found in an animal's body—whether in the eyes, the fur, or the flesh—Sheldrake suggests that DNA does not determine an animal's *form*. Since the makeup of cells in various parts of an animal varies considerably, he proposes that the cells cannot all have been "programmed" by an identical genetic code.

It is Sheldrake's theory that as the forms of living creatures have evolved, they have created a morphogenetic (form-creating) field. This field ensures that the animal's descendants will conform to the patterns established by generations of their own kind, be they cats, kangaroos, or two-toed sloths.

Thus the individuals of past generations have, in effect, created the forms of their own species. As each new individual develops, it contributes to the morphogenetic record; at the same time, the field shapes the individual.

Morphogenetic fields have not been detected in the laboratory. If they do exist, the fields do not obey accepted laws of science and would, for example, allow direct communication between the past and the present, a phenomenon that no existing scientific instrument can detect.

"Morphic resonance" is the term that Sheldrake gives to the means by which creatures are able to communicate with those that resembled them in the past. As he says, "The thing that an organism resembles most closely in the past is itself." He suggests that morphic resonance not only permits individuals to communicate with past members of their own species but also enables an individual creature to tune in its own past. Therefore, memory is a journey that the mind makes into the past via morphic resonance, not a physical record stored in the brain.

Startling implications

One of the fundamental tenets of biology is that living things can be explained exclusively in terms of physical and biochemical processes. Sheldrake's hypothesis challenges this belief, since morphogenetic fields, and memories, do not exist in any as yet measurable physical form.

Another by-product of Sheldrake's hypothesis is that it offers possible explanations for a variety of paranormal phenomena. If human beings can tune in their past, perhaps they can tune in the pasts of other individuals. Telepathy, then, would not be thought transfer but the reading of someone else's recent memory; clairvoyance would be receiving the memory of someone who is a distance away.

Sheldrake's hypothesis also offers support for the idea of a collective unconscious put forth by the eminent Swiss psychologist Carl Gustav Jung. Jung theorized that there was a pool of unconscious images and wisdom shared by all humans.

Could the collective unconscious be a form of species memory, a sum of human experience that our morphogenetic field passes on to us?

FULL OF YEARS

The oldest man in the world

SHIGECHIYO IZUMI started to drink alcohol when he was 70 years old. At the age of 91 he decided not to remarry. At 116 he gave up smoking. He died on February 21, 1986, at the age of 120 years and 237 days. Izumi was the world's oldest living man.

Others—such as Georgians in the U.S.S.R., who supposedly live to be more than 165 years old—have made more extravagant claims. But evidence to support such numbers has proved scanty. The authenticity of Izumi's great age, however, was established beyond doubt: his name and date of birth (June 29, 1865) appeared in Japan's first census, held in 1871 when he was six years old.

Recipe for life

Izumi spent all his life on a remote coral island. A sugarcane farmer, he ascribed his longevity to living a simple life and to never overdoing things.

On his 120th birthday he also credited his daily glass of *schochu,* a kind of white rum, with keeping him young. Advised by his doctor to give up drinking, he answered, "Without *schochu* there would be no pleasure in life. I would rather die than give up drinking."

Apart from his striking peace of mind, the reasons for Izumi's longevity are probably twofold: all his life he worked physically hard, and he continued to take regular exercise into his old age; he started each day with a stroll and then weeded his garden. In addition, Izumi always ate a typical Japanese diet, low in fats, with large quantities of fish and vegetables and very little meat. He suffered few serious illnesses throughout his life; he had his first heart attack at the age of 114.

Izumi's record may yet be challenged—quite possibly by one of his own countrymen. Between 1960 and 1985 the life expectancy in Japan increased by eight years. At 74 for men and 80 for women, it is today the highest in the world.

HAPPY BIRTHDAY *Shigechiyo Izumi, the world's oldest man, celebrates his 120th year.*

THE UNSURPASSED FLEA

Some great athletes have six legs, and wings

"I WAS BETWEEN time and space," said Robert Beamon in describing how he felt as he made his unrivaled long jump at the Olympic Games held in Mexico City in 1968. Beamon jumped 29 feet 2½ inches, shattering the previous world record by an astonishing 21½ inches.

It could accurately be said that Beamon also took a jump into the future, for in 33 years athletes had added only nine inches to the world long-jump record. At that rate of progress it should have taken until 2046—another 78 years—for someone to achieve Beamon's distance.

Experts say that Beamon's jump may never be equaled: the effort required is near the limit of human endurance, at which bones can break and muscles can be shredded. Yet, phenomenal as Beamon's achievement is, it does not match some by less-celebrated athletes of the animal kingdom.

RUNNING *In 1963 U.S. athlete Robert Hayes was timed at 27 m.p.h. during a 100-yard sprint—a world record. However, a cheetah can average 56 m.p.h., with short bursts of more than 60.*

HIGH JUMP *The record is held by Zhu Jianhua of China, with 7 feet 10 inches in 1984. The animal record goes to an Australian red kangaroo; it jumped over a 10-foot-high stack of lumber in 1965.*

LONG JUMP *Robert Beamon entered the record books with a 29 foot 2½ inch jump in 1968. In 1951 a red kangaroo established a 42-foot record jump in New South Wales, Australia.*

Human
27 m.p.h.

0 m.p.h.
10
20
30
40
50

Cheetah
56 m.p.h.

60

0 ft.
2
4
6
8

Human
7 ft. 10 in.

10

Kangaroo 10 ft.

12

0 ft.
10
20

Human
29 ft. 2½ in.

30
40

Kangaroo 42 ft.

50

In fact, many human athletic records look paltry next to the performances other animals put on as a matter of course. For example, whales regularly dive 3,700 feet below the surface of the sea. The human body can withstand underwater pressures to a depth of only about 2,300 feet, and even this dive would be lethal without special equipment.

Humans do little better at swimming. Even a penguin—which is a bird, not a fish—can move through the water as fast as 22 miles per hour. The human record is 5.3 miles per hour.

Humans even fail to drop out of the sky as rapidly as some birds. Although a skydiver can reach 185 miles per hour in free fall, he will still be overtaken by a peregrine falcon, which can plunge at speeds up to 225 miles per hour.

Numerous animals can outsprint the fastest athlete. Both the greyhound and the red fox race along at more than 40 miles per hour, leaving the speediest human trailing along at 27.

Finally, no human, not even Beamon, can hope to match the jumping ability of a flea. It can hop about six inches into the air and cover as much as two feet in a single leap. Weight for weight, this would be the equivalent of a man leaping a quarter of a mile in just one bound.

SKATING *Record-holder Pavel Pegov of the U.S.S.R. hurtled at 30.6 m.p.h. around a 500-yard ice rink in 1981. A seal being chased across ice in Antarctica was clocked at 11.8 m.p.h.*

WEIGHT LIFTING *The record was set in 1984 by the U.S.S.R.'s Alexsander Gunyashev: 1,025 pounds. A chimpanzee in the U.S.A. hoisted 600 pounds; in theory, a gorilla could lift 1,800.*

SWIMMING *While humans can barely manage to swim any faster than 5 m.p.h. over a short lap, many sea creatures can swim far faster over greater distances. The sailfish can average 68 m.p.h.*

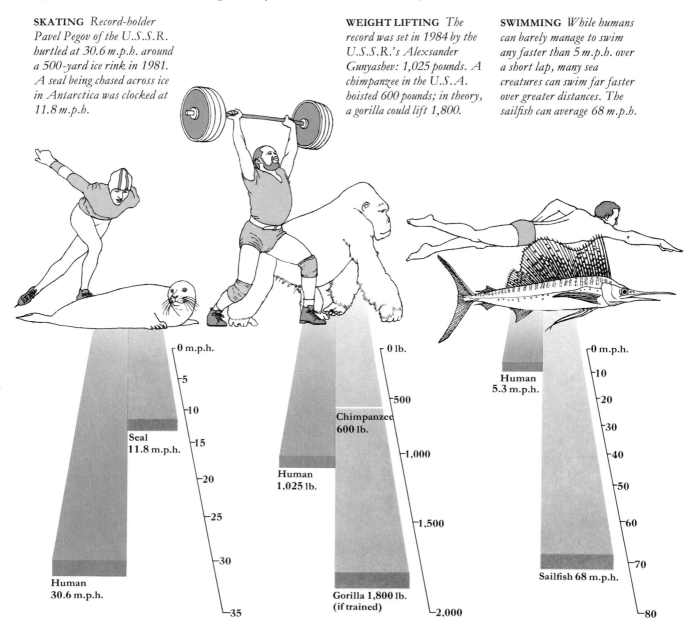

Human 30.6 m.p.h.

Seal 11.8 m.p.h.

0 m.p.h. — 5 — 10 — 15 — 20 — 25 — 30 — 35

Human 1,025 lb.

Chimpanzee 600 lb.

Gorilla 1,800 lb. (if trained)

0 lb. — 500 — 1,000 — 1,500 — 2,000

Human 5.3 m.p.h.

Sailfish 68 m.p.h.

0 m.p.h. — 10 — 20 — 30 — 40 — 50 — 60 — 70 — 80

BRAINTEASERS

What does it really take to be clever?

TREATING A MATHEMATICS STUDENT at the University of Sheffield, England, for a minor ailment, the campus doctor noticed that the young man's head was slightly larger than average: $24\frac{1}{2}$ inches in circumference. The doctor knew that one of the university's neurologists, Professor John Lorber, would be interested and sent the student to see him.

The student had an IQ of 126, well above average, and was expected to earn the equivalent of a *summa cum laude* in his studies. What astounded Professor Lorber, however, was that a scan of the man's head revealed virtually no brain at all.

A damming effect

The student suffered from hydrocephalus— literally, "water in the head." The liquid is in fact cerebrospinal fluid, which is produced in cavities in the inner part of the brain and normally circulates within and around the brain and spinal cord, and finally enters the bloodstream. But in hydrocephalics this fluid gets dammed up inside the brain.

The usual effects of hydrocephalus are malformation of the brain hemispheres, enlargement of the head, and—should the victim survive beyond the first few months of childhood—severe mental retardation. But this bright student had lived a perfectly normal life even though he had only a fraction of an inch of cerebral tissue stretched across the inside of his cranium instead of the usual brain depth of $1\frac{3}{4}$ inches.

Lorber has now identified several hundred others whose cerebral hemispheres are virtually nonexistent yet who remain intelligent people. Some, whom he describes as having "no detectable brain," have scored up to 120 in IQ tests.

Lorber does not know why this is so, since it is the hemispheres of the brain that do most of its work. In hydrocephalics, Lorber suggests, other, less-developed parts of the brain may take over. On the other hand, it may be that a normal brain operates at only a fraction of its full capacity. Whatever the reason, it is apparent that a small brain is no bar to having a fine mind.

SEEING CAN BE DECEIVING

More to vision than meets the eye

EVERYONE KNOWS how important human eyes are. A direct extension of the brain, they are among our most sensitive and vulnerable organs. Everyday speech reflects the preeminence of vision among the five senses: "I see" is synonymous with "I understand."

Surprisingly enough, the human eye is in fact a kind of radio receiver. Visible light is a form of electromagnetic radiation, which includes long, low-frequency radio waves at one end of its spectrum and short, extremely high frequency X-rays and gamma rays at the other. Light falls between these two extremes.

The eye can detect electromagnetic signals with wavelengths of far less than a thousandth of a millimeter; the frequencies lie between 0.00072 millimeter, the wavelength of red light, and 0.00038 millimeter, the wavelength of violet light. In between lie all the colors of the rainbow.

Picking up these minute vibrations are no less than 125 million light-sensitive cells in each eye. The nerve cells are divided into two separate systems: a set of cones that detect color and operate in good light, and a set of rods that see only monochromatically and come into play in poor light. The momentary blindness we experience when moving from darkness to bright light or vice versa lasts for the time it takes the eye to switch from one system to the other.

The rods tend to be scattered around the edge of the retina, away from the center—which is why it is easier to see things in the dark when one is not looking directly at them. These receptors are astonishingly sensitive; in total darkness the human eye can detect the light of a solitary candle positioned five miles away.

In dealing with the information they receive, the nerve cells in the eye perform about 10 billion calculations per second. During that same second, the eyeballs have moved around in their sockets about 100 times. This eye tremor does not blur vision, but actually improves our ability to see very fine detail; it allows the brain to process light that falls on the eye at different angles.

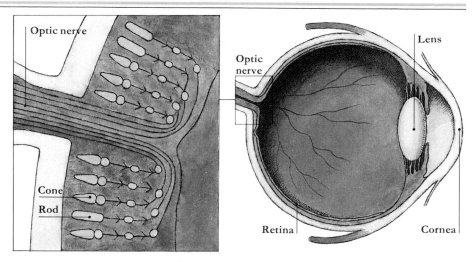

HOW THE EYE WORKS *Rays of light pass through the transparent cornea at the front of the eye. The lens then focuses them onto the retina, a region packed with light-sensitive cells called rods and cones (inset). A chemical change triggers the cells to send impulses through the optic nerve to the brain. The entire process takes about two-thousandths of a second.*

The fact that visual information reaches the eye is no guarantee that someone can see. People born with clouded corneas, who have had no visual experience at all, have been utterly confused by what they saw after surgery had restored their sight. Even the simplest geometric diagrams held no apparent pattern for them, and they had to learn to make sense of the new, visible world they had entered. Medical scientists and psychologists agree that it is the brain, not the eye, that integrates the seemingly disparate data the eye detects.

Experiments with cats show that the brain cells that are activated by vertical lines are quite different from those activated by horizontal lines, which are in turn different from those that react to diagonals.

Therefore, when we see a triangle, the brain performs two separate functions. It automatically recognizes the separate elements of the triangle, then it integrates these elements so that we see the triangle as a whole. But apparently the second function, organizing information into a coherent picture, is something that the brain has to learn from experience. Precisely how it does this remains one of the great mysteries of science.

A rosy view

Just how little we know about vision can be gauged from experiments carried out by Swiss psychologist Dr. Ivo Kohler, who has investigated the nature of color vision.

Kohler discovered that if he looked through rose-tinted glasses for long enough, two phenomena occurred. After a while his eyes "washed out" the pink, and he saw the world in its normal hues. When he took the glasses off, everything he saw was tinged with green.

The reason, Kohler theorized, lay in the way the cone-shaped nerve cells in the eye detect color.

Each cell contains a number of color-sensitive substances known as pigments. Any given color creates its own specific chemical reaction among the pigments, and this identifying information is transmitted to the brain.

Kohler reasoned that when the eye has been exposed to red for a while, as his eyes were, the pigments become overworked and exhausted. The brain no longer receives information about the color, and so someone wearing rose-tinted glasses soon stops seeing everything through a pink haze.

The aftereffect of seeing a green tint, he thought, occurred because the cell pigments were no longer able to "see" red light. Only the green portion of the spectrum was being transmitted to the brain.

Changing color

That, at least, was the theory. But Kohler's final experiment produced a startling result. He divided each lens of his glasses in half; he colored the left portion green and the right part red. If he looked to the left, his vision was shaded green; to the right, it was red. As with his earlier experiment, after a time the colors appeared to return to normal.

Then Kohler took off the glasses. When he looked to the left, he saw red; when he looked to the right, he saw green. If his previous theory were correct—that the effects were due to changes in the pigmentation of the cells inside the eye—he should have seen the same color, whether he looked to the right or to the left. But Kohler's results indicated that the changes in color seemed to depend on the position of the eyeball, not on what was occurring inside it—an altogether different matter.

To date there has been no satisfactory explanation for Kohler's intriguing results. What they do suggest, however, is that there is certainly more to vision than meets the eye.

LEFT OUT

One person in 10 has sinister leanings

MOST PEOPLE IN THE WORLD today are right-handed. In 1977 a study of works of art that ranged from cave drawings made in 15,000 B.C. to paintings of the 1950's found that an overwhelming majority of the people in them were also right-handed, regardless of their race, country, or culture.

Yet throughout the history of the human race, some people have been left-handed. Today the proportion of left-handers is 10 to 15 percent of the population worldwide.

Why are most people right-handed? And what causes some to be different?

There are no clear-cut answers to these questions, not least because human babies go through several periods of using first one hand and then the other. At about two years, a baby usually becomes either left- or right-handed.

Since there are no records of a culture or a people that was exclusively or predominantly left-handed, it would seem that right-handedness is probably biological, not cultural.

Division of labor

Studies of children have also revealed that left and right hands are complementary: each hand is used in different, but equally important, ways. For most people, the left hand is used for finding, holding,

GOOD AND BAD *The idea that there is something strange about left-handed people was present in early theology, where the "left-handed path" was the way of the devil. In this painting Italian artist Fra Angelico offers a 15th-century view of the Last Judgment: the righteous take the right-hand path to eternal life, but the damned must follow the left-hand path into everlasting punishment.*

and supporting; the right hand is used for handling and manipulating.

Scientists suggest that this division of labor could be due to the difference between the left and the right sides of the brain. The left brain, which controls the right hand, is dominant in most people and is the center of logical thinking. The right side, which controls the left hand, is stronger in the area of visual skills. One would therefore expect a high proportion of artists to have dominant right brains and to be left-handed. And research has shown that left-handedness is roughly twice as common among artists as in the population as a whole.

But there seem to be other causes of left-handedness in addition to a dominant right brain. Doctors have noticed that up to 40 percent of people who suffered severe brain damage at birth are left-handed. Medical experts reason that some left-handed people may have had very slight, unnoticed brain damage at birth. But since not everyone who suffers brain damage becomes left-handed, a genetic factor still seems to be involved.

Several complicated genetic theories have been set forth to explain left-handedness, but the simplest—and the most comprehensive—one states that most people inherit a right-hand bias. People who do not have this bias in their genes may become either left- or right-handed, as chance or their environment dictates.

Crib clues

One piece of research that supports this theory reveals that babies who usually lie with their heads to the right become right-handed; those who turn to the left become left-handed. Theoretically, both laying the head to the right and becoming right-handed are the result of the inherited bias.

An intriguing discovery is that left-handers have more fibers in the corpus callosum, the large bundle of nerves that connects the right and left sides of the brain. Many of these nerve fibers die off soon after birth, and more fibers die in right-handers. Whether an inherited right-hand bias or some other mechanism controls the extent to which these nerve fibers survive is not yet clear.

Until recently children who showed left-handed leanings ran the risk of being punished until they conformed with the majority of right-handed children. But today they have become the subjects of an engrossing scientific inquiry.

A Dream Come True

Putting the dreamworld to practical use

PSYCHOLOGIST ALAN WORSLEY, of St. Thomas's Hospital, London, has developed a special talent that most people would envy: he can control the contents of his dreams. In them, he creates magical fantasies. Snapping his fingers, he produces a flame like a cigarette lighter; he can soar through the air or pass a knife harmlessly through his wrists.

Even more remarkably, Worsley sets specific tasks to perform while dreaming, and he accomplishes them. He has counted objects, moved his eyes and arms, and spoken aloud in his dreams, just as he had predicted he would, while electrical sensors have confirmed that he is in a dream state.

Light in the darkness

Worsley's achievements are known as "lucid" dreams: the dreamer knows that he is dreaming and, with this awareness, can manipulate his dreamworld. Although many people have this experience, psychologists and philosophers have dismissed it as a fantasy or a mistake.

But Worsley has sent simple messages from his dreamworld to observers. Given a slight electric shock, he responded with a prearranged signal— five rapid eye movements. He did so in a dream, and while aware that he was dreaming. Responding in this way to an outside stimulus while still asleep seems to demonstrate that lucid dreaming does, in fact, occur.

The applications of controlled dreaming are numerous. Dream researcher Dr. Stephen La Berge of Stanford University in Palo Alto, California, has trained himself not to wake from nightmares; he wakes *in* the dream, rather than from it. Thus he can face and resolve the fears and anxieties the nightmare represents, instead of avoiding them and having them recur in later dreams.

La Berge further points out that dreams make use of the whole of our knowledge and experience, calling up facts of which we are only subconsciously aware when awake. In a dream we can give a perfect description of someone we know only slightly: he has green eyes, always wears brown shoes, and is left-handed. Asked to give such precise details when awake, we would probably be at a complete loss for an answer.

According to La Berge, lucid dreaming allows us to tap into areas of hidden knowledge when seeking a solution to a problem. The result should be better decision-making, because we have been able to review a situation in all of its detail.

Dreams of discovery

Russian chemist Dimitri Mendeleev was undoubtedly using hidden knowledge when he dreamed of a periodic table of the elements. A number of other scientists and inventors have made important discoveries as a result of dreams. American inventor Elias Howe had worked for years to perfect his design for a sewing machine; success came after he dreamed that he had been ordered, on pain of death, to finish the machine.

And physical problems have been solved too. While suffering a run of bad scores, golfer Jack Nicklaus dreamed about a different way to hold his clubs. When he tried the new method on the course, his golf scores improved dramatically.

Revelatory dreams are usually unpredictable; a lucid dreamer should be on the lookout for clues that might help solve problems. According to some researchers, a practiced lucid dreamer with a problem could set this creative process in motion, bring it under conscious direction—and accelerate it.

Perhaps the most intriguing application is healing illness through lucid dreaming. Psychologists have found that many patients with psychosomatic illnesses persistently dream about physical injuries, suggesting that such dream experiences may contribute to causing the illness in the first place. Dream researchers believe that the reverse could also be true: an ill person could help to cure himself by intentionally dreaming that he is healthy.

With sufficient training and patience, it seems possible that some of us might be capable of making our dreams literally come true.

PULLING THEIR WEIGHT

An ancient art still practiced today

IN RECENT YEARS training with weights has become more and more popular. Physical strength and stamina, epitomized by Arnold Schwarzenegger, are among the new yardsticks of health, and to many people, workouts at a health club or a gym have become part of a routine. But the interest in physical strength and stamina is not new; it is firmly rooted in the ancient world.

Great strength has always been prized. Chinese recruits during the Chou dynasty (1122–255 B.C.) had to pass weight-lifting tests before they were accepted into the army. And artifacts from ancient Egypt, India, Greece, and Rome provide ample evidence that exercises were performed with weights of stone, marble, or lead.

At Olympia, the site of the original Olympic Games, archeologists have unearthed a 315-pound block of red sandstone dating from the sixth century B.C. Its inscription states that Bybon had thrown it over his head with only one hand.

Cattle raising

The most famous athlete of ancient times was probably Milon of Croton. As part of his daily training routine he would pick up and carry a calf that originally weighed 35 pounds. He continued to pick it up each day until it had grown into an 800-pound bull. This, no doubt, contributed to Milon's 30 years of supremacy as a wrestler. Legend has it that he also carried a four-year-old heifer around the stadium at Olympia—a distance of 538 yards—and then killed it with a single blow.

The Romans, too, knew about exercising with weights, but in medieval times the practice seems to have waned. During the Renaissance weight training was again on the curricula of schools and gymnasia, and physical strength was seen as one of the qualities of the well-rounded Renaissance man.

By the 18th century, weight lifting had moved from the athletic arena into the field of entertainment. In shows and circuses, touring strongmen performed feats that sometimes relied more on skill and illusion than actual muscle power.

An Englishman nicknamed Sampson discovered that he could place his body in positions that enabled him to pull against horses and lift huge weights even though he was of only average size and strength. A German, Van Eckeberg, was renowned for lying on the ground with an anvil on his chest while an assistant struck it with a hammer.

Shows of strength

Thomas Topham of London was the genuine article. Using no artifice and with no training, he could roll up a heavy pewter plate with his fingers and lift an 800-pound boulder with one hand. Topham performed his most famous feat in 1741: he lifted three casks of water weighing 1,836 pounds over his shoulders using a rope and tackle.

In the 19th century, strongmen from Europe found a ready audience in the United States. Central European and Scottish immigrants in particular were instrumental in moving displays of strength from the stage back to the gymnasium. A German, Louis Durlacher, "Professor Attila," immigrated to New York, where he opened the first physical culture studio in 1894. Attila traveled all over the world. His training of many of the great men of his day helped to win respectability for weight lifting.

Milon's great feats were eventually equaled and even surpassed. In 1957 Paul Anderson lifted a record 6,270 pounds in Toccoa, Georgia.

But the Greeks would find much of today's sport familiar. Weight lifting is today reestablished as an athletic event and is part of the same drive for physical perfection so admired in the ancient world.

STRENGTH THROUGH THE AGES *Feats of muscular strength have been highly valued by many civilizations through the centuries. Left: An encounter between two strongmen of the classical world, Hercules and Atlas, as depicted by the 20th-century artist Walter Crane. Below: Paul Anderson of the United States tests his strength during a friendly competition with the U.S.S.R. in 1955. Anderson won first place in the heavyweight division with a lift of 1,130 pounds. Two years later Anderson lifted 6,270 pounds off a trestle — a world record unequaled to date.*

·HERCVLES·AND·ATLAS·

USE YOUR BRAINS!

Contrary to popular belief, the human brain does not necessarily lose its power through age. Constant mental activity will keep the brain young. That is what Professor Marian Diamond of the University of California says after years of research on the development of the human brain.

She bases her findings on the behavior of young rats. Instead of keeping the rats on their own in empty cages, she and her fellow researchers gave them a stimulating environment: the company of other rats, plenty of playthings such as wheels and ladders—in fact anything that would make them use their brains.

Professor Diamond found that this stimulation changed the chemistry and structure of the cortex, the brain's thin outer layer of nerve cells. Every part of each nerve cell enlarged, and the number of support cells attached to them increased. As a result, the brains of the rats became more active and the creatures were better able to cope with the number of different tasks the researchers set for them.

The team of researchers then experimented with elderly rats, aged 766 days. (In terms of a rat's potential life span, this is the equivalent of a human age of 76 years.) When stimulated, even the old rats showed a thickening of the cortex.

What do these experiments imply for the human brain? Professor Diamond interviewed a number of active people who were over 88 years old. She says: "I found that the people who use their brains don't lose them—it was that simple."

A MATTER OF TASTE

How we taste what we taste

FOR SOME PEOPLE, eating is one of the great sensual pleasures in life. The taste of a meal is one of the reasons we like or dislike our food. Yet the actual mechanics of taste are still not completely understood.

Taste is detected by minute, barrel-shaped taste buds—about 9,000 of them—located on the upper surface of the tongue. There are also a few taste buds in the throat and on the soft palate at the back of the mouth. The tip of each taste bud carries a group of 15 to 20 taste receptors—cells linked to nerve fibers that carry taste impulses to the brain.

Taste receptors have a short life: they are completely renewed every seven days or so. As we grow older, the number of taste buds decreases; thus, older people are less receptive to taste than children, a fact that may explain why some children dislike strong-tasting, spicy foods.

Discerning detectors

Taste buds can detect only four basic tastes: sweet, sour (or acid), salt, and bitter. Different areas of the tongue respond to these different tastes. The tip is sensitive to sweet things, the sides to sour, the tip and sides to salty, and the back of the tongue to bitter. Some substances, therefore, *seem* to produce different flavors depending upon which part of the tongue they stimulate. For instance, on the tip of the tongue saccharin tastes sweet; farther back, it tastes bitter.

The actual experience of taste, or more accurately, of flavor, is more complex. It involves not only the sense of taste but also other senses and qualities. These include the sense of smell and the sight, temperature, and texture of food. Smell is particularly important; anyone who has eaten food while suffering from a heavy cold knows only too well how the flavor of food may be impaired. Indeed, although a cold is said to destroy the taste of food, what it actually destroys is its smell.

Acting on impulse

Scientists still do not completely understand the taste process, but it would seem that taste is probably the result of a mild chemical reaction. The molecules of the food being tasted form a bond with the molecules of the surface of the taste cell. This excites the nerve fiber, which in turn gives rise to a nerve impulse. The central nervous system relays these sensations to the brain, which identifies the taste and associates it with a particular food.

Whatever the process, one thing is certain: without our ability to taste, food would cease to be the pleasure that it is.

THE POWER OF SLEEP

Shakespeare was probably right

Sleep that knits up the ravelled sleave of care,
The death of each day's life, sore labour's bath,
Balm of hurt minds, great nature's second course,
Chief nourisher in life's feast.

WITH THESE WORDS, spoken by the murderer-king Macbeth, William Shakespeare voiced a view taken up by poets and philosophers through the centuries: sleep is good for you. Accepted as commonplace for so long, it is probably taken for granted. However, only recently has medical science started to investigate thoroughly the restorative powers of sleep.

Serious attention to sleep began in the 1950's with the use of the electroencephalograph (EEG) to record changes in the electrical waves in the brain. By using the EEG to record the pattern of changes in brain waves during sleep, scientists distinguished two kinds of sleep: rapid eye movement sleep (REMS) and slow wave sleep (SWS), or nonrapid eye movement sleep (NREMS).

In REMS the brain waves are small, fast, and irregular, and the sleeper's eyes move rapidly as if watching events. Most dreams occur during this period of sleep. In SWS, however, the brain waves are large, slow, and regular. This is the deepest form of sleep—the sleep from which people are most difficult to wake.

The greatest breakthrough in sleep research was made in the 1970's by Dr. Ernest L. Hartmann, founder of the U.S.-based Sleep Foundation and director of the Sleep and Dream Laboratory at Boston State Hospital in Massachusetts. In addition to the two different types of sleep, Hartmann

BRAIN WAVE PATTERNS DURING SLEEP

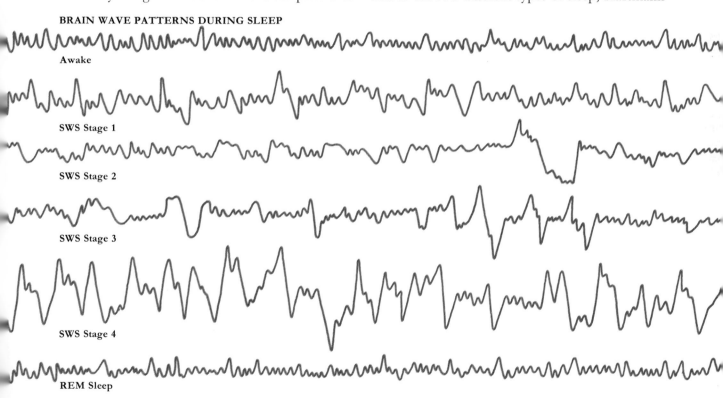

Awake

SWS Stage 1

SWS Stage 2

SWS Stage 3

SWS Stage 4

REM Sleep

BRAIN WAVES *With the help of the electroencephalograph, physicians can now measure brain waves, which tell us a great deal about the way we sleep. Above are the brain wave patterns in a typical sleep cycle. Soon after falling asleep one enters the SWS (slow wave sleep) phase which, according to some experts, restores the body physically. SWS is divided into four stages: 1) irregular brain waves; 2) bursts of activity called spindles; 3) long, slow patterns called delta waves; and 4) the deepest sleep of all, delta sleep. After progressing from Stages 1 through 4, the sleeper repeats the stages—in reverse. After again reaching Stage 1, the sleeper will enter REMS (rapid eye movement sleep)—a period of dreaming and of mentally restorative sleep, some believe. According to proponents of this theory, people repeat these cycles four to five times every night.*

also identified two kinds of tiredness: physical tiredness, following bodily activity, and mental tiredness, following intellectual activity or emotional stress.

Hartmann then took his study one step further and began to ponder if the two kinds of sleep and two types of tiredness might be related.

The long sleep

To put his theory to the test, Hartmann and his colleagues at the Sleep and Dream Laboratory gathered two groups of volunteers. The first group consisted of men who usually slept an average of $5\frac{1}{2}$ hours a night; the second, men who usually slept at least $8\frac{1}{2}$ hours. After several days of observation and tests, Hartmann discovered that both sets of sleepers spent almost exactly the same amount of time in slow wave sleep. Those who slept more spent the extra hours in rapid eye movement sleep.

From this and other research, Hartmann concluded that everyone needs roughly the same amount of SWS, but that some people need more REMS than others. The difference depends largely on the type of personality and on factors such as stress and anxiety. Thus, people who are worriers or have problems need more REMS than people with normally tranquil or problem-free minds.

The reason, Hartmann believes, is that REMS has a particular mental restorative function. It is his theory that during waking hours the nerve cells in the brain deteriorate, particularly when subjected to stress and anxiety. REMS restores the loss by producing chemicals, known as catecholamines, that repair the damaged cells. The greater the stress or anxiety, the more REMS is needed.

Vital properties

REMS, then, restores—mentally. Conversely, according to Hartmann, SWS restores physically. In the same way that brain cells undergo normal wear and tear so, too, do bodily tissues. Some recent research suggests that during SWS the body builds up supplies of protein and ribonucleic acid, which are vital for healthy cell growth. Therefore, the greater the physical activity, the more physically tired one feels and the more SWS one needs.

Not all researchers agree with Dr. Hartmann's theories, and he is careful to stress that they are only theories. But they do seem to support everything we have always believed to be true about sleep. As Shakespeare said, it seems that whenever we succumb to feelings of tiredness, we are merely invoking nature's own repair system.

A QUESTION OF SIZE

Solving the Pygmy puzzle

AN ADULT PYGMY male may grow as tall as five feet; his wife to a mere four feet six inches. Why Pygmies are so small is a question that has puzzled anthropologists ever since explorers first encountered them in the tropical rain forests of Africa. After more than 100 years of research, it seems that the mystery has at last been solved.

Anthropologists have been particularly intrigued because the Pygmies seemed to be essentially no different from the taller Bantus with whom they shared their villages—except in their size. Pygmies and Bantus enjoyed the same diet, shared the same blood groups, and even had the same levels of growth hormone. Yet on average Bantus were more than a foot taller than Pygmies.

It was not until 1981 that the breakthrough was made by Professor Rudi Froesch of the University of Zurich. Froesch is an expert on a little-known but important group of hormones known as IGF's. The two main ones—IGF-1 and IGF-2—form when

there is a reaction between growth hormone and certain proteins in the body. Their precise function is not known, but it seems that they are essential for normal growth, and growth hormone will not work properly without them.

Missing connection

Froesch suspected that the size of the Pygmies and the presence of IGF-1 were somehow linked, and he decided to see if his theory held up. To stimulate the production of IGF-1, he injected volunteers with growth hormone. Blood tests showed that the normal reaction had not taken place. There *was* a major deficiency of IGF-1; for some reason Pygmies could not produce it in the right quantities, which is why they did not grow taller.

"The riddle of the small size of Pygmies has been solved," Froesch says. However, what he has not commented on is the possibility that, with the development of artificial IGF-1, Pygmies could one day be as tall as other African peoples.

HOT BUT NOT BOTHERED

A little touch of fever may be good for you

FOR MORE THAN 2,000 YEARS physicians believed that a fever was nature's way of burning out the poisons that made people ill. But in the 20th century doctors have taken a different view, using drugs such as aspirin to reduce the temperature of feverish patients. Today, however, research suggests that the ancient doctors were right after all: fever is an important part of the body's process of healing itself.

The research was begun in 1975 by Matthew J. Kluger at the University of Michigan Medical School. Kluger decided to use reptiles, in which body heat is determined by the surrounding temperature, rather than humans, whose body heat remains constant. For his experiments Kluger chose the desert iguana, a small American lizard.

Fever pitch

Kluger infected some of the iguanas with bacteria and kept them in incubators at controlled temperatures. Those that were kept at about 104°F raised their own body temperatures to the same level and developed a fever. Subsequently they recovered from the infections induced by the bacteria. Those kept at 93.2°F were unable to develop a fever and later died from their infections.

Since Kluger reported the results of his experiments, physicians and other scientists have been applying his findings to humans. They have focused their research on the hypothalamus, the part of the brain that keeps the body's normal temperature hovering around 98.6°F. When bacteria or viruses invade the bloodstream, white

FEVERED LIZARD *The desert iguana may seem an unlikely animal to use to study fever in humans. But because it is a reptile, its body heat is determined by the environment and is easily controllable in experiments.*

blood cells rally to the defense. They release a substance called endogenous pyrogen into the bloodstream; it immediately adjusts the thermostat in the hypothalamus so that the body temperature rises. The higher temperature in turn stimulates the production of more white blood cells, which try to identify and destroy the cause of the illness.

However, not all fever temperatures are beneficial. Prolonged temperatures of around 102°F can put excessive strain on patients with heart or breathing problems, while temperatures higher than 107°F, if not reduced quickly, are generally fatal. So although a little touch of fever may be good for you, too much can be harmful.

THE BODY IN BALANCE

An amazing juggling act

WE ALL ADMIRE an acrobat balanced on a high wire, juggling dozens of objects at the same time. But such a feat of physical control is nothing compared to the internal balancing act that keeps our bodies functioning in a normal, healthy state day after day.

Scientists call this internal balance homeostasis, and its achievement involves some of the most complex and finely tuned mechanisms in nature.

To remain healthy, the human body must be maintained at a temperature neither too warm nor

too cold; body fluids must be kept at the required levels; and blood chemicals such as salts, sugars, and hormones must be present in precisely the correct proportions. A small imbalance in any one of these can quickly lead to disease, even death. Without our being aware of it, the balance is constantly monitored, adjusted, and maintained.

In hot weather, people perspire and blush— reactions that increase heat loss and keep body temperature down. In the cold, shivering and "goose bumps," respectively, increase body heat and reduce the heat loss that normally occurs with evaporation of moisture from the skin.

Such bodily responses may seem simple, yet they require that many of the body's organs work in harmony. Nerve cells on the skin that are sensitive to changes in temperature send signals to the brain, stimulating a small glandlike structure, the hypothalamus, to release chemicals into the blood. These chemicals in turn stimulate other organs.

The heartbeat may alter, the breathing rate may be adjusted, or food chemicals stored in the liver may be released to fuel increased body activity. When signals from the skin indicate that the reaction is no longer necessary, the hypothalamus ceases to stimulate the other organs.

Into action

The hypothalamus regulates many other elements of homeostasis in a similar way. When shortages of food and liquid are detected, the hypothalamus stimulates a sensation of hunger or thirst. When enough food or water has been taken in, the sensation ceases. Another important mechanism is the "fight or flight" reaction that instantly prepares the body for danger. The heartbeat increases dramatically, blood vessels dilate to reduce blood loss through wounds, and blood supply to the muscles increases rapidly. What creates these reactions is the release of adrenaline into the blood from the adrenal glands, which are first stimulated into action by chemicals produced in the hypothalamus.

Imagine a factory that could function without supervision, adjusting its output to ever-changing conditions and repairing defective parts as required. As yet, this completely self-supporting, self-regulating technology does not exist outside the human body, other than in animals. The miracle of homeostasis gets top honors for sophistication and complexity—and can probably never be duplicated artificially.

SEPARATE – BUT NOT EQUAL

Are two minds better than one?

A MAN GETS UP in the morning and begins to dress. When he tries to put on his pants, he finds his left hand pulling them up and his right hand pulling them down.

On another occasion the same man loses his temper with a tool. His right hand starts to throw it down; his left hand grabs his arm.

This man has had a commissurotomy, an operation in which the major nerve fibers that permit one side of the brain to communicate with the other are severed. As a result, the right side of his brain can be telling the left hand to pull his pants up without informing the left side of the brain, which controls the right hand, about what is going on.

At one time used to relieve epileptic fits, the operation usually has little effect on the ability of the patient to live a normal life. But an occasional bizarre occurrence indicates how independent the two sides of the brain are. Indeed, laboratory tests on split-brain patients reveal that the two halves of the brain understand the world and respond to it quite differently.

One brain, two minds

Since the right brain "sees" objects in the left field of vision, and the left brain sees objects in the right field, experimenters have been able to devise ingenious split-screen techniques to ensure that only one side of the brain receives a particular piece of information. In this way they can compare left-side and right-side responses to the same object.

In one test a woman was seated in front of a screen. It had a small black dot in the center. When a picture of a cup was flashed to the right of the dot (to her left brain), the subject reported that she had seen a cup. Then a picture of a spoon was flashed to the left of the dot, to her right brain. The subject reported that she had seen nothing. A number of objects were then hidden behind the screen. When asked to reach under the screen with her left hand (controlled by the right side of the brain) and select the object that she had seen, she chose a pencil.

In a second experiment, the subject's right brain was shown a picture of a nude woman. The subject giggled and blushed, but said that she had seen only a flash of light.

In both experiments the right brain had been aware of what it had seen, but it was, in effect, dumb; it knew more than it could describe.

In another experiment with split-brain patients, the right brain consistently matched a pair of scissors with a crossed knife and fork, and a wide-brimmed hat with a cake on a plate. The left brain, however, matched the scissors to a needle and thread, and the cake to the knife and fork. The right brain, therefore, grasped connections between the

VISUAL PATHS *When fixed on a single point, each eye sees both visual fields but sends information about the right visual field only to the left side of the brain, and information about the left visual field only to the right side. The two sides of the brain—the hemispheres—normally communicate through the corpus callosum, the nerve fibers that link the two sides of the brain. If the callosum is cut and the eyes prevented from moving, each side of the brain is, in effect, blind to what information the other is receiving. When this happens, experimenters are able to compare the abilities of each hemisphere.*

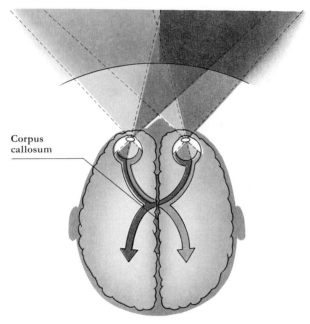

Corpus callosum

Left hemisphere   Right hemisphere

appearance of objects; the left brain could group them according to their function.

The reasoning, analytic nature of the left brain emerged with even more clarity when subjects looked at a shape, such as a cube. They then drew it, first with the left hand (right brain) and then with the right hand (left brain).

The left-handed drawings were fairly accurate representations of a cube, but the right-handed drawings consisted of rows of parallel lines, or a square with lines projecting from it. The left brain had broken the cube down into its constituent parts; the right brain had seen the cube as a whole.

It seems that the right brain is more intuitive in its understanding than the left brain, which persists in questioning what it sees. The left brain excels at analyzing the world; the right brain sees it as a whole and accepts it.

Reason and intuition

These two very different ways of interpreting all experience are reflected in our everyday lives and sometimes come into conflict with each other. The instincts and intuition of our right brain may tell us things that seem completely illogical; the powers of reasoning in our left brain are sometimes unable to help us out of an emotional crisis.

To make a clear-cut choice between two different points of view often seems impossible, especially when questions of right and wrong may be involved. Might what often seems to be a moral dilemma merely reflect the different ways in which the two sides of our brains are interpreting reality?

CRYING CLUES

Shedding different tears

THERE IS NOTHING like a good cry when one is upset, and the effect is usually beneficial. However, few people realize that the tears provoked by an irritant, such as particularly pungent onions, differ in composition from emotional tears. Science has now proved that the tears shed while preparing onions are chemically unlike those that fall in sadness.

Tears are one of the ways nature protects the body. Tears form continually in small quantities to clean and lubricate the eyes and contain a substance called lysozyme that inhibits bacteria. Some of the tears evaporate; the balance are discharged into the nose, where the antibacterial action of lysozyme also helps to prevent infection.

Until recently, research into weeping has been a matter for psychologists who have investigated what makes people cry. But today other scientists working on the physical composition of tears have arrived at some interesting conclusions.

Controlled tears

The pioneer in this research is William H. Frey II, a biochemist at the St. Paul–Ramsey Medical Center in Minnesota. Frey and a team of colleagues have been conducting a comprehensive study of tears. To obtain emotionally induced tears, they showed teams of volunteers sad movies for two or more hours and collected the teardrops that flowed from the eyes of the viewers. To obtain the tears that result from irritants, the researchers exposed the volunteers to the vapors of freshly cut onions for a mere three minutes.

Crying it out

Frey's team discovered that both types of tears contain various protein-based hormones that are known to be released by the body in response to stress: prolactin, adrenocorticotropic hormone, and leucine enkephalin, a natural painkiller. But analyses of the two groups of tears showed that the lacrimal (tear-producing) glands respond differently to emotion and to onions. The tears that were motivated by emotion contained larger amounts of proteins than did the tears induced by irritants.

Frey believes that the discovery in teardrops of prolactin, the hormone that stimulates the secretion of milk, may explain why women cry more easily than men: they have more prolactin in their blood. After menopause women tend to cry less, and their prolactin levels are lower. Frey thinks that perhaps in both men and women tears help to flush out toxic substances that accumulate in the body as a result of stress—which may explain why many people feel better after a good cry.

Tear analysis may also find application in the diagnosis of disease. Given the similarity in the composition of blood and tears, some scientists believe that analyzing tears may prove as valuable as analyzing blood.

OUR RELATIVES, THE CHIMPS?

They may be closer than we thought

CHARLES DARWIN was right: We *are* related to the great apes. But Darwin and his fellow naturalists were wrong in supposing that the apes are our remote ancestors; in fact, apes and humans are almost brothers and sisters.

We owe this new insight to the research of Professor Maurice Goodman of Wayne State University in Detroit. He and other biologists who have been analyzing the genetic makeup of humans and the great apes have come up with a startling fact: the difference between humans and the two African great apes—gorillas and chimpanzees—can be categorized as only 1 percent.

Life studies

Before scientists learned how to study the actual molecules of life, they relied on such crude features as body shape and the physical similarities between organs and limbs in order to determine how closely related two different species might be. It was little better than educated guesswork. But now that scientists can analyze the genetic material common to all plants and animals, DNA, piece by piece, they can exchange that guesswork for something more like certainty.

DNA is a kind of blueprint, a set of instructions that tells a living thing how to grow and develop,

ORIGIN OF THE SPECIES *The publication in July 1858 of* The Origin of Species *by Charles Darwin stirred up enormous controversy. Misinterpreting Darwin, many people assumed that humans were directly descended from apes—as parodied in this contemporary cartoon.*

how to repair itself, how to make the countless different molecules it needs daily. Chief among those molecules are the proteins, which are necessary for everything from muscles to the chemicals that ferry messages within and between the cells of every organism.

In studies of evolution, it has proved quicker to examine similarities between proteins rather than similarities between the DNA on which they are based. The faster method is just as reliable: if the proteins are different at one particular location, it can only be because the DNA, too, is different at the corresponding location in the blueprint.

A protein molecule is fairly easy to analyze, because it is composed of, at most, just 20 different submolecules, known as amino acids. Therefore, although some proteins may be made up of hundreds of such submolecules, there are only 20 different kinds to identify. One protein in particular—hemoglobin, the pigment that gives blood its red color—has now been completely analyzed in hundreds of different species. It proves to be a chain of 141 amino acid units.

Relative differences

In all the animals that possess this protein molecule, the sequence of the amino acid chain is similar enough for scientists to be able to say, "That's hemoglobin." But the precise details vary from species to species. For instance, when comparing the Japanese monkey with humans, we find we share 137 amino acids in identical sequence; only four are in a different order. Dogs, however, differ from humans at 23 locations along the molecule. So they are at least five times more distantly related to humans than is the Japanese monkey.

By comparing not just hemoglobins but dozens of other proteins common to many species, biologists can express the differences between any two species as a percentage. According to this yardstick, humans and apes are just 1 percent apart.

Such differences act as a kind of clock, ticking out the aeons of evolutionary time. According to our clock, this means that humans and the apes have a common ancestor who lived about 5 million years ago (or 10, say more conservative biologists). The differences between humans and the apes, and among the apes themselves, have arisen since then.

To put it another way: we could take 99 percent of a gorilla's DNA and substitute it for that of a human being's—and no one could tell the difference. Over the coming decades, that crucial 1 percent will be the focus of some fascinating research into what sets us so very far apart from our probable brothers and sisters, the apes.

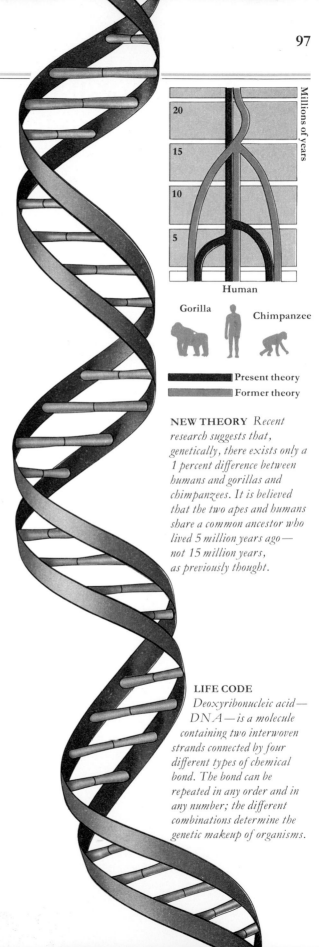

NEW THEORY *Recent research suggests that, genetically, there exists only a 1 percent difference between humans and gorillas and chimpanzees. It is believed that the two apes and humans share a common ancestor who lived 5 million years ago— not 15 million years, as previously thought.*

LIFE CODE *Deoxyribonucleic acid— DNA—is a molecule containing two interwoven strands connected by four different types of chemical bond. The bond can be repeated in any order and in any number; the different combinations determine the genetic makeup of organisms.*

LEARNING FROM THE PUPIL

Keeping an eye on what we really think

OFFER A DOORMAN a thick roll of $100 bills for just holding open a door, and his eyes will probably open wide with pleasure and surprise. In fact, they will open in two quite distinct ways. Not only will his eyelids widen, but his pupils, which control the amount of light entering the eye, will dilate as well. And they will do so even if the man shows no other emotion.

By observing the way the pupil behaves, psychologists learn much about our true reactions to events—no matter what we say we feel and however we try to disguise our feelings.

Just as the pupil dilates in pleasure, it shrinks when confronting something distasteful or frightening—a picture of a poisonous snake, for example. But watching the pupil at work can reveal even more subtle information; it seems that the pupil is a window on the way our minds work.

Nervous reaction

The pupil offers a valid indication of the state of the nervous system as a whole. Psychologists have noted that when students are given a math problem to solve, their pupils dilate, and remain dilated, until they have solved the problem and announced the answer. At the same time, their hearts beat faster and they display other signs of nervousness.

Taste or smell can also affect the behavior of the eye's pupil. A group of people were given soft drinks to taste during some market research. The degree to which their pupils dilated or constricted indicated—much more than their oral descriptions—how well each liked the different flavors.

Because humans have no control over the way the pupils behave, they are a kind of lie detector. In one test, scientists found that the pupils of the eyes of women who claimed to be unaffected by photographs of male models gave them away. Their pupils dilated when the women actually looked at the pictures.

In another test, people were asked to look at a set of modern abstract paintings. Curiously, a number of those who claimed to enjoy modern art showed a negative reaction; many of the pictures triggered signs of rejection when the subjects' pupils contracted in dislike.

Magic, motherhood, and marketing

Observing how the pupils of the eye behave has a number of applications. Some magicians may not be particularly skilled with a pack of cards but can tell when a hidden card turns up: the pupils of the person who put it in the pack dilate in recognition.

Other uses are more practical. Psychologists are employing the technique when exploring young people's attitudes toward their parents and the point at which an interest in the opposite sex emerges. Perhaps the broadest application is in testing reactions to new products, packaging, and advertising. When a new item appears on the supermarket shelves, it may be available because it made someone's eyes light up.

MIRACULOUS TRANSPLANT

The world's first heart transplant was accomplished in 1967, but legend has it that the world's first leg transplant took place in medieval times. This medical first is attributed to Cosmas and Damien, the patron saints of medicine, who were martyred in the 3rd century A.D. After their deaths many wondrous cures were attributed to their healing powers.

One story tells of a white man suffering from cancer of the leg. He had been praying at the saints' shrine in Rome and fell asleep. In his dream the two saints appeared to him and debated how to cure him. When the man awoke, he discovered that he had a new leg, taken from a recently deceased black man. The event is depicted in the painting attributed to the 15th-century Italian Girolamo da Cremona.

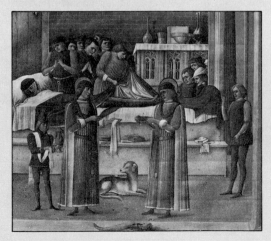

PART 2

FEATS OF BUILDING AND ENGINEERING

AN ANCIENT WONDER OF THE AMERICAS

Chancing upon the remains of a lost civilization

IN 1848 SMALL BANDS of determined men were hacking their way through almost impenetrable rain forest in the remote Peten region of Guatemala. Known as *chicleros,* the men were in search of sapodilla trees; the sap was prized as the main ingredient of chewing gum.

The inhospitable jungle was inhabited by wild animals and snakes and deluged by 200 inches of rainfall a year. It seemed impossible that anyone could ever have lived in such a place. But to their surprise the *chicleros* came upon vast edifices that towered above the green canopy of the forest— buildings long since empty and abandoned to the jungle. Unwittingly, the *chicleros* had chanced upon one of the ancient wonders of the Americas.

Rebuilding a city

The discovery soon came to the attention of archeologists, who paid the *chicleros* $15 for each building to which they were led. It was known that from about 600 B.C. a highly advanced and sophisticated people, the Mayans, had lived and built cities in the region of Peten. But the cities had disappeared long ago, and it was not known if the inhabitants had survived.

Although some preliminary excavation was carried out late in the 19th century, it was not until 1956 that a team from the University of Pennsylvania, under the direction of William R. Coe, started to excavate one of the oldest and largest of the sites, Tikal.

As laborers hacked back the forest, more than 100 specialists analyzed the discoveries. For 13 more years experts continued to sift and examine every square inch of soil, piecing together and virtually rebuilding six square miles of the magnificent city, less than a quarter of the original site.

Excavations within the area have revealed the existence of some 3,000 buildings. They formed a complex system of spectacular pyramid-temples, palaces, and monasteries that were once surrounded by verdant stretches of irrigated fields. The city appears to have been a labyrinth of multilevel, interconnecting buildings constructed with limestone and mortar. So advanced were their engineering skills that the Mayans built reservoirs and

STANDING PROUD *Named for the animal carved on its main door, the Temple of the Giant Jaguar is one of the six major temple pyramids of Tikal. Built as a burial monument about A.D. 700, it was not excavated until 1962. Inside was a skeleton surrounded by valuable jewelry and ornaments.*

aqueducts to solve the problem of providing a continuing supply of water.

Archeologists have managed to reconstruct some of the history of this mysterious people. But they frankly admit that they do not know what purpose Tikal served. Some say that the city was a political and commercial center; others, that it was solely a religious or ceremonial center.

It is also difficult to understand how a large population could have supplied food for itself in a region that today supports only about two people per square mile. Estimates suggest that during the height of the Mayan civilization some 50,000 people lived in Tikal and outlying areas—around 200 per square mile.

Means of survival

Each expert has a theory as to how the Mayans subsisted. Some authorities believe that they hunted and fished for their food. Others suggest that they practiced a highly organized and intensive form of agriculture, using advanced methods of irrigation. There are signs also of "raised field" cultivation, which would have enabled Mayans to grow crops during the rainy season when the

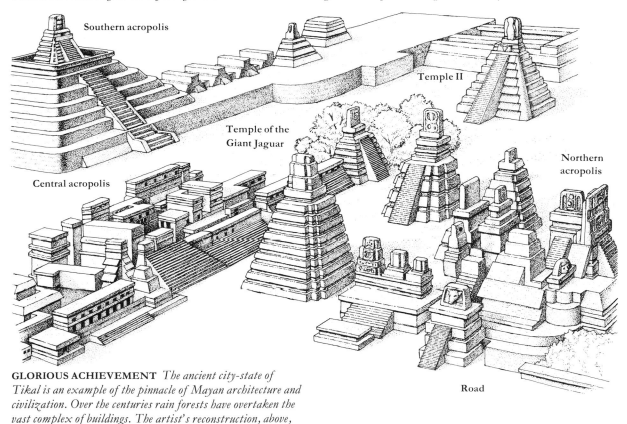

Southern acropolis

Temple II

Temple of the
Giant Jaguar

Central acropolis

Northern
acropolis

Road

GLORIOUS ACHIEVEMENT *The ancient city-state of Tikal is an example of the pinnacle of Mayan architecture and civilization. Over the centuries rain forests have overtaken the vast complex of buildings. The artist's reconstruction, above, offers an impression of how it may have looked.*

lowlands were flooded. But there is no doubt that the Mayans had to battle adverse conditions.

Complicating the puzzle is the fact that after flourishing for more than 1,000 years, around A.D. 900 the Mayan civilization mysteriously collapsed, and cities such as Tikal were abandoned. Among theories put forward to explain the mystery: the Mayans were conquered by a less advanced people; food shortages led to a rebellion against the ruling class; an earthquake, a famine, a plague—or even another disaster—decimated the population.

Whatever happened, over the years the city of Tikal became entombed by the jungle, its buildings gradually overrun by nature. Today the Peten region of Guatemala is still an isolated place, although it has been connected to the outside world by roads. Intensive searches for petroleum and minerals are under way, and the ancient Mayan sites are being developed as tourist attractions.

Yet had it not been for the invention of chewing gum, the glorious Mayan civilization might never have been discovered.

DROWNING A WATERFALL

The dam that powers two countries

ON NOVEMBER 11, 1982, President João Figueiredo of Brazil and President Alfredo Stroessner of Paraguay inaugurated the world's largest hydroelectric scheme: the building of the Itaipu Dam across the Paraná River. The ceremony also marked the drowning, forever, of the world's most voluminous waterfall.

The Paraná River forms part of the border between Brazil and Paraguay. Some 118 miles upstream from the new dam, the river formerly flowed into a deep canyon, forcing the waters from a channel 1,250 feet wide into a gorge merely 200 feet in width. This sudden compression created the Guaira Falls, known in the Portuguese language of Brazil as the Sete Quedas (Seven Falls).

The falls carried the greatest volume of falling water in the world—twice the amount of Niagara and 12 times that of the Victoria Falls on Africa's Zambezi River. The roar of the Seven Falls could be heard 20 miles away, and a permanent rainbow hovered over the river. Once a popular tourist attraction, today the falls are just cliffs hidden beneath the vast lake that the new dam has created.

Massive undertaking

Brazil and Paraguay signed an agreement to build the Itaipu Dam in 1966, but work did not begin until 1978. The first step was to divert the Paraná River. Workers dug a channel 1¼ miles long, 490 feet wide, and 300 feet deep, the largest river diversion ever undertaken.

Work on the main dam started the following year. On the Paraguayan side alone, nearly 40,000 workers toiled around the clock to meet the completion date. Some 15,700,000 cubic yards of concrete were poured and 19,700,000 cubic yards of rock and soil moved for use as an abutment.

Today the main concrete dam stands 620 feet high and is 4,050 feet long. The concrete abutment dam supporting the entire structure is 210 feet high. The artificial lake behind the dam covers 540 square miles and is nearly twice the size of the largest such reservoir in the United States, Lake Mead, which lies behind Hoover Dam on the Arizona-Nevada border.

Powerful benefits

The 18 vast turbines in the dam's powerhouse can produce 12,600 megawatts of electricity—even more than the Grand Coulee Dam in the state of Washington, formerly the world's largest hydroelectric power plant. Although Paraguay and Brazil share the electricity equally, most of it is sold to Brazil because Paraguay's few industries consume little power. The revenues help Paraguay pay its share of the $12.7 billion cost of the dam, most of which had been borne by Brazil.

When the project was at its busiest, it virtually ended unemployment in Paraguay and brought extra revenue into the economy. Even after the Itaipu Dam was completed, work proceeded on two smaller power dams downstream, constructed jointly by Paraguay and Argentina at a cost of an additional $13 billion.

Many see the Itaipu Dam as one of the great feats of engineering of the 20th century. Its effects on Brazil in particular will be enormous. Eventually the dam is expected to provide as much as one-third of the power required in her busy southeastern region, which at present consumes two-thirds of the national supply of electricity. Although the dam has been criticized as a vast financial burden on a country already heavily in debt, its low running costs may prove to be Brazil's salvation.

SECRET OF THE STONES

At Carnac in Brittany, northern France, stand some 3,000 upright stones, or menhirs, varying in height from 18 inches to 20 feet and laid out in several parallel lines. These impressive rows of local stone, created about 4000 B.C., stretch almost three miles across open countryside. One single stone, the Great Menhir, lies shattered in four pieces; intact, it would have towered 60 feet above the ground and weighed about 340 tons.

No one knows the reason these stones were placed at Carnac. Archeologists can only guess at their significance, since we have been left no clues in either words or pictures. But the presence of burial chambers, or dolmens, nearby suggests that the stones probably represented sacred monuments to the dead; in Breton, the name Carnac means "cemetery of bones."

The Carnac stones run from west to east. This has led many archeologists to speculate that the people who arranged them may have been sun worshipers; the position of the stones clearly indicates the direction of sunrise at the solstices and the equinoxes. It has also been suggested that the stones may have formed some kind of lunar observatory erected by astronomer-priests to predict eclipses of the moon. Or perhaps the stones served as powerful fertility symbols for a people obsessed with fruitful harvests and healthy offspring. Indeed, in the 19th century childless couples were told to dance naked at Carnac if they wanted children.

Investigations continue, but it seems that the stones of Carnac may never reveal their secret.

MONUMENTAL STONES *The giant stones of Carnac line the Brittany countryside. Although the significance of the stones remains a mystery, some archeologists believe that they were originally erected as monuments to the dead.*

THE TOWERING INFERNAL

It is not automatic that what goes up must come down. At least that is what a demolition company in Hackney, London, found out.

The company had been hired to demolish a 21-floor apartment building. The structure, Northaird Point, was only 20 years old but from the start had been plagued by faulty design. The main problem was that the concrete panels that formed the outside walls were not weather-resistant. They let in both wind and rain,

making the apartments cold and damp. Too expensive to repair, the building had to come down.

The cost of demolition was a staggering £391,000 ($560,000), and the preparations were very elaborate. Computers were used to site the explosive charges on the first eight floors. When detonated, the charges were to make the rest of the building collapse under its own weight.

Before demolition day, a massive safety operation was mounted. Streets were closed to traffic, and residents evacuated.

When the big day arrived—November 3, 1985—thousands of people turned up to see the

fun. At noon, the charge was detonated and there was a massive explosion. Amid much applause, the building began to collapse in a gigantic cloud of dust.

But when the dust cleared, Northaird Point was still standing—or at least some of it. The top 12 floors remained intact, leaning at an angle on top of a large pile of rubble that had once been the first nine floors. Some wits immediately dubbed the remains "the towering infernal."

Investigation revealed that what was holding the building up were the outer wall panels—the source of the trouble in the first place. Since there was nothing else they could do, the contractors sent for a wrecker's ball in order to demolish the rest of the building section by section.

But the problems were not over yet. In order to get the massive machinery close enough to start the demolition, workers had to knock down a huge wall—which was not supposed to be demolished at all.

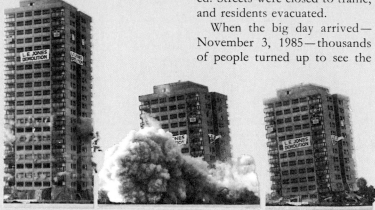

Going . . .   *Going . . .*   *Not gone.*

JOURNEY TO THE CENTER OF THE EARTH

Investigating the world below

WHILE SCIENTISTS probe the secrets of outer space, much about the world on which we stand remains mysterious. To expand our knowledge, the U.S.S.R. started a deep borehole drilling program to investigate geological theories about the formation of the earth.

The Kola Peninsula, in the northwest of the U.S.S.R., was selected, and drilling began in 1970. By the mid-1980's the borehole was more than seven miles deep—the deepest penetration of the surface of the earth yet attempted. From this depth it takes 18 hours to hoist samples to the surface.

The thickness of the earth's crust ranges from 50 miles in mountainous areas to just 6 miles beneath the ocean floor; the average around the world is 21 miles. The borehole, therefore, has already eaten its way through one-third of the earth's surface.

Russian engineers have achieved the feat with modern drilling technology. The main body of the drill, a string of metal pipes weighing more than 300 tons, can withstand the high pressures and temperatures of the earth's interior. The pipes remain stationary as a drilling turbine that protrudes below them brings up rock samples.

The Kola borehole has disproved some theories and established many new facts. Previously, the earth's three-tier structure was thought to consist of a thin sedimentary layer, a granite layer as deep as four miles, and finally a basalt layer—starting at the so-called Conrad Boundary—that descends to the core of the earth.

But the drill has revealed that the sedimentary layer reaches a depth of nearly four miles, and at seven miles the drill still has not struck the basalt layer. The discrepancy came to light because rock between three and five miles deep is less dense than that above it, and the temperature is nearly double the estimates. At five miles it is 356°F, not 212°F as believed; it increases 4.5°F every 100 yards. The heat makes the minerals in the rocks give off water; this creates still more pressure, causing the rocks to expand and crack.

In its descent, the drill has discovered fossilized microorganisms in the billion-year-old rocks at depths previously thought to have been barren of life. These fossils may well make scientists revise their opinions about early life on this planet.

Similar boreholes are being drilled elsewhere in the world, and should give future generations a better understanding of what lies beneath their feet.

PORT FOR FIVE SEAS

A 260-year-old dream comes true

IF ASKED TO NAME a city that was a port for five seas, the inland city of Moscow would probably not be the first that comes to mind. However, the completion of the V. I. Lenin Volga–Baltic Waterway in 1964 gave Moscow access to the White, the Baltic, the Azov, the Black, and the Caspian seas. Nearly 1,850 miles in length, this is the longest canal complex in the world.

In the early 18th century Czar Peter the Great dreamed of linking the Baltic Sea with the seas to the south and the cities of the interior in order to overcome Russia's major disadvantage: a small coastline that left the nation virtually landlocked.

The first canal, which linked St. Petersburg (today Leningrad) with Europe's longest river, the Volga (2,293 miles), was opened in 1709. But the canal was too shallow to be of much use. By 1810 the more elaborate Mariinsk system was in operation, and improvements continued to be made throughout the 19th century. In the 1930's an 80-mile stretch of canal was added to link Moscow with the Volga. Another canal linked the Baltic with the White Sea, shortening the water route from Leningrad to Archangel by 2,435 miles.

In the 1940's a new canal was built to connect the Volga to the Don, which flows into the Sea of Azov and then on into the Black Sea. The rebuilding of the Mariinsk system was completed in 1964.

The waterway is able to handle ships weighing up to 5,000 tons; as a result, new cities have sprung up along its route. Togliatti, with its flourishing car industry, now stands on former swampland.

Most progress, unfortunately, has its price. Part of the Volga's role is to provide reservoirs for irrigation and hydroelectricity. These demands have decreased the flow of the river so that the level of the Caspian Sea has fallen 7 feet 6 inches since 1930. This has caused an exodus of sturgeon, the source of the famous Russian caviar. Today the fish prefer the deeper waters off the coast of Iran.

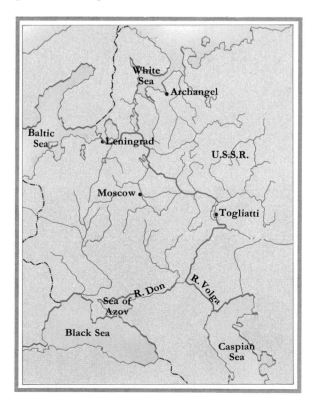

WATERY HIGHWAY *The world's longest canal complex links five seas: the Baltic, White, Black, Caspian, and Azov.*

UNBUILT DREAMS

FOR EVERY BUILDING successfully completed, at least one other fails to leave the drawing board. Existing only as plans, some are practical, everyday buildings. Others are the result of dreams in which the imagination of the architect may border on fantasy. Many unbuilt buildings were designed to celebrate or commemorate particular people or events, others to glorify the town or country in which they were to be erected. Had they been built, a stable in the shape of a cow, a pyramid enclosing the house of Sir Isaac Newton, and a tower with tributes to great Americans of history might have joined the architectural wonders of the modern world.

But today these structures, and many others like them, are known to us only on paper, testimony to the artistic genius— or, some might say, lunacy—of their creators.

MONUMENT TO THE THIRD INTERNATIONAL *A 1,000-foot-high structure designed by Russian architect Vladimir Tatlin in 1919–20 was to consist of two intertwining spirals with huge glass meeting halls suspended inside; they were to rotate at different speeds.*

ISAAC NEWTON MONUMENT *Designed by Anglo-German artist George Scharf in 1834, this truncated pyramid was to enclose Newton's house.*

UNITED NATIONS TOWER *An aluminum structure 110 stories high, designed by U.S. architect Raphael Soriano in 1969, the tower was to be erected on Alcatraz Island in San Francisco Bay as a visual reminder that San Francisco was the city where the U.N. Charter was drawn up.*

VILLA LUCIA, NAPLES *Designed by 19th-century U.S. architect Lamont Young, this leisure center, made of iron, was to contain stores, restaurants, lecture rooms, theaters, and art galleries.*

LEQUEU'S COW STABLE *The design of 18th-century French architect Jean-Jacques Lequeu, the enormous building was to be built in the shape of a cow; the hayloft was to be ventilated, and lights would shine through the eyes.*

FLOATING SPHERES
Aluminum spheres designed by U.S. architect Richard Buckminster Fuller in 1967 were to be modules for floating cities of the future. Hot air would hold them aloft.

PALACE OF THE SOVIETS, MOSCOW
Designed in 1934 by Russian architect B. M. Iofan, this massive wedding-cake structure was to rise some 1,500 feet and be surmounted by a large statue of Lenin.

BEACON OF PROGRESS, CHICAGO *A monument intended to celebrate U.S. achievements, this structure was to be erected on the site of the World's Columbian Exposition of 1893. Designed by American architect Desiré Despradelle in 1900, it was to contain exhibits acknowledging the great Americans in history.*

GREAT TOWER OF LONDON *A design submitted in a competition devised by Sir Edward Watkin, this tower was intended to rival the Eiffel in Paris.*

THE LEANING TOWER OF PISA

Why does it lean?

THE LEANING TOWER OF PISA, in Italy, is one of the world's most beautiful and bizarre buildings. Breaking every architectural rule, the tower at present leans about 14 feet from the vertical and continues to lean farther south every year. The structure, today more than 800 years old, has leaned almost since the day construction was started.

In 1174, during Pisa's golden age, a period of economic prosperity and artistic riches, the citizens resolved to build the campanile (bell tower) that their magnificent cathedral had been without for so long. The tower was to surpass all other towers being built in Italy at the time and was to symbolize the wealth and power of the illustrious Republic of Pisa.

Work in progress

The first stone was laid in August 1174, and numerous architects and master masons worked on the structure. But no sooner had the first story been completed, than the tower started to lean to the south. The culprit was settling of the foundation. To compensate, subsequent stories were built closer to the vertical in order to "straighten" the tower.

The work was very laborious, and the architects and masons either lost interest or were defeated by the problem of the lean. Meanwhile, the tower continued to tilt badly. More radical solutions had to be found for the upper stories, or the whole tower would topple.

One of the more ingenious solutions was to make the pillars on the south side higher than those on the north, so that the tower could "grow" back into line.

The tower was completed in 1350, when the bell chamber was added—also built at an angle to compensate for further settling, with the heaviest bells on the north side. But the tower still leaned southward. Fortunately, no further stories were added. Had they been, the center of gravity would have moved outside the base of the tower, and the entire structure would have fallen.

The site was the cause of all the problems. Pisa stands on a flat alluvial plain, and settling is a common phenomenon throughout the city.

The famous Leaning Tower itself is cylindrical, with eight stories of arched arcades built of white marble. Its present height is 179 feet, although it was originally taller. Not only has settling caused it to lean but also has made it sink into the ground.

Modern technology has helped to stabilize the tower and arrest its rate of lean to about one-sixteenth of an inch every year. But even at this rate, in another 175 years the tower will fall to the ground, reduced to a pile of rubble.

DECLINE—AND FALL? *The Leaning Tower of Pisa has been on a tilt since it was built more than 800 years ago. From the top of the tower, astronomer and physicist Galileo Galilei, a native of Pisa and lecturer in mathematics at the university between 1589 and 1591, conducted his famous experiments. He proved that bodies of different weight fall at the same speed.*

ENTERTAINING CURE

Hollowed into a barren mountain slope on mainland Greece is the ancient and imposing theater of Epidaurus. It was built in the fourth century B.C. by the architect Polyclitus, who made expert use of the mountainside.

As many as 14,000 people could be entertained in this perfectly proportioned auditorium. And the acoustics were excellent. The semicircle of seats was wider than at other theaters, bringing the audience close to the stage so that more sound was retained in the auditorium. Even today a whisper uttered from the circular orchestra, where the chorus danced, can be heard 74 feet higher up in the top tier.

Epidaurus warranted such a large theater because it was the hospital-shrine of Asclepius, the god of healing. It could be considered a pagan equivalent of Lourdes today. And the sacred dramas performed here were all part of "the cure."

However, with the triumph of Christianity, Epidaurus declined. Its hospital buildings fell into ruin, and its theater was eventually buried beneath rubble from the mountain encircling it.

Then, in the 19th century, excavations revealed that it was the best preserved of all the ancient theaters.

At the annual summer festivals of Greek drama held there today, Epidaurus is again crowded with theatergoers. Modern audiences seem to find its remarkable acoustics, which appear to be more magical than engineered, as reviving and stimulating as did the ancient followers of the pagan god Asclepius.

The ancient theater of Epidaurus, Greece, features extraordinary acoustics.

A BEAUTY THAT REFUSES TO DIE

The architectural triumph of the Parthenon

ON THE EVENING of September 26, 1687, a massive explosion sent a column of fire and smoke into the sky above Athens. A shell from the artillery of the Venetian general Francesco Morosini, besieging the city's Turkish occupiers, had landed in the enemy's powder store. The siege was over and the Turks defeated—but the glory of ancient Greek architecture, the Parthenon, was in ruins. It was within the walls of this temple, built 2,100 years earlier, that the Turks had placed their ammunition and gunpowder.

The Parthenon is a ruin to this day. Some of its sculptures were lost forever when collectors ransacked the site in the 18th and 19th centuries. Many more sculptures are in museums throughout Europe. Yet what still stands on the Acropolis, visible for miles around, remains an awe-inspiring monument to the Golden Age of ancient Greece.

It was Pericles, leader of Athens from 461 to 429 B.C., who proposed building a majestic new temple to the city's patron goddess. Athens was the center of an empire, and Pericles was determined that some visible symbol of its wealth and influence be erected. Not only would the new temple house a magnificent gold and ivory statue of Athena, it would also serve as the treasury of the empire.

The Parthenon consists of three basic parts: a colonnade on all four sides, the roof with its

LOOK OF GRANDEUR
The unusual architectural lines of the Parthenon are exaggerated in the illustration below. The horizontals on all four sides curve up slightly at the center. The columns lean inward and are unevenly shaped: all are slightly larger at the center than at the base and taper gently at the top.

MAJESTIC SIGHT
The imposing temple of the Parthenon on the Acropolis towers over Athens below. Above: In "Pheidias and the Parthenon Frieze," the 19th-century painter Lawrence Alma-Tadema imagines how the interior might have appeared at the time that it was being decorated.

triangular pediments at each end, and a central room called the naos. The naos was divided into two parts: one for the statue of Athena, the other for the treasury.

Such a formal arrangement of triangles and repeated rectangles could easily have ended up looking rigid and lifeless. But the columns lean inward slightly, are a little larger at the center than at the base, and gently taper toward the top. And the horizontal lines of the temple are not "true"; there is a slight upward curve toward the center on each of the four sides. These refinements not only soften the lines of the building but also enhance the grandeur of the Parthenon for the viewer standing at ground level.

Hidden features

One of the most astonishing features of the Parthenon was in fact barely visible from the ground: the perfectly detailed, brilliantly colored sculptures that decorated the outside.

The pediment at one end depicted the birth of Athena, who sprang fully formed and fully armed from the head of her father, Zeus. The other pediment illustrated the contest between Poseidon and Athena for the loyalty of the city.

In addition to the pediments, there were two distinct series of sculptures: the 92 metopes, or square panels, above the columns, and the frieze, which ran along the top of the walls of the naos. All were the work of Phidias, the sculptor who also created the statue of Athena within the temple.

The metopes depicted four symbolic battles in which men or gods defeated various agents of disorder and barbarism in the shape of centaurs, giants, Amazons, and Trojans. The frieze depicted the great procession that took place every four years in honor of Athena.

Phidias' crowning contribution to the Parthenon was the 33-foot statue of Athena. It stood in the naos and cost nearly twice as much as the rest of the temple. Athena's flesh was rendered in ivory, her eyes were precious stones, her clothing of gold. In one hand she held a gold statue of Victory. At her feet, a pool of water reflected her glory.

The movement of the stones

All work was completed by 432 B.C., just 16 years after the Athenians had decided to build the temple. Blocks of marble, each of which took 300 working days to cut and deliver, were transported from quarries 10 miles outside Athens and hauled up the steep sides of the Acropolis. Winches, pulleys, and cranes swung the stones and sculptures into place. The walls contained no mortar—each stone was cut to fit exactly. Central pins held sections of the columns together, and masons carved the characteristic fluting once each column was complete.

For nearly a thousand years the Parthenon stood in all its splendor, although every trace of the great statue of Athena had vanished by early in the sixth century. When the Christians arrived in the seventh century, they converted the building into a church. In the 15th century the invading Turks made it into a mosque and set up the arsenal within its walls—sealing the Parthenon's fate.

And yet, although just a shell today, this astonishing temple can still take one's breath away.

CONSTANTINOPLE'S CROWNING GLORY

Outshining Solomon's temple

THE HUGE CHURCH of Hagia Sophia was packed, but above the solemn chanting of the service came the boom of cannon. It was the night of May 28, 1453, and the people were praying for the deliverance of their Christian city of Constantinople from the besieging Islamic Ottoman Turks. The prayers were in vain.

With the dawn came the news that the Turks had reached the city walls. Advancing through the narrow streets, they smashed their way into the church, killing many of those inside. Later that day the Turkish sultan Mehmet II entered the city in triumph. He looked with awe at the great church and, to symbolize his victory over this capital of Christendom, ordered that it be turned into a mosque. After 900 years the ancient church was to begin a new life dedicated to a new religion.

The Byzantine masterpiece

The church had been built in the sixth century A.D. by the Byzantine emperor Justinian. The Byzantine Empire, founded in A.D. 330, was the first great flowering of Christian civilization after the fall of the Roman Empire. Its capital city of Constantinople (today Istanbul), on the site of the ancient Greek city of Byzantium, commanded the Bosporus, the narrow strait linking the Black Sea with the Dardanelles and the Mediterranean. The city

HEAVEN ON EARTH *Suffused with light, the church — and, since 1453, mosque — of Hagia Sophia may be one of the most admired buildings in the world. As the sultan Murat IV remarked: "It is the place where heavenly inspiration descends into the minds of the devout and which gives a foretaste even here below of the Garden of Eden."*

was the geographical and cultural bridge between Europe, the Middle East, and Asia. Its crowning glory was to be the Hagia Sophia (Holy Wisdom).

Justinian appointed as architects Anthemius of Tralles and Isidorus of Miletus. Their design was a masterpiece of Byzantine construction. The central dome was more than 100 feet in diameter and, at its highest point, 184 feet above the ground. With 40 windows around its base, it seemed, in the words of one observer, to be suspended from above rather than supported from below.

For the walls and floors an army of laborers and craftsmen brought marble and granite from quarries as far distant as the Atlantic coast of France. Temples and other places of antiquity were plundered for features of special interest or beauty. Dazzling and intricate mosaics covered large areas of the walls and ceiling. Gold, silver, precious stones, and ivory were lavished on the interior decoration. Some 40,000 pounds of silver were used in the sanctuary behind the altar alone.

The work was finished in the short space of five years — A.D. 532 to 537 — at an estimated cost (by today's values) of more than $180 million. Entering his church for the first time, Justinian cried, "O Solomon, I have surpassed thee!"

"A spectacle of marvelous beauty," agreed the Byzantine historian Procopius. For the scholar Michael of Thessalonica, it was "a tent of the heavens. Sunlight flashes with such brilliance that the gold seems to flow from the dome."

Then catastrophe struck. Earthquakes shook the city, and a part of the dome collapsed. Undaunted, Justinian had it rebuilt. Six centuries later, in 1204, Christian Crusaders on their way to the Holy Land to fight the infidel Turks attacked Constantinople and robbed the church of many of its treasures. In 1346 the dome partially collapsed again. By 1453 Hagia Sophia, although restored and still impressive, was a shadow of its former self.

The church as mosque

Its second age of splendor, as a mosque, was about to begin. The sultan Mehmet II repaired and strengthened the building and added a tall minaret from which, according to Islamic custom, the muezzins could call the faithful to prayer. The sultan's successors added further minarets; furnished the interior with basins of white marble, alabaster urns, and a marble throne; and suspended from the dome six large green medallions bearing the names of Allah, the prophet Muhammad, and other founders of the faith.

For another five centuries the mosque served the faithful of Islam. But in 1935, twelve years after the collapse of the Ottoman Empire and the establishment of a secular Turkish state, the mosque was converted into a museum. In the process many of the mosaics were restored to their former glory.

Today the edifice of Hagia Sophia, its dome, and minarets still tower above the waterfront of Istanbul—a monument to two great religions and more than 1,400 years of history.

GETTING AWAY FROM IT ALL

The extensive building activities of the Solomon Islanders

EVERY YEAR OR SO the Solomon Islands increase in number. In the last 300 years, 50 new islands have been added to this archipelago in the western Pacific, and the process shows little sign of abating. But the additions are not natural phenomena. The islands are artificial, the result of years of painstaking work by the people who live on them.

The new islands are situated in Lau Lagoon, a large stretch of water surrounded by coral reefs off the north coast of Malaita in the eastern Solomons. Opinions vary about the original reason for building these artificial outcroppings: some say it was to provide refuge from the aggressive bush dwellers; others, to escape from the mosquitoes on the shore; still others, to alleviate overcrowding.

According to popular belief, Sulufou was the first man-made island in the Solomons. Leo, a fisherman, built it more than 300 years ago to provide a base near the all-important fish market. Another island, Adagege, was specifically used as a maternity home, and Foubuli was constructed solely to house pigs. More recently a man created one to mark the spot where a shark killed his son.

Rocky foundations

However, most of the islands are made by young couples for their own use. The majority are built up from the floor of the lagoon, but some are constructed around existing rocks. Methods have changed little over the years.

Jagged coral boulders from the reef, or the more suitable flat rocks from the bottom of the lagoon, are transported by raft to the designated site. When the island reaches about 10 feet above the water, it is covered with sand dredged from beaches and riverbeds. A variety of trees provide shade; their roots also help to hold the loose coral foundation together. Because the walls of the islands cannot be seen, even from a short distance away the trees seem to rise out of the sea.

Room for growth

On average it takes at least a year to create an island. Initially, it will be just large enough to accommodate a few huts; some are on stilts to avoid being flooded. As families grow, the area is extended to make room for more huts.

Sulufou, 80 yards long and 30 yards wide, is the largest man-made island; it houses four principal families and has a population of 300. It lies only 700 yards from the main island, and at low tide people can wade out to it—a journey that is undertaken frequently, since firewood and fresh water must be carried out from the main island. Women are responsible for both tasks; they transport the water in long bamboo tubes that are blocked at one end.

Visitors to the islands are welcomed by the inhabitants, who are proud of where they live. After all, there are not many people in the world who have built not only their own homes but also the land on which they stand.

THE MIRACLE OF BOROBUDUR

The temple that embodied the universe

THE MILITARY ENGINEER looked around doubtfully. Purely on the strength of local rumor, he had been dispatched to this ordinary-looking hillock in central Java by the island's English lieutenant governor, Thomas Stamford Raffles. Although folklore suggested that this was the site of "a mountain of Buddhist sculptures in stone," on this day in 1814 all that H.C.C. Cornelius could see were trees, shrubs, and the odd block of stone. Reluctantly following orders, Cornelius directed his team to start digging.

PILGRIM'S PROGRESS *An aerial view of Borobudur (below) reveals the complex design of this ancient Buddhist monument. More than a place of worship, the temple's symbolic structure represents the pilgrim's spiritual journey from ignorance to the ultimate Buddhist ideal of nirvana. To achieve true enlightenment, the pilgrim travels through four distinct stages (inset) before reaching the central stupa that marks the end of his journey. The ordinary world is represented by a wide platform (1), followed by five square terraces symbolizing the preparatory stage of the pilgrim's spiritual transition (2). At the seventh level (3), enlightenment is reached, after which the pilgrim attains his spiritual goal: the state of nirvana (4).*

Tons of vegetation had to be uprooted and moved, cartloads of earth shifted. The work was difficult and tiring in the relentless jungle heat, and after two months there was little to show for it. Then one of the workmen uncovered an intricately carved stone Buddha. With renewed enthusiasm, the workmen continued to clear the site, revealing a temple far more magnificent, vast, and extraordinary than the rumors had even suggested.

A cast of thousands

The temple dated from the time of the Javanese dynasty of the Sailendra kings, who ruled from about A.D. 740. They inspired such strong religious fervor in their subjects that from A.D. 800 many thousands of men worked to construct a Buddhist monument of exceptional scale, beauty, and detail.

The temple of Borobudur (the word means "the monastery on the hill") was built around a natural hill. More than two million cubic feet of stone was

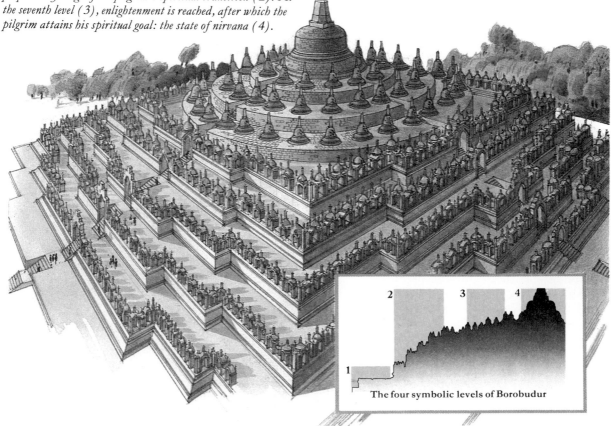

The four symbolic levels of Borobudur

VISION OF PEACE *One of the 440 statues of Buddha at Borobudur gazes over the nearby Menorah Mountains and overlooks the complex network of terraces below.*

worked by craftsmen to create a giant symbol of the universe. The symbolism can be fully appreciated only from the air—a view none of the builders could ever have had.

Covering almost four acres, the pyramid-shaped temple is built on 10 levels. Each corresponds to the spiritual stages in the life of a Buddhist pilgrim as he travels from ignorance to nirvana, the ultimate Buddhist ideal. The first six levels are square and represent the preparatory stage of the pilgrim's journey. Subsequent levels are circular, symbolizing the spiritual transition into a state of enlightenment. The highest point of the temple (the stupa), rising to a height of more than 120 feet, marks the apogee of the pilgrim's journey.

The walk through all the galleries to the top is more than three miles. Carved friezes showing scenes of Buddhist teachings decorate the maze of short, right-angled corridors. In niches all over the temple sit hundreds of Buddhas.

Entombed in ash

Once consecrated, the temple became the focal point of Buddhist worship in the Sailendra kingdom. But in A.D. 930 disaster struck. The nearby volcano, Mount Merapi, erupted with great force, spewing out tons of molten lava and volcanic ash. Overnight Borobudur disappeared without a trace, buried under layers of ash and debris.

For centuries the temple lay hidden in its subterranean tomb, until the curiosity of Raffles inspired it to be revealed once again. Unfortunately, after Raffles left Java, excavation was continued in a very haphazard way. The temple was neglected, and collectors of antiquities stole the priceless treasures. Local people used the stones to build houses. Natural elements further battered the temple, undermining the foundations and eroding the many exposed surfaces.

Restored to splendor

It was not until 1900, when Java was under Dutch administration, that action was taken to restore Borobudur. A Dutch engineer, Dr. Theodore Van Erp, was placed in charge of salvaging and reconstructing the temple, but two world wars and financial problems meant that he would never complete the work.

But in 1973 UNESCO launched the Borobudur Restoration Project. At a cost of $25 million, 700 men worked for 10 years to restore the temple to its former glory. They used the best of modern technology to ensure, as President Suharto of Indonesia said at the ceremonies marking the triumphant reopening, "that Borobudur will live a thousand years more."

A DREAM OF THE STARS

The long grind to success

ACROSS MANY PARTS of the United States in the spring of 1936, crowds gathered to watch an unusual train pass by. It consisted of just a locomotive, two cars, and a caboose. But it was carrying a very special cargo: a circular disc of glass 200 inches across and weighing about 20 tons. It was destined to become the largest telescope mirror in the world.

The train with its fragile freight required 16 days to make the 3,000-mile journey from New York to Pasadena, California. Traveling only by day, its speed was 25 miles per hour so that vibrations would not shatter the glass. For weeks railroad engineers had been surveying the track to make sure that the steel crate containing the disc would clear bridges, tunnels, obstructions, and other hazards along the lengthy route.

The 200-inch dream

Creating and transporting the mirror was but the first step in the realization of a dream for George Ellery Hale, one of the greatest astronomers in the United States. Hale had already masterminded the construction of what was at the time the world's largest reflecting telescope, atop Mount Wilson in

FRAGILE CARGO *Standing upright on its railway car, the world's first 200-inch telescope mirror made stately progress across the United States in 1936.*

California. Completed in 1918, that telescope has a mirror 100 inches across. Hale then began planning a telescope with a mirror with twice that diameter; it would be able to explore farther into space than any other telescope in the world.

Like all telescope mirrors of the time, the Mount Wilson one was made of plate glass, a material that expands and contracts with changes in temperature and causes temporary distortion. Hale sought a more stable material.

After two years of costly experiments, it was decided to use Pyrex, the heat-resistant glass. In March 1934 a 200-inch Pyrex disc was cast at the Corning Glass Works in western New York. Cooled and hardened for a period of four weeks, it proved to be imperfect. In December a second disc was cast. This time the cooling and hardening took 10 months. The result: a perfect disc.

When it reached California in April 1936, a new phase began. To hollow it to the required concave shape, five tons of glass had to be ground away. But World War II interrupted the task, and the final grinding and polishing was not completed until 1947. The underside was then coated with aluminum, making the glass a perfect mirror.

Reflecting success

Meanwhile, the mounting for the giant mirror was under construction on Mount Palomar. The tube of the telescope, a girder structure 60 feet long and weighing more than 120 tons, was to move to follow stars across the night sky. Weighing a total of 500 tons, the vast apparatus was mounted on pressurized-oil bearings, which reduce friction, and housed within a rotating dome 135 feet high.

The telescope finally became operative in 1949. It was named for Hale, who had died 11 years before. In 1969 both the Mount Palomar and nearby Mount Wilson observatories were renamed the Hale Observatories.

Today smog from the city of Los Angeles can spoil the view of distant space from Mount Palomar. Newer and larger reflecting telescopes have been built or are under construction, including the 236-inch telescope at Zelenchukskaya in the U.S.S.R.—currently the largest reflecting telescope in the world. But from the first day that observations on Mount Palomar began, the Hale telescope has been in the forefront of space research, justly earning its reputation as the workhorse of astronomy.

ON THE ROOF OF THE WORLD

Atop a hill 425 feet high in the middle of a fertile plain, surrounded by a towering mountain range, sits the Potala Palace, overlooking Lhasa, the capital of Tibet. Until China took full control of the country in 1959, the Potala was the official residence of the Dalai Lama, the Buddhist spiritual and temporal leader of more than 6 million people.

Roofed in gold, the 13-story Potala is itself more than 350 feet high and stretches 900 feet from east to west. Six gates guard the palace, which is reached by a 125-step stairway.

Started in 1645, the building took more than 50 years to complete. Two palaces—one red, the other white—make up the Potala, constructed as a combination fortress, palace, and temple by the fifth Dalai Lama.

The interior of the building is a honeycomb of galleries and halls with more than 1,000 rooms and 10,000 chapels. All are set on various levels and connected by a maze of stairways and passages.

One of the most impressive features of the interior is the tomb of the fifth Dalai Lama. Some 60 feet high and covered in half a ton of gold, it has a base of solid silver that is surrounded by many precious treasures of porcelain and jade and a belt set with 200,000 tiny pearls. The tombs of seven other Dalai Lamas are also within the Potala, and the palace contains 200,000 statues, 20,000 scrolls, 246 gold paintings, and 615 volumes of sacred Buddhist literature written in gold characters. The walls of one hall are covered with some 698 murals.

Once a secluded monastery, the Potala Palace is today a museum, its many hitherto hidden treasures revealed to the eyes of the outside world.

The Potala Palace

A SCHEME THAT HOLDS WATER

An irrigation system that goes back to ancient times

BEFORE DAWN one morning in 1848 a British writer and traveler, Sir James Emerson Tennant, set out by torchlight through the northern forests of Ceylon on an arduous journey. He had heard that in the dense jungle lay one of the engineering wonders of the ancient world.

The wilderness was difficult to penetrate. Since the path was narrow and choked with thorn trees and luxuriant climbing plants, for most of the 10-mile trek the members of Tennant's party were forced to lead their horses on foot.

Finally, Sir James reached his destination. There, stretching before him, were the remains of a huge reservoir. Its scale had Sir James searching for superlatives, for he knew that this astonishing feat of engineering, known as the Padawiya Tank, was more than 1,500 years old. The team spent two hours on horseback crossing the vast expanse from the point at which they entered the bed of the reservoir to its dam, or bund.

"The extreme breadth of the enclosed space," wrote Sir James, "may be 12 or 14 miles, narrowing to 11 at the spot where the retaining bund has been constructed across the valley, and when this enormous embankment was in effectual repair, and the reservoir filled by the rains, the water must have been thrown back along the basin of the valley for at least 15 miles. The dam itself," he added, "is a prodigious work, nearly 11 miles in length, 30 feet broad at the top, about 200 at the base, upwards of 70 high, and faced throughout its whole extent by layers of squared stone."

Ahead of their time

Padawiya is known to be just one of thousands of reservoirs and elaborate waterworks built from the 1st to the 12th centuries A.D. on the island today called Sri Lanka. The waterworks range from the ponds designed to serve individual villages to vast man-made lakes. The largest, the 6,000-acre Parakrama Sea, was enclosed by a barrier almost nine miles long and 40 feet high.

Sri Lanka's climate made the construction of an elaborate irrigation system necessary. For much of the year up to two-thirds of the island is threatened by drought and must have water if rice is to grow. The ancient Sinhalese kings recognized the need for an irrigation system and ordered the building of tanks, dams, and canals to trap the monsoon rains. Said one king after surveying his kingdom: "Truly in such a country, not even a little water that comes from the rain must flow into the ocean without being made useful to man."

Mass construction

The historians of ancient Sri Lanka (Taprobane) maintained careful records of the achievements of each ruler. Vasabha (65–109) is credited with the construction of 12 tanks and 12 canals; Mahasena (274–302) commissioned 16 tanks, including Minneri, which covered 4,670 acres. In the reign of King Dhatusena (460–478) a canal 40 feet wide and 54 miles long provided water for the capital city of Anuradhapura in the north. Most energetic of all, however, was Parakrama Bahu I. From 1153 to 1186 he was responsible for the construction of 770

tanks and 534 canals, and for the successful repair of 2,300 tanks and 3,621 canals.

The tanks and canals were a spectacular success. Crops flourished, and the money they brought paid for great temples, pleasure gardens where fountains played, and cities with palaces as high as nine stories. Between harvests, the people worked on the vast construction projects; their labor was a form of *rajakayira,* a tribute paid to the king.

Although wars, the encroaching jungle, and the deaths of the great engineer-kings brought ruin to many of the tanks, the tradition of great irrigation projects still survives in Sri Lanka. Many of the tanks rediscovered by 19th-century explorers have been restored, and vast new undertakings, such as the Mahaweli Diversion Scheme, are under way, bringing water to hundreds of thousands of acres of arid land and doubling the country's supply of electric power.

With the aid of bulldozers and computers, the comprehensive irrigation system of Sri Lanka, initiated by the kings of ancient times, continues.

MONUMENTAL MINIATURIZATION

A palace built for a queen

ENGLAND'S WINDSOR CASTLE is a triumph of medieval architecture, with its massive walls, imposing battlements, and turrets towering over the surrounding countryside.

Within the huge walls of the castle stands another great building, but of quite different proportions. Standing a mere 92 inches high and covering just 40 square feet, this miniature miracle is Queen Mary's dollhouse.

British architect Sir Edwin Lutyens designed the house in 1920. Intended as a gift to Queen Mary, the reigning monarch, it was exhibited in 1924 and has been on display ever since.

A work of art

The dollhouse is not a toy but a working model of a contemporary royal home. Built by 150 craftsmen with the utmost attention to detail, it is in the Georgian style on three levels. The walls, made of wood carved and painted to resemble stone, form an outer shell that can be raised electrically to reveal the opulent interior. The floors are of real marble or parquet, the decoration a profusion of the most sumptuous materials: gold and silver, velvet and lace. Everything works just as it would in a real house. The windows slide open, operated by

threadlike cords and miniature weights. The doors are fitted with working locks turned by keys a quarter of an inch long. Silver faucets deliver hot and cold water, which is carried away by a functional drainage system.

Faithful replicas of Chippendale and Queen Anne furniture fill the rooms. More than 700 drawings and watercolors decorate the walls. The wood-paneled library has a collection of 200 books. And the wine cellar would satisfy the most discerning connoisseur: each tiny bottle contains a few drops of some of the finest vintages of the time.

Beneath the house is a garage with a fleet of limousines and a fully equipped mechanic's workshop. A garden with a lawn of green velvet and beautifully kept flower beds is laid out to the east, where it will catch the morning sun. And to ensure the security of the palace, miniature sentries stand eternally at attention around the grounds.

FIT FOR A QUEEN *Designed by Sir Edwin Lutyens in 1920, Queen Mary's dollhouse is a remarkable feat of craftsmanship. Visible in the view of the west front on the facing page are the underground garage and a variety of rooms, including the library, for which specially bound leather volumes were made.*

PRINCESS ROYAL'S ROOM   SITTING ROOM   NIGHT NURSERY   NURSERY BATHROOM

MAID'S ROOM   MAID'S ROOM

KING'S WARDROBE   KING'S BEDROOM   KING'S BATHROOM

A PRINCELY EXTRAVAGANCE

England's Taj Mahal by the sea

A FAIRY-TALE PALACE of pinnacles, domes, and minarets has been astonishing visitors to the English seaside resort of Brighton for more than 160 years. The Royal Pavilion was the brainchild of the wild and extravagant prince of Wales, later to become King George IV. Admirers call it an architectural delight; critics say it could have inspired Disneyland.

Today the Royal Pavilion gives no hint of its modest beginnings as a farmhouse where the 24-year-old prince and his secret bride, the twice-widowed Mrs. Fitzherbert, played at living the simple life.

Fashionable friends from London came to visit the prince, and soon Brighton, once a little fishing village, became one of the most popular resorts in Europe. The prince's opulent lifestyle demanded something grander than a farmhouse. For the next 35 years—from 1786, when he first moved in, until 1821—the house was designed and redesigned by several of England's leading architects. The various stages of refurbishment cost more than $750,000—an amount that would be astronomical in today's terms. In the end the prince's subjects reviled him for the extravagance.

The house of debt

The history of the pavilion's transformations is a record of imagination, skills, and bankruptcy. Several contractors were ruined when the prince ran out of money.

ARCHITECTURAL FOLLY? *The Royal Pavilion in Brighton, England, with its bizarre mix of architectural styles, reflects the extravagant, whimsical nature of the prince regent who later became King George IV. Originally an unpretentious farmhouse, the property was acquired by the prince who then commissioned several leading architects to enlarge the building. The final version (above) is based on a design by the celebrated 18th-century architect John Nash, whose plans for the Royal Pavilion (below) represent a flamboyant combination of styles.*

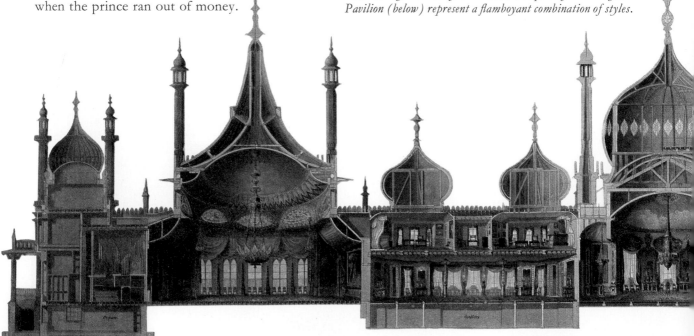

The fashionable architect Henry Holland was the first to convert the farmhouse into a neoclassical villa. He repeated the design of the farmhouse and linked the new building to the original one with a domed central rotunda, producing an elegant bow-windowed house with ironwork balconies. It took 150 workmen less than a year to complete the work. Later, green canopies were erected over the balconies.

Inspiration from the East

Another well-known architect, William Porden, then turned his creative thoughts to refurbishing the pavilion. His instructions were to make it look Chinese. The prince had been given some Chinese wallpaper, which had inspired him to furnish the palace in oriental style. Fake bamboo furniture, bright colors, and Chinese silk wall hangings were to replace the more restrained French furnishings.

Porden drew up the plans but shelved them to deal with a more urgent matter—the building of the royal stables next to the pavilion. To the prince's astonishment, a magnificent domed structure was erected—not in the Chinese tradition, but in the picturesque style of Islamic India.

The prince was so delighted with the novelty that he now wanted the pavilion to be redesigned in the same style. Humphrey Repton, a respected landscape gardener, was asked to submit a design. His plans, too, had to be set aside, this time because of lack of money. The prince's debts had again increased considerably.

By 1815 the prince had become regent, taking over the royal duties from his father, the ailing George III. Because his new position brought him more income, the prince again turned his thoughts to completing the palace in Brighton. He commissioned John Nash, his favorite architect, to make the dream come true. Nash embellished the pavilion with more domes, miniature pagodas, slender columns with lotus flower tips, and a few unexplainable Gothic features.

The interior was even more overpowering. Nash had added at least two magnificent chambers: the music room and the banqueting room. Both were enormous and featured elaborate domed ceilings and rich color schemes of red, gold, and blue. Painted dragons glided across the ceilings and curled around doors. One supported a bejeweled chandelier that weighed almost a ton. Nash provided a huge kitchen for lavish entertaining: in each corner a tall, slender cast-iron column, crowned with palm fronds made of copper, supported the ceiling—one of the first times that cast iron was used in a British building.

The empty dream

After the prince became king in 1820, he seldom visited his dream palace. He died in 1830, and the pavilion was rarely used by his successors. His niece, Queen Victoria, thought it inconvenient for her growing family. During her reign the pavilion was stripped of its furnishings and stood empty and forlorn until it was bought by the residents of Brighton in 1850.

Today carefully restored to its early splendor, the Taj Mahal by the sea sits majestically in the now bustling resort. Each year thousands of visitors tour this bizarre architectural folly, a prince's dream that became a reality.

A LONG, LONG TRAIL A-WINDING

Building the Alaska Highway

ON THE AFTERNOON of October 25, 1942, Pvt. Al Jalufka was nosing his 20-ton bulldozer north through a forest a few miles from the border between Alaska and the Yukon Territory, Canada. Above the roar of the machine he could hear the sound of another engine coming slowly toward him.

At the same moment, Corp. Refines Sims, Jr., was hearing similar sounds as he worked *his* bulldozer south through the bush.

Both men crashed their huge machines through the trees toward each other. Stopping with the great blades of their land movers just inches apart, the two leaped out, oblivious to the −30°F cold, and shook hands in delight. The two soldiers had made the final link in the long and winding Alaska Highway, one of the most astonishing engineering feats of the 20th century.

The threat from Japan

Less than 10 months before, Japan had catapulted the United States into war with the surprise attack on Pearl Harbor—and raised the specter of an invasion of the American mainland. The danger was driven home when, in June 1942, the Japanese succeeded in occupying a far corner of the United States: three of the Aleutians, islands that string out from the Alaskan coast into the North Pacific.

Alaska had always been the most likely—and most vulnerable—point of attack, since it was the U.S. territory closest to Japan. At the time, the only route for transporting men and supplies to the virtually undefended outpost was by sea, after running the gauntlet of enemy shipping. A road to connect the states south of the Canadian border with Alaska had to be built—and built quickly.

The Alaska Highway is that road. For 1,523 miles it snakes through forests, across swamps, around mountains. It crosses 133 permanent bridges and five mountain ranges, in country where some of the world's most inhospitable terrain joins forces with some of the world's worst weather. And yet from the arrival of the first workers to official opening, it was built—by 10,000 military personnel and 7,500 civilians—in an incredible seven months.

The temperature was well below freezing on March 13, 1942, when the first road builders arrived at Dawson Creek in British Columbia, Canada. From there the road was to join an existing highway to Edmonton, Alberta, and then connect with the main road south into the United States. Meanwhile,

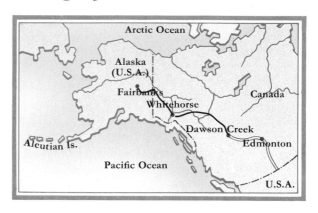

INTO THE WILDERNESS *Completed in 1942, the Alaska Highway (in red, above) winds through more than 1,500 miles of forests, swamps, mountains, and rivers. The road was built to link Alaska with the northwestern United States as a defense against possible Japanese invasion.*

other units were making their way by boat and train to two more points: the northernmost end of the new road in Fairbanks, Alaska, and the headquarters of the operation in the Canadian town of Whitehorse, about halfway along the route. Engineering units at each point were to push the road toward each other.

Just one step ahead

The first task was to plan the road's exact route. Surveys were made by airplane and on foot, with dog teams and pack trains. So urgent was the task, the surveyors worked only a few miles ahead of the construction teams.

The surveying party marked the center line of the route with rag streamers or small fires. Down this line, a 20-ton bulldozer carved a pathway, followed by others clearing trees and brush.

Then came a construction company to build wooden bridges—one spanned a river 2,000 feet wide—and culverts. Another company installed drainage ditches, and standardized the width of the road to 24 feet. Most of the backbreaking labor was done by men wielding a shovel or ax, with only sweat and muscle to help them.

It has been said that the reason the Alaska Highway twists and turns so much was to render attacks from Japanese aircraft ineffective. The real reason—hardly less of a nightmare for the army engineers—was the muskeg, the centuries-old swampland along the route. Efforts to bypass it created the turns in the road. When muskeg was unavoidable, the road was "corduroyed": layer upon layer of pine trees were laid down so that the road could "float" across the marsh on top of them.

Working conditions were often appalling. In winter the temperature could sink so low that steel piling would crystallize and shatter; the Canadian summer, however, was notorious for its sticky, near-tropical heat and legions of bloodthirsty insects. And there was never enough to eat. At the beginning, army rations were supplemented with local wildlife. Supplies were so difficult to come by

EPIC FEAT *The men who built the Alaska Highway worked tirelessly around the clock against challenging odds. Despite the rigors of weather and inhospitable terrain, they completed the link in only seven months.*

that one unit shot most of its own food throughout its entire tour on the highway. Yet the work went on, day and night, seven days a week.

At last, on November 20, 1942, a short ceremony declared the Alaska Highway open. Ironically, the road was never used for military purposes. By the time it was completed, the tide of war had turned against the Japanese, who were coming under increasing pressure from the onslaught of advancing U.S. forces throughout the Pacific.

Yet the road remains a monument to the skill, stamina, and dedication of the men who built it. Most were raw recruits, few of whom were prepared for the unbelievable conditions in which they worked. Yet the road was built at a rate of nearly eight miles a day. In normal times, the job could have taken five years.

NINE-DAY WONDER

The airplane that made a dream come true

FOR 31 MINUTES a slim, white, oddly shaped aircraft circled the dry lake bed at Edwards Air Force Base in California. Gradually the strange plane lost altitude, then swooped down to land safely on the desert floor. It was 8:06 A.M., December 23, 1986.

When the two pilots emerged from the craft shortly afterward, they could barely walk; they had been crammed into a cabin the size of a bathtub for nine days. Not once during those nine days had the team stopped or refueled their delicate aircraft. Col. Richard G. Rutan and Jeana Yeager had just flown around the globe and into aviation history.

Such an achievement had been the dream of pilots and designers since the days of Lindbergh. Viewed as the last great record to be won in aviation, the nonstop round-the-world flight had never before been attempted; no aircraft had been capable of carrying enough fuel to complete the trip without stopping.

Paper airplane

The beginnings of this milestone flight go back to 1981, when Richard's brother, Burt, an innovative aircraft designer, sketched a revolutionary design on the back of a paper napkin. For five years thereafter, with the help of numerous dedicated volunteers and a tiny core of paid staff, the Rutans and Yeager worked to fund, build, and fly the dream plane they called the *Voyager*. The project ultimately cost $2 million, much of which was donated by various aerospace companies.

The aircraft had to be light in order to conserve fuel, and tough enough to withstand turbulence, since most of the flight path would lie in the storm-prone tropics. Burt constructed the plane almost entirely out of panels of a graphite composite a quarter inch thick—20 percent lighter and seven times stronger than aluminum, the material used for conventional aircraft.

Tough as it was, the composite was extremely flexible. *Voyager*'s slim, 110-foot wings could "flap" in a 30-foot arc, and gave the craft the sleek aerodynamics of a sailplane. Although *Voyager* had two engines, they were to be used together only in an emergency; the rear engine was for cruising at an average speed of 115 miles per hour.

Burt created the plane's distinctive H-shape both to add rigidity to the overall design and to provide more space in the long tail booms for fuel. In fact, *Voyager* was little more than a flying fuel tank: a day

and a half were required just to fill its 17 tanks with the 1,000 gallons of fuel needed to power the plane during its round-the-world trip.

The long haul

Voyager's long-awaited mission started on the morning of December 14, 1986. As the airplane rolled down the runway in California, the wingtips, bent by the weight of fuel, scraped along the ground. However, despite small tears in the aircraft's skin, the damage was insignificant.

With the aid of both NASA and the U.S. Defense Department satellite navigation and communications systems, the crew was kept up-to-date on weather conditions. Storms did force them 2,000 miles farther north than planned, and to avoid turbulence over Africa they had to climb from 10,000 to more than 20,000 feet. These changes consumed extra fuel—but instrument failure made it impossible for the team to determine exactly how much remained.

Fortunately, unexpected tail winds compensated for the unplanned use of fuel. In just two days *Voyager* was able to travel from Kenya, East Africa, to the coast of Central America—some 8,000 miles.

Mechanical mishaps were few, although one engine almost burned out due to a problem with the oil supply. On the last night of the flight, one of the fuel pumps failed and the rear engine stopped. To restart it Richard had to go into a challenging 3,500-foot dive.

Nevertheless, Richard Rutan and Jeana Yeager were back in the United States a day ahead of schedule. The exact flight time for the 25,012-mile journey was 9 days 3 minutes 44 seconds. The aircraft's fuel tanks were almost dry: a scant 20 gallons remained when *Voyager* landed.

CIRCLING THE EARTH NONSTOP *Unexpected rough weather from the southern Pacific to central Africa forced* Voyager *to alter course and fly the route indicated in red on the map— much farther north than originally planned.*

RECORD BREAKER *The experimental aircraft sits on the runway at Edwards Air Force Base in the Mojave Desert after completing the first flight around the world made without refueling.*

THE LONG-LIVED LION

How the Great Sphinx survived the sands of time

WINDBLOWN, battered, and threatened on every side by shifting sands, the Great Sphinx has majestically stood guard over the royal pyramids at Giza, in Egypt, for nearly 5,000 years. Yet for much of its history, this colossal monument lay half buried in sand, attacked and vandalized by human and natural forces. Its very survival has often been in doubt.

The human lion

The fortunes of the Great Sphinx were for a long time interwoven with those of the Egyptian pharaohs. From the earliest period of Egyptian art, it was customary to represent the pharaoh as a lion to symbolize his power and strength. The concept of the pharaoh as both human and animal resulted in the creation of the sphinx, a hybrid creature with a lion's body and a human head. Since the pharaoh was believed to be both human and divine, the sphinx, too, came to be seen as superhuman.

Many sphinxes were built in ancient Egypt, but the Great Sphinx at Giza was the first. It dates from the reign of Khafre in the 26th century B.C. and lies south of the Great Pyramid complex.

An impressive 66 feet high and 240 feet long, it guards the causeway leading to the Second Pyramid, also built during Khafre's reign.

The reasons for the construction of the Sphinx can only be guessed. It is thought to be the work of an unknown sculptor who carved it out of a block of limestone left in a quarry after other stones had been used for the nearby pyramids. Since the unsightly knoll of limestone interrupted the view of the Second Pyramid, rather than remove the massive eyesore the sculptor transformed it into a monument to Khafre, whose face it depicts.

GREAT SPHINX *The giant man-headed lion that guards the entrance to the pyramids at Giza.*

RESTORED TO GLORY
For most of its 5,000 years, the Sphinx lay buried in sand up to its neck. It was not until the 1920's that the true majesty of the great statue was revealed. The sand was cleared away and the structure cleaned. Only then could work begin to repair the damage caused by centuries of neglect.

The origins of the Sphinx had been forgotten by the time of the New Kingdom (about 570 B.C.). The priests believed it to be an incarnation of the sun god Ra, and worshiped it accordingly. By this time, too, the sands had buried the body of the Sphinx; only the majestic head remained visible.

According to legend, Thutmose, young son of the pharaoh Amenhotep II, was hunting on the Giza plateau and took a rest in the shadow of the Sphinx. Thutmose dreamed that Ra spoke to him, complaining that the sand was making breathing difficult. If the prince would clear the sand, the god assured him that he would inherit the kingdom. Thutmose obliged, and in due course ascended the throne of Egypt. To prevent future encroachment of sand, Thutmose erected a series of mud-brick walls around the monument and ordered the story

of his dream inscribed on a granite slab that still stands between the feet of the Sphinx.

The fortunes of the Sphinx began to improve. As the center of the sun-god cult, it attracted visitors and pilgrims from all over the ancient world who left numerous offerings to the Sphinx. Some of these were clay tablets and bore prayers to the sun god. During the time of the Roman Empire many travelers visited the Sphinx; the graffiti they left can still be seen on its paws.

Up to its neck

Over the succeeding centuries the Sphinx again fell prey to the drifting desert sands that piled up against its flanks, burying all but its head. The wind eroded its exposed surfaces, and vandals carved pieces out of it.

Legend has it that Napoleon turned his guns on the Sphinx because he thought its smile was mocking him. The truth is more prosaic. The face had been disfigured and the nose broken off in the late 14th century by Saim-el-Dahr, a religious zealot who regarded the mere presence of the statue as pagan and idolatrous.

Not until the 19th century was the Sphinx again freed from the encroaching sand. Then archeologists began painstaking excavations and research into the history and significance of the Sphinx. During the 1920's the huge monument was finally cleared of sand, and cement supports were erected to hold up the head. Today the Sphinx is being restored to much of its former glory as guardian of the pyramids. The face of the pharaoh Khafre will continue to gaze out across the desert.

THE TAJ MAHAL

A monument to love, or to power?

ON THE BANKS of the Jumna River, near the old Mogul capital of Agra, stands India's most celebrated monument. With its white marble dome, cupolas, minarets, and exquisite mosaics, the Taj Mahal has justly earned its place as one of the Seven Wonders of the Modern World. Its fame owes as much to the romance of its origins as it does to the beauty of its architecture.

Mumtaz Mahal, the wife of the fifth Mogul emperor, Shah Jahan, died in childbirth in 1631. According to legend, the emperor was so distraught that to express his eternal love, he pledged to build the most beautiful tomb in the world. He commissioned a Turk, Ustad Isa, to design the

building, and the following year work began on the construction of the tomb. To ensure that no other monument would ever be built to surpass the magnificent Taj, when it was completed Shah Jahan cut off the architect's head, as well as the hands of the craftsmen.

A paradise on earth

The entire monument—consisting of Mumtaz Mahal's tomb, two mosques, four minarets, a gateway, and ancillary buildings—was conceived as a single, harmonious unit. Rising to a height of nearly 250 feet, the mausoleum towers magnificently over the river. Covering 42 acres, the landscaped gardens, with splendid water channels and fountains, reflect the Mogul vision of paradise on earth.

The entire complex is said to have taken 22 years to complete, using a labor force of 20,000. Stonemasons, goldsmiths, sculptors, and calligraphers embellished every surface, inside and out. As many as 43 types of precious stone, including jade, crystal, topaz, sapphires, and diamonds, were used to create elaborate designs. Silver candlesticks, gold lamps, and the finest Persian carpets filled the interior, and a solid gold balustrade was erected around the sarcophagus.

After the collapse of the Mogul Empire in 1857, marauders plundered the tomb, taking silver, gold, and jewels. The monument, however, has remained intact, standing for centuries as a symbol of spiritual purity and love. But contemporary accounts paint an altogether different picture.

In pursuit of power

According to European travelers in India in the 17th century, Shah Jahan was a man whose excessive vanity was matched only by his lust for power. Far from being a faithful husband, he is reputed to have had an insatiable sexual appetite: it is even claimed that he committed incest with his eldest daughter. His ruthless pursuit of the throne is said to have led him to murder his elder brothers and five other male relatives.

Most of Shah Jahan's life was spent fighting. His beautiful wife, Mumtaz Mahal, who accompanied him on his military campaigns, appears to have been as bloodthirsty as her husband. Fanatical in her hatred of Christianity, it was she who urged Shah Jahan to raze the Portuguese colony at Hooghly on the northeast coast of India. The inscription on her sarcophagus reads, "Lord defend us from the tribe of unbelievers."

Throughout his reign, Shah Jahan was obsessed with power. He commissioned many buildings during his lifetime, and the Taj Mahal, with all its riches, can be seen as yet another way to display the glory of his empire. The very purity and perfection of its design perhaps hints at a supreme conceit: the desire to rival God. The romantic myth that has intrigued travelers for centuries may mask the true purpose of the Taj Mahal: to immortalize the most powerful of Mogul emperors, Shah Jahan.

THE GREAT STONES OF BAALBEK

Superhuman strength or supernatural power?

SITUATED AT BAALBEK on a lush, high plain, 53 miles from Beirut in Lebanon, stand the ruins of a group of Roman temples famous for the beauty and grace of their architecture.

Constructed in the first century A.D., the temples stand on a raised platform and command magnificent views of the countryside below. But it is not only the setting that is spectacular; surrounding the temples is a massive stone wall that baffles experts even today.

At its western end lie three of the largest cut blocks of stone in the world. Transporting and placing them in their horizontal position would pose an insurmountable problem even to modern engineers using the most sophisticated machinery technology can provide. Yet these stones have been in position for almost 2,000 years. Despite the technical expertise of the Romans, there is no similar example of such astonishing skill anywhere else in their former empire. The great stones of Baalbek are unique.

The three colossal stones are known as the Trilithon. If stood on one end, each stone would be as high as a five- or six-story house. The largest stone is about 64 by 14 by 12 feet and weighs some 800 tons. Cut from a quarry about a mile away, each block was transported to the site at Baalbek, and lifted up some 25 feet to its final position onto the top of a platform of smaller stones.

The devil's stones

Today few industrial cranes would be capable of such a feat, yet the three stones were placed so precisely, it is impossible to insert the blade of a knife between the joints. No wonder that in earlier times people speculated that the stones must have been hewn and positioned by the devil. Even today some people believe that there must be a supernatural explanation.

The mystery deepens when one learns that in the quarry lies another great block, larger than the stones forming the Trilithon and weighing approximately 1,000 tons. No one knows why this last block was never used in the construction of the temples. To this day the explanation that it was just too heavy for the people who had already cut, moved, and placed the largest blocks in the history of the world remains unsatisfactory.

TALES FROM THE CRYPT

Legend has it that Saint Swithin, the English bishop of Winchester who died in 862, instructed that his body should be buried outside the cathedral, where the rain from heaven could fall upon his remains. A century later, after the body was exhumed for burial inside the building, the bishop's spirit was angered and made it rain for 40 days and 40 nights.

To this day some people believe that if it rains on Saint Swithin's Day (July 15), 40 days of rain will follow.

With such a patron saint, it is not surprising that Winchester, one of Britain's finest cathedrals, should become a victim of serious flooding. But the way in which the cathedral was saved is unique.

In 1905 it was discovered that part of the cathedral wall was leaning dangerously. The massive weight of the medieval building—40 tons per square foot — was found to be resting on tree trunks on a bed of peat, which had been steadily compressing below the water table. In effect, the cathedral was sinking into a peat bog and in desperate need of concrete underpinnings. To make matters worse, the foundations were completely submerged.

Plumbing the depths

In 1906 the authorities decided that a revolutionary approach was needed to solve the problem: they recruited the services of William Walker, an experienced deep-sea diver. For nearly six years visitors were greeted with the incongruous sight of a man working in the cathedral wearing a diving suit.

Walker spent six hours every day diving beneath the water.

Steadily he dug away the layer of waterlogged peat and gradually replaced it with more than 25,000 sacks full of concrete, 115,000 concrete blocks, and some 1 million bricks.

THE DIVER *Wearing a 200-pound diving suit, William Walker works to save Winchester Cathedral.*

By 1912 Walker's task was completed, and at a thanksgiving service in the cathedral, England's King George V personally thanked him for his work.

As if to acknowledge that the curse of Saint Swithin had been averted through modern technology, the service was held on Saint Swithin's Day.

FANTASY BY DESIGN

The unfulfilled vision of a unique architect

ONE EXHIBIT in the Paris Exhibition of 1910 stole the show. It was a plaster model of a church designed by the Spanish architect Antonio Gaudi — a design so daring and outrageous that it was difficult to believe anyone would seriously consider building it.

An extraordinary fusion of Gothic and Art Nouveau in style, the model was painted in vibrant colors that further enhanced the exuberant design. The plans called for spotlights to direct shafts of light into parts of the interior. Three sets of bell towers, housing both manually operated and electronically controlled tubular bells, were to be topped by stone statues of cherubim with wings that would move in the wind.

One man's vision

Not only was this unconventional design approved and commissioned, but at the time of the exhibition the church was already under construction. Gaudi himself had been working on the Church of the Sagrada Familia (Church of the Holy Family) in Barcelona since 1883. He continued to work on it until his death in 1926, when he was run over by a trolley. The church is still unfinished today.

What there is of it is breathtaking. Many of Gaudi's more unusual ideas have not been carried out, partly because his models and plans were destroyed during a fire in 1935 and, more importantly, because the church was one man's vision and was eclipsed upon his death.

The role of the cast

The Sagrada Familia is a dominant feature of Barcelona. The building stands on a terrace nearly 12 feet high, surrounded by a dry moat. Its highly decorated towers, with turrets that one critic compared to "termite hills or crustaceous creatures," soar into the sky, dwarfing nearby buildings.

Although Gaudi's plans for the central section of the church were never realized, the three main entrances are complete, decorated with elaborate sculptures depicting biblical scenes, animals, flowers, and trees.

All the sculptures were based on life models. Ordinary inhabitants of Barcelona were carefully picked according to age and physique to match their biblical counterparts. A tableau depicting the Massacre of the Innocents (King Herod's attempt to destroy Jesus by killing all children under the age of two) included a Roman soldier, modeled on a local waiter. Gaudi was excited to discover that the man had six toes on each foot. Although the sculptor, Lorenzo Matamala, had wanted to

CREATIVE WORKPLACE
Antonio Gaudi's workshop in the Sagrada Familia demonstrates his vision as both architect and sculptor. Not only were the architectural lines of the building meticulously planned in miniature, but careful attention was devoted to making the statues. First, plaster casts of the faces and bodies of live models were made and then modified before being reproduced in stone.

UNFINISHED MASTERPIECE *The Church of the Sagrada Familia, still uncompleted, towers above the Barcelona skyline.*

disguise the deformity, Gaudi insisted that it be seen: "It is an anomaly, just as it is an anomaly to kill children!"

Hundreds of photographs were taken of the models posed in front of mirrors so that every angle of the body could be captured realistically. To obtain the exact position of the body Gaudi wanted to achieve, his team also studied skeletons. The faces and bodies of all the models were molded in plaster, a dangerous procedure that could result in death if the plaster were left on too long.

True dedication

The same attention was shown to all detail. The birds Gaudi chose were killed and then arranged into the required position for the sculptor to copy. They too would be photographed and a plaster cast created. Stillborn babies from the local hospital were used in the same way. Every leaf, flower, and grain of corn was photographed; even inanimate objects were given the same treatment.

The Sagrada Familia shaped Gaudi's life. At the beginning of the project, he was a 31-year-old dandy who enjoyed the pleasures of life and had had some quarrels with the established church. Ten years later he was deeply religious and a vegetarian who chose to live a life of severe austerity. Toward the end of his life he dedicated himself to the cathedral, living on the site in uncomfortable conditions. Gaudi became so obsessed by the project that he was driven to beg for donations.

Since Gaudi's death, work on the church has continued in a slow, spasmodic way, based on his original plans; many people feel that the building will never be finished. Gaudi had planned that the building would take generations to complete, but his vision was perhaps too personal and did not consider the fact that few others would continue with the same forceful conviction.

Today the architectural world remains divided. Should the cathedral be completed in a less ambitious contemporary style? Or should it be left, unfinished, as an original creation?

MADE IN HONG KONG

An ancient art collaborates with modern technology

ON APRIL 7, 1986, executives of the Hong Kong and Shanghai Banking Corporation welcomed more than 3,000 people to the opening of their prestigious new headquarters in the heart of Hong Kong's thriving commercial district. Designed by British architect Norman Foster, the new bank had been hailed as the architectural achievement of the century. At an estimated cost of $750 million, it was also the most expensive building in the world.

But it was not all Western sophistication. Eastern mysticism played a part, too. One of the consultants on the project was a practitioner of the ancient art of *feng shui;* it was his job to ensure that the building was protected against evil.

Internal sunlight

The new bank is a masterpiece of technical innovation. Eight steel towers—four of them 850 feet high—clad with thousands of aluminum panels form the main structure: the balance of the building is literally suspended from these towers.

The centerpiece of the design is a giant atrium, a soaring space 150 feet high surrounded by open galleries housing banking facilities and offices. At ground level a glass ceiling covers the public plaza that stretches the entire width of the building. At the summit of the atrium a canopy of mirrors reflects shafts of sunlight caught by a giant "sunscoop" affixed to the outside of the building.

Part of Foster's assignment was to give the bank the flexibility that would allow a rapid response to changes in technology. A partitioning system that can be completely dismantled makes the office space so adaptable that an entire department can be shifted in days rather than weeks. All essential services—cabling for computers, electricity, and communications as well as the air-conditioning ductwork—run beneath the floors.

The entire building was constructed to the most demanding standards and had to be assembled, with pinpoint accuracy, from more than 10,000 components manufactured on three far-flung continents. The sheer engineering perfection and the high degree of built-in flexibility were extremely costly. The official completion figure of $750 million is probably conservative: the true cost is more likely closer to $1.1 billion.

The success of the project was not left entirely in the hands of Western technological wizards. The Chinese believe that people are affected, for good

FOLLOWING THE SUN *The giant "sunscoop" on the south face of this bank building in Hong Kong contains 24 computer-controlled mirrors; they track the sun and reflect its rays to the top of the atrium (at far right). From there the light is projected down into the building.*

or ill, by mysterious earth forces known as *feng shui* (literally, "wind and water"). The way in which every wall, door, and window of a building faces wind and water determines the health, prosperity, and good fortune of its occupants. *Feng shui* experts abound in Chinese communities throughout the world, advising on all aspects of the environment from the orientation of a new house to the shape of a new bed and its position in a room.

Good luck and prosperity

Even before presenting his initial proposals to the bank, Foster consulted a *feng shui* expert; a *feng shui* sketch, showing alterations that would deter "bad spirits," is included in the architectural drawings for the new building. The *feng shui* authority determined the angle of the two escalators that link the plaza to the banking area and even changed an inauspicious furniture layout in Foster's Hong Kong office.

The most important task of the *feng shui* expert was to supervise the positioning of two bronze lions, Stephen and Stitt, in front of the building. The lions have acted as sentinels for the bank's headquarters since 1935 and play a crucial part in the economy of Hong Kong; it is said that as long as they stand guard, Hong Kong will prosper.

When it was time for the lions to be installed, the *feng shui* authority specified their exact position—to guarantee good fortune in the years ahead.

香港上海滙豐銀行

OUTSIDE AND IN *The
"outboard" structure of
architect Norman Foster's
50-story skyscraper consists
of eight steel masts from
which the rest of the building
is suspended. The advantages:
enormous, unobstructed areas
inside, as above. Decks with
offices line the sides of the
cathedrallike space of the
atrium, which rises 170 feet
above the public banking
facilities. In a building this
size, the atmosphere could be
chillingly impersonal. But
Foster has organized the
bank into zones and created
a series of "villages." The
23 express elevators stop
only at every fifth floor; 62
escalators offer service to the
floors in between. The name
of the bank in Chinese
is at top.*

FROZEN ASSETS

Engineering in ice

THE AMOCO CORPORATION built one of the largest oil-exploration platforms ever in 1986. Known as Mars I, it took only seven weeks to complete, with all the construction work performed on the site in the remote frozen wastes of the Beaufort Sea, off the northern coast of Alaska. Amoco had good reason to be pleased with its achievement: the cost of the new platform was one-third that of comparable drilling rigs.

Other companies prospecting for oil in Alaska have been eager to follow Amoco's lead, since the techniques used may help to transform a high-risk venture into an economically viable project. No shipyards were needed to build the new platform, and the building material cost nothing; it was available locally in abundance. Unlike traditional platforms, Mars I was built not of steel but of ice.

SPRAY ICE *In the Beaufort Sea five miles off the northern coast of Alaska, a temporary ice island provides an economical "onshore" drilling site. The island consists of layers of compacted ice crystals; they are produced by spraying highly pressurized seawater into the subfreezing Arctic air.*

Engineering in ice has its origins in World War II, when British engineers drew up plans for an aircraft carrier built of ice. Experiments demonstrated that ice could be strengthened by adding a compound material, such as sawdust. No aircraft ever actually landed on a frozen warship, but after the war, in the winter of 1952–53, planes did touch down on an ice runway built on the sea off the Alaskan coast by the U.S. Navy.

The location of the runway was the natural ice sheet off Point Barrow, Alaska. A confined area 3,000 feet long and 150 feet wide was flooded with seawater through a system of dikes, until an ice block 16 feet thick had formed. Although navy aircraft made several landings and takeoffs on the runway, the trials were considered only partially successful. Problems with the freezing process left pockets of water that weakened the structure.

By 1979 further mastery of the technique enabled engineers to construct an offshore ice road nine miles long for use by Alaskan oil prospectors. Work on the project showed that tougher surfaces could be made by freezing wooden cross members into the ice, a process similar to steel reinforcement in concrete. A form of "ice concrete" was also produced by mixing crushed ice with fiberglass.

Ice in the air

To build Mars I, the Amoco engineers devised a new ice-making method. They called the result spray ice, because it was formed simply by spraying water high into the subfreezing air. Before it hit the

surface, the water froze into tiny ice granules, which compacted under their own weight to form a tough but flexible material.

The engineers used four water cannons to spray 265 million gallons of water drawn from the sea beneath the ice. As new layers of ice formed, the platform grew; eventually its increasing weight sank the natural ice sheet on which it rested to the seabed 25 feet below. The spraying continued until an island 950 feet in diameter and 50 feet high was sitting half in and half out of the water.

A drilling rig and accommodations for 40 workers were then installed on top of the platform. For seven weeks the men sank exploratory boreholes to a depth of 8,300 feet; then the wells were capped. As the spring thaw approached, the island was abandoned. Not long afterward it melted and disappeared forever.

Meltdown

At present, ice structures are suitable only for winter drilling. Even then, the temperature must remain below 16°F. If not, the water droplets will not freeze properly and will hit the surface as slush. Warm spells can cause costly delays.

But there may come a time when ice islands can withstand the warmth of summer. Scientists have discovered a bacterium, *Pseudomonas syringae,* that encourages ice to form at higher temperatures. A small number of the bacteria added in powdered form to spray water assists the making of ice at marginal temperatures. (*Pseudomonas* has already proved effective by helping to make the artificial snow used at some ski resorts.)

Another experiment has produced ice capable of remaining solid in searing heat. When ice is compressed, some of it melts. But the remainder fuses into a solid lump. If the process is repeated several times, it forms a substance called Ice 9, which only a blowtorch can melt.

Oil companies believe that the use of ice islands may lead to the granting of exploration permits in environmentally sensitive areas of the Arctic. After all, they argue, who is going to protest the construction of an industrial complex that simply melts away after it has been used?

WARM AS ICE

Lighting a fire inside an igloo may seem foolish. But rather than melting the building into slush, the heat from a small fire or seal-oil lamp actually strengthens and insulates the structure.

Until recent times Eskimos built their snow houses not only as permanent dwellings but also as temporary shelters for use on long hunting trips. Often, igloos were occupied for just one night and then abandoned. This is not as wasteful as it may seem. In just 45 minutes an experienced builder could make an igloo large enough to house two people.

The largest problem facing an igloo builder is to find enough of the right kind of snow. It must be firm and compact but not too icy, and ideally, produced by a single storm; snow that has fallen on separate occasions will not hold together well.

To make his igloo, the builder uses a long knife to cut blocks of snow. He then arranges them in a circle to form the base. Working from within the circle, he lays successive levels of blocks, creating a spiral that tilts inward at an ever-increasing angle until it forms a dome. The builder then fills any gaps with soft, fresh snow. The final task is to cut an opening and to shape a block of snow for a snug fitting door.

Although almost ready to move into, the house must first be "iced" to make it strong.

With the door firmly in place, the owner lights a seal-oil lamp. Almost at once the igloo begins to melt. But the walls act like blotting paper and draw the interior moisture to the outside, where it then freezes.

The interior is iced next. The builder bores a hole in the roof of the dome and removes the door block. As the warm air rushes upward, cold air enters through the doorway; soon the walls are coated with a thin film of ice.

Although made of ice, the finished igloo is not particularly cold. Indeed, the structure is so well insulated that one can sit inside without a coat, while outside the temperature could well be as low as −50°F.

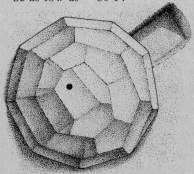

An igloo made from compacted snow

AMAZING INVENTIONS

ANOTHER MAN'S POISON

A lethal venom, a boon to medicine

THE SLIGHTEST SCRATCH by a poison-tipped dart from the blowpipe of an Indian in the Amazon Basin will kill in minutes. Yet, incredibly, doctors have been using the same poison to help save lives.

The power of this substance, curare, both to kill and to save lives lies in its ability to totally immobilize those muscles in the body that can be consciously controlled.

Tree power

The "flying death," as curare was commonly called, has been used by the Indians of South America for thousands of years. When absorbed into the bloodstream, its lethal properties are undisputed. The heart is unaffected, but as the poison reaches the muscles that control breathing, it totally paralyzes them. Victims suffocate, fully aware of their fate. Working with relentless efficiency, curare kills a small bird in seconds, a man in five minutes, and a 1,000-pound ox in less than 30 minutes. To date no wholly reliable antidote has been found.

Great pains are taken to ensure the effectiveness of the poison. An early traveler to the Amazon claimed that in one tribe the task of making the poison fell to the ugliest and oldest women; the hunters deemed the poison sufficiently powerful only when at least one of the women had died from inhaling the fumes. Perhaps more credible is the tale that many Amazon tribes grade curare according to the number of trees a monkey can jump to before falling dead from a poisoned dart. One-tree curare is considered strong enough for hunting; three-tree curare is too weak.

Curare is made by masters of tribal poisons; they have been known to include a multitude of bizarre ingredients in the mixture: the fangs and livers of venomous snakes, large hairy spiders, wings of bats, and even the stingers of ants.

Lethal vine

But the lethal element comes from the bark of *Strychnos toxifera,* a climbing vine. First the Indians strip off the bark and pound it. They then filter cold water through the fibrous pulp and boil the

resulting liquor to concentrate it. Finally, they add the juice of the kiracaguero tree to produce a tarry syrup that sticks to the tips of darts.

The Indians of the Amazon Basin use the darts in 10-foot-long blowpipes made of reeds encased in bamboo. Each dart is about nine inches long, needle-sharp at one end and bound with wild cotton—to create a tight fit in the tube—at the other. A good blowpipe marksman can propel a dart that will kill at a range of 100 yards.

From poison to anesthetic

Curare had been notorious in Europe since explorers in the 16th century reported its effects. Yet so inaccessible were the jungles of the Amazon that scientists were unable to investigate it thoroughly until the mid-19th century. By 1847 experiments had shown how curare worked and how a victim of curare poisoning could be kept alive by artificial respiration. But the active ingredient was still unknown, and the strength of curare imported from South America was too variable to give predictable results.

FLYING DEATH *Amazon Indians blow their curare-tipped darts through pipes made from 10-foot-long reeds that are encased in bamboo for extra rigidity. The strength of the poison is tested by the number of trees that a wounded monkey can jump to before dropping down dead.*

Finally, in 1935 Harold King, an English doctor, identified the main paralyzing agent in curare; that same year Guillermo G. Klug, a German botanist, identified the plant that was the source of the agent. After that, drug companies were able to produce a standard-strength curare, and the way was open to apply the powerful drug in medicine.

The first modern use of curare was as a relaxant in treating paralysis. Then in 1942 Dr. Harold Griffith of Montreal administered it as an anesthetic in surgery. Since then it has been used in many operations. Not only does curare relax muscles, making the surgeon's work easier, but the patient needs less anesthetic and can recover more rapidly.

After centuries as a murderously efficient poison, curare has become one of the more trusted weapons in modern medicine.

THE PIG ORGAN

A chorus fit for a king

KING LOUIS XI OF FRANCE was noted for his cruelty. He often tortured his enemies to death and organized manhunts in which a victim was covered with a deer skin, chased, and torn to pieces by hounds.

Louis was also fascinated by animals. He kept a large menagerie that included an elephant, monkeys, and bears, and he often traveled throughout his kingdom with a tame lioness.

On one occasion Louis contrived to combine his two preoccupations in a wager with one of his clerics. As the 17th-century English writer Nathaniel Wanley described it:

"The Abbot of Baigne, a man of great wit, and who had the art of inventing new musical instruments, being in the service of Louis XI, king of France, was ordered by that prince to get him a concert of swine's voices, thinking it impossible. The abbot was not surprised, but asked for money for the performance, which was immediately delivered him; and he wrought a thing as singular as ever was seen. For out of a great number of hogs, of several ages, which he got together, and placed under a tent or pavilion, covered with velvet, before which he had a table of wood, painted, with a certain number of hogs, he made an organical instrument, and as he played upon the said keys, with little spikes which pricked the hogs he made them cry in such order and consonance, as highly delighted the king and all his company."

Some 400 years later the abbot's highly original instrument was adapted by the inventor of the so-called Porco-Forte. The *Musical World* of November 1839 described the device as having been invented in Cincinnati. It operated on a principle similar to the abbot's device: a number of pigs were placed in a partitioned box, with their tails projecting through holes. By means of a keyboard mechanism, the pigs' tails were pinched to elicit what was hoped would be a harmonious range of squeals.

WHO'S ON FIRST?

Inventions ahead of their time

Baby incubator A Frenchman named Budin is credited with having invented, in 1880, a crude baby incubator: a wooden cabinet heated by pans of hot water. In 1891 Budin's countryman, Dr. Alexandre Lion, introduced a more sophisticated incubator, or *couveuse,* which both filtered air and kept it at a constant temperature.

Blood transfusion The principle of blood transfusion was understood as early as 1665, when an Englishman, Richard Lower, transfused blood between animals. Two years later, Jean-Baptiste Denys, physician to King Louis XIV, transfused two pints of blood from a sheep to a young man.

But so great was the danger of a patient's receiving blood incompatible with his own that transfusion was rarely attempted. Although Dr. James Blundell of Guy's Hospital, London, gave human blood to a patient in 1818, transfusion did not become safe until 1900, when Karl Landsteiner, an Austrian pathologist, identified the four different types of human blood. He developed the groupings (known today as the ABO system) that made it possible to match donors and patients.

Contact lenses Although first suggested in 1827 by the British astronomer Sir John Herschel, contact lenses were not manufactured until 1887, when a Swiss doctor, Eugen Frick of Zurich, devised a means of producing precision lenses. The Zeiss factory in Jena, in what is today East Germany, manufactured the first contact lenses.

Credit card Credit cards for the purchase of gasoline were common in the United States in the 1920's. However, it was not until May 1950 that Diners Club introduced the first general-purpose credit card.

Guillotine The guillotine was named for Joseph Ignace Guillotin, the French physician who had proposed its use during the Revolution. But Guillotin was not the inventor.

A beheading device is known to have been used in Ireland in 1307, and in 1587 William Harrison, an English historian, described the "Halifax gibbet," a guillotinelike instrument that had a horizontal blade rather than a slanting one; it had been in use since very early times. In 1581 a version known as

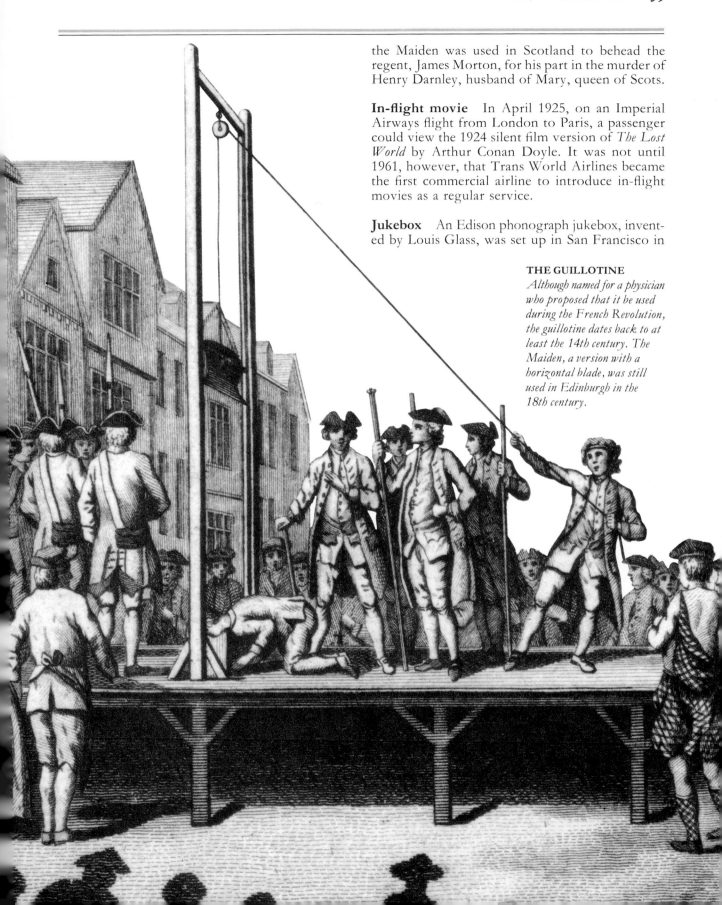

the Maiden was used in Scotland to behead the regent, James Morton, for his part in the murder of Henry Darnley, husband of Mary, queen of Scots.

In-flight movie   In April 1925, on an Imperial Airways flight from London to Paris, a passenger could view the 1924 silent film version of *The Lost World* by Arthur Conan Doyle. It was not until 1961, however, that Trans World Airlines became the first commercial airline to introduce in-flight movies as a regular service.

Jukebox   An Edison phonograph jukebox, invented by Louis Glass, was set up in San Francisco in

THE GUILLOTINE
Although named for a physician who proposed that it be used during the French Revolution, the guillotine dates back to at least the 14th century. The Maiden, a version with a horizontal blade, was still used in Edinburgh in the 18th century.

1889. John C. Dunton's 1905 invention was the first to offer a choice of 24 cylinder recordings. The first jukebox using disc recordings was made in Chicago a year later.

Space travel Although evidence is scanty, it appears that four monkeys were the first animals to enter the earth's stratosphere via a V-2 rocket launched from White Sands, New Mexico, in 1951. The next year Aerobee rockets with monkeys and mice on board were frequently launched to test the effects of weightlessness. But usually the U.S.S.R. is credited with having started the age of space travel by launching the dog Laika into orbit on board *Sputnik 2* on November 3, 1957.

Stereo Within five years of Alexander Graham Bell's invention of the telephone in 1876, Clement Adler, a French engineer, had devised a primitive form of stereophonic transmission. He linked telephone receivers in a hotel to transmitters on the stage of the Paris Opera, four miles away. But more

than 50 years passed before the technique became practical for domestic use. In 1933 British inventor Alan Dower Blumlein patented the stereophonic phonograph. However, the first stereophonic records did not go on sale in the United States until 1958 — 25 years later.

Tooth care Strong evidence suggests that the first toothbrush was made in China in 1498. It was certainly in use in Europe in the 17th century, and various pastes and powders were sold for use as cleaning agents.

The first toothpaste to be sold in a collapsible metal tube was Dr. Zierner's Alexandra Dentifrices, marketed in Britain in 1891.

Videodiscs Major Radiovision of London began selling videodiscs in June 1935. Each side of a disc offered six minutes of sound and pictures; they were reproduced by means of a device linked to a primitive television set. The discs were never commercially successful.

WATER ON TAP

The ultimate in military headgear

THE NOVEMBER 1901 issue of the British *Strand Magazine* featured an article entitled "Military Novelties." Its author, James Scott, described and illustrated a number of recent inventions that the British Army, at war in South Africa at the time, should consider adopting.

Most prominently featured in the article was the "reservoir hat," which apparently had been patented

DUAL PURPOSE *Constructed with a rim to collect rainwater, the reservoir hat both cooled its wearer's head and allowed him to quench his thirst.*

in Germany several years earlier. After reviewing the effect of thirst upon the fighting man in warm climates, Scott acknowledged that the proposed invention "appears at first to be an outrageous and ludicrous one."

The reservoir hat was a tropical helmet. A wide brim at the crown acted as a deep gutter in which rainwater could be collected. A ring of carbon inside the brim was to purify the water. Scott assured readers that a filled helmet could also serve as a "beneficial cooling agent to the throbbing head of the soldier wearing it." He neglected to suggest that the throbbing head could have resulted from the weight of a helmet filled with pints of water.

After a march — assuming it had rained — a soldier had only to remove his helmet and turn a tap to release the "life-sustaining liquid." Scott also proposed an extra refinement: a detachable cup mounted on top of the helmet.

Any thoughts of an army of marching water barrels were soon dispelled, however. Trials of the helmet in Africa showed that despite the purifying carbon, the water was quickly contaminated with amoebas, and soldiers drinking it frequently came down with dysentery. Nothing more was ever heard of the reservoir hat again.

CLOTHES FOR STEPPING OUT

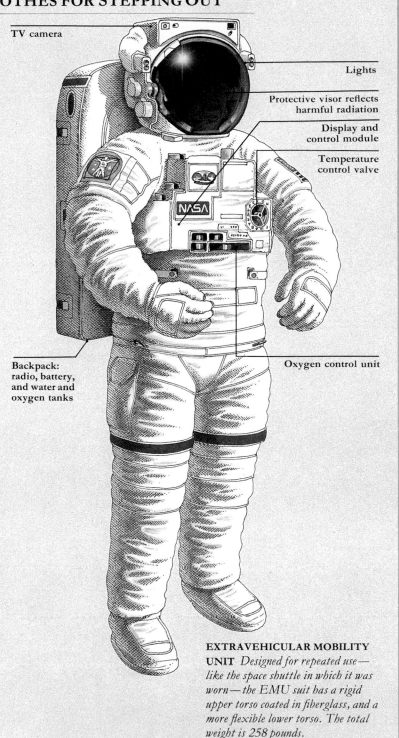

TV camera

Lights

Protective visor reflects harmful radiation

Display and control module

Temperature control valve

Backpack: radio, battery, and water and oxygen tanks

Oxygen control unit

Inside a space shuttle an astronaut travels in relative comfort: he works in shirtsleeves if he wants, and can even wear shorts. But when an astronaut ventures outside the craft, a space suit is an essential item.

Outer space is the most hostile environment in which humans have ever attempted to work. Because no atmosphere filters the rays of the sun, temperatures vary between 250°F in direct sunlight and −250°F in the shade.

A space suit must protect its occupant from these extremes, and modern versions have 11 layers of insulating material. The first layer, next to the skin, functions as a cooling system. Otherwise, it would very soon become unbearably hot inside.

The suit has to be filled with oxygen to allow the wearer to breathe and to keep the body itself under pressure. Without this pressure, oxygen in the astronaut's blood and lungs would expand in a reaction similar to the bends experienced by deep-sea divers who surface too rapidly. However, the pressure must also be maintained at a level that will prevent the suit from ballooning out in the vacuum of outer space, making movement for the person inside it impossible.

Because it takes about 12 hours for a person to adjust to this low pressure—too long in an emergency—NASA is in the process of developing a new suit. An astronaut will be able to step into it and immediately head out into space. It is called the zero-prebreathe suit, or ZPS, because it will relieve astronauts of the lengthy decompression process before they go into space.

EXTRAVEHICULAR MOBILITY UNIT *Designed for repeated use— like the space shuttle in which it was worn—the EMU suit has a rigid upper torso coated in fiberglass, and a more flexible lower torso. The total weight is 258 pounds.*

FINGER OF SUSPICION

The telltale mark that we carry to the grave

EARLY IN JULY 1892 Inspector Alvarez of the police force in La Plata, Argentina, arrived in nearby Necochea to help investigate a particularly unpleasant murder. Two children had been found battered to death in bed in the shack where they lived with their mother, 26-year-old Francisca Rojas. Although suspicion had fallen on Francisca herself, the police had failed to extract a confession from her.

A bloody thumb

Alvarez searched the shack for clues and on the door found the print of a bloody thumb. Removing that piece of the door with a saw, he took it to the police station, then sent for Francisca and had her fingerprinted. When she learned that the print on the door matched that of her own right thumb, she broke down and confessed to the crime.

With Francisca's confession the case was closed, and Inspector Alvarez became the first detective in history to solve a murder by finding a fingerprint at the scene of the crime.

Alvarez had studied the work of his colleague Juan Vucetich, head of the bureau of statistics for the La Plata police. Vucetich had discovered a method of analyzing and classifying fingerprints that made them easy both to file and, equally vital, to retrieve. Until then, the police authorities had largely ignored his work. But because of the Rojas case and subsequent successes, Argentina adopted fingerprinting as its sole method of identifying criminals—the first country in the world to do so.

INDIVIDUAL PRINT *Every fingerprint is unique, but all share common characteristics. The fingerprint classifications established by Edward Henry in 1896, and still in use today, grouped them into the five basic types below. Henry's codes appear next to each.*

The use of fingerprinting in detective work had actually begun more than 30 years earlier. In 1858 William Herschel, a British civil servant working in India, had impressed an illiterate local builder with the importance of a contract by making him sign it with the print of his entire palm. As he was examining the contract later, Herschel noticed the print's characteristic lines.

He was fascinated by his observation and began collecting fingerprints from everyone he knew. He soon realized that each print was unique. After years of collecting, Herschel made another crucial discovery: fingerprints remain the same throughout a person's lifetime.

Independent inquiry

When Herschel returned to London in 1880, he read an account in the journal *Nature* by Dr. Henry Faulds that detailed his own work on fingerprints. A Scottish missionary working in Japan, Faulds had observed that for centuries local people had been using fingerprints as signatures. He also had established the individuality of fingerprints, and discovered that the sweat from the pores on the tips of the fingers leaves a print as clear as any left by a bloodstained or inked palm. In his article, Faulds suggested that the police search for fingerprints at the scene of every crime.

Although Herschel wrote to *Nature* to describe his own work, very little notice was taken of his discoveries or those of Faulds's until 1888. Then, while investigating methods of identifying criminals, the eminent British scientist Sir Francis Galton remembered the claims of the two men and soon became an ardent proponent of fingerprinting. But he made it clear that a simple system of classifying prints was vital if the technique was to be of any practical use to the police.

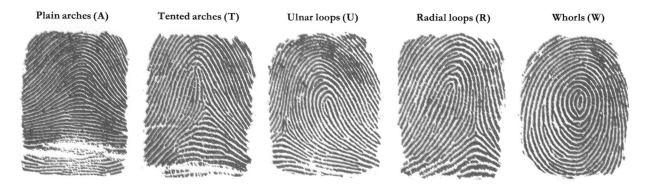

| Plain arches (A) | Tented arches (T) | Ulnar loops (U) | Radial loops (R) | Whorls (W) |

In 1896 Edward Henry, then inspector general of the Bengal police in India, solved the problem. By 1901 his classification method—which he insisted be called the Galton-Henry system in recognition of Galton's contribution—had been adopted by Scotland Yard.

Fingering the crime

Henry divided fingerprint patterns into five basic types: plain arches, tented arches, ulnar loops (which slope toward the little finger), radial loops (which slope toward the thumb), and whorls. These he coded A, T, U, R, and W. By also counting the number of lines in a print and mapping the position of the triangles that formed where the lines divided, he produced a system of identification that not only was easy to learn but also made filing and retrieving a rapid process. Any print could be located in minutes.

So successful was the system that during the next few years police forces throughout Europe and North America followed Britain's lead and took up fingerprinting. It was not until the 1920's, however, after J. Edgar Hoover took charge of the FBI, that a nationally effective system operated in the United States.

Today the files of the FBI contain more than 140 million sets of fingerprints. Not all are the prints of criminals: every government employee and serviceman is routinely fingerprinted. Scotland Yard's pioneering files are now computerized and contain 3.6 million sets—all belonging to convicted persons. With the exception of China and South America, where the system developed by Vucetich is still used, police forces throughout the world file their prints by the Galton-Henry method. In those files are countless prints that bear nature's own unique, unchanging, ineradicable calling card.

A DIVINE DRINK

How a goat led to a discovery

THE FIRST CREATURE to enjoy the invigorating effects of coffee was a goat—if popular legend is to be believed.

Many years ago Kaldi, a young Arabian goatherd, was tending his flock when he noticed the goats leaping around in a strange fashion. As he watched he saw that this odd behavior began after they had eaten the red berries of an unfamiliar tree. His curiosity aroused, Kaldi ate some of the fruit himself—and began to dance with his animals.

Prophetic dream

One day a Muslim holy man stopped to stare at the cavorting group. He listened to Kaldi's story and puzzled over it as he returned to his mosque. That night, after many hours spent praying to Allah, he dozed off. The prophet Muhammad appeared to him in a dream and told him to collect Kaldi's berries and boil them in water; the resulting potion would keep awake those who came to worship at the mosque. The great god Allah was angry at hearing not the prayers of the faithful but only their snores as they slept, said Muhammad.

The holy man did as Muhammad instructed, and the brew proved to be a great success: the mosque became famous for its lengthy and unflagging devotional sessions.

The fame of the elixir spread beyond the temples of Islam; before long the drink could be found in almost every Arab household. Because Muhammad had forbidden the drinking of wine, the delicious beverage was indeed a godsend; Arabs named it the Wine of Araby. The Arabic for wine is *qahway*, a word that eventually became *coffee* in English.

By the 16th century Arabs had discovered that the coffee tree held another secret: the red berry contained green beans, or seeds. These they dried, roasted, ground, and simmered in water; the liquid was then strained through silk and poured into an earthen pot. Portions were reheated and served in china cups with cinnamon or cloves.

Soon throughout the Islamic world the faithful were neglecting the temples in favor of coffeehouses, which also offered singing, dancing, and gambling. Much alarmed, prominent religious leaders decided that coffee was as unholy a beverage as wine and decreed that the drinking of coffee was forbidden.

But no less a personage than the caliph of Cairo, a descendant of Muhammad and ruler of much of the Islamic world, had become a passionate coffee drinker. When news of the decree reached him, he immediately revoked it.

Thanks to his prompt action, coffee drinking again flourished. In due course the beverage was discovered by European traders who, in the 17th century, started to bring it back in quantity to refresh—and invigorate—the West.

PATENT APPLIED FOR

Some inventions that were never heard of again

THE PRINCIPLE that inspires many inventions is to find a solution to a problem. But in some instances the problem proves not to have been worth the solving, or the solution itself is so complicated or unreliable that it cannot be applied. And some inventions have not provided the breakthrough their creators envisioned.

For example, in 1878 Thomas Alva Edison obtained a patent for a voice-activated motor for sewing machines and other appliances. Edison had developed the idea after a friend told him that her pedal-operated sewing machine tired her.

With Edison's invention all the operator had to do was to maintain a constant stream of sound, which a "vocal engine," or "phonomotor," converted into power. Edison's friend, however, found constant talking even more fatiguing than pedaling.

Rude awakenings

Other inventors have tackled the problem of waking up every morning. Proposed solutions have ranged from devices that tip one out of bed to those that shower a person with cold water.

A more gentle approach was adopted by Samuel S. Applegate of New Jersey in 1882. He devised an alarm clock that was connected to a frame by a series of gears. From the frame dangled 60 cork blocks "sufficient to awaken the sleeper, but not heavy enough to cause pain." When the alarm rang, the corks fell on the sleeper's head.

Getting the baby to sleep was solved in 1971 by a Californian, Thomas V. Zelenka. His invention, to be attached to the side of the crib, was an electric motor that operated a rod with a gloved hand to pat the baby's bottom.

Other domestic problems have also merited the attention of various ingenious inventors. In 1897 a British-designed, pedal-driven shower was on display at the Paris Bicycle Exhibition. The harder one pedaled, the stronger the gush of water that flowed from the shower.

"Make a better mousetrap and the world will beat a path to your door," wrote Ralph Waldo Emerson in 1871. In 1908 Joseph Barad and Edward E. Markoff of Providence, Rhode Island, attempted to fulfill Emerson's prediction with the humane "bell-rat."

The invention consisted of a framed structure, pulleys connected to bait, and a collar with a bell. As the rodent nibbled the bait, it activated a device that slipped the noisy collar around the creature's neck. In theory, the rat would return to the nest and frighten away other members of its family.

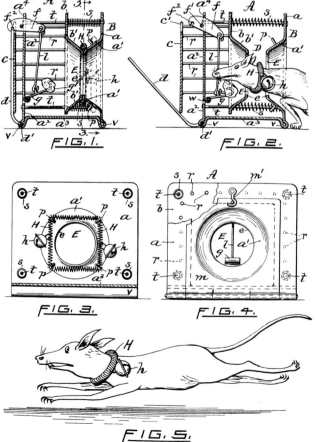

Barad and Markoff's bell-rat

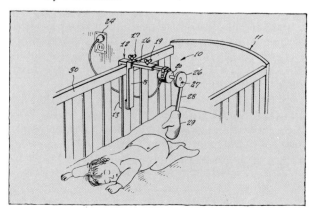

Thomas V. Zelenka's baby soother

And what if the house caught fire? Benjamin B. Oppenheimer of Trenton, Tennessee, offered his aid in 1879. Anyone trapped in a blazing building could strap Oppenheimer's patented parachute to his head, slip on the accompanying heavily cushioned shoes, and jump fearlessly out of the window to safety.

Benjamin B. Oppenheimer's fire escape

Turn-of-the-century security devices included a burglarproof bicycle seat. Invented in 1900 by Adolph A. Neubauer, the seat sported a sharp spike that projected through it. Naturally, the owner could unlock the lethal-looking weapon, but a would-be thief received a salutary lesson. A similar principle was employed in Frank P. Snow's 1914 hat protector. Unaware of the presence of a spike inside the rim, a hat thief could receive a shock.

Simple but strange

Some of the simplest inventions are nonetheless the most extraordinary. In 1903 Andrew Jackson, Jr., of Munich, Tennessee, was granted a patent for spectacles for chickens. Not intended to aid eyesight, they were described as eye-protectors "so that [fowls] may be protected from other fowls that might attempt to peck them."

Military requirements have resulted in innumerable strange gadgets, but few are as

Andrew Jackson's chicken spectacles

WITHOUT CHARGE

There has never been any stipulation that a patented invention *has* to work. One that could not be proved was a "method of collection and putting to practical use the electricity from the interplanetary ether." This fanciful scheme was patented in 1903, both in the United States and in Great Britain, by Albert Gallatin Whitney of Chicago.

Whitney's plan was to send a 150-mile-long cable up into the atmosphere, either by shooting it from a cannon or by attaching it to an airship. Whitney was convinced that this feat would not be as difficult as it seemed. After the first 17 miles "the ether itself will raise the furthest end of the cable through the miles remaining without the necessity of employing any extra force."

Electricity that passed down the cable would be collected on the ground and the power used for heating and lighting.

unusual as that made by Jones Wister of Philadelphia. During World War I, Wister devised a weapon intended to revolutionize trench warfare: a rifle that could shoot around corners. Its curved extension would fit the barrel of a conventional rifle; a periscope replaced the standard sights.

Although there is no evidence that Wister's invention was ever used, a similar attachment that appeared during World War II, the *krummlauf,* was actually used by German troops.

Comfort for all

An odd device patented in Britain in 1904 by a Prussian count, Vladimir Skorzewski, was a compressed-air walking assister. It consisted of a seat and handlebars, shock absorbers, and leg extensions and soles attached to stirrups. The count's notion was that the shock absorbers at the contraption's joints would function much like a series of miniature pogo sticks. The user could bound along the street and still enjoy the comforts of sitting down while "walking."

Should a user's feet become heated, Miguel y Villacampa of Argentina had the answer. In 1905 he introduced the ventilated shoe heel; it contained a pump that circulated air around the foot.

Inventors have often attempted to devise novel forms of entertainment. A device patented by a Belgian, Eduard Wulff, in 1904, was described as an "acrobatic apparatus for animals." An animal was to be led onto a platform and strapped into a quick-release body belt; when the spring was released, the creature would be launched upward and turn a somersault in midair.

Wulff specified the animals for which the apparatus was designed. The list included monkeys (they might have performed the feat); horses (which could have sustained serious injury); and elephants. Apart from the problems involved in constructing an apparatus capable of catapulting so large a pachyderm, the idea of an animal that weighs five or more tons performing an airborne somersault and then landing on its feet is mind-boggling.

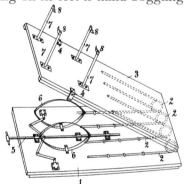

Eduard Wulff's acrobatic apparatus for animals

Another circus invention, also dating from 1904, was the loop-the-loop bicycle of Karl Lange of Berlin. It resembled two bicycles, with one inverted on top of the other. The rider, wedged between the two seats, was to hurtle down a ramp, shoot off it, and then land on a nearby platform—upside down. There is no evidence that any daredevil ever put Lange's invention to the test.

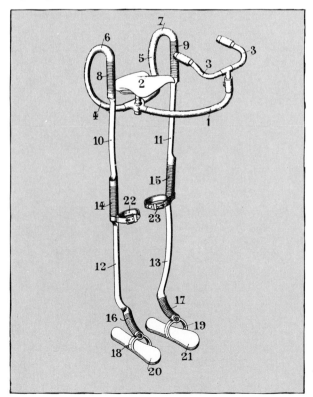

Count Skorzewski's walking assister

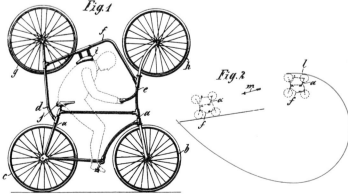

Karl Lange's loop-the-loop bicycle

FLYING HIGH

In 1972 the engineering division of British Rail, the national railway system in Britain, applied for a patent for a flying saucer. Powered by nuclear fusion, it would be capable of transporting 22 passengers either on earth or in outer space. The fact that the technology to construct such a revolutionary vehicle did not exist failed to deter its inventors. But by 1976 they seemed to have

A successor to the train?

lost faith in its practicability and allowed the patent to lapse.

In 1981 Florentine inventor Alfredo Bizzarri also took out a patent for a flying saucer. Meant to operate like a Hovercraft, it was, nevertheless, unworkable.

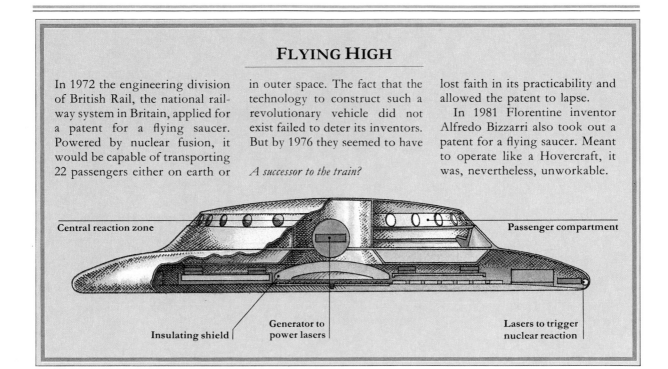

Central reaction zone

Passenger compartment

Insulating shield

Generator to power lasers

Lasers to trigger nuclear reaction

"NEEDED INVENTIONS" THAT CAME TO BE

Others are still awaited

IN 1933 the British Institute of Patentees offered inspiration to would-be inventors by publishing *What's Wanted,* a helpful list of "895 needed inventions." All were devices for which the institute imagined a demand, but none of them had yet been invented. In the United States 13 years later, Raymond Francis Yates, an authority on inventions, published *2100 Needed Inventions.* By 1951 this had been expanded to *3100 Needed Inventions.*

Both books suggested an extraordinary selection of both useful and absurd items, ranging from simple domestic articles to complex industrial machines. Browsing through them today offers an eye opening picture of the technology of a period that for many is still within living memory.

With hindsight it is easy to note that certain "needed inventions" either turned out to be completely unnecessary or were overtaken by other developments. A unique "method of resharpening hypodermic needles," for example, became redundant when cheap disposable needles were invented, as did a "cloud-disperser for pilots," once radar and automatic guidance systems for airplanes were introduced in the 1930's.

In general, however, the challenge was taken up, and many of the items on the "wanted" lists were eventually invented on one side of the Atlantic or the other. Progress was rapid: a large number of inventions that are now commonplace either were not even on the drawing boards in the years surrounding World War II or existed only in a very primitive form.

Fact and fantasy

There are some inventions on the lists that have yet to make their appearance, either because they are too ludicrous or because there is still no way to create them. Some, such as the "bulletproof stroboscope" and the "illuminated collar stud," are so whimsical that it is difficult to believe that anyone would ever have wanted them. Others, such as "improvements in neckwear," are so vague as to defy strict interpretation.

Some of the inventions, though desirable, were clearly not serious: an "indicator of the wife's frame of mind on returning late from the office"; an "appliance to wake, shave, bathe, and dress a man ready to catch his train to town in the morning"; a "simple way of making money." Even the multi-functional Swiss Army knife does not offer a "combined pen, pencil, penknife, eraser, paint-brush, ruler, compass, magnet, sparking-plug tester, toothbrush, nailfile, razor, adjustable watch-key, cigarette holder, automatic lighter, corkscrew, monogram, toothpick, fitted with a clip for the waistcoat pocket."

Home improvements

Among the many household items listed by Yates as "needed"—and today generally available—were waterproof dishwashing gloves and a mechanical dishwasher, along with a waterproof adhesive bandage, a transparent oven door, a pop-up toaster, a mechanical hedge trimmer, and a biodegradable wrapper.

The world is still waiting, however, for a machine for peeling bananas and one for peeling onions without causing tears, as well as for nondrip ice cream cones, a mousetrap that disposes of rodents' bodies, and "a method of opening oysters by electric shock."

Likewise, there is no sign yet of a "deck chair in which one can sit sideways," while a "machine for the home which gets rid of unwanted books and papers by pulping them" and a bed with a trapdoor in the middle (so that the occupant can put his legs down in order to sit up when eating a meal) are still awaiting any enthusiastic inventor's attention.

A "cheap replacement for silk or woollen stockings," much in demand in 1933, was found four years later when nylon was patented; but "lipstick-proof linen," spectacles that enable one to see in

LIQUID CRYSTAL DISPLAY

The very black numbers displayed on modern pocket calculators and digital watches are formed from a remarkable group of natural substances. At normal temperatures, the substances are not quite liquid nor quite solid. They are called liquid crystals.

Liquid crystals were first observed and studied in detail by the Austro-Hungarian scientist Friedrich Reinitzer in 1888, but scientists and businessmen have capitalized on them only in the past 20 years. Liquid crystals are complex organic chemicals with molecules that can flow like liquids but also form regular patterns like solid crystals.

In a liquid crystal number display, the crystals are sandwiched between two transparent electrodes that transmit the electric current. The electrode on top is divided into seven different segments; together the segments form a figure 8.

Numerals other than the 8 are created when a charge is not sent to one or more bars of the 8, as directed by a silicon chip.

On a digital watch, four such arrangments of electrodes, side by side, provide the full digital display of hours and minutes.

HOW THE NUMERAL 3 APPEARS *In a digital watch, the battery sends low voltage to the five segments of the upper transparent electrode that will create the numeral 3. Light that falls on the display is filtered through those liquid crystals directly underneath the charged electrodes. The angle is such that the polarizing sheet beneath the crystals prevents the light from reaching the mirror and reflecting back to the display. The result: the segments of the electrode that create the numeral 3 are black.*

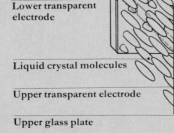

Mirror

Polarizing sheet

Lower transparent electrode

Liquid crystal molecules

Upper transparent electrode

Upper glass plate

Polarizing sheet

Digital display

Charged segment of electrode

Light beam

the dark, and cigarettes that do not release smoke from the lighted end have defied the ingenuity of inventors for more than 50 years.

On the road

The suggested device that makes recommendations to the driver of an automobile can be found today in some models. Light-sensitive devices for turning headlights on and off, turn indicators, and automatic windshield washers are often available.

Nonskid road surfaces have been longer in coming, and a "car that can be converted into an airplane" still sounds like a futuristic daydream—as does an airplane so simple to operate that it can be flown by a child.

High-tech

The high-tech office of today could scarcely function without devices that were once listed as wanted, such as the typewriter eraser key and the telephone-answering machine. A "method of keeping fingers clean when changing typewriter ribbons" has been effectively taken care of by the introduction of the ribbon cartridge, and a "method of printing multiple copies of a document," with the advent of photocopiers and word processors. The suggestion half a century ago for a "device for converting the spoken word into the written word" has also proved prophetic, with the introduction of word processors that respond to the sound of the human voice.

New sources of energy have been developed from proposals for wind-powered electric generators and a "practical method of using the power of the tides." And a "new fuel to replace coal" has been realized in the form of nuclear power.

A "method of avoiding collisions at sea by detecting the presence of other vessels" came into existence when radar was developed in the 1930's; so have self-inflating life jackets, folding baby carriages, inexpensive color photography, instant color photographs, and machines for milking cows automatically.

Meanwhile, the demand for "phonograph records that last 100 percent longer" has been exceeded by the invention of the virtually indestructible laser-read compact disc.

There remains plenty of scope for a "what's needed" list today; inventors are no nearer than the list compilers of a generation ago in producing an electric blackboard eraser or a silent pneumatic drill. "Dog silencers" still do not exist; no one is close to finding "an efficient substitute for an umbrella, or an umbrella that is impossible to leave behind"; and a "device for screening off gravitation" remains a science fiction fantasy.

RIGHTS OF PASSAGE

From ancient token to modern passport

IN ORDER TO travel today, everyone crossing national boundaries must have a passport—an official document confirming the bearer's identity and authorizing that person to move freely from one country to another. A vital document easily taken for granted, the modern passport is younger than the 20th century. Its origins, however, date back thousands of years.

Official protection

Before the advent of railroads, passenger ships, and airplanes, few people made international journeys. The merchants and diplomats who did travel carried tokens of recommendation from their rulers. These sometimes took unusual forms. For example, in ancient Egypt official couriers were given a cartouche—a small oblong shield—on which the pharaoh's name was inscribed; elsewhere in the Middle East, rulers issued a ring bearing the official seal to their envoys.

Roman emperors came closer to the equivalent of the modern passport by giving envoys certificates of safe conduct throughout the empire and through foreign territories. The blunt wording on a document Caesar Augustus issued to the philosopher Potamon some time in the first century B.C. left no doubt as to its importance: "If there be anyone on land or sea hardy enough to molest Potamon, let him consider whether he be strong enough to wage war with Caesar."

The dangers of travel

In medieval Europe passports took the form of personal letters that a person in authority gave the traveler. The handwritten letters served both as a means of identification and as a guarantee of personal protection.

In those times travelers of humble means faced many hazards, one of which was the chance of being driven out of a town as a vagrant. As protection against such a fate, pilgrims who jour-neyed to the religious shrines of Europe carried a kind of passport called a *testimoniale,* issued by ecclesiastical authorities.

The 11th-century English king Canute took a special interest in the welfare of English pilgrims en route to Rome; he provided elaborate letters requesting free "ingress, egress, and regress" in foreign monasteries, cities, and villages. As a reward, when they reached their destination pil-grims promised to pray for those who had respect-ed the bearer of Canute's letters.

Although such individually signed letters from rulers and other high-ranking officials were the main form of passport for centuries, without secure frontiers or efficient border controls many traveled without any documentation at all. As recently as 1890, only a few countries—including Persia, Romania, Russia, and Serbia—required foreigners to have passports to cross their borders; almost no country required its own nationals to have appropriate documents to travel abroad.

FREEDOM TO MOVE *As these examples of 19th- and early 20th-century passports demonstrate, passports over the years have taken many forms and served many purposes, from allowing travelers to enter and leave a country to letting messengers cross military lines in times of war.*

Saxony passport, 1866: early example of the booklet passport

Fold-out British passport, 1917

American Civil War pass, 1861: issued by the Union Military Headquarters, Washington, D.C.

Austrian passport, 1845: enabled a visitor from Brussels to visit the country

In the United States, in the early days of independence, passports were provided by a local authority or notary. But faced with the refusal of foreign countries to accept them as valid, in 1856 the government confined the issue of passports to the secretary of state. Until 1918, foreigners could enter the United States without one.

Document of state

The number of countries issuing passports, and requiring visitors to have them, increased considerably during and after World War I. The passport soon became a recognized state document, confirming both the citizenship and the identity of its bearer. To control immigration, some countries added the requirement that passports be endorsed with entry visas as well.

Faced with a profusion of documentation and the large variety of styles and wording from country to country, in 1921 the League of Nations introduced a uniform 32-page format to be used by all countries (it has since been modified).

The passport has become universal, its authority recognized in every country. Eventually the booklet format may be replaced by a plastic, computer-readable card. But whatever its form, the modern passport still has the same force as the precious official rings and cartouches of old.

DOUBLE FIRST

Just 20 years after making the first powered flight, near Kitty Hawk, North Carolina, in 1903, Orville Wright came up with another flying machine.

The gadget consisted of a tiny wooden figure, a catapult, and a trapeze. After being placed in the catapult, which was pulled back by an adjustable spring, the wooden doll was released. It performed a midair somersault and its hooked arms caught the bar of the trapeze, which then spun around several times.

Perhaps not as revolutionary as the Wright brothers' *Flyer 1*, the doll was a novel and entertaining toy nonetheless.

Orville Wright's flying doll

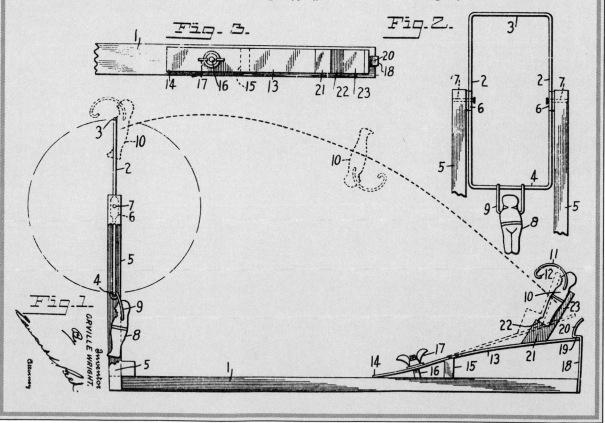

MOOD MEDICINE

Flowers that may improve your health

IN THE LATE 1920's a middle-aged physician turned his back on conventional medicine in order to search for an alternative way to cure chronic ailments. He began to study plants, hoping to discover treatments that would not be harmful, unpleasant, or addictive.

That man was Edward Bach, and several decades later his gentle flower remedies are still used by devoted followers all over the world.

Bach qualified as a doctor at University College, London, in 1912. For the next 16 years he worked as a pathologist and bacteriologist, setting up his own practice and laboratory and eventually formulating vaccines based on intestinal bacteria. These proved to be extremely effective in treating certain chronic illnesses and won Bach some renown in medical circles.

Despite his success, Bach became more and more dissatisfied with orthodox methods of treatment. He began to investigate homeopathy, the medical practice developed by a German physician, Samuel Hahnemann, at the beginning of the 19th century. It treats a disease with the administration of minute doses of a drug that in a healthy person would produce the same symptoms as the disease itself. Bach was convinced that what was important was to treat the patient, not the disease.

Unlike homeopathic practitioners, however, Bach believed that the mental state of the patient was the basis for a correct diagnosis—not the physical symptoms of illness. In his practice he had made the important observation that patients with the same disease did not respond the same way to the same treatment.

Bach abandoned London in favor of the countryside, where be began to observe his surroundings in detail. The result of his travels was the beginning of the Bach Flower Remedies—38 tinctures derived from wildflowers.

Positive thinking

With his remedies Bach hoped to cure the negative states of mind that he believed were responsible for the body's susceptibility to illness. By reversing the negative mood, one could cure, or even prevent, disease. In Bach's view, complete healing came from within, from the soul itself.

Bach divided negative emotions into seven main categories: fear, uncertainty, insufficient interest in the present, oversensitivity to influence and ideas, despondency and despair, loneliness, and excessive interest in the welfare of others. Bach made distinctions within each group, based on observations of personality types gathered in the course of his work. Each of his 38 remedies is designed to treat a specific emotion.

Bottling nature

To make the medicine, the best blooms of a particular species are picked, immersed in pure water, and left in full sunlight for a minimum of three hours. The liquid is then bottled. The recommended dosage is two drops of tincture diluted in a glass of water or juice and sipped slowly. The duration and frequency of treatment varies, and if more than one problem exists, remedies can be taken in combination.

In addition, Bach devised a "rescue remedy," comprising five different tinctures: star-of-Bethlehem, rockrose, impatiens, cherry plum, and clematis. The rescue remedy was intended as a form of emergency first aid to be used in all cases of "panic, sorrow, shock, terror, sudden bad news, and accidents." Many alternative-health therapists have advocated it for coping with childbirth. The remedy can be applied externally to the temples, lips, or affected part, or taken internally.

The effectiveness of the Bach Flower Remedies depends on accurate diagnosis—but in a way that stands conventional medicine on its head. Because the underlying emotional state is seen as the cause of illness, the same treatment can be prescribed for sufferers with complaints as different as asthma, alcoholism, and paralysis—as long as the patients display the same character traits.

Despite the skeptics

The publication of Bach's findings in 1930 attracted considerable public interest, and many people traveled great distances to try the flower cures. Satisfied patients were convinced by his philosophy, and many case histories support the success of the remedies. Medical opinion remains one of skepticism, however.

Although Bach died in 1936 at the age of 50, his innovative ideas have not been forgotten. Today the Bach Centre still operates out of a country cottage in Oxfordshire, England.

No matter what people think of his philosophy, many remember Bach as a man with an intuitive understanding of human nature and a sincere desire to help people regain their health.

A CASE OF PLANTS

The chance discovery that led to worldwide growth

SOME 640,000 TONS OF TEA are grown in India each year. It is an enormous industry, today worth more than a billion dollars annually, yet it owes its existence to an accidental discovery made in 1829 by a family doctor from London's grimy East End.

Dr. Nathaniel Bagshaw Ward's house was, as he put it, "surrounded by, and enveloped in, the smoke of numerous factories." A very dedicated amateur naturalist, Ward did his best to grow plants in the neighborhood's polluted atmosphere but was usually defeated. The breakthrough, when it came, was in a most unexpected fashion.

A moth in a bottle

Ward was conducting an experiment with the chrysalis of a sphinx moth, which he had buried in some moist earth in a glass bottle covered with a lid. As he watched the development of the insect, Ward was fascinated to observe that in the heat of the day moisture from the soil condensed on the sides of the bottle. Because of the lid, the moisture did not evaporate but returned to the soil. He was even more intrigued to see two tiny green shoots—one a fern, the other a grass—growing in the soil.

Ward duly retrieved his moth from the bottle, but his attention was now fixed on the two shoots that were flourishing despite the fact that they had not been watered. Ward concluded that the plants did so well because the air in the bottle was clean and the conditions were stable. All that the plants needed was light; their water was being automatically recycled.

In 1833 Ward tested his theories in a dramatic fashion. He filled two specially made glass cases with ferns and grasses and loaded them onto a ship bound for Australia. The plants arrived in perfect condition despite the lengthy journey.

But Ward had prepared an even tougher test. The cases were refilled with native Australian plants, some of which had never before reached England alive. After a nine-month voyage, during which they endured very extreme changes in the weather and temperatures ranging from 20°F while rounding Cape Horn to 120°F at the equator, the plants arrived in London in good health.

Wardian cases

The great potential of Ward's invention was immediately recognized by his fellow scientists. Wardian cases, as the covered containers came to be

PORTABLE GREENHOUSE *An ornate example of the Wardian case that revolutionized the plant trade during the 19th century.*

known, were soon being used to transport plants all over the world. They revolutionized the trade in plants and transformed several national economies in the process of doing it.

So it was that in 1848 the British Empire's favorite beverage, tea, came from China to India. Wardian cases also took rubber trees from Brazil to Ceylon (today Sri Lanka) and Malaya and coffee bushes from Africa to Brazil. Medicine benefited too: by means of the Wardian case, the cinchona tree—the source of quinine, at the time the sole antidote to malaria—was successfully carried from its native Peru to India.

In size Wardian cases ranged from no bigger than a shoe box to the massive constructions that once brought a shipment of trees from Tierra Del Fuego in South America to London and weighed nearly 350 pounds each. Most cases looked like conventional greenhouses. All were made to the highest standards of craftsmanship with glass and seasoned wood, perfectly fitted to keep air in and seawater out. Elaborately ornate versions called "terrariums" later appeared in thousands of respectable parlors, filled with the endless varieties of fern that so delighted Victorian England.

Nathaniel Ward has a permanent scientific memorial: a species of South African moss is named after him. But Ward was no inhuman scientist. For 20 years he tried to persuade the landlords of London's overcrowded slums to put his cases in tenement windows in order to give tenants at least a glimpse of nature's greenery. So perhaps the memorial that would have pleased him most are the millions of terrariums that today brighten homes all over the world.

STUMBLING INTO SUCCESS

Accidental discoveries that endured

WHILE MANY of the important inventions and discoveries that are today taken for granted came about after years of patient study and experiment, some were the result of a single accident or chance observation.

The stories behind several are probably apocryphal: For example, Joseph-Michel Montgolfier is said to have conjured up the idea of ballooning when he saw his wife's chemise, drying by the fire, rise up as it became filled with hot air. A number of other such stories, however, are known to be true.

Aniline dye During his summer vacation, William Henry Perkin, an 18-year-old student at the Royal College of Chemistry in Britain, was experimenting in his garden shed. While trying to make synthetic quinine from coal tar, he inadvertently created a sticky purple substance. Its principal virtue seemed to be the ability to dye cloth surprisingly quickly. What Perkin had hit upon was the world's first synthetic dye, aniline. After a dispute as to whether anyone under the age of 21 could, legally, be granted a patent, the boy succeeded in obtaining one in 1856. The properties of mauveine, as the dye became known, revolutionized the textile industry.

Chewing gum In the early 1870's an American schoolboy, Horatio Adams, was assisting his father, Thomas, in experiments with chicle, the dried sap of a Mexican jungle tree. Thomas originally tried to make rubber out of it. When this failed, he and young Horatio idly chewed pieces of chicle—and discovered its most promising use. They soon established a business to manufacture it for chewing. Although various types of tree gum and even flavored paraffin wax had been chewed in the United States since the mid-19th century, chicle-based gum soon replaced all others.

NEWFOUND DYES *Two of the aniline dyes invented by William Henry Perkin. Mauveine, at right below, was the first synthetic dye in history. On the left is alizarine, a substitute for a red dye obtained from the madder root.*

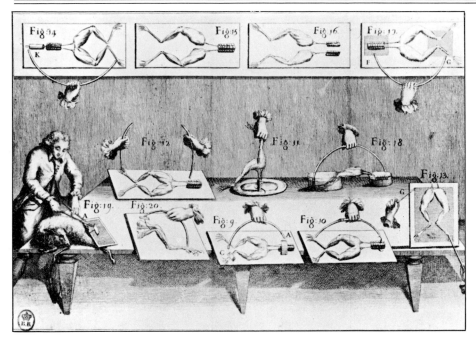

SHOCK TREATMENT
After applying electric shocks to make frogs' legs twitch, Luigi Galvani, professor of anatomy at the University of Bologna, thought he had discovered "animal electricity." Subsequently, however, his views were disputed.

DDT Quite by chance, a 19th-century Austrian chemist, Othmar Ziedler, invented dichloro-diphenyl-trichloro-ethane, or DDT, in 1874. But he ignored it since he could envision no practical value for it. It was not until 1939 that Paul Müller of Switzerland observed its insecticidal properties. It was patented by the German company J. R. Geigy A-G in 1942 and within a few years became the most widely used insecticide in the world.

Dry cleaning Jean-Baptiste Jolly of Paris inadvertently spilled camphene, a type of fuel, onto a dress. The garment, which he feared would be ruined, was instead cleaned. In 1855 Jolly established the world's first known dry-cleaning company.

Electric current Italian scientist Luigi Galvani was working in his Bologna laboratory in the 18th century when he accidentally touched a steel scalpel to a frog's leg that was lying on a zinc plate. The leg twitched, and Galvani believed he had discovered "animal electricity." In following up Galvani's research, his countryman, Count Alessandro Volta, showed that it was the two metals that were responsible for generating the electric current—and established the principle of the battery.

Float glass The float-glass process, which creates a high-quality surface, is today used to produce 99 percent of the glass manufactured in the United States. The method was developed in 1950 after Alastair Pilkington, a British glassmaker,

observed the way that a film of fat formed on the surface of his wife's dishwater. Sensing that molten glass could also be floated on a molten metal such as tin in order to produce a smoother finish, Pilkington's company invested seven years and $16.5 million to perfect the process.

Lithographic printing The technique of lithography was discovered about 1796 by Johann Nepomuk Aloys Senefelder, an aspiring Czech playwright. He is said to have copied his mother's laundry list onto a piece of limestone, using a wax pencil. When he accidentally spilled water on the stone, he noticed the waxed portion did not become wet. Senefelder realized that the same principle would enable printing ink to be selectively transferred to paper or cloth. The process he developed and patented in 1801 marked a major development in the history of printing.

Matches In 1825 John Walker, a 44-year-old chemist from the English town of Stockton-on-Tees, was busy making a "lighting mixture" of antimony sulfide and potassium chlorate for use with a flint and steel. When he accidentally rubbed some of the mixture against his hearthstone, he discovered that it lit spontaneously. He could light the friction matches he developed from this discovery by drawing them through a piece of folded sandpaper. Walker's invention, sold only locally, was never patented. It was Samuel Jones who copied and patented the matches in 1828 under the trade name Lucifer. The invention of the modern friction match is attributed to Sir Isaac Holden of Keighley, Yorkshire; in 1829 he produced a match of phosphorus and sulfur that, being more efficient than Walker's, superseded it by 1833.

Penicillin   In 1928 the Scottish bacteriologist Sir Alexander Fleming observed the effect of an antibacterial agent when the cover on a culture in which he was growing staphylococcus bacteria was accidentally removed and the culture became contaminated by a mold from the atmosphere. Fleming noticed that the mold—a strain of a fungus called penicillium—had destroyed the bacteria. Its potential for combating bacterial disease occurred to Fleming, but isolating and stabilizing the bactericidal substance, which he called penicillin, proved beyond his resources.

Between 1939 and 1941, however, two other researchers, Howard Florey and Ernst Chain, working at Oxford University, resumed Fleming's initial work. Penicillin was eventually patented in 1943. In recognition of their work, the three men shared the 1945 Nobel Prize in medicine.

Synthetic fibers   The centrifugal method used to twist thread evenly in the manufacture of synthetic fibers was invented in England at the turn of the century by Charles Topham, who, while cycling, noticed the way in which mud was thrown off the wheels of his bicycle. His "spinning box," patented in 1900, facilitated the commercial manufacture of cellulose and artificial yarns.

Transfer printing   John Sadler, a Liverpool engraver, used to give his children spoiled engravings while the paper was still wet with ink. After noticing that the children amused themselves by transferring the impressions from the paper onto pieces of broken pottery, Sadler conducted a series of experiments. He finally perfected the transfer of printing onto pottery and porcelain—a process that revolutionized pottery design.

Vulcanized rubber   Pure rubber has a tendency to harden in cold weather and soften in warm. In 1839 Charles Goodyear, the son of an American storekeeper, accidentally dropped rubber with sulfur onto a hot stove. Because the resulting mixture did not react to temperature changes in the same way, it was ideally suited to the manufacture of tires and other rubber products; indeed, it became the foundation of the rubber industry. Goodyear patented his discovery in 1843, but he was compelled to spend the rest of his life in legal battles against the many firms that infringed his patent. The Goodyear Tire & Rubber Company commemorates his name, but he had no connection with it: it was established in Akron, Ohio, in 1898, 38 years after his death.

FLASH OF INSPIRATION

An electrifying event

ON APRIL 18, 1777, as storm clouds gathered above, the people of Siena, Italy, looked anxiously toward their cathedral. For 500 years it had stood on the town's highest hill. Now, they were sure, it was about to be destroyed by lightning as punishment for the sacrilege committed by its priests: the installation of a lightning conductor on its spire.

The people believed that lightning was a direct expression of the wrath of God, and that any attempt to divert it was a defiance of His will. Far from saving the cathedral, the "heretical rod" could only attract a worse retribution.

Just as they had feared, a massive bolt struck the spire. But a few minutes later, a ray of sunshine broke through the clouds: the cathedral was intact. The astonished people rushed into the building to join a service of thanksgiving.

While the people of Siena were thanking God, some priests were perhaps remembering Benjamin Franklin in their prayers; Franklin had invented the lightning conductor 25 years earlier. Others had noted that lightning and the newly discovered electricity had similar properties; their flashes even released the same sulfurous smell. But Franklin was the first to conclude that lightning *was* electricity.

The kite and the key

Franklin decided to test his belief by flying a kite into a storm cloud. A metal spike fixed to the kite would attract a lightning bolt and the control cord, wet with rain, would conduct the lightning downward. Franklin tied a key to the cord and attached it to an early form of electrical condenser, a Leyden jar. If lightning was electrical, the thunderbolt would charge the Leyden jar.

On July 4, 1752, Franklin flew his kite into a Philadelphia thunderstorm. The effect, literally, was electrifying. Just as Franklin had hoped, the Leyden jar became heavily charged. Although Franklin had proved his theory, he was lucky not to have been killed. A flash of lightning can discharge 20,000 amperes at a temperature of 54,000°F.

Earthquakes and experts

With the "wrath of God" identified as electricity, Franklin set out to show that a metal rod fixed to the top of a high building could attract lightning. He reasoned that if the rod was attached to a cable made of a good conducting material, and if its end was buried firmly in the ground, lightning would be carried safely to the earth and would leave the building completely untouched.

Although no one doubted the truth of Franklin's theory, his brilliant invention was surprisingly slow to catch on. Churchmen condemned it as a heretical interference with the will of God. A French scientist thought that conductors were dangerous because they attracted lightning that might otherwise have passed by. And a Boston preacher claimed that an earthquake in Massachusetts in 1755 had been caused by excess electricity being driven into the ground.

But people gradually were convinced when they saw the conductors at work. For the first time church steeples and spires were safe from possible destruction in storms.

Were it not for the inspired notion of Benjamin Franklin's, today's skyscrapers might never have been made safe for humans.

FASHIONABLE CONDUCT *The experiments that Benjamin Franklin conducted in 1752 finally convinced people that lightning was a form of electrical discharge. Many buildings were equipped with lightning conductors to spare them from damage, and the idea soon spread to fashionable Paris. In 1778 some women attached conductors to their hats as protection against electrocution.*

SKIP BOMBS

Bouncing their way to success

IN 1942, partway through World War II, a British aeronautical designer and inventor, Barnes Wallis, was faced with one of the greatest challenges of his career. He had to create a bomb that would destroy the dams of the West Ruhr valleys in order to flood and cripple the heart of the German armament industry.

It *was* quite a challenge. The bombs would have to explode below the waterline immediately adjacent to the dams in order to produce shock waves that would cause maximum damage. Conventional bombs could not be dropped with sufficient accuracy: when released from an airplane, they tended to fall forward. And torpedoes were unsuitable because of antitorpedo nets in the lakes behind the dams.

As Wallis pondered the problem, he remembered skimming stones across the surface of a lake. He knew that naval gunners had long used the same principle, skimming cannon balls to increase their range and cause devastating waterline damage. Would it be possible, Wallis wondered, to create a massive water-skipping bomb?

Lengthy experiments

Wallis had long been fascinated by the ballistic properties of spheres, and in the belief that a spherical bomb might be the answer, he used a catapult to fire marbles across a tub of water. From this simple beginning, Wallis progressed to scale models in large water tanks and ultimately blew up Nant-y-Gro, an unused dam in Wales. But Wallis soon discovered that a true sphere was an unsuitable shape because, like a ball, it rotated in unpredictable directions.

Wallis realized, however, that if the bomb could be rotated like a wheel, it would maintain forward momentum. To keep the bomb skipping smoothly on course, he flattened the sides. The result was a barrel-shaped bomb five feet long and just over four feet in diameter. Each bomb contained 6,000 pounds of high explosive; together with its reinforced case, it weighed a total of 9,250 pounds.

Airplanes were converted to carry the special bombs, which were mounted under the fuselage and rotated by a chain drive attached to an electric motor. Just before release the motor was switched on to rotate the bombs to a speed of 500 r.p.m. When the bombs hit the water, the backward spin prevented them from plowing beneath the surface or breaking apart.

Lighting the way

Wallis's "bouncing bombs" encountered a great deal of skepticism in official circles. Successful demonstrations, however, convinced the British Air Ministry of the potential effectiveness of the bombs. A new unit, Bomber Squadron 617, was specially formed for the dam-bombing mission under Wing Commander Guy Gibson.

In order to achieve the correct launching angle, Gibson had his pilots fly at precisely 60 feet, a height that no instrument of the time was capable of measuring accurately. This problem was solved with a simple device: two flashlights mounted at preestablished angles, one in the airplane's nose, one in the tail. When the two beams of light converged on the surface of the water, the pilot knew that he was at the required height and could release the bomb.

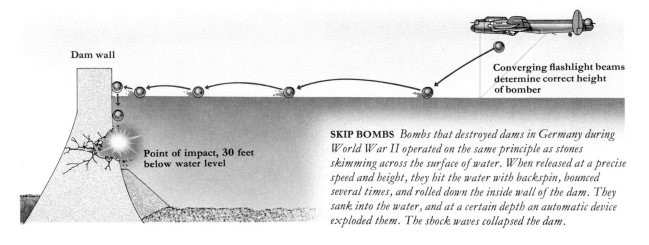

Dam wall

Converging flashlight beams determine correct height of bomber

Point of impact, **30 feet** below water level

SKIP BOMBS *Bombs that destroyed dams in Germany during World War II operated on the same principle as stones skimming across the surface of water. When released at a precise speed and height, they hit the water with backspin, bounced several times, and rolled down the inside wall of the dam. They sank into the water, and at a certain depth an automatic device exploded them. The shock waves collapsed the dam.*

On the night of May 16, 1943, 19 bombers set out for Germany. A clear, moonlit sky aided the pilots, and water levels at the dams were at their peak. Despite several aborted attempts and some losses, most of the bombs were set spinning and released, skipping across the lakes and against the walls of the dams, where they sank 30 feet to be exploded by preset triggers.

The result was everything that Wallis had anticipated: the dams on the Möhne and Eder rivers were breached and the Ruhr valleys flooded; power stations, factories, and railway lines were washed away; and the German war machine suffered a catastrophic blow.

Curiously, the patent for the dam-buster bomb was not published until 1963, more than 20 years after it had been used successfully and nearly 10 years after a feature film, *The Dam Busters,* had both celebrated Barnes Wallis and demonstrated how the bombs worked.

THE ORGONE ACCUMULATOR

Storing life-forces to heal the sick

IMAGINE A CUBICLE, about the size of a telephone booth, that a sick person could enter, sit in for a while, and leave feeling healed. In 1940 Austrian-born psychoanalyst Wilhelm Reich believed that his newly invented orgone box could achieve such magical results.

Reich built the box to attract and store a new kind of energy he claimed to have discovered. Reich maintained that this energy, which he called orgone, was a cosmic life-force composed of tiny particles that fell to earth from space. He claimed that in concentrated doses it could be used to cure all human ailments, from depression to cancer. Although no one ever saw orgone, Reich asserted that it was an eerie blue color. Once trapped inside the box, orgone had an effect like that of a small electrical charge and could be measured by an orgone energy field meter.

The box itself was about five feet high and two and a half feet square. Its six-inch-thick walls were made of alternating layers of wood and metal; in later models Reich added layers of both glass and steel wool to increase the box's effectiveness. According to Reich, to work properly the inside of the box had to be metal and the outside wood or another organic material.

The patient inside the box absorbed the collected orgone and experienced a feeling of warmth, although the metal walls were cold to the touch. There was nothing frightening about the box: the patient could look out through a small square opening cut in the door.

Miracle cure

Born to Jewish parents in Vienna in 1897, Reich was a qualified physician. His ideas may appear to be farfetched, but he based them on solid scientific training. As a medical student, he became a member of the group of psychoanalysts in Vienna presided over by Sigmund Freud. But Reich disagreed with Freud's focus on childhood as a source of adult problems and soon left Freud's circle to develop his own theory of sexuality as a major cause of adult neuroses. Against orthodox medical opinion, he claimed that there was no difference between mental and physical illness. Both, he maintained, were the result of unreleased sexual energy—a blockage that orgone could treat.

Reich took his radical ideas to Germany, which he left when the Nazis came to power in 1933, and then to Scandinavia, where he was frequently ridiculed by his fellow practitioners. He finally settled in the United States in 1939, establishing a laboratory in Rangeley, Maine, for the scientific study of orgone and its practical uses.

Reich thought orgone might cure cancer in the early stages of the disease, although no one else shared his enthusiasm. He claimed some success with 15 terminal cases, all of whom showed some improvement. Several lived two years more than expected, although none was permanently cured.

Reich's ideas were well received in the United States. By the summer of 1947, he was renting out nearly 200 orgone boxes at $10 a month to patients anxious to try his miracle cure. But in 1954 the U.S. Food and Drug Administration obtained an injunction to prevent his sending the boxes across the state lines: they called the boxes fraudulent devices. Refusing to comply, Reich was sent to prison, where he died of a heart attack in 1957.

It was a sorry end to a controversial career. Since his death, Reich's ideas have usually been scorned by doctors and psychoanalysts alike. The orgone box and the claims he made for orgone have largely been ignored. It seems unlikely that anyone will try to accumulate orgone again.

SAFETY COFFINS

The ultimate protection against premature burial

IN 1906 Frederick J. Harvey, the 20-year-old son of a millionaire Kansas restaurateur, died suddenly after a short illness. When his fiancée, Lily Godfrey, visited the family tomb, she became convinced that Frederick was only sleeping and arranged for the body to be taken home. Four months later Frederick emerged from his trance. He married the faithful Lily soon afterward.

Premature burial was a serious danger in the days when doctors did not fully understand such conditions as comas and catalepsy, because it was not always possible to declare with certainty whether a person was truly dead or merely unconscious.

Because top medical authorities considered the only sure sign of death to be "putrefactive decomposition," clauses in wills frequently stated that bodies should not be buried until a week after apparent death. "Waiting mortuaries" were once widely advocated; some were even built. Cremation was promoted as a certain way of ensuring that no one risked waking up in a coffin, and in Ireland it was once customary to slit a corpse's jugular vein. The 19th-century writer Harriet Martineau went one step further: her will left her doctor a sum of money if he would ensure her death by cutting her head off.

Grave concern

Short of such drastic methods, other means were sought to guard against the risk of premature burial. One of the most popular was the safety coffin. Built to allow periodic examination of a body, it provided either a means of escape from the coffin or ways to summon attention. In the second half of the 19th century, when premature burial had become a major concern and numerous pamphlets and books had been published, there was a flurry of patents for such devices.

Franz Vester's patented coffin of 1862 had an air tube and a bell, with a

JUST IN CASE *Safety coffins were popular in the 19th century, when premature burial was a possibility. In the coffin at right, proposed in 1892 by A. Kwiatkowski of Germany, the "deceased" could operate a lever to trigger a brush that, hopefully, would attract attention above ground when it moved.*

ladder to facilitate exit from the grave. In 1882 Albert Fearnaught designed a coffin in which the slightest hand movement would make a flag wave.

Perhaps the most sophisticated safety coffin was designed by Count Karnice-Karnicki, chamberlain to the emperor of Russia. The apparatus consisted of a pipe from the coffin that extended four feet above the ground. Below ground the pipe was fixed to a glass ball that rested on the chest of the deceased. With the slightest movement, the ball activated a spring, and an iron box at the top of the pipe flew open; a lamp would be lit, a flag raised, and a bell would ring. The same pipe could also be used to communicate with the revived corpse.

Signs of life

Various other ways of sounding alarms have also been suggested. In 1903 Emily Josephine Jephson of Cambridge, England, applied for a patent on her invention, announcing: "Jephson's improved Coffin for indicating the burial alive of a person in a trance or suffering from a comatose state so that same may be released or rescued, has means for admitting air to the coffin and for giving an audible signal by means of an electric bell, which may be placed either on the grave or in the cemetery house.

"There is a glass plate in the lid, and a small shelf attached to one side of the coffin which may hold a hammer, matches, and candle so that, when the person wakes, he can light the candle and with a hammer break the glass, thus assisting to liberate himself when the earth . . . is removed."

J. J. Toolen's coffin of 1906 combined a sprung lid with a battery that would power a light for 150 hours. E. V. Blacker's design offered two novel features. The body was chained to the spring-loaded lid and the coffin buried only in shallow earth. Any movement would raise the lid and the occupant could free himself. A tube extending from the coffin contained litmus paper: when it changed color, indicating that decomposition was taking place, the grave was filled in.

The latter was one of the last safety coffins to be patented. With the outbreak of World War I, the real horrors of sudden death put an end to any interest in the somewhat remote possibility of premature burial, and improved medical techniques increasingly made the certification of death a more precise science. The era of the safety coffin had ended.

SETTING THE WORLD ALIGHT

The bright story of the streetlight

ON JUNE 4, 1807, London's well-known Pall Mall was the scene of a singular event: the world's first street with gas lighting. The man behind this marvel was a German-born entrepreneur, Frederick Winsor. The lights were part of the celebrations honoring the birthday of King George III; soon they would become a part of daily life in all major cities.

Today it is probably difficult for most of us to imagine what life was like before the introduction of streetlights. Once night fell there was complete darkness, except for the occasional candle shining through a window or the torch carried by a lone traveler. The main source of light was the moon, and it offered strong illumination for only a few days each month.

Most people stayed indoors after dark. It was a challenge to find one's way, and the dark also provided cover for criminals. Indeed, so dangerous was the darkness that the Roman writer Juvenal warned that it was careless in the extreme to go out for supper at night without having first made a will.

Not until the 15th century was street lighting introduced in Europe to any significant degree. In 1416 the lord mayor of London, Sir Henry Barton, ordered householders to hang lanterns outside their houses on winter evenings, and in 1461 King

BRIGHTER FUTURE *By the 19th century, electric streetlights were established in most major cities. In this engraving lights illuminate La Place du Carrousel, Paris.*

Louis XI of France issued similar instructions to the citizens of Paris in the interests of safety.

Even by the end of the 17th century the situation in England had improved little. In London only 1 of every 10 houses was lit by an oil lamp. In most places streetlights were not used at all.

In the United States, the main streets of New York and other cities were lit by lamps of whale oil tacked up on posts. Although liberally distributed throughout the city, numerous complaints were recorded that the lights were very inefficient and barely made the darkness visible.

Illuminating ideas

The invention of gas lighting in the 19th century altered the situation considerably. At last, here was a technology that gave people the freedom to travel more safely at night. Despite objections from those who claimed that it would frighten horses, by 1830 gas street lighting had been adopted on a large scale in New York as well as in most European cities.

Experiments with electricity that began in the mid-19th century made possible even brighter street illumination. Although many people had been producing electric lamps from 1845 onward, it was the work of Joseph Swan in England and Thomas Alva Edison in the United States that was to revolutionize street lighting.

Independently of each other, both scientists had invented the incandescent filament electric lamp—Swan in 1878 and Edison in 1879. Using an improved vacuum system within the glass bulb containing the filament, the lamps were brighter and lasted longer than existing ones, making them ideal for street lighting.

Soon Edison's lights were appearing in the streets of New York, powered from the Pearl Street Power Station. Established in 1882, it was the prototype of every generating station in the world today. For the first time, the public had a supply of electricity available on demand.

The invention of electric light had a strong impact in the United States, especially in reducing street crime. And by 1884 New York, in particular, was illuminated so well that the British electrical engineer Sir William Preece was moved to write: "I know of nothing more dismal than to be transplanted from the brilliantly illuminated avenues of New York to the dull and dark streets of London."

However, despite its advantages, electric light superseded gas very slowly. But the advent of automobiles demanded brighter street lighting, and by the 1930's mercury and sodium lights were in general use.

Today we take inexpensive, efficient lighting for granted. And those who complain of the cost of electricity should note that it would cost 500 times more to produce the same amount of light from candles than it does from one fluorescent tube.

TO BE OR NOT TO BE

The world's oldest almanac

IS IT A GOOD DAY to have a haircut? Is that cat good or evil? What is the best cure for an earache? What does last night's dream signify? For the millions of Chinese around the world the answer to these and other everyday problems is found in their almanac—the *T'ung Shu* ("Book of Myriad Things"). According to tradition, the almanac was first produced in China in 2256 B.C. It was probably one of the first books to be printed by the block printing press, invented in the seventh century A.D. By the beginning of the ninth century a writer commented that "these printed calendars have flooded the empire."

They have been on sale ever since. The *T'ung Shu* has the longest continuous printed history of any book in the world—more than 1,200 years.

Inquire within

The almanac today is a unique blend of some folk remedies, astrological charts and predictions, moral teaching, divination, palmistry, popular sayings, and practical farming advice. It also contains full details of all Chinese festivals, a complete calendar with the significance of each day explained, astronomical details, advice on etiquette, and a pronunciation guide to English.

Yet the almanac has not always been so varied in its content. Legend has it that it was originally drawn up as a calendar for the emperor Yao, and for much of its life the *T'ung Shu* has been regarded as a sign of the emperor's power. In imperial China the ruler's authority was strengthened by the ability of his court astrologers to produce an accurate calendar. By predicting eclipses and good harvests, the emperor could show that he was in command of the heavens and the seasons.

Over the centuries the *T'ung Shu* has been revised and updated by Taoist, Buddhist, and Muslim astrologers. Between 1629 and 1687 Jesuit missionaries in China controlled the bureau of astronomy, and thus were responsible for the almanac. With the aid of more sophisticated astronomical instruments than those possessed by the Chinese, they reformed the Chinese calendar as published in the almanac and brought it into line with Western practice. The date of the Chinese New Year is still set by the method the Jesuits established.

After the Communist takeover in 1949 the almanac was suppressed on mainland China, and it is difficult to estimate how widely it is used today in the People's Republic. But it is still published by Chinese communities in Taiwan, throughout Southeast Asia, and particularly in Hong Kong. There the governor is presented with a new copy at each New Year, and the old almanac is ceremoniously burned. One million copies are sold in Hong Kong each year, although such is the almanac's complexity that many users need to consult a professional astrologer in order to understand the ancient mysteries of the *T'ung Shu*.

A SNAPPY LITTLE INVENTION

For centuries man's battle against the mouse has raged as new methods have been devised to outwit the tiny creature. The most effective method of elimination—as lethal as it is simple—has been the mousetrap. But over the years, even this device has had to become more complex, as the ingenious mouse has found ways to evade it.

Although mousetraps are believed to have been invented by the Romans, traps first came into their own in Europe in the 15th century, when mice were particularly numerous. The medieval moneylenders were among the first to use traps in order to prevent the mice from nibbling the paper of their customers' pledges—often a moneylender's only record of transactions.

The first of the designs included hinged metal traps, wooden gates with doors operated by release levers, and "deadfall" traps that slammed shut, killing the prey. Much later the Victorians were responsible for a wealth of inventions, including the guillotine, perpetual, folding breakback, and seesaw traps.

In the 20th century, poisons have been used, but since the evolution of a supermouse that is resistant to chemical control, the traditional baited mousetrap is very much back in style.

A BETTER MOUSETRAP *A selection from the many ingenious mousetrap designs through the centuries. 1) English; drops a wooden block on the creature. 2) Tunisian terracotta; imprisons the rodent. 3) English; slips a noose around the mouse's neck. 4) Medieval wooden; squashes the mouse. 5) U.S. tinplate; catches five mice. 6) Medieval wooden; encloses the animal. 7) English wire rat and mouse trap combined; once inside, a rodent's feet become tangled in the wire. 8) Folding trap; breaks the mouse's back.*

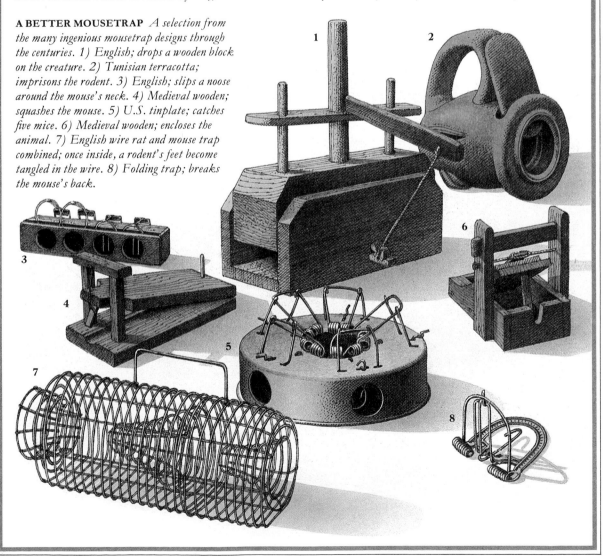

PET PATENTS

The retractable dog leash is not the only gadget designed with pets in mind. In 1973 French inventor Georges Richard developed a dog bone that fought back. Made of plastic, it was sufficiently soft so that when a dog bit into the bone, an electric circuit inside was completed. This started a small motor, and the bone vibrated to entertain the dog.

Bertha Dlugi of Milwaukee had the answer for people who enjoy letting pet birds fly free around the home. In 1959 she patented a bird diaper, a minuscule triangle of fabric that was to be held in place with tapes.

In 1961 Robert Oropei Martino proposed that fish in public aquariums be fitted with small waterproof shirts, to earn extra income. How would they do so? With restaurants in mind, it was his thought that advertisers would buy space to display their messages on the shirts.

A TASTE OF HISTORY

The world's classic dishes

Apple Charlotte Known as "the king of cooks and the cook of kings," the French master chef Marie Antoine Carême served such distinguished patrons as the statesman Charles Talleyrand, Czar Alexander I, and George IV. While employed by the English prince regent at Brighton Pavilion, from 1816 to 1819, Carême created a new dessert: layers of apple and sugar baked between slices of buttered bread. He named it Apple Charlotte in honor of the prince's daughter.

Oddly enough, Carême named another dessert for the English princess while working for Czar Alexander in 1819. A custard decorated with ladyfingers, it was christened Charlotte Russe.

Baked Alaska The invention of this famous ice cream dessert is credited to physicist Benjamin Thompson. Although born in Massachusetts, Thompson worked chiefly in England and Germany. He was made a count in 1791 as a reward for his services to the elector of Bavaria. In Britain, in 1799, he founded the Royal Institute, for the "promotion, diffusion, and extension of science and useful knowledge."

As if this were not enough, Thompson was also the inventor of one of the first efficient cooking ranges and of a revolutionary coffee percolator. In the course of his research Thompson conducted many experiments with heat. It was probably one of these that led to the invention of the dish that eventually became known as Baked Alaska, a meringue topping and a cake base that insulate an ice cream center from the heat of the oven.

Chateaubriand Originally a method of cooking meat, but today a specific cut, steak called chateaubriand was named for François René, viscount of Chateaubriand, who fled from France soon after the Revolution. After exploring the United States, René returned to Europe and in 1822 was appointed ambassador to Britain. It was while he was living in London that his chef, Montmireil, devised a method of preserving the tenderness of a steak during cooking by placing it between two lesser pieces of meat. The chef duly named the dish for his employer.

Coquilles Saint-Jacques In French this is the term for scallops; and although *coquille* means shell, why *Saint-Jacques*? Legend has it that the body of Saint Jacques was being carried by sea from Joppa (Jaffa today) to Galicia, in northwest Spain. As the boat passed the Portuguese village of Bonzas, a marriage ceremony was taking place onshore. When the horse the bridegroom was riding was frightened and dashed into the sea, the saint's companions saved the groom from drowning. In gratitude the groom converted to Christianity on the deck of the vessel.

When he returned to shore, the groom found that his clothes were covered with scallop shells. And so, when the groom converted the other villagers to Christianity, they ever after used the scallop shell as the symbol of Saint Jacques.

Mayonnaise The origin of mayonnaise is one of the most disputed in culinary history. The French duke of Mayenne is one of the first to whose name it was attached, allegedly as early as 1589.

Another version claims that it was discovered by the French marshal Richelieu. After seizing Fort St.-Philippe at Mahon, Minorca, on June 28, 1756, Richelieu celebrated his victory with a feast. Since no butter or cream was available on the island, his chef made a dressing from eggs and oil. When the recipe was taken back to France, it became known as *sauce mahonnaise.*

Some historians even place the origin in the town of Bayonne, in southwest France, claiming that it was once known as *bayonnaise.* The truth may be simpler: it may be derived from the French verb *manir,* "to stir," or perhaps from *moyeu,* an Old French word meaning the yolk of an egg.

Oysters Rockefeller   A dish created by billionaire John D. Rockefeller? Not exactly. Jules Alciatore of Antoine's restaurant in New Orleans devised these elaborately stuffed oysters in 1899. A customer proclaimed the dish "as rich as Rockefeller"—and thus it acquired its name.

Praline   César de Choiseul, the count of Plessis-Praslin, led the French Army against Spain in 1650 and devoted his life to royal service. Yet he is remembered not so much for his military achievements as for the fact that his chef prepared a confection composed of sugar and almonds. It became known as *praslins,* and ultimately as praline.

THE SIEGE THAT GAVE BIRTH TO THE CROISSANT   *Although commonly thought of as French, croissants were, in fact, first made in Austria. In 1683 Vienna was under siege from the Turks. Working through the night, Viennese bakers heard the Turks tunneling beneath the city, raised the alarm— and thus prevented a Turkish victory. To commemorate the occasion, the bakers devised the croissant, basing the shape on the crescent moon of the Turkish flag, below. Bottom: An 18th-century engraving celebrating the liberation of Vienna.*

EXPRESS MAIL

A special way to deliver letters

IN THE 1920's AND 1930's, visionaries talked of sending rockets to the moon. More practical men set their sights lower, however, and pioneered what is today an almost forgotten chapter in the lengthy annals of the world's postal service: rocket mail.

The idea of using rocket-propelled cylinders to carry messages originated with an Austrian engineer, Friedrich Schmiedl. In July 1928 he attempted a series of six experimental firings of rockets between Mount Schoeckl and the nearby village of St. Radegund in the Austrian Alps, a distance of some four miles.

The crude rockets consisted of a fuel chamber containing an explosive propellant, not unlike gunpowder, and a nose cone fitted with a parachute; the latter acted as the delivery vehicle. Although the primary purpose of the tests was to gather scientific data from instruments carried on board, the rockets also contained a few pieces of mail as mementos for the scientist's supporters.

None of these tests was very successful, and when the sixth rocket exploded in flight, Schmiedl abandoned the project.

But in 1931 Schmiedl resumed his experiments on Mount Schoeckl. He organized the world's first rocket flight dedicated solely to carrying mail. Two successful flights carried a total of some 300 letters. But a change of government in Austria led to a withdrawal of Schmiedl's only means of financing the project—the right to issue and sell postage stamps—and the flights ceased.

The big splash

Schmiedl's experiments were not in vain, however; his ideas were taken up by the young German rocketeer Gerhard Zucker. In 1933 Zucker conducted a series of rocket experiments near Hasselfelde, today in East Germany; none was successful.

The London Air Post Exhibition in May 1934 gave Zucker the opportunity to demonstrate his skills in England. Although part of the program was canceled, the visit encouraged Zucker to carry on with his work in England. His ambition: to establish a cross-Channel rocket mail service. Zucker calculated that at 960 miles per hour, the journey would take 50 seconds.

The first rocket experiment Zucker conducted in England took place in 1934 on the South Downs, overlooking the English Channel. Shaped like a shell with tail fins, the rocket was launched from a primitive rack lubricated with butter. It was fortunate that the rocket carried no letters, since on a trial run it crashed into the Channel.

On the second attempt the rocket flew about half a mile. The 1,000 letters on board were recovered and taken to the nearby Brighton post office for delivery. Unfortunately, neither flight succeeded in crossing the Channel.

In an attempt to enhance the reputation of his rocket mail system. Zucker moved to Scarp, an island off the Scottish coast. Storms often isolated it in the winter months and deprived residents of regular mail delivery. However, both firings from the site resulted in explosions and the loss of all the mail; the second burst almost killed Zucker.

Controlled rocket flight

The next major development in the troubled history of rocket mail took place in the United States. In place of a crude fuel such as gunpowder, a more sophisticated liquid propellant, based on liquid oxygen, was employed in a continuous-combustion engine. But Willy Ley's experimental version—set off in Greenwood Lake, New York, on February 9, 1936—failed to get off the ground. A second attempt, on February 23, covered a distance of 300 yards.

In 1936 a local American Legion post launched rockets from McAllen, Texas, to Reynosa, Mexico. They carried mail with special stamps designed for the occasion. But the flights were unsuccessful. The first rocket exploded just over the Rio Grande; five others that were launched soon afterward never reached their destination.

Subsequent flights were a little more successful, but not enough to attract official backing. Since the carrying of mail and the selling of postage stamps was controlled by the U.S. government, interest in rocket mail as a practical public service soon died.

But rocket mail has been revived for limited use in outer space. Increasing interest in space technology in the 1940's and 50's led to more sophisticated rocket techniques. In 1959 a U.S. Air Force officer sent a letter from Florida to Ascension Island, in the South Atlantic, on an airborne missile—the first intercontinental missile mail. In more recent years mail has sometimes been carried on space flights, a fitting end, perhaps, to the efforts of Zucker and the other early rocket pioneers, even if outer space had not been part of their original vision.

AIRMAIL WITH A DIFFERENCE *In the early days of rocket development, many believed that rockets held the answer to fast, efficient mail service. In the 1930's one of the earliest pioneers in the field, Gerhard Zucker, conducted many rocket experiments in Scurpa, Scotland. Above: Zucker and his companions prepare the rocket for launching. Left: The hopefuls share their disappointment.*

MARVELS OF SCIENCE

HEART SURGERY AND STAR WARS

The many uses of a light beam

THE LASER HAS BEEN one of the most glamorous symbols of modern technology since 1960, when the first one was constructed in California. Originally the laser was described as a solution looking for a problem, for no one was quite sure to what uses it could be put. But today the laser is in the forefront of scientific, medical, and military research. Within the next decade a laser will be able to destroy individual human genes or blast missiles out of space.

How a laser works

A laser is a device that stores energy and then releases it in the form of a very intense beam of light. Its heart is a tube filled with gas or liquid, into which energy is pumped, stimulating the atoms of the substance inside to produce light. Mirrors at each end reflect the light backward and forward, concentrating and amplifying it into a high-energy beam. This beam is able to penetrate solid objects and can be projected over great distances.

Because the length of a laser's beam can be controlled with great accuracy, it is an ideal measuring instrument. A very precise measurement of the distance between the earth and the moon has been achieved by firing a laser beam from the McDonald Observatory in Fort Davis, Texas, onto a mirror placed on the moon by the *Apollo 11* astronauts in 1969. Because a laser beam travels at the speed of light, a constant speed of 186,281 miles per second, the time taken by the beam to reach the moon and then be reflected back to Texas has given a mean distance between the moon and the earth of 240,250 miles.

Measuring the world

Another experiment, originated by NASA, is currently using lasers to measure movements in the earth's crust. Laser beams are fired from various sites in the world, such as the Goddard Space Flight Center in the United States and the Royal Greenwich Observatory in England, and bounced off a satellite back to their place of origin.

Although the satellite remains in a fixed position above the Atlantic Ocean, the earth-based sites move slowly as the continents drift. By making a

HEALING LASER *Lasers have been in the forefront of medical research since they were first produced in 1960. The scientist (left) is testing the power of an infrared laser; the beam is invisible to the human eye. Such lasers are used to remove tumors and unblock arteries.*

EYE SURGERY *Such is the precision of lasers that they are now employed to correct retina detachment, cut out tumors, and remove cataracts in eye surgery. Above: A complex operation has corrected a fault in the iris and restored the patient's sight.*

series of measurements over a period of time—usually for at least 10 years—scientists are able to assess where the crust of the earth is moving, and by how much each year.

Lasers in medicine

One of the most exciting breakthroughs in medical science in the last few years has been the use of lasers in combating blood circulatory diseases. A pioneering team led by Dr. David Cumberland at the Northern General Hospital in Sheffield, England, has been using a laser to unblock the arteries of patients suffering from atherosclerosis of the leg, a condition in which fatty deposits line the artery walls and inhibit circulation. Without such an operation, patients in the severest cases would have to undergo amputation.

In 1986 Cumberland's team successfully used a laser to remove a blood clot from the coronary artery of a 39-year-old man; left unattended, it would have caused a heart attack. If this operation proves successful in the long term, lengthy and often dangerous heart bypass operations could be a

thing of the past. The research team is hoping that a laser will be able to remove a clot during a heart attack itself, possibly saving the patient's life.

In operations such as these, a laser beam passes along optical fibers inserted into the artery and cuts through the fatty deposits and blood clots. Then a tiny plastic balloon is inserted into the artery: it is pushed along with the blood flow, cleaning the artery walls and facilitating easier circulation.

Tumors and genes

Another example of the precision of lasers is in the removal of otherwise inoperable tumors of the brain and spinal cord, where surrounding tissue must be left undisturbed. With conventional surgery it is usually impossible to remove all the malignant cells, which often spread to other parts of the body. Although such operations are still in the experimental stage, it is hoped that before long even the most inaccessible tumor will be within reach of a laser's cutting beam.

Researchers in genetic engineering are speculating on the use of lasers to destroy individual genes in order to correct such genetic abnormalities as cystic fibrosis and hemophilia. Such ideas, which at one time sounded like science fiction, are now entering the realm of science fact.

Throughout medicine, lasers are often proving to be more successful and cost-effective than established methods of surgery. It may not be long before treatment by laser will become an everyday event for those requiring surgery.

Star Wars

The laser was initially envisaged as a futuristic wonder weapon. The Strategic Defense Initiative, or "Star Wars" project, has since furthered that warlike image.

High-energy lasers are at the forefront of Star Wars technology. A laser beam is powerful enough to burn a hole through a steel block several inches thick. Traveling at the speed of light, it could burn a hole in a ballistic missile or its warhead and render it ineffective. But to turn this science fiction idea into an effective defense system requires that a vast array of technical problems be overcome— particularly, how to generate enough energy to project the laser through the turbulence of the earth's atmosphere and still ensure its accuracy.

The most ambitious Star Wars weapon is the X-ray laser being developed at the Lawrence Livermore National Laboratory in California. This device would use a small nuclear explosion to produce a short, intense burst of X-rays to destroy missiles or satellites. Like other Star Wars developments, this research is highly controversial, and many scientists consider it technically impossible, even in the long term.

Laser technology has an exciting future, particularly in medicine and industry. The image of the laser as an all-purpose tool now has substance, its actual and potential uses spanning a vast range. It remains to be seen whether lasers will be developed more as instruments to cure disease or as weapons of defense.

METALS WITH MEMORIES

The changing shapes of modern alloys

GREENHOUSE WINDOWS that open when the temperature rises and close when it falls. Fine filters to keep blood clots away from the heart. Hydraulic-fluid pipes in airplanes. All these make use of a group of wonder metals: alloys with memories.

These alloys—compounds of different metals— are known as shape-memory alloys: if shaped at one temperature and then distorted at another, they recover their original form when the original temperature is restored.

Changing shape

The first stage in the discovery that alloys have memories came at the beginning of this century. Metallurgists had observed that the hardness of hard steel, an alloy of iron and carbon, is the result of a change in its crystal structure that occurs when the alloy cools down after molding. They named this process of change the martensite phase for the 19th-century German metallurgist Adolph Martens. It was subsequently discovered that other alloys assume a martensite phase.

The shape-memory effect itself was first noticed in 1938 when Alden B. Greninger of Harvard University and V. G. Mooradion of the Massachusetts Institute of Technology observed that the martensite phase in brass could be induced by cooling the alloy rapidly or by putting it under stress. When it was reheated, the alloy reverted to its original, parent phase. Subsequent experiments demonstrated that most alloys can be trained to form two different shapes, one in each phase, by repeated heating, cooling, deforming, and reheating. Once trained, a shape-memory alloy "remembers" both shapes and can change from one to the other indefinitely.

Today shape-memory alloys have many uses in engineering and medicine. One of the first practical applications was in couplings for hydraulic-fluid pipes for airplanes. Deliberately made too small, the couplings are then cooled to well below room temperature and stretched until they slip over the pipes. When they again warm up, they return to their original size—with a secure grip on the ends of the pipes. Shape-memory alloy couplings are today used in ships, automobiles, and on underwater pipes.

Shape-memory alloys are used in thermostatic devices such as control valves for central heating systems and automobile engines, electric circuit breakers, and window openers in greenhouses. The window opener contains a spring that contracts when the metal is cool, keeping the window shut.

When warmed by the heat from the sun, the spring expands and the window opens.

Saving lives

Perhaps the most exciting application of shape-memory alloys has been in medicine. The alloy used is nitinol, named for nickel, titanium, and the Naval Ordnance Laboratory in Silver Spring, Maryland, where it was first developed in 1962.

Fractured bones are commonly bridged with nitinol plates. The plates are first chilled so that they can be stretched before being screwed into place. As the plates are warmed by the heat of the body, they shrink, pulling the two ends of bone tightly together. A nitinol tube performs a similar function in hip-replacement surgery. Body heat expands the tube connecting the thighbone and the artificial hip to form a tight grip, locking the new hip firmly in place.

Spinal curvature can be corrected by inserting nitinol rods into the spine; the constant pressure they exert works to straighten it.

Nitinol in wire can be used for dental braces, and when made into a fine-mesh filter it can stop blood clots from reaching the heart. First the filter is chilled and then collapsed so that it can be inserted into the main vein leading to the heart. When warm blood flows through the filter, it heats up and assumes its meshlike state again.

Current research into shape-memory alloys is concentrated on their possible use in energy production. In 1973 the Lawrence Berkeley Laboratory at the University of California designed an engine in which lengths of nitinol wire alternately bend and straighten as they are dipped into warm or cold water. A nitinol engine of the future could be powered by making use of the distinct layers of water of different temperatures that exist in deep lakes and reservoirs: the nitinol rods would perform like pistons as they react to temperature changes. With the approaching depletion of the fossil fuels on which modern technology depends, shape-memory alloys may hold a key to future energy requirements.

A Brand New Suit of Skin

Tailor-made in a test tube

IN 1984 a six-year-old boy was rushed to the Massachusetts General Hospital with appalling burns. Nearly 98 percent of his skin was destroyed, 89 percent by third-degree burns; only tiny patches on his scalp and armpit remained. But the boy is alive today, thanks to an accidental discovery in a cancer research laboratory at Harvard Medical School.

When the boy was admitted to the hospital, a team of plastic surgeons gradually cleaned away his burned skin. Then, in six separate operations, they covered the boy with skin taken from dead bodies. But it was only a temporary covering; the surgeons were waiting for the boy's skin to grow—in a test tube in a laboratory down the hall.

After his admission, surgeons had taken two square centimeters of the boy's precious remaining armpit skin. They divided it up into separate cells, and put the cells into a liquid that would provide ideal conditions for growth. It took only 10 days for a new sheet of skin to form. The surgeons divided it up again, and used it to grow still more new skin, this time for grafting onto the boy.

Three weeks later the doctors grafted nine sheets of the boy's own cultured skin onto his lower abdomen, replacing some of the cadaver skin.

More operations followed, including a few conventional grafts, using skin taken from the boy's scalp. After six months his wounds were 85 percent healed and more than half of his body was covered with his own, laboratory-grown skin. Not long afterward his suit of grafted skin was complete.

Skin support system

Two cancer research doctors had made the achievement possible. At the Harvard Medical School in the late 1970's, Dr. Howard Green and Dr. James Rheinwalk were trying to grow cancer cells from a type of mouse tumor. Although they had failed, during the experiments they noticed an unexpected growth of skin cells. Recognizing the importance of this growth, the doctors concocted a rich broth to nourish the cells; within a month the cells had multiplied 10,000-fold.

Skin grown in a laboratory is remarkably like natural skin. It has the same constituents—even pigment cells and blood vessels. Its one drawback is that it does not have the same elasticity: it does become tight over knees and elbows, for example. But research is continuing, and scientists hope that it will not be long before they can provide patients with a new suit of skin that will fit perfectly.

SETTING THE WORLD TO RIGHTS

A new map for a new world

OST OF US have at one time or another pored over a map of the world; most of us know what it looks like. But today a radical and highly controversial new map is proving our perception of the world quite wrong—and completely out of date.

For more than 400 years maps of the world have been based on the Mercator projection of the globe, first produced in 1569 and named for the Flemish-born cartographer Gerhard Kremer (in Latin, Gerhardus Mercator), who devised it. Mercator was confronted by the problem that bedevils all global mapmakers: because the world is a globe of three dimensions, how can it be depicted accurately on the flat surface of a two-dimensional map?

Projecting the world

Mercator's method was to project the features of a globe onto a flat map. To fully understand the procedure, imagine wrapping a piece of paper around a transparent globe; there is a light bulb in the center of the globe. The light projects the globe's lines of latitude and longitude onto the paper. When the paper is unrolled, the lines create a grid on which the map of the world is then drawn.

Using this procedure, Mercator "stretched" the world horizontally at the two poles so that they

GERHARDUS MERCATOR *The 16th-century Flemish cartographer's map of the world is only now being superseded —after more than 400 years.*

GERARDI MERCATORIS RVPELMVNDANI EFFIGIEM ANNOR. DVORVM ET SEX – AGINTA,SVI ERGA IPSVM STVDII CAVSA DEPINGI CVRABAT FRANC. HOG. CIƆ. IƆ. LXXIV.

became lines at the top and bottom of the map. As a result, on Mercator's map the meridians of longitude, which on a globe converge at the poles, are parallel to each other, while the lines indicating latitude, which on a globe are equal distances apart, are spaced farther and farther as they recede toward the poles from the equator.

The old world

Mercator's map—the first projection to put the entire world onto a rectangular map—was designed for European navigators whose remarkable voyages of discovery were at that time opening up the southern continents to European trade and colonization. And as a navigational aid it has never been surpassed. Any vertical line plotted and drawn above a point on a Mercator projection will always run due north.

But what Mercator achieved in accuracy of direction and shape, he sacrificed in terms of area, for his map distorts the relative sizes of the world's continents and countries.

The effect is most pronounced near the poles. Greenland, which is 800,000 square miles in area, looks as large as China, which is 3.6 million square miles; Europe, which is 3.7 million square miles, appears to be larger than South America, which in reality is almost twice as big (6.9 million square miles). Most dramatic of all, although the equator in actuality divides the world into two halves, on Mercator's map the equator is so low that the northern hemisphere occupies two-thirds of the map. This distortion places Europe—in reality, quite far to the north of the equator—in the center of the world.

Despite these distortions, Mercator's projection has survived and is today still the most commonly used of all map projections. It is the view of the world with which most people are familiar, but its many inaccuracies, errors, and distortions have long troubled cartographers.

A new world

The first radical challenge to Mercator's map has come from a German, Arno Peters. He argues that Mercator's projection reflects the view of an age in which Europe dominated the rest of the world. The distortions and misplaced equator on Mercator's map give the impression that the U.S.S.R. and the industrial nations of North America and Europe are vastly more important than the larger but

TWO VIEWS OF THE WORLD

MERCATOR'S PROJECTION *Drawn in 1569, this projection, while accurate in terms of direction and shape, distorts toward the poles; Greenland looks almost as large as North America and Africa. The off-center position of the equator exaggerates the size of the Northern Hemisphere.*

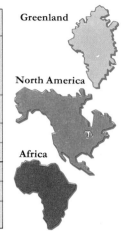

PETERS'S PROJECTION *Drawn in 1974, this projection depicts all areas of the world according to the actual area they encompass and places the equator in the center. But the resulting distortion of distance and shape makes Greenland appear to be short and fat, and North America and Africa elongated.*

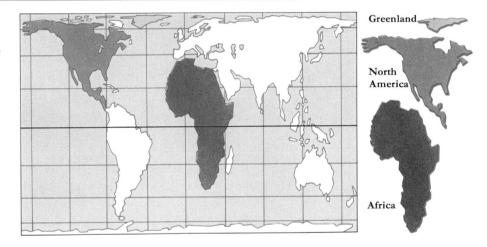

economically disadvantaged Third World countries of Asia, Africa, and South America. Today this traditional view is not only geographically misleading but, politically, increasingly unacceptable to many people.

Peters set out to correct the imbalance by producing a map that showed the world as it really is. His new map was first published in 1974—and created an immediate controversy. One glance at the map reveals why.

Like Mercator, Peters depicts the entire world on a rectangular map. But in contrast to Mercator, Peters elongates the world on both sides of the equator and flattens it out at the poles. This shows all areas according to their actual size: China no longer appears smaller than Greenland, South America no longer smaller than Europe. And since the equator runs through the middle of the map, no longer do countries in the Southern Hemisphere

appear to be overshadowed in size by those to the north. The result is startling, and a very different view of the world emerges.

The issue, however, is not yet resolved. Peters has put the world to rights in one way, but his map has the effect of distorting it in others—namely distance and shape. Whereas Mercator's map distorts near the poles, Peters's projection distorts around the equator. Africa and South America appear to be extraordinarily long and thin, when in reality Africa is roughly as wide as it is long.

The fact remains that despite the sophisticated surveying techniques available in the late 20th century, a three-dimensional world cannot be accurately and neatly depicted on a two-dimensional plane. Some distortion is inevitable. Peters has presented the world with a radical new view of itself, but a map that is accurate in every respect has yet to be created.

PREHISTORIC PUZZLES

Rocking the cradle of civilization

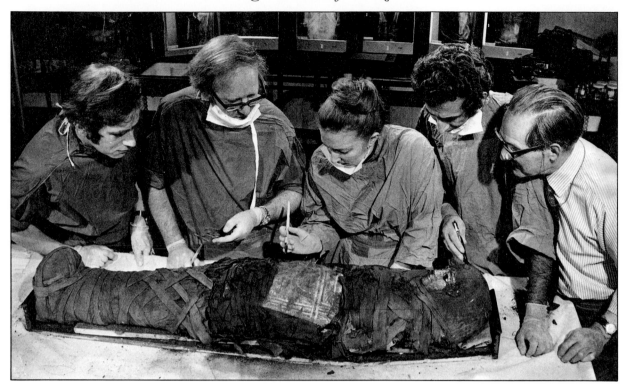

PUZZLING REWRAPPING *Egyptologists examine a 3,500-year-old mummy. Carbon-14 dating established the age of the mummy—and the fact that it had been wrapped in new bandages 1,200 years after the body had first been embalmed.*

F OR MORE THAN a century, archeologists were convinced that the cradle of civilization lay in Greece, Crete, Egypt, and Mesopotamia. The learning of the advanced peoples of this region, it was thought, gradually moved west into Europe.

But in the last few decades these theories have been overturned, thanks to Nobel Prize–winning physicist Willard F. Libby and a substance known as carbon 14.

Carbon 14 is a radioactive substance that exists in minute quantities. In the late 1940's Libby discovered that all plants and animals absorb it. When they die, the carbon—like all radioactive substances—begins to decay at a regular rate. Libby was able to measure this rate and could thus use carbon 14 as an archeological calendar. Today it is known that half of the carbon 14 in any living organism disappears in 5,730 years, half of what remains in an additional 5,730 years, and so on.

How old is old?

Many of the items found at prehistoric sites are made of organic material. By measuring the amount of carbon 14 remaining in the shaft of an old ax or a piece of pottery, for example, scientists can accurately determine its age.

Radiocarbon dating has proved to be phenomenally accurate: it can date to within 100 years going back to 50,000 B.C. It is particularly useful on wood because it can be checked against dendrochronology, dating by tree rings. A new ring forms every year in the trunk of a tree as it grows: counting the number of rings enables one to determine the age of any tree.

Where did civilization begin?

Before radiocarbon dating, written records were the historian's only clue to the age of the civilized world. Prior to written records, different events could be dated relative to one another, but not absolutely. The earliest surviving written records come from Egypt; they date events fairly accurately back to 3100 B.C. Other ancient events had to be slotted into these known chronologies.

The huge stone temple at Tarxien, in Malta, has decorations that resemble some at Mycenae, in Greece. Since the ones at Mycenae are known to date from around 1600 B.C., historians thought that the Maltese temples, deriving from the Greek, could not have been built any earlier.

Similarly, Stonehenge, in southern England, has been given the same "latest possible" date, while the stone tombs at Carnac, in Brittany, France, have been dated earlier, at around 2200 B.C.

But radiocarbon dating, checked against dendrochronology, now proves that the Maltese temples were built in 3100 B.C.—1,500 years *before* the Mycenaean structures that were supposed to have inspired them. Stonehenge was created long before the first Egyptian pyramid, which was constructed about 2650 B.C.; and the tombs at Carnac are now believed to date from around 4000 B.C.—the oldest monuments in the world.

The theory that culture began in the Near East and gradually spread west seems to be in error. European culture came first. So historians today are asking whether Europe was perhaps the true cradle of civilization.

MEDICAL MISSILES

Homing in on disease

MEDICINE HAS OFTEN been something of a hit-or-miss affair. Such lifesaving drugs as penicillin were discovered by accident, and no one knew at first how or why they worked.

But today this ignorance may, for the most part, be a thing of the past. With increased knowledge of how the body fights disease, scientists are able to design drugs that work in ways similar to those of the body's natural defenses. These "target drugs" home in on invading organisms and destroy them.

Target drugs

The key to the body's defense against disease lies in the antibodies of the immune system. These components recognize antigens—substances foreign to the body that live on the surface of invading viruses and bacteria—by their particular chemical characteristics. The antibodies then chemically "lock on" to the antigens and make them inactive—and the viruses and bacteria on which they exist as well.

In 1975 two scientists, César Milstein and Georges Köhler of Cambridge University, England, developed antibodies in the laboratory as effective as those the human body itself produces. They reasoned that if a powerful toxin were attached to these artificial antibodies, then the antigen could be killed without affecting other cells. In addition, the two scientists observed that certain cancer cells also had particular chemical characteristics that could be targeted for destruction the same way.

The scientists called the new wonder drugs monoclonal antibodies, and the idea seemed very promising. Milstein and Köhler received the 1984 Nobel Prize in medicine for their pioneering work.

However, during clinical trials the two scientists ran into problems. The monoclonal antibodies were nowhere near as effective as the team had hoped: a patient's immune system would identify the drugs, manufactured from mouse cells, as invaders themselves. Therefore, the immune system was producing anti-antibodies in response, and the monoclonal antibodies were being destroyed before reaching their targets.

To overcome the problem, Milstein and Köhler turned to the Trojan-horse technique. The idea was to disguise the monoclonal antibodies so that they could enter the body unnoticed by the immune system. Genetic analysis of the mouse cells had identified the small fragment of the gene that was responsible for manufacturing the active part of the monoclonal antibody. It was removed and spliced into the equivalent place in the human gene where the code for producing human antibodies is carried. In theory the immune system would then not "see" the foreign invader, and the active part of the monoclonal antibody would reach its target.

Toward an all-in-one drug

Trials are not yet advanced enough to determine if the Trojan-horse technique will succeed, and further modifications to the drug may be necessary. But Milstein and Köhler are confidently advancing this line of research. One idea involves finding a way to link different monoclonal antibodies together to form an all-in-one strike force to combat an array of diseases. The elements of this compound drug would attack individual viruses and tumor cells as each is encountered.

Unforeseen problems may lie ahead, but research on monoclonal antibodies may be laying the foundations for the one-shot wonder drug that both doctors and patients have dreamed about.

PROBING THE DEPTHS

Mechanical submariners

ON SEPTEMBER 1, 1985, 400 miles southeast of Newfoundland, video screens on board the U.S. Navy research vessel *Knorr* picked up a large metal object. It was clearly a boiler from a large steamship—but no ordinary ship. Scientists on the *Knorr* had found the wreck of the ill-fated *Titanic,* 73 years after it had collided with an iceberg and sunk, with the loss of 1,500 lives.

The extraordinary discovery was made possible by ARGO, ANGUS, and ALVIN, three underwater robots. They are just part of the wide range of mechanical substitutes for human divers developed for marine research and exploration by a sophisticated technology.

The advantages of these submersibles, as they are called, are considerable. They record and relay detailed video images of objects found on the seafloor; some of the cameras they carry are so sensitive they produce clear pictures under conditions where the human eye cannot see at all.

Broadly, undersea craft are divided into two categories: manned vehicles and remotely operated vehicles, or ROV's. Some are free swimming, powered by batteries. Others are tethered to the

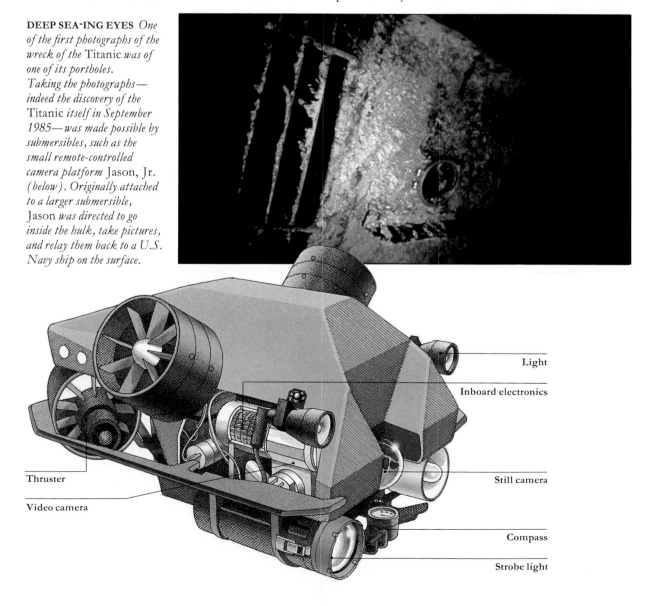

DEEP SEA-ING EYES *One of the first photographs of the wreck of the* Titanic *was of one of its portholes. Taking the photographs— indeed the discovery of the* Titanic *itself in September 1985—was made possible by submersibles, such as the small remote-controlled camera platform* Jason, Jr. *(below). Originally attached to a larger submersible,* Jason *was directed to go inside the hulk, take pictures, and relay them back to a U.S. Navy ship on the surface.*

Light

Inboard electronics

Thruster

Video camera

Still camera

Compass

Strobe light

mother ship by an umbilical cord—a line composed of a suspension wire and electric cables that power the thrusters, lights, camera gear, and special tools. Manned vehicles carry, in addition, hoses for heating and an air supply for the crew.

Submersibles were developed to offer more range and endurance than that of human divers, who can operate safely at a maximum depth of approximately 1,000 feet. A manned submersible protects its crew from the harmful effects of high pressure and rapid changes in pressure, so that divers can move to different depths in total safety.

The ROV has gained increasing popularity in recent years. Since it carries no crew, it can operate for indefinite periods at no risk to human life.

Useful aids

Submersibles are used in all areas of underwater research and industry. They collect mineral samples from the seabed to help in the search for valuable ores and metals. Sonar-equipped vehicles are used to monitor fish stocks by measuring the size of different shoals. In one recent mapping project, a sonar ROV surveyed 250,000 square miles of seabed in only 102 days.

The size of submersibles varies. Typically, a manned craft is about 28 feet long, carries a crew of three, and can dive to a depth of about 3,000 feet. ROV's, on the other hand, tend to be smaller, averaging about six feet in length; but they can operate at much greater depths.

Automatic dexterity

Until recently, the main disadvantage of both types of submersible was that they lacked the manual dexterity of a human diver. But modern technology has devised a substitute: arms called manipulators.

The arms are equipped with a variety of tools, depending on the type of work required. Motor-driven wrenches, screwdrivers, and cutting gear can be complemented by hydraulic gripping claws much stronger than a human hand. The vehicle may also carry ultrasonic probes to detect corrosion in welds and steel structures.

The offshore oil industry has been a major beneficiary of the new technology. As shallow-water oil fields become depleted, and greater depths must be explored, the use of human divers has become increasingly expensive and dangerous. Submersibles may soon be the only means used in the exploration, construction, and maintenance of deep-water oil platforms. Sophisticated ROV's will do the job, and men will no longer have to risk their lives to reap the rich harvests under the sea.

THE FIFTH GENERATION

Speak, and it shall be done

IT IS COMMON KNOWLEDGE that computers are stupid. As some computer programmers put it, GIGO, or "Garbage in, garbage out," means that if inaccurate or insufficient information is entered into a computer, the machine will produce rubbish in return.

The reason: computers cannot think. Given the information that a table has four legs and that a dog has four legs, the machine might include a dog when producing a list of suggested dining-room furniture. Within the limits of what the computer knows, this is perfectly logical.

But today groups of computer scientists in the United States, Japan, and throughout Europe are working on a new generation of machines that will be incapable of making such elementary errors.

Instead of being programmed with a mass of unrelated pieces of information, the new computers will contain reams of knowledge about a subject that are connected. From an immense body of data and a set of complex rules as to how the data fit together, the machines will compare and contrast items of information, and be able to reject illogical or senseless conclusions.

The new "fifth generation" computers will already know that dogs are the mammals that eat bones, bark, wag their tails, and chase other mammals called cats. Comparing this knowledge with the attributes of dining-room furniture, the computer will infer that in this case the dog is an inappropriate selection.

Even a present-day computer could make this deduction if given enough information and enough time. But, because it has to consider alternative solutions one at a time before selecting the best, it would take days for even the most powerful computer to arrive at a simple conclusion.

Speed is the essence

Computers now being planned will be able to work on many clusters of facts simultaneously. And, not unlike the human brain, the more work the computer of the future does, the more it will be able to "learn" from past experience.

The new computers will also be able to understand human speech. By dealing with large quantities of related facts and rules about grammar, syntax, and vocabulary, they will, for example, be able to distinguish between similar-sounding words such as *bear* (to carry), *bear* (the animal), *bear* (to tolerate), and *bare* (to uncover).

The technology required to perform these calculations is astounding. Computer experts call a single comparison between two sets of information a "logical inference"—each one requires up to 300 separate calculations. The new machines should be able to perform 100 million logical inferences per second. In order to do so, the computers need newly designed circuits.

Enter the hypercube

One new circuit design is the hypercube; it employs several electronic processors working in parallel on the same problem. Conventionally, a computer has had to search backward and forward through its memory to locate the information it is seeking. The hypercube puts several such processes into operation at once; its design also enables each process to be aware of what is happening in the others.

The way a computer usually searches its memory is similar to a messenger's collecting and delivering packages in several different skyscrapers. To take a package from a room on the 96th floor of one building to a room on the 96th floor of a neighboring skyscraper, the messenger has to take the elevator all the way to the first floor, cross the street, and take another elevator up—even though the windows of both rooms may be within shouting distance of each other.

In its parallel processing systems, the hypercube circuit design builds electronic bridges and corridors between such "rooms," or memory cells, drastically reducing computing time. Hypercube computers process data up to 600 times more quickly than conventional supercomputers.

But perhaps the most promising development for speeding up computers is the optical chip. In conventional computers, information in the form of electrical impulses travels along wires at about 930 miles per second, 1/200 the speed of light. But microchips that use laser beams to encode information will operate at the speed of light itself: about 186,300 miles per second.

Understanding spoken words

Computer programs already exist that can recognize up to 5,000 words of spoken English. Experts in Japan are eager to create their own voice-recognition programs; they would free Japanese computer operators of the need to learn English. (Computer keyboards cannot accommodate the 5,000 characters of Japanese script.)

By the end of the century the new generation of computers should be serving the general public. Anyone should be able to approach one to check facts, or even to ask for advice, simply by speaking to it in everyday language. The machines will be able to tell us why they have arrived at their decision, and suggest alternatives. Certainly, they will not address the dining-room table as "Fido."

PICTURES WITHOUT FILM

Traditional photographic film works on the principle that molecules of silver oxide darken when exposed to light. Patches of silver not exposed are removed during processing; the lighter areas on the film correspond to dark parts of the subject being photographed, and the dark areas to the bright parts of the subject. This negative, or reverse, image produces a positive print.

But a process that could very well revolutionize the world of photography is in an advanced stage of development. In the latest generation of cameras, a small magnetic disc is substituted for a roll of film.

On the outside the new camera resembles a traditional one. But inside, behind the usual lenses and mirrors, is a light-sensitive, charge-coupled device—a CCD.

As light from the image falls on the CCD, it analyzes the light, codes the variations as a series of electronic signals, and transmits them to a floppy disc for storage—much as information is stored on a computer disc.

Once encoded on the disc, the image can be viewed instantly on a television screen by inserting the disc into a special player; videotape can then record the image for future viewings. A print can also be made. And since the image is stored electronically, it can be sent on a telephone line to a similarly equipped receiving station anywhere in the world.

A GLOWING EXPERIMENT

A key step in genetic engineering?

TOBACCO THAT LIGHTS UP by itself sounds like a fantasy. Yet such a plant exists. It is a product of the science of genetic engineering and a potentially important step toward understanding how genes work.

Genes consist of strands of deoxyribonucleic acid (DNA), the complex molecule that controls the behavior of cells in living organisms. Every organism starts life as a tiny cluster of identical cells. In theory, each cell has the potential to serve any function. For example, a cell that becomes part of a kidney also contains the instructions necessary for it to become hair; cells in hair could potentially be brain cells.

As cells reproduce, the DNA in each one instructs it to alter its makeup so that it can perform a specific function—to become, say, part of an arm bone rather than part of a nerve. But scientists still do not know what elements in the structure of DNA are activated to create cells that are so different from one another. The self-lighting tobacco plant may help them find out.

Genetic technology

The plant is the work of biochemists at the University of California at San Diego, who created it by adding to tobacco cells a gene from a firefly. The idea for the experiment came from the study of luciferase, the enzyme in fireflies that produces light. Extracting the luciferase itself from fireflies, however, proved to be a laborious task; instead, the scientists isolated the appropriate gene from the DNA of the firefly and grafted it onto a bacterium, *Escherichia coli*. The bacterium proceeded to multiply and produce large quantities of luciferase.

Having successfully harnessed the enzyme, the research team wondered if the substance might be put to some use. Could it perhaps act as a visible marker? The researchers reasoned that if they could fuse the firefly gene to specific plant or animal genes, they would likely be able to monitor the behavior of those genes simply by looking at what parts of the organism lit up and when.

The team tested their theory with a tobacco plant. They spliced the luciferase gene to a gene from a plant-infecting virus, then grafted the double gene onto a bacterium and bred quantities of it. Then they incubated the bacterial gene with tobacco-leaf cells, which they nurtured into plants.

When watered with a solution containing luciferin, another chemical from fireflies that reacts

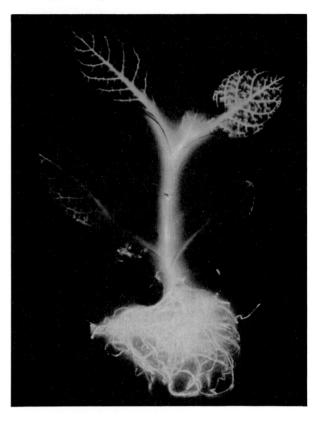

LIGHT FUSE *This self-lighting tobacco plant was produced by fusing the gene of a firefly with that of a tobacco plant. For decades scientists have been experimenting with genetic engineering, hoping to discover exactly how genes work.*

with luciferase to produce light, the tobacco plants glowed in the dark—faintly, but enough to be detected by sensitive film and video equipment and by human eyes accustomed to the dark. And as the researchers had hoped, it was possible to identify which parts of the genetic mechanism were operating: they glowed more strongly.

Cures of the future?

Already scientists are planning to use the technique to study genetic behavior in other organisms. By knowing how genes pass on instructions and why the instructions sometimes become garbled, eventually it may be possible to introduce new genetic information into cells and correct defects.

One day, scientists believe, genetic engineering may provide a cure for gene-influenced cancers and other diseases as well.

THEY CAME FROM OUTER SPACE

Lift-off to a better life

MILLIONS OF PEOPLE watch a rock concert relayed to opposite ends of the world. A fire fighter wearing breathing apparatus spends 25 minutes in a burning building rescuing a trapped child. A prospective buyer watches as a mechanic runs a complete check on a used car. On a remote Texas ranch, water is heated with solar panels. An orthopedic surgeon analyzes the muscle movements of a victim of cerebral palsy. A student in a college dormitory spots an intruder and triggers a portable alarm.

These seemingly disconnected events have all been made possible by an advanced technology that has made a radical difference in day-to-day life on earth: they are all spin-offs from NASA's space exploration programs.

Instant communication

Satellite communications that enabled millions to instantaneously see pictures of a rock concert in aid of famine relief are today being used to monitor the state of vegetation in remote parts of Africa. The hope is to be able to forecast crop failures and avert the need for future emergency aid. Satellite technology has also given us live news coverage of world events, intercontinental telephone links in which every word is usually crystal clear, and information on weather around the globe.

But not all the spin-offs from space technology come from such highly sophisticated equipment. For example, the fire fighter's breathing apparatus was developed from basic lightweight materials used in the casings of rocket motors. Introduced in 1971, the breathing apparatus replaced equipment so cumbersome that it actually hampered the firemen who used it.

The need for NASA ground personnel to know exactly what is happening to the vital parts of a spacecraft at all times led to the installation of computerized sensing systems—first in spacecraft

SPACE SPIN-OFFS *A running shoe with a new type of cushioned sole and a breathing system for fire fighters are but two of the many by-products to emerge from technology developed for the U.S. space program.*

and later in used-car lots. In 25 minutes a system named Autosense now checks all the working parts of an automobile against factory specifications, identifies faults, and even suggests remedies.

Although still very expensive today as a source of heat, solar panels were originally designed to tap the sun's energy in order to power the electrical systems of satellites and spacecraft. Anticipating the day that conventional fuels will have been exhausted, one of NASA's most visionary programs is to research ways to pick up solar power in space, convert it to microwaves, and beam it back to earth. Meanwhile, NASA has built Tech House at its Langley Research Center in Virginia to explore and publicize recycling techniques derived from space technology.

Medical aid

Some of the most remarkable advances in modern medicine have their origins in space technology. During a mission the physical condition of astronauts is constantly being monitored by tiny lightweight sensors glued to the body; each contains a miniature transmitter.

The same sensor technology today enables doctors to make precise diagnoses of patients with severe nervous and muscular problems.

A NASA engineer also invented a supersensitive device to record the impact of micrometeorites on satellites. With modifications, the sensor is used today to detect the invisible but ominous muscle tremors that may be an early indication of the onset of Parkinson's disease.

But possibly the most famous medical advance made possible by space technology is the rechargeable heart pacemaker. In recent years the instrument has been further refined so that physicians can monitor the functions of the heart by radio telemetry and reprogram the pacemaker if necessary — without the need for further surgery.

Alarming results

Electronic miniaturization, whether in calculators no thicker than credit cards or in personal computers, is a direct result of the need to keep the weight of rocket payloads to an absolute minimum. Today this technology has been freshly applied in a pen-size personal alarm. A tiny transmitter sends an inaudible ultrasonic signal to a nearby receiver that alerts a central control room as to the exact location of the device.

The applications of space technology seem endless, and infinitely varied, ranging from aiding U.S. Forest Service surveyors and keeping the oil flowing through the Alaska pipeline to helping blind merchants read dollar bills. According to recent reports, the Russians have started to export products derived from their space technology to the West. These include biodegradable, drug-impregnated contact lenses for eye diseases as well as new implements for setting broken bones.

Space exploration has come down to earth.

BLOOD SIMPLE

The search for the right solution

BADLY INJURED in an automobile accident in the Netherlands in October 1980, a Jehovah's Witness was dying from loss of blood. Since his religious beliefs prevented him from accepting blood from another human being, it seemed that there was little hope of survival.

But his life *was* saved, thanks to an artificial blood substitute flown in from Britain.

Available to all

It is not only people with certain religious beliefs, and their children, who reap the benefits of this marvel of modern science. Artificial blood can be given to anyone, regardless of blood group; there is no need for time-consuming checks to ensure that the donor blood matches that of the patient. The substitute can be manufactured in large quantities at times when blood supplies run short. And chemically manufactured blood is completely free of bacteria and viruses.

Despite 20 years of research, however, blood substitutes are not perfect. Natural human blood is a miracle of chemical engineering, and very difficult to emulate. Among its many functions, blood absorbs oxygen in the lungs and releases it into the body; at the same time, it collects carbon dioxide from the body tissues and releases it into the lungs, where it is exhaled.

Most forms of artificial blood are derived from fluorocarbon emulsions; the primary use of this group of chemicals is as propellants in aerosol sprays. They effectively carry oxygen and carbon dioxide — the main requirements of substitute blood — and have been used with great success in emergency transfusions. However, the patient must be able to breathe deeply in order to provide a higher than normal supply of oxygen to the blood.

A second type of blood substitute uses a hemoglobin solution to transport oxygen. In natural blood the hemoglobin is enclosed in cell membranes so that it does not escape and damage organs, such as the kidneys. In artificial blood, the hemoglobin molecules are joined in clusters; they are not contained in cells.

Hemoglobin in this form does not damage the kidneys, but it is less efficient in carrying oxygen. Another drawback is that natural blood is used in manufacturing the hemoglobin solution; this makes it unacceptable to those with religious objections to blood transfusions.

Substitute blood of any kind can be used only as a temporary measure; it tends to depress the immune system, increasing the risk of infection. And within a day or so the substitute must be replaced by natural blood—either created by the body or from a transfusion.

Nonetheless, the development of blood substitutes has proved a lifesaving boon in emergency operations. For example, hemorrhaging from internal injuries often causes death. But operations using blood substitutes have raised the survival rate from 17 to 80 percent in recent years.

Although a great deal of painstaking research lies ahead, scientists are optimistic that they will be able to create a true equivalent for what is probably the body's most vital fluid.

EYES IN THE SKY

How satellites can help fishermen

THE LIFE OF A FISHERMAN is often dangerous and uncertain. Despite modern sonar and radar equipment on their boats, men can waste days in a fruitless search for fish. Even after a catch is located, sudden storms may disrupt or prevent fishing and, at worst, threaten vessels and claim lives.

While there will never be a substitute for experience at sea, modern technology can help improve the chances of finding a good catch. Satellite observation of the oceans may soon make life both safer and surer for the fisherman.

Fishy preferences

It has long been known that certain types of fish prefer certain types of water. The Pacific albacore, for example, usually favor clear blue oceanic water, particularly if the water forms a front with greener, plankton-rich seas. The plankton attract the small marine creatures on which the albacore feed.

Sea temperature is important too. Salmon live in waters with a temperature of around 50°F, while tropical tuna prefer a temperature of 80°F. In the past it has been extremely difficult to identify and locate these waters.

But satellites can. The experimental satellite *Seasat,* launched in 1978, demonstrated that it could provide constant monitoring of the seas, day or night, whatever the weather conditions below. Infrared cameras enabled *Seasat* to "see" through clouds and create a picture of temperatures at the ocean surface. The success of *Seasat* led to the launching of several operational ocean observation satellites, such as *Nimbus-7* and *NOAA-7.* These satellites are currently giving fishermen off the west coast of the United States up-to-the-minute information on a range of ocean conditions.

Locating the best waters

Surface water temperature is measured by infrared cameras that detect the heat rays from the sea; the readings are plotted on charts showing the major bands of temperature variation. *Nimbus-7* also carries a coastal zone color scanner, which gives computer-enhanced images of the color of the water in four bands, from green to clear blue. The point at which two such bands meet often indicates a large fish population. Other satellite data indicate wind speed and wave height, two factors fishermen take into account when deciding where the fish are.

Temperature observations are backed up by on-the-spot measurements that research and weather ships take at depths of 50 to 150 feet. This provides important additional information about the depth of the surface layer of water, helping fishermen to decide how deep to trawl their nets.

Relaying the information

The information recorded by the satellites is broadcast to receivers on earth and sent to the Navy-Fleet Numerical Oceanography Center (FNOC) at Monterey, California. There computer analysis uses the data to create detailed charts that are then transmitted to the fishermen by radio. The charts show fishermen where the major commercial species of fish are likely to be found. The information is useful for about two days; after that, ocean conditions have changed enough to warrant a completely new set of charts.

Preliminary results of the program are encouraging. Fishermen are reporting increased catches and more efficient fishing. It seems likely that the system will be adopted by other countries, and that the satellite is here to stay as part of the modern fisherman's equipment.

Although some people fear that overfishing could result from the new technology, the satellites also offer a more reliable way to monitor fish stocks and understand the ecology of the sea. Not only can they make the fisherman's life at sea less hazardous, but the satellites may also help us to manage the ocean's increasingly scarce resources of fish more effectively in the future.

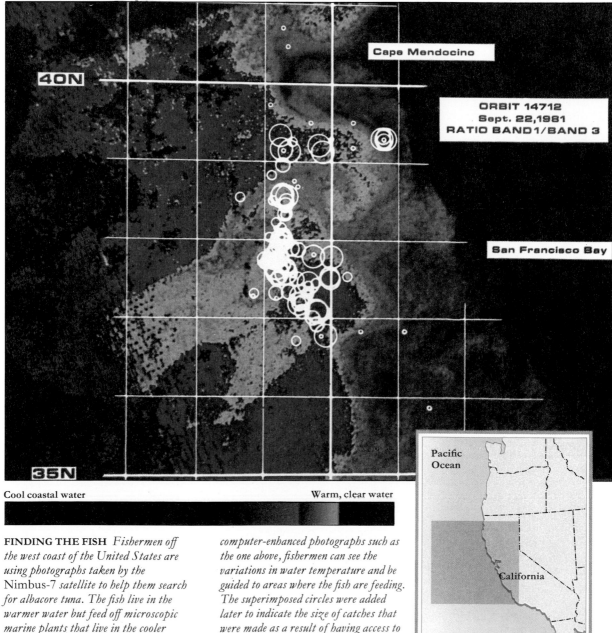

Cool coastal water   Warm, clear water

FINDING THE FISH *Fishermen off the west coast of the United States are using photographs taken by the Nimbus-7 satellite to help them search for albacore tuna. The fish live in the warmer water but feed off microscopic marine plants that live in the cooler coastal waters. By carefully checking computer-enhanced photographs such as the one above, fishermen can see the variations in water temperature and be guided to areas where the fish are feeding. The superimposed circles were added later to indicate the size of catches that were made as a result of having access to this information.*

SLICES OF LIFE

A giant magnet can see through the body

AT ONE TIME the only way to inspect the interior of the human body was to cut it open and look. Although the advent of X-ray technology enabled doctors to see bones clearly, it provided only a blurred impression of softer tissues. Besides, the rays themselves were potentially harmful.

Ultrasound scanning, a major step forward, made it possible to create images of soft tissues and of organs such as the liver and kidneys. But the technique could not achieve the microscopic clarity that doctors need to detect and treat many illnesses.

And so doctors have again started to slice into patients. The difference: today there are no blades and no blood; a magnet, a radio, and a computer do the work once reserved for the surgeon's knife. In tandem, these highly sophisticated instruments can produce superbly clear images, packed with details of the inner workings of the body.

Magnetic resonance imaging (MRI) is one of the biggest breakthroughs ever in medical diagnosis. It achieves extraordinary clarity because it is able to probe farther even than the surgeon's knife: MRI reaches into the very atoms that constitute flesh.

The product of protons

The secret of MRI lies in the fact that protons, which make up part of the nuclei of atoms, are magnetically sensitive. Furthermore, protons of different chemical elements react differently to magnetism, and to radio signals as well. In the 1970's Professor P. C. Lauterbur of the State University of New York at Stony Brook speculated that it ought to be possible to take advantage of

BODY WATCH *Thanks to a revolutionary technique, doctors can examine parts of the human body in minute detail. Known as magnetic resonance imaging (MRI), the technique can produce images of an entire organ or of the atoms within an individual cell. Entirely safe for the patient, the method has many diagnostic applications.*

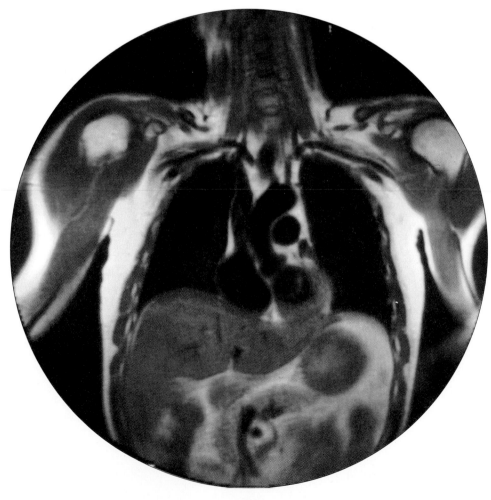

these differences in behavior, translate them into pictorial terms, and use them to create a map of the human body. Dr. William Edelstein, working with Dr. John Hutchison of Aberdeen University, Scotland, discovered how to do this.

Scientists at Aberdeen had realized that virtually every tissue in the body contains water, which is a combination of hydrogen and oxygen. It was hydrogen that held the key, since the behavior of the hydrogen atom's single proton in a magnetic field was the easiest to detect.

Their work was further refined by Dr. Ian Young in the United States. Young developed a way to distinguish the behavior of hydrogen protons in different tissues; his method made possible a clear, easily readable "photograph" of the interior of the body.

Inside a magnet

As finally developed, MRI works this way: First the patient is put inside a metal cylinder—in fact, a huge magnet—large enough to surround the body. When the magnet is switched on, all the hydrogen protons in the patient's body fluids line up in one direction, parallel to the magnetic field. A radio signal then "flips" the protons so that they lie at 90 degrees to the magnetic field. As they flip over, the protons generate an electric current.

When the radio signal is turned off, the magnetic field tugs the protons back into line. As they realign, their electric current fades: the more complex the tissue, the faster the protons turn and the faster the current recedes.

To create a picture of the tissues, a computer analyzes a "slice," or flat section, of hydrogen protons throughout the body as they are reverting to the direction of the magnetic field. The time that it takes the current in different protons to fade, and the number of protons in a given area, are digitized to show as either darker or lighter in the final "map" of the slice. For example, a quick realignment by protons in brain tissue shows up as a bright area; slower-moving protons in cerebrospinal fluid show up as a dark area.

Pinpoint pictures

Because there are so many protons in even a small volume of body tissue, they provide extremely detailed information. Unlike X-rays or ultrasound, MRI can create perfect images of any organ in the human body. MRI techniques have even produced pictures of single cells. And the greatest boon is that the system is totally harmless to the patient.

The applications of MRI seem limitless. To date its most important uses have been in monitoring the blood supply in the brains of stroke victims, detecting tumors at the earliest stage of growth, and examining heart conditions without surgery. It is also proving to be a vital tool in detecting the first signs of a disease with an unknown cause, such as multiple sclerosis. As it quickly reveals the telltale evidence of a disease, the technique also provides highly detailed data about the whole of the body. By coordinating all of this information, medical scientists hope that they may at last find the causes of some of our most serious illnesses.

TOWARD A 24-HOUR DOCTOR?

A possible new way to control disease

MANY MEDICAL conditions can be controlled if patients take regular medication. For example, diabetes.

Diabetes is an illness that occurs when the body fails to produce enough insulin, an enzyme. In healthy people insulin helps the body break down glucose. Without it, glucose builds up to dangerous levels, which can cause coma and even death.

To prevent this from happening, diabetics must daily make tests of the amount of glucose in their blood or urine and take measured injections of insulin to stabilize their condition. In this way diabetics can lead relatively normal lives. But if the tests are not conducted correctly or if the diabetic misses an injection, problems arise.

The ideal solution for the diabetic would be to have a supply of insulin implanted into the body and introduced into the blood in regulated amounts as glucose levels begin to rise. Current medical research into devices called biosensors and infusers is trying to achieve such a solution—and not just for diabetics but for sufferers of other diseases as well.

Chemical care

Biosensor is the name given to any device that measures biological activity. At the simplest level, a thermometer is a biosensor, since it measures body temperature. Electrocardiograms that measure the heart rate of premature babies and stroke victims, and sound the alarm when dangerous fluctuations occur, are a more sophisticated example. But at the forefront of the research are chemical biosensors that can detect the levels of specific substances, such as glucose, in the bloodstream.

A glucose biosensor for diabetics has been developed by scientists at the University of Michigan. Measuring less than one-fiftieth of an inch across, it can be implanted with little discomfort into the vein of a patient. Shaped like a capsule, the biosensor is connected to the outside of the body by a tiny optic fiber. When a beam of light is directed down the fiber, a dye inside the capsule emits varying amounts of light, depending on the amount of glucose in the blood. Any change in the intensity of the emitted light indicates a change in the glucose level—long before it can be noticed in the usual way by the diabetic or a physician.

Continuous control

Accompanying the work on biosensors has been research into infusers—miniature pumps implanted in the body to deliver drugs when and where they are needed. Clinical trials of an infuser for diabetics that releases insulin began at the University of New Mexico in 1981. The infuser was controlled by microchip circuits that physicians activated with a small hand-held radio control unit.

The goal of this research was to develop a "closed-loop" system, in which a biosensor detects a dangerous condition and automatically activates the infuser that corrects it. The doctor would intervene only for routine maintenance and replacement of the implant.

Pioneering work is also taking place at the University of Washington. The hope: to have an insulin infuser contained in a membrane that will open or close in response to glucose levels and release the required amount of insulin. Such a system would copy the way in which insulin is released into the blood in healthy individuals.

Wider applications

Although much of the work on biosensors and infusers was done to benefit diabetics, the principles can be applied to other conditions. High blood pressure could be controlled by a closed-loop system rather than by daily medication.

Cancer patients could benefit too, with infusers delivering controlled amounts of anticancer drugs and painkillers to the sites in which they were needed. This would reduce dosage and help minimize some of the severe side effects that most patients currently suffer.

For biosensors, other applications suggest themselves. Defective genes could be detected in the earliest stages of pregnancy, for example, while signs of other diseases may be caught long before damaging symptoms appear. Increasingly, an internal 24-hour physician becomes a possibility.

NATURE'S POWER SOURCE

In search of an elusive phenomenon

IN JANUARY 1984 the pilots of a Soviet Ilyushin-18 aircraft flying over the Black Sea were astonished and terrified to see a fireball, about four inches in diameter, in front of their airplane.

Then, as the Soviet news agency Tass reported, the fireball "disappeared with a deafening noise, but reemerged several seconds later in the passengers' lounge, after piercing in an uncanny way through the airtight metal wall. The fireball slowly flew above the heads of the stunned passengers. In the tail section of the airliner, it divided into two glowing crescents, which then joined together again and left the plane almost noiselessly."

The Russians had witnessed one of nature's rarest and most mysterious phenomena: ball lightning. Detailed reports date back many centuries. Diane de Poitiers, mistress of Henry II of France, is said to have been burned by a ball of lightning that chased her around her bedroom on her wedding night in 1557. One year earlier, eight people in England were reported to have been killed by a "fiery, sulfurous globe" that rolled through a door.

Source of inexpensive energy?

Today, ball lightning is no longer a phenomenon of purely natural interest, for scientists are now studying it as a possible new source of energy. In Rotterdam, in the Netherlands, researchers have begun an elaborate experiment that may lead to the production of electricity from artificially created ball lightning.

The leader of the Dutch team, Gerard C. Dijkhuis, has proved that the lightning ball is held together by forces that fuse its atomic particles. If this fusion reaction could be controlled, ball lightning could be used to generate inexpensive electric power.

The first step: produce ball lightning to order. Dijkhuis had heard that sailors often report seeing the phenomenon following short circuits occurring in submarine batteries, and bought from the Dutch Navy an old system of 400 individual batteries.

Dijkhuis installed them in a shed on a dock in Rotterdam, linked them together, and then short-circuited the system. Success came in 1985, although the apparatus produced fireballs only four inches in diameter and they lasted no more than a second. In subsequent experiments the scientists hope to sustain the ball indefinitely and create a continuing source of power.

A lightning character sketch

One of the greatest problems the Dutch team faces is that no one can offer an easy explanation for ball lightning. Some researchers have even suggested that it is an optical illusion, no more than an image left on the retina of the eye following a conventional lightning flash. But the many reports of seeing it inside buildings, where no conventional lightning was visible, argue against this theory.

Two British investigators, Mark Stenhoff and Dr. E. R. Wooding, have made a list of the characteristics of ball lightning, based on more than 50 reports. Their analysis confirmed many properties of ball lightning that scientists had previously only suspected.

For example, they found that in 69 percent of the cases ball lightning is seen out-of-doors, although it can also occur in enclosed spaces, such as the room of a house or, as the Ilyushin-18 passengers discovered, an airplane cabin. In 89 percent of the cases the phenomenon appears during a thunderstorm. But, intriguingly, the researchers found that about a third of the witnesses had not seen it come from a conventional lightning flash.

A ball itself, Stenhoff and Wooding concluded, is about 10 inches in diameter, lasts about five seconds, and is as bright as a 40-watt light bulb. Occasionally it seems to leave a pungent smell. In about a quarter of the cases the ball lightning caused damage—a broken window, for example, or scorched grass. More than half of the people who took part in the survey said that the ball seemed to explode as it disintegrated.

Key to the universe?

But ball lightning remains a mystery, and a tantalizing one. Some scientists see it as far more than a possible source of energy. Ball lightning, they contend, is plasma, rare on earth but common in the sun and the stars beyond our atmosphere. Close study of its properties may offer a key to a greater understanding of the universe itself.

However, such projects are likely to mean little to those who happen to encounter the phenomenon. One lady in Florida did not pause to theorize when a sphere of lightning "the size of a basketball" rolled into her house. Instead, she hit it firmly with her flyswatter.

NATURE'S FIREBALL
Ball lightning has long been a source of wonder. Usually encountered outside, it has been observed indoors, as depicted in this engraving of 1901. Today scientists are studying ball lightning as a possible source of energy.

HATFIELD THE RAINMAKER

The man who courted nature

THEY CALLED Charles Hatfield a commander of nature, the greatest rainmaker of modern times. For more than 30 years he practiced his art and won a name for himself by filling lakes, saving crops, and breaking droughts, from the Yukon to Guatemala. He offered to clear London of its fogs and to water the Sahara. But the scene of his most spectacular achievement was San Diego, California.

Hatfield approached the city council in December 1915 with a simple offer. For a fee of $10,000, he would fill the vast city reservoir at Morena Dam; if no rain fell, he would expect no pay. The council's amused reaction: if he did fill the reservoir, they would pay him, with pleasure.

It seemed a safe bet. The reservoir could hold a staggering 15 billion gallons and had never been more than one-third full since it was built. Besides, as one member of the council pointed out, if Hatfield did succeed, he would supply them with 10 billion gallons of water at a cost of one-tenth of a cent per 1,000 gallons; if he failed, the attempt would have cost them nothing.

Drawing the clouds

On January 1, 1916, Hatfield arrived at Morena Dam, some 60 miles east of San Diego, and set to work. First he erected a wooden tower about 20 feet high. On top of it he placed large galvanizing trays containing his special moisture-attracting mixture. Then, through a process of chemical evaporation—the details of which he kept a closely guarded secret—he began "coaxing, wheedling, and courting" nature.

By January 5 there was already rain at the reservoir. By January 10 heavy, almost continuous

GREAT FLOOD *Members of the town council of San Diego, California, got more than they bargained for when they agreed to let Charles Hatfield make enough rain to fill the local reservoir. The resulting downpour led to widespread flooding and devastation.*

rain fell throughout the county. Then the down-pour began in earnest—and continued for 10 days.

To the inhabitants of San Diego, it seemed the rains would never end. As torrents of water rushed through the streets, business stopped and all normal life was suspended. Highways were closed and rail connections flooded. The telephone and telegraph were cut off. Rivers overflowed their banks, washing away houses and barns.

There was a brief respite. For a few days the sun shone weakly through the clouds, and repair work began. But on January 26 the storm returned. At Morena Dam rain fell heavily and steadily all day. By midnight the level of the lake was rising at the rate of two feet per hour. It finally stopped just five inches from the top of the dam, and disaster on a massive scale was averted.

Wall of water

Other districts were less fortunate. The nearby Lower Otay Dam disintegrated, releasing a wall of water 40 feet high. The water plowed 12 miles to the sea, demolishing everything before it.

Altogether, an estimated 50 lives were lost, more than 200 bridges were washed away, and miles of track were destroyed; trains were halted for 32 days. The floods left scars on the mountains and hills for years, and in some places the landscape was changed permanently.

There was no doubt in Hatfield's mind that he had lived up to his promise to fill the Morena Reservoir. But when he went to claim his money, the city council refused to pay.

Hatfield had proceeded on the basis of an oral agreement, without a signed, legal contract. Now the council was maintaining that the deluge was an "act of God," unless Hatfield could provide evidence that he was the one responsible. And, of course, Hatfield could never prove that it was he who had brought forth the rain.

Many people thought that Hatfield had been treated unfairly, although the episode did much to enhance his reputation as King of the Cloud Compellers. He filed a suit against the city, but did little to pursue it; it was finally dismissed in 1938 for lack of prosecution.

But the city of San Diego remembered Hatfield for years to come: in 1948, when they hired a cloud seeder to make it rain, they took out substantial damage insurance.

A LIFE AFTER DEATH

The bequest of Henrietta Lacks

ONE DAY in February 1951, a black American woman named Henrietta Lacks was examined by doctors at the Johns Hopkins University Hospital in Baltimore. Cells from a suspicious purplish spot on her cervix were analyzed and identified as cancerous. They multiplied so quickly that, despite treatment, Mrs. Lacks died eight months later, at the age of 31.

Today, however, her cells are still alive and are being used to help combat a wide variety of diseases all over the world.

Test tube success

The resident gynecologist at the hospital was the first to take an interest in Henrietta Lacks. Intrigued by the extraordinary rate at which her cells multiplied, he sent a sample of them to Dr. George Gey, a friend and colleague at Johns Hopkins University. A distinguished cell biologist, Gey was particularly interested in the science of tissue culture; cells cultivated in a special medium in the laboratory can be studied or used to grow viruses so that vaccines can be tested against them.

Tissue culture is usually a difficult task, since few cells grow easily once they are removed from the body. In this case, however, the cancer cells in the culture were so vigorous that they continue to reproduce themselves to this day.

Rapid growth

Called HeLa cells—a combination of the first two letters of Henrietta and Lacks—the tumor cells have been used in numerous medical experiments. One of the earliest was in the culture of polio viruses, which, for the first time, could be grown rapidly in a laboratory instead of slowly in animals. This advance paved the way for development of a polio vaccine. The HeLa cells have also proved invaluable in research on bodily protein synthesis and genetic engineering.

Today there is not a cancer-research laboratory or vaccine-promotion center in the world that does not owe something to the tenacious longevity of HeLa cells. In addition, scientists hope that the well-traveled cells of Henrietta Lacks might one day lead them to a cure for cancer.

THE NUMBERS GAME

THE SEARCH FOR PI

The work of centuries

IN 1873 THE MATHEMATICIAN William Shanks was a contented man. He had completed his life's work: he had calculated pi to 707 decimal places—a more exact calculation than anyone before him had produced.

Pi (from the name of the Greek letter π) is familiar to all geometry students. It represents the ratio of the circumference of a circle to its diameter, and it appears in numerous mathematical and scientific processes, from measuring distances and volumes to studying the behavior of electromagnetic radiation. Extended to five decimal places, it equals 3.14159.

But the task of writing out pi is endless, for it does not have an exact numerical equivalent; the figures go on forever.

Fortunately for Shanks, it was not until long after his death that anyone challenged his calculations. In 1945 the most advanced mechanical calculator of the time was assigned the task of calculating pi—and showed that in the 527th decimal place Shanks had made a mistake that threw out all the rest of his hard-earned figures.

The desire to determine the value of pi as exactly as possible is an ancient one. The Greek scientist and engineer Archimedes tackled it in the third century B.C. But he had a slight problem: he did not know how to calculate the circumference of the circle. He overcame this, however, by approximating the circle with a polygon—a straight-sided figure—of 96 sides. Archimedes could put only upper and lower limits on the value of pi: he found that it lay between $3\frac{1}{7}$ and $3\frac{10}{71}$. The fraction $3\frac{1}{7}$, which as 3.14 is accurate to two decimal places, is still used by students today. A more accurate value, correct to six places, is equivalent to $3\frac{6}{113}$, which was known to the Chinese mathematician Tsu Chung-chi in A.D. 500.

A random selection

But why do mathematicians continue to calculate pi to such degrees of accuracy, using computers to take the sequence to millions of decimal places?

One purely mathematical question that interests them is whether the sequence of numbers is as random as it looks. For example, do all the digits from 0 to 9 crop up equally often? The first 10 million figures have been thoroughly analyzed. Logically, each digit would be expected to occur 1 million times. But this is not the case. Seven, for example, occurs 1,000,027 times, while 8 comes up only 999,814 times. These comparatively small differences are probably due to chance. But mathematicians would like to have some definite proof, one way or the other, as to whether the entire infinite sequence is random or determined.

In the meantime they can always study the output of the computers. The first true electronic computer, ENIAC, calculated pi to 2,036 decimal places in 1949; it required about two minutes for each digit. In 1973 pi was calculated to a million places for the first time. That computer took a little longer than 23 hours, an average of one-twelfth of a second for each figure.

But even this record was beaten. In 1986 NASA used a Cray-2 supercomputer to calculate pi to 29,360,000 figures—more than 463 miles of numbers if typed at 10 figures per inch. The results were known in just under 30 hours, less than four-thousandths of a second for each digit.

The feat was not only a demonstration of the computer's virtuosity but also a practical test. The calculation was immediately done again by a different method, and the two sets of results were compared. They agreed. NASA scientists breathed a sigh of relief: their expensive new machine worked.

PROVING ELUSIVE

The enigma of Fermat's last theorem

IN A BOOK belonging to the 17th-century mathematician Pierre de Fermat, there is an intriguing scribble: "I have found a truly wonderful proof which this margin is too small to contain."

Fermat's note referred to the equation $a^n + b^n = c^n$. He wrote that although it has any number of solutions when n is equal to 2, the equation has no solutions at all if the power is greater than 2.

It is a pity that Fermat's book had such small margins. Every mathematician since has wondered what that "truly wonderful" proof might have contained, and every great mathematician has attempted to prove Fermat's assertion. All have failed, and the theorem has become one of the great unsolved problems in modern mathematics.

Even the most sophisticated computers have not been able to provide the answer. They have revealed that the statement is true for particular sets of numbers, and they have never found a set of numbers for which the theorem does *not* hold true. But computers cannot *prove* it.

Mathematicians continue to believe that it is *probably* true. In every other case, when Fermat said he had proved a theorem—even when his work did not survive—its correctness was eventually established. But what has come to be called Fermat's "last theorem" remains an enigma.

TEASING LEGACY *Surrounded by the tools of his trade in this 19th-century engraving, French mathematician Pierre de Fermat bequeathed to his successors one of the more tantalizing problems in mathematics.*

OCCULT NUMBERS

The secret power of numerology

SECRETLY, many people are a little superstitious about numbers. Thirteen is unlucky; for some, Friday the 13th is an inauspicious day and there should never be 13 at table. On the other hand, three is a lucky number—except that bad luck always comes in threes.

Many people also have their own personal lucky number: the number of the house they were born in, or the date on which they were married, or a number that has proved lucky before and may bring more good fortune in the future.

Few people would admit to taking these beliefs seriously. But they are relics of the ancient and once highly regarded art of numerology—the belief that numbers hold some hidden knowledge about the world, that they can reveal the future or concealed aspects of a person's character.

A significant assignation

Numerology originated among the Jews of biblical times and among the mathematicians of ancient Greece. Those who practice it today use what is known as the Hebrew system, in which each letter is assigned to a number between 1 and 8:

1	2	3	4	5	6	7	8
A	B	C	D	E	U	O	F
I	K	G	M	H	V	Z	P
Q	R	L	T	N	W		
J		S			X		
Y							

To find the number associated with a word, the numbers corresponding to the letters are added together. Each time the resulting number is more than 9, the two digits are added together. For example, if the total is 15, 1 and 5 are then added together to give 6.

According to numerologists, each number between 1 and 9 has its own significance. The number one signifies dominance and leadership; two, gentleness, kindness, and lack of ambition. Three is the most "extrovert" number, denoting intelligence, creativity, and wit. Four is the number of fairness,

organization, dependability, and attention to detail. Five is brilliance, cleverness, and impatience. Six is perhaps the "happiest" number, signifying tranquillity, balance, loyalty, sincerity, and conscientiousness. Seven is the number of the loner, the philosopher, the mystic. Eight represents worldly success—and egocentricity. Nine stands for the height of intellectual and spiritual achievement.

What's in a name?

Numerologists believe that when this system is applied to an individual's full name, it reveals the true nature of the personality, the characteristics that influence decisions taken throughout life. Applied to a nickname, it indicates what other people think of the individual. And if a married woman compares the numbers of her maiden and married names, she can find out how marriage has changed her.

Finally, the sum of the numbers corresponding to consonants, called the personality number, indicates the impression made on others; the sum of the numbers corresponding to vowels, the heart number, is a measure of inner character.

Shakespearean sums

William Shakespeare's number was 5, signifying that he was clever, fast-moving, and impatient. Shakespeare's friends, however, called him Will, which corresponds to 4, showing a completely different side to his character—perhaps the side only his good friends knew. His personality number, showing the impression he made on the world, is 3—the number of a proud, extroverted, ambitious, and pleasure-loving man. But his heart number is 2, showing his true nature to be gentle, kind, and unassuming.

Numerologists believe that individuals should apply their personal number in every aspect of life. People whose number is 6, for example, should arrange to make difficult decisions or perform important tasks on days of the month that also add up to 6: the 6th, the 15th, and the 24th. People whose names add up to 8 should make sure they eat oranges—or any other food that adds up to 8.

Numerology can be applied to dates as well as to names. It gives an indication of what will happen on a particular date or in a particular year. For example, the digits of 1988 add up to 26, and 2 plus 6 equals 8—which suggests that the year 1988 is one of success and good fortune.

SWEET NOTHINGS

In search of zero

IS ZERO A NUMBER? If so, it is a very peculiar one. It does not behave like an ordinary number at all. It is not used in counting, and if it is added to or subtracted from a "normal" number, it makes no difference. Zero barely exists.

But put it to the right of another number and that number increases tenfold. Multiply it by any number and the answer is always zero. If dividing by zero on an electronic calculator, the calculator will play peculiar tricks. Calculators do not allow division by zero and will register an error.

Zero made its debut in Babylonian mathematics as early as 1000 B.C., and it shows up in the mathematical systems of the ancient Egyptians, Greeks, and Mayans as well. The concept may have arisen because of the need to notate the result when two equal numbers were subtracted from each other, leaving no positive remainder. It was not until the Arabs adopted the Hindu system of numerals and in turn passed it on to Western mathematicians in the ninth century A.D. that zero achieved widespread recognition.

But even then documents referred to 9 numbers, not 10—implying that zero still had not achieved the status of a number. Indeed, the peculiar behavior of zero led some people to believe that it had magical powers. Secret societies used one of its many names, *cifra,* as a password.

Today mathematicians usually take a pragmatic approach to zero. They use it, even though they do not fully understand it. And most of the time it behaves like a regular number. For example, zero belongs to the sequence . . . $-3, -2, -1, 0, 1, 2, 3$ . . . . But the paradoxes remain.

GREAT GOOGOLS

How many grains of sand are there on the beach at Coney Island in New York City? How many raindrops fall on London in a year? What is the number of words that have been spoken in all the history of mankind? How many electrons are there in a thimbleful of air?

In order to answer questions such as these, mathematicians often have to deal with very, very large numbers. To help them do it, the American mathematician Edward Kasner coined a name for a very, very large number: the googol. A googol is a hundred billion billion, which is a 1 followed by 100 zeros.

How large is a googol in real terms? The number of grains of sand lying on the beach at Coney Island has been calculated at about 100,000,000,000,000,000,000— 1 followed by only 20 zeros. Much smaller than a googol!

The number of raindrops that fall on London in a year, or even a century, is also less than a googol. The total number of words ever spoken out loud by mankind is somewhere in the neighborhood of 10,000,000,000,000,000, substantially less than a googol.

The number of electrons in a thimbleful of air is a slightly different matter. Electrons are so small that the number passing through the filament of an ordinary 40-watt light bulb in a minute is equal to the number of drops of water flowing over Niagara Falls in a century. One might expect, therefore, that the number of electrons in a thimbleful of air could be expressed in googols. But it cannot be. The theories of Albert Einstein enable astrophysicists to estimate the number of electrons in the entire universe, and even that is less than a googol—about 1 followed by 79 zeros (to be as precise as scientists dare). In fact, the googol is just larger than the very largest numbers used in physics and chemistry.

And the googol is not the largest number. The googolplex is larger still: a 1 followed by a billion billion zeros.

It is hard to imagine how much room it would take to write out a googolplex, but to get some idea, there would not be enough room for it if, starting at the farthest known star, one took the most circuitous route back to earth, writing zeros all the way.

10, 000 000 000 000 000 000 000 000 000 000 000 000 000
000 000 000 000 000 000 000 000 000 000 000 000 000 000
000 000 000 000

PRIME CONSIDERATIONS

The continuing search for the indivisible

IN 1903 FRANK NELSON COLE gave a wordless lecture to the American Mathematical Society—and solved a problem that had troubled mathematicians for centuries.

On one blackboard Cole wrote out a 21-digit number. On a second blackboard he wrote two numbers, one with 12 digits, the other with 9. Still in silence, Cole proceeded to multiply the two together in the usual way. At the end of the lengthy process, he obtained the same huge number that he had written on the first board and won spontaneous applause—unprecedented at the dignified sessions of the society.

For 200 years mathematicians had suspected that the 21-digit number was "prime": one that cannot be divided without a remainder by any number other than itself (and, of course, the number one). But this number was so large that it was difficult to find its divisors, if it had any. Cole's performance proved that the number was not prime.

Record breakers

Today number theorists compete to find ever larger primes, much as athletes continue to try to break records. Although computers have produced lists of millions of primes, no one has found any pattern or predictability in the way they occur. A formula that will automatically produce an endless supply of primes is one of the most sought-after goals of mathematics. Until it is found, candidates must be tested individually.

In 1874 the English mathematician W. Stanley Jevons stated that it was unlikely that anyone but himself would ever know the divisors of 8,616,460,799; he had obtained the number by multiplying together what at that time were two large prime numbers. He spoke rashly.

Today anyone with a computer can program it to find Jevons's two primes: 96,079 and 89,681. But in the 19th century the difficulty of finding divisors was a huge obstacle to checking whether or not a given number was prime. Nevertheless, the largest prime discovered without the help of computers had 39 digits. Its reign lasted from 1876 to the middle of the 20th century.

With the advent of the computer, the discovery of primes surged forward. In 1983 a 39,000-digit monster was the largest known. In 1986 the title was held by one containing 60,000 digits.

Sophisticated mathematical procedures have been devised to determine whether or not a huge number is prime. No longer can the method of successively dividing it by small numbers be used to determine if there is a remainder. By this process, the fastest supercomputer today would not have had time to explore all possibilities for a number with a mere 50 digits—even if the computer had been running constantly for 15 billion years.

SUBWAY SIMPLIFICATION

A mathematical solution for travelers

CONSTRUCTION OF LONDON'S subway began in the 1860's. Over the next 70 years, as demands for public transportation grew, the system developed haphazardly until by the 1930's it had reached much the form it has today: a network as sprawling as the city it serves.

Drawing the system on a map was feasible—but the map was almost impossible for users to follow. Planning a trip with it was about as easy as finding one's way into and out of a maze—and more difficult if the trip involved changing trains.

Then, in 1931, draftsman Henry C. Beck found a brilliant solution, which led to the London Underground map so widely used today. Whether he knew it or not, Beck was applying the principles of topology, an exotic branch of mathematics in which, for example, a doughnut and a teacup can be regarded as the same thing.

Topologists say that any two objects are the same if you can take a model of one—made of clay—and twist and mold the soft material into the shape of the other without tearing or breaking the clay or making new holes in it. According to topologists, a teacup and a doughnut are the same because both have a single hole through them. The hole in the center of the doughnut is equivalent to the hole in the handle of the teacup; and a doughnut made of modeling clay could, with a little skill, be twisted into a passably realistic cup.

Beck's proposal for a usable subway map was to abandon the idea that it should be a literal representation of how the lines ran underground. Instead, it should show the *relationships* between the stations. After all, what the underground traveler needed to know was which station he wanted to get to and whether he needed to change trains.

To make it easier to read, Beck also proposed enlarging the central, most complex part of the system in relation to the simple parts at the outskirts. And for further simplicity, he would use only horizontal, vertical, and diagonal lines to represent the routes.

Revolutionary designs

The transport authorities were dubious, fearing that many people would find the new design just as difficult to follow as the old one. But early in 1933 a few experimental copies of the new map were printed. They were an immediate success.

The simplification of the London Underground map was not the only spectacular success for topology. It has similarly revolutionized the design of networks for electricity, water, and gas; for automated assembly lines; and for traffic control.

Even the circuit diagram that accompanies a transistor radio is drawn according to topological principles. It may be meaningless to a layman, and look quite different from the mass of wires and semiconductors visible when the equipment is opened up, but the topological diagram conveys everything an expert needs to know about the relationships between the different components. And it makes a repairman's task as simple as seeing where to change subway trains in London.

TANGLED LINES
London's subway system is not easily understood on a conventional map. However, a diagrammatic representation (below) helps travelers find their way.

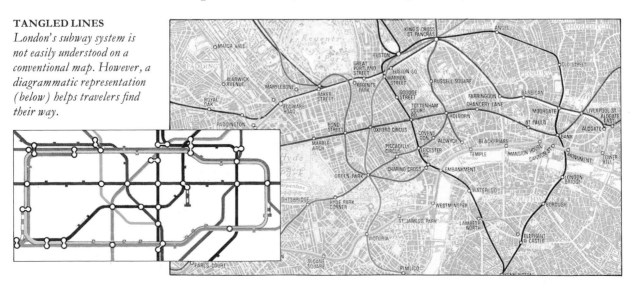

PERFECT, FRIENDLY NUMBERS

Mathematical puzzles that still challenge

WHAT PUZZLE has been worked on continually for more than 2,000 years, has no practical application, and will probably never be solved? The answer: the search for the definitive list of perfect and friendly numbers.

The mathematicians of ancient Greece attributed characters to numbers and awarded some the status of perfection. For Euclid, one of the founding fathers of modern mathematics, a perfect number was one that equaled the sum of its own divisors—that is, the numbers that will divide into it without leaving a remainder. The first perfect number is 6: its divisors are 1, 2, and 3, which add up to 6. The second is 28 $(1 + 2 + 4 + 7 + 14)$. The Greeks knew only two other perfects: 496 and 8,128.

Quantum jump

More than 1,500 years later, in the 15th century, the existence of a fifth perfect number was announced: 33,550,336. Four additional perfect numbers were discovered in the next three centuries. But such was their rarity that in 1811 the mathematician Peter Barlow confidently stated that the ninth perfect number, one with 37 digits, "is the greatest that will ever be discovered. . . . It is not likely that any person will attempt to find one beyond it." But in 1876 Barlow was proved wrong when a 10th perfect number was found—one with 77 digits.

Today the list has been greatly extended and is still constantly growing. The largest known perfect number, the 27th, has a staggering 26,790 digits; it was revealed, with the help of a computer, in 1979.

But many puzzling aspects of perfect numbers remain. Why, for example, are all the known perfects even numbers? Are any odd ones yet to be discovered? Is there a largest perfect number? Or will there always be others to find?

Friendly numbers

Related to perfect numbers are amicable, or friendly, numbers. The Greek mathematician Pythagoras regarded two numbers as friendly if each was the sum of the other's divisors. The Greeks were aware of just one such pair, 220 and 284. The divisors of 220 (1, 2, 4, 5, 10, 11, 20, 22, 44, 55, 110) add up to 284, while the divisors of 284 (1, 2, 4, 71, 142) add up to 220.

Not until 1636 was another pair of friendly numbers—17,296 and 18,416—discovered by the French mathematician Pierre de Fermat. However, by the middle of the 19th century, the number of known friendly pairs totaled more than 60. Incredibly, the second-lowest pair of all had been missed. In 1867 a 16-year-old Italian, Nicolo Paganini, demonstrated that 1,184 and 1,210 are friendly.

There are questions associated with friendly numbers too. All known examples consist of either two odd or two even numbers. Are pairs consisting of an odd and an even number possible? Why are all the odd friendly numbers multiples of three?

Mathematicians will continue to puzzle over the mysterious properties of perfect and friendly numbers for some time; with the aid of computers, the list continues to grow.

NATURAL TIMING

Reading the signs of the seasons

HUNTERS, FARMERS, and fishermen always relied upon natural signs to indicate the passing of the seasons. These signs make up a "natural calendar" that takes precedence over the solar year in governing the lives of certain peoples around the world.

In 700 B.C. the Greek poet Hesiod wrote that sailors feared the days when the star cluster called the Pleiades, or Seven Sisters, first appeared in the sky just before dawn: this was the time (at the end of May today) that marked the beginning of the storms that heralded summer.

In Egypt the ancients watched for the first appearance of Sirius, the Dog Star that heralded the flooding of the Nile River during the summer months. The event was welcomed by the Egyptians because the floodwaters brought rich silt deposits into the valley, improving the fertility of the soil.

Down to earth

Not only were signs in the sky significant, events on earth were also guides to the progress of the year. Hesiod wrote that when water snails climbed the reeds, it was time to stop digging in the vineyards. When cranes migrated south, it was time to begin plowing and sowing in the fields.

When the euphorbia trees produced new shoots, the Banyankole people of Uganda were confident that the rains were imminent. And the Indians of the Orinoco River in Venezuela relied on various signs to help them determine the onset of the rainy season: the piercing screams of the Araguato monkeys at midnight or just before sunrise, the sudden appearance of blossoms on certain trees, and the sprouting of new leaves on the yam plants.

In the lore of the Indians of Pennsylvania, the time to plant corn was when the leaf of the white oak tree was the size of a mouse's ear and the call of the whippoorwill could be heard.

Even today similar events are used by many peoples to regulate their lives. When the leaves of the mahogany and sala trees unfold and certain flowers blossom, the Thonga people of southern Africa know that the warm weather is imminent, prompting them to prepare the fields for sowing.

The Dyaks of southeast Borneo rely on the appearance of large quantities of a particular mushroom to remind them that the time has come to plant their rice. And in southeast Australia, the Bigambul tribe reckon the height of summer to be when there are no longer blossoms on the trees: "the time when the ground burns the feet."

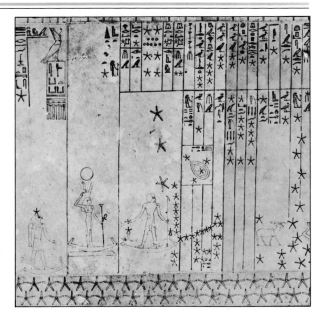

PREDICTING THE FLOOD *Ancient Egyptians observed that the flooding of the Nile River began each year when the star Sirius appeared in the sky before sunrise. Using their sound knowledge of mathematics, Egyptian priests were able to calculate when the annual flooding would occur by plotting the course of the star. Some of the positions of Sirius throughout the year are depicted in the 16th-century B.C. tomb painting above.*

THE MÖBIUS BAND

Any strip of paper joined at the ends to form a continuous round band has two edges and, as one would expect, also two surfaces, one interior and one exterior. However, twisting this strip of paper once before joining the ends changes the two-surfaced, two-edged figure into a single-surfaced, single-edged band.

This strange phenomenon was first described by the 19th-century German mathematician August Ferdinand Möbius, for whom the band has been named.

It is easy to demonstrate its properties by drawing a pencil line down the middle of the band without lifting the pencil from the paper. The result: "both"

The Möbius band

surfaces have a continuous pencil line running around them, proving that the band has only one surface. Likewise, running a finger along the edge of the band reveals that it has only one edge.

Additional properties of the band are revealed if one cuts along the pencil line drawn down the middle of the paper. One longer band results—not two as might be expected.

This new strip has four twists, instead of the original one, and two surfaces and two edges. As such it is no longer a Möbius band. But cutting this new, larger strip down the middle results in two interlocking bands, each one a Möbius band.

MAGIC SQUARES

Counting up the numbers

MATHEMATICS MAY BE POWERFUL, but can it work magic? It may seem a fanciful notion today, but for thousands of years people were so impressed by numbers that they believed they had supernatural effects on every aspect of daily life.

"Magic" squares—thought to be endowed with particularly strong powers—are patterns of numbers such as this:

1	15	14	4
12	6	7	9
8	10	11	5
13	3	2	16

The 16 consecutive numbers start at one, and any horizontal row, vertical column, or diagonal adds up to the same sum: 34. This particular square was engraved on talismans in 16th-century Europe to protect their owners from the plague and other diseases. It is still used today in the Far East.

The oldest known magic square appears in the *I Ching,* an ancient Chinese book of divination dating from about 2200 B.C. The square looks like this:

4	9	2
3	5	7
8	1	6

Each vertical column and horizontal row, plus each diagonal, adds up to 15. This square became widely known throughout the ancient world; the Chinese regarded it as an especially powerful mystical symbol. It was of great significance, too, to the ancient Hebrews, for it represented the name of God. In Hebrew, the letters of the alphabet have

NUMBER MAGIC *Special properties have been attributed to number squares throughout history. The 16-number square that appears in Albrecht Durer's 1514 engraving "Melencolia I" is still used today in India and China to protect against disease.*

numerical values; the first two letters (YH) of God's name, YHWH (which is pronounced Yahweh), represent the number 15.

Magic squares of different sizes represented different things. In medieval Europe the squares were believed to enshrine in some way the secrets of turning base metal into gold—the alchemist's dream. Some people held, too, that the squares concealed some of the secrets of the heavens; individual squares were made into amulets representing astrologically significant planets. The 16-number square illustrated on the left was for Jupiter, and the 9-number one for Saturn.

When a square was used as an amulet, it was important for it to have been drawn up when the planet in question was displaying a favorable aspect; otherwise the square would bring misfortune instead of wealth and happiness.

ARITHMETIC ON A DIFFERENT BASE

Not all counting systems add up to 10

THE NUMBERING SYSTEMS of many societies and cultures around the world today are based on either 5 or 10, the number of fingers on one or both hands. Among the exceptions: the systems used by the Bolans of West Africa, who were said to have counted in 7's, and by the Maoris of New Zealand, who traditionally used a numbering system based on 11.

But other numbering systems of the past also featured numbers other than 5 or 10. For example, the ancient Babylonians worked with a system based on 60. They did not have the Arabic numbering system in use today, but instead used the end of a stick to draw a cuneiform, a vertical wedge-shaped symbol, on a soft clay tablet. This symbol represented one unit. A horizontal wedge represented 10 units.

The wedge shapes were then grouped together in columns. Wedges were placed in the first column until they added up to 59; a single wedge in an adjacent column to the left symbolized the numeral 60. A wedge in the third column to the left represented 60 times 60 (3,600), and a wedge in the fourth column 60 times 60 times 60 (216,000).

The Babylonians are not the only people who employed a different system. The Mayas, an ancient people of Central America, used a number system based on 20. The first column contained symbols that totaled 20; in the column to the left a single symbol represented 20. In the third column to the left a symbol represented 18 times 20 (360). The number was again multiplied by 20 in each of the columns to the left. The Mayas may have given 360 this special place in their system because it was close to the number of days in the year and therefore made calculations for their remarkably advanced calendar easier.

One-two counting

The familiar base-10 system in use throughout the world today has been superseded. An overwhelming number of calculations are now carried out by computers, in which every number is symbolized by sequences of just two numbers: 0 and 1.

Called the binary system, the value of a 1 doubles each time that it is moved one place to the left. Therefore, 1 = 1, 1 and 0 = 2, 1 and 0 and 0 = 4, and 1 and 0 and 0 and 0 = 8. The binary system is essential for computers; the 0's and 1's are represented by the opening and closing ("on" or "off") of the switches in an electronic circuit: 0 when the switch is closed, 1 when it is open.

However, many computer experts find it difficult to move back and forth between the decimal and the binary systems, and use still another system as an intermediate step between the two: the hexadecimal, or "hex," which is based on 16. Hex uses the numerals 0 through 9—together with the letters A through F to represent the numbers from 10 to 15; 16 is represented as 10.

While the hexadecimal system may baffle adults accustomed to more traditional ways of counting, many young computer buffs around the world consider it merely child's play.

MARKING TIME

How the world dates itself

WHEN MIDNIGHT ushers in January 1, A.D. 2001, Christian countries and many others that have adopted the Christian calendar will celebrate the beginning of a new century and a new millennium. But in large areas of the world, that day will have no significance.

In Jerusalem it will be Tevet 6 in the year 5761. In Buddhist Colombo, in Sri Lanka, the year will be 2545. In Delhi the Hindu calendar will be showing the date of 6 Paush in the year 1922. In Mecca the date by the Muslim calendar will be 5 Shawwal in the year 1421. And to the world's astronomers, who do not mind using large numbers to escape the confusion of dating systems, January 1, 2001 (Greenwich time), will be Julian 2,451,910.

How did these diverse starting points for the world's calendars first arise?

The Christian calendar

In the sixth century A.D. a monk, Dionysius Exiguus, reputedly abbot of Rome, is said to have proposed that Christians should count years from the birth of Christ. From various sources he had calculated that Christ was born in the 28th year of the reign of the Roman emperor Augustus, and it is still regarded as close to the true date.

But Exiguus made a mistake in working out just which year this was: A.D. 1 should have been the year he called 4 B.C. Since we perpetuate the error to this day, the new millennium should in actuality occur in 1997.

The Jewish calendar

During the reign of King Solomon in the 10th century B.C., Jewish scholars calculated the date of the Creation and started counting the years from then. So, by that reckoning, in the year 2001 the world will be celebrating its 5,761st birthday.

The Buddhist calendar

The starting point for Buddhist calendars is the year of Buddha's death, which is generally believed to have occurred in 544 B.C.

The Hindu calendar

Various Hindu calendars that were in use until 1957, each with a different starting point, created considerable confusion throughout the Hindu world. The Indian government then decided to rationalize the system by adopting the Official Hindu Calendar, using a starting point of A.D. 78.

This is reputedly the first year of the reign of Kaniska, a semilegendary king who ruled over much of what is today modern India.

The Muslim calendar

Muslims date their calendar from the Hegira—the flight of the prophet Muhammad from Mecca to the city of Medina, which took place on Friday, July 16, A.D. 622. Muslim years follow the movements of the moon, not the sun, and are therefore 10 or 11 days shorter than the years of the Christian calendar. So the 1,379 years in the Christian calendar from the Hegira to the end of this century correspond to 1,421 Muslim years.

The Julian date

In the 16th century, Joseph Justus Scaliger, a scholar and physician, suggested that astronomers should use a cycle of 7,980 years. This length of time can be divided into 15-, 19-, and 28-year periods that are often used in calculations of the intricate movements of the sun and moon. Scaliger took the start of one such cycle to be January 1, 4713 B.C., when the celestial bodies were conveniently placed. It is believed that he called this date "Julian" in order to commemorate his own father, Julius Caesar Scaliger.

CLOCKING IN

Keeping the world punctual

FINDING OUT the time of day was tricky for the mid-19th-century traveler. For example, on entering the main railroad station in Pittsburgh, he would see no fewer than six clocks. One clock displayed Pittsburgh local time; the other five, the time at the head office of each of the railroad companies that had trains running into the station. Changing trains at European frontiers could be just as confusing, since each railroad generally adhered to the time in the capital city of its own country.

Time traveling

Such problems arose because, until the mid-19th century, the time in any given location was determined by the position of the earth relative to the sun. When the sun was directly overhead, it was noon, but it was still morning to the west and already afternoon to the east. This meant that local time varied from place to place, causing considerable confusion for everyone.

The problem became more pressing with the expansion of the national and transcontinental railroads in the 1840's. At first, the local time was retained, and the passenger going from Bristol, in the west of England, to London had to remember to set his watch forward 10 minutes when he arrived. In Germany, signs next to the railroad tracks informed the traveler where each one-minute adjustment was to be made.

But by 1843 all major British railroad companies were using Greenwich time, established by the Royal Observatory at Greenwich, just outside London. At first, companies took the time from chronometers transported from Greenwich. But after 1852, time signals were distributed throughout the United Kingdom by "lines of galvanic communication"—the telegraph.

Abraham Follett Osler, a Birmingham businessman, had long advocated that Greenwich time be enforced by law throughout the country. He ingeniously advanced the cause in his own city by raising money for a clock to be placed outside the Philosophical Institution. After the townspeople came to rely on its accuracy, Osler surreptitiously altered the clock one Sunday morning from local to Greenwich time. One by one, church and public clocks were brought into agreement. And by 1860 most towns and villages in Great Britain were operating on Greenwich time.

From time to time

The United States was too large to employ a single standard time. Again it was the railroads that took the initiative by establishing, in 1888, the time-zone system that today remains virtually unchanged. All railroad clocks within the same zone maintained the same time, which was an even number of hours earlier than Greenwich time. The changeover to the new system was made on Sunday, November 18, and public clocks eventually followed suit.

The following year, an international conference recommended a system of time zones, based on the Greenwich meridian, that was gradually adopted around the world. A few countries were very late in joining: Saudi Arabia did so only in 1962, and Liberia not until 1972.

THE WORLD'S TIME *Time changes in different parts of the world according to the time zone. Roughly, each of the 24 zones spans 15° of longitude, starting from the Greenwich meridian (center, in red). One zone differs from its neighbors by one hour, although some, in yellow below, differ by only half an hour.*

National pride did not always permit the relationship with Greenwich to be acknowledged. In 1911 French civil time was legally defined as being 9 minutes and 21 seconds later than the local time in Paris; no mention was made that French civil time was, in fact, precisely Greenwich time.

Coordinating the world's time

Today Paris is the heart of the world's time system. Since 1920, times around the world have been coordinated with superaccurate atomic clocks. Readings from the clocks in dozens of countries are collected in Paris and averaged.

In atomic clocks, spinning electrons inside the atoms of the element cesium flip over or reverse direction when they are bathed in radio waves. When the electrons flip at regular intervals, they are at the correct frequency to activate a quartz crystal. The vibrations of the crystal control the mechanism of each clock with no greater variation than one second in 800,000 years—more predictable than the rotation of the earth itself.

Atomic clocks have revealed that the earth's rotation slows and then speeds up throughout the year as polar ice melts and refreezes and as air masses warm and cool over oceans and continents. As a result, the day varies in length about one-thousandth of a second per year—a degree of accuracy that the modern-day airplane traveler is unaware of as he speeds through different time zones. The times have indeed changed.

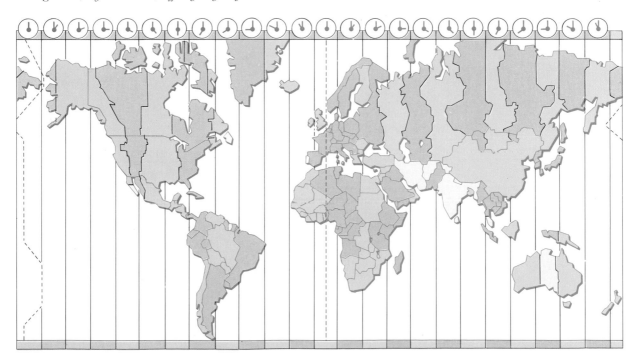

THINK OF A NUMBER

Games with mathematics

THINK OF A NUMBER (6). Double it and add 2 ($6 \times 2 = 12 + 2 = 14$). Triple the result and add 3 ($14 \times 3 = 42 + 3 = 45$). Subtract the original number ($45 - 6 = 39$). Subtract 4 from the result ($39 - 4 = 35$). Subtract 5 and divide by 5 ($35 - 5 = 30 \div 5 = 6$). Surprisingly you are back where you started!

Nearly everyone at some time has participated in a similar mind-reading act. Usually, one person is asked to think of a number and then instructed to do a little arithmetic with it. At the end of the routine the performer may announce, as if by magic, that the answer is the number the person originally thought of.

Guessing games

The secret of such tricks is a series of operations, too complicated for the uninitiated to follow, that cancel themselves out until the original number is reached. In the game above, the instructor never discovers what the original number was—only that after a series of instructions (always the same) the participant will return to the number he first thought of. (Some games do allow the instructor to "guess" what the original number was.)

One of the more advanced routines starts with the instruction to think of any three-figure number in which each succeeding figure is smaller than its predecessor (752). Reverse that number (257). Now subtract the smaller from the larger ($752 - 257 = 495$). Reverse that number (594). Add the two together ($495 + 594$). The answer: it is always 1,089—no matter what three-figure number was first thought of.

The mathematics behind this game is even more complex than that in the first game. Even if you do not understand it, the game is still entertaining—and can impress other people.

LIGHTNING CALCULATORS

The natural number crunchers

ASKED HOW MANY SECONDS he had lived when he was 70 years, 17 days, and 12 hours old, one man supplied the answer in a minute and a half. When his questioners challenged his answer, he corrected them by pointing out that they had omitted to take into account leap years.

The man who demonstrated this astounding arithmetical ability was Thomas Fuller, the Virginia Calculator. Born in West Africa in 1710 and later shipped to America as a slave, he remained illiterate all his life.

Ready reckoners

There have been other lightning calculators. Some have not only lacked formal education but have been idiot savants, with little intellectual ability in other fields. Jedediah Buxton, another prodigy of the 18th century, could remember for a period of at least a month the calculations needed to solve a complex arithmetical problem. Yet he remained illiterate, in spite of having a schoolteacher father, and seemed to have little intellectual inclination apart from his fascination for figures. On the one occasion that he attended a Shakespearean play, the only things that interested him were the number of words that each actor spoke and the number of entrances and exits each made.

Vito Mangiamele, son of a Sicilian shepherd, was a 19th-century arithmetical wonder with a limited education. In less than a minute he could tell a questioner that the cube root of 3,796,416 was 156. (The larger number is equal to $156 \times 156 \times 156$.) This he did as a child of 10, under examination before the French Academy of Sciences. Even more amazingly, he was able to calculate the 10th root of 282,475,249 in his head. (The answer is 7.)

Some calculating prodigies have been gifted mathematicians. Carl Friedrich Gauss, who was born in 1777, was one of the world's most remarkable mathematical geniuses. His brilliant aptitude for figures was evident from an early age. On his first day in an arithmetic class at school he provided the answers to a series of problems before the teacher had finished dictating them. He published his theory of numbers in 1801 and later became a foremost mathematician of his age.

Born in 1887, Srinivasa Ramanujan was an Indian mathematician with extraordinary abilities in manipulating numbers. On one occasion his fellow mathematician G.H. Hardy recalled the time that he visited Ramanujan in the hospital. Hardy said that his taxicab had the number 1729, and remarked that it was a very dull number.

Ramanujan instantly replied that it was in fact very interesting: it was the smallest number that could be expressed as the sum of two cubes and in two differents ways (as 12 cubed plus 1 cubed or as 10 cubed plus 9 cubed).

All in the head

Such calculating geniuses have sometimes been of service to mathematicians as "human computers." One 19th-century prodigy, Zacharias Dase, could multiply 100-digit numbers together mentally and create mathematical tables with the greatest of ease. Yet Dase was not able to comprehend even the most rudimentary of mathematical formulas. The Hamburg Academy of Sciences gave him financial support to create further mathematical tables that would shorten the labors of his fellow mathematicians and scientists.

Lightning calculators have not been able to explain their gifts, but they seem to share some common traits. When confronted with numerical calculations, they possess exceptionally capacious memories and demonstrate remarkably rapid recall. Such arithmetical ability enables them to carry out complicated calculations without pen or paper and remember the results for use in future problems.

It seems that most have been left-handed. Left-handed people rely more on the right hemisphere of the brain, which controls spatial judgment, perception, intuition, and artistic ability. Perhaps the secret of the lightning calculators lies there.

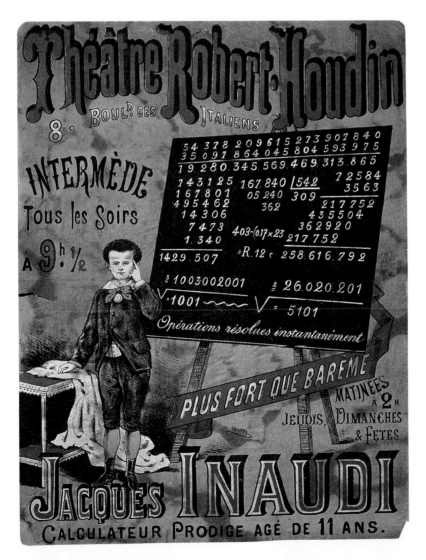

CALCULATING PRODIGY *During the 1880's young Jacques Inaudi (on the poster at left) traveled all over Europe and the United States to demonstrate his remarkable agility with mental arithmetic. A typical performance involved completing five complex calculations in only 10 minutes. Inaudi would stand with his back to the blackboard. As members of the audience called out numbers, his manager would write them on a blackboard in chalk and Inaudi would repeat them in order to engrave them on his mind before beginning his calculations.*

SCIENTIFIC GENIUS *Carl Friedrich Gauss (above) was a lightning calculator who went on to become a brilliant scientist and mathematician.*

FAMOUS FOUR

The minimum number of colors needed on any map so that no two adjoining areas are the same color has been a bothersome question for cartographers over the years.

Experts have long suspected that the answer must be four; experiment had proved that three colors were not enough and that five were probably more than were needed. But *proving* that just four colors would be sufficient for any map had not been easy.

Then, in 1976, two mathematicians at the University of Illinois in Urbana claimed to have established the proof with the aid of a computer.

The proof they constructed is voluminous. It consists of almost 600 pages. Text and diagrams occupy 50 of them; nearly 2,500 supplementary diagrams take up 85 more; and 400 microfiche pages contain more diagrams and proofs of subsidiary theorems used. The proof required some 12,000 hours of computer time.

PUZZLE *If you were painting this map, and instructed not to use the same color on any two adjoining states, how many different colors would you need?*

Just one problem remains: the proof is so long and so complicated that only a computer can check its accuracy. To date no mathematician has been able to verify it, and therefore no one is absolutely sure that it is valid.

RANDOM THOUGHTS

Taking a chance

IMAGINE THAT YOU ARE in a casino in Las Vegas, betting at the roulette table, and that 10 consecutive spins of the wheel produce even numbers. How would you bet on the next spin—that the number will again be even? Or odd?

Many would be prepared to stake a lot of money that the next number will be odd. They believe that the "law of averages" will soon compel the wheel to turn up some odd numbers to compensate for the freak run. Statisticians call this the Monte Carlo Fallacy, and it has been responsible for some heavy losses at gambling tables all over the world.

In fact, the law of averages does not exist. There is no unseen influence that somehow balances out the wheel's past and future results to guarantee that odd and even numbers turn up equally. If the wheel is indeed totally unbiased, there is still a fifty-fifty chance that the next spin—and all subsequent spins—will turn up an even number. If anything, the run of even numbers makes it *slightly* more likely that the bias is toward even numbers—which might justify staking a very *small* amount that the number turned up by the next spin of the wheel will be *even,* not odd.

Chance selection

Whenever an event occurs that is completely unpredictable based on its context or the history of such events—such as a particular number coming up in a game of chance—it is called random.

Randomness is obviously important in many games: the deck of cards must be well shuffled before the next hand is dealt, the space invaders in a video game must always pop up in unpredictable places on the screen, the dice must not come up double-six too often.

In science, too, randomness is often essential. For example, when people are selected for a survey or for a psychological experiment, they must be picked at random, or the results may be misleading.

It is not an easy job to get a truly random sequence of events or numbers. Simply trying to think up random numbers will not work—we all have psychological quirks that bias us, say, toward odd numbers or away from 7's. And for most scientific purposes, the shuffling of a deck of cards is not truly efficient.

Computer know-how

An obvious solution might seem to be to use computers. True, computers can certainly produce apparently random numbers if needed. But in reality these are only "pseudorandom" numbers. They are obtained by complicated arithmetic—and if the sequence includes a large enough number of digits, it will repeat itself. Also, the same sequence will be obtained every time that the computer is commanded to produce the random numbers. Ultimately, the sequence will no longer be random; it becomes completely predictable.

One activity that depends on obtaining the most random numbers possible is a state lottery, for which the draw must be scrupulously fair. In some cases the winning numbers are selected by electronic equipment. The choice depends on the behavior of individual atoms—according to present scientific theories, the most perfectly unpredictable happening of all.

THE FIBONACCI SERIES

A natural growth of mathematics

REGULAR PATTERNS IN NATURE are common, but sometimes they occur with a mathematical precision of an astonishingly high order. One such pattern was discovered by an Italian mathematician, Leonardo Fibonacci, at the beginning of the 13th century.

Fibonacci lived in Pisa, where he was tutored by an Algerian in the Arabic art of mathematics—at the time, the most advanced system of mathematics in the world. In addition to writing a number of books on mathematics and geometry, Fibonacci is credited with having encouraged the use of Arabic numerals throughout Europe.

How many rabbits?

In one of his books Fibonacci discussed the following problem: "A certain man put a pair of rabbits in a place surrounded on all sides by a wall. If it is supposed that each pair begets a new pair every month, beginning in its second month, how many rabbits will there be in a year?"

The answer: one pair will be born in the second month, one pair in the third, two in the fourth, three in the fifth, five in the sixth, and so on, in a series that has come to be known by Fibonacci's name. When written out, the series runs 0, 1, 1, 2, 3, 5, 8, 13, 21, 34 . . . , each number after 1 being equal to the sum of its two predecessors. So the number of pairs of rabbits born in each month equals the sum of the pairs born in the preceding two months. (In a year there will be 233 pairs.)

This series is often found in nature. The petal-like florets in the head of a sunflower, for example, form two overlapping spirals, one clockwise and the other counterclockwise. There are 21 florets in the clockwise spiral and 34 in the counterclockwise spiral—and both 21 and 34 are found in the Fibonacci series.

Spirals can also be seen in the structure of pinecones. Usually there are eight clockwise spirals and five counterclockwise ones. Again, five and eight come from the Fibonacci series. On the outside of a pineapple there are normally 8 spirals in one direction and 13 in the other.

Functional relationships

The way in which shoots are arranged on plant stems also seems to be in accordance with the Fibonacci series. Compared with the one beneath it, each shoot is offset so that it does not shade its neighbor. The angle between one shoot and the next, expressed as a fraction of the circumference of the stem, is generally found to be given by two numbers from the Fibonacci series: $\frac{1}{2}$ for grasses and for elm and linden trees; $\frac{1}{3}$ for sedges, beech, and hazel; $\frac{2}{5}$ for oak and fruit trees; $\frac{3}{8}$ for poplar and rose; $\frac{5}{13}$ for willows, almond trees, and leeks.

As the Fibonacci series progresses, the ratio of each number to its predecessor is close to 1.62:1. Since the time of the ancient Greeks, this has been known as the golden ratio—also called the golden section—and regarded as being aesthetically pleasing. The ratio can be seen in the proportions of many classical buildings, such as the Parthenon in Athens. Even architects as modern as Le Corbusier have incorporated the proportions based on the Fibonacci series in their work. In this way art imitates life, and the golden ratio is used the world over by countless artists and architects to whom Fibonacci's rabbits mean nothing.

THE PEA AND THE PLANET

To most people, the world of mathematics is a fairly unfamiliar place, and much of what is discussed in it is accepted by the layman without question.

But occasionally some mathematicians come up with an idea that defies common sense.

Probably one of the most startling examples is the theory put forward early in this century by the distinguished Polish mathematicians Stephen Banach and Alfred Tarski.

To nonmathematicians, the theory appears quite incredible. It states that there is a way to divide a pea into separate parts and rearrange them so that they fill all of planet earth without leaving any holes. The opposite is also true. The earth can be divided into separate parts and arranged so that, without squeezing or distorting the parts in any way, they can fit into a coat pocket.

There are no holes in the logic that led Banach and Tarski to their startling conclusion. Both the pea and the planet are spheres, and mathematicians have a fundamental difficulty establishing a way to measure the surface area of a sphere. (Seemingly simple notions can sometimes become complex when the ideas behind them are explored.)

According to the mathematical logic of the two Poles, it *is* possible that a sliced-up pea could fill the whole planet, and the planet could fit into a pocket.

IRRATIONAL NUMBERS

The square root of wonderful

FOLLOWERS OF the Greek mathematician Pythagoras in the sixth century B.C. viewed numbers with reverence and awe. They believed that the truths of arithmetic, together with those of geometry, were the most perfect that could be attained. Among their cherished convictions was the concept that whole numbers, or integers, held the key to understanding the universe.

Pythagoreans were therefore shaken when a strange type of number, which they dubbed "irrational," was discovered.

Shocked by numbers

Pythagoreans thought that any number was either whole or could be represented as a ratio of two whole numbers—$\frac{11}{12}$, for example, or $\frac{583}{820}$. This meant that a measurement such as forty-three fiftieths of an inch could be regarded as 43 lengths, each one-fiftieth of an inch long. It came as a shock when they found that the square root of 2 could not be represented with a ratio of two whole numbers.

The number that multiplied by itself equals 2 occurs throughout mathematics, particularly in geometry. For example, if the four sides of a square are each 1 inch long, the length of the diagonal, in inches, is equal to the square root of 2.

The value of the square root can be calculated to many degrees of accuracy: $\frac{14}{10}$, $\frac{141}{100}$, and $\frac{1414}{1000}$ approach the correct value. But no matter how large the numbers in the fraction, the square root of 2 can never be revealed. The same is true of many other numbers: the square roots of 3, 5, 6, 7, 8, and 10 are not exact squares of a whole number.

Pythagoreans were forbidden, on pain of death, to reveal this discovery. When one mathematician in fact did so, his subsequent demise in a shipwreck was regarded as divine retribution.

Stretching the imagination

Ever since Pythagoras the history of mathematics has been punctuated with the discovery of other types of numbers that defy the imagination—such as the square root of −1. As most students learn, when a positive or a negative number is multiplied by itself, the result is always positive. But what are the numbers that, when multiplied by themselves, result in a negative, such as −1?

Girolamo Cardano, a 16th-century Italian, was one of the first to discuss so-called imaginary numbers, which he described as "ingenious but useless." Mathematicians, however, use them to make calculations that would otherwise be impossible. Imaginary numbers, which once confused the best minds in mathematics, are now found in every high school curriculum—even though some students may still find them baffling.

PART 3

ODDITIES AND ECCENTRICITIES

EXTRAORDINARY FEASTS

Strange meals in peculiar places

AMERICAN FINANCIER George A. Kessler had a passion for unusual parties. All of the wealthy guests at a "hobo dinner" were required to wear tattered clothing and eat out of cans. On another occasion his guests sat down to dinner in an airship hovering over the Atlantic. His most extravagant party, however, was held at the Savoy Hotel in London on June 30, 1905, to celebrate his birthday.

Taking Venice as his theme, Kessler flooded the courtyard of the hotel with water dyed blue to resemble the sea. Magnificent painted backdrops provided the setting, and the entire scene was illuminated by 400 Venetian lamps. His two dozen guests sat inside a huge silk-lined gondola bobbing on the "canal," surrounded by 12,000 carnations and an enormous number of roses. They ate food prepared by 15 master chefs and served by waiters dressed as gondoliers.

The evening's entertainment featured the great opera singer Enrico Caruso; he performed an aria while a baby elephant with a five-foot-high birthday cake strapped to its back was led across a gangplank to the gondola and 100 white doves flew overhead. Unfortunately, the dye used in the water poisoned the swans that had been scheduled to swim around the gondola.

Four years later Kessler converted the garden of the Savoy into an Arctic paradise. Plaster "snow" covered the ground, huge white chrysanthemums decorated the walls, and an enormous metal nail represented the North Pole. Held to celebrate Robert Peary's achievement in having reached the pole in 1909, the dinner was a unique affair. But still it was his gondola dinner that Kessler regarded as "the most novel little party I have given."

Eccentrics all

One of the most macabre meals of all time was organized by the eccentric French culinary expert Grimod de la Reynière in 1820. He staged it in the Paris mortuary, with a coffin behind the seat of each diner and, as the centerpiece, a catafalque—the raised platform on which a body lies. Reportedly, some 300 spectators watched the feast from the mortuary gallery.

In the same year, in London, the height of fashion for dining in unusual places was established by a group of builders. They lunched 365 feet above the ground, inside a new cross and ball erected on the top of St. Paul's Cathedral.

Also in London, in 1843, two weeks before the statue of Horatio Nelson was to be hauled to the top of its column in Trafalgar Square, 14 men sat down to a feast of rump steak on the slab at the top, a mere 166 feet above the ground.

Monster meal

A number of eminent British scientists received a bizarre invitation to a dinner party in December 1853. The invitation itself—printed on a replica of the wing of a pterodactyl—was as unique as the site. The invitation read:

> Mr. B. Waterhouse Hawkins solicits the honour
> of Professor ———'s company at dinner,
> *in the Iguanodon,*
> on the 31st of December, 1853, at 4 P.M.

The iguanodon was one of 29 life-size plaster-covered brick-and-iron models of prehistoric creatures designed by animal sculptor Benjamin Waterhouse Hawkins. They were to be displayed at the Crystal Palace, the gigantic glass building that had housed the Great Exhibition in 1851.

The 22 distinguished guests who attended the dinner on New Year's Eve found themselves seated inside the creature's body. There they were served a sumptuous meal by a team of waiters who had to clamber to the dining table after crossing a platform supported by scaffolding.

Following the superb banquet, according to the *Illustrated London News,* the party returned to London by train, "well pleased with the modern hospitality of the iguanodon, whose ancient sides there is no reason to suppose had ever before been shaken with philosophic mirth."

EQUESTRIAN EPICURES *On March 28, 1903, at Louis Sherry's elegant New York City restaurant, 36 formally attired gentlemen attended dinner as the guests of C. K. G. Billings, a wealthy businessman. The novel feature of the occasion: all were on horseback. Sod had been laid on the floor, and the horses were brought to the dining room by elevator. Feed bags were used as dinner plates; rubber buckets as decanters for champagne. The reputed cost of the horseback banquet was $50,000.*

THE WATERLORD

Fresh air and water gave him long life

MATTHEW ROBINSON-MORRIS, who became the second Lord Rokeby in 1793 at the age of 81, was an intelligent, widely read Englishman. He was highly democratic in his political views and a great believer in the equality of mankind. But he had a number of eccentricities that puzzled his contemporaries.

Rokeby was in his day the only peer, and possibly the only well-born gentleman in all of Britain or Ireland, with a beard. At one time it almost reached his knees.

He also had many peculiar beliefs, such as that the Bank of England would fail in his lifetime; he even took bets on it. The effect would not have been of much consequence, since he also believed that the earth would soon be consumed by fire.

He was opposed to excessive cultivation of the land and allowed his vast estate to revert to nature. Birds and animals of every kind roamed the grounds in perfect freedom.

Rokeby was well ahead of his time with some of his diet and health fads. A lover of the countryside,

he took long walks "such as would tire a quadruped," and was passionate about fresh air. Discouraging the consumption of "exotics" of every description, he despised sugar and instead used honey, rejected coffee and alcohol, and appeared to live on a diet of beef tea and vast quantities of water (although some of his neighbors thought that he was possibly a cannibal).

Obsessed with the virtues of water, Rokeby kept a pocketful of change to reward anyone he met drinking it. He adopted a semiaquatic way of life, spending hours swimming in the sea long before it became a popular pastime and bathing in a specially constructed tub in a glass-fronted thatched house. He had designed his solar-heated pavilion, where he received guests and took his meals, himself.

Rokeby despised all doctors, and when he was ill threatened to disinherit his nephew if he called a doctor. Despite this—or perhaps because of it, in view of the crude methods of most 18th-century physicians—Lord Rokeby lived to what at that time was the remarkable age of 88.

MAKING HAY

A kingdom built on books

ON APRIL FOOLS' DAY 1977, a small country town on the border between England and Wales declared its independence. Passports were issued and stamped for Hay-on-Wye in each of the town's two taverns, and the Hay national anthem was sung. Leading citizens were appointed to top government jobs, and aristocratic titles—dukedoms, earldoms, and knighthoods—were available for a price. Ambassadors were dispatched to the International Court of Justice at The Hague in the Netherlands, and a rowing gunboat patrolled the meandering river Wye.

A town of books

Events like these might seem out of place in such a rural community, but Hay is no ordinary town. It is the home of the largest secondhand bookstore in the world. Every available building is full of books, and every year this flourishing enterprise attracts visitors from all corners of the globe.

The man responsible for turning Hay into a mecca for the bibliophile is the self-proclaimed

king of Hay, Richard Booth. When Booth started his first secondhand bookstore there in 1961, Hay was a picturesque but dying town of fewer than 2,000 people. The town had gradually declined along with the local farming economy, and many of its businesses had closed. Booth began to pack the many empty buildings with books. In due course he filled up the old workhouse, a chapel, a movie theater, and even Hay Castle, where he lives today.

An estimated $8\frac{1}{2}$ miles of book shelving wend their way through Hay-on-Wye's unusual bookstore. The Booth empire boasts an enviable turnover of more than a million books a year. Unlike most dealers in old books, Booth has never specialized in one subject. He buys books in bulk—entire private libraries whenever possible—in the belief that no book is worthless, that "someone in the world wants it." Prices are low and there is something for everyone, the casual browser and the collector of rare books alike.

It was Booth's battles against the rules and regulations of government agencies that led him to declare Hay-on-Wye an independent kingdom in 1977. He is passionately committed to the survival of rural communities such as Hay and firmly believes in encouraging the revival of traditional crafts. He even delivers books around town in a horse-drawn cart. Horse transport, he says, relieves the energy crisis and provides work for local saddlers, wheelwrights, and blacksmiths who might otherwise be unemployed.

The people of Hay are fond of their eccentric and amiable king, who has brought prosperity to their town. And although not everyone thinks that his ideas are realistic, his new industry does employ about 10 percent of the local population. All the merchants in Hay benefit from the regular invasions by bookworms, and the townspeople have every reason to be proud of the books that have placed their town so firmly on the map.

THE EMBALMING DENTIST

Preserving his marriage to further his career

OF ALL THE GIMMICKS dreamed up to attract customers, few can be as extraordinary as the one employed by Martin Van Butchell, a dentist in London.

A student of surgery and anatomy, he turned his attention to dentistry in the 1760's. His advertisements in *St. James's Chronicle* announced: "Real or Artificial Teeth from one to an entire set, with superlative gold pivots or springs, also gums, sockets and palate formed, fitted, finished and fixed without drawing stumps or causing pain."

Such advertisements, however, were not sufficiently effective for Van Butchell. Then, with the death of his wife, Mary, on January 14, 1775, he devised an ingenious method that could not fail to draw the crowds: he decided to have her body embalmed and put on display in his London home where he practiced.

Van Butchell turned to Dr. William Hunter, under whom he had studied, and Dr. William Cruikshank. They took on the task, injecting the body with preservatives to which coloring had been added to give Mary's cheeks a rosy glow. A pair of "nicely matched glass eyes" completed the effect. Mary was then dressed in a fine lace gown and embedded in a thin layer of plaster of paris in a glass-topped coffin with curtains.

Dear departed

People came from all over London to gape at the embalmed woman, whom Van Butchell introduced as "my dear departed." But Van Butchell attracted much criticism for exploiting Mary's demise; some people even claimed that a clause in their marriage settlement provided an income for him as long as Mary was aboveground. On October 31, 1775, Van Butchell advertised again in *St. James's Chronicle*:

"Van Butchell (not wishing to be unpleasantly circumstanced and wishing to convince some good

MARTIN VAN BUTCHELL *His eccentricities even extended to painting his white pony with spots. He changed the color of them daily.*

minds that thay [sic] have been misinformed) acquaints the Curious, no stranger can see his embalmed wife unless (by a Friend personally) introduced to himself, any day between Nine and One, Sundays excepted."

Not long afterward Van Butchell remarried. His second wife, Elizabeth, was perhaps understandably distressed that Mary was still in residence, and insisted that she be removed.

Reluctantly Van Butchell presented Mary's embalmed body to Dr. Hunter's brother John for his museum. The embalming process was far from perfect, and a century later a writer described Mary's body as "a repulsive-looking object." It was exhibited until 1941, when a German incendiary bomb fell on the museum and Mary was finally cremated—166 years after her death.

THE JARI PROJECT

The billion-dollar dream of the world's richest man

DANIEL K. LUDWIG is a typical billionaire. Born in a small town in Michigan in 1897, he entered the shipping business at the age of nine by salvaging a sunken boat. He had made his fortune 30 years later. After building the first of the petroleum supertankers in the early 1950's, Ludwig then diversified into mining, oil, gambling, and property. By 1957 he was reckoned to be the fifth wealthiest person in the world. When J. Paul Getty died in 1976, Ludwig inherited his unofficial title: the world's richest man.

As such, however, Ludwig appeared to enjoy none of the trappings of wealth. Wearing inexpensive, nondescript clothes, he was the despair of tailors. He clung to an anonymous lifestyle, refusing to grant interviews, avoiding photographers, traveling economy-class, and living in a modest house in Connecticut.

Ludwig had a prodigious appetite for work, and it showed no sign of diminishing with his advancing years. As he approached his 70th birthday, he undertook his most ambitious project yet.

Vision of the future

Ludwig had always prided himself on his ability to think a generation ahead. He foresaw world food shortages in the 1980's and beyond, and he predicted a simultaneous shortage of paper created by the explosion of global communications. To capitalize on his foresight, Ludwig needed to find a considerable amount of land on which to grow timber and crops. His eye turned to Brazil and the virtually limitless tracts of the Amazon basin.

Amazonia is almost as large as Australia. It contains the world's largest stands of timber and the largest known deposits of iron ore, as well as untold quantities of tin, manganese, bauxite, and gold. The region was also home to the "Amazon factor": a combination of climate, isolation, soil, pests, and disease that has bedeviled every attempt to exploit its wealth.

Ludwig had little difficulty persuading the Brazilian government that he was the man to tame the Amazon and tap its resources. His plan was to clear a few million acres of forest and then to plant fast-growing trees—to transform the jungle into tree farms, in effect. These would provide the raw materials needed to feed the huge pulp and paper mills that he envisioned. At the same time, Ludwig saw great possibilities for rice production and cattle farming on a massive scale.

CLOUDED VISION *A rare photograph of the reclusive American billionaire Daniel Ludwig. His ambitious scheme, the Jari project, ended in costly failure.*

In 1967 he purchased some 4 million acres of the upper Amazon by the River Jari for less than $1 an acre. Thus the Jari project was born.

Man against nature

Ludwig tackled the Amazon factor head-on. He brought in the world's mightiest machines to clear the jungle. He laid 2,600 miles of road and 45 miles of railroad track. He shipped an enormous pulp mill, complete with its own power plant, from Japan and anchored it in the Jari; this alone cost $269 million. He planted 250,000 acres of fast-growing gmelina, pine, and eucalyptus trees. He planted rice and raised cattle, at the same time mining kaolin and laying plans to exploit the huge bauxite reserves. To accomplish all this he imported and accommodated an army of technical experts; a shantytown housing 35,000 laborers sprang up on the outskirts of the new town.

But the Amazon soon began to retaliate. By the late 1970's Ludwig's grand campaign was foundering. The gmelina trees, imported from Indonesia, did not flourish on Jari's soil. Ants and termites devoured crops and supplies. Malaria and meningitis plagued the workforce. Ludwig's response was to spend his way out of trouble—at an average rate of $180,000 a day.

Final defeat

As if the Amazon factor were not enough, Ludwig was being criticized increasingly for the autocratic manner in which he fired experts, refused to talk to the press, and ignored the sensibilities of the Brazilian authorities. Scientists all over the world condemned the scheme and its threat to the delicate ecological balance of the region.

In 1982 Ludwig, 84 years old and in failing health, finally abandoned the fight. A consortium of 27 Brazilian corporations reluctantly bowed to government pressure and took over the Jari project. The new owners immediately began to scale it down to more manageable proportions. Ludwig went back to the United States and into complete seclusion.

Ludwig had plenty to brood about: 15 years of unremitting toil had resulted in almost total failure and had netted him a loss of more than $1 billion.

TAMING THE JUNGLE *Located in the heart of Brazil's Amazon basin (inset), the Jari project of the late 1960's covered 4 million acres. Vast tracts of jungle were cleared to create a massive agricultural and industrial complex, primarily for the production of wood pulp and rice. Some 35,000 men were hired to turn the dream into reality, but ambitious production targets were not met. After investing $1 billion and 15 years of his life, Daniel Ludwig was forced to concede defeat.*

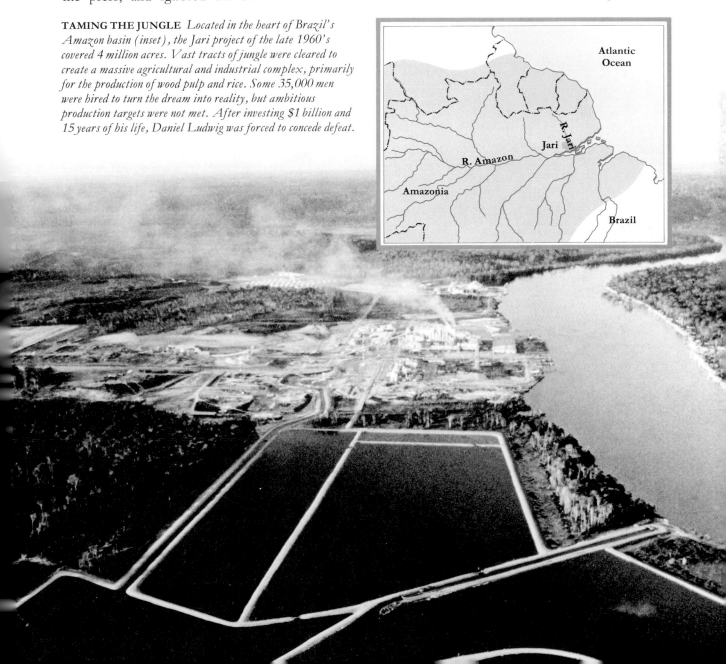

NOUVELLE CUISINE

When the Parisians became more adventurous in their eating habits

THRIVING BUSINESS *In the Franco-Prussian War of 1870–71, starving Parisians turned to dogs, cats, and even rats for food. In the 19th-century engraving above, a butcher plies his trade. The main fare: cats and dogs, with an occasional rat thrown in for good measure.*

DURING THE WINTER of 1870–71, Paris was under siege by the Prussian Army. The city was totally surrounded; it was sealed off from the outside world. As no supplies were getting through, prices of existing food stocks soared and a black market was rapidly established. Within weeks, shops were emptied and the inhabitants of Paris, accustomed to the finest foods, were compelled to consume whatever edible goods they could obtain.

Although horseflesh was customarily eaten in France, the horses that were now slaughtered were those that not long before had pulled the carriages of the wealthy. Two trotting horses that had been a gift from the czar of Russia to Emperor Napoleon were among the estimated 65,000 horses eaten during the siege. As food supplies became scarcer and scarcer, the Parisians were forced to consider alternative sources of meat. Gourmets were soon turning their hungry gaze toward dogs and cats.

Culinary skills were severely tested and many imaginative new recipes devised to disguise the taste of such novel ingredients.

As the bleak winter wore on, with no end to the siege in sight, rodents were added to the list. A rat market was set up in the center of Paris; large rats dangled from hooks on the market stalls, and local residents argued over the best ways to prepare them for the table. Even ornamental goldfish were gathered from the ponds in Parisian parks. On December 4, 1870, *Les Nouvelles,* a French daily newspaper, published the menu (see the next page) created from the ingredients that circumstances had forced upon the food-loving Parisians.

Consommé de cheval au millet
(Horse soup with millet)

Brochettes de foie de chien à la maître d'hôtel
(Dog liver kebabs)

Émincés de râble de chat sauce mayonnaise
(Sliced saddle of cat with mayonnaise sauce)

Épaule de filet de chien sauce tomate
(Shoulder of dog with tomato sauce)

Civet de chat aux champignons
(Cat stew with mushrooms)

Côtelettes de chien aux petits pois
(Dog chops with peas)

Salmis de rats à la Robert
(Rat stew)

Gigot de chien flanqué de ratons
(Dog leg with small rats)

Plum pudding au jus et à la moelle de cheval
(Plum pudding with horse-marrow sauce)

By the end of the year the Paris Zoo was no longer able to feed its animals and reluctantly agreed to sell them for food. The zoo thought it too dangerous to attempt to slaughter the lions and tigers; the monkeys, too, were spared because they were closely related to humans. A hippopotamus was offered for sale at 80,000 francs, but no one was prepared to pay such an exorbitant price for an animal that might prove to be inedible.

Prime steaks

However, Monsieur DeBoos, a butcher on the Boulevard Haussman, had a roaring trade selling steaks derived from buffalo, zebra, and yak, and reportedly paid 27,000 francs for two elephants, Castor and Pollux, that ended up on his slabs. Their trunks, regarded as a special delicacy, sold for as much as 40 francs a pound.

By the end of January 1871, the siege was over, and it was with much relief that Parisians returned to more conventional fare.

PRESERVED FOR POSTERITY

The immortal life of Jeremy Bentham

ON JUNE 6, 1832, the eccentric English philosopher Jeremy Bentham died at the age of 84. Two days later eminent scientists and literary figures received a remarkable invitation—not to Bentham's funeral but to his dissection at a London medical school.

Bentham had been fascinated with the problem of usefully disposing of the dead. Until just prior to his own death, he had been preparing a pamphlet with the bizarre title *Auto-Icon; or Farther Uses of the Dead to the Living* (it was eventually published in the 1840's). In it he suggested that everyone should become his own memorial, or "auto-icon," by having his body preserved after death and exhibited in some suitable viewing spot.

The philosopher even went so far as to suggest that "if a country gentleman had rows of trees leading to his dwelling, the Auto-Icons of his family might alternate with the trees." Bentham proposed having them varnished as a protection against the weather. Alternatively, preserved heads could be exhibited in a specially designed cabinet.

A museum was another possibility; auto-icons of prominent people might be manipulated like puppets in theatrical tableaux, or "Dialogues of the Dead . . . for the moral edification of the lower orders." Bentham foresaw the possibility of legal problems, however, and speculated that an auto-icon might be seized by the deceased's creditors as an asset, or even pawned.

Bentham's will, dated a week before his death, left his body to his friend Dr. Thomas Southwood Smith. In the will was the request that Smith use Bentham's body as the subject of a scientific lecture and then preserve the skeleton and head according to a carefully designed plan.

Smith duly sent out invitations, and at 3 P.M. on June 9, guests arrived at the School of Anatomy and Medicine in London to witness the dissection.

Macabre scene

Smith addressed the assembled audience while Bentham's body lay on a slab before him. The scene must have resembled the gothic excesses of Dr. Frankenstein's laboratory: as Smith began his lecture, a violent thunderstorm erupted, and it continued to rage while he performed the task of dismembering Bentham's cadaver.

Later Smith attempted to mummify the head, but it became so dark, leathery, and expressionless that he had a wax model made by the skillful French artist Jacques Talrich. Topped by a wide-brimmed hat, the wax head was attached to the skeleton, which was padded out with hay and dressed in

Bentham's own clothes; his favorite walking stick, nicknamed Dapple, was placed across his knee.

For 18 years Smith kept Bentham's auto-icon in his apartment. Then in 1850 he presented it to University College, London, which Bentham had been instrumental in founding.

An examination of the auto-icon in 1898 revealed that Bentham's imperfectly mummified head, wrapped in tarred cloth, was nestling within his rib cage. For many years the head was exhibited between his feet, until the authorities pronounced it too grisly to display and had it locked away.

A second examination took place in 1939, and Bentham's moth-eaten vest was replaced, his clothes laundered, and the stuffing renewed. To reduce the risk of his being bombed during World War II, Bentham was evacuated to Hertfordshire. When the war was over, the great man was returned to a new glass-fronted case in University College, where he sits to this day.

THE KING OF THE MISERS

How mean can you get?

DANIEL DANCER was the son of a miser and the grandson of another. He lived with his sister, who was also a miser. His entire life was devoted to miserly pursuits, which he carried to such an extreme that he may truly be regarded as the king of the misers.

Dancer inherited a tract of land north of London and with it a considerable annual income. His food, however, consisted of one meal a day: a meager scrap of meat and a single cold dumpling. On one occasion he found a dead sheep in a field. Despite the fact that it was beginning to decompose, Dancer took it home and had it made into mutton pies—which he kept locked in a trunk.

Another time, his neighbor Lady Tempest sent him a gift of a trout cooked in claret. The weather was frosty, and the trout arrived frozen. Too stingy to go to the expense of heating it, Dancer sat on the fish until it had thawed enough for him to eat it.

Dancer slept in a sack, and his clothes consisted largely of rags and bundles of straw. He did have one sartorial extravagance: once a year he would buy a secondhand shirt, which he would then wear until it fell to pieces. When his supplier of shirts overcharged him by threepence, he took her to court. He avoided any danger of being sued himself when his dog began worrying sheep: he took it to the local blacksmith and had its teeth filed down.

Once, on a rare visit to London, Dancer was mistaken for a beggar and given a halfpenny. "Every little helps," he commented as he pocketed it. If offered a pinch of snuff, he would take it and put it in a box. When the box was full, he used it to barter for candles. If he had insufficient snuff for candles, he preferred to sit in the dark.

Brotherly love

In 1766 Dancer's sister, who worked as his housekeeper, was dying. He refused to call a doctor, saying: "Why should I waste my money in wickedly endeavouring to counteract the will of Providence? If the old girl's time is come . . . she may as well die now as at any future period."

Miss Dancer was looked after by Lady Tempest, to whom she intended to leave her fortune. However, when Miss Dancer died, it was found that she had not left a will, and Dancer managed to acquire two-thirds of her estate by claiming 30 years' back rent for her accommodation and food.

Dancer delighted in hiding his money in obscure places, such as under piles of farmyard manure. He was so terrified he would be robbed that he barricaded himself in his house.

Dancer died in 1794. The kindly Lady Tempest inherited his estate. Unfortunately, while she had been nursing Dancer on his deathbed, she had taken ill. Within four months she, too, was dead.

Engraving of Daniel Dancer, made soon after his death

THE MAN WHO LIVED IN A BOX

A cozy little place in the country

TO MOST PEOPLE the thought of living in a small box only three feet wide, four feet long, and five feet high would be enough to bring on an attack of claustrophobia, the fear of confined spaces. Yet this is exactly how one Englishman, Alexander Wortley, chose to live until his death at the age of 80 in 1980.

The green box Wortley called home looked like a minitrailer. Except for an arched metal roof, it was made of wood and sat on four small wheels. Inside were an old bus seat—with an extension for Wortley's feet—and a few shelves for his food and possessions.

Despite the apparent drawbacks of such a small home, to Wortley it had its advantages. For one thing, he was able to pull this bizarre, homemade structure all over the country, stopping wherever he pleased. By adopting this alternative lifestyle, Wortley could also avoid the unwanted attentions of government. A fiercely independent man, he had no wish to pay local or national taxes; in return, he expected no welfare or pension benefits.

Wortley was a man of singular ideas. His many idiosyncrasies included a deep suspicion of zippers. He would invariably take them out of any trousers he was given because he did not relish having a lightning conductor near any sensitive area.

His eccentricity also extended to his speech, since he suffered from a disorder known as Klang Association. The sound of one word would remind him of another, usually unconnected, and his conversation would veer off in strange directions, making little sense to anyone but himself. On one occasion, when asked why he did not like telephones, he answered: "It's all that copper wire, all those coppers, all those policemen, it's all those poles, all those foreigners. Then it's the numbers, puts you in mind of black Humbers—police cars again, you see."

Wortley spent the last 20 years of his life as the caretaker of a secluded cottage in Buckinghamshire. Having a regular job did not make any difference in his lifestyle: he simply parked his box at the bottom of the garden.

COUNTRY COMFORTS

Getting away from it all in style

IN THE 1870's, guests at the holiday home of Cornelius Vanderbilt II in Newport, Rhode Island, could choose to wash in running water that was hot or cold, salt or fresh. They sat down to eat in a dining room two stories high, browsed in a library paneled in walnut and leather, and heard recitals in a music room that had been created in its entirety in France, dismantled, and then shipped to Newport for reassembly.

Vanderbilt, who with his younger brother William had inherited the family railroad fortune, referred to his summer house in Newport as a cottage. Called The Breakers, it contained some 70 rooms and cost around $5 million to construct. But Vanderbilt hardly used it.

Rebuilding the past

The Breakers was only one of a number of palatial cottages built along the cliffs facing the Atlantic Ocean in Newport—which by the 1890's had become one of the most fashionable resorts in the United States because of its pleasant summer climate.

Most of the Newport "cottages" were imitations of European aristocratic palaces. The Elms, built by Philadelphia millionaire E. J. Berwind, was modeled on the Château d'Asnières near Paris, although it also contained a Venetian-style dining room and a breakfast room decorated with 17th-century black and gold lacquer panels from China. Vernon Court featured a reproduction of a garden in England created by King Henry VIII for Anne Boleyn. Château-sur-Mer was English Victorian, and boasted a mirrored ballroom. Rosecliff, which featured a heart-shaped staircase, was inspired by the Grand Trianon at Versailles in France.

The earliest of the most extravagant Newport palace-cottages was Ochre Court, completed in 1891. Its interior was festooned with ornate sculptures, crystal chandeliers, marble fireplaces, stained glass, and carved and gilded wood. It cost $4.5 million to build, and its owners, the Goelet family, used it a mere eight weeks a year.

Marble House was completed in 1892 as a birthday gift from William Vanderbilt to his wife,

Alva. Modeled on the White House in Washington, D.C., with details borrowed from the Petit Trianon at Versailles, the 50-room house cost $2 million, the furnishings and interior decoration another $9 million.

The furnishings—including marble of all kinds and colors and a $75,000 fireplace with a mantel from ancient Pompeii—arrived by the boatload from various parts of the world. A special warehouse, wharf, and 10-ton derrick were constructed in Newport harbor to handle them.

Fit for the gods?

Marble House has bronze-and-steel front doors weighing a ton and a half each. Most of the rooms are decorated in a variety of French styles, while the medieval living room boasts original Gothic stained-glass windows. Most elaborate is the ballroom, smothered in gold, with bronze figures as candelabra and a ceiling depicting Greek gods at a banquet. Mere mortals wishing to sit down to eat needed the servants to help pull the solid bronze dining chairs up to the table.

Four years after seeing her birthday gift completed, Alva Vanderbilt left it—and her husband—for another millionaire, Oliver H. P. Belmont. His grandiose cottage, Belcourt, was constructed between 1891 and 1893 at a cost of $3 million. The design, based on a hunting lodge, was basically that of a stable, with elegant 60-room living quarters above. Belmont kept 13 live horses on the ground floor, and two stuffed ones upstairs.

The walls of Belcourt's central courtyard are clad in the half-timbering of Shakespeare's England. The banquet hall, with a floor of marble mosaic, accommodates some 300 guests. The 75-foot-long ballroom is French Gothic in style, with a vaulted ceiling, a musicians' gallery, and an organ loft.

Today these extraordinary buildings, some with original furnishings, are open to the public, who may be entertained by the sight of what a few spare million dollars could once make of a "cottage."

PLAYGROUND OF THE WEALTHY *The opulent home of the Vanderbilt family in Newport, Rhode Island, contained more than 70 sumptuously decorated rooms. The music room (above) was created in France, dismantled, and then shipped to the U.S.A. Lavish lawn parties, such as the one below, made The Breakers prominent in Newport society.*

CAREFULLY CHOSEN WORDS

The minor American author Ernest Vincent Wright had started his literary career modestly enough with fairy stories such as *The Wonderful Fairies of the Sun*, published in 1896, and *The Fairies That Run the World and How They Do It,* which appeared in 1903.

However, Wright's output was not prodigious, and it was another 15 years before he wrote *Thoughts and Reveries of an American Bluejacket*. The author then rested for another 20 years before producing his pièce de résistance in 1939, a novel called *Gadsby*.

The book took 165 days to write, and it was unique: not one single word of the 50,000-word text contained the letter *e*.

Books in which certain letters of the alphabet were deliberately omitted had been written before, and there is even a name for them: lipograms. But what Wright had achieved was indeed astonishing. The novel was nearly 300 pages long, and *e* is by far the most used letter in the English language. Wright taped down the *e* key on his typewriter to make it impossible to use, and by choosing his words carefully, succeeded in writing prose that, remarkably, is not noticeably forced.

But the strain was too much for him: Wright died on the day of publication. After his death copies of *Gadsby* were to become highly prized by collectors of rare books, and today they can be sold for more than $1,000.

FOR THE RECORD

A new meaning for "sight reading"

ARTHUR LINTGEN has an extraordinary talent that makes him well-known beyond the town of Rydal, Pennsylvania, where he is a physician. Hand him a long-playing record with the label concealed, and within seconds Lintgen will identify the piece of music featured on the disc. As an encore he can sometimes even name the orchestra and the conductor—without ever having played the record.

Lintgen does not claim to be infallible. He can identify classical music only from the time of Beethoven to the present, and only music he has heard before.

His performance has impressed the most expert critics. One challenge was held in the presence of two reputable musicians from major American orchestras. Devoting 15 to 30 seconds to each record, Dr. Lintgen managed to identify Bruckner's Fourth Symphony, Orff's *Carmina Burana,* Rachmaninoff's "The Bells" and Second Symphony, and the Saint-Saëns "Organ" Symphony.

Finally, Dr. Lintgen correctly identified Richard Strauss's Alpine Symphony, mentioning in passing that Strauss himself was conducting it. In each case he only looked at the surface of the record to help him make his identification.

Lintgen claims neither psychic powers nor X-ray vision. How, then, does he explain his talent?

It seems that Lintgen has learned to interpret the pattern of the grooves that are cut into the surface of a disc. He can "see" whether the music itself is loud or soft, and which instruments are playing when. This he does by recognizing the pattern that, say, a bass drum creates on a record groove as opposed to that of a violin.

An eye for detail

When the magazine *Discover* investigated Lintgen's talent, the doctor passed with flying colors. He identified all of the classical recordings shown to him, adding that one, Schubert's Fifth Symphony, was being played by a German orchestra. He also detected two "controls" that had been included in the test: one recording with spoken words and one with popular music. He called the two records "gibberish" and "disorganized."

How could he tell that a German orchestra was performing the Schubert work? He noticed that the recording had an upturned edge, which only Deutsche Grammophon records have, and he knew that that company records only German orchestras.

So far, Lintgen has confined his record reading to vinyl discs, but he is confident that he can keep pace with technology and read the grooves on compact discs. But since the grooves on a CD are closer together, he may have to use a microscope.

THE STORE WINDOW AFFAIR

The wrath of an artist

NEW YORK'S prestigious Fifth Avenue is home to many of the city's famous department stores. Many people go there to shop, others just to look at the window displays. But on a warm summer's day in 1939, one store window had attracted most of the attention.

The store was Bonwit Teller and the theme of its window display was Night and Day. But this was no ordinary depiction. A four-poster bed covered with black sheets, scarred with burn marks, symbolized night. The canopy over the bed was a buffalo; in its mouth was a pigeon dripping blood. The feet of the bed were the four feet of the buffalo. Across the bed, covered in cobwebs and dust, lay a wax mannequin, its head propped up on artificial burning coals.

The depiction of day was even more extraordinary. A bathtub lined with ermine and filled with water occupied most of the window. A mannequin in a voluminous ballgown was stepping into the tub, her features reflected in a mirror held in front of her by two wax arms that reached up from the floor. Flowers sprouted from every available surface of the display.

The famous window dresser

Bonwit Teller may have gotten more than it bargained for, but management might have anticipated the interest the window would create. The man who designed the display was one of the most famous and notorious painters of his day, Salvador Dali.

The Spanish-born Dali first came to the public's attention as a member of the surrealist group of painters whose art dominated Europe and the United States between the 1920's and World War II. The surrealists rejected the realistic portrayal of subject matter in their paintings and sculptures and instead used the fantasy world of dreams and illusions as inspiration for their work.

The brilliantly imaginative Dali became the movement's leader. His bold, sometimes stunning pictures often shocked and assaulted the art world, and his natural flair for publicity introduced him to a wide audience. When Dali arrived in New York City in early 1939 to attend the World's Fair, society lionized him. He was interviewed in many of the newspapers, his exhibitions were sellouts, his lectures packed. *Time* magazine featured him on the cover. So it was perhaps a piece of inspired

PROFESSIONAL ECCENTRIC *With his upturned mustache, wildly staring eyes, and bizarre dress, Spanish painter Salvador Dali has long been famed for his eccentric behavior. Here Dali poses with a drooping pocket watch on his knee, an image he used in many of his paintings.*

publicity for Bonwit Teller to have hired him to design a window display.

Once the display was set up, Dali left the store for the night. But when he returned the next morning, he could not believe his eyes. His precious work had been tampered with by an over-zealous employee concerned that the window display did not focus on the ballgown. The bed had been removed, the decor altered, and the wax mannequin stepping into the tub had been repositioned so that her gown could be seen to better effect from the street. Dali felt that the whole display had been ruined.

Storm in a bathtub

So enraged was Dali that, without waiting for an explanation, he stormed through the store and forced his way past the store assistants into the window display. In protest he tried to overturn the tub of water, but his foot slipped. In the ensuing melee, Dali and the bathtub crashed through the plate glass window out onto the sidewalk, shower-ing the watching crowd with cold water and splinters of glass. The police were summoned and Dali was arrested on charges of willful destruction.

Brought into court, Dali was given a suspended sentence. The incident made the front page of many newspapers, and Dali remained the center of attention and gossip the entire length of his stay in New York.

Not that this was the only time that the eccentric Dali had attracted publicity. His trip to New York had started off on the wrong foot when his design for a pavilion at the World's Fair, with the Dream of Venus as the theme, was censored. When the fair's organizers objected to Dali's plan to decorate the facade with an enormous representation of Botticelli's naked *Venus,* her head replaced with that of a fish, Dali withdrew from the exhibition in a fury. A few years previously, Dali had made the newspapers when he had attended an exhibition in London wearing a diving suit complete with heavy-duty helmet. He had almost suffocated when his air supply ran out and his helmet could not be removed for some time.

Such events conspired to keep Dali in the headlines all over the world, his name a byword for eccentric and outrageous behavior. But few events in his life made as large a splash as the time he drenched Fifth Avenue.

PUBLICITY SEEKER
Salvador Dali was notorious for the lengths to which he went in order to attract publicity. At a press conference in Paris in 1963 (above), Dali reenacted the story of Salome. On an earlier occasion, the opening of a surrealist art exhibition in London in 1936 (right), he wore a diving suit — in order to descend into the depths of the unconscious, he said.

SNUFFED OUT

At one time in Ireland, anyone wishing to taunt another by threatening to outlive him would say: "I'll get a pinch of snuff off your belly yet!"

This expression derived from the custom of inviting mourners at a wake to partake of a pinch of snuff from a dish inside the coffin.

In London in the late 18th century—the heyday of snuff taking—Margaret Thompson, a fanatical snuff addict, decided that a mere dish of snuff was not enough. In her will she stipulated that her coffin should be filled with Scotch snuff: "Nothing can be so fragrant and refreshing to me as that precious powder."

The coffin was to be carried to its final resting place by six pall-bearers, the leading snuff takers of the parish, wearing snuff-colored beaver hats. It was to be accompanied by a priest carrying a quantity of snuff, and six elderly ladies, each with a box of snuff to sustain them during the procession. Liberal quantities of snuff were to be scattered among Miss Thompson's friends and neighbors by her maid, Sarah Stuart; at a party at her house afterward an additional two bushels (16 gallons) of snuff were to be distributed among the guests.

Apparently, Margaret Thompson's bizarre funeral instructions were carried out in full.

THE WORLD TURNED UPSIDE DOWN

Comyns Beaumont's unique view of the past

IN A SERIES OF BOOKS published between 1946 and 1949, British journalist William Comyns Beaumont astonished the world with the following extraordinary revelations:

Jesus of Nazareth had been crucified just outside Edinburgh, Scotland—the site of the ancient city of Jerusalem.

Satan was a comet that collided with the earth and caused Noah's Flood.

The ancient Egyptians were in fact Irishmen.

Hell is to be found in western Scotland.

The Greek hero Achilles spent his childhood on the Isle of Skye.

Galilee, birthplace of Jesus, was Wales.

Ancient Athens was in reality Bath, England.

Legacy of Atlantis

Comyns Beaumont started his radical revision of history with the belief, innocuous enough, that the lost island of Atlantis might be Britain. According to the legend, Atlantis had vanished beneath the waves around 9000 B.C.

Comyns Beaumont claimed that the native Celts had colonized many countries of the world, notably in Europe, the Middle East, and South America. Then, he said, a comet had collided with the earth, destroying a huge landmass in northern Britain. The survivors spread the news of this calamity to the Celtic—or Atlantean—colonies, and so today we find the legend of a cataclysmic flood in many widely scattered cultures.

So far Comyns Beaumont had done little more than add another eccentric book to the pile of speculation about the location of Atlantis.

The old and the new

But then he noticed the similarities between modern British place names and those in the ancient world, and concluded that many of these places had, in reality, been in Britain itself. Loch Carron in Scotland, for instance, and the nearby village of Erbusaig sounded to his ears strangely like Acheron, the Greek river of hell, and the mythical purgatory Erebus. Achilles, the Greek hero, grew up on the island of Skyros—which could be none other than the Isle of Skye. Bath *had* to be Athens; the names of the two cities were too similar for it to be otherwise.

Then, reasoned Comyns Beaumont, if the Flood had occurred in northwestern Europe, it was surely likely that Noah—and every other biblical character—had lived there too. The British Isles were the true cradle of world civilization.

Once inspired with that idea, Comyns Beaumont was not to be distracted by the facts. For his theory to be consistent, all the other peoples and places of the classical world had to be in or near Britain. With unending energy he redrew the map so that the ancient countries of the Mediterranean and North Africa fit neatly into the map of Britain. It was irrelevant that Athens or Jerusalem, Crete or Ethiopia, persisted in occupying their habitual sites in modern times.

Reading between the lines

The impeccable illogic of Comyns Beaumont insisted that historians had distorted the truth in order to glorify their own countries. It was clear from a "true reading" of the records that Ethiopia was Ireland, Sodom was Bristol, Crete was just another name for the Shetland Islands.

As for Edinburgh and Jerusalem, the unique vision of Comyns Beaumont found many parallels.

The Dung Gate in Edinburgh was the King's Stables Gate in Jerusalem. Edinburgh Castle was King David's citadel, and Edinburgh's Nor' Loch was the Pool of Bethesda. Both cities had streets called Water Gate. The Mount of Olives was the hill just outside Edinburgh, named Arthur's Seat.

All this was consistent with Comyns Beaumont's lifelong belief in the innate superiority of all things British. His career as a journalist had been dogged by his frustration with newspaper owners and editors who, he believed, failed to represent British interests adequately. His new theory of history restored the balance, to his satisfaction at least — and to the amazement and entertainment of all those who read his books.

GRUBBY EATING HABITS

A feast of delicacies to tickle the palate

IN 1885 VINCENT HOLT, an eccentric English author, wrote an extraordinary book entitled *Why Not Eat Insects?* In it he attempted to overcome what, to him, was an unaccountable prejudice against eating insects and other unappetizing creatures. Taking the Bible as his starting point ("These of them ye may eat: the locust . . . the beetle . . . the grasshopper" — Leviticus 11: 22), he surveyed the world of insect eaters and suggested that people who declined to eat insects were missing out on something.

Tasty morsels

As Holt outlined, the consumption of insects is worldwide: Hottentots eat grasshoppers, grasshopper egg soup, and white ants, which are said to taste like sweet almond paste. Ants are used to make ant squash; its acid flavor is said to be similar to lime juice. Queen white ants are eaten in parts of southern Africa; the queen ant resembles a sausage in shape, and is even reputed to taste like one when fried. Zanzibar white ant pie is made from termites, sugar, and banana flour ground together to form a sort of honey-nougat paste.

The larvae of weaver moths spin nests — hence their name — and are considered a delicacy in central Africa, where they are eaten *with* the nest. In Mexico a giant water bug — so huge that it eats frogs and fish — is eaten as a delicacy. In North America the 17-year locust, or periodical cicada, was boiled and eaten by the Indians; less adventurous white settlers used it to make soap. Even in the West today, many people, perhaps unwittingly,

eat insects in the form of cochineal, the red food coloring derived from the dried bodies of *Dactylopius coccus,* a Mexican cactus-eating insect.

After examining such geographical precedents, and scouring history for examples of people who were partial to insects, Holt offered ways of preparing everything from stag beetles to caterpillars, termites to butterflies. He strongly advocated this rich source of protein for the workingman: "What a pleasant change from the laborer's unvarying meal of bread, lard, and bacon, or bread without lard or bacon, would be a good dish of fried cockchafers [beetles] or grasshoppers."

As a means of ridding agricultural crops of insect pests, he suggested that "these insect devourers should be collected by the poor as food." He was sensitive to the potential objections of the average person to such a revolution in diet; in order to tempt the jaded palate, Holt concluded his treatise by proposing such irresistibly mouth-watering menus as the following:

Fried Soles with Woodlouse Sauce
Curried Cockchafers
Fricassee of Chicken with Chrysalids
Boiled Neck of Mutton with Wireworm Sauce
Cauliflower with Caterpillars
Moths on Toast

While such a menu might seem outlandish, the eating of insects is nutritionally sound. But individuals will have to decide for themselves if they are adventurous enough to try grasshoppers as a substitute in a shrimp cocktail.

A CHANCE ENCOUNTER

Stumbling across Nauru's wealth

JUST AS ALBERT F. ELLIS was leaving the offices of the British Pacific Island Company in Sydney, Australia, one day early in 1899, he stumbled over the doorstop—a curious lump of wood that his manager had brought back as a souvenir from the Pacific island of Nauru, which he had visited a year or so earlier.

Ellis stopped to examine the doorstop carefully, for to him it did not look at all like wood. He carried out various tests and discovered that it was, in fact, a rock of almost pure phosphate.

Once believed to be formed from the droppings of countless generations of seabirds, but today considered to be the remains of ancient sea creatures, phosphate is prized as a fertilizer. And when Ellis visited Nauru in May 1900, he found that the island was virtually made of phosphate.

Treasure island

The eight-square-mile republic of Nauru—the world's smallest republic—lies in the western Pacific, nearly 200 miles from its nearest neighbor. Today, because of the phosphate that the island exports, Nauru's economy produces $21,400 per capita every year—nearly twice as much as the American economy. The tiny nation is one of the richest in the world, ranking just after the United Arab Emirates, Qatar, and Kuwait.

But the island's riches had not been won easily. For nearly 70 years after Ellis's discovery, the Nauruans were exploited by German, Japanese, and Australian administrations. Only when Nauru gained its independence from Australia in 1968 did the islanders begin to reap the full benefits of their store of mineral treasure.

The 4,600 citizens of Nauru pay no taxes. And they enjoy superb medical care (anywhere in the world), schools, telephone calls, and public transportation entirely free of charge. When Nauruans marry, a house is placed at their disposal in which they can live rent-free for as long as they wish, with all bills and maintenance costs paid.

Consumer goods are abundant, and many families have three or four cars—despite the fact that the round trip on the island's single road takes only 20 minutes.

Not that this wealth has changed the islanders much. Most live in simple houses, sleeping on mats woven in a pattern unique to each of the island's 10 tribes. It is forbidden for a member of one tribe to copy the patterns of another, just as legends and songs of one tribe may not be told or sung by someone from another—no matter how well known they are to everyone.

And Nauruan hospitality is legendary. The custom of *bubutsi* still flourishes: anyone expressing admiration for something—a car, a boat, a refrigerator—is given it immediately.

Planning ahead

The Nauruans are fully aware that the phosphate cannot last forever. Since it is estimated that the source of the island's present good fortune will run out by the end of the century, the government has made investments abroad: Nauru owns Australia's tallest skyscraper (the 52-story Nauru House in Melbourne), as well as hotels and office buildings around the world, and it has set up five long-term trust funds. And the island has become a tax haven for those who need one—a kind of Switzerland of the Pacific Ocean.

All this is designed to produce enough capital by the year 2000 so that, without the phosphate, Nauruans will still enjoy a tidy income. One estimate puts that income as high as $500,000 for each and every year of every Nauruan's life.

WEALTH UNDERFOOT
The tiny island republic of Nauru (below) — a mere eight square miles — owes its wealth to its vast resources of phosphate. Inhabitants mine (at left) and then export enough of the mineral every year to make the country one of the world's richest nations.

THE HERMITS OF HARLEM

They lived and died in a house full of junk

ON MARCH 21, 1947, the 122nd Street police station in New York City received a call from a man claiming that there was a dead body at 2078 Fifth Avenue. The police knew the house, a decaying three-story brownstone in a rundown part of Harlem, and its inhabitants, Langley and Homer Collyer, two eccentric recluses.

No one could recall having seen Homer for years. There were even rumors that his dead body was in the house. Langley was seen only when he went out on furtive sorties, usually after midnight. He had earned himself the nickname of "the ghostly man."

The day after the call, patrolman William Barker broke into the second-floor bedroom. What he found there took his breath away. The room was filled from floor to ceiling with objects of every shape, size, and kind. It took him several hours to cross the few feet to where the dead body of Homer lay, shrouded in an ancient check bathrobe.

The autopsy revealed that Homer had not eaten for several days and had died of a heart attack. There was no sign of Langley, and the authorities immediately began to search for him.

A full house

It took three weeks to sift through the estimated 136 tons of junk with which the house was filled. The bizarre collection of objects included 14 grand pianos, two organs, and a clavichord; human medical specimens preserved in glass jars; the chassis of a Model-T Ford; a library of thousands of medical and engineering books; an armory of weapons; the top of a carriage; six U.S. flags and

LEGACY OF A LIFETIME *New York City police sift through the mountains of trash that filled the home of Homer and Langley Collyer. At the time Homer's body was discovered in the house, his younger brother, Langley (at right in a rare photograph taken in 1945), was still unaccounted for.*

one Union Jack; a primitive X-ray machine; and 34 bank deposit books with the balance totaling $3,007.18.

Gradually the story of the Hermits of Harlem unfolded, and the presence of some of the contents of the house began to be explained.

Homer Lusk Collyer and Langley Collyer were born in 1881 and 1885, respectively. Their father, Dr. Herman L. Collyer, was an eminent gynecologist and their mother, Susie Gage Frost Collyer, a well-born lady noted for her musical abilities.

The family set up home at 2078 Fifth Avenue in then-fashionable Harlem. But around 1909 Herman left. When he died in 1923, all the furniture, medical equipment, and books that he had collected over the years were taken back to Fifth Avenue and crammed into his wife's house.

Life in early Harlem

Langley had been trained as an engineer; Homer became a lawyer. Both were eccentric in innocuous ways—increasingly so when left to fend for themselves after their mother's death in 1929. Langley apparently never had a job, but was always tinkering with inventions, such as one for vacuuming the insides of pianos, and attempting to make the Model-T engine run the electric lighting.

In the 1930's Homer became blind, crippled with

WEIRD HOUSE *The Collyers' mansion inspired many bizarre tales, but their macabre story is stranger than fiction.*

rheumatism, and progressively paralyzed. Langley devoted the rest of his life to caring for him. Distrustful of doctors, but with access to his father's extensive medical library, Langley devised odd "cures" for his brother's illnesses, subjecting him to such regimes as a diet of 100 oranges a week, black bread, and peanut butter.

The house was already cluttered with the contents of two large homes, but Langley stuffed it with yet more objects picked up on his nightly excursions. After all windows were boarded up, and the gas, electricity, and water cut off, one small oil stove served all their cooking and heating needs; Langley collected water from a standpipe four blocks away.

On more than one occasion thieves tried to break in to steal the fortune that was rumored to be kept in the house. Langley responded by building booby traps, intricate systems of trip wires and ropes that would bring tons of rubbish crashing down on any unwary burglar. A honeycomb network of tunnels carved out in the mountains of junk enabled Langley to grope his way to where Homer sat.

A trap is sprung

As the world's newspapers revealed the secrets of 2078 Fifth Avenue, there was a final, grisly twist. On April 8, Artie Matthews, one of the workmen commissioned to clear the place, raised a pile of newspapers, tin boxes, and other debris near the spot where Homer had been found. His horrified gaze fell first on a foot, then on the remains of a body. It had been gnawed by rats, but there was no doubt that it was Langley Collyer.

In death, as in life, Langley was wearing a strange collection of clothes that included an old jacket, a red flannel bathrobe, several pairs of trousers, and blue overalls. An onion sack was tied around his neck; another was draped over his shoulders.

Langley had died some time *before* his brother, suffocated under the garbage that had cascaded down upon him when, in the dim light of his warren of tunnels, he had sprung one of his own burglar traps.

Homer's death was now easily explained. Blind and paralyzed, and totally dependent on Langley, he had died of starvation and shock.

The house was gradually emptied, and its more valuable contents sold at auction. But despite the Collyer brothers' lifelong hoarding, the 150 items raised only $1,800.

The house, too, has gone. Condemned as a health and fire hazard, number 2078 Fifth Avenue was razed to the ground. Today it is a parking lot.

ROLLS-ROYCES OF THE RAJ

Vast wealth reflected in automobiles

THE WEALTH OF THE Indian princes of days gone by is legendary. The maharajas chose to display their wealth in terms of fabulous palaces, enormous feasts, and vast collections of jewels and gold. Then, in the 20th century, many turned to that modern symbol of wealth and superior craftsmanship, the Rolls-Royce.

Between 1907 and 1947—the year of India's independence as a nation and the end of the absolute power of the princely states—a total of 36,000 Rolls-Royces were produced in Great Britain; about 1,000 were exported to India. In 1908 a six-cylinder Rolls-Royce christened the Pearl of the East won first prize at the Bombay Motor Show. The car went on to win the grueling 620-mile Bombay to Kolhapur rally and was later bought by Maharaja Scindia of Gwalior.

Custom built

Within a few years the reputation of Rolls-Royce had spread among the Indian ruling classes; its members vied for preeminence in acquiring quantities of these superbly appointed vehicles. The maharaja of Patiala, who died in 1938, owned no fewer than 38, while the maharaja of Mysore was

ROLLING IN MONEY *To the Indian princes of the British Raj, a Rolls-Royce was a conspicuous symbol of their wealth. The raj of Monghyr commissioned a Calcutta silversmith to decorate his Rolls (below), but not every car was so well looked after. Before being rescued in 1969, the Rolls above sat abandoned for years.*

the last of the notable bulk buyers, placing orders in 1947 for 8 Rolls-Royces as well as 9 Bentleys. The maharaja Jamsaheb of Nawangar had a garage that could accommodate 450 cars, including 8 Rolls-Royces. Each automobile had its own chauffeur as well as its own cleaner.

Various body shops altered Rolls-Royces to create many bizarre and extravagant vehicles that satisfied the sometimes eccentric whims of their clients. For example, J. W. Brooke of Lowestoft, England, fulfilled the order of the maharaja of Nabha, who demanded a car in the shape of a swan. Brooke made it in such a way that the exhaust discharged through the beak of the giant bird.

The maharaja of Patiala, on the other hand, preferred a 1911 Rolls-Royce upholstered in salmon-pink silk, with the bodywork painted to match. The diamond-studded dashboard was so valuable that whenever the car was serviced, it had to be protected by four armed guards.

Multipurpose luxury

The remarkable durability of Rolls-Royce cars under the toughest conditions created a demand for them in some of the most mountainous regions of the Indian subcontinent. A Rolls-Royce acquired by one of the ranas of Nepal was carried across the Himalayas to Kathmandu by porters, who used rafts to transport it across rivers. The maharani of Udaipur converted her 1934 Thrupp & Maberly Rolls-Royce into a jeep, and a number of vehicles were converted for use on tiger hunts.

The nawab of Bahawalpur (who also had a 1928 Mercedes S specially converted with lamps and gun racks for these safaris) even relied upon Rolls-Royces for his personal safety. He had a Silver Ghost converted into an armored car, complete with gun turret. And it is said that the maharaja of Alwar, after a dispute with Rolls-Royce over some modifications to his six automobiles, ordered all of them converted into garbage trucks.

An export ban introduced in 1969 meant that these opulent cars could no longer be taken out of India. Some remain in princely hands, and a number have survived to this day in excellent condition. The nizam of Hyderabad's 1913 Silver Ghost has only 345 miles on its odometer.

Other Rolls-Royces have been allowed to fall into disrepair. Many rare and priceless vehicles sit forlornly in ramshackle garages, while others lie in fields, their woodwork eaten away by termites, trees sprouting through their bodywork.

THE DETERMINED BIBLIOMANIAC

"One copy of every book in the world"

WEALTHY ENGLISH landowner Sir Thomas Phillipps had several strange ideas. They ranged from his refusal to allow either cheese or vinegar in his house to his desire to have as many servants and tenants as possible who bore the same surname as himself.

Sir Thomas also had two abiding loathings: the Roman Catholic Church (he was convinced that the Jesuits were intercepting his mail) and his son-in-law, James Orchard Halliwell. But his principal preoccupation was to acquire and hoard rare books and ancient manuscripts.

Paper weight

Born in 1792, Sir Thomas from childhood was obsessed with the idea of obtaining virtually anything written or printed on paper, including cartloads of documents from wastepaper merchants and the entire inventories of booksellers.

"I wish to have one copy of every book in the world," he declared to a friend. He very nearly succeeded. His collection ultimately grew to more than 100,000 books and at least 60,000 manuscripts—larger in its day than the holdings of all the libraries of Cambridge University.

As a result of his extravagant purchases, Sir Thomas was permanently on the verge of bankruptcy and was constantly pursued by creditors. Although his three daughters owned only one dress each, at one time his country house, Middle Hill, was filled to the bursting point as box after box of books was delivered. So many arrived that it was impossible to unpack his acquisitions, much less keep pace with them.

Visiting scholars, driven to distraction, would spend days hunting for an elusive text in the dusty heaps that filled every room. Because Sir Thomas had a morbid dread of fire, most of his collection was housed in coffinlike boxes that could be carted away quickly. Visitors to Middle Hill were struck, too, by the presence of numerous logs, a ploy he used to lure beetles away from his books.

As Sir Thomas relentlessly pursued his passion, the house itself began to crumble and its floors started to sag under the vast weight of hundreds of tons of paper. His neglect of Middle Hill was partly deliberate, however.

Sir Thomas's chief enemy in life, James Halliwell, had married his daughter, Henrietta, against his wishes. It appears that Halliwell was, in Sir Thomas's eyes, the worst kind of criminal, a book thief who had stolen valuable works from university libraries and even from his father-in-law. Having no sons, Sir Thomas was unable to prevent Halliwell from inheriting his estate.

To ensure that his detested heir would never receive anything of value, Sir Thomas's solution was to allow Middle Hill to fall into complete disrepair. He even went so far as to chop down and sell for lumber the centuries-old oak trees that lined the majestic mile-long drive to his home.

Room for expansion

In 1863 Sir Thomas decided to move—in order to accommodate his books. With the aid of 160 men, 103 wagonloads of books and papers, drawn by 230 horses, lumbered from Middle Hill to their new repository in nearby Cheltenham, Thirlestaine House. Still, thousands of rare and valuable volumes remained behind.

It is said that for years afterward the countryside was littered with the remains of carts that had collapsed under the sheer weight of the Phillipps collection. At Thirlestaine, Sir Thomas supervised the construction of room after room of shelving, riding from one to another on horseback. He was determined to achieve his aim and continued to add to his massive library until his death in 1872.

In bidding sometimes outrageous prices for early manuscripts, Sir Thomas greatly inflated their price. That was apparently part of his master plan. "Nothing tends to the preservation of anything so much as making it bear a high price," he announced with confidence.

A lengthy sale

Yet the ironic fate of perhaps the greatest library ever assembled by a private individual was that it would never find a home where scholars could have access to it. Sir Thomas's tempestuous dealings with leading British libraries made it impossible for one of them to take it over. His family had to dispose of the collection.

So vast was the library, however, that although individual items and large sections were sold privately or through numerous auction sales, the Phillipps collection is *still* being sold more than a century after the death of its owner.

In the course of these sales, many treasures have come to light. As late as 1964, part of a long-lost and unique medieval manuscript of the Roman poet Ovid's *Metamorphoses* appeared and was subsequently reunited with its other half at Magdalen College, Oxford.

Once destined for destruction as worthless wastepaper, this and many other priceless works were saved by the single-minded obsession of the greatest known bibliomaniac of all time.

EATEN OUT OF BUSINESS

Situated just off the fashionable Champs-Elysées in the heart of Paris, the Nova Park Elysée was until recently the most expensive hotel in the world. The lowest rate for some of its 73 rooms was $250 a night; the top rate was $7,000—without breakfast.

For $7,000 a visitor occupied the Thousand and One Nights Suite, with rooms on three floors, a private garden, and a swimming pool. A chauffeur-driven Rolls-Royce for the evening was complimentary. The Royal Suite, at $4,500 a night, consisted of five bedrooms, a reception room, seven bathrooms, a meeting room, and an office. Even the most inexpensive of the single rooms was luxuriously equipped.

The manager would personally greet guests with a bottle of his champagne and a bouquet of flowers. Visitors had the use of a gym, several bars, a disco, and a business service center equipped with secretaries, telex machines, and up-to-the-minute financial reports from around the world. With such facilities, the hotel seemed guaranteed to succeed.

But the Nova Park Elysée became a victim of the popularity of its restaurant. Designed to attract outsiders to the hotel, the restaurant established such low prices that clerical workers found they could afford them. The result: the restaurant was packed, but the hotel remained largely empty. The dwindling number of guests objected to the unpretentious restaurant and resented the intrusion of the clientele into the exclusive hotel.

In January 1986, five years after it opened, the hotel closed.

GUT FEELINGS

An iron-rich diet

THE ANNALS OF MEDICAL SCIENCE contain many cases of people who have tried to devour metal objects. Usually they injure themselves, and sometimes they die.

Yet there is one man who has devoted his adult life to metal-eating on a grand scale and seems none the worse for wear. His name: Michel Lotito, a Frenchman from Grenoble, whose stage name of Monsieur Mangetout means "Mr. Eat-All."

Lotito has given "eating performances" all over the world, including North and South America, and Japan. In recent appearances he has chewed his way through supermarket carts, television sets, aluminum skis, and several bicycles ("the chain is the tastiest part," he is reported to have said).

Apart from these substantial objects, he has consumed hundreds of razor blades, plates, coins, glasses and bottles, cutlery, beer cans, bullets, nuts and bolts, knitting needles, lengths of chain, and phonograph records. His major achievement to date: a Cessna 150 light aircraft. He started munching it in Caracas, Venezuela, in June 1978, and transported the dwindling plane with him on a tour of North America. At the rate of a few snacks a day, it took him until 1980 to finish his meal.

Lotito's remarkable eating habits began when he was a child. Mocked by other children because he had rickets, he came to win their admiration by chewing glass and proving his resistance to pain; he would invite them to beat him with bats and to stick needles into his body. Even today, sidelines of his act include using his body as a dart board and letting his chest be punctured with staples.

Lotito's technique is to cut objects into bite-size portions and to eat about two pounds of metal a day. He likes to first lubricate his digestive tract by drinking mineral oil, and then consume large quantities of water while he is eating.

Disbelieving doctors have frequently subjected Lotito to detailed examination, including X-ray, and have concluded that at least part of what he consumes is broken down by unusually powerful digestive juices. Specialists have also found that the linings of his stomach and intestines are twice as thick as average. As a result, while he can eat metal and other apparently indigestible objects, his digestive system does not cope efficiently with soft foodstuffs, such as eggs and bananas.

Lotito believes that the time of his birth—midday on June 15, 1950, exactly halfway through the middle day of the middle month of the middle of the 20th century—has given him mysterious superhuman powers. In 1981 he was attacked and stabbed, receiving severe internal injuries. He underwent major surgery and recovered rapidly. Three weeks later he ate a robot.

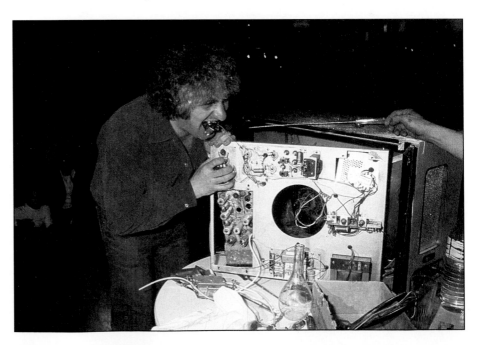

MR. EAT-IT-ALL *Iron, steel, aluminum, glass, and vinyl are among the staples in the unique diet of Michel Lotito. Known as Monsieur Mangetout, he has consumed many common household goods —including television sets— as well as an airplane.*

GAMES PEOPLE PLAY

Laughs at the expense of others

Barrel of fun   It is said that in the 18th century the American general Israel Putnam once invited a British general to a novel test of nerves. Both were to sit on barrels of gunpowder, and the fuses were to be lit. The last man to run away would be the winner. The unnamed British general accepted Putnam's challenge. But as the fuses burned, he became increasingly fidgety while Putnam sat calmly, smoking his pipe. At the last moment the British general fled. Putnam stayed seated; he knew that both barrels were filled with onions.

Washing the lions   For several hundred years the Tower of London was home to a menagerie of wild animals, including a number of lions that later became the basis of a hoax. *Dawks's News-Letter* for April 2, 1698, announced: "Yesterday being the 1 April several persons were sent to the Tower of London to watch the annual lion-washing ceremony." This fictitious event continued to attract gullible visitors. Indeed, 158 years later, in 1856, many bought tickets to attend the ceremony. They were unaware of the significance of the date, April 1, or that the lions had been moved to the London Zoo 21 years before.

TOTAL WASHOUT *One of the tickets sold for the "annual ceremony of Washing the Lions" hoax at the Tower of London in 1856.*

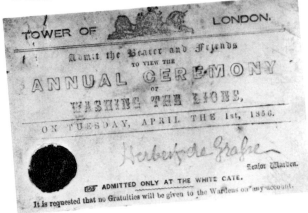

Artistic license   In 1935 the Museum of Modern Art in New York City held a major exhibition of works by Vincent van Gogh. Assuming that some visitors to the show were more interested in the sensational aspects of Van Gogh's life than in his paintings, American artist Hugh Troy contrived a simple practical joke.

He molded a piece of beef and placed it in a velvet-lined box with a label that read: "This is the ear which Vincent van Gogh cut off and sent to his mistress, a French prostitute, Dec. 24, 1888." Troy smuggled his supplementary exhibit into the museum and placed it on a table. Until authorities were alerted, the ear stole the show.

Small talk   Franklin D. Roosevelt, who was the 32nd president of the United States, was a notorious practical joker. Since he had to attend many functions at which he was inevitably introduced to hundreds of strangers, Roosevelt came to realize that most of those he greeted paid little attention to the brief pleasantries that were exchanged.

Roosevelt once put his theory to the test at a party in the White House. As he shook hands with each guest he muttered, "I murdered my grandmother this morning." Only one person responded to this confession: an eminent Wall Street banker. His reply: "She certainly had it coming!"

Swift end   In his book *Predictions for the Year 1708,* a soothsayer who used the name Isaac Bickerstaff made an unusually precise pronouncement: John Partridge, a cobbler turned astrologer and editor of a rival almanac, *Merlinus Liberatus,* would "infallibly die upon the 29th of March next, about 11 at night, of a raging fever."

On March 30 Bickerstaff published a pamphlet claiming that his prediction had come true and that Partridge had died within four hours of the time given by Bickerstaff; on his deathbed he had even confessed that he was a charlatan.

Still very much alive, Partridge protested that the report was entirely false; he even advertised the fact in newspapers. But Bickerstaff, together with other writers, continued to insist that Partridge had died and that the man who claimed to be Partridge was an impostor.

Partridge lived another seven years but spent most of them struggling to prove his existence and discover the identity of Bickerstaff. The latter, it turned out, was none other than Jonathan Swift, the author who would later write *Gulliver's Travels.* But Partridge died before knowing the truth.

Nothing but hot air   In April 1844 the *New York Sun* carried a detailed account of the first transatlantic balloon trip that had just been undertaken by eight men, including Monck Mason, a balloonist;

FLIGHT OF FANCY *A report in the* New York Sun *in 1844—that the first lighter-than-air balloon had crossed the Atlantic—was greeted with great acclaim. However, the account was soon discovered to be fraudulent. The* Double Eagle *(left) made the first official balloon trip—134 years later.*

William Samuel Henson, the inventor of the unsuccessful "aerial steam carriage," who in 1843 had attempted to launch the Aerial Transit Company; and William Harrison Ainsworth, a British novelist. The newspaper story told how the men set out from Penstruthal in North Wales in a gigantic 40,000-cubic-foot gas balloon named *Victoria*. Less than 75 hours later they had landed on Sullivan's Island, near Charleston, South Carolina.

Filled with technical detail, the description of the voyage was said to have been derived from Mason's journal, with footnotes by Ainsworth; the participation of such well-known figures added authenticity to the story. It was, however, a total fabrication—a hoax perpetrated by American novelist Edgar Allan Poe.

Despite a number of genuine attempts to cross the Atlantic after 1873, it was not until 1978 that three intrepid U.S. balloonists succeeded.

Spaghetti harvest On April Fools' Day, 1957, *Panorama,* a highly regarded BBC Television current affairs program, carried an unusual news item. Narrated by a distinguished broadcaster, Richard Dimbleby, the report told of the annual spaghetti harvest in Ticino, on the border of Italy

and Switzerland. Women were seen picking strands of spaghetti from trees and laying them in the sun to dry. Dimbleby assured viewers that "there is nothing like real, homegrown spaghetti."

Many responded favorably to the humor of the spoof; others complained that a serious program such as *Panorama* should not employ absurd jokes. But many viewers wrote to ask for further details so that they, too, could attend the harvest festival.

Family affair In the 1860's philanthropist Horace Norton, founder of Norton College, was given a cigar by Ulysses Simpson Grant, the 18th president of the United States. It is said that Norton decided not to smoke the cigar but to keep it as a memento of the meeting. On his death the cigar passed to his son and then, in turn, to his son's son, Winstead.

In 1932 Winstead attended a Norton College reunion in Chicago. As he delivered a speech to the audience, he lit Grant's cigar, remarking: "As I light this cigar with trembling hand, it is not alone a tribute to him whom you call founder, but also to that titan among statesmen who was never too exalted to be a friend, who was—" *Bang!* The cigar exploded. It had taken some 70 years, but Grant had finally played his joke.

THE BIZARRE BILLIONAIRE

The strange, secret world of Howard Hughes

HOWARD ROBARD HUGHES was already a legend by the time he was 30. A successful movie producer and daring flying ace, he was also one of the richest men in the world—with a lifestyle that was glamorous beyond dreams.

He was to spend the last years of his life as a crazed eccentric and to die in squalor, degraded and completely isolated.

Howard Hughes was born in 1905. At the age of 18 he inherited the Hughes Tool Company from his father, who had patented the only effective bit for oil drills. Worth $750,000 on paper when Hughes took it over, the company had made a cumulative profit of $745 million by 1972. By then his empire included a number of hotels and casinos in Las Vegas, Reno, and the Bahamas; mining interests; real estate; and the Hughes Aircraft Company — the ninth largest military contractor in the United States. Trans World Airlines (TWA) had been sold for $546 million in 1966.

Public and private

It was not only for his wealth that Hughes was famous. In 1942 he designed and built the largest airplane in the world: a cargo plane nicknamed the Spruce Goose because spruce was used in its construction. He took great pleasure in flying, and insisted on being the test pilot for the Hughes Aircraft Company. Hughes broke a number of aviation records; in 1938 he flew around the world in record time, returning to a hero's ticker-tape welcome in New York.

His exploits in other areas were equally noteworthy. Hughes became a Hollywood movie producer, with successes such as *Hell's Angels, Scarface,* and *The Outlaw.* It was while making *The Outlaw,* with actress Jane Russell, that he designed a special, cantilevered brassiere for her. He also frequently made newspaper headlines because of his considerable reputation as a playboy.

Then, in 1958, at the age of 53, Hughes mysteriously went into hiding.

His desire for privacy was absolute. From then on he saw no one from the outside world. All his messages were passed through a "palace guard" of personal aides—to whom he wrote more often than he spoke. Even daylight was too much for him. The drapes in the hotel room where he lived were always black and taped shut. When he moved into the ninth-floor penthouse of his Las Vegas hotel, the buttons on the elevators were altered to indicate only eight floors. Hughes managed to travel the world without a passport, thanks to the ingenuity of his aides—the same ingenuity that had kept his 1949 marriage to the actress Terry Moore out of the official records.

Strange obsessions

Hughes had curious eating habits. Sometimes for weeks on end he would eat nothing but canned soup. It would take him hours to get through just one can, since he would repeatedly send the soup back to the kitchen to be reheated. At other times he ate only steak sandwiches—and occasionally he ate nothing at all.

For months Hughes insisted on having banana-nut ice cream with every meal, and his aides panicked when they discovered that the manufacturer had discontinued the flavor.

The solution was one that only great wealth made possible: the manufacturers were asked to make up a special batch. They agreed, but the minimum order would have to be 350 gallons. Hughes's staff could breathe again, even if they had to find somewhere to store the ice cream.

The next day Hughes finished his habitual two scoops of banana-nut and then said: "That's great ice cream, but it's time for a change. From now on I want French vanilla."

Perhaps his greatest and strangest obsession was with germs—or what he called "contamination." Hughes once wrote his staff a three-page memo—one of hundreds concerning hygiene—detailing the nine separate steps he wanted taken in opening a can of fruit so that no germs would come in contact with the contents.

Long before his retreat from the world, Hughes had ordered that any document for his personal attention should be typed by a secretary wearing white cotton gloves and handed to him by someone similarly clad. Toward the end of his life, anything an aide handed to him had to be wrapped in 8, even 15 or 20, layers of paper towel. The aide himself first had to undergo a 30-minute cleansing ritual. Hughes put paper towels on the floor rather than walk on the carpet, and the sheets on his bed were covered in more paper.

Riches to rags

For all his wealth, Hughes did not surround himself in his later life with the trappings one might expect. When he died his wardrobe consisted of an

HIGH FLYER *Howard Hughes, a billionaire and eccentric obsessed with flying, regularly piloted his private airplane (above). In 1942 Hughes designed the largest aircraft ever built: the Spruce Goose (top). Built as a World War II freight carrier, it flew only once. Today it is a tourist attraction in Long Beach, California.*

old bathrobe, some pajamas, a Stetson hat, and several pairs of drawstring shorts. Sometimes he did not bother to wear clothes at all.

Despite his obsession with cleanliness, Hughes was living in appalling squalor. His blacked-out bedrooms were never cleaned, the bedsheets rarely changed; dust, dirt, and wastepaper were everywhere. He seldom bathed and never brushed his teeth. In 10 years his full-time barber gave him only three haircuts. The nails on his fingers and toes were inches long, leading one of his aides to remark that he "looked like a witch's brother." He was also addicted to codeine and injected it with a hypodermic that was never cleaned.

Hughes had four doctors in his entourage, yet refused to let them treat the sores that developed from sitting—and frequently sleeping—all day in an old lounging chair. Toward the end of his life, the sores were so widespread that the shoulder bone kept breaking through his weakened skin.

On April 5, 1976, Howard Hughes died of kidney failure. In his prime he stood 6 feet 4 inches tall and weighed 160 pounds. At the time of his death he had shrunk three inches and weighed only 90 pounds. With an estimated fortune of between $1.3 and $2 billion, he died the richest man in the United States—and probably the loneliest.

WHAT'S IN A WORD?

NAMES BEHIND WORDS

Some common terms from some uncommon people

Bloomers Amelia Jenks Bloomer, editor of an American magazine, the *Lily,* was a fervent supporter of dress reform for women. In an attempt to be free of the tightly laced corsets and voluminous dresses in vogue in the mid-19th century, Amelia Bloomer advocated wearing a jacket and knee-length skirt; beneath the skirt was a pair of trousers tucked into boots.

The outfit—which had in fact already been designed and worn by a contemporary dress reformer, Mrs. Elizabeth Smith Miller—caused a storm of controversy. "Bloomer girls" were refused entry to churches and other public buildings, and the *New York Herald* went so far as to declare that "those who have tried it will very likely soon end their career in the lunatic asylum, or perchance, in the state prison."

It was not long, however, before "bloomer dress" became popular on both sides of the Atlantic, particularly as a practical outfit for the newly popular pastime of bicycling. And the term *bloomers* was soon applied to just the trousers or any sort of long undergarment.

Bowdlerize In 1807 a four-volume *Family Shakespeare* was published in Bath, England. *Family* was part of the title because, as its anonymous editor explained, "those words and expressions are omitted that cannot with propriety be read aloud in a family." In *Macbeth,* for example, "Out, damn'd spot!" had become "Out, crimson spot!" and in *Romeo and Juliet,* the heroine's speech declaring her love for her suitor was reduced to less than half its original length.

In 1818 an expanded 10-volume edition of the *Family Shakespeare* appeared with the name T. Bowdler listed as editor. Dr. Thomas Bowdler was a retired English medical practitioner and a leading light in the Society for the Suppression of Vice. An expurgated version of Edward Gibbon's *Decline and Fall of the Roman Empire* was issued under Dr. Bowdler's name in 1825, and although he died the same year, within a decade *bowdlerize* was being used to describe any absurdly prudish form of literary censorship.

There is strong evidence, however, that this term may have been derived from the wrong

Bowdler. The doctor's sister, Harriet, a middle-aged spinster, was probably responsible for the work, which may explain why the first edition of the *Family Shakespeare* was published anonymously. Once the work was a proven success, her brother stepped forward as its supposed editor, and so it is Thomas rather than Harriet who is today remembered as the originator of bowdlerizing.

Celsius In 1742 Anders Celsius, a Swedish-born astronomer, invented the thermometer that today bears his name, in order to provide a simpler version of the already existing Fahrenheit instrument (named for Daniel Gabriel Fahrenheit). Celsius designated 0° as the boiling point of water at sea level, and 100° as the temperature at which water freezes; but after his death the 0° and the 100° were transposed. For more than 200 years the scale he devised was called centigrade, but in 1948 scientists honored him by renaming it Celsius.

Dahlia Prized by the Aztecs, the dahlia, a native flower of Mexico and Central America, was introduced into Europe at the end of the 18th century by the German naturalist Friedrich von Humboldt. Its name honors a Swedish botanist who had died in 1789, Anders Dahl; allegedly, the bloom of the plant resembled Dahl's untidy hair.

Jacuzzi The whirlpool bath widely known as a Jacuzzi is named for Candido Jacuzzi, an Italian immigrant to the United States. His family was originally involved in aircraft production, but in 1921 the death of one of Jacuzzi's brothers in the crash of a prototype monoplane influenced his mother to ground the family and urge a change of direction into a less hazardous field: manufacturing hydraulic pumps.

Later, the senior Jacuzzi had the idea of using one of the firm's jet pumps for hydromassage for his son, who was crippled with rheumatoid arthritis. Perfected in the 1950's, the revolutionary bath started the fad of the hot tub. Particularly popular in California, it became the basis of a multimillion-dollar manufacturing empire.

Nicotine In 1559 Jean Nicot, a young French scholar and diplomat, was sent to Portugal to negotiate the marriage of six-year-old Princess Marguerite de Valois to the five-year-old King Sebastian of Portugal. Although his mission failed, Nicot took back to France tobacco plants that had recently arrived from Florida.

By the year of Nicot's death, his name had become associated with the plant, which was called

THE LEOTARD *Jules Léotard, a successful French trapeze artist of the 1860's—and reputedly the first to turn a somersault in midair—was celebrated during his lifetime in the popular song "The Daring Young Man on the Flying Trapeze." After his death, Léotard's name lived on in the tight-fitting garment he devised for acrobats and dancers.*

MAE WEST *"I've been in* Who's Who *and I know what's what, but it's the first time I ever made the dictionary!" is attributed to the inimitable Mae West when she learned that the inflatable life jacket (below) had been named for her.*

Nicotiana. But by the 19th century the word *nicotine* was assigned exclusively to the poisonous active ingredient of the tobacco plant.

Rastafarian   A movement that arose on the island of Jamaica in the Caribbean in the late 1930's, Rastafarianism acquired its name from Prince Ras Tafari of Ethiopia, who in 1930 became Emperor Haile Selassie. Rastafarians believe Selassie to be a deity and the leader whose spirit will guide adherents back to their promised land of Africa.

Stetson   John Batterson Stetson, a hatmaker born in New Jersey in 1830, established the John B. Stetson Manufacturing Company of Philadelphia, which made the famous 10-gallon cowboy hat. Before acquiring the better-known name of stetson, the hat was often called a John B.

Tawdry   Princess Etheldreda, the daughter of a seventh-century Anglo-Saxon king named Anna,

was the founder of a monastery at the Isle of Ely, England, and was canonized as Saint Audrey. She died of a throat tumor, which she believed was a punishment for her vanity in wearing necklaces.

To commemorate her, the fashion grew up in medieval times of wearing Saint Audrey silk ribbons around the neck. Stallholders at medieval fairs, however, were all too aware that the country girls could not afford real silk and began to offer cheap substitutes. As the years went by, the quality of these "Seynt Audries" or "tawdry" collars declined so much that the name came to be applied to anything cheap and inferior.

Tureen   Henri, viscount of Turenne, marshal of France, and commander of the French Army during the Thirty Years' War, once used his helmet as a soup bowl, thus giving the name *tureen* to any large serving vessel—or so the story goes. A more likely explanation is that the word derives from *terrine,* French for an earthenware container.

WHEN GIRLS COULD BE BOYS

How some meanings have been reversed

Backlog Once a word that indicated a desirable state of affairs, a *backlog* was a reserve—the back log placed on a fire to keep it going. Today it usually means a pile of work that has been neglected.

Girl In the 13th century *girl* meant any young person, female or male. To distinguish between the two, a female was sometimes known as a gay girl and a male as a knave girl.

Idiot Once used to describe an ordinary person, *idiot* gradually came to mean a layman, as contrasted with a clergyman. Since few people outside the church were educated, the term became associated with an uneducated person, hence an ignorant or foolish one, and ultimately with a person who was mentally deficient.

Nice The Latin *nescius* ("ignorant") was the root of the English word *nice,* meaning "foolish." In the 15th century *nice* came to mean "coy"; and in the 16th century, "fastidious," as in such expressions as "a nice distinction." By the 18th century, *nice* had come to mean "good" or "agreeable."

Prevent In the 15th century *to prevent* meant to act in anticipation of some occurrence. By the 16th century its sense had shifted to mean "to keep from happening."

Quilt At one time the term for the bedding under a person, from the Latin *culcita* ("mattress"), *quilt* by the 19th century had come to mean the covering on top of the sleeper.

Sophisticated Until relatively recently, *sophisticated* meant "false." To sophisticate a substance was to add artificial ingredients; a sophisticated document was one that had been altered by forgery. In its current meaning, the word suggests refinement and culture, without any remnants of its original sense of deception.

Upset Up until the 17th century this term meant to set up or erect something. Today it means the opposite: "to capsize."

With At one time *with* meant "against," a meaning preserved in such phrases as "to fight with."

THE WORDS TO SAY IT

It is curious that so many words that English-speaking people take for granted have no equivalents in some other languages.

It seems obvious that a flight attendant, a pterodactyl, and a space shuttle are very different things. But in the language of the Hopi Indians of Arizona all three are "things that fly that are not birds"—along with bats, skydivers, and airships.

In Greece the word *xenos* can mean "foreigner," "stranger," and "guest." The Greeks see no difference between them and, accordingly, are justly famous for their hospitality.

But other languages can sometimes leave all of us speechless— literally. We have one word for snow; the Eskimos, whose lives are ruled by it, can distinguish three kinds of snow, and they have a word for each of them.

Some tribes of Indians in Brazil have no word for parrot and none for palm tree. But they do have a word for each *kind* of parrot or palm that they know.

The number of words a language has for apparently identical objects is one measure of how familiar and important those things are to the speakers. In the United States, English offers a host of words for an automobile: *car, sedan, coupé, hardtop, convertible, cab, crate, roadster, van, compact, dragster, limousine, jalopy.* Some of these words are not found in any other language in the world, not even in Britain.

Equally interesting are the different pictures of the world that different languages reveal. The Chinese word for railroad train means "fire cart." In the language of the Shawnee Indians, a person does not say he "cleans a gun with a ramrod": instead, he says he "moves a tool to make a dry space inside a hole." And since the Hopi language has no way of presenting the past, present, or future, a Hopi speaker can only indicate how true he believes his statement to be. Thus in Hopi, "he will jump" translates as "I expect jumping."

BRAVE WORDS

Unique weapons during World War II

THE EARLY HOURS of December 7, 1941, marked the dawn of what President Franklin D. Roosevelt called "a date which will live in infamy." The day that the Japanese launched a surprise attack on the U.S. fleet anchored at Pearl Harbor in the Hawaiian Islands was the day that brought the United States into World War II.

For the next three and a half years, many islands in the Pacific Ocean became a vast, fragmented battlefield. Allied soldiers, unaccustomed to guerrilla warfare, fought for weeks to gain a few yards in desperate attempts to force back the Japanese.

An incident on the island of Saipan was typical. One night the enemy retreated a few hundred yards and a unit of U.S. marines moved forward. But in the darkness and confusion, members of the unit immediately found themselves under artillery fire—from their own countrymen. The marines urgently radioed headquarters to explain their plight. But the gunfire only intensified; their message was being considered a Japanese ruse.

Finally the marines received a curious request: "Do you have a Navajo?" Fortunately they had. He transmitted a message in Navajo—and convinced headquarters that the unit was one of their own. The firing ceased immediately.

Hidden weapons

The Navajos—from Arizona, Colorado, New Mexico, and Utah—had been recruited into the U.S. Marine Corps in 1942 at the instigation of Philip Johnston, the son of missionaries who had lived with the tribe. They were trained to communicate in a code that no enemy was able to break.

The qualifications of the Navajos for this specialized task were unbeatable: their language was totally incomprehensible to anyone who had not lived among them and studied it in depth. The Navajos were the only Indian tribe that German philologists had not studied prior to the war. In 1942 it was estimated that only some 28 non-Indians could understand what Navajos said.

As with other Indian tongues, Navajo is a "hidden" language, one with neither native alphabet nor written symbols, and it is spoken with extraordinary precision and subtlety of inflection and pitch. Depending on how it is stressed, one word can have several meanings.

At first 29 Navajo recruits worked out the code that, by the end of the war, some 420 of their fellow tribesmen would use. The code's vocabulary—411

LANGUAGE BARRIER *The unwritten language of the Navajo Indians was used as the basis of a cryptic code that the Japanese never deciphered throughout the Pacific campaign.*

terms—was based on association: dive-bomber became chickenhawk; fighter-plane, hummingbird; battleship, whale; submarine, iron fish. The Navajos used imagination and humor too. They called ammunition "all sorts of shells," and antitank missiles "tortoise shooters"; Australia was "rolled hat," and China, "braided hair."

They also devised a code for the alphabet in order to spell out words not included in the 411-term vocabulary. For example, the letter *A* became *wol-la-chee,* the Indian word for ant; *B* was *shush,* the word for bear. To make the alphabet more complicated, the most common letters—*A, E, I, O, N,* and *T*—had several coded alternatives.

Total success

Crouched over radios and field telephones, the Navajo code-talkers became familiar figures from the Solomon Islands to Okinawa. They sent messages at lightning speed in a series of rapid, guttural, singsong sounds that were incomprehensible to their fellow soldiers and the Japanese alike.

The Navajos needed no time-consuming codebooks or charts. They had memorized the entire code and carried it in their heads. Japanese cryptographers tried every known technique to crack it. They never succeeded.

CURIOUS ORIGINS

The unusual origins of some familiar words

Carat The word *carat,* a measure of weight for precious stones, derives from the carob bean, which grows on the *Ceratonia siliqua* tree. The bean is remarkable for its consistent weight of 0.2 gram; therefore there are approximately 142 carats, or carob beans, to the ounce (one ounce equals 28.35 grams). One carat is divided into 100 points, with each point equivalent to the weight of only about three bread crumbs.

Cattle rustling The term was not applied to stealing until 1882. The word *rustle* evolved in the 19th century as a variant of *hustle,* meaning energetic or pushing. It then came to be used as a synonym for *wrangler,* a cowhand. In the days when numerous unbranded cattle roamed wild, a rancher might order his hands to "rustle up" some of the mavericks, which he then branded as his own.

Dandelion The name comes from the supposed resemblance of one of the leaf spikes of this plant to the tooth of a lion—or *dent de lion,* in French.

Disaster and **influenza** At one time it was widely believed that most events on earth were controlled by the stars. A *disaster* was thus an unfortunate occurrence attributed to the unfavorable aspect of a star (*astrum* in Latin); *influenza,* likewise, was a disease resulting from the influence (*influenza* in Italian) of the stars. That word's first use in English was in 1743 in the *London Magazine,* which reported "news from Rome of a contagious Distemper raging there, called the Influenza."

Dodo When Portuguese sailors first encountered a large flightless bird on the island of Mauritius, they were struck by its ludicrous clumsy appearance and the ease with which they were able to catch it. They christened it the *doudo,* the Portuguese word for stupid. Even the bird's Latin name (*Didus ineptus*) emphasized its silliness. Since *doudos,* or dodos, tasted delicious, they were hunted, and by the end of the 18th century they were extinct— hence the origin of the expression "as dead as a dodo."

Film The word *film* is derived from the Old English word *filmen,* "skin," which in turn came from the Greek *pelma,* meaning "the sole of the foot."

Halcyon According to ancient Greek legend, Zeus saved Halcyone and her husband from death by turning the couple into kingfishers (halcyons). To give Halcyone quiet days for brooding her eggs, Zeus also ordered the winds not to blow for two weeks during the winter solstice. Thus, *halcyon* came to signify peace and calm, which led to *halcyon days* in contemporary usage.

Kamikaze During World War II, Japanese suicide pilots adopted the name *kami kaze,* or "divine wind," after a storm that had destroyed an invading Mongol fleet in 1281.

Knickerbockers Washington Irving published *A History of New York From the Beginning of the World to the End of the Dutch Dynasty* in 1809 under the pseudonym Diedrich Knickerbocker. The English illustrator George Cruikshank produced a series of drawings for a later edition of Irving's book. In them, the supposedly Dutch author, Knickerbocker, wore the loose-fitting knee breeches that subsequently acquired the name.

Mews The buildings known as mews are derived from the medieval hawk houses in London, stablelike barns in which hawks molted. (The word *mew* means to molt.) Known as the royal mews, the later adaptation of the barns for human habitation started a fashion for converting stables into houses that were then called mews cottages.

Normal The Latin word *normalis* meant that something had been checked against a carpenter's square, or *norma.* So anything that had had its trueness verified was held to be normal.

Sabotage The use of *sabotage* in English dates from about 1910. Used in France around 1887 to mean industrial warfare, it is believed to come from the French word *sabot,* which has two meanings: a heavy wooden shoe, and a kind of metal peg that is used to secure a railway track.

It is uncertain which really gave birth to *sabotage.* Did French workers smash machinery with their clogs, or did railway workers uproot the *sabots* to disrupt the trains? Since the first recorded use of *sabotage* in England related to a description of a rail strike that took place in France, the latter seems to be the more likely explanation.

Spoof The Victorian era was the golden age of the parlor game, and *spoof* was one of them: a hoaxing game invented in the 1880's by a British comedian, Arthur Roberts. The word soon came to mean any amusing prank or parody.

Tabloid The British drug company Burroughs, Wellcome & Co. registered the trademark *Tabloid* on March 14, 1884. Derived from the word *tablet,* it was originally applied to various concentrated types of drugs marketed by the firm.

By the end of the 19th century, the word had acquired a secondary meaning: almost anything small and compressed came to be called tabloid. The phrase "tabloid journalism," which described small-format newspapers (as contrasted with large "broadsheet" papers), became so established that by 1903 Burroughs, Wellcome & Co. instigated legal proceedings in an attempt to protect the trademark. It was concluded that the independent use of *tabloid* had become so much a part of the language that no damaging infringement could be claimed. Since then, the media usage has superseded the first meaning of the word.

ENIGMA VARIATIONS

Cracking Hitler's "unbreakable" code

O N JULY 25, 1939, six weeks before the German invasion of Poland and the outbreak of World War II, three British Secret Service men met with their Polish counterparts in an underground room deep in the Molokov-Pyry forest outside Warsaw. There the Poles offered the British the Third Reich's most precious secret: the phenomenally complicated Enigma machine that encoded and decoded all German military messages. It was a gift that would change the course of the impending war.

By the end of the following day the machine was in England, together with everything the Poles had discovered about its operation. The British immediately established a special center at Bletchley Park, a rambling country mansion, and gave the operation the code name Ultra.

Soon it became apparent just how complex the Enigma machine really was.

A fiendish device

Battery-powered to facilitate complete mobility on the battlefield, the Enigma machine resembled an electric typewriter. But when one key was pressed on the keyboard, a complex system of three parallel rotating wheels went into action.

Each wheel displayed a full alphabet. The accompanying plugboard, similar to a telephone switchboard, ensured that a different letter would light up on a panel containing 26 bulbs—one for each letter of the alphabet. The devious way in which the different letters could be conjured up made Enigma fiendishly difficult for an outsider to crack, even if he had had a machine.

The message-sender and the recipient organized the machine in a different way each time that a message was sent. Both followed instructions in an operating manual. Before the war the instructions were changed monthly; toward the end this was done three times daily. The result: any message could be garbled into any one of a possible 10,000,000,000,000,000,000,000 different codes. To crack it would require exceptional ingenuity.

Cracking the uncrackable

Living and working at Bletchley Park were some of the foremost code-breaking brains in the world, including Alan Turing, one of the greatest mathematicians of the time. He invented a 10-foot-high electromechanical device that could test combinations of coded letters from Enigma at high speed. The device contained more than 30 sets of rotating wheels; each set could sift 17,576 combinations at one time.

Unknowingly, the Germans themselves helped the British by repeating in their messages certain phrases, such as "by order of the Fuehrer," "with reference to," or "commanding officer." Once deciphered in one code, the message offered vital clues to the structure of other codes using the same phrases. Consistently, German operators would also align the three rotating wheels with the same three letters—such obvious combinations as ABC or XYZ—over and over again. This knowledge reduced the number of possibilities the code breakers had to consider.

The machine itself also had some limitations. For example, it was incapable of encoding any letter of the alphabet as itself—*W*, for instance, would never appear in code as *W*.

The British used this knowledge to their advantage. Occasionally they would send an aircraft out to bomb an insignificant target. Experts could then find the name of the place in the coded Enigma traffic that reported the incident; they searched for groups of letters that did not contain any of the letters of the real name in the same position. This was a way into the balance of the code.

Turning the tables

Soon the British were reading Enigma messages, and Bletchley Park was able to relay enemy bombing plans, U-boat positions, and the strength and deployment of ground forces on to the commanders in the field—often with disastrous results for the Germans.

Fighter squadrons could concentrate around British cities well before a German attack started; at the same time the settings of the radio-navigation system for German bombers, learned from Enigma traffic, could be disrupted. In the Atlantic, convoys carrying vital supplies to Britain were able to avoid packs of U-boats—as RAF bombers destroyed the vessels supplying the U-boats.

In 1940 Enigma revealed that Hitler had abandoned Operation Sea Lion, his planned invasion of Britain; the next year Enigma helped British warships destroy the battleship *Bismarck*. When British and American commanders discovered Rommel's plans, Allied bombers were able to destroy some of the ships carrying Rommel's troops to North Africa. And in 1944, thanks to Enigma, the Allies knew that the Germans expected the main D-Day invasion forces to land at Calais, not Normandy—and learned exactly what opposition would be waiting for them.

Careless talk costs lives

Because Allied intelligence was so good, the greatest fear at Bletchley Park was that the Nazi high command would realize that their code had been cracked. Instead, however, the Germans believed they were the victims of an informer or, in the U-boat war, that tracking techniques had improved. So closely was the secret of Enigma guarded that many of the Allied commanders were unaware of the source of the uncannily accurate information they received. Indeed, no intelligence was ever released that could not plausibly be attributed to some alternate source.

The breaking of the Enigma code remained a secret until the late 1970's; even to this day, many details of the equipment and techniques used are not known. But no future historian of World War II can ignore the crucial part the Enigma machine played in the defeat of Germany.

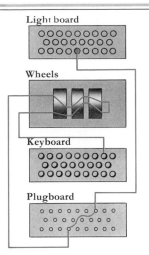

Light board

Wheels

Keyboard

Plugboard

UNBREAKABLE CODE
Despite its compact size, Germany's Enigma machine was capable of complex encoding. When an operator pressed any of the 26 letter keys on the keyboard, a signal passed through a system of wheels and a plugboard before lighting up a letter on a light board in its coded form. It was almost impossible to decipher a message encoded by the machine.

FLORAL TRIBUTES

The time-honored language of love

RED ROSES, boxes of chocolates, valentine cards, diamond rings. . . . In every age, lovers have found many symbolic ways to express their deepest feelings.

One of the most curious and complicated examples of lovers' language evolved in 18th-century Turkey. There, the passionate sender would assemble an entire ragbag of items; when painstakingly decoded by the hopeful recipient, they revealed elaborate thoughts and sentiments.

Some of these love packages, secretly delivered by a peddler woman, could easily be mistaken for wastebaskets. In addition to certain flowers, with their own traditional meanings, the parcels contained other objects, such as charcoal (meaning "May I die and you live long") or wax ("I perceive that all the ice of your heart cannot diminish the heat of the fire you have kindled in mine").

LOVE IN THE MAIL *Flowers as symbols of love have survived into the 20th century, as indicated on this French postcard of the 1930's.*

A well-known traveler and letter-writer of the time, Lady Mary Wortley Montagu, learned about this extraordinary language during her stay in Constantinople. She wrote to a friend: "There is no colour, no flower, no weed, no fruit, herb, pebble or feather that has not a verse belonging to it."

A blossoming trend

No one seems to know who introduced such language into Western Europe, but within a few years it had become the craze of fashionable lovers in Germany, France, and England. By that time, however, the objects had been eliminated from the packages and only the flowers remained.

Until the end of the 19th century, this romantic and colorful flower language captivated young and old. Many books were devoted to the subject, and publishers vied with each other to produce the most up-to-the-minute dictionary.

One such volume, published in England in 1866, boasted the inclusion of several new entries and their meanings—including 30 blossoms

from the conservatory and greenhouse, so that lovers would not be "condemned during the long winter months to floral silence."

Unfortunately, the dictionaries did not always agree on definitions, and decoding a bouquet involved many potential traps and misunderstandings. For example, it was often difficult to be certain that the yellow rose meant "infidelity," and a spray of orange blossom, "Your purity equals your loveliness."

By the 1880's the fashion for using flowers as a language had died out. Today many would argue that, like Latin and ancient Greek, it is dead. But even after all these years, red roses—recently adopted as the official flower of the United States—are still often given as expressions of love.

And no doubt in a spring meadow somewhere in the world today, a young girl is stripping petals off daisies while musing "He loves me. . . . He loves me not. . . . He loves me."

THE PLEASURES OF PARADOX

Some classic twists of logic to challenge the brain

LIKE RIDDLES, paradoxes such as the ones that follow have intrigued, baffled, and entertained people since ancient times. The reason: paradoxes are sentences or tales that make sense at first glance or first hearing, but they can also have another meaning that may contradict one's first impression. For example, the statement "This sentence has three erors" contains a trick.

The result can be a tangle of contradictions and irreconcilable opposites. Usually, first one meaning, and then another, becomes clear, until realization finally dawns.

The village barber

A man visits a village that has a single barber. The barber proudly tells the visitor that he shaves only those, and all those, in the village who do not shave themselves.

The stranger leaves the village and next day wakes up preoccupied by a problem that perplexes him for the rest of his life. He has remembered that the barber himself was a clean-shaven man. Who, then, shaves the barber?

At first it seems clear that the barber shaves himself. But if he does, he breaks his own rule: that he shaves *only* the men in the village who do not shave themselves. But if someone else shaves him, the barber cannot shave *all* those who do not shave themselves. Who shaves the barber?

The Cretan liar

Since the sixth century B.C., philosophers have wrestled with one sentence spoken by a Cretan named Epimenides: "All Cretans are liars."

If, as he says, all Cretans *are* liars, Epimenides is telling the truth. But if he is telling the truth about Cretans, he must be lying, since all Cretans are liars and he is a Cretan.

It is said that the poet Philetas became so perplexed trying to work out whether or not Epimenides was lying that he died of frustration.

Give a man enough rope . . .

A prisoner on death row was visited by his jailer, who was known to be an honest man. "You will hang one day between Monday and Friday next week," said the jailer, "but it will be on the day you least expect it."

The condemned man thought over the jailer's words and, after a while, his face brightened. He explained to the jailer that he had concluded that he was not to be hanged after all.

"I can't be hanged on Friday," he reasoned, "because if I am still alive on Thursday I will certainly be expecting the noose on Friday.

"But I can't be hanged on Thursday either. First, I know it can't be Friday. If I am still alive on Wednesday night, then Thursday will be the only day left. So I can't be hanged on Thursday.

"The same is true for Wednesday, if they haven't hanged me by Tuesday night.

"Then, by Monday night, there will be only Tuesday left, which means it cannot happen on Tuesday either. That leaves Monday, but because I now expect to be hanged on Monday, the execution cannot be held then, or your word will be broken. The truth is, you are playing a trick on me."

The jailer looked thoughtful, then said: "I can promise you that I am telling you the truth."

Thursday dawned, and the indignant prisoner was dragged from his cell to the gallows. "You are a liar," he shouted at the jailer.

"Not at all," replied the jailer calmly. "You convinced yourself that you would not be hanged. As a result, *any* day we set for the hanging would be unexpected. Which is no more than what I said."

A TWITTERING OF BIRDS

The inscrutable world of jargon

ORIGINALLY A FRENCH WORD meaning "the twittering of birds," *jargon,* in English, was applied to the codes used by criminals who did not want law-abiding citizens to know what they were saying.

Today jargon words are coined not to confuse outsiders but because the objects, jobs, or situations they describe may have no equivalents outside a particular profession.

Computer language

In the fast-growing computer industry, new words are born almost as fast as the machines come off the production line. Terms such as *bit, byte,* and *nybble* (half a byte) are now fairly common, but there are many less familiar ones.

Originally, homemade computers were nicknamed *kludge,* which may have been derived from *klug*— German for clever. Today some people use the word as a term of endearment for a computer, especially enthusiasts.

The opposite of a kludge—a large, unfriendly piece of computer equipment—might be called a *moby,* probably for the dangerous white whale in Herman Melville's novel *Moby Dick.*

Data assembled in such a computer might well be destroyed, or MUNG-ed ("*m*ushed *u*ntil *n*o *g*ood"). It may be necessary to *gronk,* or free, a jammed computer. But an operator who tells you about his "flops" is not describing setbacks but "*f*loating point *o*perations *p*er *s*econd," a method of measuring the power of a supercomputer.

Some of the easiest computers to use employ devices known as WIMP's, an acronym for *w*indows/*i*cons/*m*ouse/*p*ull-down menu. And "windows" are the areas on a computer screen in which graphic representations of certain functions are displayed—for example, a trash can to symbolize the disposal of data. With some computers the "mouse," or pointer, is used to select the needed function; and a list of operations may be seen on the screen by "pulling down a menu."

Movie madness

It is not only the real world of computers that makes use of jargon. At the end of a detective movie, usually the villain is caught, the red herrings explained, and the hero and heroine united. But for many the mystery may just be beginning. As the credits roll, some strange terms may appear on the screen. What is a gaffer? A best boy? A key grip?

Like many professions, the movie and television industries have their own jargon, a very private language often impenetrable to outsiders. A gaffer is, in fact, the chief electrician. The word is derived from *granfer,* or *grandfather;* it came to mean "foreman" before acquiring its present-day use on a movie set.

A best boy assists a gaffer, or a key grip— someone whose strength or gripping power is important because he erects and dismantles scenery or puts down the tracks on which the camera can move. A gaffer should not be confused with a gofer, an apprentice so called because he is constantly told to "go for this," "go for that."

Movieland jargon does not stop with the production team. There are many terms relating to distribution and publicity. For instance, a highly successful film may be known as a "gorilla," a heavyweight. It may even be fortunate enough to have "legs," or staying power; in other words, it is a film that will "run and run."

Social practice

Back in the real world, sociologists and the media have invented some terms to identify groups of people who share certain patterns of behavior. Some of the terms are euphemisms, such as POSSLQ (pronounced "puzzlecue"), an acronym for "*p*ersons of the *o*pposite *s*ex *s*haring *l*iving *q*uarters." This term is used by the U.S. Bureau of the Census to describe a man and a woman living in what sociologists have termed "couplehood."

Researchers studying poor communities have devised words such as *slurb dweller:* a California term that is derived from "*sl*um" and "sub*urb*an," hence one who lives in a suburban slum.

The 1980's saw the emergence of *yuppies*— "*y*oung *u*rban *p*rofessional *p*eople," who might be further identified as *dinks,* a term meaning "*d*ual *i*ncome, *n*o *k*ids," which is applied to professional, childless couples with much discretionary income. Yuppie couples who do have children could also be *taffies,* members of a *t*echnologically *a*dvanced *f*amily—a wealthy household with a home computer and many other electronic appliances.

Even people who drop out of conventional society cannot escape the sociologists' labels. If they decide to leave full-time employment to work for themselves, they may become *droppies,* "*d*isillusioned, *r*elatively *o*rdinary *p*rofessionals *p*referring *i*ndependent *e*mployment *s*ituations."

THE LIGHTNING LINE

"Electric intelligence" is born

ON MAY 26, 1844, an uproar broke out during the Democratic Party convention in Baltimore, Maryland. Twice in 10 minutes, Senator Silas Wright of New York had turned down his nomination as candidate for the vice presidency of the United States. At first the delegates did not think it authentic. After all, Wright was nearly 60 miles away, in Washington, D.C.

In fact, Wright had sent his message to Baltimore by telegraph from a room under the Senate Chamber on Capitol Hill. But so new and so unfamiliar was the "lightning line" and its powers of instant communication that a committee was put on a train to Washington to make sure that Wright had sent the message.

A flash of inspiration

The operator and the inventor of this marvelous new apparatus, America's first electromagnetic telegraph, was Samuel F.B. Morse. The occasion was a triumph for his perseverance. Only two days earlier Morse had officially opened the Washington–Baltimore telegraph line. But for 12 years prior to that he had struggled to make telegraphic services a reality.

The idea of an electric telegraph had occurred to Morse in 1832 when he was returning to the United States from France on the S.S. *Sully*. Some passengers were discussing the fact that electricity travels instantaneously through wire. In one intuitive leap Morse grasped a way to exploit a combination of electrical and magnetic effects to create the telegraph. He spent the rest of the voyage making notes for his invention and developing the code that remains in use today, almost unchanged.

On the same voyage, Morse also designed a device for producing and recording his electrical code—"making the presence of electricity visible," as he put it. The Morse recorder, or embosser, that was used in the Washington–Baltimore demonstration in 1844 scored the dots and dashes on a strip of paper tape unreeled at a constant pace by a clockwork mechanism. But the impressions left by the recorder were sometimes indistinct, and in 1854 Thomas John of Vienna invented a system using an inked wheel and paper tape.

In practice, however, operators learned to decipher messages from the distinctive clacking of the

LISTENING IN *The development of the telegraph in the 19th century was as astonishing to most American pioneers as it was to the indigenous tribes of the western plains. Henry Farny's contemporary painting, "The Talking Wires," evokes the changing face of the land.*

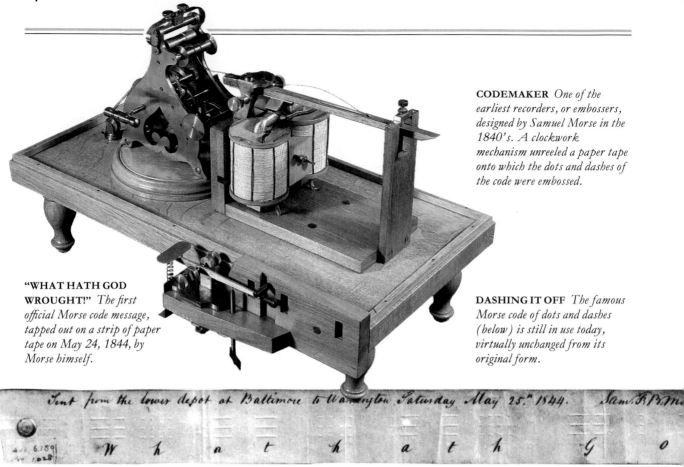

CODEMAKER *One of the earliest recorders, or embossers, designed by Samuel Morse in the 1840's. A clockwork mechanism unreeled a paper tape onto which the dots and dashes of the code were embossed.*

"WHAT HATH GOD WROUGHT!" *The first official Morse code message, tapped out on a strip of paper tape on May 24, 1844, by Morse himself.*

DASHING IT OFF *The famous Morse code of dots and dashes (below) is still in use today, virtually unchanged from its original form.*

telegraph key, rather than read the paper tape. So Morse developed the sounder to amplify the signals that were received.

After five years of experimentation and development, in 1837 Morse applied for a U.S. patent. By that time he had cleared the greatest hurdle to cross-country signaling—the weakening of the signal over long distances—by inventing the relay. It boosted the electric current and overcame the natural resistance in the wire.

Summoning up support

At the same time that he applied for his patent, Morse asked Congress for financial assistance in building a telegraph line. The proposition aroused enthusiasm but no cash. Morse then spent nearly a year in Europe trying, unsuccessfully, to persuade other governments to back his idea. He returned to New York in 1839, destitute.

For four more years Morse continued to petition Congress. At last, in February 1843, the House of Representatives voted him the funds by a tiny margin, and not before one member had suggested that the money would be better spent on a railroad to the moon. On March 3, 1843, in the very last

THE INTERNATIONAL MORSE CODE

ALPHABET

a	·—	h	····	q	——·—
ä	·—·—	i	··	r	·—·
å	·——·—	j	·———	s	···
b	—···	k	—·—	t	—
c	—·—·	l	·—··	u	··—
ch	————	m	——	ü	··——
d	—··	n	—·	v	···—
e	·	ñ	——·——	w	·——
é	··—··	o	———	x	—··—
f	··—·	ö	———·	y	—·——
g	——·	p	·——·	z	——··

NUMERALS

1	·————
2	··———
3	···——
4	····—
5	·····
6	—····
7	——···
8	———··
9	————·
0	—————

PUNCTUATION MARKS

,	·—·—·—
..	··——··
,	——··——
-	—····—
()	—·——·—
?	··——··
"	·—··—·

DISTRESS SIGNAL (SOS)

··· ——— ···

hour of the 27th Congress, the Senate passed the bill to President Tyler, who signed it.

Morse himself had already left the public gallery, convinced that his hopes were doomed. The good news was delivered to him next morning by Annie Ellsworth, daughter of the commissioner of patents. Overjoyed, Morse promised to let her choose the first message to be transmitted when the telegraph was completed.

The final hurdle

Understanding the need for publicity, Morse immediately started to build his experimental service between Washington and Baltimore, the site of both of the forthcoming Whig and Democratic party presidential conventions. If his telegraph could transmit news of nominations to Washington faster than the train could deliver them, the worth of his invention was assured.

Morse very nearly overspent his $30,000 by running the wires through lead pipes buried in the ground. Water entered the pipes and destroyed the wire. The wires were then strung between wooden poles erected next to the railroad linking the cities.

By May 24, 1844, the world's first intercity electromagnetic telegraph line was ready. From the chamber of the Supreme Court in the Capitol, Morse tapped out the first official message, selected, true to his promise, by young Annie Ellsworth: "What hath God wrought!" In Baltimore, Morse's assistant Alfred Vail received the message and speedily sent it back to Washington.

Within days of Morse's official recognition at the Democratic convention, the telegraph was being hailed as the wonder of the age; it was soon to spread with the railroads across the continent.

Although Morse was not alone in conceiving the electromagnetic telegraph, he did so independently of other inventors. And it was he who made the concept a practical reality. Even today, when the telegraph has given way to computers, and satellites bounce audiovisual signals around the world, his code remains an internationally recognized method of communication.

SPEAKING FREELY

Capitalizing on the First Amendment

FAREWELL YOU POMPOUS CLOWN, read a banner unfurled by some citizens of Baltimore, Maryland, celebrating the departure in 1987 of their mayor, William D. Schaefer, for higher office elsewhere.

Refreshingly direct as this message was, it seems fairly limited when compared to the range of abusive terms available in the English language as recently as the 19th century. These insults, if revived, would add color and variety to any political campaign.

Why settle for calling someone a fool when available words include *fopdoodle* and *alcatote,* both meaning simpleton, and *doddypoll,* derived from "dote," meaning stupid, and "poll," meaning head. In Baltimore they could even have called the mayor a *grobian*—a character from German literature known for being clownish, slovenly, and boorish—or a *mobard,* meaning much the same thing.

Are the morals of the candidate open to question? Brand him as a *cockabaloo* (a bully or a ruthless boss). Or expose him as a *waghalter*—a rogue so reckless he risks ending his days in a noose. Does he lack charm or good looks? Revile him as a *humgruffin*—a repulsive, goblinlike creature. Does he miss the best-dressed list? Label him as a *slubberdegullion* (a dirty fellow) or as a *tatterdemalion,* a beggar so scruffy that he wears more holes than clothes.

Since many politicians today are women, masters of historical insult might want to have in their arsenal such affronts as *besom* (old hag), *bronstrop* (lewd), and *ronyon* (a mangy or scabby creature). Or possibly *blobtale, long-tongue,* and *chattermucker;* all three are gossips.

Someday rival politicians may once more vilify each other as *dandiprat dogberries*—contemptible, insignificant, ignorant officials.

What opportunities the Baltimoreans missed.

What's in a Cliché?

Yesterday's quote, today's cliché

MOST OF US use clichés—phrases that are convenient because they describe in a graphic or shorthand way a particular meaning we wish to convey. However, many people regard clichés as indications of lazy thinking or writing because they are overused. In fact, clichés have become so much a part of the English language, often the original sources are forgotten.

Some clichés derive from proverbs or popular sayings, while others are of literary origin. An additional group of clichés comes from writers or famous people whose words or reported sayings have become part of everyday speech.

Absence makes the heart grow fonder These six words appeared in print for the first time in an anonymous poem that was published in *A Poetical Rhapsody,* a collection of "divers sonnets, odes, elegies, madrigals, and other Poesies." The book was printed in 1602 by two English brothers, Francis and Walter Davison. The sentiment achieved the status of a cliché when, early in the 19th century, it was used in a popular song, "Isle of Beauty," by Thomas Haynes Bayly.

And so to bed Samuel Pepys often used this phrase to sign off entries in his *Diary,* which he kept from 1660 until 1669. It came into common usage in the 19th century, when the special system of handwriting that Pepys used was deciphered.

Ax to grind This clichéd phrase is often attributed to the statesman and scientist Benjamin Franklin, who wrote a story called "Too Much for Your Whistle." In it, Franklin describes the way in which a boy is persuaded to sharpen an ax by a man who pretends he cannot operate the grindstone.

Although he introduced the idea, Franklin did not actually use the phrase "an ax to grind." The first to do so was probably the editor and congressman Charles Miner. In a piece entitled "Who'll Turn Grindstones?," which was published in a Pennsylvania newspaper, the *Lucerne Federalist,* on September 7, 1810, Miner retold a story from his childhood, when, as in Franklin's tale, he was flattered into grinding an ax for a man but received no payment or thanks. Henceforth, noted Miner, "when I see a merchant over-polite to his customers, begging them to taste a little brandy and throwing half his goods on the counter—thinks I, that man has an ax to grind."

The best-laid schemes of mice and men The full version appears in the 1785 poem "To a Mouse" by Robert Burns. ("Gang aft a-gley" in the second line below means "often go awry.")

> The best laid schemes o' mice an' men
> Gang aft a-gley;
> An' lea'e us nought but grief and pain,
> For promis'd joy.

The female of the species is deadlier than the male Rudyard Kipling's poem "The Female of the Species" contained the following lines:

> When the Himalayan peasant meets the
>   he-bear in his pride,
> He shouts to scare the monster, who
>   will often turn aside.
> But the she-bear thus accosted rends the
>   peasant tooth and nail,
> For the female of the species is more deadly
>   than the male.

Gone with the wind In *Le Complainte Rutebeuf,* the 13th-century French poet Rutebeuf remarks:

> Friendship is dead:
> They were friends who go with the wind,
> And the wind was blowing at my door.

The phrase "gone with the wind" became a cliché, of course, after Margaret Mitchell published her romantic Civil War novel in 1936. The book became a best-seller, and the film version, released in 1939, won 10 Academy Awards.

Hell hath no fury like a woman scorned John Fletcher and Colley Cibber were among several 17th-century English dramatists who wrote plays that included similar sentiments. But it was William Congreve who, in his extremely popular tragedy of 1697, *The Mourning Bride,* wrote the lines that included a phrase that soon entered the language as a cliché.

> Heaven has no rage like love to hatred turned,
> Nor hell a fury like a woman scorned.

Hold the fort "Hold the fort! I am coming!" was the message Gen. William Tecumseh Sherman sent from Kennesaw Mountain to Gen. John Murray Corse at nearby Allatoma, Georgia, during a Civil War battle in October 1864. "Hold the fort" was later popularized as the title of a religious song in a compilation published in 1874.

In the doghouse In James Barrie's famous play *Peter Pan* (1904), the irascible Mr. Darling punishes the dog-nursemaid, Nana. As a result, the Darling children—Wendy, John, and Michael—leave home. As a penance, Mr. Darling lives in the doghouse until the children return. Mr. Darling was based on Arthur Llewelyn Davies, the real-life father of the boys on whom Barrie based two of the characters; Nana was Barrie's Newfoundland dog, Luath.

Keeping up with the Joneses A comic strip called "Keeping Up With the Joneses," by the cartoonist Arthur R. Momand, was first syndicated in U.S. newspapers in 1913. Momand originally wanted to entitle it "Keeping Up With the Smiths," but he decided on Joneses just before the strip was to appear. Publication ceased in 1931, at the peak of the Depression. But the cliché lives on.

Mad as a hatter Lewis Carroll may have popularized the phrase, but it was already a widely used cliché before the Mad Hatter made his appearance in Carroll's classic *Alice in Wonderland* (1865). In 1836 Nova Scotia-born Thomas Haliburton, in *The Clockmaker,* referred to someone being "as mad as a hatter," and William Makepeace Thackeray used the phrase in his novel *Pendennis* (1850). A variety of explanations have been put forward for the origin of the cliché: that it derives from "mad as an adder" (as dangerous or poisonous as a snake); that hatters were traditionally driven mad by the effect of poisoning by the mercurous oxide used in the process of felt tanning; or that it refers to a particular 17th-century English mad hatter, Robert Crab.

Throw the baby out with the bathwater This cliché was probably originated by George Bernard Shaw, who used the same image several times. For example, in his *Pen Portraits and Reviews* in 1909 he wrote: "Like all reactionists, he usually empties the baby out with the bath."

Variety is the spice of life In *The Time-piece,* the second book of his six-volume epic nature poem, *The Task,* published in 1785, William Cowper included the lines:

> Variety's the very spice of life,
> That gives it all its flavour.

CLICHÉS FROM THE IMMORTAL BARD

The works of William Shakespeare have given pleasure to many generations. But they have also provided us with a number of phrases that have become such common, everyday expressions, few realize their source. Among some of his best-known sayings:

Be-all and end-all While musing on the assassination of his rival Duncan, Macbeth describes its potential significance as "the be-all and end-all."

Lend an ear "Friends, Romans, countrymen, lend me your ears" opens one of Shakespeare's most famous speeches (by Mark Antony in *Julius Caesar*).

Greek to me In *Julius Caesar,* Casca describes having heard a speech by the orator Cicero. But as Cicero has spoken in Greek, and not Latin, Casca has not understood it and comments: "It was Greek to me."

Eaten out of house and home In *Henry IV* Part II, Mistress Quickly complains that the gluttonous and overweight Sir John Falstaff "hath eaten me out of house and home."

More in sorrow than in anger Hamlet's close friend Horatio describes the ghost of Hamlet's father as having "a countenance more in sorrow than in anger."

More sinned against than sinning As a storm rages around them, a distraught King Lear describes to the earl of Kent his feelings that he is "a man more sinn'd against than sinning."

A pound of flesh In *The Merchant of Venice,* Antonio's pledge of a pound of flesh to Shylock, the moneylender, is regarded as a jest—until Shylock insists that he be paid according to the letter of the law. In the play the phrase is repeated nine times.

Murder most foul The ghost of his father appears to Hamlet and reveals the circumstances of his death. Hamlet's father describes how he was poisoned by Claudius as "murder most foul."

Gild the lily In *King John,* the earl of Salisbury refers to the fact that King John has had two coronations and remarks that this "double pomp" can be compared with other extravagant displays, such as, "To gild refined gold, to paint the lily."

THE MEDIUM IS THE MESSAGE

Communications from the sky

ON NOVEMBER 28, 1922, residents of New York City witnessed an unusual spectacle in the skies. As a solitary plane performed a series of elaborate maneuvers, it left behind a trail of letters in smoke. They spelled "Hullo U.S.A."

Created by British pilots Maj. J. C. Savage and Capt. Cyril Turner, the greeting was the first skywritten message in the United States. The two Englishmen had devised the technique only a few months before and had quickly realized its potential as an advertising medium. The first writing to be seen in the sky was the name of an oil company, Castrol, which Turner spelled out over London.

Although by no means universally welcomed at first (the magazine *Flight* described it as a "terrible prospect"), skywriting rapidly gained acceptance. Soon Savage was training other pilots in the technique—by having them ride bicycles, outlining the letters one by one on the ground.

In-flight problems

Skywriting with smoke was eventually outlawed in Britain, but it is still sometimes used for advertising in the United States and other countries. Today teams of flyers are usually sponsored by businesses. The Pepsi-Cola Company once claimed that its name had appeared in the skies above 5,000 different locations, from Canada to Venezuela.

As an occupation, skywriting does have its drawbacks. On one occasion Suzanne Asbury Oliver, who joined the Pepsi team in 1980, was writing the firm's name above Chicago when she was warned that a Boeing 747 was approaching her flight path. The potential danger so unnerved her that she wrote "PPEPSI."

And there are tales of competition between pilots. When one pilot writes "Buy Such-and-Such," a rival has been known to fly up and add the word "Don't."

A major disadvantage of conventional skywriting is that the wind quickly disperses the letters; by the time the last one is formed, often the first has disappeared. This is one of the reasons that a faster method, known as sky typing, was devised in 1949. Several airplanes fly in formation, and the smoke emissions, electronically synchronized, form a series of dashes that join to create letters.

In 1986 pilot George Sanborn, of Portland, Oregon, devised an even more economical method. A single airplane tows a 300-foot-long cable; attached to it are several cylinders containing a fogging agent. A computer controls the release of the fog at a rate of as many as five bursts every two seconds; words can be created quickly.

Voices from on high

Skywriting is not the only form of aerial advertising that has been employed over the years. In the 1930's sky shouting had a brief vogue in the United States, Sweden, and Italy. Advertising slogans were broadcast through powerful loudspeakers mounted on the plane's fuselage. However, some people were alarmed to hear voices from above, and the practice never became popular.

A machine that projected slogans onto overhead clouds was first demonstrated at the World's

Columbian Exposition in Chicago in 1893. A similar device was later set up on the roof of the Pulitzer Building in New York to advertise various publications. On one occasion, when the sky was cloudless, rockets were fired and the slogans projected onto the smoke that trailed behind.

Sky projection enjoyed a brief revival in the 1930's when Alfred Ganthier of New York City experimented with beaming advertising slogans onto clouds overhead.

Unfurled banners

Towing banners behind airplanes became the most widely used means of exploiting the skies. In 1928 the pioneering French aviator Louis Blériot patented a banner that could be unfurled and rolled up while the airplane was in flight; unfortunately, the device made the craft unstable.

A Pennsylvania engineer, Mark Sylvan du Pont, perfected the use of detachable letters on towed banners. Six-foot-high canvas letters were attached to lengths of tape, and a piece of netting served as a stabilizing fin to make the banner trail in a straight line. The banner was laid out in a U-shape on the ground: as the plane taxied down the runway, the banner was lifted into the air gradually.

Among the more bizarre devices for displaying an aerial message was the V-Liner, dreamed up by the Central American Manufacturing Company in 1964. What was intended to be the world's longest fixed-wing aircraft—it measured 378 feet from nose to tail, whereas a Boeing 707 is 145 feet—was also its slowest. A V-Liner was to fly at only 50 miles per hour. The extra length was added by extending the body of the plane with an elaborate framework to which illuminated signs with 3,000 or more light bulbs were to be attached.

The company had estimated that there would be a demand for 400 V-Liners throughout the world, and planned to launch the prototype in Britain in 1969. The British Air Registration Board's response to the contraption consisted of just three words: "It won't fly."

As it turned out, the board was correct.

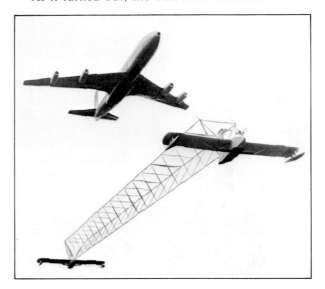

AERIAL ADVERTISING *In an attempt to display lengthier messages in the sky, in 1964 the Central American Manufacturing Company designed the V-Liner, which never flew. For comparison, a model of a Boeing 707 flies above it in the illustration. Below: A more conventional plane was used to spell out in smoke the name of a well-known soft drink.*

WORDS FROM NOWHERE

Common words—but where did they come from?

MANY WORDS in the English language have defied attempts to trace their origins. Even such common words as *blizzard, flare, freak, pad,* and *puzzle* are listed in dictionaries as being of "unknown origin." It is not even that their roots have been lost with the passage of time: no one can explain the appearance of certain contemporary words, such as *hijack,* which was first recorded in the 1920's.

The investigation of the source of such words has led to many different explanations, some more farfetched than others. Here are some examples.

Balderdash   The English satiric writer Thomas Nashe has the honor of being the first person known to have used the word *balderdash*—in his book *Have With You to Saffron Walden,* published in 1596. He used it to mean a foam or froth, but the sense was soon lost.

During the next century it was used to describe an odd mixture of drinks, such as wine and beer, but by about 1660 it had also come to mean a nonsensical jumble of words. *Balderdash* became popular in the United States in the 1920's. The satirist H. L. Mencken often used it to describe the speeches of politicians of the day.

But where did the word come from? There is a Medieval Latin word, *balductum,* meaning a curdled milk drink, that may be connected to the original sense. An Old English dialect word, *balder,* meaning coarse language; the Dutch *balderen,* "to roar"; and the Welsh *balldordus,* "idle chatter," are among the numerous sources that have been suggested for the later meaning. But to this day no one has discovered the origin of *balderdash.*

Ballyhoo   As a description for a sensational piece of publicity, *ballyhoo* was first recorded in the United States in 1913. Etymologists have been arguing about its origin ever since.

One possibility is Ballyhooly, the name of a village in Cork, Ireland. Another, that the word comes from *B'allah hoo* ("Through God it is"), a cry heard among the dervishes who appeared at the World's Columbian Exposition in Chicago in 1893. Still another belief suggests that it comes from *ballahou,* a two-masted sailing ship used in the West Indies, which in turn is derived from the name of a Central American wood used in making boats. An alternative suggestion: *bally,* a euphemism for *bloody,* was joined to *hooey,* meaning bunkum. A popular 19th-century music-hall song contained the phrase "the ballyhooly truth," or "whole bloody truth."

Butterfly   Is a butterfly so named because it "flutters by"? Does the name perhaps come from the butter-yellow color of the wings of some common butterflies? No one knows. But perhaps the most appealing explanation points to an ancient belief that butterflies stole milk and butter. In a number of folktales, butterflies are witches in disguise.

Gremlin   Gremlins were apparently hard at work during World War II, when pilots blamed them for everything that went wrong with airplanes. *Service Slang,* compiled by J. L. Hunt and A. G. Pringle in 1943, defined gremlins as "the pixies that are supposed to haunt aircraft and persuade the pilots (especially learners) to do strange things. They sit on the wings and make faces at air crew, thus taking their minds off the job in hand."

The idea that gremlins were grinning goblins may account for the origin of the word. In Ireland a *gruaimin* was an ill-tempered goblin. There is also an Old English word, *greme,* meaning "to vex"; the Danish *gram,* "a devil"; and the Old Norse, *gramr,* "angry." Farfetched theories have even claimed a connection with the Kremlin in Moscow.

The jinx of gremlins may have been exorcised, however. Steven Spielberg's 1984 movie *Gremlins* was one of the most successful films of all time.

Hobo   "Bums loafs and sits. Tramps loafs and walks. But a hobo moves and works, and he's clean." That is how Godfrey Irwin explained the difference between bums, tramps, and hoboes in *American Tramp and Underworld Slang,* published in 1931. So hoboes were originally itinerant workers, not tramps.

Could the name have come from *hoe boy,* a migratory farmhand? Or from the warning "Ho, boy!" shouted by American railworkers as they tossed mailbags from trains in the Northwest? French lumberjacks in Canada were known to shout *"Haut bois!"* ("High timber!")—the equivalent of "Timber!" in English—and thus they may have come to be called hoboes.

An alternative suggestion: the French musical instrument *hautbois* became *hautboy* or *hoboy* (and later the oboe) in English. The wandering minstrels who played the hoboy may have been hailed as the original hoboes.

TRAMPING AROUND
Although today the word
hobo *is generally applied to*
a tramp, at the turn of the
century the word meant
itinerant worker, not an
idle vagrant.
The exact origin of the
term is unknown. Some claim
that it might be derived from
hoe boy, *a migratory*
farmhand—or even from
wandering minstrels in
Europe who played the
*hautboy (*hoboy *in*
English), an early
form of the oboe.
The newspaper that hobo
F. A. Clarke holds (at
left) is a descendant of The
Hoboes Jungle Scout,
first published in 1913. In
addition to political news and
articles on labor and social
issues, it included
contributions from hobo
writers on the road.

Hoodlum The only aspect of the origin of *hoodlum* on which all the experts agree is that it first appeared in San Francisco in the 1870's.

Some believe that it arose from a newspaper article in which the name of Muldoon, leader of a street gang, was spelled backward. Thus the word became *noodlum,* which in turn was eventually changed to *hoodlum.*

Alternatively, the Pidgin English *hood lahnt,* or "lazy Mandarin," was used about the Chinese inhabitants of San Francisco. The street cry of "Huddle 'em!" has been suggested. Lastly—and perhaps most likely—the Bavarian word *hodalump,* meaning "rogue," was brought by German immigrants to San Francisco in the 1860's.

Posh Early in the 19th century, *posh* came into use as a slang word for a low-denomination coin, apparently derived from the Gypsy word *posh* ("a half"). Later in the century—and no one knows why—it came to connote a dandy. *Posh* was then subsequently used to mean stylish. It was first recorded in its modern sense, smart, in the English periodical *Punch* on September 25, 1918.

The most commonly repeated account of its origin is that *posh,* standing for "port(side) out, starboard home," was stamped on the luggage labels and tickets of passengers sailing from Britain to India. Since their cabins were on the side of the vessel away from the sun, these passengers paid a higher fare—and were termed *posh.* The truth of this is uncertain. Not a single ticket or label on which *posh* had been stamped has survived.

Yankee This nickname for a New Englander dates from the mid-18th century, when many sailors visiting New England were of Dutch origin. *Yankee* may have come from a Flemish nickname for Dutchmen, *Jan Kees* ("Johnny Cheese"). Alternatively, it may be derived from *Janke* ("little John" in Dutch). And James Fenimore Cooper, author of *The Last of the Mohicans,* suggests that *Yankee* comes from *Yangees,* an Indian pronunciation of *English.*

THE COUNTESS AND THE COMPUTER

Destroying a legend

IN 1975 the U.S. Department of Defense (DOD) announced its plans to develop a single computer language meant to replace the 1,500 or so languages—many of them mutually incompatible— in use at the time. A new, custom-made language would streamline all operations, simplify work schedules, and save millions of dollars every year.

By 1979, designs for the new language were complete, and the DOD was seeking a name for its latest creation. It decided on ADA. To computer buffs, it seemed a logical choice.

A place in history

In the story of computing, Augusta Ada King, the countess of Lovelace, for whom the new language was named, was a well-known name. Born in 1815, she was the only legitimate daughter of the poet Lord Byron, whom one former admirer had described as "mad, bad, and dangerous to know."

Ada Lovelace did not, in fact, know her father; but she was a friend of Professor Charles Babbage's

MECHANICAL THOUGHT *In 1834 the English scientist Charles Babbage drew up plans for an analytical engine—the world's first computer. His assistant, Ada Lovelace, was an enthusiastic proponent of the machine; to honor her, a present-day computer language has been named ADA. However, Babbage failed to complete the project before his death. The complex machine below is only a model of part of the mechanism.*

and, significantly for those working on the DOD project, an admirer of his analytical engine, a forerunner of today's computer.

A complex arrangement of more than 1,000 wheels and gears, Babbage's engine was designed to add, divide, multiply, and subtract with perfect accuracy to 20 decimal places. Like an early computer, it received initial data on punched cards. The system incorporated mechanical devices that, supposedly, enabled it to make the same kinds of complex mathematical calculations as are made by digital computers today.

According to popular belief, Ada Lovelace wrote the first program for this invention, which was far ahead of its time. Even the historian of the ADA project claimed that Ada Lovelace suggested the idea of programming Babbage's engine with punched cards, had recognized the potential power of the machine, and had explained its workings in a lengthy paper published in 1843.

Unfortunately the truth is different. Enthusiastic as she was, Ada Lovelace seems to have had a poor understanding of mathematics and an even weaker grasp of the feats that Babbage's innovative engine could accomplish.

Extravagant claims

Ada maintained, for example, that the engine could perform algebraic calculations and could even compose music. It could do neither. The commentary that she wrote was attached to her translation of a paper written in French by an Italian military engineer, extolling the virtues of the engine. On occasion the translation is nonsense: printer's errors, for example, were converted into meaningless mathematical terms. And the program credited to Ada Lovelace was supervised, if not actually set out, by Babbage himself.

Although Ada Lovelace had her difficulties in working out mathematical problems, her belief in Babbage and his invention is not in doubt. Part of the basis for her extravagant claims may lie in the fact that the engine itself was never completed; for years Babbage had campaigned for funds from the government to allow him to continue to develop it. Much of Ada Lovelace's spurious information was undoubtedly approved by Babbage in the hope that it would impress authorities.

Historical inaccuracies aside, however, reportedly the Department of Defense is pleased with the way its computer language performs.

GHOST WORDS

Words without meaning

SOME WORDS DO NOT DESERVE a place in a dictionary. Known as spurious or ghost words, they are there, complete with convincing definitions, as the result of error. The 19th-century scholar William Walter Skeat savagely described them as "coinages due to the blunders of printers or scribes, or the perfervid imaginations of ignorant or blundering editors."

Some common words are former ghosts that have become accepted through widespread usage. *Gravy,* for example, originated from a misreading of the Old French word *grané* ("containing grain") as *gravé.* Other words have been evicted from their lexical home once their origins were discovered.

Abacot   Up to the end of the 19th century, *abacot* was defined in many dictionaries as "the cap of state formerly used by English kings, wrought into the figure of two crowns." Some dictionaries even contained an illustration of an abacot taken from the great seal of the 15th-century king Henry VII.

It was Sir James Murray, editor of the *Oxford English Dictionary,* who in 1882 revealed the true origin of the word. In a 1548 history of the kings of England by Edward Hall, the printer mistook the words *a bicocket* (a kind of helmet) for *abococket.* This was then misread by other writers, changed to *abacot,* and copied by dictionary compilers.

MISNAMED HAT   *This royal hat has been wrongly named the abacot for centuries.*

Dord   The 1934 edition of *Webster's Second New International Dictionary* gives the definition of *dord* as "density." The reason: in the files of the publishers, G. & C. Merriam of Massachusetts, the abbreviation for density was listed as "D or d." Somehow the spaces between the letters were lost and *Dord* appeared. The mistake was spotted in 1939 but not changed until the 1947 edition.

Howl   An interesting dialect word that really never was, *howl* was at one time defined as "a house," allegedly derived from the Scottish spelling of *hovel.* This can be blamed on the printer responsible for setting into type Robert Louis Stevenson's unfinished novel *Weir of Hermiston* in 1896. Stevenson had been working on the book when he died in Samoa in 1894. The manuscript was sent to England, where the printer saw the word *howf,* meaning a shelter or hiding place, and set it as *howl.*

Kime   In 1808 Sidney Smith, editor of the *Edinburgh Review,* described the "savage customs" of Hindus, telling how "some run kimes through their hands, and widows burn themselves to death." In a book published soon afterward, John Styles took issue with Smith for not being sufficiently critical of self-mutilation with kimes, which he assumed to be dreadful instruments of torture. As Smith pointed out, he had simply written *knives,* but it had been misread by the printer.

Morse   "Hardened wretch, art thou but this instant delivered from death, and dost thou so soon morse thoughts of slaughter?" So says Father Eustace in many early editions of Walter Scott's novel *The Monastery.* What did Scott mean by *morse?* It had nothing to do with Morse code: his book was written 17 years before the code was invented.

One authority explained that it came from the Latin word *mordere,* "to bite"; another, that it was derived from *amorce,* an Old French word meaning "to prime." Then someone looked at Scott's manuscript. The word he had written was *nurse.*

Slughorne   In "The Battle of Hastings," the 18th-century poet Thomas Chatterton wrote "Some caught a slughorne and an onsette wounde." He was using *slughorne* to mean "a battle trumpet."

Even though Chatterton was known to be a forger of medieval works, other writers copied him, and slughornes were soon appearing in other epic poems—in Robert Browning's 1855 poem "Childe Roland to the Dark Tower Came," for instance. In fact, Chatterton had misunderstood the meaning of the Gaelic word *slaugh-ghairm,* "a battle cry" (from which the English word *slogan* comes). An instrument called a slughorne never existed.

Tweed   The cloth known as tweed is really tweel, the Scottish equivalent of *twill,* which refers to a fabric made with two threads. It became *tweed* because it was confused with the river of that name, which happened to flow through the area where the cloth was traditionally made.

TOKEN AFFECTION

The story behind an ancient custom

O N VALENTINE'S DAY in medieval times, choosing a sweetheart was literally in the luck of the draw. A girl might find herself paired up with the local buffoon for an entire year because he happened to draw her name in the annual village lottery. On the other hand, she might be joined with her heart's desire—and live happily ever after.

But the celebration of this special day, sacred to sweethearts and greeting-card manufacturers alike, goes back much earlier. Its origins are a confused mixture of nearly 2,000 years of fact and fancy.

Saint Valentine himself certainly existed. An early Christian martyr, he is said to have been beheaded on February 14, 270. What is not clear is how he came to be associated with romance and lovers. The connection is probably accidental. February 14 was also the eve of the Lupercalia, an important Roman fertility festival.

Old habits die hard

As Christianity gained influence in Rome, the church fathers replaced the fertility rites of Lupercalia with the feast of Saint Valentine, who ever

You'd like to be a Swell, I see,
But really it won't do;
The right is what you wish to be,
The left, my love, is you!

No. 30.

AFFECTIONATELY YOURS *It was not until the mid-18th century that the custom of exchanging valentine cards became popular. Cards ranged from exquisitely decorated, handmade tokens of affection (above) to cruder specimens (left) that were far from complimentary.*

after was to be the patron saint of lovers. But though the date was given a new name, the sentiments and customs of the pagan festival remained, with variations added gradually.

By the 16th century, lovers were giving their dear ones love tokens—in particular, gloves and garters. A special gift from a sweetheart sailor might be a corset stay that he had carved out of wood and decorated with hearts, flowers, and a highly flattering self-portrait.

In the 17th century the Puritans tried to put a stop to such frivolous behavior but without much success. Even John Winthrop, Puritan governor of the Massachusetts Bay Colony, wrote to his wife on February 14, 1629: "Thou must be my valentine, for none hath challenged me."

After the restoration of the Stuart monarchy in England in 1660, the customs of Saint Valentine's Day returned as ardently as before. Curiously, however, they survived only in England and France; they had died out in Italy and Germany.

Love calls

The French village of Corcières carried on the tradition of publicly shouting for valentines. After suitable inquiries about those they believed to be eligible for marriage, the elders of the community would divide into two groups and enter houses on opposite sides of the narrow streets.

Then, with the lower-floor windows open, the elders called out the names of eligible boys and girls from one window to another. If the paired couples took a liking to each other, the girl would prepare a feast for her new beau and he would bring a bottle of wine; they ended the evening at a dance attended by all the people from the village.

But woe to the girl whose valentine snubbed her: she had to spend the following week at home—alone. Vengeance would be exacted at huge bonfires in the village square, where effigies of those who had spurned their appointed valentines were burned. All ended in 1776, however, when a law was passed banning such behavior.

Hearts and flowers

The good saint's breakthrough came with the popularity of the newly fashionable valentine card about the middle of the 18th century. In the beginning, cards were handmade, decorated with gold letters and paper lace, and inscribed with handwritten love poems. More ambitious cards contained satin hearts hiding small perfumed sachets or tiny mirrors.

By the 1850's, however, machine-made valentine cards were being sold, and suddenly the expression of love became big business. For those who had difficulty expressing their feelings, invaluable volumes such as *The Young Man's Valentine Writer*—published in both the United States and England—were at hand.

Victorians favored cupids and flowers and cards embellished with shells. By the turn of the century, stand-up cards were in fashion, and comic, insulting cards had appeared.

Today, in the United States and England, Valentine's Day is still very much a commercial occasion. Millions of valentines continue to be exchanged, and some collectors are willing to pay substantial amounts for old cards.

For the foreseeable future, the celebration of Saint Valentine's Day seems here to stay. Its namesake would probably be nonplussed.

GOLDWYN GEMS

The late Hollywood producer Samuel Goldwyn—whose name was originally Samuel Goldfish—was noted for making garbled and self-contradictory statements. While the Polish-born immigrant is known to have uttered some gems, so many have been attributed to him that it is not certain which are authentic. The next two columns contain some of his most frequently quoted statements.

"Why did you name your baby John? Every Tom, Dick, and Harry is named John."

"A verbal contract isn't worth the paper it's written on."

"In two words: impossible."

"Anybody who goes to see a psychiatrist ought to have his head examined."

"I want you to know that a Goldwyn comedy is not to be laughed at."

"What we want is a story that starts with an earthquake and works its way up to a climax."

"Include me out."

"They are always biting the hand that lays the golden eggs."

"The trouble with this business is the dearth of bad pictures."

"Why only 12 disciples? Go out and get thousands."

"If Roosevelt were alive today, he'd turn over in his grave."

UNUSUAL IDEAS, UNUSUAL CUSTOMS

SHOCKING REVELATIONS

An outlandish theory on disease

FOR MANY YEARS the cause of cholera was unknown. Theories accounting for the disease ranged from pollution by foul air to one's elevation above sea level. Even hair color was suggested as a possible culprit.

But perhaps one of the most bizarre notions was set forth in a book published in Dublin in 1849. The work of Sir James Murray, a physician, it bore the extraordinary title *Electricity as a Cause of Cholera, or Other Epidemics.*

Based on a series of articles he had written the previous year for the British medical journal *The Lancet,* Murray's book expounded his remarkable theory in great detail. Essentially, he argued that there was no such thing as a germ (he dismissed the idea as "absurd"). All contagious and infectious diseases were caused by one factor: electrical disturbances, with the degree of the disturbance determining the nature of the illness.

Expanding on his theme, Murray explained that diseases such as malaria were caused by "disturbed electro-galvanic currents . . . causing a want of electrical equilibrium in human bodies." Taking the arbitrary figure of 10,000 as a "natural" level of electricity, he showed, with the help of a detailed chart, that a disruption of +10 would result in acute rheumatism, +70 epilepsy, +100 "mania," +120 tetanus, and +130 "fatal lightning." On the negative side, −10 would cause influenza, −90 bubonic plague, and −130 "fatal thunder."

Murray also explained that clouds of positive charges were inclined to hover over people, attracting their negative charges. These two "elementary fluids" would then "rush towards each other into the centre of the body"—often with lethal results.

Potent remedy

The Irish cholera epidemic of 1832, Murray maintained, was caused by "the disturbed galvanic state of earth and air," and he came up with a number of suggestions to "lighten the density and pressure of the atmosphere around cholera patients." For example, he had found through experiments that a potion made from liquid camphor mixed with "fluid magnesia" was effective against the electrically induced cholera.

Murray also advocated wearing silk (or, in the case of the poor, flannel) next to the skin. Sleeping under silk sheets, he claimed, would assist "in warding off the mysterious and all-pervading currents of irregular electricity." Damp floors, he thought, should be covered with quicklime to dry them out, and baskets of lime placed all around the patient's house "to abate untoward galvanism."

Murray had proposed further defenses: houses should be built on insulated platforms, beds balanced on glass bottles, and huge batteries positioned around cities to absorb charges. Quarantine, he insisted, was a waste of time.

Murray was not without his supporters in this view of the association between electricity and disease. And he was hardly the first nor the last to promulgate such ideas. Some 50 years earlier a U.S.

quack named Elisha Perkins had marketed two expensive rods that he called "tractors." Each was made of three metals: one of iron, silver, and platinum, the other of copper, zinc, and gold. When the rods were drawn over the body, claimed Perkins, the electricity they generated discharged all known diseases.

Similarly, late in the 19th century, the London Medical Battery Company sold electric corsets, claiming that they would cure everything from gout to consumption.

However outlandish these ideas may seem, in some ways we are not entirely free of such notions today. Many people still believe that car sickness can be cured by grounding automobiles with metal contact strips that drag along the road and drain away static electricity.

THE DEVIL'S COACH

Deep in the wilds of the Scottish Highlands, the devil himself is at work. On the darkest, coldest nights of winter, his jet-black coach has been seen racing at high speed across the moors. It is pulled by a team of jet-black horses and carries its load of mortal passengers to a land beyond the grave.

According to local tradition, the marks of the coach wheels are often seen in the middle of frozen lakes, clear and unmistakable in the snow that covers the ice. The tracks start and stop suddenly; they are never seen on land. No trace of human footprints, nor any sign of the horses, has ever been found.

As Otta F. Swire, who saw the tracks with her husband, writes: "I have been told that there are no hoof marks because the devil's horses are spirits, whereas his coach, used to carry mortals, must have earthly substance; but if so, why do the wheels leave tracks only on ice? And whom does he carry off? And why?"

LAND AHOY!

The floating islands of the Sargasso Sea

THE FIRST TIME Christopher Columbus crossed the uncharted Atlantic, not knowing precisely where he was going nor when he would land, his apprehensive crew was comforted to see a quantity of drifting weeds. To them it was a sign that land was near. The men were vastly relieved when they saw crabs among the weeds, for such creatures were unheard of in mid-ocean.

Day after day the ships sailed on waters that were unusually warm and deeply blue, often cutting through weeds so thick and matted that it was similar to navigating a meadow. However, it would be weeks before the sailors saw land. In reality, they were thousands of miles from the nearest coast.

This was man's first reported contact with the Sargasso Sea, a unique, weed-covered, oval-shaped area in the North Atlantic. It was so named by Portuguese sailors, who thought the weeds looked like the grapes they called *salgazo*. The phenomenon of a sea covered by weeds was so strange that it soon gave birth to legends of hidden monsters that preyed on ships and of weeds so dangerous that ships passing through them would be dragged to a watery grave many fathoms below.

Delving into the deep

These stories so fascinated William Beebe of the New York Zoological Society that in 1925 he decided to investigate the sea for himself.

At first he was disappointed. Far from the "golden-yellow undulating meadows" he had expected, he found patches of weeds rarely bigger than a man's head, an average of one every 100 yards. It did not take him long to realize that this was autumn in the Sargasso Sea; in spring and summer these small floating islands would join together to form the fields that had astounded and puzzled early sailors.

Beebe's investigations proved that the Sargasso Sea was far more fascinating than the myths had suggested. He found that this strange sea, covering about 2 million square miles, had developed its own unique population of bizarre creatures.

Invisible threads

While studying the nature of the weeds and the various inhabitants, Beebe became aware of the presence of numerous small eels in the water. He caught some and placed them in a laboratory aquarium—where they were all but invisible.

Nevertheless, Beebe plunged his hand into the tank until he felt something and drew out "a 12-inch piece of flexible water." All he could see was a pair of gleaming eyes—but no evidence of bodily structure. Upon closer inspection the eel appeared to be shaped like a long, thin leaf, formed of many delicate segments. The gills were barely visible.

Ideal grounds for breeding

Over thousands of years, the fish, crabs, shrimps, and worms that live in the Sargasso Sea have developed camouflage that has made them indistinguishable from the weeds that give them sanctuary.

Even more remarkable is the fact that the Sargasso Sea is also the breeding ground for American, Mediterranean, and European eels. When the time comes to spawn, the eels leave their safe homes in the continental rivers, drawn by the call of the warm, still waters of the Sargasso Sea. The eels embark on a journey of many thousands of miles — a journey in which they are exposed to attack from various marine predators. Once the mature eels have spawned in the Sargasso, they die, and their offspring then start the marathon journey back "home" — wherever that might be.

Today scientists understand much more about the Sargasso Sea. Bounded by the major Atlantic currents, the water has been forced up so that it is about three feet higher than the surrounding seas. It rotates clockwise, very slowly. And in these calm blue waters the free-floating weeds are able to multiply very rapidly to form the characteristic meadows of the Sargasso.

We now know that no mysterious monsters lurk beneath the surface, and that the waters are not as treacherous as they were once believed to be. Nevertheless, the Sargasso Sea, with its curious weeds and compelling lure for eels, remains an intriguing phenomenon.

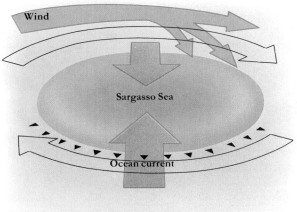

UNIQUE SEA *The warm, deep blue waters of the Sargasso Sea cover some 2 million square miles of the North Atlantic. A complicated combination of ocean currents and winds makes the sea a huge eddy that rotates slowly in a clockwise direction.*

WEEDY CAMOUFLAGE *Sargassum weed, which floats on the still waters of the Sargasso Sea, hosts a variety of unusual creatures that have adapted to their unique marine environment. A Sargassum anglerfish* (Histrio histrio) *is almost indiscernible in the weeds.*

THE FIRST COWBOYS

Tending cattle had little to do with their job

THE HARD-RIDING cowboys of the Wild West have left a deep and lasting impression on American folklore. Burned by the sun, driven by rain and snow, surviving attacks by hostile Indians, the cowboy presents an ideal of physical courage, and fair play.

But the cowboys of popular imagination are a far cry from the first men who went by that name. The term may indicate their vocation, but the only connection they had with cattle was stealing them.

Guerrilla war

When the British seized New York City in 1776, after the beginning of the American Revolution, the rest of the province was thrown into turmoil. Both sides formed guerrilla outfits that were sanctioned to commit acts of robbery and murder.

The Westchester Light Horse Battalion was an irregular British Army corps under Col. James de Lancey. De Lancey's horsemen soon gained the nickname of "Cow-boys" from their success as cattle raiders. They also acquired a reputation as ruthless killers of men, who used cowbells to lure their unsuspecting victims into the woods before doing away with them. As a result of their activities, the term *Cow-boys* became synonymous with terror throughout the neutral areas of Westchester County, a large tract of land that stretched north of New York City for some 30 miles and separated the lines of the opposing forces.

Westchester County became the common hunting ground for the irregulars on both sides. While the Cow-boys swooped from the British position, the "patriot" brigade of New Jersey Volunteers, led by Gen. Courtland Skinner, operated from the American lines. With horses and cattle as their main targets, the aptly named Skinners were even more vicious and unprincipled than the Cow-boys.

Although the Skinners professed allegiance to the American cause, and the Cow-boys to the British, the distinction was lost on the unfortunate inhabitants caught in the cross fire. The marauding bands pillaged Westchester County and spread terror throughout neighboring Connecticut and nearby New Jersey and Long Island.

The Skinners and Cow-boys often banded together, and they had a working agreement for the disposal and distribution of their plunder, sharing the profits more or less equally. New York was the main market for such goods, but since the city was

---

HOW POPEYE GOT IT WRONG

Popeye the Sailor has done more for spinach than any salesman could ever have dreamed possible. When Popeye made his first appearance in the 1930's, spinach consumption in the United States rose by 33 percent.

Why? It was spinach that gave Popeye his mighty strength and bulging muscles, because it was so full of iron.

But the belief that spinach promotes strength was based on a very simple mathematical error. Nutrition researchers in the 1890's put a decimal point in the wrong place, thus giving spinach 10 times more iron than it actually contains.

Modern nutritionists believe that as a source of iron, spinach is no better—and no worse—than any other green vegetable. Its iron content is only average, and the little iron it does have is virtually ineffective, because the body cannot absorb it directly.

Ironically, however, in the 1940's nutritionists discovered that folic acid in spinach *does* give strength. Perhaps *that* is how Popeye got his muscles after all.

VEGETABLE POWER *Since the creation of Popeye the Sailor, it was thought, erroneously, that spinach contains more strength-giving properties than other vegetables.*

in British hands, it was out of bounds for the anti-British Skinners. They therefore exchanged their plunder with the Cow-boys, who gave them contraband articles in return. The Cow-boys then disposed of both sets of goods in New York.

In order to disguise this illicit trade, the Skinners would go through the charade of a skirmish with the Cow-boys near the American lines. The Skinners would emerge victorious. They would then return to their own lines with their booty, pretending it had been captured from the enemy.

With the cessation of hostilities in 1781, General Skinner changed sides and escaped on a British man-of-war, one day ahead of the American soldiers who had come to arrest him. He spent the rest of his life in England. De Lancey fled to Nova Scotia, where he settled as a farmer.

It was several generations before the cowboy as we know him today emerged on the western plains at the end of the Civil War. He has been celebrated ever since, most of his fans oblivious to the brutal way in which he first gained his name.

PARENTAL CHOICE

Can you choose the sex of your baby?

TODAY, DOCTORS can tell the sex of a baby before it is born. But no foolproof method of *choosing* the sex of a baby has as yet been found, although scientists have tried for centuries.

Many weird theories about the way sex is determined have developed, and people all over the world have evolved numerous customs in an attempt to have a child of the sex they want. Since there is always a 50 percent chance of success, it is not surprising that some of these methods are thought to work to some degree.

Early attempts

In the fifth century B.C. it was believed that women had two wombs, and that boys developed in the right one and girls in the left; therefore, complicated maneuvers were performed to produce the "correct" baby.

The Roman naturalist Pliny the Elder, writing in the first century, advocated eating the testicles, womb, or rennet of a hare for sons; he made no mention of what to eat when a girl was preferred.

Many later folk beliefs center around food. In one, if a woman wanted a girl, she was advised to eat cakes and candy throughout pregnancy; if she wanted a boy, red meat.

Other methods seem even less scientific. For example, in some parts of Austria peasants believe that a good nut harvest means that more boys will be born that year, and in the rural areas of Pennsylvania some men reportedly still believe that they can decide the sex of a baby by hanging their pants on either the right or the left side of the bed.

Recent years have produced many pseudoscientific theories. Earlier in this century it was thought that males were produced by eggs from the right ovary, girls from eggs made by the left ovary. This idea was based on the mistaken belief that for each month of the menstrual cycle, ovulation took place from alternate ovaries. Therefore, after the birth of the first child, the "little girl" and "little boy" months could be determined.

Today it is known that chromosomes are the crucial factor. Each one of us has 23 pairs of chromosomes; one pair are sex chromosomes. In females, these are both X, which together form the female XX combination. In males, the pair are X and Y chromosomes, which together give the male XY combination. It all depends on which sperm reaches the egg first. If it is the Y-bearing sperm, this will combine with the X chromosome in the egg to produce an XY combination—a boy. If it is the X-bearing sperm, the resulting XX combination will produce a girl.

Current methods

Nowadays, chiefly two methods are used to try to predetermine sex. One relies on the theory that "male" or "female" sperm can be encouraged by appropriate douching (vinegar if a girl is wanted, bicarbonate of soda for a boy). Like many folk remedies, the second method involves food—but near the time of conception rather than during pregnancy. Thus, plenty of meat, salt, and vegetables are advocated for a boy, and dairy products for a girl. Some claim an 80 percent success rate for this diet; others say that it has no effect.

Many of these ideas may sound absurd, but researchers believe that determining the sex of a child before conception could have implications for medical science. Assessing the sex of a child correctly may, they believe, make it possible to avoid certain genetic diseases, such as hemophilia, which are carried by females but affect only males.

LAUGHTER: THE BEST MEDICINE?

A hilarious cure

IN AUGUST 1964 the American editor Norman Cousins was struck down by a seemingly irreversible disease. The connective tissue between his bones was degenerating rapidly. Within a week of the appearance of the first symptoms, he was lying in the hospital, unable to move his limbs and in terrible pain. Sleep was impossible.

But he refused to believe that his condition was incurable. Cousins knew that such diseases were often caused by adrenal exhaustion. In his case, it could have been the result of the emotional and physical stress of a hectic trip to the Soviet Union.

He reasoned that if negative emotions produce negative chemical changes in the body, perhaps positive emotions would bring about positive changes. If he could reverse his emotional state, he might restore the functioning of his adrenal glands. Then his body would start to cure itself.

Laughter, he decided, was the best medicine, and Cousins started to watch classic episodes of the television program *Candid Camera*. "I made the joyous discovery," he wrote later, "that 10 minutes of genuine belly laughter . . . would give me at least two hours of pain-free sleep."

Next Cousins left the hospital for a hotel room, where he could enjoy comic movies, television programs, and readings from humorous books—and sleep whenever he wanted.

Eight days after his move, the pain had gone from one thumb and he was sleeping well. Three weeks later he was jogging on a Puerto Rican beach, and the tissue in his spine and joints was beginning to renew itself. Within a few months he had returned to work.

Cousins is convinced that his refusal to give in, coupled with his regimen of laughter, was crucial to his recovery. "What we are talking about essentially," he says, "is the chemistry of the will to live." Living and laughing, according to Cousins, very much go hand in hand.

MODERN FOLKTALES

Some strange goings-on

IN THE 1930's A CURIOUS CRAZE swept across the United States. Americans started to buy baby alligators, which they reared as pets in their city apartments. But the novelty soon wore off, and as the pets grew too large and fierce, they were flushed down the toilet.

As a result, some people claim that a race of giant sewage-feeding alligators—probably albino, since they live in permanent darkness—is thriving in the sewers of many a city.

This may be a familiar story. But although it has been circulated as true for decades, there is very little truth in it. There is some evidence that a few small alligators were found in the New York City sewers during the 1930's, but the authorities soon eradicated them—at least that is what we are led to believe. The notion that subterranean tunnels are teeming with monstrous reptiles has very little foundation in fact.

The alligator story is one of many modern folktales (frequently with an ironic or horrific twist) that are retold as true, with embellishments to make them seem plausible. They appear in varying forms in different parts of the world and, like many stories, travel rapidly on the grapevine. Certain modern folktales have become classics. Among the most frequently recited:

Spiders in bubble gum

The story once spread that Bubble Yum, a brand of bubble gum, contained spiders' eggs, and that children who chewed it would wake up to find spiders crawling on them. In the 1970's the manufacturers of the brand, E.R. Squibb & Sons, launched a $100,000 advertising campaign to reassure all customers that their gum was "clean, wholesome, pure, and great fun to chew."

Hong Kong surprise

A European couple dining out in Hong Kong went to a restaurant where they had difficulty making themselves clear. Only after much sign language did they make their choice of meal understood.

Next came the problem of getting food for their dog, which was also hungry. The couple pointed to it and to their mouths. That seemed to convey the message, and the dog was led away. A few hours later the high point of the meal arrived when a large platter was brought to the table and the cover removed with a flourish. Beneath the lid: their succulently roasted dog.

The disappearing matriarch

A British couple, their children, and a grandmother were on a camping vacation in Europe when the grandmother passed away. Reluctant to have her buried in a foreign country, or to bear the expense of having the body shipped home, the family decided to keep the corpse with them until the end of the vacation. Bundling the deceased in a rug, they strapped her to the roof rack of the car.

After stopping at a restaurant for lunch one day, they returned to discover that the car, with their late grandmother on top, had been stolen. They never saw either again. Continue some versions of the story: since the body was never found, the family could not claim the proceeds of a substantial life insurance policy.

BEARING FALSE WITNESS

When the hunters of the Ostyak tribes in Siberia have trapped and killed a bear, they cut off its head and hang it on a tree. Then, with much sorrow, the hunters tell the bear that they were not responsible for its death: the Russians were to blame.

A Russian ax beheaded it and a Russian knife skinned it, they say. And they pay the skin of the bear the respects they would usually pay to a god.

The Ostyaks perform this ritual in the hope of appeasing the bear; otherwise, they believe, the ghost of the bear will wreak its vengeance on them, and the tribes' future bear hunts will not be successful ones.

The hunters have no qualms about blaming the Russians, who first conquered the Ostyaks as long ago as 1583. Little love is lost between the two peoples even to the present day.

BEAR WORSHIP *To the Ainu people of the island of Sakhalin, off the Pacific coast of Russia, the bear is a creature to be respected—even after death. A bear is killed with great ceremony, and its head positioned so that it can witness the honors that follow. The Ainus hope that the spirit of the bear will tell other bears how well it has been treated so that they too will approach the tribe to sample the hospitality for themselves.*

EXECUTION *IN ABSENTIA*

Observing your own demise

IN 1655 THE MARQUIS de Canillac was sitting by an upper window of a house in Toulouse, France. He was watching an execution taking place in the square below. He was no innocent bystander, however. The person being executed was himself—in effigy. As the executioner struck off the head of the dummy, the live marquis remarked that he did not even have a headache.

The marquis enjoyed a good meal and a sound sleep after his death sentence had been carried out. That he was heavily fined and all of his property confiscated was indeed a small price to pay for having had his life spared.

Symbol of justice

The origin of a hanging or a beheading in effigy is unknown. The first case on record was in the 13th century, when a nobleman, Thomas de Marle, was condemned to death by Louis VI for treason. This form of punishment remained an important weapon in the French judicial armory for more than 400 years. According to French law, a person accused of a crime but not yet caught could be tried even if he was not present. If convicted and then sentenced to death, the judgment could be carried out on the effigy of the condemned.

The legal fiction behind this symbolic form of punishment was that the condemned person had run away and could not be found. If arrested within 30 years, he could be executed in person. In practice, this rarely happened.

Execution in effigy was not regarded as a mere formality, however. People so punished were considered in such disgrace that they might as well be dead. And because any influence they might have had in public affairs was lost, the punishment was often used with powerful noblemen who had abused their position.

One advantage of execution in effigy was that it provided an enjoyable public spectacle without involving bloodshed. At times French citizens were treated to the sight of 30 or more effigies being executed in the public square simultaneously. The effigies themselves were then kept on public view for a day, as an example to others.

Contemporary French law still retains an echo of the old custom: fugitives from justice can still be tried in their absence. If they are found guilty, the text of the judgment is to be displayed in the main square of the town where the crime was committed. Symbolic executions with effigies, however, are no longer carried out.

FATHER MOON

Astronauts have set to rest the myth that the moon is made of green cheese. But no matter how many future lunar expeditions there are, earthlings may never be willing to surrender their notions about the powers of the moon.

As a symbol of fertility, the moon plays a part in the ancient folklore of people all over our planet. According to the legends of Greenland, the moon is a young man who pays amorous visits to married women careless enough to sleep lying on their back. In this Arctic land, young girls dared not stare at the moon for fear of becoming pregnant.

In northwest France, some Breton peasants believe that women who expose their bodies to the moonlight risk giving birth to monsters. And the members of one tribe in Borneo hold that albinos are sired by the moon; their paleness reflects the pallor of their father.

Because the duration of a woman's fertility cycle, in general, coincides with the 29-day cycle of the moon, some cultures believe that the moon is a woman's true husband. The Maoris of New Zealand maintain that marriage between a mortal man and woman is of no real importance because the moon is the permanent husband.

Animals and plants are also thought to be subject to the moon's cycles. Apis, the sacred bull of ancient Egypt, was said to have been sired by moonbeams falling on a cow.

Even in our own time, some farmers the world over sow a crop during a certain phase of the moon, just to be on the safe side and ensure germination.

Whatever scientists and visiting astronauts may discover, the moon will no doubt continue to exert its influence on the peoples of the earth.

DIVINE ANOINTMENT

An ancient art with an attractive aroma

EVERYONE KNOWS how a familiar aroma can bring back a rush of memories: the delicious smell of chocolate chip cookies baking in the oven may be a reminder of childhood, the heavy perfume of gardenia may recall the senior prom, and the powerful, evocative perfume of orange blossoms may be linked with a wedding. But how many people are aware that plant fragrances have been used for thousands of years as a means of curing illness?

Aromatherapy, the art of healing with aromatic oils of plants, was known to the ancient Egyptians, Romans, and Greeks. Centuries ago "wise" men and women treasured the secrets of the precious oils and applied them with great skill. Not only were the oils used to cure a variety of ailments, they also formed an essential part of many important daily beauty treatments.

The Romans massaged themselves with sweet-smelling unguents before plunging into their elaborate baths. The Greeks assigned a godlike virtue to each plant; by inhaling the fragrance, they could assume the god's attributes. For example, if they inhaled the fragrance of the poppy, a flower sacred to the god of war, courage would not desert them. The scent of the shy violet, on the other hand, had a calming influence.

Some practitioners saw a resemblance between parts of the human body and the shapes of certain plants—for example, lungwort or liverwort—and treated the affected area with the appropriate plant.

Mind over matter

Today aromatherapists seek to treat the patient, not the disease. In the belief that the mind plays a major role in certain bodily ailments, powerful fragrances

AROMATHERAPY TREATMENTS FOR SOME COMMON AILMENTS

Sage	Peppermint	Eucalyptus	Rosemary	Chamomile	Lavender
Asthma	Asthma	Asthma	Asthma	Burns	Burns
Burns	Bronchitis	Bronchitis	Burns	Depression	Cystitis
Diarrhea	Colds	Burns	Colds	Diarrhea	Depression
Eczema	Colic	Cough	Constipation	Eczema	Diarrhea
Fainting	Indigestion	Cystitis	Diarrhea	Fainting	Eczema
Flatulence	Influenza	Diarrhea	Fainting	Fever	Headache
Indigestion	Mental fatigue	Indigestion	Headache	Headache	Nausea
Influenza	Nausea	Influenza	Indigestion	Indigestion	Nervous tension
Sore throat	Shock	Rheumatism	Influenza	Nervous tension	Rheumatism
Toothache	Toothache	Sore throat	Rheumatism	Rheumatism	Sore throat

Marjoram	Fennel	Thyme	Basil	Juniper	Hyssop
Asthma	Colic	Asthma	Bronchitis	Colic	Asthma
Bronchitis	Constipation	Bronchitis	Colds	Cough	Bronchitis
Colds	Cystitis	Cystitis	Depression	Diarrhea	Colic
Colic	Flatulence	Fainting	Fainting	Eczema	Eczema
Constipation	Indigestion	Indigestion	Fever	Flatulence	Fever
Headache	Nausea	Rheumatism	Indigestion	Hemorrhoids	Indigestion
Indigestion			Mental fatigue	Indigestion	Influenza
Nervous tension			Nausea	Rheumatism	Rheumatism

are used to alter the patient's emotional state and thus leave the way open for a beneficial cure.

Aromatherapy is said to be useful in the treatment of stress-induced illnesses, such as asthma, headache, and depression. Skin ailments, respiratory diseases, digestive problems, and backaches sometimes respond to aromatic oils as well. Usually inhaled or massaged into the skin, the oils are always extracted from plants and the dosage is measured very carefully.

The medical fraternity has not yet endorsed aromatherapy—with the exception of many French physicians, who use it in conjunction with orthodox medicine. However, for most people aromatherapy remains a fringe medicine and a costly treatment.

Meanwhile, many ordinary people are practicing a time-honored form of aromatherapy each time they take a bouquet of fragrant flowers to cheer up a friend or relative who is ill.

A Shipload of Dreams

The extraordinary cults of Melanesia

IN 1919, in the Vailala district of Papua New Guinea, Melanesia, the local people were suddenly seized by mass hysteria. Violent shaking fits, ecstatic trances, visions, speaking in tongues, and other symptoms of "spirit possession" were rife. People had abruptly refused to work on the plantations and tend their crops. They began to destroy all signs of their traditional religion and were instead holding elaborate feasts.

The feasts were being held in honor of their ancestors who, according to one of the local prophets, would soon be returning on a huge steamer. It would be laden with all kinds of goods—food, knives, cloth, soap, rifles—free for everyone to use. A golden age was about to begin. Crops would grow unattended, no one would work, and everyone would have plenty of money.

This was the Vailala madness, just one of numerous religious movements that have arisen in Melanesia since the middle of the 19th century. Collectively called cargo cults, many are still prevalent today.

Return of the gods

Cargo cults share some common beliefs, which is surprising because each began independently of the others across the entire Melanesian Archipelago. The central idea of the cults is that the ancestors will return, often on a specified date, bringing with them an abundance of the material goods the Melanesians have seen in the possession of the European colonists of the islands. The ancestors will have white skins, and the people themselves will turn white. Together they will drive out the Europeans. In some cults it is believed that this great day will be heralded by an earthquake or other terrible natural disaster that will swallow up the white settlers.

The Europeans must be expelled, say the cultists, because the colonists are diverting the cargo that is rightfully the people's. The cargo cannot belong to the Europeans because it arrives on boats and airplanes from somewhere else. The goods are in fact made by the ancestors for the people, but the Europeans are intercepting them. One cult prophet, Batari, claimed that he could prove this. In a ship's hold he had seen boxes addressed to him—labeled "batteries"—but they had never been delivered to him.

Acts of faith

Members of the cults try to attract the attention of their ancestors—and the cargo—in a number of different ways. They disguise themselves as Europeans, adopting Western dress and imitating Western behavior. They perform elaborate rituals with flagpoles, believing that through them they will be able to communicate with the spirits.

Some cults build docks for the expected steamer, and construct ships or aircraft of wood or palm thatch to be ready to receive the cargo. Others await a fleet of aircraft, similarly laden with the bounties of the West.

What lies behind the cargo cults? Most contain muddled elements of Christianity: one cult worshipped a faded portrait of King George V of England, declaring that it was a picture of *Ihova,* or God. When white colonists first arrived on the islands, the Melanesians believed that they were returning ancestors who had acquired white skins in the afterlife. And the people were overwhelmed by the religion, power, and material wealth of the Europeans, whose presence they resented. So cargo cults were the result—a mixture of national pride, local and Western religions, and a sincere desire for independence and justice.

THE COMING OF JOHN FRUM

Since the 1930's the people of the island of Tana in Vanuatu in the South Pacific have been anticipating the arrival of John Frum, king of America and savior of the world.

It is said that when Frum does arrive, the mountains will fall down and fill the rivers, the land will be fertile, and the people will prosper. Frum will provide new schools and the money to pay for the white man's goods; everyone will have everything he wishes.

But Frum does not really exist. Although many claim to have seen him, he is a figment of the islanders' imagination, appearing in firelight and in shadows to men under the influence of *kava,* the local narcotic drink.

The John Frum movement reached its zenith during World War II, when the U.S. Army arrived on the island. There were many blacks among the visiting troops, and it was the first time the Tanaese had seen black men dressed the same as whites—and with so many belongings. Believing the soldiers to be sent by Frum, the islanders immediately began to imitate their behavior: they drilled with enthusiasm, carrying bamboo rifles and wearing improvised uniforms.

When the war ended, the soldiers left, taking their belongings with them. But the islanders did not lose faith in Frum. In 1976 there were reports that most of the population was still eagerly awaiting his arrival.

FACE OF A SAVIOR *People of the island of Tana gaze at a photograph of the man they believe to be king of America, John Frum.*

THE OPENING KNIGHT

Being of noble birth may bring some curious privileges. Should an English lord be condemned to death, he can choose to be hanged with a silken rope. In olden days the French nobility paid no taxes, despite their vast wealth. And it is said that all over medieval Europe, lords of the manor enjoyed *jus primae noctis,* the right to be the first to sleep with a bride on her wedding night.

About A.D. 875 King Ewan III of Scotland decreed that "the Lords of the ground shall have the maidenheads of all the virgins dwelling in the same." This is how the law stood until it was abolished by King Malcolm III in the 11th century.

In Spain the practice was not abolished until 1486. Elsewhere it thrived. Even monks who owned estates as large and powerful as any aristocrat's were allegedly able to enjoy this singular right. In the South Tyrol and Switzerland the custom was officially illegal, and some nobles were exiled for maintaining the old ways. In France it probably continued until the Revolution in 1789, as Charles Dickens suggests in *A Tale of Two Cities.*

The "right of the first night" died out in most countries as the serfs were freed. But an echo of the old feudal order remained: it became traditional for the lord of the manor to stride over the bride as she lay in bed on her wedding night waiting for her husband.

ALL TIED UP

The hidden power of knots

THE PROPHET Muhammad, founder of Islam, was taken mysteriously ill one day. No one could diagnose his affliction and no one could find a remedy. According to legend, the archangel Gabriel then appeared to Muhammad and revealed that one of his enemies had bewitched him. The ill-wisher had tied nine knots in a piece of string and thrown it down a well.

Immediately, Muhammad's servant was sent to fetch the knotted string. Muhammad then recited nine magic verses over it; at each verse a knot untied itself, until the prophet was cured.

Muhammad was perhaps the most celebrated person to fall victim to the magic of knots, which has been known all over the world since the dawn of time. All knot magic derives from the idea of tying things up: imprisoning, constricting, or entangling something or someone, whether for good or for evil. At certain times, therefore, it is important to tie knots to achieve a particular objective. At other times, it is vital to *untie* them.

So strong was the belief in the power of knots in Scotland that sick people would pray to the devil to loose the hidden knot that lay behind their illness. In ancient Babylon sorcerers could seal a man's lips—making him tongue-tied—merely by tying the knots in a cord and casting a spell over it. In Togo, West Africa, witch doctors would claim to "bind up the life" of their enemies by knotting a piece of grass. In Bordeaux, France, in 1718 one person was burned alive for ruining the life of an entire family with curses involving knotted cords.

The marriage knot

In many societies it is taboo to tie knots during a wedding service. In some places in medieval Europe, anyone doing so could be punished by law and excommunicated from the church, for the consequences could be twofold: barrenness in the bride or impotence in the groom.

In places as far apart as Morocco, Greece, and Scotland it was formerly the custom to insist that any knot in the clothing of the bride or groom should be undone during the wedding. In contrast, in some churches it is still traditional for the priest to knot his stole (a long embroidered silk scarf) around the clasped hands of the couple once they have made their vows.

To ease the pains of childbirth, it was customary to untie all knots, unlock all doors, and even unbraid the plaits in a woman's hair in any house where a child was being born. A medieval Scandinavian couple who wanted no more children would call the last-born Knut ("knot"). When someone died, knots were loosened so that the soul would encounter no obstacle in leaving the body.

Not all knots had ill effects. Pliny the Elder reports that in the first century A.D. people would heal diseases of the groin by tying seven or nine knots in a thread and naming a widow for each knot. An old German cure for warts involved tying knots in a length of string and leaving the string under a stone. The first unfortunate person to tread on the stone caught the warts.

In Gujarat, India, a man could be released from fever if someone took seven cotton threads to a place where an owl was hooting. He was to tie a knot at each hoot, and then return and tie the thread around the right arm of the sufferer.

A knot could therefore protect life. Fathers in the Masai tribe in East Africa would tie a knot in their hair for each son going out to battle, with a prayer to keep their bodies and souls as tightly bound together. Russian hunters tied knots in thread to prevent themselves from being shot: knots had the power to lock guns and entangle bows. Zulu hunters in Africa would tie a knot in the tail of every animal they killed to make certain that the flesh did not give them stomach pains.

Even the weather could be controlled by knots. In the Shetland Islands, fishermen used to buy the wind—tied up in a handkerchief—from old women who claimed to rule the elements. Early in the 20th century, women were still selling wind to sailors—in the shape of a string with three knots. The more knots the sailor untied, the stronger the wind would blow for him.

KNOT OF FAITH *A Parsee high priest in India ties the sacred girdle of faith, or* kushti, *around the waist of a young initiate into the Zoroastrian religion. After the ceremony the boy will adopt the girdle as part of his everyday dress to remind him of his religion. To the accompaniment of prayers, he will untie and reknot the cord several times daily to express his determination to defeat the forces of evil and his dedication to the worship of God.*

ROUGH JUSTICE

One night in May 1950 a cacophony of clattering, banging, insults, and abuse erupted outside a small inn in the Basque country of northern Spain. Behind the shuttered windows, two lovers, each married to someone else, hid in shame: their guilty secret had been discovered. Eventually the din abated and the perpetrators dispersed in the darkness.

This was more than local outrage at immoral behavior; it was part of a tradition that has survived for more than a thousand years in many rural areas of Europe.

Charivari, or "confusion of noises," is a type of popular justice, the means by which members of a community register their disapproval of marriages or partnerships that threaten the values of their society. Targets include adulterers, men who are dominated by their wives, and widows and widowers who remarry too hastily or who take a new, much younger partner.

A chorus of disapproval

The chorus of disapproval usually takes the form of a raucous symphony played on pots and pans, horns, bells, whistles, and drums, accompanied by coarse chants and by insults. Sometimes the victim is paraded through the streets sitting backward on a donkey, heckled by onlookers and occasionally even pelted with tripe.

A peculiar variation known as the Devon Stag Hunt has been recorded in the south of England. A man dressed as a stag is pursued by yelping companions dressed as hounds. When the "hunting party" reaches the house of the culprit, its members daub the doorstep with blood.

Originating in France as a noisy accompaniment to wedding celebrations, charivari has been practiced, in varying forms and under different names, in most European countries and has spread to Canada and the United States, where it is commonly known as shivaree.

The carnival pranks of charivari have their serious side. Passions often run high, sometimes with violent consequences. After the Basque incident, a farmer named Agarra took up his gun. He killed one man and wounded two others. Then he hanged himself. The police later discovered that Agarra himself had suffered the shame of charivari. On this occasion he had been provoked beyond endurance to see others punished with similar "justice."

NEIGHBORLY CONCERN
Members of a small community in England in 1909 perform a mock serenade to show their disapproval of an adulterous couple. This form of popular justice was an effective way to ostracize offenders. Many left the district altogether; for some it even had violent consequences.

RETURN OF THE LEECH

The bloodsucking horror is back in favor

FEW IMAGES CONJURE UP the horrors of primitive medical practice more powerfully than that of the leech. This parasitic worm was used to suck blood from the veins of sick people in the belief that it could draw out the "evil vapors" responsible for their disease. Large numbers of leeches were employed. In 1837 alone, 96,000 leeches were applied to 50,557 patients at St. Bartholomew's Hospital in London. Their use was so common in England that British-bred leeches became scarce, and foreign leeches had to be imported from India and Mexico.

Early in the 20th century doctors discarded leeches as having no place in modern medicine. But today leeches are back, helping to heal skin grafts.

One of the main problems in plastic surgery occurs after the new skin has been grafted. Blood is unable to circulate freely through the graft until the healing process is complete. Congestion results,

and the blood flow in the arteries slows down. This reduces the supply of oxygen brought to the new skin, and the graft sometimes fails.

Plastic surgeons studying this problem suggested using leeches to improve the blood flow. The hungry leech is attached to the grafted skin and drinks its meal of up to two fluid ounces of blood in 10 to 20 minutes, drawing blood into the graft. The leech can increase its own dry weight by as much as six times. After feeding, it drops off, but the patient continues to bleed for as long as two hours. With the blood now circulating freely through the graft, congestion is alleviated and the skin graft usually takes successfully.

In the 19th century more than 50 leeches were sometimes applied simultaneously to a patient. In modern-day plastic surgery usually only one or two leeches are used at one time. But if the arteries to the grafted area take a long time to develop, leeches may be applied at six-hour intervals over a week — some 28 leeches in all.

Such is the demand for leeches today that in 1983 they were declared an endangered species. Leech farms were set up to ensure a regular supply. Because leeches have a long life — they can survive for up to a year without eating (and the hungrier they are, the greater their effectiveness) — they can be stocked in hospital pharmacies and made available on short notice.

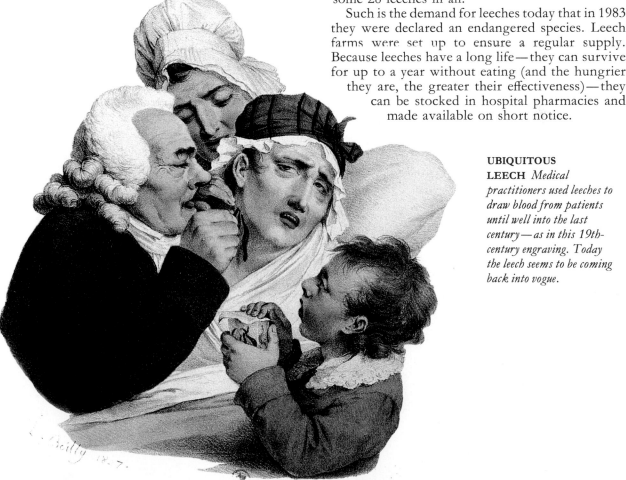

UBIQUITOUS LEECH *Medical practitioners used leeches to draw blood from patients until well into the last century — as in this 19th-century engraving. Today the leech seems to be coming back into vogue.*

THE HIGHEST OFFICE

Who was the first president of the United States?

ASK ANYONE TO NAME the first president of the United States and "George Washington" is the likely reply. But it could be argued that in 1781 a lesser-known American, John Hanson from Maryland, became the first president. After Hanson, seven other men held that high position before Washington was elected and took office on April 30, 1789.

The reason: although the office of president as it is known today was not created until 1789, the office of "President of the United States in Congress Assembled" has existed since 1781.

The Maryland delegate

John Hanson was born in Charles County, Maryland, in 1721. He first attracted public notice in 1757 when he was elected to the Maryland House of Delegates, or General Assembly, where he sat until 1779. A staunch patriot, Hanson established himself as a prominent leader in the growing discontent and agitation about British rule over the Thirteen Colonies.

To represent their interests, in 1774 the colonies established the Continental Congress, with delegates sent by each colony. Although reticent at first, a year later the Congress responded to the outbreak of hostilities by creating the Continental Army under the leadership of George Washington, and on July 4, 1776, issued the Declaration of Independence. John Hanson was elected to the Congress as a Maryland delegate in 1779.

UNFAMILIAR FACE? *Had George Washington not been on the scene, this face might have become as famous as his. John Hanson can lay claim to having been the first president of the United States. The portrait was by Charles Willson Peale.*

A need for unity

Apart from conducting the war against Britain, Congress was also concerned with the creation of a federal constitution. There was a pressing need both to maintain unity between the newly independent states and to define the relative powers of the Congress and of the states themselves. A committee, with one member from each state, was created to examine the problem. In July 1776 the committee issued what became known as the Articles of Confederation. From 1781 until 1789 these 13 articles were the law of the land, until superseded by the Constitution.

One of the articles stated that a delegate could be appointed "to preside" over the Congress. John Hanson was elected to this office on November 5, 1781. He served in the post for one year. During his tenure, peace terms with Britain were drawn up, treaties with foreign powers signed, and government departments instituted.

Presiding officer

Although George Washington himself congratulated Hanson, stating that he held the "most important seat in the United States," Hanson's role, and that of the seven men who followed him, was to preside over Congress. He lacked the executive powers the Constitution would invest in Washington and his successors, and he was powerless to enforce the measures of Congress, which were often ignored by the individual states.

By 1786 the political weaknesses of the Articles were identified, and in 1789 the new Constitution established a more effective central government.

But for eight years the Continental Congress had ruled the newly united states, and John Hanson, largely forgotten today, had the honor of being its first president.

MILK TABOOS

Not everyone believes that milk is good for you

FOR MANY YEARS, it was not uncommon for milk-loving Americans to swallow a quart a day of the white elixir in order to ensure strong bones and pearly teeth. But in many other parts of the world, taboos and rituals discourage or prohibit the drinking of an animal's milk.

Most people seem to agree that mother's milk is the perfect food for infants, but attitudes about its use after the weaning stage differ sharply. In many cultures milk from a variety of domesticated animals, such as cattle, goats, sheep, camels, horses, buffalo, and reindeer, is considered either forbidden food or, less often, a sacred one.

A distasteful drink

One widespread belief is that characteristics of the animal are passed on to the person who drinks its milk; the notion even persisted regarding human milk. In Italy, for example, great care was taken to select wet nurses of untarnished reputation.

In some world cultures milk is viewed with abhorrence. In areas of China many regard milk as a form of excrement and shudder at the idea of drinking it, and the Lengua Indians of Paraguay forbid young people to drink milk, fearing that it may impair their physical and mental health.

Among the Bangala people of the Upper Congo in Africa, anyone drinking milk is considered unclean and is not allowed to eat with other people. For the same reason, milk is rarely featured in the diet of Japanese, Polynesians, and Melanesians.

Some taboos against drinking milk are intended to protect the well-being of the animal and its newborn. Such a belief is held by the Bahima and Masai peoples of Africa; they claim that if milk is boiled, the cow that produced it will die.

Prejudices against the drinking of milk are sometimes associated with religious attitudes. For example, among the Toda tribes of India the milk of sacred buffalo may not be used for human consumption; such an act is considered profane.

Changing attitudes

Recent research indicates that an aversion to milk may not be due solely to cultural superstitions.

Many people from societies in which the drinking of milk is frowned upon have difficulty digesting the milk sugar (lactose) in cow's milk. The intolerance to milk is attributed to a deficiency of the enzyme lactase, which converts the milk sugar into a simpler form so that it can be absorbed into the bloodstream.

"ACT PROMPTLY AND WITH A PURPOSE"

Mystery writers of the 19th century loved quicksand. The villain foundering in a cold and clammy morass that would eventually and inevitably engulf him almost guaranteed a dramatic climax to any story.

But the notion that getting caught in quicksand means certain death is a complete fallacy.

Quicksand is most often found at the mouths of large rivers where the shore is of clay or other impervious material. Quicksand looks much like the ordinary sand that surrounds it, but it has one crucial difference: it is suspended in water. Since the sand cannot support any weight, anyone stepping on it will sink as if in water, only more slowly. The real trouble begins when the victim struggles to escape.

For example, when the person lifts a leg the sand and water mixture will not flow readily into the new void; instead, a partial vacuum will form and hold the leg in a vicelike grip.

But lying down on the quicksand is like lying down in water: the body floats. So for anyone unfortunate enough to get caught in quicksand, the best method of escape is to lie down and roll over it toward firm ground.

Gerard H. Matthes, who was an engineer with the United States Geological Survey at the turn of the century, had to learn the technique based on practical experience.

A victim of quicksand, he said, "should act promptly and with a purpose." If he has a cane or a stick, he should place it on the sand at right angles to his body and work it down his back as far as his hips.

From this position he should be able to extricate his legs gradually, and then roll slowly across the quicksand to firm ground—and safety.

AN ALL-AROUND HIT

To most people, baseball is as American as apple pie or Independence Day. Most written records state that the first baseball game in history was played at the Elysian Fields in Hoboken, New Jersey, on June 19, 1846, between the New York Nine and the Knickerbocker Baseball Club. In 1907 a commission established to investigate the origins of the game declared categorically that it had been invented in 1839 by an American general named Abner Doubleday in Cooperstown in upstate New York.

But much evidence suggests that baseball originated much earlier—in Europe.

A game called base ball is referred to by Jane Austen in her novel *Northanger Abbey,* published in 1818. And a woodcut illustrating John Newbery's English children's book *A Little Pretty Pocket-Book* (1744) reveals that a ball game involving bases was being played in England even earlier in the 18th century.

Many early games, in fact, involved the use of bats and balls and running between different kinds of bases. One such game

FIRST STRIKE? *In a manuscript dating from about 1344, monastic players seem to be watching a team member prepare to hit a ball, which a nun is about to toss. Some historians think they are playing an early form of baseball.*

became formalized as rounders, first described in detail in William Clarke's *The Boy's Own Book,* published in 1828. And in *Ball, Bat and Bishop,* a history of the origin of ball games, a connection between rounders and baseball is established fairly conclusively.

But it may be that rounders and baseball, as well as cricket, are all derived from a game that dates back to even earlier times.

A TOUCH OF CLASS

The king's cure for the king's evil

IN MEDIEVAL TIMES, when doctors' cures were often more dangerous than the illnesses themselves, people who were sick commonly sought help by praying to various saints. They believed that the saints would intercede with God, whose divine mercy and forgiveness could restore the afflicted to health.

Each disease had its patron saint: Saint Vitus for chorea, or "Saint Vitus' dance," Saint Maur for gout, Saint Anthony for skin diseases, and Saint Pius for paralysis. At least six saints, among them Saint Valentine, were invoked in prayers to ward off the greatest terror of the age, the plague.

In France and England, however, there was one extraordinary variation on this practice. Anyone suffering from scrofula, a disfiguring form of tuberculosis, could pray to Saint Marcoulf—but could also go to the reigning king to seek relief. It was thought that his royal touch could by itself cure the affliction, and therefore "king's evil" became the common name for scrofula.

A gift for a gift
Marcoulf, who died in 558, was said to have had a healing touch. The French king Childebert honored Marcoulf with a grant of land, and according

to the legend, God showed His pleasure in this generosity by passing Marcoulf's gift of healing scrofula on to the kings of France.

The first French monarch actually recorded as having exercised the gift is Robert the Pious, who reigned from 996 to 1031. From then on the "king's touch" was practiced by all French sovereigns until the Revolution in 1789.

The first English king said to have cured scrofula was Edward the Confessor. Edward was later canonized; whether he acquired his healing power from his royal ancestors or through his own holiness was a matter of dispute among medieval chroniclers. In any case, his successors continued the tradition of healing the "king's evil."

Hands-on training

The healing was thought to occur when the monarch touched the affected part of the sick person's body: the swollen glands in the neck. At first the ceremony was simple. The king would place his hand on the swellings, pray, make the sign of the cross, and send the sufferer away with a little money. But by the late 15th century an elaborate ritual had evolved.

In England a special order of religious service was used. Sufferers were brought before the king one at a time. As the service was read, the king stroked the affected part with an "angel," a coin specially minted for giving to the sick. The diseased person would wear the coin around the neck until the cure was complete.

In the French ceremony, the king first celebrated mass. Then he would move among the assembled victims, sprinkling holy water on them, touching the swellings, and making the sign of the cross. After they had been touched, the sufferers received money from a court official.

Healers of thousands

In both England and France the healing rituals were held on important holy days, especially on Good Friday. At the height of their popularity, the ceremonies attracted thousands of the afflicted.

Between 1660 and 1664 Charles II of England reputedly touched more than 92,000 victims. On one occasion in 1684 such a huge crowd of sufferers gathered around him that seven people were trampled to death.

But belief in the efficacy of the king's touch was beginning to wane. Following the accession of George I in England in 1714, the custom was abandoned in the face of popular skepticism. Although as late as 1774, Louis XVI of France touched 2,300 scrofula victims on the day of his

ROYAL TOUCH *In France and England, people unlucky enough to be suffering from scrofula tuberculosis could seek a cure from the monarch, who would lay his hands on the neck of the afflicted. In this illustration the 17th-century English monarch Charles II performs the royal cure.*

coronation, after the French Revolution only one attempt was made to revive the ritual, by Charles X in 1825. But the ceremony was performed only once, on the day the king was crowned.

Divine right

Did the king's touch actually heal scrofula? To some people, it must have seemed that way, because the symptoms of the disease are erratic; severe outbreaks alternate with temporary remissions lasting a few months.

The king's touch may have had a political advantage too. By continuing the practice, a monarch was underlining his authority, reminding the populace that his right to rule, not unlike the gift of healing, was God-given and did not derive from the people.

WITH A LOVING KISS

Seals of love

KISSING IS A time-honored way of showing affection. But, say the scientists, it may also *induce* bonding, or even love, between people. Recent medical research has shown that during the act of kissing, certain chemicals may be exchanged. One of these chemicals is sebum, a greasy substance secreted through the skin by the sebaceous glands; it helps to lubricate the skin and keep it supple.

Some of the largest concentrations of sebaceous glands are found on the lips, face, and neck—parts of the body associated with kissing. Since sebum dissolves in water, the moistness of kisses helps to transfer the substance from one person to another. As heat increases the production of sebum, the warmth of the passion boosts output.

Sebum is a pheromone—a chemical substance that attracts other members of the same species, such as the scent female insects emit to lure males.

Possibly the interchange of pheromones plays a part in the bonding between humans. Sebum transfer by kissing, for example, is thought to be a factor in a mother's devotion to her baby. If scientists are right, then one aspect of love could be defined as the addiction to, or recognition of, another person's pheromones.

Perhaps Shakespeare was right when he described kisses as the "seals of love."

A LITTLE LIGHT RELIEF

New remedy for an old disorder

DARLENE BARRY, a freelance writer living in Washington, D.C., used to experience a crisis every fall. She would gain weight—as much as 30 pounds over the winter—due to an obsessive craving for food. She also became depressed, irritable, and unable to concentrate on her job. She was constantly tired and slept as much as possible. Miss Barry had a classic case of the winter blues—known today as seasonal affective disorder, or, appropriately, SAD.

Only recently have doctors started to understand SAD, although the winter blues have been recognized medically since the 1930's. Victims of the condition (80 percent are women) find their energy levels drained to the point where leading a normal life becomes difficult. In children, SAD has sometimes been confused with "growing pains." Although long regarded as untreatable, SAD may soon become less of a problem.

Story of the blues

A team led by Dr. Norman E. Rosenthal at the National Institutes of Health (NIH), in Bethesda, Maryland, concluded that the shorter days and sparse sunlight of fall and winter were responsible for the onset of winter blues. The remedy: for two or three hours a day sufferers should sit in front of bright ultraviolet-balanced lamps that duplicate sunlight; ordinary electric bulbs emit little light at the blue and the ultraviolet end of the spectrum.

The result: symptoms of depression disappear after a few days because of the increased hours of "daylight." After her successful treatment at NIH, Miss Barry installed her own set of lights at home.

Although this cure may seem simple, the causes of SAD are difficult to discern. One theory suggests that the condition is related to the production of melatonin, a hormone produced by the pineal gland deep in the center of the brain.

Melatonin is secreted only in darkness; through the optic nerve, daylight triggers a reaction that halts its production. The hormone's function is uncertain, although it seems to affect sleeping patterns and emotional states. Its purpose may be to keep the energy levels of the body in rhythm with the cycle of night and day.

However, some researchers believe that melatonin may be but a partial cause of the winter blues. Patients who took drugs that completely suppressed production of melatonin continued to suffer from depression and other symptoms of SAD. Other hormones acting in concert with melatonin may be involved.

While the causes of SAD are being investigated, its cure has found several new applications. Light therapy may help relieve the effects of jet lag, the result of an upset in the body's normal rhythms due to changing time zones. Workers on night shifts and insomniacs may also benefit. The future for the new therapy looks bright.

TIGER BONES TWICE DAILY

Medical prescriptions in the Far East, often different from those in the West, include an extraordinary range of remedies—many based on animal and mineral substances. Despite Western skepticism, many seem to be effective.

High on the popularity poll is earthworm liquid, a concentrated solution of the body fluids of worms. It is used in treating a wide range of ailments, from high blood pressure to kidney failure. A chemistry teacher in one major Asian city devised a new way to brew this traditional remedy without its equally traditional unpleasant odor.

Bones are popular too. Those of leopards, lynxes, and tigers are regularly prescribed as tonics, as are "dragon's bones," which are in fact fossil ivory and include the bones of dinosaurs. For ailments as different as skin diseases, fevers, and ulcers, other remedies include turtle shell, anteater scales, snake skins, dried scorpions, and even toad venom.

Perhaps equally strange to most Western tastes are the drugs prepared from dried human placentas and the genitalia of the male sea lion; they are used as cures for infertility. And the dung of sheep, goats, bats, magpies, white pigeons, and of some other creatures finds application in healing nervous disorders and eye diseases.

For asthma some Asian doctors recommend a cure consisting of the tails of one male and one female spotted lizard. Powdered human hair is considered a perfect cure for bleeding gums.

Many of the prescriptions are remarkably detailed, such as "powdered licorice root that has

been enclosed in a bamboo case and buried in a cesspool for one winter." Among the most esoteric is "the hardened earth found on the interior bottom of wood-burning kitchen stoves after several years of use." This is intended to keep the patient from feeling sick.

HOME CURES *Despite the introduction of Western medicines into the Far East in recent years, many people still rely heavily on traditional remedies made from animal bones and skins, which they sometimes purchase from a vendor.*

BREAKING THE SILENCE

Dispelling myths about the world's first talkie

WHEN *THE JAZZ SINGER,* starring Al Jolson, opened at the Warner Theater in New York City on October 6, 1927, crowds flocked to see it. It was a momentous event, the screening of the world's first talking picture.

But although *The Jazz Singer* was the first *full-length* feature film containing vocal sound, it was not the first film to present sound to the public.

Mixed reception

As strange as it seems today, "talking" films were not universally welcomed in the 1920's, despite their novelty. Silent films were highly respected as an extension of the art of mime, since actors had to resort to exaggerated gestures to help convey what was happening. Also they could immediately be understood by audiences in any country regardless of language. So the advent of sound was even resisted to some extent; in some quarters it was viewed as a potential threat to both an actor's skill and his marketability.

Despite the objections, within a few years of the invention of cinematography in the 1890's a number of pioneers were experimenting with ways to combine sound and vision. Early attempts with phonographs were unsuccessful, largely because of the problems of amplifying the sound enough for the entire audience to hear it.

A prototype talking picture was demonstrated on June 8, 1900, at the Phono-Cinéma-Théâtre during the Paris Exposition. It was a primitive synchronized-disc system and featured such well-known performers as Sarah Bernhardt delivering a range of short speeches and songs. During the rest of the decade a number of short films were shown; they featured music-hall stars, accompanied by their recordings of popular songs.

A sound-on-film process, with the sound actually recorded onto the film, was demonstrated by French-born Eugène Lauste in London in 1912, but further development was temporarily halted by World War I.

In 1918–19 a system known as Tri-Ergon was developed in Germany. It advanced and refined the technology for recording sound on film photographically—later to be perfected by the American inventor Lee De Forest in his Phonofilm system. By the 1920's, sound-on-film was being used concurrently with films accompanied by records. In the years following World War I, several short films were made containing both dialogue and music.

Sound effects

In 1921 D.W. Griffith's silent film *Dream Street* was rereleased with two added audio sequences—a song and a series of sound effects, but no spoken dialogue. *La Muchacha del Arrabal,* made in Argentina in 1922, contained short segments of dialogue.

On September 17, 1922, at the Alhambra Cinema in Berlin, a film with dialogue, *Der Brandstifter (The Arsonist),* became the first movie made as a talkie to be shown to an audience. Based on a play of the same name by Von Heyermann, the film featured a cast of three; one actor, Erwin Baron, played seven different parts.

ALL THE WAY WITH LBJ

In 1964 the inhabitants of New Hanover, off New Guinea, found a novel way of expressing their discontent with the Australian government, which administered their territory: they established a fund to buy President Lyndon B. Johnson from the United States.

More than 2,000 of the island's 7,000 inhabitants supported the scheme, which reportedly raised nearly $3,000 toward installing the U.S. president as their leader. Many of the islanders withheld their taxes, instead paying the money into the Johnson fund. They made a down payment on the president, which they deposited with a local missionary, and refused to take part in local elections because Johnson's name did not appear on the ballot.

The movement to buy the president continued for two years without success; more than 500 of the islanders were jailed for failing to pay taxes. The affair ended with the appearance of an Australian regiment that visited the island to reassert the government's authority.

It was President Johnson's lot never to run on New Hanover.

Also in 1922 a U.S. film, *Lincoln's Gettysburg Address,* presented a monologue delivered by Ellery Paine. It was made for experimental purposes, however, and was not shown commercially.

The following year several short talkies were made by the Phonofilm process and shown at the Rialto Theater in New York City. In 1924 a talking-film recording was made of President Calvin Coolidge speaking during his reelection campaign. That same year a ballet, Balieff's *Chauve-Souris (Bat),* was filmed in Technicolor with a sound track; in 1925 it became the first color sound-on-film subject shown to an audience in Britain. Also in 1925 the De Forest Phonofilm Company produced *The Gentlemen,* a short comedy film with sound.

Sweet success

The decades of experiment led to the making of *The Jazz Singer* in 1927, filmed by Warner Brothers with its newly developed Vitaphone system. Although the film contained very little dialogue—its two spoken sequences have just 354 words—and the musical accompaniment was on a record, its phenomenal success assured its place in popular legend as the "first" talkie.

Prophetically, one of the first ad-libbed lines spoken by Jolson in the film was "You ain't heard nothin' yet, folks!"—an expression that came to symbolize the Age of the Talkies.

A SOUND SUCCESS *Released in 1927,* The Jazz Singer *has become legendary as the world's first talking picture. However, it was not the* first.

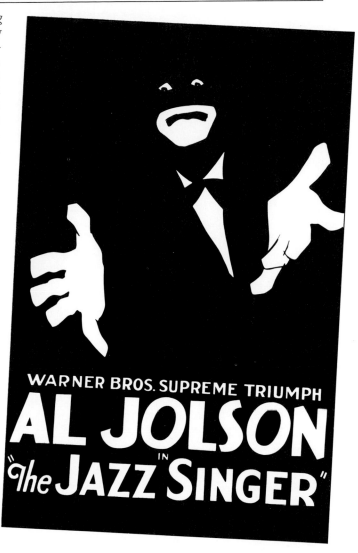

DIVERSIONARY TACTICS

It is against Buddhist teachings to kill other creatures, but that has not stopped Buddhists in the past from executing wrongdoers. To avoid transgression, some Buddhists would devise ingenious methods of bringing about the death of an intended victim without administering the fatal blow.

In Tibet, Buddhists would often imprison victims in dungeons—such as the notorious Cave of Scorpions in the Potala Palace in Lhasa—or throw them into a well and leave them to their fate, as in the case of the Christian missionary Sundar Singh early in this century.

At other times Buddhists would sew up the unfortunate wretch in a wet yak skin; when it dried and shrank in the sun, the sufferer would either suffocate or be crushed to death. Binding the arms and legs of the victim and throwing him into a river to drown was another method of carrying out an execution.

Such apparent brutality is difficult to reconcile with the Buddhist belief in the sanctity of life, but it helped to ensure that Tibetans remained law-abiding.

ESCAPE BY VERSE

It may seem difficult to believe that simply by memorizing the first verse of Psalm 51 in the Bible, a murderer could escape the hangman's noose. But that was the law in medieval England.

In those days English secular courts meted out severe punishments; the death sentence applied to anything from treason to horse stealing. But in the church courts the death sentence did not exist. Having a connection—however tenuous—with the church meant a trial in an ecclesiastical court, which could save a life.

Proving the connection was easy. If a person could read, he was obviously a Christian cleric entitled to claim "benefit of clergy," a church law that exempted the lawbreaker from the most severe punishment.

Those who could not read—the majority of the population at the time—avoided the test of their literacy by memorizing what popularly became known as the "neck verse."

By reciting the first verse of Psalm 51—"Have mercy upon me, O God, according to thy loving-kindness: according unto the multitude of thy tender mercies blot out my transgressions"—the lawbreaker claimed benefit of clergy. While this exemption led to much corruption, it also saved the neck of many a petty criminal.

By the time Henry VIII came to the throne in 1509, so many people were claiming a connection with the growing number of cathedrals, colleges, and monastic houses that many hundreds of thousands of lawbreakers were eligible for the benefit-of-clergy privilege. Apart from the nuns, however, until 1692 women could not claim the privilege, and then only if they were married.

When the literacy test was revoked in 1705, anyone convicted of a first felony could claim benefit of clergy without having to prove it. However, many subsequent laws that were passed expressly stated that punishment was to be "without benefit of clergy." The law was finally abolished in England in 1841.

In the United States, where early English colonial settlers had introduced the law, it was abolished in 1790 for all federal crimes. By the middle of the 19th century it had disappeared from U.S. courts altogether.

THE FEAST OF FOOLS

A grotesque parody

ONCE A YEAR in medieval France the world turned upside down. On January 1 the great cathedrals and churches were the setting for uproarious revels that mocked the foundations of faith and poked fun at holy rites.

The singing of the magnificat at vespers was the signal for the burlesque to begin. On the words "He hath put down the mighty from their seat and exalted the humble and meek," the *baculus*, or staff of office, was handed to a representative chosen from the ranks of the lower clergy to be "Bishop," "Pope," or "King" of Fools. Then revelers dressed in pantomime costume, wearing animal masks and decked in flowers, invaded the higher stalls, the preserve of their superiors. Sometimes they put church vestments on inside out, dressed up as women, or took their clothes off.

There was dancing, off-key singing, eating, drinking, whipping, and ducking—even playing dice on the altar. Often, an ass was brought into the church and a parody called the "Prose of the Ass" was chanted, complete with braying responses.

Instead of incense, sausages, black pudding, and burning shoes were waved in the air; sermons were conducted in gibberish, and satirical verses performed. Finally, at the end of the "service," the participants would proceed out of the church on a manure wagon, regaling the winter night with their lewd songs and obscene antics.

Role reversals

The Feast of Fools was most popular in France, Germany, Spain, and England. Strictly speaking, it took place on the Feast of the Circumcision, on January 1, but festivities often continued for days.

The origins of this bizarre custom probably date back to pagan times. The Roman festival Kalends took place at this time of year and included remarkably similar activities. It persisted well into the Christian era, finally disappearing just as the Feast of Fools began, early in the 12th century. Aspects of the revelry are related to other Christian celebrations at the same time of year—the festival of the choirboys on Holy Innocents' Day (December 28) and the Feast of the Asses (January 14).

What all these events had in common was the inversion of status, with the lesser clergy—subdeacons, vicars, chaplains, and choir clerks—assuming the role of higher officials. The Feast of Fools was their holiday, a chance to overturn the rules they had obeyed the rest of the year.

Although the church generally viewed the feast with indulgence, attempts were made to curb its worst excesses. One such edict specified that no more than three buckets of water could be poured over the "Bishop." Finally, in 1435, the Great Council of Basel issued a decree prohibiting the feasts altogether. In France this law was enforced by Charles VII, with parliament given the power to impose heavy penalties.

Despite these measures, the irrepressible spirit of mayhem of the Feast of Fools refused to die. When forbidden by the church, the topsy-turvy tradition was adopted by lay people, who managed to preserve it, in modified form. It eventually petered out sometime during the 16th century.

STREET LIFE *Although the annual Feast of Fools was banned by the church in 1435, the festivities associated with it—as depicted in this contemporary engraving—continued in towns and villages until the 16th century.*

The Good and the Bad

WILD BILL HICKOK

Villain or hero?

THE EXPLOITS of James Butler Hickok are legendary. During his short life (he died at 39) he was a federal scout, army spy, Indian fighter, professional gambler, and U.S. marshal. Somewhere along the way he also acquired the nickname Wild Bill and a reputation as a fearless hero, peerless gunfighter, and charming womanizer, renowned for his fashionable clothes.

Wild Bill Hickok died in 1876, shot through the back of the head by a coward—a coward who had so feared Hickok's reputation as a gunfighter that he felt it would be suicide to meet him face to face.

But shortly after Hickok's death, rumors started that his great reputation was founded on exaggeration, and sometimes downright lies.

Hickok first became famous in 1867, when *Harper's New Monthly Magazine* published an article about him. It told of an incident in 1861 when Hickok had pitted himself against a man called McCanles and his gang of "desperadoes, horse thieves, murderers, and regular cut-throats." It was said that Hickok had killed six men with the six bullets in his gun, then the remaining four with a

knife. He had survived, despite being riddled with bullets and stab wounds. The article was the foundation of Hickok's heroic reputation; afterward he was constantly besieged by journalists who wanted more tales of his daring deeds.

To some people, however, the "McCanles massacre" raised some doubt as to Hickok's behavior. Hickok had met McCanles when he was at Rock Creek Station, working for the Pony Express Company, which owed McCanles money. McCanles was putting pressure on Wellman, the station superintendent, to pay up.

On July 21, 1861, McCanles went to Wellman's ranch house with his 12-year-old son and two employees to demand a settlement. Wellman, suspecting trouble, summoned Hickok to the house.

During an argument outside between McCanles and Wellman, Hickok stepped inside the house and behind a curtain. When McCanles yelled at him to come out, Hickok shot him through the curtain. The McCanles gang came to help, and Hickok shot them too. McCanles died from his wounds, but the others were killed by Wellman and his men.

But another version of the story claims that it was Wellman who shot McCanles, and that Hickok killed the other men. There was also some dispute as to the part played in the affair by McCanles. Some people believed that he was a bully, but not a killer, and that he had been unarmed when Hickok shot him. And why should a man expecting trouble take his son along? Others argued that McCanles had always been armed before; why not then?

At the trial it was the word of McCanles Junior against Hickok that his father had been unarmed. The truth was never conclusively established, but the court accepted the plea that Hickok, Wellman, and another man had acted in self-defense in the protection of company property.

Hickok's detractors may say that he acted like a coward. But the general view is that the original story was essentially true, if exaggerated. To most people Wild Bill Hickok is still a hero of the Wild West—brave, fearless, and honest to the end.

HERO OR COWARD? *The reputation of Wild Bill Hickok as a fearless and invincible gunfighter was widespread in the Wild West. After his death at the age of 39, however, rumors began to circulate that cast doubt on his reputation.*

THE ATTORNEY AND THE SERVANT

An offer he could not refuse

AT 4:30 P.M. on May 2, 1962, Mrs. Robert Lee Kidd walked into the offices of the *San Francisco Examiner* and placed the following personal advertisement in the paper:

> I don't want my husband to die in the gas chamber for a crime he did not commit. I will therefore offer my services for 10 years as a cook, maid or housekeeper to any leading attorney who will defend him and bring about his vindication. 522 Hayes St. UN 3–9799.

Mrs. Kidd's husband was accused of the torture and murder, 18 months previously, of Albert Clarke, a 71-year-old San Francisco antiques dealer. Kidd's bloody fingerprints had been found on the murder weapon, an ornate sword. But Mrs. Kidd insisted that her husband had been at home with her on the night of the slaying.

Kidd had already been tried twice for the murder. He had been convicted the first time, but the State Supreme Court ordered a new trial because the court had admitted prejudicial evidence. The second trial had ended in a hung jury. And now funds had run out. So Mrs. Kidd made her extraordinary offer to pay an attorney with a decade of domestic work.

Mrs. Kidd's advertisement appeared on May 3, 1962, along with an unexpected bonus: the *Examiner* featured the Kidds' story on its front page. As a result of the publicity, one of San Francisco's most eminent attorneys, Vincent Hallinan, took up the case.

Innocent or guilty?

In court, Hallinan first proved that the sword was not, in fact, the murder weapon. Then he showed how Kidd's bloody fingerprints had gotten on it. Kidd and a friend had visited the antiques shop some time before the old man's death, and Kidd had been accidentally hurt while fighting a mock duel with the weapon.

After 11 hours of deliberation, the jury found Kidd not guilty. Both husband and wife went free: Hallinan graciously refused to take up Mrs. Kidd's offer of 10 years of service.

THE UGLY DUCHESS

During her adventures in Lewis Carroll's *Wonderland,* Alice meets a very sour-tempered duchess who treats a baby badly, sings "Speak roughly to your little boy," and—much to Alice's dismay—commands, "Chop off her head." John Tenniel's classic illustration in the first edition of *Alice* portrays the duchess as a grotesque, wide-mouthed old woman in medieval dress.

This unpleasant character is not purely the product of a vivid imagination: she is almost certainly modeled on a real duchess who was one of the most evil women of all time.

Duchess Margaret of Tyrol was born in 1318, the daughter of Henry, duke of Carinthia and of Tyrol, a claimant to the throne of Bohemia. Since Duke Henry had produced no sons, Margaret was eventually to inherit his dukedom. In the meantime, in order to strengthen his family's claims to the throne, the duke arranged the marriage of 12-year-old Margaret to John Henry, son of the king of Bohemia.

Brief affair

It was not long before Margaret decided to divorce Prince John on grounds of his impotence, resulting in a sensational (and in its day, rare) court case and the threat of excommunication from the church by the pope.

Even before the case was concluded, Margaret married Louis, the son of the emperor of Germany. This, too, appears to have been an unsatisfactory partnership: Margaret openly conducted numerous liaisons with young peasants, whom she frequently rewarded with titles and lands.

As a result of her involvement in many sex scandals and political intrigues, Margaret was regarded by her contemporaries as the most "wicked and licentious" woman in Europe.

Her chief political weapon seems to have been the poison bottle. She is reputed to have poisoned many of her opponents as well as her husband and her son—just as the latter was about to wrest power from her.

Margaret's many love affairs are all the more remarkable when one considers her unattractive appearance: she had a vast gaping mouth that led to her being nicknamed Margaretha Maultasch ("Pocket-mouthed Meg") and the reputation of being one of "the ugliest women in history."

GROTESQUE PORTRAIT *John Tenniel's well-known illustration of the Ugly Duchess (above) appeared in the first edition of* Alice in Wonderland. *It is probably based on a sketch of Duchess Margaret of Tyrol attributed to Leonardo da Vinci (left).*

DEAR DIARY

One of the most extraordinary frauds in history

ON THE MORNING of April 22, 1983, the telex machine at the West German magazine *Der Stern* in Hamburg began sending an astounding message to news agencies around the world: *Stern* had acquired the original manuscripts of the long-lost private diaries of Adolf Hitler. Publication in *Stern* would begin the following week, and the diaries would be serialized in publications all over the world.

It was to be the greatest journalistic scoop of all time and would give an unparalleled insight into the mind of the German dictator. Historians, former Nazis, and newspapermen expressed grave doubts about the authenticity of the documents, but *Stern* remained adamant that they were genuine. Then, on May 5, West German forensic scientists announced that the precious manuscripts had failed their tests. The 62 volumes of Hitler's diaries were fakes.

How had *Stern* been so deceived? And who was behind a fraud of such spectacular proportions?

Trail of obsession

Gerd Heidemann, the *Stern* researcher who had procured the diaries, was an obsessive collector of Nazi memorabilia and an acquaintance of several high-ranking former Nazis. He was also aware that in the last days of World War II an airplane carrying material from Hitler's underground bunker in Berlin had crashed near Boernersdorf, in what is today East Germany. Hitler had been appalled when he heard of the crash. The aircraft, he had said, had been carrying personal documents of enormous importance to posterity.

Early in 1980 Heidemann met another collector who showed him his prize possession: a volume of Hitler's personal diary which, he claimed, had come from the wreck at Boernersdorf.

Through another contact, Heidemann eventually traced the source of the diary: a man calling himself Konrad Fischer, living in Stuttgart. Late in 1980 the two men met. Fischer said that his brother, a general in the East German border guard, had acquired the diary from the Boernersdorf villagers who had taken it from the crashed airplane. Furthermore, the diary Heidemann had seen was only the first of 27 volumes.

Heidemann was ecstatic. He immediately began negotiations with Fischer to smuggle the rest of the diaries into West Germany, together with the manuscript of an unpublished volume of Hitler's *Mein Kampf*. For this, Heidemann told *Stern*'s management, Fischer wanted 2.5 million deutschmarks (just over $1 million at the time).

Heidemann urged against bringing experts in to examine the material. Absolute secrecy was essential: if the existence of the diaries became known, the East German general would stop sending them across the border. *Stern*'s management agreed that it was a small price to pay.

Genuine belief

What the executives at *Stern* overlooked, however, was the nature of Heidemann's obsession with the Nazis. He had already spent a large amount of the magazine's money in a fruitless search for Martin Bormann, Hitler's aide, who had vanished at the end of the war. Heidemann's own collection of Nazi relics was full of fakes, although he believed every item to be genuine. And his determination to restore the yacht that had belonged to the Luftwaffe commander, Hermann Goering, had plunged Heidemann into debt.

Nevertheless, *Stern* accepted all of the conditions that Heidemann laid down. Heidemann was the only person to have contact with Fischer. A special bank account was set up from which he could draw the large sums of cash he would need to pay Fischer on *Stern*'s behalf.

First sight

Early in February 1983 Heidemann presented the *Stern* executives with the first of the diaries: three notebooks, each about half an inch thick, bound in black imitation leather, embossed with the initials "A.H.," and with a red wax seal on the covers. A label signed by Hitler's deputy, Rudolf Hess, testified that they were Hitler's property. The pages of the notebooks were filled with an old-fashioned German script. No one present had any doubts about their authenticity.

Heidemann met no resistance when, after delivering only 12 of the diaries, he said that the price had risen to 100,000 marks ($40,000) per volume. Six volumes later the price rose again, to 200,000 marks each. Heidemann also persuaded *Stern* to pay him a fee of 1.5 million marks ($615,000) for his part in finding the diaries. And, he announced, many more than the 27 volumes first mentioned had been saved from the crash.

Fischer was to receive considerably smaller sums than these for his part in bringing the diaries into

West Germany: Heidemann kept a large portion of *Stern*'s money for himself. But then, Fischer's own efforts were slightly less dangerous than he had led Heidemann to believe.

Fischer's real name was Konrad Kujau, and his brother the general was in reality a railway porter. Kujau had become expert at forging Nazi relics. His specialty was producing paintings by Hitler, which he sold at astronomical prices to gullible but wealthy collectors. He turned out hundreds over the years, each with a certificate confirming its authenticity. Then he decided to try forging a diary. It was to prove the simplest, and most lucrative, work he had ever done.

Story of a forgery

Kujau amassed a library of more than 500 books and periodicals to provide details of Hitler's day-to-day existence. Once his research was completed, it took him less than five hours to write a volume in Hitler's handwriting. The notebooks he used were old schoolbooks he had found in East Germany. To age them he bent and beat them, and splashed them with tea.

The content of the diaries is in general so banal that no one familiar with Hitler's real thoughts could possibly have been taken in. Page after page is devoted to some detailed accounts of official engagements and Nazi Party announcements. One five-page entry, for example, consists of nothing more than a list of promotions in the German Army. But Heidemann was convinced that the diaries were genuine.

Incontrovertible evidence

Under mounting international pressure, *Stern* finally had the diaries rigorously tested. The forensic evidence was indisputable: *Stern*'s great scoop was nothing but a forgery. But the management of *Stern* had no one but itself to blame. Eager for a massive journalistic coup, executives had ignored the fact that Heidemann had in the past shown himself to be exceptionally gullible, and they had initially allowed only the most cursory examination of the diaries. Because of fears that the story would leak out, only a few key executives knew of the transaction, despite its enormous cost.

The magazine had paid out 9.4 million marks (almost $4 million) through Heidemann, of which 5 million are still missing today. Other liabilities brought the total cost of the fiasco to 19 million marks. After their conviction, Heidemann and Kujau went to jail for fraud.

The trade in Nazi mementos, real or otherwise, continues to thrive. The grim figure of Adolf Hitler still fascinates the world long after his death.

A MASTER OF HIS ART

How one man fooled a nation's art dealers

ON SEPTEMBER 10, 1984, more than 1,000 people crowded into the salesroom at Christie's, London's famed auctioneers, and pushed up the bidding for 204 paintings and drawings enough to bring in seven times the amount Christie's had estimated. Even more surprising was that, without exception, these particular works of art were acknowledged fakes.

They were the work of Tom Keating, perhaps the greatest art faker of the 20th century. As with so many artists, his paintings had made far more money after his death than they had in his lifetime.

For more than 25 years Keating produced paintings in the styles of some of the most renowned artists in history, including Constable, Rembrandt, Degas, Gainsborough, Goya, Renoir, Turner, Toulouse-Lautrec, Modigliani, Monet, and Van Gogh.

Yet Keating never faked these pictures for financial gain. He did it, he said, "simply as a protest against merchants who make capital out of ... artists, both living and dead." And he added: "I've given away a lot more than I've sold."

Tricks and clues

Keating always left a clue in his pictures to show that they were not genuine. Sometimes he would write "This is a fake" or "Ever been had?" in white lead paint on a canvas before starting work on it. Such messages were guaranteed to show up if the paintings were X-rayed—a standard procedure in testing suspected forgeries. On other occasions he would paint a detail in the wrong style, or use modern paper for a drawing purportedly made in the 19th century.

Nonetheless, Keating's methods were often painstaking. He had learned many of them as a picture restorer. He would spend hours in junk shops looking for old paintings with mountings and frames that he could use. He sometimes managed to acquire the wooden stretchers to which the canvases of genuine old masters had been fixed, with Christie's catalog numbers stenciled on them. Keating would call Christie's to find out which painting by which artist had been on the stretcher. Then he knew what to paint.

Keating made ink for "Rembrandt" drawings by simmering walnuts in water for 10 hours and straining the resulting liquid through silk. Other effects were simpler to achieve. Keating faked foxmarks (stains caused by mildew) on paper by first soaking the paper in water and then scattering a few granules of instant coffee over it.

Keating ascribed his ability to create such expert fakes to something more than sheer technique. "I couldn't paint a Goya, Rembrandt, or even a Samuel Palmer for a million pounds or to save my life," he explained, "but I often felt their spirits actually guiding my hand." When that happened, the images would "flow out onto the canvas without the slightest effort on my part."

Suspicions mount

It was Keating's imitations of the 18th-century artist Palmer that finally unmasked him in 1976. In 1970, some 13 previously unheard-of Palmer drawings began to circulate in the salesrooms. Several art dealers became suspicious because all 13 pictures were supposedly of Shoreham, England, where Palmer had spent only a few years. It seemed incredible that so many drawings should emerge so quickly from such complete obscurity.

When the London *Times* published an article doubting the authenticity of the drawings, Keating wrote to the newspaper confessing not only to faking them but also to producing more than 2,000 other imitations.

In 1977 Keating was arrested on charges of conspiracy and criminal deception, but the trial was stopped after a defense plea that Keating was too ill to stand the strain. He died seven years later, aged 66, still unrepentant.

Keating did, however, leave the art world a legacy by refusing to name all his fakes. So today when an old master comes up for sale, with an asking price perhaps running into millions of dollars, the auctioneer always has to wonder if the painting before him might be one of Keating's.

OLD MASTER *Countless works of the celebrated art counterfeiter Tom Keating have passed under the hammer at Christie's, the prestigious London auctioneers. Although most were acknowledged fakes, Keating's paintings have been known to sell for remarkably high prices.*

THE FASTEST GUN

The fighter who rarely fought

WILLIAM BARCLAY "BAT" MASTERSON was one of the most feared gunfighters in the Old West. Born in Illinois in 1853, he was a hero by the time he was 23.

Masterson first attracted attention as one of a party of 35 buffalo hunters and plainsmen who, for five days in June 1873, held off a ferocious attack by some 500 Indians at Adobe Walls in the Texas Panhandle. Masterson's standing rose even further in the spring of 1875 when, as a U.S. Army scout, he helped rescue two sisters whom the Cheyennes had been holding hostage.

Masterson's first gunfight took place in Sweetwater, Texas, in 1875; it sealed his reputation as a man to fear. His relationship with saloon girl Molly Brennan so angered her former lover, Sergeant King, that King came gunning for Masterson. As King fired, Molly threw herself in front of Masterson. The bullet killed her instantly, then smashed into Masterson's pelvis. Staggering, he drew his gun and killed King.

In 1877, when he was 24, Masterson was elected sheriff of Ford County, Kansas, home of the unruly cow town, Dodge City. Saloons, gambling houses,

TWO RAVENS AND A MIRACLE

Nestled in a lakeside valley some 30 miles southeast of Zurich, Switzerland, lie the town and Benedictine monastery of Einsiedeln. Every year, the town plays host to thousands of pilgrims who come to pay homage to the monastery's Black Madonna, an unusual black statue of the Virgin Mary. Visitors also hear the story of how the holy icon came to be there.

In A.D. 840 Meinrad, a monk from the Benedictine abbey of Reichenau, went into the mountains to become a hermit. He took with him a statue, the Black Madonna (a gift from the abbess of Zurich), and settled in a remote cave overlooking Lake Sihl.

Meinrad lived in this simple cell for more than 20 years. Legend says that he befriended two ravens, so loyal they would bring the holy man food to eat.

Simple as Meinrad's life was, a pair of thieves suspected that the monk was hiding something of worldly value greater than his treasured icon. In 863 they attacked Meinrad in his cell and killed him. Their greed turned to

terror when two candles in the cave lit of their own accord, and the two ravens began to shriek, cry, and harass them.

Although the thieves fled as far as Zurich, the ravens pursued them, pecking at them and flapping their wings until the two villains were arrested.

In 940, in memory of Meinrad, the Benedictines established a monastery near the site of Meinrad's cave, and in 948 a new church was built to house the Madonna. But as Bishop Conrad of Constance began the service of consecration, a great voice sounded three times throughout the

church: "Stop, stop, brother! God Himself has consecrated this building," it commanded.

In 964, Pope Leo VIII issued a papal bull pronouncing the event a miracle, blessing all who made the pilgrimage to Einsiedeln.

Meinrad was canonized in the 13th century. In memory of the ravens, for many years afterward the brothers at Einsiedeln used to catch a raven each fall, feed it through the winter, and set it free in spring.

HOLY PLACE *The Chapel of Grace, with the famous statue of the Black Madonna, is inside the church of the Benedictine monastery of Einsiedeln in Switzerland.*

and ladies of the night did a roaring trade in the spring and summer as hundreds of cowboys arrived with herds of Texas cattle for shipment to Chicago stockyards by rail.

Bat by name

The name Masterson was guaranteed to strike terror into the heart of most seasoned desperadoes. Masterson had his own rather unusual way of dealing with troublemakers—a method that earned him his famous nickname. The fracas in Sweetwater had left Masterson lame, and he always carried a cane. Not only did it help him walk, he soon found that using it to give a smart bat on the head quickly subdued most ruffians.

Masterson was not the cold, dedicated killer of Western legend. Gregarious, mild-mannered, and good-humored, he arrived in Dodge City sporting a gray sombrero with a rattlesnake band; a silver-studded belt and holsters, with two ivory-handled, silver-plated pistols to match; a crimson Mexican sash; and a red silk kerchief at his neck. Marveling at his flamboyant appearance, one bystander even wondered whether Masterson was hoping to blind, not shoot, any potential adversary.

And rarely did Masterson have to pull his gun to win an argument. Instead, he would spend hours shooting at targets before a crowd of admiring onlookers. As word of his phenomenal speed and accuracy spread, Masterson's mere presence was usually enough to keep the peace.

On one occasion the notorious James brothers, Jesse and Frank, sneaked out of Dodge City quietly rather than face him. In the 1880's the town of Trinidad, Colorado, reputedly paid Masterson $1,000 a month simply to be sure that he was seen wearing his marshal's badge. Trinidad remained a quiet town. Although folklore puts the figure between 20 and 30, throughout his long career as a professional gunman, Masterson killed only three men in gunfights.

To die with his boots on

Masterson felled two of his opponents in 1878, when he saw his brother Ed, marshal of Dodge City, shot dead at point-blank range by two drunken cowboys. From 60 feet away, Masterson downed one of the men with one shot. Three more bullets riddled his companion.

Masterson rarely used his guns again, other than in self-defense. He supplemented his livelihood as a gambler by promoting prizefights; eventually he became sports editor of the *Morning Telegraph* in New York City. This living legend and frequent guest of President Teddy Roosevelt's died of a heart attack in 1921 while working at his desk.

ROOT CAUSES

Violence may go to the head

PEOPLE HAVE LONG puzzled over what factors go into the making of a criminal personality. In the past, some psychiatrists, psychologists, and criminologists have attributed it to a deprived upbringing. But recent studies indicate that violent and antisocial behavior can be caused by chemical imbalances in the body.

How did this line of investigation start? Surprisingly enough, with a chess game.

When a team of scientists challenged a team of long-term offenders at Stateville State Prison, Joliet, Illinois, to a friendly game of chess in 1972, they did not expect the inmates to beat them. Nursing their sore egos, the experts—all from the Argonne National Laboratory at the University of Chicago—demanded a rematch. Other games followed, and friendships between the two sides sprang up. One of the scientists, chemist William J. Walsh, began to wonder "why such nice people could have done such terrible things."

Abandoning some long-held "bad environment" theories, Walsh mustered a group of 20 volunteer chemists, statisticians, physicians, and computer analysts, and began to search for clues to violent behavior in body chemistry. The question the group asked was: Do violent people have biochemical characteristics that are different from those of nonviolent people?

Metal tracing

At first the scientists searched for answers by analyzing blood and urine. But the results were too inconsistent to be useful, since these fluids are affected by diet.

The breakthrough came in 1976, when the Walsh team began to use hair analysis, a method also being employed by scientists at McGill University in Montreal. Convinced that hair was the ideal medium for his work—he believed that it would retain a higher concentration of trace metals than blood would—Walsh and his colleagues spent several years collecting hair samples and analyzing them in terms of their metal content.

When funds from the Argonne Laboratory ran out in 1980, Walsh and his fellow scientists set up their own specialized unit, the Health Research Institute. Their first experiment was a controlled study involving 24 pairs of brothers, ages 8 to 18. Each pair consisted of one delinquent and one nondelinquent boy. All the subjects lived with their parents and ate the same food, so environmental distinctions were minimized.

Hair samples were taken from each of the 48 boys and tested for 11 elements: calcium, magnesium, sodium, potassium, copper, zinc, iron, manganese, phosphorus, lead, and cadmium. Concentrations of these trace metals were found to be 10 to 100 times higher in hair than they had been in blood or in urine.

Violent patterns

The violent subjects had far higher levels of metals in their hair than the nonviolent ones, as had been anticipated. But the results of further tests were extremely surprising.

Expecting to find two patterns of behavior, one for the violent and one for the nonviolent, the scientists instead uncovered two patterns for the violent brothers alone. Those in the Type A category (also observed in hyperactive children) appear to be law-abiding until something snaps, and they can commit vicious violence. The Type B pattern was different. Those with this behavior are antisocial and chronically in conflict with authority.

Armed with these results, the Walsh team decided on a more complex experiment involving 96 former convicts, prison inmates, and delinquent youths with extremely violent histories, and 96 nonviolent males. This time the results were consistent with those of the previous experiment.

Hair analyses divided the violent group into either Type A or Type B personalities, supporting the theory that these people suffer from two types of chemical imbalances. Since that time Walsh has added a Type C and a Type D category to include patterns found among the mildly violent.

The gentle approach

The implications of Walsh's analysis were far-reaching. If a link was found between chemical imbalances in the hair and violence, a similar correlation might exist between such imbalances and hyperactivity, alcoholism, or learning disabilities, for example. Biochemical screening in conjunction with other methods might, therefore, be used to diagnose such problems.

Walsh has now turned his attention to the therapeutic possibilities of his work. At the Brain Bio Center, near Princeton, New Jersey, Dr. Carl Pfeiffer has been combining Walsh's data with his own therapy, prescribing vitamin and mineral supplements in place of drugs to correct chemical imbalances in criminals.

Although no formal study of the results has been made, encouraging reports have come back from those treated for violence. As interest in Walsh's pioneer work grows, science may one day help transform violence into constructive behavior.

THE FAMOUS FORMOSAN

The man who invented a nation

EARLY IN THE 18TH CENTURY a mysterious stranger captivated London's fashionable society with spellbinding tales of human sacrifice and cannibalism. He called himself George Psalmanazar, a native of the far-off land of Formosa. History knows him as one of the greatest impostors of his age.

Aristocrats, churchmen, and scientists competed to wine and dine the strange young man, just to hear his stories. Formosa was an exotic place, and few could have located it on a map. Today it is known as Taiwan, an island in the China Sea.

Psalmanazar had appeared with a letter of introduction to the bishop of London from the Reverend William Innes, who was attached to a Scottish regiment stationed in the Netherlands. The letter had unfolded the amazing story of how Jesuits had kidnapped the youth from his Formosan homeland and taken him to France. Despite threats of torture, he had bravely resisted conversion to Catholicism and escaped to Holland, where he had met the chaplain whose zeal and dedication had brought the youth into the Protestant church.

The story was pure fantasy, invented by Psalmanazar and elaborated upon by the mischievous chaplain. But the bishop—and every one of his associates—believed every word. Almost overnight Psalmanazar became a celebrity.

The visitor was undoubtedly talented. He could converse with the bishop in Latin and could also speak a number of other languages. As a gift, he had brought the Church of England catechism translated into "Formosan."

Island customs

Psalmanazar's patrons were agog listening to the descriptions of Formosan religious practices. He told them that at one festival it was commanded that every day for nine days 2,000 boys should have their hearts burned out upon an altar.

When someone pointed out that such a custom would soon leave Formosa with no population, Psalmanazar explained that his countrymen were polygamous and that the eldest sons were exempt from sacrifice. The life span on the island, Psalmanazar claimed, was 120 years; his own grandfather

SUPERHOAX *Illustrations from* An Historical and Geographical Description of Formosa *by the 18th-century literary trickster Psalmanazar.*

had lived to 117, remaining as vigorous as a youth thanks to the local custom of sucking the warm blood of a viper every morning.

Psalmanazar's audience sighed with pleasure over the surplus of gold and silver on Formosa: it was used not only for decorating the temples but also for covering the roofs and walls of houses in every town and village in the land.

Since the bishop thought it important to spread the news of this fascinating nation, he and his friends raised enough money to send Psalmanazar to Oxford University for six months. They wanted him to lecture to the students and teach them the basics of the Formosan language, in the hope that they would return with him and become Christian missionaries in far-off Formosa.

A fabulous place

Psalmanazar was encouraged to write an account of his exotic homeland. Published in 1704, *An Historical and Geographical Description of Formosa, an Island Subject to the Emperor of Japan* contained marvelous descriptions of the natives of Formosa, their dress, their architecture, and their religious ceremonies. The book also included the Formosan alphabet and Psalmanazar's translations of the Apostle's Creed, the Lord's Prayer, and the Ten Commandments. Almost immediately the book became what we would today call a best-seller, and was reprinted the following year.

However, Psalmanazar had made his first serious error in the title of the work: Formosa was a province of China, not of Japan. Various accusations of fraud were leveled at him, but Psalmanazar made it a point never to retract his claims.

In a second edition of the book he dealt with his critics severely, accusing them of lying. There had always been some who doubted the truth of his stories, but now the skepticism was growing.

Soon Psalmanazar was being scorned and ridiculed. Nor did he have the comfort of his partner in the hoax: the chaplain had been awarded an important post in Portugal.

Telling the truth

Psalmanazar withdrew from the public life he loved so much and had to support himself with menial jobs. After a serious illness in 1728, he totally rejected his past life and in a book of memoirs that was to be published only after his death, decided to tell the truth.

Psalmanazar died on May 3, 1763; he was about 84. His memoirs were published the following year. But to this day, his true name and native land remain an intriguing mystery.

KING OF THE GAMBLERS

The law of averages says that you cannot win at gambling: the odds are always against you. One man who spent most of his life proving that the law of averages was wrong was Nick the Greek Dandalos, also known as the King of the Gamblers.

During his lifetime Nick won more than $50 million. The secret of his success? He combined a passion for gambling with a businesslike approach. He became a specialist, playing only games such as poker and craps, which he felt confident he could win. Nick became so expert at judging the odds that he would think nothing of betting $60,000 on one roll of the dice.

Even when he was a multimillionaire and enjoying a lavish lifestyle, Nick could not resist the lure of a big game. In 1949, in front of thousands of spectators in a Las Vegas casino, he played his archrival, Johnny Moss, in what turned out to be the most dramatic poker game of all time.

The game lasted five months in all, with breaks every four or five days for sleep. At one point Nick won $1 million in a single hand. But eventually fortune smiled on Moss, and Nick reputedly lost about $2 million.

Convinced that the game was crooked, Nick brought a lawsuit against the casino, but in the end he lost the case.

Whatever the truth, it was the beginning of a terrible losing streak for Nick, and he was soon heavily in debt. His reign as King of the Gamblers was over.

Nick the Greek ended his days playing $5 poker games in the bars of California.

THE PRINCESS AND THE PIRATES

Tales from the East

ON THE EVENING of April 3, 1817, a very exhausted young woman knocked on a clergyman's door in the village of Almondsbury, in Gloucestershire, England. She spoke no English, and her tattered, exotic clothing gave her an Asiatic appearance. Bewildered by the girl, the clergyman took her before his friend Samuel Worrall, a local magistrate.

Worrall and his wife gave the girl shelter for the night, and the next day questioned the mysterious foreigner about her circumstances. The young woman answered their questions, using signs and gestures. She made it clear that her name was Caraboo, and that she was a princess from the Far East. She had been kidnapped by pirates and sold to the captain of a ship bound for Europe. When the ship reached England she had escaped and was now wandering the countryside begging for food.

The Worralls decided to care for Caraboo while they tried to solve the mystery of her nationality.

Feathers and a tambourine

The girl's behavior was indeed odd. She insisted on cooking her own food, would rarely eat meat, and drank only tea and water. Reluctant to sleep in a bed, she preferred to lie on the floor. She put feathers in her hair and walked around the gardens beating a tambourine. She often jumped into the lake fully clothed, and one time was found perched in a tree—with a bow and arrow.

News of the Worralls' exotic guest spread. Men who had traveled in the Far East came to interview her and observe her unusual habits. Although her language was gibberish to all, it was generally agreed that she must be from the East Indies.

After 10 weeks Caraboo disappeared. She was soon traced to the city of Bath, where she had become a celebrity in fashionable society. Mrs. Worrall went to Bath to collect her wayward charge and bring her back to Almondsbury.

The great pretender

Not long afterward Mrs. Worrall heard from a Mrs. Neale in Bristol, who had read about Caraboo in a local newspaper. Mrs. Neale believed that she could shed some light on the mystery. Caraboo seemed remarkably like Mary Baker, a former lodger of Mrs. Neale's. When confronted by Mrs. Worrall, the girl admitted to the deception and revealed her true identity.

Caraboo's real story was almost as remarkable as the made-up one. Born Mary Willcocks, she was from a poor family in Devon. Put to work at the age of 8, she was harshly treated and ran away from home when she was 16. She traveled to London with a band of Gypsies, from whom she acquired her odd behavior and dress.

Desertion and disguise

In London Mary met and married a widely traveled man named Bakerstendht (which she shortened to Baker). From her husband Mary picked up the smattering of Arabic and Malay that formed the basis of her strange language. When Bakerstendht deserted Mary after only a few months, she retreated into a fantasy world, eventually assuming the guise of the foreign princess.

Mrs. Worrall was moved by the hardship Mary had endured. When the girl expressed a desire to go to the United States, the kindly woman paid for her passage and put her on a ship in the care of a party of missionaries.

But during the voyage the ship skirted St. Helena, the island where Napoleon Bonaparte was living in exile following his defeat at Waterloo. Mary became Caraboo once more, stole a boat, and rowed ashore. She apparently enchanted Napoleon and became his companion.

Nothing more was ever heard of the mysterious Caraboo, although a rumor some years later maintained that she had returned to London, where she made her living selling leeches.

WOLF IN SHEEP'S CLOTHING

The most infamous pope in history?

OCTAVIAN, THE COUNT OF TUSCULUM, was barely 18 when he was consecrated pope on December 16, 955. His reign as Pope John XII was one of the worst in history.

Few were less suited to the office. As described by contemporary chronicles, John's major preoccupations were fighting (he donned armor and led an unsuccessful expedition against rival princes), mutilating enemies, arson, hunting, and gambling. He also frequently indulged in affairs with married women, and rewarded his many mistresses with gifts plundered from St. Peter's.

Power struggle

Threatened by the advance of Berengar, a local warring prince, in 962 John summoned to his aid Otto I of Saxony, whom John crowned Holy Roman Emperor. Otto subsequently tried to make John swear an oath of allegiance. When John refused, Otto summoned a council on November 6, 963, and leveled further charges against the pope. Among them: that he had ordained a deacon in a stable; consecrated a 10-year-old boy as bishop of Todi; converted the Lateran Palace into a brothel; raped female pilgrims in St. Peter's; stolen church offerings; drunk toasts to the devil; and, when playing dice, invoked the assistance of Jove, Venus, and other pagan gods and demons.

John refused to answer his accusers, however, and on December 4 was deposed by the emperor, who replaced him with Pope Leo VIII.

But as soon as the emperor left Rome, John returned and Leo fled. John then wreaked savage revenge on all who had opposed him, maiming many by cutting out their tongues, chopping off their noses, and hacking off their hands.

But John did not live to enjoy his return to power, and it was an affair with a married woman that led to his downfall. Caught in the act by the woman's outraged husband, he was severely beaten. He died of his injuries a few days later, on May 14, 964. John's brief reign had ended.

John XII was probably the most notorious pope in history.

INSCRUTABLE OR UNSCRUPULOUS?

The double life of Sir Edmund Backhouse

INSCRIBED ON a marble roll of honor on the wall of the Bodleian Library at Oxford University in England are the words "Edmundus Backhouse, baronettus." The inscription pays tribute to the eminent scholar Sir Edmund Backhouse, whose gift of more than 27,000 rare Chinese books and scrolls made the Bodleian into Europe's finest repository of Chinese scholarly materials.

The Backhouse Bequest arrived at the Bodleian Library in batches between 1913 and 1923. It proved to be an invaluable source of information about a still-mysterious land. The scholars and librarians had every reason to be thankful to their benefactor, an English gentleman-scholar who was born in 1873 and lived in Peking for many years until his death in 1944.

But had scholars known then what is known today about the baronet, they might have had second thoughts before inserting his name on that marble roll of honor. For in 1973 Sir Edmund Backhouse lost his respectability and earned notoriety as one of the greatest charlatans the world has ever known.

In that year Hugh Trevor-Roper, professor of modern history at Oxford University, acquired Sir Edmund's memoirs from one of the baronet's friends. It was Trevor-Roper's task to examine these memoirs before placing them in the Bodleian alongside the Backhouse Bequest.

Friend of the famous

To his surprise Trevor-Roper found himself reading an "unutterably pornographic" account of Sir Edmund's erotic adventures with dozens of the celebrities, male and female, of his day. There were detailed descriptions of liaisons with the poet Verlaine, the British prime minister Lord Rosebery, an Ottoman princess, and even the dowager empress of China. Backhouse also claimed to have acted with Sarah Bernhardt in Paris, chatted with the czarina in Moscow, gone drinking with Henry James in London, and visited Tolstoy on his country estate in Russia.

These anecdotes were so sensational that Trevor-Roper was immediately suspicious. He quickly discovered a significant mistake. Backhouse stated that his affair with Verlaine occurred in 1896, but the poet was not in England that year as Backhouse claimed.

Trevor-Roper then meticulously checked every detail and came to an inescapable conclusion: the

EMINENT FRAUD *Sir Edmund Backhouse long enjoyed an unrivaled academic reputation based on his two books about China and his magnificent bequest of books to the Bodleian Library in Oxford, England. Yet his revealing memoirs— which came to light in 1973—cast doubt on every aspect of his life and suggest that he was a fraud.*

memoirs were pure fantasy. Almost nothing in them was true. A new portrait of the Bodleian's benefactor began to emerge.

Fraud and forgery

One of the most startling discoveries made by Trevor-Roper about Backhouse's life concerned his business dealings in Peking. Backhouse had used his position as professor of law and literature at Peking University to make contacts at the imperial court in order to gain lucrative contracts for Western companies that were all too anxious to trade with China.

In 1916 Backhouse had negotiated a 13-year contract for the American Bank Note Company of New York City to supply bank notes to China, a contract supposedly signed by the Chinese prime minister. Officers of the company were so delighted that they readily paid Backhouse's large expenses and were happy to honor their agent's request that everything about the deal be kept secret.

However, no order from the Chinese government followed that contract. Meanwhile, the British shipbuilding company John Brown negotiated a contract through Backhouse to build seven warships for the Chinese. That contract also failed to receive confirmation. When the desperate companies tried to confront Backhouse, they found that he had left the country. On his return to Peking in 1921, he lived as a complete recluse and constantly refused to discuss the contracts.

Through careful investigation Trevor-Roper was able to establish that the contracts had been forged by Backhouse and that the Chinese government had never ordered any bank notes or battleships. Since the two companies had been sworn to secrecy, nothing emerged about the contracts, and Sir Edmund's reputation remained untarnished.

That reputation had been built on two classic books about imperial China—*China Under the Empress Dowager* (1910) and *Annals and Memoirs of the Court of Peking* (1914)—that Backhouse wrote with the London *Times* journalist J.O.P. Bland and published in England. The first book was based on the diary of a high-ranking court official, giving an insider's view of the turbulent events in turn-of-the-century China. By the 1930's academic critics had decided that the diary was a forgery that had been foisted upon an innocent Backhouse by a devious Oriental. But following up on clues in the Backhouse memoirs, Trevor-Roper discovered that no such diary had ever existed; Backhouse had invented the diary in order to give his work scholarly credibility.

But what of the treasures lodged at the Bodleian Library? Most of the books are authentic, but many of the thousands of calligraphic scrolls are undoubtedly fakes. Obviously, Backhouse could not have forged them all himself, but he must have been completely aware that they were not genuine when he donated them to the library.

Only detailed investigation of each book and scroll of the bequest will establish whether it is authentic or not. Meanwhile, Backhouse's name as a great scholar has been tarnished forever, and he has earned himself immortality as one of the greatest rogues of all time.

BE WELL...GOOD LUCK

What a symbol originally signified

THE 20TH CENTURY has been dominated by the swastika, one of the most feared symbols in the modern world. It represented Hitler and Nazi Germany and the horrors of 12 years of destruction, oppression, persecution, and mass murder on a hitherto undreamed-of scale.

Hitler made the swastika his emblem. He had chosen it in 1920 when he assumed leadership of the National Socialist (Nazi) Party. He wanted, he said, to give the party a flag that would draw people to it like a magnet. He chose the *hakenkreuz* —the "hooked cross," or swastika—and had it depicted in black in a white circle on a blood-red background. It was a stroke of evil genius.

Ancient origins

The design of the flag was his own. The swastika that dominated it was not. It had existed for thousands of years, its precise origin unknown.

In the book in which he set forth his political creed, *Mein Kampf* (My Struggle), Hitler wrote this about his flag: "In red we see the social idea of the movement, in white the nationalistic idea, in the swastika the mission of the struggle for the victory of the Aryan man." To Hitler the Aryans were the personification of racial purity, and he identified them with the fair-skinned, blue-eyed Nordic peoples of northern Europe.

In this belief he was actually wrong, for originally the Aryans were a tribe of Asiatic nomads that had invaded India in about 1500 B.C. and later forged strong racial and cultural links with all the peoples of the Middle East and Europe. Whatever else they might have been, they were hardly Hitler's ideal pure race. But they did provide him with the symbol of the swastika.

The word *swastika* is Aryan in origin. In Sanskrit, the ancient language spoken by the Aryans, the word *svasti* meant "Be well," or more colloquially, "Good luck." It is from *svasti* that the word *swastika* comes. The Aryans first associated the symbol with the fire god Agni, which may indicate

MALIGNED SYMBOL *Despite its notoriety, the swastika was originally a sign of good luck. As seen in the 12th-century carving (above) from a church doorway in Essex, England, Christians used it as a symbol of Christ's Resurrection and Second Coming. The swastika acquired its evil reputation when Hitler adopted it as the symbol of the Nazi Party. It was featured on objects from flags to propaganda posters, as in this fund-raising appeal by the Hitler Youth Movement (right).*

that the swastika predates the Aryans and is of prehistoric origin. Some scholars believe that it may at first have symbolized the spindle-drill, one of the oldest methods of making a fire: a spark was created by spinning a small stick inside another piece of wood—and hence "Good luck" was needed, since acquiring the skill was one of prehistoric peoples' greatest achievements.

Universal significance

Whatever its origins, the sign of the swastika spread across most of the ancient world to the other peoples of the Middle East and the Mediterranean, including the ancient Egyptians, Greeks, and Romans. With the passage of time the swastika assumed other meanings related to the revolving sun, the four winds, the four quarters of the moon, and the progression of the seasons. It was commonly depicted in two forms: left-handed (counterclockwise) and right-handed (clockwise). In China, where it was introduced by Buddhist missionaries from India in the sixth century A.D., the two forms stood for the *yin* and the *yang* — the balance between solar and lunar forces in the universe.

The swastika was used by early Christians as a symbol of Christ's Resurrection and Second Coming. It is also found in ancient Nordic and Teutonic mythology as the symbol of Thor, the god who hurled thunderbolts down from heaven. Quite independently from the rest of the world, many of the peoples of pre-Columbian America devised a form of the swastika for religious and ritualistic

purposes. In places as distant as Tibet and Peru, the swastika has been found on altars, urns, vases, swords, spears, shields, clothing, paintings, coins, and mosaics. Until it was adopted by Hitler, the swastika had assumed a meaning that was holy and usually benign, a universal religious symbol.

Hitler was no historian, but he knew of the swastika's ancient meanings as a sign of fire, of strength, and of power—attributes that he wanted to claim for his party. But it was his manipulative skill that turned such a revered symbol into the mark of oppression it has come to be today. Thus did Hitler corrupt and defile one of the oldest and most fascinating of human symbols.

STAGE FIGHT

A regular occurrence in the Wild West

WHEN THE TRAIN pulled into Palisade, Nevada, a junction town on the Central Pacific Railroad, passengers could hardly believe their eyes.

As they disembarked to stretch their legs after the long train ride, a gaunt cowboy with a .45 revolver rounded the side of the railroad depot and crossed the main street to the town saloon. Eyeing another man across the street, he shouted: "Ah bin lookin' for ya, an' now ah'm gonna' kill ya." He then pulled out his gun and fired.

The other man slumped back, apparently dead. The passengers hastily climbed back onto the train. Out on the street, an angry mob hustled the gunslinger away to the town jail.

This was not an isolated occurrence in Palisade in the 1870's. Indeed, it was so common that a train rarely pulled into the station without its passengers witnessing some similar manifestation of Wild West violence. Very soon Palisade was notorious as one of the toughest towns west of Chicago. Passengers on the Central Pacific would draw into Palisade with a mixture of excitement and trepidation, taking some comfort in the knowledge that no passengers had yet been involved in the carnage.

On show

There was, however, a bizarre twist to lawlessness in Palisade. Originally the town was no more than a watering stop on the railroad. But when a branch line was built to the nearby iron-ore mines at Eureka, Palisade became a boomtown. Saloons and stores sprang up to cater to the influx of passengers, many of whom were easterners visiting the West for the first time; they were prepared to believe everything they had heard about the wild area.

Inspired by the gullibility of their visitors, the inhabitants of Palisade decided to promote their town by reenacting the fabled Wild West behavior in front of the passengers. Each time a train pulled in, they turned Palisade into a theatrical stage and acted out an elaborate drama; beef blood from the local slaughterhouse added authenticity.

Main attraction

At one point or another, every resident of the town played a part: sometimes a gunslinger, sometimes a victim, a frightened passerby, or a lawman. The favorite performance of all, the one that most terrorized railroad passengers, was the bank robbery. This reenactment involved robbers, sheriff's deputies, and even a few Indians.

The violent charade ceased only when the town's fortunes declined, after the ore-mine railhead to Eureka was abandoned, unfinished, in 1876. Surprisingly, no one had given the secret away.

But despite its reputation as one of the most lawless towns of the West, the greatest irony was that in Palisade not a single crime had been recorded during the entire time the theatrics continued. Indeed, so law-abiding were its citizens, the town did not even have a genuine sheriff.

MOON RESCUES THE SUN

Tales that captivated a city

IN AUGUST 1835 citizens in New York City received extraordinary news. According to the *New York Sun,* the British astronomer Sir John Herschel had found proof of life on the moon.

Using an enormously powerful telescope able to magnify objects 42,000 times, Sir John had distinguished a wide range of flora and fauna with astonishing clarity. In just one area of the moon, the newspaper disclosed, he had observed 38 species of forest trees, twice that number of other plants, and 16 different creatures, including small reindeerlike animals, elks, moose, bears with horns, and beavers with no tails and only two feet.

Each issue of the newspaper brought new revelations, reported by journalist Richard Adam Locke and based on Sir John's accounts in the highly respected *Edinburgh Journal of Science.* Day after day Locke told astonished readers of lunar amethysts more than 60 feet high, immense fields of poppies, a great temple made of sapphire, and herds of buffalo with fleshy appendages over their eyes that protected them from the damaging extremes of light and darkness.

Even more intriguing was the discovery of lunar inhabitants that were semihuman in form: they stood four feet tall, were covered with glossy, copper-colored hair, and, from the expression on their yellowish faces, were clearly intelligent. They also had wings on their backs. They talked in an animated fashion, bathed in lakes, and flew.

Over the moon

The articles created a sensation. The circulation of the *Sun*—which hitherto had been suffering a dwindling readership—soared, giving it the largest sales of any New York daily of the time. The reports were reprinted in other newspapers throughout the United States and Europe. Printed in pamphlet form, an edition of 60,000 copies quickly sold out.

But what was so extraordinary about this journalistic coup was that few of the words in Locke's articles were true.

In a bid to boost the declining circulation of the *Sun,* Locke had fabricated the entire story. It was true that Herschel's newly constructed Cape Town observatory contained a remarkably powerful telescope. Locke, however, had made it 10 times larger and thousands of times more powerful than it actually was. And although there had in fact been an *Edinburgh Journal of Science,* it had ceased publication two years earlier. Everything else was pure invention—but well written and with just the right amount of scientific detail to make it convincing.

Not everyone was taken in, however, and American astronomers were highly skeptical. One day a delegation of scientists from Yale University appeared unannounced in the newspaper offices and demanded to see the original reports.

With all the charm he could muster, Locke explained that the reports, unfortunately, were at the printer's. The suspicious scientists persisted until Locke was forced to give them the printer's name and address. The group started off at once.

But Locke managed to arrive before they did. He persuaded the printer to tell the scientists, when they arrived, that the material had been sent elsewhere. It was the start of a wild-goose chase as Locke sent the scientists from one printer to another, while he took shortcuts through lanes and alleys to tell his printer friends where they should direct the scientists next.

The final truth

It may seem amazing today that such a hoax could ever succeed. But in a world without mass communications, without airplanes or telephones or television, it took many weeks for the truth to emerge. It was some two or three months before Sir John Herschel even learned of his "remarkable discoveries" and was able to deny them. Once exposed, Richard Locke was forced to resign from the *Sun* in disgrace.

Although New Yorkers were soon reading different stories in their newspapers, probably few easily forgot that fabulous world in the sky.

ENGLISH AS SHE IS SPOKE

The world's most misleading phrase book

ONE OF THE MOST EXTRAORDINARY books ever published appeared in Paris in 1815. Its simple if slightly ungrammatical title, *The New Guide of the Conversation in Portuguese and English,* revealed little of the nature of its truly remarkable contents.

Pedro Carolino—of whom virtually nothing is known—had collaborated with Jose da Fonseca, the respected author of a Portuguese-French phrase book first published in 1836, in converting his book into a Portuguese-English phrase book. There was just one problem: Carolino did not know a word of English.

Imagine translating Portuguese, a language you speak, into French, a language of which you have a rudimentary grasp, and then, via literal translation from a French-English dictionary, into English, a language of which you have not the slightest knowledge. You will have *some* idea of the likely outcome, but nothing can prepare you for the credible, surreal, and often hilarious contents of Carolino's *New Guide.*

"The care what we wrote him"

In the preface Carolino presents his book "clean of gallicisms, and despoiled phrases," proclaims "the care what we wrote him," and decries the "corelessness" of his rivals. It serves as a delightful introduction to the fabulously inaccurate and extensive sections that follow: "Vocabulary," "Familiar Phrases," "Familiar Dialogues," and "Idiotisms and Proverbs."

The world of Pedro Carolino is one in which people's jobs include those of "harbinger" and "parapet." They suffer from such ailments as "the vomitory," "a bald," and "an ugly," and have as everyday items of tableware "some crumb." Contained in their comprehensive list of popular fish are the hedgehog, snail, and wolf. They play such games as "gleek" and "keel."

Students of Carolino use commonplace English phrases such as, "I shall not tell you than two woods"; "He laughs at my nose"; "You hear the bird gurgling?"; "Let us prick go us more fast"; "Take that boy and whip him to much"; and "Who lhat [sic] be too washed, too many soaped, and the shirts put through the buck."

Carolino's dialogues ensure that his readers can discuss any aspect of the weather, having rehearsed such observations as: "There is some foggy"; "The sun rise on"; and "It is light moon's."

A transaction with a "furniture tradesman," for example, might run as follows: "Which highness want you its?" "I want almost four feet six thumbs wide's, over seven of long."

Anyone with the intention of going fishing could make good use of:

"That pond it seems me many multiplied of fishes. Let us amuse rather to the fishing."

"I do like-it too much."

"Here, there is a wand and some hooks."

"Silence! there is a superb perch. Give me quick the rod. Ah! there it is. It is a lamprey."

"You mistake you, it is a frog!"

A certain humor

Although we cannot be sure that Da Fonseca died of shame, we do know that he passed away in 1866 and that his name did not appear on the next edition of the book.

Within a few years of publication the completely unintentional humor of Carolino's bizarre book was widely recognized. In 1883 in Britain selections from the book were published as a 60-page pamphlet, *English As She Is Spoke*, which ran to 10 editions. A pirated American edition was equally successful. In the same year, Mark Twain, a devoted fan of Carolino's, published a facsimile of the original. Referring to "its delicious ridiculousness," Twain wrote: "In this world of uncertainties, there is, at any rate, one thing left which may be pretty confidently set down as a certainty: and that is, that this celebrated little phrase-book will never die while the English language lasts."

PLEADING THEIR BELLIES

Impersonation on the high seas

THE PRESIDENT of His Britannic Majesty's Vice Admiralty Court seemed delighted. Before him in the dock of a courtroom in St. Iago de la Vega, Jamaica, stood Capt. "Calico Jack" Rackham and his notorious band of pirates. The pirates had been captured by a British merchant sloop commissioned by the governor of Jamaica to bring the elusive brigands to justice. They now faced statutory death by hanging.

"Is there any reason," asked the president before imposing sentence, "why death should not be pronounced upon you?"

"My lord," replied two of the prisoners, "we plead our bellies."

The plea was a common one in the 18th century, when the law forbade a pregnant woman to be hanged. However, surely this point of law was not applicable in the present case?

But an examination confirmed that the two rough sea-brigands were indeed women, and that

THE GENTLE SEX *The notorious 18th-century female buccaneer Anne Bonny, disguised as a man, in a contemporary engraving.*

they were pregnant. Their names were Anne Bonny and Mary Read, and under law they had to be spared the gallows.

Another notorious buccaneer, Capt. Charles Johnson, wrote about the two women in his book *A General History of the Robberies and Murders of the Most Notorious Pyrates*. It was published in 1724, just four years after Anne Bonny and Mary Read were captured. According to Johnson, the pair had decided upon their murderous maritime careers independently, but fate had thrown them together.

Spirited runaway

The brief factual reports that exist state that Anne's father was an Irish lawyer who left his wife and sailed from County Cork in order to establish a new practice in Carolina, an immense domain of land in America. His high-spirited daughter ran away from home with an unscrupulous sailor named James Bonny, whom she married. Deserted by her husband shortly afterward, she joined Jack Rackham and his band of pirates.

Mary, an English girl, had been deserted by her mother; possessing a keen sense of adventure, she disguised herself as a boy in order to fight with the British Army in Flanders.

After distinguishing herself in the wars, Mary wed a fellow soldier. But their union was short-lived, as her husband soon died. She once more donned men's clothes and joined the crew of a ship that was bound for the West Indies.

That ship was seized by pirates; by chance, Anne was one of Mary's captors.

Accepted into the fold

Normally, pirates did not carry women to sea. Indeed, they had a custom that strictly forbade such practice. But the evidence is that Rackham and his gang accepted Anne and Mary as equals. According to the accounts of two French captives, the women usually wore dresses on board ship: "When . . . we gave chase or attacked, they wore men's clothes; at other times they wore women's."

At the trial of Rackham and his crew on November 28, 1720, Thomas Dillon, the master of a sloop captured by the pirates, told the court that the women were both "very profligate, cursing and swearing much."

Because of their condition, the two women escaped the fate of the rest of the crew, whose lives were shortened by the hangman's noose.

When Anne saw Rackham on the gallows, she is said to have remarked that "had he fought like a man, he need not have hanged like a dog."

Ironically, Mary died in childbirth. But according to legend, Anne had her baby in jail, was reprieved, and finally returned to Carolina, where she vanished into obscurity.

THE SPEAR OF LONGINUS

The dark past of the double-edged sword

IN 1909 IN THE Hofburg Museum in Vienna, a thin, pale, shabby young man stood before the treasures of the House of Hapsburg. Jeweled crowns glittered in their cases. But what transfixed the observer was one small item: the remains of a spear, dull and black with age. The unprepossessing visitor was Adolf Hitler. The object he worshiped was the Spear of Longinus.

The spear is reputed to be the one that pierced Christ's side as He hung upon the cross. Hitler discovered that there were at least three other "holy" spears in Europe at that time. One was in the Vatican. A second had been taken to Paris at the time of the Crusades. Another was to be found in a church in Cracow, Poland. But the Spear of Longinus, named after the Roman centurion who wielded it, had commanded most attention. The reason: attached to its handle is a nail reputedly used in the Crucifixion.

The spear is said to have acted as a powerful talisman or charm for Constantine the Great, first Christian emperor of Rome; Charles Martel, who drove the Arabs out of eighth-century France; the emperor Charlemagne; and the Holy Roman emperor Frederick Barbarossa. According to tradition, all who possessed the spear were victorious. It was the mystical qualities of the Spear of Longinus that so fascinated Hitler.

An occult obsession

The man who revealed Hitler's obsession with the Spear of Longinus was an Austrian scholar, Dr. Walter Stein. He struck up a friendship with Hitler prior to 1914 and came to know the man well.

According to Stein, Hitler's belief in the supernatural powers of the spear led him into the darker realms of magic and the occult. He saw himself as a reincarnation of Landulf II of Capua, a terrifying ninth-century Sicilian tyrant who was also supposed to have obtained possession of the spear. Stein believed that Hitler's rise to power was aided by black magic and the Spear of Longinus.

When Hitler annexed Austria into the Third Reich in 1938, one of the first things he did was to revisit the Hofburg Museum, to claim his "Spear of Destiny." He arranged for it to be taken by special train, under armed guard, to Nuremberg. There it was placed in a church that, on his instruction, was turned into a Nazi shrine.

When the Allies bombed the city, Hitler ordered the spear hidden in a special-purpose vault deep within the foundations of Nuremberg Castle.

Finally, on April 30, 1945, U.S. troops, who had fought their way into Nuremberg in the face of fierce resistance, entered the vault and came upon the spear. Hitler, by then isolated in his bunker in Berlin, did not know this had happened. But only hours later, he shot himself.

Today, the spear is back in the Hofburg Museum, an ancient relic with a notorious past.

SPEAR OF DESTINY *In his 17th-century painting "The Crucifixion," Rubens depicted the Roman centurion Gaius Cassius Longinus piercing Christ's side with his spear, giving rise to the legend that the spear had acquired great mystical power. In later years it was to become a lifelong obsession for Adolf Hitler, who believed that its possession would make him master of the world. Hitler was certain that the spear below, in Vienna, was the Spear of Longinus.*

FORTUNE AND MISFORTUNE

STRANGE DEATHS

Some unusual and unfortunate exits

Shell shock In 456 B.C., at the age of 69, Aeschylus, known as the father of Greek tragedy, was living in retirement in Gela, Sicily. When he was out walking one day, an eagle hovered above him, seeking a rock on which to smash open the shell of the tortoise it carried in its talons. Presumably mistaking Aeschylus' bald head for a rock, it released the tortoise, which killed the playwright instantly. Friends recalled the irony that some years earlier an oracle had prophesied that Aeschylus would be killed by a blow from heaven.

Grapes of wrath Calchas was regarded as one of the greatest of the ancient Greek soothsayers. According to a widely reported account of his death, another soothsayer saw Calchas planting vines and predicted that he would never drink wine pressed from the grapes. When the vines matured, Calchas made the wine. He then invited his rival to a party in order to disprove the prophecy, which the rival repeated even as Calchas raised a goblet to his lips. Overcome with mirth, Calchas began to laugh uproariously—and choked to death.

Wheel of ill fortune In September 1927 dancer Isadora Duncan happened to express her admiration for a Bugatti sports car owned by Benoit Falchetto, a garage owner in Nice. Anticipating that Isadora's interest might extend to purchasing it, Falchetto offered to take her for a test drive. Since Isadora was lightly dressed, with only a silk scarf around her shoulders, Falchetto offered her his leather driving coat. But she declined. "Goodbye, my friends, I am off to glory," she called out, theatrically throwing her scarf behind her as the Bugatti pulled away. Seconds later the trailing scarf became entangled in one wheel of the car, and Isadora was strangled.

Bad timing One of the tricks performed by the magician Harry Houdini involved tensing his muscles so that he could be punched in the stomach without ill effect. On October 22, 1926, Houdini was resting his fractured ankle by lying on a sofa in his dressing room at the Princess Theatre in Montreal. One of the three visitors he received was the amateur boxer Joselyn Gordon Whitehead, who casually asked Houdini whether he really could withstand stomach punches. No sooner had Houdini answered than he received several fierce blows—before he had had the chance to tense his muscles. The next day, a Saturday, Houdini began to feel ill. While onstage in Detroit the following Monday, he collapsed; he had a ruptured appendix and peritonitis. He died six days later.

And carry a short stick In 1687 Jean-Baptiste Lully, Italian-French composer and operatic director for King Louis XIV, was conducting the Te Deum for the king by beating time with a large stick. He accidentally stabbed his foot with it, developed blood poisoning, and soon died.

Means to an end Wealthy French wine maker and miser Samuel Tapon had only two interests in life: his substantial vineyards in Cognac, where he also owned several châteaus, and money. In October 1934 he suffered a loss of approximately $75,000 in a speculative venture. Inconsolable, Tapon went to a village and bought a length of rope—after haggling over the price. He then went home and used his cut-rate rope to hang himself. The value of his estate: $2 million.

FLIGHT TO THE FINISH *In 1785 French ballooning pioneer Jean-Pierre François Blanchard became the first person to cross the English Channel by air. His equally intrepid wife, also a well-known balloonist, made a number of balloon ascents to celebrate national events, notably the marriage of Napoleon in 1810. In the 19th-century engraving at left, Mme. Blanchard plunges to her death after fireworks set her balloon on fire in 1819. Her husband had been killed in 1809, while using the parachute he had invented.*

A PRESIDENTIAL SECRET

An operation to save the nation

ON AUGUST 29, 1893, a startling report appeared in the *Philadelphia Press.* According to the writer, Elisha J. Edwards, U.S. President Grover Cleveland had recently undergone major surgery while on board a friend's yacht, the *Oneida,* on New York's East River. A large portion of his upper jaw had been removed, together with many of his teeth. The operation had been necessary, Edwards stated, because the president had been suffering from cancer.

The report was strenuously denied. At the time it appeared, Cleveland was in the White House in Washington, D.C., and seemingly in good health. His speech was normal and he displayed no signs of any recent operation. All that his aides would admit

WELL-KEPT SECRET *Despite many rumors, the operation on President Cleveland's jaw remained unpublicized during his lifetime. The surgery left no visible scar on his face, but the payment of a $50 fee by the president to William Keen, one of the surgeons who performed the operation, confirms the story.*

was that the 56-year-old president had indeed been on the yacht and had suffered a slight toothache, which was the reason that a dentist had been summoned on board. Most people were satisfied with the official explanation. The argument caused by the report raged briefly but soon died down. The affair was quickly forgotten.

The need for secrecy

Many years later the truth came out. A major operation on the president's jaw had indeed been performed. Everyone involved in the incident had been sworn to secrecy and the affair skillfully covered up (despite the leak to Edwards), since the future health of the whole nation, not just of its president, was at stake.

In 1893 the United States was suffering a severe economic depression. Some 200 banks had failed or suspended operations, a number of businesses had declared bankruptcy, and at least 20 percent of the population was unemployed.

The cause of the panic had been a run on banks after Congress passed the Sherman Silver Purchase Act in 1890. The legislation enabled investors with paper or silver assets to exchange them for gold. Mistakenly, people feared that the act would empty the U.S. Treasury and leave the government with insufficient reserves of gold to back up its currency or pay its debts.

President Cleveland believed that the only road to economic recovery lay in repealing the act. But even his own Democratic Party was deeply split on the issue. The vice president, Adlai Stevenson (grandfather of the U.S. presidential candidate in 1952 and again in 1956), was a stubborn opponent of repeal—as were many other influential members of the party. The president knew that unless he remained available to lend active support, the reform program in which he so deeply believed had little chance of being implemented, and the United States might be plunged into further chaos.

That is why it was crucial that Cleveland's ill health and any possible absence from Washington be kept a closely guarded secret.

A matter of urgency

Surgeons had found a malignant cancerous growth in Cleveland's upper jawbone on June 18 and recommended immediate treatment. Any wait for the operation during what could be a long-drawn-out political battle over repeal might well prove fatal. So on June 30, 1893—the very day that Cleveland announced a special session of Congress to meet on August 7 to discuss repeal—the president disappeared from public view and that evening secretly boarded the yacht.

A team of doctors and surgeons welcomed him on board. Among them were a well-known surgeon and a friend of the president's, Dr. Joseph D. Bryant, and a dentist, Dr. Ferdinand Hasbrouck.

Hasbrouck administered an anesthetic to the president and removed several of his teeth. The surgeons then went to work, and one of them, Dr. W. W. Keen, used a "cheek retractor," an instrument that enabled him to operate inside the president's mouth while leaving no external scar. Cleveland's upper jawbone was then removed.

The operation was a brilliant success in every respect but one: it left the president without the power of coherent speech. As a remedy, a vulcanized rubber jaw was designed and fitted in his mouth. He was then able to speak without impediment. On August 5 the newly invigorated president was back at his desk in Washington ready for the new session of Congress. The reforms were soon approved and the economy restored.

The real story

In 1917, long after Cleveland and many of those involved in the affair had died, Dr. Keen published his account of what happened. It vindicated the *Philadelphia Press* report by Edwards, who for 24 years had suffered public abuse as a "calamity liar," and substantiated the story for the first time. It had to be a secret, wrote Dr. Keen, for on its successful conclusion "hung not only the life of a human being and an illustrious ruler, but the destiny of the nation."

BEST FOOT FORWARD

The 4,000-mile walk to freedom

IN MARCH 1942 six Indian soldiers on patrol in the Himalayas were startled to see a small group of men wearing animal skins stumble down a mountain trail toward them. The soldiers were even more amazed when the four emaciated strangers—who a few moments before had scarcely been able to walk—began to laugh and dance, hugging each other and singing.

The four had every reason to rejoice: they had just completed a 4,000-mile trek on foot from a Soviet labor camp in Siberia.

Secret adviser

The leader of the group was Slavomir Rawicz, a young Polish officer sentenced to 25 years of hard labor for spying. He had been sent to Camp 303, 400 miles south of the Arctic Circle, in February 1941. His first thought had been of escape.

Rawicz received help and advice from an unexpected source: the wife of the camp commandant, Mme. Ushakova, who virtually planned the escape for him. Once away from the camp, she told him, Rawicz should head south, toward Afghanistan or India. It was a long and treacherous route but the safest; he would face certain capture if he were to take the shortest route east toward the Pacific.

Following her instructions, Rawicz recruited six other like-minded prisoners. They stole the skins of animals that had been trapped by their guards and made them into clothing and moccasins. In secret they devised fire-lighting tools, knives, and other necessities. Meanwhile, Mme. Ushakova stole an ax for the group and filled a sack for each man with a few days' provisions.

During a snowstorm on the night of April 9, 1941, Rawicz and his six companions slipped under the wire and clambered over the outer fence of the camp. For two nights they ran cross-country without pause, hiding by day to snatch bits of food and a few moments of sleep. There were no signs of pursuit; the snow had covered their tracks, and the choice of a southern route seemed correct.

The first real rest for the escapees came after they crossed the Lena River, where they ate the only fresh food they had had in nine days: fish they caught by smashing through the ice covering the river. The next objective was Lake Baikal, 500 miles farther south. Seven weeks later they had crossed the lake and entered Outer Mongolia, 1,200 miles from Camp 303. By then the party was eight strong, for they had met a Polish girl, Kristina, who had escaped from another labor camp.

Traveling in Mongolia was relatively easy. The friendly population let the little band work in exchange for food. It was apparent, however, that they would be safe only when they reached India, 2,500 miles away on the other side of the Gobi Desert and the Himalayas.

The journey across the Gobi, a grim expanse of bare rock that burns by day and freezes at night, claimed the lives of Kristina and one of the men. By then they had finished their meager rations; for three weeks the remaining fugitives survived by eating snakes. In October 1941 they reached Tibet, where, once again, the local residents helped them on their way. The next stage of the journey took the group into the Himalayas, where another died in his sleep of the cold. In crossing the mountains, the five survivors forced themselves to remain awake day and night to avoid the same fate.

Encountering yeti

At last the group started the descent toward the Indian border. Then a bizarre incident occurred: two apelike creatures, seven feet tall, barred their path. In his book *The Long Walk,* Rawicz shared his belief that they were the elusive "abominable snowmen" of the Himalayas. To avoid the strange creatures, the group made a treacherous detour. Unfortunately, one man fell into a huge crevasse.

Rawicz and his three fellow survivors were to endure another eight days without food until at last, nearly a year after their escape, they surprised the Indian Army patrol.

The men were taken to a Calcutta hospital, and only after sleeping almost continually for four weeks did Rawicz believe he was a free man. He then rejoined his Polish regiment, and fought with the Allies during World War II.

LONG WALK *In April 1941 Slavomir Rawicz and three fellow prisoners from Soviet Labor Camp 303 in Siberia walked 4,000 miles to freedom. Their route is in black on the map.*

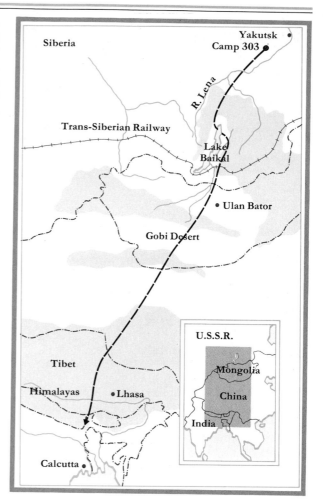

TRIAL BY ORDEAL

One man's fight for justice

WHEN LONDON DEMOLITION contractor Alfie Hinds was framed by the police for a robbery, he vowed that he would clear his name, no matter how long it took. And he did just that—after serving 11 years of a 12-year sentence.

Hinds's nightmare began in 1953 after a London furniture store had been robbed of a large quantity of cash. A short time before the robbery, Hinds had met a man who offered to sell him a carpet for a low price. Unfortunately for Hinds, however, the man was not only a disreputable dealer, he was also a member of the gang that was about to rob the store. When the two met a few days after the burglary to discuss the carpet transaction, the police arrested Hinds along with the real thief.

Convinced that Hinds was involved but unable to prove it, the police persuaded another member of the gang to give evidence against him in return for a lenient sentence. Other evidence that could have saved Hinds was not presented, and Hinds was sent to jail for 12 years; the informer, for 1.

Legal battles

Hinds then started his fight for justice, which was to make him the scourge of the courts as the man who knew more about the law than lawyers. It would also make him a public hero—as an escapee.

Over the years Hinds tried all the legal methods he could find to have his case reviewed. It was only after every one had been systematically blocked that he decided to escape to Ireland. He thought that if he could attract enough publicity there, English authorities would eventually give in.

The first time he escaped, he followed a fellow inmate over the prison wall. Hinds had discovered that by using another prisoner's escape route rather than planning his own, he was not, in the eyes of the law, committing a crime. This was important. Hinds did not want to prejudice his case by committing one crime in order to prove that he was innocent of another. Within a few months he was rearrested and brought back to London for trial.

To the embarrassment of the prosecution, the legal loophole Hinds had discovered was upheld. In addition, Hinds won his legal victory without benefit of a legal defense. The lawbooks he had studied while on the run in Ireland proved as useful as he had hoped.

Hinds continued to fight his case from his prison cell and paid frequent visits to the lawcourts. During one of these visits he made another escape attempt. A fellow inmate who was going to court agreed to leave a padlock taped under a table in the cafeteria. When Hinds visited the cafeteria, he pocketed the padlock.

When Hinds and his two guards went to use the rest room, Hinds politely held the door open. But instead of following them, he closed the door, snapped on the lock, and calmly walked out of the court, leaving the two guards behind.

Within hours Hinds was back behind bars, but not for long. His third escape was a carbon copy of his first. Moments after jumping off the wall of Chelmsford prison, another prisoner was surprised to hear a heavy thump behind him. Hinds had followed him. Although he had injured his leg in the fall, Hinds managed to limp away, and he again took refuge in Ireland.

For two years Hinds ran a company that exported automobiles to England via Northern Ireland. When he realized that his business would be more lucrative if he did not have to pay duty for sending vehicles across the border, Hinds started to smuggle the cars across the border illegally. He was caught and sent back to prison.

Lucky break

Then luck smiled on Hinds. Herbert Sparks, the detective who had secured his conviction, retired. The milestone was noted in articles in a Sunday newspaper. One said that Hinds was guilty of the furniture-store robbery. This was what Hinds had been waiting for, and he sued Sparks for libel. What followed was in effect a retrial of the original case, but this time all evidence was heard.

When Sparks broke down under cross-examination, the police revealed the conspiracy for the first time. Hinds had won his case.

Although he had convinced a jury that he was innocent, authorities were less easily persuaded; they dismissed yet another appeal to have Hinds's conviction set aside and refused to grant him a pardon. But the one thing they could not deny him after the libel verdict was his freedom.

After 11 years Hinds was again out of prison. This time it was official.

THE FISH THAT CHANGED A LAKE

Thanks to a misguided ecological experiment, the Nile perch—introduced into Africa's largest lake in 1960 to boost the availability of protein for local inhabitants—has devoured most of the 300 other fish species in Lake Victoria.

Capable of reaching a weight of more than 200 pounds, the perch has become the villain in a major environmental catastrophe. During its years of easy living, it has all but wiped out the lake's indigenous fish, upset the delicate balance of the food chain, and also left the ecology of Lake Victoria unstable.

The "elephant of the water," as the perch is sometimes called, has not only gobbled up rare species of ornamental fish, it has also preyed on a valuable species that helped to control schistosomiasis, a potentially dangerous parasitic disease.

Residents of the hundreds of fishing villages that border Lake Victoria have also seen their traditional livelihood disappear. There are no small fish left in the lake, and the villagers cannot compete with the large trawlers, with their stronger nets, that have monopolized the perch catch.

There are other problems too. Because of its exceptionally oily flesh, the big perch cannot be sun-dried. It must be smoked, and firewood is scarce.

Unless conservationists can devise a radical new approach, or nature intervenes, it seems likely that the Nile perch has changed Lake Victoria forever.

A WHALE OF A TALE

A fisherman's tale — with a difference

IN FEBRUARY 1891 a whaling ship, *Star of the East,* was operating near the Falkland Islands in the South Atlantic when a large sperm whale was sighted three miles away. Two smaller boats were launched. As the men on board were trying to harpoon the whale, it flicked its tail and overturned one of the boats. One man drowned; another, James Bartley, disappeared and presumably died.

Eventually the whale was killed and brought alongside the ship. When the crew cut open the creature's huge stomach, they found Bartley inside. He was doubled up and unconscious — but, miraculously, still alive.

Bartley was placed in the captain's quarters, where, over a period of several weeks, he gradually recovered from his extraordinary experience. But the gastric juices in the whale's stomach had bleached his skin a deathly white — a condition that was to remain for the rest of his life. All that Bartley could recall of the incident was that although he could breathe, the heat in his temporary prison had been almost overpowering.

The story of James Bartley, first published in England in the Great Yarmouth *Mercury* in October 1891, has appeared in many books and periodicals since. Strangely enough, no one ever managed to interview Bartley about his ordeal; nor, as might have been expected, did the bleached-skinned sailor become a celebrity as a real-life Jonah who lived inside a whale.

The truth will out

But perhaps these facts are not so surprising; it is unlikely that a single detail of the tale is true.

An indefatigable researcher of popular fallacies, A. S. E. Ackermann, decided to investigate the incident after reading about it in a 1924 book, *Sixty-three Years of Engineering.* In answer to Ackermann's inquiries, Canon A. Lukyn Williams, a clergyman, told Ackermann that he had examined the evidence in 1906, when most of those associated with the *Star of the East* were still alive. He had concluded that it was "a canard, pure and simple."

And on February 17, 1928, one Albert R. Stegall wrote to the London *Daily Telegraph* to point out that although the captain of the *Star* was now dead, his wife had denied the story.

Ultimately, there is not a shred of evidence that James Bartley — if he existed at all — was swallowed by a whale. Yet nearly a hundred years after the supposed event, the story is usually repeated as if it were completely true.

THE FINAL CURTAIN

The performance of a lifetime

ON MARCH 23, 1918, the illusionist Chung Ling Soo, "the Marvelous Chinese Conjurer," appeared in a London theater to demonstrate the feat that had made him famous: his escape from death at the hands of a firing squad.

A small army of Soo's assistants, dressed as Boxers (the Chinese nationalists who had rebelled against foreign rule in 1900), marched onto the stage. Wearing magnificent oriental robes, Soo invited two members of the audience to come up and inspect a pair of ancient muzzle-loading rifles.

Meanwhile, Soo's wife, Suee Seen, went into the auditorium and asked two people to scratch their initials on two lead bullets. She then put the marked bullets in a cup and brought them back to the stage.

After supervising the loading of the guns, the voluntary inspectors shook hands with Soo and returned to their seats. Soo then held a china plate in front of his chest as two of his assistants stepped forward, took the rifles, raised them to their shoulders, and aimed at the magician. At a signal, they opened fire.

Midair miracle

At previous performances it seemed that Soo had miraculously stopped the initialed bullets in midair by catching them on the plate. He would then offer them to the audience for identification. But events took a different course this time.

When the two deafening shots rang out, the Chinese conjurer crumpled onto the stage floor as blood poured from a bullet wound in his chest. He was rushed to a hospital but died the next day.

Soo's tragic death gave newspapers sensational headlines. Then rumors began to circulate that he had been murdered, or had even committed suicide, and that the fatal bullets had mysteriously disappeared. The truth, however, was in this case far more mundane.

At the inquest into Soo's death, Suee Seen explained that her husband always hid the initialed bullets in the palm of one hand; after the guns were fired, he would produce them as if he had caught them. Duplicate bullets were loaded into the guns; a secret mechanism inside prevented them from discharging the bullets. Her husband had never allowed anyone else to inspect the guns; only he knew how the mechanism worked.

DEATH-DEFYING ACT *A celebrity in theaters and music halls the world over, Chung Ling Soo was renowned for catching live bullets on a plate. The front and back of the coaster below advertise one of his shows at the Palace Theatre in Bristol, England, in about 1913.*

Robert Churchill, an expert gunsmith, was called in to investigate, and revealed the secret of Soo's death-defying act for the first time. The barrel of each rifle had been sealed, making it impossible to ignite the charge that propelled the bullet. Instead, the detonating spark was diverted to the ramrod tube beneath the barrel, where it fired a harmless charge of powder that Soo had secretly placed there.

Fatal spark

On the fateful night of March 23, however, one of the rifles was so worn that some of the gunpowder in the main barrel came into contact with the percussion cap. As the marksman pulled the trigger, the spark ignited both the blank charge in the ramrod tube and the lethal charge in the barrel. The bullet had then passed through the magician's body; the police later recovered it from the stage. After assessing the evidence, the coroner returned a verdict of death from misadventure.

Chung Ling Soo was not the first victim of the bullet-catching trick. At least 10 stage illusionists had died performing it in one variation or another, and the entire fraternity of magicians recognized its dangers. The celebrated Harry Houdini once warned Soo: "Be careful with your bullet-catching trick, as your method is certainly daring." Chung Ling Soo had trusted his luck once too often.

BUNGLED BURGLARIES

A catalog of misfortunes

AT ONE TIME "the perfect crime" was an often used expression. But some attempts seem doomed to failure from the start. Whether the result of poor planning, bad luck, inept perpetrators, or a combination thereof, some crimes deserve a lesser superlative.

Poor judgment

In March 1978 a New York City burglar attempted to rob a supermarket by entering through the skylight. Finding the window too small, he shed his bulky clothing and hurled it through the window, intending to follow. Unfortunately, the window was still too small. After some two hours on the roof on that chilly evening, the shivering burglar was forced to hail two passing police officers. They retrieved his clothing—and then arrested him.

On January 20, 1979, David Goodall, an accomplished shoplifter from Barnsley, England, entered a general store. Having helped himself to what he wanted, he made for the door—only to be stopped by no fewer than eight detectives. Unknown to him, the shop he had raided had been selected as the site for a convention of store-detectives.

Not cut out for the job

Some burglars are just not up to the demands of their profession. A burglar in Detroit was so attached to his dog that one night in 1968 he took it to work with him. Unfortunately, while making a hasty getaway, he had to leave the hound behind. To the delight of the police, all they had to do was say "home, boy," and the faithful creature led them straight to their suspect.

And in 1971, after a reckless, drunken drive through town following his most recent robbery, Philip McCutcheon of Yorkshire, England, made his 20th appearance in court. An exasperated judge outlined McCutcheon's nonqualifications for a life of crime. "Whoever heard of a burglar succeeding with only one leg, a withered hand, and a glass eye? It's time you gave it up. You are a rotten burglar. You are always being caught."

Overdrawn and out

Robbing a bank has usually been a popular way to obtain cash, although unsuited to the timid. This was illustrated by the case of the would-be bank robber in Portland, Oregon, in 1969. Instead of stating his demands, the diffident man wrote on the piece of paper that he handed to the cashier: "This is a holdup and I've got a gun. Put the money in a paper bag." The cashier wrote back, "I haven't got a paper bag." The burglar fled.

And David Rich of London encountered similar resistance when he tried to rob the local branch of his bank on March 15, 1978. Wearing three stocking masks and a scarf over his face, Rich announced that he had a gun and ordered the staff and the customers to lie down on the floor. But so complete was his disguise that Rich could hardly see; in place of a gun he produced his glasses case. After several minutes of brandishing this weapon at the highly amused hostages, Rich realized that

SOME YOU WIN . . .

On one summer day in 1982, Toronto hairdresser H. André Nader decided to try his luck on the horses. He put $140 on the Sweep Six, a system offered by the local Greenwood and Woodbine racecourses.

In order to succeed in the Sweep Six, the bettor must name the winning horses in six specific races. Winnings from the first race become the stake for the second, and so on. The odds on all six horses coming in first are long, but the winnings are potentially enormous.

Nader won. The only person to name all six winners, he collected $140,000.

The next day, Saturday, July 31, Nader left a customer under the dryer at his salon near the Woodbine track in order to place another bet. Once again he chose six horses for the Sweep Six. This time he forked out $3,400.

All six horses he picked had romped home, each one in first place. Once again only Nader had picked the winners and he was richer by $117,000. In just two days Nader had collected more than $250,000.

As for the woman he had left under the dryer, he set her hair for free the next time.

something had gone wrong and he made for the door. He was arrested several minutes later, hiding behind a nearby car.

Unsuitably dressed

On November 4, 1933, a Parisian burglar attempted to rob the home of an antiques dealer. Hoping, no doubt, to blend in with the background, he donned a 15th-century suit of armor. Effective as this may have seemed, it proved restrictive for carrying out his work—not to mention his escape.

The unlucky burglar had been in the house only a few minutes when the owner was awakened by the sound of clanking metal. He got out of bed, saw the suit of armor climbing the stairs, and promptly knocked the burglar off balance. The homeowner left the felon pinned under a heavy sideboard and telephoned the police. This was not the last of the downed burglar's problems, however. The pressure of the sideboard dented his breastplate so much that the armor could not be removed for 24 hours; he had to be fed through the visor.

Court in the act

One of the most ill-fated crimes of all time involved 75 convicts who were attempting to break out of Saltillo Prison in northern Mexico. Undetected, the gang had spent six months digging a tunnel to take them beyond the prison walls. Unfortunately, the tunnel led directly to a nearby courtroom. As each escapee appeared, the astounded judge immediately ordered him back to jail.

A THIRST FOR LIFE

In the shadow of death

GEOFFREY PRESCOTT is alive and well and living in London—something of a miracle for a man who plunged hundreds of feet down the crater of an extinct volcano. There he lay for three days—bleeding, with several broken bones and a fractured skull—under the broiling African sun without food, water, or medication.

In 1985 Prescott had been working as a teacher in Nyala, in the western part of the Republic of Sudan, when he and fellow teacher, Noel Smith, decided to hike across the Marra Mountains, a distance of 65 miles. In a village in the foothills the two were joined by Mik Iadt, a Dane. On November 27 the trio set off on the three-day trek to Mount Gimbala, the extinct volcano that dominates the region.

Into the crater

Although their water was running low, on the morning of the third day the travelers decided to keep going up over the hills surrounding the rim of the volcano. Their maps indicated that there were springs on the floor of the crater, which would take another half a day to reach.

The three men had started their descent into the crater when, at about 3:30 P.M., Prescott lost his footing on the treacherous terrain. Exactly how many feet he fell is uncertain, but it took Iadt and Smith an hour to reach him. All that time Prescott remained unconscious.

When he regained his senses, Prescott was in extreme pain, unable to move, and bleeding profusely from a number of deep cuts. Iadt decided to go for help, although by even the shortest route it would take him a week to reach Nyala.

Prescott knew that he would probably be dead before Iadt and a rescue party could return. With only a few pints of water and temperatures exceeding 100°F, Prescott felt that he would die of dehydration if not from loss of blood (he feared that he was bleeding internally).

Waiting for death

Smith stayed with him until the next morning, and then he too decided to move on; he lit a fire as a rescue signal before leaving.

But the flames soon leaped across the dry scrub, and Prescott had to inch away from the threat posed by yet another danger. Fortunately, the flames came no closer than a few feet—but they did consume his remaining medical supplies and the food that Smith had left him.

For two days and two nights, Prescott waited to die. Although his injured body was in torment from lack of water, he managed to drag himself farther down the mountainside, hoping that he might find water on the crater floor.

Waters of the heart

Around 10 A.M. on the fourth day of his ordeal, he heard a shout. Incredibly, Iadt was back—with expert medical help. Iadt had been able to reach Nyala in three days. By jeep and by horseback, he and a nurse and doctor had returned immediately. The rescuers heaved Prescott into the saddle for the first stage of his return journey—but not before he had gulped down four pints of water.

A small airplane took Prescott from Nyala to Khartoum, where he spent eight days in a hospital before being flown back to England. Not until the night before he left was Prescott able to sleep—the first time in 11 days.

Only when he was examined in a London hospital did the full extent of his injuries come to light. Prescott and his doctors were astonished to discover that he had ridden a horse and bounced in a jeep across the desert with a cracked skull, a broken wrist, three smashed vertebrae, and the ligaments torn away from the muscles of one knee.

Once back in normal health, Prescott decided to study nursing. His own totally unexpected survival, he said, had convinced him that he should help others to face, and perhaps defeat, death.

SONNY BOY

The joke that became a hit

ONE NIGHT AT A PARTY in Atlantic City, New Jersey, veteran songwriters Buddy DeSylva, Lew Brown, and Ray Henderson received an urgent long-distance telephone call. The year was 1928 and the caller none other than Al Jolson, the singer who had dubbed himself "the greatest entertainer in the world."

Jolson was still enjoying the overnight success of *The Jazz Singer*. Released the previous year, the movie had launched Jolson's meteoric rise to stardom. Now he had a favor to ask.

In his next film, *The Singing Fool,* Jolson was to play the part of a brash entertainer who is heartbroken at the death of his little boy. Although the movie had to include a song on this theme, no one had been able to come up with the right one. In desperation, Jolson had decided to track down the three buddies who had written so many hit songs for him in the past.

Sentimental melody

Jolson was not noted for his tact, and the three songwriters were piqued by this last-minute, long-distance order. They were amazed that Jolson could want a song on such a sentimental theme. As DeSylva said: "Who could take a thing like that seriously?"

Reacting to the request as if it were a joke, between them, amid hysterical laughter, the three put together "Sonny Boy," a song containing just about every musical cliché imaginable. So ridiculous did they feel the song to be that they could not bring themselves to put it in the mailbox but instead asked a bellboy to do it for them.

Jolson did not see the joke. Instead of throwing the song into the garbage can, he gave it everything he had as a performer. The result: "Sonny Boy" was among the first recordings to sell a million copies, and *The Singing Fool* became the greatest box-office success of all time, unsurpassed until *Gone With the Wind* opened in 1939.

DeSylva, Brown, and Henderson had laughed as they wrote the song. Al Jolson laughed too. All the way to the bank.

SINGING HIS WAY TO SUCCESS *The original British cover of the sheet music of "Sonny Boy," the song that was to confirm Al Jolson as one of the world's leading entertainers.*

THE PLAGUE OF EYAM

The village that died to save its neighbors

EARLY IN SEPTEMBER 1665 George Viccars, a tailor, opened a consignment of cloth in his cottage in Eyam, a village near Sheffield in northern England. He found that the cloth was damp and hung it in front of his fire to dry.

With that innocent act, Viccars unleashed upon his community the most feared disease of the age. The package had come from London, where bubonic plague had been raging for months, and the cloth harbored fleas that carried the disease.

Lice and fleas were man's constant companions in the 17th century, and the unfortunate tailor thought little of the bites he received from the newcomers. A few days later he fell desperately ill with fever, headaches, and swollen glands. His skin was covered with open putrid sores, and he became delirious. He died within one week.

By the end of September, five more people in the neighborhood had died, and in the first three days of October there were four more deaths. At the end of the month the toll had reached 23. The plague had come to the remote village of Eyam.

A desperate solution

Treatment for the plague was crude and ineffective, and the pestilence was known to sweep through towns and villages without check. The first sign of the symptoms signaled certain death.

The terrified villagers began to panic. Many prepared to leave Eyam for healthier surroundings. Fearing this would only spread the plague across the countryside, the village clergymen, William Mompesson and Thomas Stanley, decided to act to stop the exodus.

In a joint sermon they urged their fellow citizens to recognize that it was their duty to stay until the scourge was over. Inspired by the courage and example of the clergymen, the villagers sealed themselves off from the world.

They lined up stones to mark the village boundaries, and no one was allowed beyond them. Supplies of food and clothing brought to the village from the outside were left at the boundary stones and were paid for with coins placed in a disinfectant of vinegar and water.

The horror increased as the months passed. By the end of August 1666, two-thirds of the original population had perished. Formal burial services were no longer held. When the cemetery became full, the dead were buried in gardens and fields.

The church was closed in an attempt to reduce contagion. Instead, the pitiful flock, which became smaller every day, gathered at a peaceful spot in the open air, where they prayed for relief from their appalling suffering.

Their prayers were answered by November 1666, when no more deaths from plague were recorded. Of the 350 villagers, only 90 survived, among them the two clergymen who had held the beleaguered group together.

The self-imposed isolation of the villagers of Eyam was an extraordinary act of heroism. But tragically, it was in vain. Had the villagers followed their instincts and abandoned their homes in the early stages of the epidemic, they would have deprived the plague-infested fleas of the human blood on which they thrived—and most of the community would probably have survived.

IN FOR A SHOCK

In August 1890 an inmate in Auburn Prison, New York, was executed in an electric chair, the first time this method of execution had ever been used. When Emperor Menelik II of Abyssinia (Ethiopia today) heard about this example of modern technology, he was suitably impressed. He was certain that this was exactly what Abyssinia needed to move into the 20th century.

Determined not to allow his country to fall behind, Menelik promptly ordered three electric chairs from the U.S. manufacturers. The chairs arrived and were duly unpacked.

But Menelik was in for a shock; no one had told him that the chairs needed an outside electrical source to work.

The revelation presented him with a major difficulty: Abyssinia had no electricity.

A lesser man might have been devastated by such a disaster, but not Menelik. He immediately found a use for one of the chairs—as his imperial throne.

A GIFT FROM THE HEART

As 14-year-old Donna Ashlock lay in bed at the Pacific Medical Center in San Francisco, recovering from a heart transplant operation, her anxious father gave her some astonishing news. Donna owed her life to the devotion of her 15-year-old boyfriend, Felipe Garza, who had given his own heart to save her.

A few days before Christmas 1985, Donna had been told by doctors that she had just four months to live. Her heart muscle had degenerated so severely that a transplant was essential. When Felipe heard of his girlfriend's tragic plight, he announced to his family that he would die so that she might live.

Since Felipe was apparently in perfect health, his parents had dismissed the notion as a romantic fantasy. But on January 4, Felipe collapsed, due to a blood clot in the brain. He was rushed to a hospital in Modesto, California, where doctors pronounced the young boy brain-dead.

Felipe's parents had never met Donna, but they remembered their son's pledge and contacted the Ashlock family. That night, Felipe's body was flown to San Francisco; in a five-hour operation surgeons transferred the boy's heart to his girlfriend.

So successful was the operation that Donna was well enough to leave the hospital after just a two-week convalescence. She went home a celebrity, with movie companies vying for the rights to tell her story.

Yet the miracle of Felipe's sacrifice is still unexplained. What had caused his sudden, fatal hemorrhage? Did the love-sick boy have a premonition of death? Or did he will himself to die to save his beloved Donna?

NO REST FOR THE WEARY

The astonishing sequel to a mutiny

TWENTY-FOUR DAYS out from Tahiti, on April 28, 1789, the crew of the H.M.S. *Bounty* mutinied, leaving their captain, Lt. William Bligh, and a few companions to fend for themselves in an open boat in the middle of the Pacific Ocean. Bligh survived his ordeal to become an admiral, but the tale of what happened to the ship and its mutinous crew is one of the most bizarre in the annals of the sea.

Led by the second-in-command, Lt. Fletcher Christian, the mutineers hoped to find an island where they could settle down beyond the reach of the Royal Navy, which was scouring the Pacific for the renegades. But the mutineers' every attempt to find a home ended in disaster.

Two-thirds of the original mutineers insisted that they return to Tahiti, where the remaining nine kidnapped a party of Tahitian girls and weighed anchor. By then the ship's company included 3 Tahitian men and 12 native women. The balance of the sexes was upset when three more Tahitian men emerged on deck.

For four months the *Bounty* searched the vast ocean for a place to rest. At last, at sunset on January 15, 1790, the *Bounty* and her motley crew sighted Pitcairn Island in the South Pacific. Here, they hoped, their troubles would end.

Once settled, the mutineers decided to avoid discovery by destroying all visible evidence of the *Bounty*. Having set the ship on fire, the nine white males then divided the land among themselves. For all intents and purposes, the six Tahitian men were treated as slaves. Furthermore, while each white male had a woman to himself, the six Tahitian males had to share three girls between them.

Mounting tension

Within a year two of the mutineers' women died. Tensions in the little community mounted when the two bereaved men abducted two of the women who lived with the Tahitians. The Tahitians reacted by plotting to kill the white men and retrieve the women. The dispute ended with two Tahitian men dead and a third in chains.

In September 1793 the four remaining Tahitian men again rebelled. Two stole up on five of the mutineers as they were working their fields and slaughtered each one, including Fletcher Christian.

Further intrigues and jealous disputes ended in the murder of the four remaining Tahitian males.

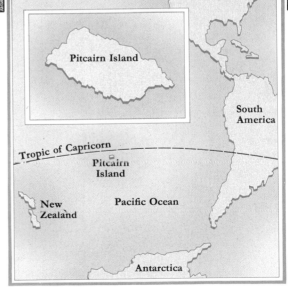

After six months of peace, one of the mutineers discovered how to distill alcohol from an island plant. Within a year he had reached such a state of intoxication that, in a fit of delirium, he threw himself off a cliff. Another's drunkenness drove his woman to suicide and so terrorized the other women that two former shipmates, Edward Young and Alexander Smith, split his skull with an ax.

Possibly in reaction to the chronicle of horrors they had shared, the two surviving mutineers instituted a sober, industrious regime. The 20 or so children that the colony now supported received regular instruction, and prayers were held twice daily—just the simple, straightforward life that Fletcher Christian had envisioned.

In 1800 Young died of a lung disease—the first man on the island to die a natural death. When the little colony was discovered in 1808, Smith was the sole surviving mutineer; he died of old age in 1829.

Today, Pitcairn's few inhabitants continue to live a simple, pious existence. Their local dialect, a mixture of English and Tahitian, is a living reminder of the origins of their forefathers.

ISLAND HOME *Colonized in 1790 by the* Bounty *mutineers and their Tahitian hostages, Pitcairn Island lies some 1,350 miles from Tahiti in the South Pacific. The 19th-century engraving above the map offers a highly romantic view of life on the island.*

THE BOOKIES' NIGHTMARE

Gambling on a dream

ON THE NIGHT OF Friday, March 8, 1946, John Godley, a student at Oxford University, dreamed that he was reading the racing results in Saturday's newspaper and saw the names of two winners: Bindal and Juladin.

The next morning he told a friend about his dream, and together they consulted the sports pages in Saturday's newspapers. The two horses were running, in separate races, later that day. Godley backed both horses, as did other friends he had told about his dream. Both horses won.

It was the first of many such dreams that Godley was to have in the coming years—and the beginning of the bookies' nightmare.

Just a few weeks later, on April 4, Godley was at his parents' home in Ireland when he had his racing dream again. This time he was looking at a list of winners. When he woke up, he could recall only one of them: Tubermore. He discovered that a horse called Tuberose was running in the Grand National the following day. The similarity of the two names was good enough for Godley and his family. They backed the horse. Tuberose won.

The next dream occurred on July 28, 1946. In it Godley was calling his bookmaker from a pay phone, and his bookmaker was saying that Monumentor had won. Next morning Godley checked the newspapers. There was a horse called Mentores running that day. He backed it and it won.

True colors

A year later Godley had his fourth special dream. This time he was at the races and saw that the winning horse carried the distinctive racing colors of the gaekwar of Baroda, an Indian prince, and that the jockey was an Australian, Edgar Britt. Godley also heard the crowd shouting the name of the favorite for the next race: The Bogie. Godley checked the newspapers and found that the prince's horse was running that afternoon and that the jockey was Edgar Britt. He also discovered that the favorite in the next race was named The Brogue.

By now Godley took the matter seriously and wanted to be able to provide evidence that he could accurately predict the outcome of the races. He deliberately told two close friends about the dream, wrote down his predictions, had them witnessed, and left the statement at the local post office for safekeeping. He backed both horses. They both won.

The news spread around the world. The dreamer became racing correspondent on the London *Daily Mirror*. Fortune continued to favor him with strange dreams from time to time—on October 29, 1946; January 16, 1949; and February 11, 1949. And in 1958 he again dreamed correctly about the winner of the Grand National.

But then his very special gift left him.

John Godley's astonishing experience raises a number of questions. Since he had only a slight interest in horses, why should he have had such a series of dreams? Was this strange chapter in his life no more than a string of lucky coincidences? If not, how was it that he could acquire information about events that had not yet taken place?

Could it be that the future is already here, running in tandem with the present, and that some people—like John Godley—have the remarkable ability to cross the barrier between them?

THAT PLAY

The real-life drama of Macbeth

"THE COMEDY OF GLAMIS," "The Scottish Business," or simply "That Play" are just a few of the euphemisms actors use to avoid mentioning the title of William Shakespeare's *Macbeth,* one of the most ill-starred plays in theatrical history.

Indeed, many professionals believe that "The Unmentionable" (another of its nicknames)—with its bloodshed, ghosts, and witchcraft—is one of the darkest dramas ever written.

If an actor does happen to mention the name, or quotes from the play while he is backstage, tradition requires him to leave the dressing room, turn around three times, spit, and then knock for reentry. Theatrical history is littered with the many misfortunes of those who have chosen to ignore these rites of exorcism.

Macbeth seemed doomed from the beginning. It was first performed before James I, a descendant of both the historical Duncan and Banquo, who are killed in the play. The curse apparently struck during that original performance on August 7, 1606, when Hal Berridge, the boy actor cast as Lady Macbeth, collapsed from a fever and later died. Shakespeare himself had to step in and play the role on short notice.

The play was rarely performed again for nearly a century. The day of its London revival in 1703 was noteworthy for one of the most severe storms in English history. Because of its blasphemous content, the play was blamed for the storm's calamities, and Queen Anne ordered a week of prayer during which all theaters were closed.

A catalog of disasters

Over the next two centuries the disasters continued, the curse taking its greatest toll after the Astor Place riots in New York City in 1849. During a performance of *Macbeth* by British actor William Charles Macready, supporters of his American rival, Edwin Forrest, clashed with police. Twenty-two people were killed and some 36 more injured.

Probably the most famous person to suffer the Macbeth curse was not an actor but a U.S. president. *Macbeth* was Abraham Lincoln's favorite play, and he spent the afternoon of April 9, 1865, reading passages aloud to a party of friends on board the *River Queen* on the Potomac River. The passages Lincoln chose happened to follow the scene in which Duncan is assassinated. Five days later Lincoln was shot.

In the 20th century numerous other calamities associated with the fatal play have been recorded. In the early 1920's Lionel Barrymore's portrayal of Macbeth received such harsh reviews that Barrymore never performed on Broadway again.

In 1937 the career of 30-year-old Laurence Olivier almost came to an abrupt end when a heavy weight crashed down from the flies while he was rehearsing at the Old Vic in London. It missed him by inches. And during the dress rehearsal, the theater's proprietor died of a heart attack.

Out in the open

In a 1953 open-air production in Bermuda, starring Charlton Heston, the soldiers storming Macbeth's castle were to burn it to the ground onstage. On opening night the wind blew smoke and flames into the audience, which fled in terror.

And troubles started early during the four month pre-Broadway road tour of a 1988 production, starring Glenda Jackson and Christopher Plummer. More than a dozen cast members came down with the flu at the same time, and Plummer twisted his knee and tore ligaments, had a front tooth knocked out, and pulled his back. Behind the scenes, three different directors were called in, and completely new scenery, lighting, and costumes were created before the production reached New York.

At one point the despairing cast invented the Revolting Thanes Award, and gave it every night to the actor who had committed the worst faux pas.

A CHAOTIC FIGHT

Of all the heavyweight prizefights in history, few can have been so poorly organized as the 1923 bout between the holder of the title, Jack Dempsey, and his challenger, Tommy Gibbons. The match took place on July 4 in Shelby, Montana, a small town of only a few thousand people. The residents staged the fight in hopes of putting their town on the map.

The promoters had borrowed heavily to build an arena that would seat 45,000 people. But they were barely able to raise the first $100,000 installment of the advance, payable to Dempsey, by selling shares in a local oil exploration company. They then had to resort to considerable arm twisting of the town's storekeepers and the members of the local American Legion chapter to raise the second installment of $100,000. They never raised the final $50,000, and Dempsey never saw anything of his promised half of the income from the gate.

The actual fight was chaotic. Only some 8,000 turned up to watch, most of whom got in free after local cowboys used lassos to pull down the perimeter fence. Dempsey was probably more afraid of getting hurt by the violent spectators than by Gibbons. Even Dempsey's bodyguard, Wild Bill Lyons—a tough New Yorker with a lawless past in the Wild West—decided to take refuge under the ring during the entire 15 rounds.

When the fight ended, with Dempsey the winner, the champion got out of town fast, worried that the bankrupt promoters might pursue him and try to reclaim some of their losses. As for Tommy Gibbons, he received nothing. It was a most inglorious end to a totally disastrous affair.

A MATTER OF LIFE AND DEATH

An epic of survival — a mystery of medicine

IN JANUARY 1912 a three-man party of explorers from the Australasian Antarctic Expedition set out from their base at Commonwealth Bay, Adélie Land, to chart a huge section of the largely unknown continent. A year later two team members were dead, and the expedition leader, Douglas Mawson, had barely survived both an epic lone journey across the Antarctic wastes and an appalling, mysterious illness that was to baffle medical science for the next 50 years.

Disaster first struck the team on December 14, 1912, when Lt. B.E.S. Ninnis vanished into a seemingly bottomless crevasse. With him had gone his team of dogs and a sledge carrying most of the party's provisions.

Mawson and Xavier Mertz, a Swiss scientist, faced a 315-mile journey back to the base at Commonwealth Bay. The trip would take weeks; they had food for only 10 days. To survive, the two men knew they would soon have to start eating the six remaining dogs.

The long march

For the first two weeks, Mawson and Mertz made good progress despite eating no more than 14 ounces of food a day, most of it dogmeat. To make the tough, stringy flesh palatable, they boiled it for hours. "It was a happy relief," noted Mawson in his diary, "when the liver appeared, even if little else could be said in its favour. It was easily chewed and demolished."

On New Year's Eve, Mertz began to feel ill. The next day he was worse, complaining of acute pains in the stomach. In a few days bizarre and distressing symptoms began to affect both men. Skin was falling off their bodies in strips and their hair was dropping out in handfuls.

A week later Mertz fell into a delirious sleep—a sleep from which he never woke. Mawson was now alone, still 160 miles from Commonwealth Bay and with very little food. His health continued to deteriorate: open sores on his skin refused to heal and he was perpetually on the point of collapse. "My whole body is apparently rotting from want of proper nourishment," he wrote. "Frost-bitten fingertips, festerings, mucous membrane of nose gone, saliva glands of mouth refusing duty, skin coming off whole body."

Mawson's solitary journey lasted 28 days. Crevasses, suicidal depression, and his terrible sickness all failed to claim his life. Against all odds, Mawson would survive.

The killer

Although Mawson's diary contained a graphic account of the gruesome illness that had plagued him and killed Xavier Mertz, no one could offer a diagnosis. The first clues did not begin to emerge until 25 years after Mawson's return to Australia.

Dr. Kaara Rodahl, a Norwegian medical researcher, had long been intrigued by the fact that Eskimos refused to eat the liver of the polar bear. During the winter of 1939–40, he decided to find out why. Analysis of two polar bear livers revealed no unusual substances, but it did reveal a massive concentration of vitamin A. Rodahl also established that several animal livers the Eskimos avoided carried similar concentrations of vitamin A. And his experiments proved that such huge amounts of vitamin A were poisonous.

By the late 1960's, doctors recognized two forms of vitamin A poisoning. Symptoms of the acute variety are stomach pains, vomiting, diarrhea, the shedding of skin, and an irresistible sleepiness. Milder forms of the same symptoms characterize the chronic form—the result of some smaller but consistent overdoses—although mental depression replaces the desire to sleep.

Not until 1969 did anyone ask whether Xavier Mertz and Douglas Mawson could have been victims of vitamin A poisoning. That year Professor John Cleland of the University of Adelaide and Dr. R.V. Southcott, a zoologist, pointed out that the symptoms displayed by Mertz matched the acute form of the disease and those of Mawson, the chronic form.

But two questions remained: What was the source of the vitamin overdose? Why had Mertz suffered more than Mawson?

The answers were supplied in 1971 with experiments that proved that the livers of huskies contain dangerously high concentrations of vitamin A. The reason for the difference in the condition of the two men: Mertz, a near vegetarian, was unable to stomach the husky meat and had eaten far more of the liver than Mawson.

Ironically, today high doses of vitamin A are proving useful in combating certain kinds of cancer. The next challenge to medical science: find a way to overcome the vitamin's grim side effects.

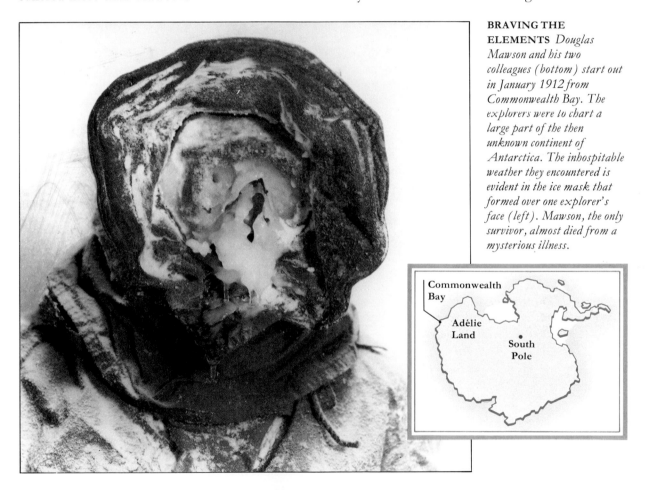

BRAVING THE ELEMENTS *Douglas Mawson and his two colleagues (bottom) start out in January 1912 from Commonwealth Bay. The explorers were to chart a large part of the then unknown continent of Antarctica. The inhospitable weather they encountered is evident in the ice mask that formed over one explorer's face (left). Mawson, the only survivor, almost died from a mysterious illness.*

THE END IS NIGH!

1,000 years of predictions

FOR CENTURIES there have been innumerable theories as to when and how the world might end. Possibilities put forward have ranged from nuclear war to destruction by a giant meteor—and even invasion from outer space. Some believers predict the coming of a Messiah, at which time all but they will be annihilated.

Here are some highlights gleaned from prophecies spanning a millennium.

992   In 960 Bernard of Thuringia, a German theologian, calculated 992 as the most likely year. As the time approached, panic was widespread.

1000   It has been said that the coming of the year 1000 (the "thousand years" referred to in the Book of Revelation) was greeted with alarm, and that many people emigrated to Jerusalem in anticipation of a holocaust that never came. Recent research, however, suggests that the scale of the panic, if it existed at all, was greatly exaggerated.

1410   It was once believed that the world was created in 5590 B.C. and would last 7,000 years; therefore, its date of destruction would be 1410. The significance of this date was not noticed until 1645, however.

1524; 1588   German astrologer Johann Stoffler predicted an overwhelming flood on February 20, 1524. Believers promptly started constructing arks; one man is said to have been trampled to death by a mob attempting to board his specially built vessel. When nothing happened, the calculations were revised and a new date given: 1588. That year also passed without any unusual rainfall, although it did see the Spanish Armada—a somewhat different watery phenomenon.

1665   Solomon Eccles was jailed in London's Bridewell Prison in 1665 for striding through Smithfield Market stark naked, carrying a pan of blazing sulfur on his head, and prophesying doom and destruction. Although the end of the world did not follow, the Great Fire of London did, in 1666.

1761   When two minor earthquakes were felt in London 28 days apart, former soldier William Bell predicted that a third would take place 28 days after the second, on April 5. So powerful would it be, he

SAVING THE WORLD *In 1962 members of the Aetherius Society in England—known for their interest in extraterrestrial life—were convinced that the end of the world was approaching. In February that year eight believers climbed a 2,600-foot peak in the Lake District in northern England to pray for the world and prevent the impending disaster.*

declared, that the world would undoubtedly end— or perhaps be consumed in a flood. Reportedly people left London in great numbers, some taking to boats. Not even the slightest tremor was felt.

1882; 1911; 1928; 1936; 1953   Basing his calculation on measurements of the Great Pyramid, Charles Piazzi Smyth, the astronomer-royal for Scotland, reckoned that the world would end in either 1882 or 1911. In the 1924 edition of their book *The Great Pyramid: Its Divine Message,* pyramidologists David Davidson and Herbert Aldersmith corrected the date to May 29, 1928. In the 1940 edition, the date was revised to August 20, 1953. Another pyramidologist, George F. Riffert, who had established the crucial date as September 6, 1936, later explained that it was the abdication of Edward VIII that the Great Pyramid was revealing, not the end of the world.

1914   After studying both the Bible and the mystical messages of the Great Pyramid, in 1874 Charles Taze Russell, founder of the sect that became Jehovah's Witnesses, concluded that the Second Coming had already taken place. He declared that people had 40 years, or until 1914, to enter his faith or be destroyed. Later he modified the date to "very soon after 1914."

1919   Albert Porta, a newspaper weatherman, was noted for the accuracy of his predictions of earthquakes in San Francisco. Therefore he was taken very seriously when he claimed that on December 17, 1919, flaming gases from the sun would consume the earth. When the sun continued shining, Porta resumed his weather forecasting.

1967   Anders Jensen, the Danish leader of a sect known as the Disciples of Orthon, convinced his followers that the world would end in a nuclear holocaust on Christmas Day, 1967. Jensen even appeared on the *David Frost Show* to announce this fact to millions of television viewers. After spending Christmas in their underground bunker, Jensen and 50 disciples emerged.

1972   Herbert W. Armstrong, publisher of the magazine *The Plain Truth,* declared that January 7, 1972, was undoubtedly the date to watch. The utter failure of his prediction has not diminished his zeal.

Toward the millennium   Based on complicated cabalistic calculations, some have offered 1997 as the "definite" year. The number arrived at after multiplying 666 by 3—both of which have magical connotations—is 1998, which has also been predicted. Moreover, Christ is said to have been crucified in the 1,998th week of His life.

However, the 16th-century seer Nostradamus is said to have favored 1999—the year of a Martian invasion—while an 18th-century French prophetess, Jeanne Le Roger, established the year 2000 as the definitive one.

Since the predictions of the past have been notably inaccurate, most people take these with a small grain of salt. Unless . . .

FROM RAGTIME TO RAGS

A second hearing — 57 years late

"THE AUDIENCE tonight went out of its mind," said the critic from *The New York Times.* He was describing the reception accorded the opera *Treemonisha* at its opening on January 28, 1972, in Symphony Hall in Atlanta Georgia. However, for the composer and librettist of *Treemonisha,* the acclaim was 57 years too late.

Artist in despair
When the opera's one and only previous performance took place in 1915, the press and the public alike had totally ignored it. Two years later its creator—one of the most popular American composers of the 20th century—died in despair in a mental hospital. His name: Scott Joplin.

Little in Joplin's earlier career as a composer would have suggested such an end. Born in 1868 in Texarkana, on the Texas-Arkansas border, Joplin began playing piano in the saloons and brothels of St. Louis, Missouri, at the age of 17. During the next 10 years he perfected his formidable technique that led to the musical form known as ragtime. From 1896 to 1900 Joplin studied at the George R. Smith College in Sedalia, Missouri, so that he could write down the music that came so easily to him as a performer. His first ragtime piece, "Maple Leaf Rag," was published in 1899.

The following year ragtime, a unique American blend of African and European musical forms, took the country by storm. Joplin had made only

$4 when "Maple Leaf Rag" was first published; but in 1900 it became a huge success, and Scott Joplin eventually became the first composer in the world to sell more than 1 million copies of the sheet music of a single tune.

Black music, white ears

For the next 11 years a stream of astonishing music poured from Joplin. But the King of Ragtime was not content to spend his life writing popular music. A serious and dedicated artist, he was pained by the tendency of white Americans to dismiss his music as trivial simply because it had black origins.

It became Joplin's mission to prove the validity of ragtime and, by implication, the worth of black Americans. In writing an opera, he was demanding direct comparison with the greatest European composers. Opera gave him the scope not only to demonstrate the artistic seriousness of his music but also, through the dramatic story, to make a claim for his race.

Treemonisha is the story of a black foundling girl educated by whites. By defeating three black magicians, she frees her people from superstition and becomes their acknowledged leader. The music integrates elements of black work songs, gospel music, and ragtime into the traditional operatic structure. When Joplin published it at his own expense in 1911, the sole reviewer called *Treemonisha* "an entirely new form of operatic art."

But the timing was wrong. Joplin had invested his hopes in a work based uncompromisingly on black music just as ragtime was on the wane in popularity. The one disastrous performance in New York City in 1915 broke him. The few, mostly invited, people in the audience at the Lincoln Theater in Harlem were unenthusiastic. The production had been staged hurriedly: there were no costumes, scenery, or musicians, and Joplin played all of the orchestral parts at the piano.

Prophetic words

Joplin had spent five years, in increasing poverty, struggling to sell his opera to music publishers and promoters. Already suffering from recurrent bouts of mental and physical instability, his health now deteriorated rapidly.

In February 1917 he entered Manhattan State Hospital, where he died two months later. The rediscovery of his genius in the 1970's—when his song "The Entertainer" formed part of the sound track for the movie *The Sting*—proved the truth of his own words: "Maybe 50 years after I am dead my music will be appreciated."

FORTUNE IN A TEACUP

A hoard of riches from the ocean floor

ON MAY 2, 1986, 46-year-old Capt. Michael Hatcher had every reason to feel pleased with himself. In the past five days he had made $12 million at Christie's auction house in Amsterdam. He had expected only a quarter of that amount from the sale of 18th-century Chinese porcelain and gold.

It was a happy ending to a tragedy that had taken place shortly after the *Geldermalsen,* owned by the Dutch East India Company, had set sail from Canton, China, on December 21, 1751. The ship's main cargo was tea, Ch'ing dynasty porcelain, and silks. She also carried a chest of gold ingots, which was to be transferred to another Dutch cruiser in the Sunda Strait between the Indian Ocean and the South China Sea.

Once the transfer had been made, the cruiser was to sail, with the gold, for Batavia (today Djakarta) on Java in Indonesia; the *Geldermalsen* was then to return with the tea and porcelain to Holland via the Indian and Atlantic oceans.

The *Geldermalsen* never arrived at the rendezvous. On January 3, after only two weeks at sea, she ran into a coral reef and sank. Of the 112 crew members aboard, only 32 escaped. The only provisions on their two small open boats were a barrel of ship's biscuits and a live piglet, but no water.

After a week of hardship and suffering, the survivors reached Batavia, where they were greeted not as heroes but with angry accusations of theft and cowardice. The Dutch East India Company officials charged boatswain Christoffer van Dijk, the senior surviving crew member, with stealing the gold and leaving his captain and shipmates to drown. Deny it as he might, Van Dijk was branded a villain and sent home.

Treasure hunt

The *Geldermalsen* and her treasures lay forgotten on the seafloor until Hatcher and his 10-man diving crew happened upon her 233 years later. Hatcher had spent 25 years in the Far East, salvaging cargoes from wrecks sunk during World War II. Purely by chance, in 1982 he had found the wreck of a 17th-century Chinese junk at the bottom of the South China Sea.

She was laden with porcelain—a treasure that spurred him on to explore again in the same area. While diving one day in the spring of 1985, he chanced upon a cannon and a few bricks sticking out of the sand. Unknowingly, he had found the wreck of the *Geldermalsen*.

A miraculous survival

To clear the wreck, Hatcher put a vacuum pump to work. For months nothing but tea came out. And then the pump began to spew fragments of porcelain onto the seafloor. The wreck contained an astonishing haul. Of a cargo of 239,000 pieces of porcelain, some 168,000 were still intact—truly remarkable in light of the fact that the ship had suffered such devastation.

A short distance from the wreck, one member of Hatcher's team also found 125 of the 13-ounce gold ingots, proving that the maligned Van Dijk had been telling the truth.

More valuable to Hatcher was the cargo of the blue-and-white porcelain. Miraculously, it was preserved, its color and glazing still pristine.

Among the surviving unbroken items were 18 complete dinner services (the largest contained 380 pieces), 2,263 cups and saucers for chocolate, 63,623 teacups and saucers, 522 teapots, 19,535 coffee cups and saucers, 1,286 soup plates, 245 cuspidors, 495 chamber pots, 681 beer mugs, and 606 receptacles mysteriously labeled "vomit pots." Gone were the 5,240 items of silk.

The 306 tons of tea that Hatcher had pumped out of the ship was, at that time, the most valuable part of the cargo by far, representing 60 percent of the invested capital. The porcelain had been packed in the tea to protect it from the rigors of the voyage; ironically, not only had the tea prevented damage, it had also helped to preserve the china's original splendor. Ruined as it was, in the end the tea had proved far from worthless.

SEAFOOD PLATTER
Scattered on the seabed in the South China Sea (above): 18th-century Chinese porcelain. Most of the cargo salvaged from the Geldermalsen *was found to be remarkably well preserved.*

A SMALL WORLD

Some odd coincidences

Sons, beware   Robert Todd Lincoln, the son of Abraham Lincoln, was present at Ford's Theater in Washington, D.C., on April 14, 1865, when his father was assassinated. He was also nearby on July 2, 1881, when President James Garfield was shot at the Baltimore and Potomac railroad station in Washington. And on September 6, 1901, he just happened to be a few feet away when President William McKinley was shot at the Pan-American Exposition in Buffalo, New York.

Prophetic play   Early in 1938 playwright A. J. Talbot published a one-act comedy, *Chez Boguskovsky,* in which a man named Boguskovsky steals a painting from the Louvre in Paris. On August 15, 1939, a painting was stolen from the Louvre. The name of the thief: Boguskovsky.

Lost and found   One day in 1952 the oboist Léon Goossens lost his pocket diary in a field near his home. A year later he was walking across the same field and discovered the diary, by then battered by wind and rain. Goossens noticed that newspaper had been used to stiffen the covers. When he pulled it out, Goossens found himself reading an extract from a gossip column. The subject: his own marriage, 19 years earlier.

Class conscious   In 1906 six babies were born on board the German ship *Grosser Kurfurst,* sailing from Bremen to New York: one in first class, twins in second class, and triplets in third class.

Heralding disaster   Film writer and producer Irwin Allen has made a specialty of disaster movies, and their production has often coincided with real-life versions of the disasters they feature. In *The Poseidon Adventure* an ocean liner capsizes. The movie opened late in 1972, the same year that the luxury ship *Queen Elizabeth* capsized. In 1974, the year that *The Towering Inferno* premiered, three skyscrapers in Brazil caught fire. And in 1980 Allen's film about a volcanic eruption, *When Time Ran Out,* coincided with the eruption of Mount St. Helens in Washington.

Too sweet   In 1974, at the Pepperidge Farm plant in Downingtown, Pennsylvania, an employee was killed when he fell into a vat of chocolate. His name was Robert C. H. Hershey.

Family affairs   On February 13, 1746, a Frenchman, Jean Marie Dubarry, was executed for the murder of his father. Precisely 100 years later, on February 13, 1846, another Frenchman, also named Jean Marie Dubarry, was executed—for the murder of his father.

Circumstantial evidence?   English politician and justice of the peace Sir Edmund Berry Godfrey was found murdered on October 17, 1678. His body had been left in a ditch on Greenberry Hill in London. Three men were arrested and tried for the crime. Their names were Robert Green, Henry Berry, and Lawrence Hill.

Survivors   On December 5, 1664, a boat sank while crossing the Menai Strait in the Irish Sea. Just one of the 81 passengers survived, a man named Hugh Williams. On December 5, 1785, another boat sank in the same place. The only survivor: a man named Hugh Williams. On August 5, 1820, 24 passengers in a stricken vessel drowned. One man was saved. His name was Hugh Williams.

IF AT FIRST . . .

After a bitter six-year battle to win a divorce from his wife, Suleyman Guresci walked away from the Turkish courts in November 1986, free at last.

Undaunted by the failure of his first marriage, Guresci was eager to find a new wife. But he was not about to make the same mistake again. This time he was determined to find the right partner. He turned to a computer service to find the ideal wife. Of 2,000 possible candidates, the machine selected only one as the most suitable: Nesrin Caglasas, his former wife.

Before remarrying Nesrin, Guresci said: "I decided to give her another try by being more tolerant toward her."

PART

4

INTRIGUING AND UNSOLVED MYSTERIES

THE STRANGE CASE OF KILLER GREEN

Was Napoleon murdered by accidental design?

ALMOST FROM the moment that Napoleon Bonaparte drew his last breath in May 1821, medical experts and historians have argued about the cause of his death at the age of 51.

Was it cancer, as officially reported? At least one doctor present at the postmortem examination disagreed, claiming it was hepatitis. Other experts have suggested syphilis or tuberculosis or malaria. Some even believe that the former emperor was assassinated—poisoned by an enemy.

It now seems likely that none of these illnesses caused his death, and there is no evidence that anybody did, or tried to, kill him. In 1982, however, more than 160 years after Napoleon's death, a respected British chemist unearthed evidence that the great man was indeed poisoned—but by a thing, not a person. And that thing may well have been the wallpaper in his house on St. Helena, where the British had exiled Napoleon in 1815.

Isolation and despair

St. Helena is a hot and humid volcanic rock jutting out of the Atlantic Ocean some 1,200 miles off the west coast of Africa. Longwood House, where

DEADLY DESIGN *The chance preservation of this scrap of wallpaper from Napoleon's house on the island of St. Helena has led scientists and historians to reconsider the cause of his death.*

DEATH OF AN EMPEROR *Did Napoleon die from natural causes, or at the hands of a skillful enemy? Or was he the victim of some nonhuman agency? Such speculation has been rife ever since he died in 1821 (above). His tranquil death mask (right) gives us no clues.*

Napoleon resided with his French officers and servants, was a single-story building so damp that the paper on its walls was moldy and peeling.

At first, life on St. Helena seems to have been tolerable for Napoleon, who enjoyed gardening and riding horseback. As time went on, however, his custodians permitted him less and less freedom. Increasingly deprived of companions and outdoor activity, he became depressed, spent much of his time indoors, and lapsed into chronic ill health. He suffered from chills, nausea, fevers. At times his legs would swell so that he could not walk without pain, and he had pain in his shoulder and in the region of the liver. In addition, he suffered frequent spells of vomiting and complained of headaches, lethargy, and dizziness. His skin began to take on a yellowish tinge.

Attendant doctors were puzzled. Medicines occasionally relieved some of the pain and anguish, but Napoleon remained sick, his condition further weakened by each bout of illness. One or two doctors decided that he was, quite simply, a hypochondriac; others diagnosed his ailment as chronic hepatitis.

Whatever was wrong, it could not be cured. Eventually the former emperor was confined to a small bed in the damp living room of Longwood House. There he slipped into a coma from which he never awoke.

On May 6, 1821 — the day after Napoleon died — his body was dissected and the internal organs carefully examined by a group of British physicians. Their report, that the renowned French prisoner had succumbed to a "cancerous ulcer" of the stomach, must have gratified the authorities in London, for it apparently absolved them of any blame or negligence. Cancer then, as today, was considered a killer disease; moreover, Napoleon's father had died of it.

The controversy over that diagnosis stems in part from suspicion of a cover-up by the British. But many medical experts are also convinced that the details of Napoleon's symptoms, as well as the recorded condition of his internal organs at the postmortem, are incompatible with a diagnosis of cancer. They would not be incompatible, however, with the effects of an accumulation of poisonous arsenic on the human system.

A lock of hair, a scrap of paper

It was in 1961 that Dr. Sten Forshufvud of Sweden jolted historians with his theory that Napoleon had died of arsenic poisoning. Forshufvud came to this conclusion after analysis of a lock of Napoleon's hair (believed to have been cut on the day of the postmortem) revealed concentrations of arsenic.

Even so, this did not prove that Napoleon had been murdered. Limited amounts of arsenic were a common ingredient of medicines in Napoleon's day. The ailing exile must have taken more than a fair share of them, which could account for the presence of arsenic in the hair. There is no reason to assume that a clever assassin laced the man's tonics with additional amounts in order to hasten his demise. But it now seems probable that additional amounts *were* "supplied." A British chemist, Dr. David Jones, has discovered what he calls "a neat chemical answer to a small historical mystery."

In the late 18th and early 19th centuries, a type of pigment known as Scheele's green was extensively used to color fabrics, paints, and wallpapers. The pigment contained arsenic, but was generally harmless in fabrics and paint. It was also safe in wallpaper on a dry wall. In a damp room, however, Scheele's green could become moldy and would release arsenic in the form of a vapor, which occupants of the room would unknowingly inhale.

Like so many Napoleonic relics, a sample of wallpaper from the Longwood House living room at the time of Napoleon's residence has been preserved. Noting its green design, Jones gained permission to submit the sample to laboratory tests; it contained a substantial amount of arsenic.

So was the emperor an unwitting victim of a nonhuman enemy? In view of the extraordinary humidity of St. Helena and the dampness of the room where he died, moldy, green-patterned wallpaper cannot be excluded as a prime suspect.

The poisonous properties of Scheele's green were recognized early in the 1800's. The pigment was used much less extensively in room decorations as the century wore on. According to Jones, however, by 1900 Scheele's green had given symptoms of arsenic poisoning to "hundreds of luckless householders." In fact, in the 1950's a bedroom in the palatial Roman residence of Mrs. Clare Boothe Luce, who was the U.S. ambassador to Italy, was redecorated. Why? Because Mrs. Luce felt unwell and her symptoms were eventually attributed to arsenic poisoning from the flaking paint on the ceiling, which had been decorated with roses. Her health improved after the ceiling was repainted.

ON THE TRAIL OF A KILLER DISEASE

The unlikely source of cholera

ON SEPTEMBER 4, 1854, the narrow courts and streets of London's usually bustling district of Soho were strangely deserted. Yellow flags hung at each street corner, and milky-white puddles of lime chloride lay everywhere. There was a ghostly calm.

In the preceding few days hundreds of people in Soho had died from the ravages of cholera, one of the most devastating and least understood diseases of the age. The yellow flags were a traditional plague warning, the lime chloride a desperate attempt at disinfection. Having made an effort to arrest the disease, most of Soho's terrified inhabitants had fled. Local hospitals were overflowing with the dying. At the height of the epidemic, 143 deaths were recorded in a single day. Corpses were so numerous, they were unceremoniously piled on carts and taken away for burial.

The mystery disease

At that time opinion in the medical profession was divided as to the cause of cholera. Most doctors favored the theory that it was spread by foul air in the overcrowded quarters of the poor. Others suggested that height above sea level was significant: the higher the altitude, the purer the air.

One authority solemnly concluded that people with dark hair were more vulnerable than blonds or redheads. But the grim fact was that no one knew how to prevent or cure the disease.

Dr. John Snow, who lived near Soho, had become involved in the argument about cholera in 1848, during the previous epidemic in Britain. Snow was an acknowledged authority on respiration and doubted that cholera was something people inhaled. In fact, he was convinced that he knew how and why this latest outbreak of the disease had occurred.

Snow's reasoning was simple enough. Cholera, he pointed out, first manifests itself as a stomach disorder; therefore, it was reasonable to conclude that what he called the cholera "poison" had to be swallowed. The major symptoms were vomiting and diarrhea, followed by spasms and cramps in the limbs. People tended not to wash before eating, and anyone in contact with a victim could easily take in the "poison" with food. And in a district full of leaking privies and overflowing cesspools such as Soho, there was every chance the disease passed directly into the local supply of drinking water.

But why had cholera broken out in such epidemic proportions in Soho?

Snow noticed that the Soho outbreak was confined to a small area. In the center, at Broad Street, stood an old water pump that supplied drinking water to the community.

Ironically the Broad Street pump, which was served by a well, had an excellent reputation for the purity of its water. Despite the availability of a supply from water mains, many people still preferred to use the local pump. And many families depended on the pump on weekends, when the water mains were shut off. Concluding that the pump must be responsible for the cholera outbreak, Snow persuaded the local authorities to take it out of service by removing the handle. They reluctantly did so on September 7.

Detective work

By September 11 the epidemic was almost over, having claimed more than 500 lives. At this point the authorities decided to launch an investigation into the causes. Their most dedicated investigator was the local curate, the Reverend Henry Whitehead. Wholly unconvinced by Snow's theory, Whitehead was determined to prove Snow wrong.

Snow had noticed that the cholera reached only so far down certain streets: "The deaths . . . diminished, or ceased altogether, at every point where it becomes decidedly nearer to send to another pump than to the one in Broad Street." Snow drew attention to the local brewery, where no one had fallen ill. It had its own well, and most of the workers quenched their thirst with free beer. The nearby workhouse, which had its own pump as well as water from mains, also remained unaffected. Residents in the single house visited by death in an otherwise unaffected street had been the only ones to use water from the Broad Street pump.

But at a factory in Broad Street itself, 18 workers had died—and so had the widow of its founder, who lived a few miles away. Partial to the pump water, she had had a bottle a day sent to her home.

The final proof

It was Whitehead, Snow's opponent, who provided the final statistics. Of 137 people who lived in Broad Street and used the pump, 80 had died. Of the 297 who did not take water from the pump, only 20 had contracted cholera. Faced with this evidence, the honest curate abandoned his opposition and sided entirely with Snow.

Despite the evidence, the medical establishment remained unconvinced that the area's privies were the root of the problem. It was Snow's new convert, Whitehead, who uncovered the final proof. He noticed that a day before the epidemic had struck the neighborhood, a baby girl had died of the disease at No. 40 Broad Street. Her mother had washed diapers in the house privy. Whitehead discovered that the privy leaked into the well that fed the Broad Street pump.

It was not until 1866, when another cholera epidemic threatened Britian, that the medical profession finally accepted Snow's theory. By that time Snow was dead. Then in 1884 the German microbiologist Robert Koch discovered the direct cause of cholera: *Spirillum cholerae,* a germ with a behavior that matched the hypothetical cholera "poison" described by Snow. The way was open to begin to attempt control of the disease.

DEATH'S DISPENSARY *Until the theory of a London doctor was finally accepted by the medical profession in 1866, the carrier of cholera—contaminated water—remained unknown. Unfortunately, many people died after drinking from communal water pumps in the 1854 cholera epidemic that swept London.*

NEW WORLD VIEW

Mapping ancient lines

IN 1966 PROFESSOR CHARLES H. HAPGOOD of the University of New Hampshire published his remarkable claim that the world had been mapped before history began to be written. Navigators and geographers, he asserted, had visited and charted the New World centuries before Columbus. More controversially, he argued that the Antarctic mainland—not sighted until 1820, according to most historians—had actually been mapped at least 6,000 years before.

Hapgood based these assertions on the study of a map drawn in 1513 by the Turkish admiral Piri Re'is. The map had some obvious errors in it: the Amazon River appeared twice, and 900 miles of South America's east coast had been left out. But it seemed to show part of the coastline of Antarctica without any ice cover—as it would have appeared when the region was warmer, thousands of years earlier. Hapgood believed that the admiral had compiled his map from several earlier versions, some possibly dating back to Alexander the Great.

MYSTERIOUS OUTLINES *The Piri Re'is map was first investigated by Charles Hapgood in 1956.*

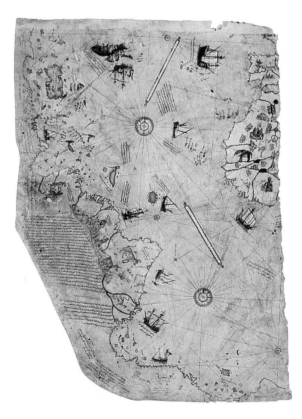

The theory could be tested only by comparing all the topographical features on Re'is's map with their equivalents on a modern map. After three years' work, Hapgood and his students replotted the map, using a grid invented by medieval sailors to chart the Black Sea and the Mediterranean. At last, a true comparison could be made.

It seemed at first that the research was not going to aid Hapgood's cause. Piri Re'is had left out the Drake Passage, which divides Antarctica and South America. However, the "Antarctic coast" on the ancient map turned out to lie roughly in the correct place and seemed to match the present-day outline of Queen Maud Land in Antarctica.

Further proof

To strengthen his case, Hapgood turned to a map drawn in 1531 by a cartographer named Oronteus Finaeus. Hapgood claimed that this map provided further proof that the ancients had possessed a detailed knowledge of Antarctic geography.

"The general shape of the continent was startlingly like the outline of the continent on our modern map," he wrote. "The position of the South Pole, nearly in the center of the continent, seemed about right. The mountains that skirted the coasts suggested the numerous ranges that have been discovered in Antarctica in recent years."

Later Hapgood claimed to have identified dozens of matching geographical features. He also maintained that the Finaeus map—like that of Piri Re'is—had been drawn from charts made in prehistory, before Antarctica was covered with ice.

Who, then, might these precocious explorers and mapmakers have been? According to Hapgood, they must have belonged to a lost civilization of "ancient sea kings," whose forgotten skills had to be rediscovered by later generations.

Other experts have greeted Hapgood's claims with skepticism. They point out that medieval cartographers often drew an imagined southern continent simply to make the world appear symmetrical, and that many ancient maps are wildly inaccurate, with countries and coastlines hundreds of miles from where they should be. One critic has even suggested that Finaeus's "Antarctica" is simply an extra outline of Africa.

Will history be rewritten? Charles Hapgood died in 1982, leaving others to decide whether his legacy is a cartographic wild-goose chase or an important clue to the wisdom of the ancients.

SECRETS OF THE AGES

Do ancient monuments shed light on a modern mystery?

WHILE SIFTING THROUGH thousands of reports from the United States and Britain on unidentified flying objects (UFO's), British researcher Paul Devereux started to observe certain patterns.

Sightings of UFO's seemed to occur most often in certain areas where an unusually high number of geologic faults—breaks between layers of different kinds of rock—made them subject to earth tremors and variations in the earth's magnetic field. In Britain, noted Devereux, the areas are also the sites of ancient earthworks and stone monuments.

Aliens at Stonehenge?

Devereux knew that some writers have suggested that the stone monuments at Stonehenge in England, at Carnac in France, and at other places around the world were not the work of humans but of extraterrestrials whom the people believed to be gods. Proponents of the idea also pointed out that sightings of UFO's have been especially frequent near these ancient sites.

But Devereux's work led him to offer a different explanation for the sightings—and some new theories as to why the monuments were built.

At the time that Devereux had completed his study of UFO's in 1975, however, he was no nearer to an explanation—despite the intriguing geologic correlations that he had discovered. An extraterrestrial agent could still have been responsible for the ancient structures.

Pinpoints of light

Meanwhile, other scientists had been conducting some seemingly unrelated research. Data compiled by psychologists Michael Persinger and Gyslaine Lafrenière of Laurentian University in Sudbury, Ontario, Canada, suggested that a combination of seismic and electrical forces might be responsible for UFO events.

And at the U.S. Bureau of Mines in Denver, Dr. Brian Brady had been investigating the effects of geologic and seismic disturbances. During experiments involving the breaking and fracturing of rocks, Brady noticed that intense emissions of light would erupt as the rocks broke apart. Inside

STANDING PROUD *Harold's Stones in Wales are one of many early European monuments that some people believe were created by extraterrestrials.*

the laboratory the lights were no more than tiny, short-lived pinpoints—but out of doors they might be seen as objects moving along a fracture.

Brady felt that movement in a fault zone in the earth might generate emissions of light along the active portions of the fault. When Persinger and Lafrenière contacted Brady, they concluded that he had created what might be UFO's in miniature.

Full circle
Bringing together all of these findings, Devereux felt that he might now have found a scientific explanation to support his statistics: *Could* UFO's be natural phenomena?

If so, the electromagnetic nature of UFO events would explain many effects that frequently accompany sightings: burn marks on the ground, buzzing noises, and the failure of automobile electrical systems. But what was the relationship between the "earthlights" from geologic fault lines and the ancient megalithic sites?

It is Devereux's supposition that the people of the New Stone Age saw the earthlights and

regarded them as holy; they then built temples and observatories at points where the lights were seen most frequently. Devereux goes on to propose an even more startling theory: perhaps the lights actually assumed the shapes that witnesses believed they were seeing.

According to Devereux, the prehistoric priests might have been able to manipulate the forms the lights took, giving them the shapes of pagan deities. Priests might have accomplished this through the power of suggestion or some process we as yet cannot comprehend.

If so, claims Devereux, it would help to explain myths and legends found throughout Europe that tell of gods that walked the earth and communicated directly with man. But the UFO's themselves may have come from the earth, not another planet, and ordinary human beings, not gods, built the magnificent structures that remain to this day.

Devereux's theories offer much food for thought to people wishing to explore various beliefs about the possible relationship between gods, UFO's, and ancient sites.

THE OUTLAW WITH A PAST
The search for Robin Hood

ROBIN HOOD is a familiar figure in history. The medieval outlaw who robbed the rich to give to the poor, outwitted the cruel sheriff of Nottingham and bad King John, and dwelt with his band of merry followers in Sherwood Forest has long been celebrated in prose and poetry. On stage and screen, he has captivated countless generations.

Yet behind the character lurks an enigma: Who, exactly, was Robin Hood? Did he exist at all?

Fact and fantasy
The evidence for his existence is flimsy. In 13th-century England there were a number of people who answered to his name or to something close to it: Robert Hood of Wakefield or Barnsdale in Yorkshire; Robyn Hode, a humble servant to King Edward II; Roberd Hude, an almost illegible name on a gravestone at Kirklees, also in Yorkshire; and Gilbert Robynhod of Sussex, from another part of England altogether.

There is also an obscure manuscript record that in 1225 a certain Robert Hood was outlawed for nonpayment of a debt or fine. However, despite exhaustive searches of local records of the time by

historians, there is little that definitely connects any of these men with the legendary Robin Hood of Sherwood Forest.

But if the real Robin Hood cannot be traced, his story should not be dismissed as a work of pure fiction; within every legend there is usually some grain of truth.

In medieval England lived many a true outlaw. Most famous was Hereward the Wake, the last Anglo-Saxon chieftain to resist the Norman Conquest of 1066. And countless other, less well known people fled the harsh and punitive justice of the day to take refuge in the thick forests that covered the English countryside.

Their exploits formed the basis of many stories, exaggerated and embellished as they were told and retold. Thus, tales about an outlaw named Robin Hood readily found an audience, and incidents and events concerning real-life outlaws were added to elaborate the original Hood legend.

By the beginning of the 14th century, the adventures of an outlawed Hood were being celebrated in ballad and poem throughout the country. By the end of the same century Hood was sufficiently well known to be mentioned in William

ELUSIVE HERO *Although the legend of Robin Hood has persisted for centuries, no one knows if he ever really existed. The earliest visual representation of him, below, is in a "biography" entitled* A Lyttell Geste of Robyn Hode, *probably written about 1400. In the more recent portrayal in the Victorian stained glass window at right, the famed outlaw shoots his last arrow.*

Langland's epic poem, *Piers Plowman,* one of the most famous works of early English literature. Around 1400 his life was celebrated in *A Lyttell Geste of Robyn Hode,* written by an unknown author. Not "lyttell" at all, this poem is a 456-verse description of Robin's "gestes," or adventures, as an outlaw. It also contains details about his fellow renegades Little John, Will Scarlock (later Scarlett), Much the Miller's Son, and Friar Tuck.

Into history

By the 16th century, Hood was an established historical figure. Henry VIII knew of him, as did William Shakespeare, who set much of *As You Like It* in the Forest of Arden, where the exiled duke and his court "live like the old Robin Hood of England." Hood was also becoming an important part in the celebrations marking May Day: Robin was associated with the character of the May King, and Maid Marian with the May Queen.

As stories about Robin Hood spread through word of mouth in taverns and at fairs and markets, they evolved and changed. Hood's status was transformed from lowly yeoman, or small farmer, to disinherited earl of Huntingdon.

And as the great forests of England were gradually cleared, the romance of Hood's abode in the "greenwood" and his dress of lincoln green—linking him to the supernatural realm of elves, fairies, and other magical forest folk—were added to the legend. Some scholars have even suggested that "Hood" may have been derived from the Old German word for a forest sprite or elf, *hodeken.*

To this day, the figure of Robin Hood remains elusive. Whether he actually existed as a real person or was a fictional representation of one or more real-life outlaws, his origins will remain obscure. What is certain is that the colorful legends of his merry band of men will continue to entertain and intrigue young and old alike.

THE EXTRAORDINARY ELECTRICIAN

One man's "little creatures"

THE TIME: the early years of the 19th century. The setting: an ancient manor house in an isolated valley in the west of England. A scientist is engaged in a very elaborate series of experiments with electricity.

Outside the laboratory, copper wires suspended on poles run for more than a mile into the countryside. Inside, mysterious equipment—coils of wire, weirdly shaped jars, strange crystals, saucers of murky liquid—glows and pulsates. The few local people who dare to approach the mansion tell of explosions, of bolts of lightning that strike when no storms are near, and of the reclusive, secretive nature of the scientist himself.

One day comes news that confirms everyone's darkest suspicions: their sinister neighbor has created life in one of his jars.

As strange as fiction

Despite its gothic trappings, the tale is true. Andrew Crosse was a gentleman-scholar who devoted his life to the study of the new science of electricity. In 1837 one of his experiments brought him attention and created a mystery that has excited controversy among scientists ever since.

The sequence of events that culminated in the experiments for which Crosse became notorious began around 1807. After visiting a cave covered with crystals, Crosse was determined to discover the process by which they had formed. He was convinced that "the crystalline matter which lined the roof of this cave was caused by some peculiar upward attraction; and . . . I felt assured that it was electric attraction."

Soon Crosse was growing a wide variety of crystals in his laboratory and could eventually claim that he had produced about 200 varieties of minerals, exactly resembling in all respects similar ones found in nature, as well as some others never before discovered in nature or formed by art.

In 1837 Crosse began still another crystal-growing experiment using an electrified stone and a chemical solution. After two weeks he noticed "a few small whitish excrescences, or nipples, projecting from about the middle of the stone." During the next few days the projections grew until, on the 26th day of the experiment, they "assumed the form of a perfect insect, standing erect on a few bristles which formed its tail. . . . On the 28th day these little creatures moved their legs. I must now say that I was not a little astonished. After a few

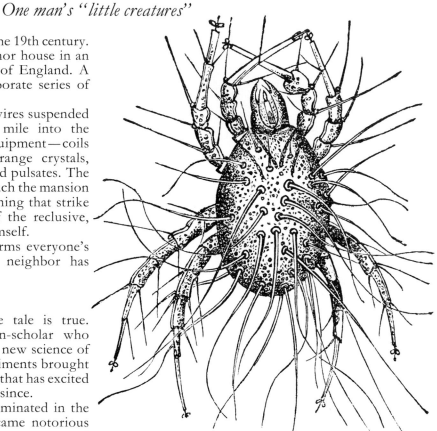

CREATION OF LIFE *One of the "perfect insects" that emerged from experiments with electricity by the 19th-century English scientist Andrew Crosse. Many people believed that Crosse had in fact created the insects, or* acari, *but the truth was never discovered—even by Crosse.*

days they detached themselves from the stone, and moved about at pleasure."

Within a few weeks some 100 insects appeared on the stone. The creatures turned out to be acari, or tiny mites. But what puzzled Crosse was how they had gotten there.

Had they been present in the water he had used in the experiment? Or had the eggs of passing insects fallen into his apparatus and then hatched? Neither explanation seemed likely. Had he somehow created the mites himself? The implications were staggering and disconcerting. So the determined scholar decided to try the experiment again.

Life in the laboratory

The next time Crosse set up seven glass cylinders, each with a different chemical solution. He passed an electric current through them. Then he waited.

After many months his patience was rewarded. Mites had developed in all but two of the cylinders. By now, confused and rather frightened by his findings, Crosse sought a rational explanation. But then another scientist, W. H. Weeks, repeated the experiments and confirmed Crosse's results. Even the physicist Michael Faraday claimed that he produced insects by following Crosse's method.

Despite the support of his fellow scientists, publication of his results brought Crosse only scorn and ridicule. Accused of meddling in God's work, he became the center of a bitter controversy and retired to the seclusion of his laboratory. Although he continued his study of electricity, he restricted his experiments to purifying seawater and preserving food with "electrified water."

Had Crosse somehow stumbled upon a recipe for the creation of life? The possibility of a hoax can be ruled out: such behavior was not in his character. Crosse himself put forward, then dismissed, another explanation: "The simplest solution of the problem . . . was that they arose from ova deposited by insects floating in the atmosphere and hatched by electric action. Still, I could not imagine that an ovum could shoot out filaments, or that these filaments could become bristles, and . . . I could not detect . . . the remains of a shell."

The question still has not been answered.

THE PULL OF THE LAND

The curious phenomenon of magnetic roadways

MOTORISTS DRIVING along Croy Brae in Strathclyde, Scotland, sooner or later usually slow down—or stop completely—in utter confusion. For Croy Brae is one of the most disorienting places on earth.

Approaching the brae ("hill") from the north is an uncanny experience. The road appears to slope downward, and drivers assume that the slope will accelerate the vehicle. Yet if they slow down, they are likely to grind to a complete halt. Despite every appearance to the contrary, the road runs uphill, not downhill. Unable to believe what has happened, many motorists stop—only to find that their cars begin to slide backward, "uphill."

Travelers who are approaching from the south experience a similar topsy-turvy sensation. Thinking they are heading uphill they accelerate—only to discover that they are speeding along faster than they had intended. The road actually goes *down*.

Powerful force

No one has yet been able to come up with a totally satisfactory explanation of what causes these strange effects at Croy Brae. It was once believed that magnetic forces induced by surrounding iron-rich rocks exerted such a strong attraction that they could actually pull automobiles uphill.

This explanation is now generally dismissed, but another theory suggests that the sensations are due to an optical illusion caused by one of two factors: local variations in the earth's magnetic field—to which our sense of balance may somehow be connected—may alter our perceptions; or the unusual topography of the land.

Whatever the explanation, the phenomenon is not unique to Croy; there are similar places all over the world. One example can be found on the road to Jerusalem near the village of Djabal Moukaber, Israel. And on Mystery Hill, a small area between Boone and Blowing Rock, North Carolina, a river reportedly flows north and apple trees grow *into* the prevailing winds, seemingly in complete defiance of the laws of nature.

In a letter to a magazine, a British visitor to Canada described how an uncle had taken him to "a rather unusual but fascinating place" near Vancouver. "He parked his huge station wagon on a bumpy road with a steep gradient, and then took the key out of the ignition and released the handbrake. There were eight of us in the car but, to my astonishment, it nevertheless began to move— *uphill*. My uncle then poured some water from a nearby stream onto the surface of the road, and this too began to flow uphill."

The best-known example in North America is Magnetic Hill at Moncton, New Brunswick, Canada. According to local legend, its mysterious properties were first noticed in the 1930's when a milkman stopped his horse and cart at the bottom to make a delivery. When he returned, to his astonishment he found that both horse and cart had drifted halfway "up" the hill.

No description can possibly convey the experience on these roads. They have to be driven to be believed. Whether or not the truth about them can ever be explained, such conjuring tricks of nature are a magnet for tourists and for all lovers of the strange and bizarre.

A STRAIGHT AND NARROW PATH

The puzzle of the lines that mark the earth

HIGH IN THE BOLIVIAN ANDES, straight pathways run for miles across the mountains and the plains that lie in between. In Vermont, Massachusetts, Ohio, and California, long-forgotten stones, put in place in the distant pre-Columbian past, mark lines that are just as long and just as true. Across Europe the lines march undeviatingly through the landscape, linking hilltop to church spire to pagan monument.

What the lines are, who laid them out and why, are puzzles that have taxed the ingenuity of researchers from fields of study as diverse as mathematics, archeology, and dowsing. There are many clues but no final answers to the numerous questions they pose.

Frequently, such lines are visible only to the trained eye, although their presence can be calculated with the help of detailed maps. However, it was purely by intuition that lines of this sort were first detected, by a brewer named Alfred Watkins, from Hereford, England, in 1921.

At age 65, Watkins had been intimately familiar with his local landscape since childhood. One day, while stopping his horse on a hilltop, he suddenly saw that the prominent features of the locality were linked as if by a network of straight tracks.

Checking on maps, Watkins found that his intuition was correct. The oldest signs of human habitation were strung out across the countryside in straight lines. The features he noticed were circles of stones, Stone Age burial mounds, forts, hilltops, and churches built on the sites of former pagan temples. Watkins further realized that they seemed to be aligned with the paths of stars across the heavens, or with points on the horizon where the sun would rise or set at certain significant times of the year—midwinter, midsummer, or during the spring and autumn equinoxes.

Watkins noted too that the places through which the lines passed often had names that ended in *ley,* or *leigh,* and frequently contained the word *salt* or *white*. He named the lines "leys" and concluded that they were, in fact, pathways—routes along which salt, a highly valued commodity in ancient times, had been moved from place to place.

Support from the stars

Orthodox archeologists long regarded Watkins as an eccentric. But his observation that the leys corresponded to astronomical events was confirmed late in the 1960's by the work of Alexander Thom, an eminent mathematician and engineer.

Thom's observations revealed that many ancient sites in Britain, especially that of Stonehenge, were aligned with astronomical phenomena. Stonehenge itself lies on Britain's longest ley.

THE WORLD ON ITS BACK

On the plains of Saskatchewan, Canada, lies the mysterious effigy, in stones, of a huge turtle. Known as the Minton Turtle (because of its proximity to the town of the same name), it is 135 feet long from head to tail.

Its origins and the identity of its builders remain a mystery to archeologists. However, similar stone effigies in the area are known to have been built by tribes of Plains Indians within the last 500 years.

The turtle held a very special place in Indian folklore and tribal

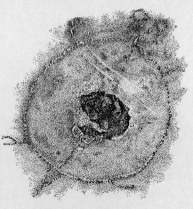

MOCK TURTLE *This effigy is said to be an ancient Indian symbol.*

ceremony. Many of the American Indians believed that before the existence of the earth as it is known today, only a great turtle floated in an enormous sea, and all other animals lived in its shell.

As various animals brought mud up from the bottom of the sea, the turtle's shell became the foundation of the world.

To date, no excavations have been carried out at the site, but archeologists believe that the Minton Turtle effigy may be an ancient Indian symbol of fertility and long life.

Soon other curious facts about the mysterious lines began to emerge. Dowsers, supported by geologists, found that both leys and ancient sites coincided with "blind" springs, where water wells up but does not break the surface. Researcher Francis Hitching discovered magnetic anomalies in the sites and along the leys. Watkins's original idea that leys were simply tracks or trade routes began to seem inadequate.

For trade or religion?

Research in the United States revealed equally elaborate networks of straight lines joining rock formations, Indian artifacts, and solitary standing stones clearly put in place by human beings. And a correspondence to blind springs also emerged.

During the 1970's zoologist Tony Morrison discovered pathways in the Bolivian Andes that ran unswervingly for miles from population centers to tiny shrines in the wilderness—and they too followed directions that were astronomically significant. This seemed to confirm the suspicion of many researchers that there was a religious aspect to leys, wherever they were found.

Some speculated that there were "earth energies" with which all the prehistoric engineers were somehow in touch. Others, backed by further evidence from Europe, held to the notion that these were trading routes; perhaps salt was a sacred commodity and had to travel along certain ritually prescribed paths.

Still, a number of questions remain unanswered. Why did so many different cultures, so distant from one another, find satisfaction in crisscrossing their landscape with straight lines? What is the significance of the invisible springs or the local magnetic anomalies, and were the ancients aware of them? How does all this relate to the astronomical alignments to which leys conform? Perhaps only a time machine can ever provide the true answers.

A VOLUME OF SPECULATION

The most mysterious manuscript in the world

AT THE BEINECKE RARE BOOK and Manuscript Library at Yale University in New Haven, Connecticut, hardly a day passes without an inquiry about a small volume known as the Voynich Manuscript.

The Beinecke contains countless rare books. What makes the Voynich Manuscript of particular interest is that no one has yet been able to read it in full; the text is written in a code that some of the world's greatest cryptographers and linguistics experts have failed to decipher.

The manuscript measures $5\frac{3}{4}$ by $8\frac{1}{2}$ inches and is some 200 pages long. Its vellum leaves are covered with extraordinary flowing writing—extraordinary because its author has used a completely unknown alphabet. The illustrations accompanying the text are equally odd—they seem to represent plants, women, and astronomical configurations. Since neither the words nor pictures are easy to interpret, the book has been called the most mysterious manuscript in the world.

Discovering the manuscript

It was in 1912 that a New York book dealer, Wilfrid M. Voynich, announced that he had discovered the curious volume in the library of Mondragone College, a Jesuit foundation in Frascati, Italy. Voynich bought it, and after returning

CLOSED BOOK *In 1912, U.S. book dealer Wilfrid Voynich acquired a mysterious manuscript that continues to baffle the world's leading cryptographers and linguistics experts.*

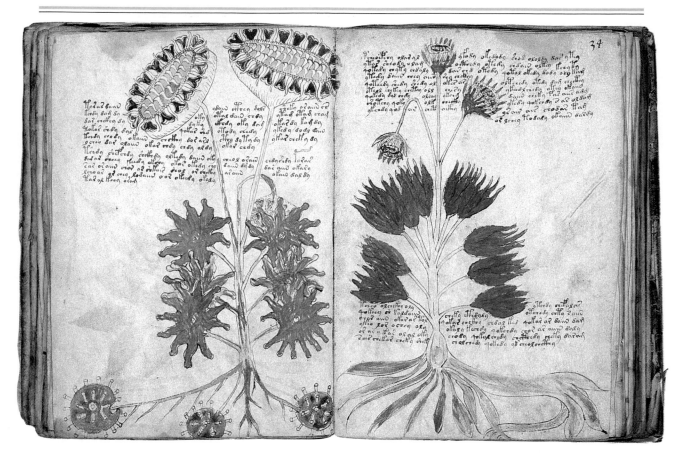

34

SECRET FORMULAS? *Two pages of the intricate and confusing Voynich Manuscript. Although the number of botanical illustrations has led many investigators to suggest that the manuscript may be some sort of treatise on the medicinal or curative powers of plants, speculation continues.*

to New York City began to unravel its history — a task simplified by an old letter included in the sale.

Written in 1666, the letter was from Marcus Marci, rector of the University of Prague and one of the leading scientists of his time, to another prominent scholar, Athanasius Kircher.

Marci wrote that he had acquired the manuscript from "an intimate friend" and was sending it to Kircher, his former tutor, "for I was convinced it could be read by no one except yourself." Marci added that he had been told on good authority that it was once owned by Rudolf II, the Holy Roman emperor, who died in 1612. Rudolf had paid 600 ducats for it, a large sum of money at the time.

Marci's most important revelation, however, was that Rudolf had believed the author of the manuscript to be "Roger Bacon, the Englishman."

Bacon, who lived in the 13th century, was one of the leading figures in the world of medieval learning. Known as Doctor Mirabilis, he was centuries ahead of his time in predicting many of the features of 20th-century life, such as cars and airplanes. His knowledge of mathematics and of physics was formidable; he was also a renowned philosopher and alchemist.

Could the Voynich Manuscript be Bacon's greatest work, a scientific treatise containing theories too revolutionary to be set down in plain language? In an attempt to find out, Voynich gave copies to interested scholars. Most, however, were completely baffled. They had expected to have a fairly simple code to crack, but the manuscript defied their efforts.

Brumbaugh's breakthrough

Real progress did not come for nearly 60 years until, in the 1970's, Robert S. Brumbaugh at Yale tackled the problem. Professor Brumbaugh noticed that some of the symbols in the Voynich Manuscript reminded him of a diagram he had come across in another document. In that case the symbols represented numerals.

A close look at some of the margins of the Voynich Manuscript revealed doodled calculations that suggested that a similar number code might have been used. In one margin Brumbaugh discovered a chart with 26 symbols, the number of letters in the alphabet. The symbols and the order in which they were arranged matched those in the doodled calculation almost exactly.

Was this, then, the key to the code? Did each of the numerals 1 to 9 represent three letters of the alphabet? Brumbaugh wrote out this box:

1	2	3	4	5	6	7	8	9
A	B	C	D	E	F	G	H	I
J	K	L	M	N	O	P	Q	(US)
	R		S		T		U	
V	W	X	Y		Z			

Since much of the language of the manuscript turns out to be a kind of simplified Latin, the words frequently end in *us*. In the code, Brumbaugh used the figure 9 as shorthand to denote this.

But was this the code? On one page of the manuscript was an illustration of a plant that resembled a pepper. Brumbaugh substituted numbers for the symbols written beneath it. He got 757752. Then he referred to the box and found that it could read PEPPER. The names of other plants and stars were also deciphered by the same method.

Yet the mystery of the Voynich Manuscript has by no means been solved. For example, the main text is repetitive and often nonsensical. Professor Brumbaugh has suggested that it may well be the disconnected outpourings of an alchemist, a follower of the ancient art that tried to turn base metals into gold through the action of a secret substance, or elixir. If this is so, could the formula for an elixir be concealed in the manuscript's puzzling pages? More work remains before the Voynich Manuscript yields up all of its secrets.

COMET CONTROVERSY

Do diseases come from space?

THE COLDS AND FLU many of us suffer regularly each year may be passed to us not by our neighbors down the street but by our neighbors in space: comets. What's more, even deadly diseases, such as the plagues that devastated medieval Europe, may arrive the same way—and will ravage the earth whenever comets appear.

This is the controversial thesis put forth by two eminent astronomers, Professor Chandra Wickramasinghe and Sir Fred Hoyle of Great Britain. Hoyle and Wickramasinghe claim that the dust that fills space between the stars consists of minute living organisms. Formed when the solar system was born, comets are made up of interstellar dust mixed with ice and frozen gases. When a comet visits our solar system, some of its dust drifts into the earth's atmosphere, where the tiny organisms, they say, multiply in the congenial environment.

Marshaling the evidence

Hoyle and Wickramasinghe can cite examples of diseases they believe to have come from space; they even link them to a specific comet. Halley's, for example, takes between 75 and 78 years to complete its orbit around the sun. A worldwide outbreak of Asian flu in 1957 followed a similar one 77 years earlier. The two men think that the outbreaks were caused by clouds of debris from the comet.

The World Health Organization (WHO) has declared that smallpox has been completely eradicated. But past epidemics seem to have followed definite cycles of a few hundred years. Hoyle and Wickramasinghe believe that smallpox will reappear, carried by an as-yet-undiscovered comet that returns every few centuries.

Although organisms from space may play havoc with life on earth, they are also responsible, claim the scientists, for the very appearance of life on this planet as well as for its continuing evolution.

According to the accepted view, complex molecules necessary for life appeared on the earth when elements in the "primeval soup" of the early oceans reacted together; these evolved into primitive, viruslike creatures. Hoyle and Wickramasinghe find it incredible that chance alone could have been responsible: life must have come from outside our planet.

To test their theory, the two astronomers studied flu outbreaks in British boarding schools. They found that flu did not spread from dormitory to dormitory, as one might think. Instead, outbreaks began randomly in different dormitories, as they might if they had been caused by organisms drifting through the atmosphere. In addition a flu epidemic in Sardinia in 1948 followed the same pattern. Once established on earth, according to the astronomers, an invading virus can bring about a permanent change in the genetic material of its host. This change is inherited by later generations. In this way, evolution occurs.

Other astronomers disagree with this theory. They claim that the effects of interstellar dust on starlight are not what would be expected from clouds of minute living organisms. And epidemics do not seem to result from annual meteor showers—the result of dust shed by comets—that should, according to Hoyle and Wickramasinghe, be disease-bearing.

For a while it seemed that the two astronomers were battling almost alone against the scientific world. Then, in 1986, space probes flying close to Halley's comet revealed that the dust that the comet gave off contained carbon and hydrogen—two elements vital to life. And the probes discovered what were probably fragments of molecules of the type produced by living things: the core of the comet was coated with a layer of a dark, carbon-containing substance.

Man's closest look at a comet may help support the theories of Hoyle and Wickramasinghe.

VENGEANCE ON THE HIGH PLAINS

The dread rider who terrorized Texas

IN THE MID-19TH CENTURY the area around the Rio Nueces in southwest Texas was known for its wild mustangs. It was also renowned for the spectral figure who roamed around on the back of a black mustang stallion.

The rider was dressed in the clothing of a Mexican vaquero: rawhide leggings, a buckskin jacket, a tattered shawl about his shoulders. But above the shoulders, where the head should have been, there was nothing. Instead, what appeared to be a head wearing a wide sombrero was tied to the horn of the saddle, from where it stared blankly out across the plains. This grisly apparition and its mount could appear at any time of day, racing across the open range. It was always alone; the other mustangs shunned it.

There was no doubt that it existed; too many people had seen it. Some had even shot at it; many local frontiersmen claimed that their bullets had gone straight through the mustang. Apparently the creature was impervious to bullets. What could the mysterious apparition be?

Demon in disguise

Some people claimed that the rider was alive— perhaps an outlaw who intended his ghostly disguise to repel the inquisitive. Some said it was the devil. Others maintained that the vaquero was a ghost, guarding the lost gold mine of the abandoned Candelaria Mission on the Rio Nueces.

A more mundane suggestion was that the figure was a kind of scarecrow that mustang hunters had tied to a stallion. The frightened horse would head for the mares, which would flee at the sight of the rider. The panic could spread through the herd; once the horses had stampeded themselves into

exhaustion, they would be unable to offer much resistance to the men who came to round them up.

Eventually some of the riders of the Nueces range decided to put an end to the mystery and hunt down the phantom rider. Half a dozen rode to a local watering hole and lay in wait for the gruesome figure, not knowing what to expect.

The truth revealed

When the mustang finally appeared, the men opened fire and the horse fell to the ground, dead. The riders approached the dead animal with trepidation. The riddle of the headless horseman would at last be solved.

When they examined the horse's back, they found the dried-up corpse of a Mexican, riddled with bullets. Under the tattered sombrero was a skull, shriveled from the sun. The ghostly vaquero was no ghost. But who was he?

Reportedly, the men were informed that his name was Vidal, a horse thief who operated from the Rio Grande into Louisiana and beyond. One day in 1850 Vidal stole some horses belonging to Creed Taylor, a hardened veteran of the Mexican War. Taylor pursued Vidal halfway across Texas before ambushing him near the Rio Nueces.

One of the men riding with Taylor, Bigfoot Wallace, suggested that Vidal's corpse be strapped to an untamed mustang stallion and, as a warning to other rustlers, be left to ride out wild on the range. Supposedly Wallace added a final gruesome touch by decapitating the corpse, tying a sombrero to the head, and fixing it firmly to the saddle.

Then the half-wild horse, bucking and rearing, was sent on its way, taking the corpse of Vidal on a last, long ride into legend.

ALL WASHED UP

The phenomenon of stranding

IN OCTOBER 1986 a beach in Reykjavik, Iceland, was the scene of an apparent massacre: 148 pilot whales lay dead on the shore. They died because in following their leader, or pilot, they swam onto the beach and could or would not escape back into the sea.

What is mysterious about this destructive behavior is that it has often happened before. In September 1975 more than 200 pilot whales were found on the beach at Bonavista Bay, Newfoundland. In January 1983, 87 killer whales stranded themselves on a beach in eastern Victoria, Australia. And from 1963 to 1980 at least 169 whales of different species stranded themselves on the coast of southern Africa alone.

Stranding, or beaching, is common behavior in whales and dolphins worldwide, and scientists are struggling to explain why these otherwise intelligent mammals, either knowingly or accidentally, kill themselves in this manner.

ON THE BEACH *This dying whale was one of 44 that stranded themselves on a beach in Oregon. Many theories have been proposed as to why whales act like this, but such behavior continues to puzzle both scientists and laymen.*

The Greek philosopher Aristotle, writing in the fourth century B.C., mentioned the stranding of dolphins but offered no opinion as to why they might do it. In the second century A.D. the poet Oppian of Corycus suggested that dolphins did this "in the hope some men may find them and . . . stay to fling a mound of shingle o'er them." Since then more scientific theories have been advanced, but no single one has been proved.

Mass suicide or primitive insecurity?

The most popular explanation among laymen is that the whales are committing suicide intentionally: when attempts have been made to head them off, or return them to deeper water, they still struggle to reach the shore. But scientists reject the idea of the whales' committing suicide.

Research from the University of Georgia suggests that stranding may be a primitive response to stress, and that the whales follow an instinct to return to the security of the land from which, as mammals, they originally came. There is little concrete evidence to support this theory, however, and other scientists see stranding as an example of social behavior; they believe that it occurs when one whale becomes ill and is followed ashore by concerned members of the group.

Disorienting theories

Explanations of stranding are extremely varied and numerous. Some blame environmental factors, such as high tides and electrical storms; others make much of the ability of whales to navigate and communicate with each other by means of sonar, a highly sensitive system of beaming sounds and interpreting echoes. For example, it has been suggested that certain beaches with very gentle slopes do not return a true echo, and so the whales become disoriented. Similar disorientation may result from ear infections that cause the sonar system to malfunction.

British scientists at Cambridge University believe they may have found the solution: that whales may strand when they have become confused by abrupt variations in the earth's magnetism. Although the earth's magnetic field varies considerably in strength from place to place, lines of equal magnetic strength run for many miles under the sea.

Whales sense these lines easily and tend to follow their direction. The magnetic lines usually follow the coastline, but occasionally they run onto the shore, confusing the whales.

This theory has been borne out by cases of stranding in Britain, which have always occurred where the magnetic line runs into the land. Unfortunately, few maps of magnetic fields from other parts of the world are available for comparison, and so the theory cannot be adequately tested.

The guessing continues

While each of these theories may partially help to explain the reason for stranding, none has proved completely satisfactory. In 1977 the Stranding Workshop was set up by the U.S. Marine Mammal Commission to study the phenomenon. There is clearly no shortage of suggestions for the commission to explore.

So far we can only guess as to why these creatures sometimes destroy themselves, and the mystery of this puzzling behavior may never be solved.

ATTACK OF THE BLUES

A case for medical detectives

AGED VAGRANTS living in the streets have long been a common sight in many cities. Accordingly, commuters in New York City paid little attention to an old man slumped against a wall one morning in late September 1944.

When a policeman became suspicious and took a closer look, to his amazement he saw that the man's nose, lips, ears, and fingers were bright blue. The patient was rushed to Beekman Downtown Hospital; by the time the ambulance arrived, the blueness had spread over all of his body.

The doctor who examined the vagrant noted that he was in a severe state of shock and suffering from diarrhea. The doctor concluded that the patient's blue color was due to an insufficient supply of oxygen in the blood, probably the result of carbon monoxide poisoning from an automobile engine or a gas pipe.

During the next nine hours, 10 more sufferers were brought to the hospital with the same peculiar symptoms. Following heart massage, stomach pumping, and oxygen, most recovered; the last to arrive was blue all over and could not be saved.

All victims were elderly down-and-outers and had fallen ill in different locations around the city. Finally it was established that all had eaten breakfast at the same run-down cafeteria, the Eclipse.

Selective poison?

Meanwhile, Dr. Morris Greenberg and Dr. Ottavio Pellitteri of the health department had become increasingly dubious that carbon monoxide poisoning was the explanation, since the men had suffered no dizziness or headaches. And if there had been a gas leak at the cafeteria, which had served more than a hundred breakfasts that morning, the city hospitals should have been filled with other victims of the mysterious illness.

Over the next two days Greenberg and Pellitteri followed the leads like true detectives. They visited the Eclipse. They were not surprised to see that its standards of hygiene were low, but there was no sign of a gas leak.

Perhaps, then, it was food poisoning? Since all the men had eaten oatmeal for breakfast, the doctors took samples of the ingredients used in its preparation. They found a can of saltpeter (sodium nitrate), a food preservative, sitting next to a can of salt. When questioned, the cook agreed that he might have added it to the oatmeal by mistake; saltpeter looks and tastes like salt. Since saltpeter is harmless, this did not worry Greenberg and Pellitteri. But they took a sample for testing anyway.

Yet something still did not seem correct about their theory. Food poisoning takes several hours to show up, but all the patients had been taken ill within half an hour of breakfast. Perhaps they had accidentally been given a toxic dose of some drug?

A crucial difference

Then came the breakthrough. Tests on the saltpeter from the Eclipse revealed that it was not sodium nitrate, but sodium *nitrite,* which looks and tastes much the same. Commonly used in manufacturing dyes and in drugs prescribed for heart conditions and high blood pressure, sodium nitrite is also a food preservative that may be used only in very small quantities. It is highly toxic and can starve the blood of vital oxygen. Tests on blood taken from each victim provided the required corroborative evidence: the presence of nitrites.

Greenberg and Pellitteri seemed to have solved the mystery of the sky-blue men. But they were still baffled as to why only 11 of the Eclipse's customers had been affected. With the help of the cook, they prepared a batch of oatmeal and analyzed individual portions. Each contained slightly less than the toxic dose, which explained why other diners had been unhurt. But why were the 11 vagrants any different?

An unnatural craving

The final clue was a medical one. Recent studies had revealed that heavy drinkers have an abnormally low level of salt in their blood. The affected down-and-outers were all alcoholics, and they craved salt. When served their breakfast oatmeal, they automatically reached not for the sugar but for the saltshaker.

The Eclipse had 17 shakers, one for each table. Tests revealed that 16 contained ordinary salt; the other was filled with more of the dangerous sodium nitrite. All of the men must have sat at a particular table and used the same shaker. The extra "salt" they sprinkled on their cereal was just enough to make the dose of sodium nitrite toxic. Since their blood was starved of oxygen, slowly but surely the 11 men turned bright blue.

DAY OF THE DOUBLE DAWN

"In the spring of the first year of the reign of King I of the Western Zhou dynasty, the day dawned twice at a place called Zheng" reads the cryptic record in an ancient Chinese chronicle known as the *Bamboo Annals.*

Zheng (today Zhenghou in Henan province) is 400 miles south of Peking. But exactly what happened on that day, or when King I began his reign, remained unknown for centuries. Then, in 1986, British and American scientists solved the mystery.

Dr. Kevin Pang, employed by the Jet Propulsion Laboratory in Pasadena, California, and Hunghsiang Chou of the University of

California at Los Angeles, suspected that a solar eclipse might have been responsible for the double dawn.

The team then contacted Dr. Kevin Yau at Durham University in England; he agreed to run a computer simulation of the past positions of the sun and moon as they would have been observed from Zheng.

The researchers learned from the computer that on April 21, 899 B.C., the day did indeed dawn twice for all the inhabitants of Zheng. Just before sunrise that morning, when the sky was already light, there was a total eclipse of the sun.

"The city would have been plunged back into darkness," said Pang. "It would have lasted only a minute or two."

Historians as well as astronomers should be grateful to the Anglo-American team. The first year of the reign of King I is now known precisely.

But the computer program also revealed something unanticipated. The day, nearly 3,000 years ago, was forty-three thousandths of a second shorter than a day is now. For the citizens of Zheng, one day was made even shorter when a second brief night descended, and the dawn was mysteriously delayed.

MOZART'S REQUIEM

Were secrets hidden in a common grave?

ONLY A HANDFUL of mourners attended the funeral at St. Marx churchyard outside Vienna on December 7, 1791. Sewn into a plain shroud that was coated with quicklime, the deceased was placed in a communal pauper's grave. No grave marker of any kind graced the final resting place of one of the world's greatest musicians, dead two months before his 36th birthday: Wolfgang Amadeus Mozart.

Although by 20th-century standards the composer's interment seems inappropriate, both the absence of mourners and the communal grave were consistent with Viennese custom of the 18th century. His former patron, the Baron van Swieten, was a notorious miser, and at the time of his death, Mozart was a pauper.

Rumors and reality

Shortly after Mozart's death, however, rumors about the circumstances of his illness began to circulate: An angel of death had been pursuing him. Mozart had been poisoned. The husband of a favorite piano pupil had attacked Mozart.

Following the September 1791 premiere of his opera *The Magic Flute,* Mozart *had* been working obsessively on a requiem. The commission, from a count who hoped to pass the work off as his own, had been delivered to Mozart by a "mysterious stranger." That the youthful composer was working on a requiem as his own death approached may have fueled the idea that Mozart perceived the messenger as an angel of death.

Of the stories that Mozart had been poisoned by various rivals or detractors, the most enduring was popularized in the play and movie *Amadeus.* It alleges that Antonio Salieri contrived the composer's early death because of an insane jealousy of Mozart's superior musical gifts.

However, it must be remembered that Salieri's confession was recorded 34 years later—when Salieri was in an asylum. Moreover, physicians at Mozart's deathbed put down as the cause of death a description of symptoms rather than a diagnosis. Later the official cause of death was registered as rheumatic inflammatory fever. Neither Mozart's family nor his friends contested this.

In addition, the composer's letters from this period reveal high spirits inconsistent with the popular notion of a man morbidly preoccupied with the fear of being poisoned.

As for tales that Mozart was killed by the jealous husband of a female student, who was pregnant, evidence points to nothing more debauched in Mozart's life than a liking for billiards. Such spicy tales, of course, are not easily laid to rest.

Although the straitened circumstances of Mozart's life stand in stark contrast to the exquisite music that was his gift to eternity, those who seek answers may have to take comfort in an old proverb: "Those whom the gods love die young."

THE CYCLE OF DEATH

What made the dinosaurs die?

ABOUT 65 MILLION years ago, three-quarters of all species alive on earth at the time died out within the space of a few hundred thousand years. The dead included every one of the mighty dinosaurs, which had dominated for some 60 million years. Their passing paved the way for the rise of the birds, mammals, and, ultimately, the emergence of humankind.

Intriguingly, a similar mass extinction had ushered in the reign of the dinosaurs. Indeed, over the last 600 million years of life on earth, there seems to have been a cataclysmic change roughly every 60 to 70 million years, and smaller changes roughly every 30 million.

As soon as scientists who study the early history of life—paleontologists—identified this pattern, they began to search for a cause. Many theories have been put forward, but in 1980 the geologist Walter Alvarez and his Nobel Prize–winning father, Luis, startled the scientific world with a new theory that, for a time, swept all others aside.

Heavenly marauders?

In 1977 Walter Alvarez, working at Gubbio in Italy, had discovered a puzzling layer of clay in rock strata that were around 65 million years old— puzzling because the clay was much too rich in the rare metal iridium to have come from the earth's

TIMETABLE OF DEATH

Fossil evidence suggests that roughly every 60 to 70 million years a major catastrophe causes a mass extinction of most living things. Less severe catastrophes occur approximately every 30 million years. Although the fossil evidence of such extinctions is often incomplete, it is clear that the last major catastrophe, 65 million years ago, eliminated dinosaurs. However, scientists disagree about the cause of these extinctions. Some have suggested meteorites; others, volcanoes. Still others maintain that mass extinctions never took place.

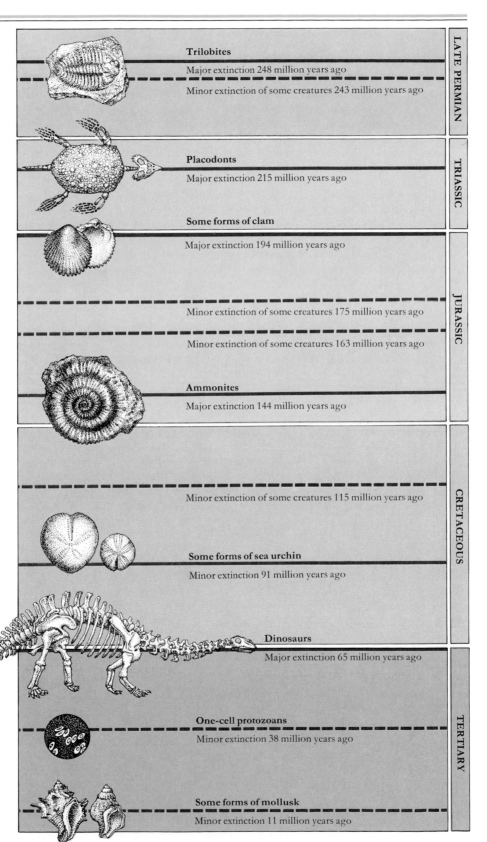

Trilobites

Major extinction 248 million years ago

Minor extinction of some creatures 243 million years ago

Placodonts

Major extinction 215 million years ago

Some forms of clam

Major extinction 194 million years ago

Minor extinction of some creatures 175 million years ago

Minor extinction of some creatures 163 million years ago

Ammonites

Major extinction 144 million years ago

Minor extinction of some creatures 115 million years ago

Some forms of sea urchin

Minor extinction 91 million years ago

Dinosaurs

Major extinction 65 million years ago

One-cell protozoans

Minor extinction 38 million years ago

Some forms of mollusk

Minor extinction 11 million years ago

LATE PERMIAN

TRIASSIC

JURASSIC

CRETACEOUS

TERTIARY

crust. The Alvarezes suggested that the clay might have come from outer space.

The theory was not as farfetched as it sounds. The debris of the solar system, which sometimes comes to earth as meteorites, is known to be rich in iridium. If a chunk of such debris 10 miles in diameter had hit the earth at around 100,000 miles per hour, it would have produced just such a layer.

First it would have unleashed more energy than all the nuclear warheads held in the world's arsenals today—perhaps 10 times as much. That energy, mostly in the form of heat, would have swiftly vaporized part of the meteorite, as well as the surface of the earth, for miles around. Then as the vapor cooled it would have again condensed into a fine dust that would have fallen to earth and settled as a layer of iridium-rich clay.

However, before the dust fell, it would have been dense enough to blot out the sun, creating a decade-long "meteorite winter," in which few plants could have survived. Fewer plants would have led to fewer herbivores and fewer carnivores.

Even if the dust were not dense enough to have had such an effect, hot debris from the meteorite would have traveled far beyond the point of impact and could have ignited fires on several continents. The resulting pall of smoke would certainly have wreaked havoc among prevailing life-forms.

Worldwide search

Following the Alvarez announcement, geologists around the world searched local rock layers at the 65-million-year level and found a layer of iridium-rich clay—a striking confirmation for the meteorite theory, even if no specific meteorite event could be pinned to that date.

But even the present surface of the earth, young as it is, bears the scars of dozens of such impacts.

Some are hard to recognize, such as the Everglades swamp in Florida. Others, such as the crater near Winslow in Arizona, about 570 feet deep and 4,150 feet across, could hardly be explained in any other way. And the surface of the moon, where there is no weather to remove the evidence, is riddled with impact craters.

Still, paleontologists remain skeptical. They point out that the mass extinctions did not occur in the decade-long or century-long time scale of the meteorite winter, but over hundreds of thousands of years. And geologists have pointed out that there *is* a source of iridium much closer to home; it is not in the earth's crust but deeper down, in the mantle. Research has shown that emissions from Kilauea volcano on Mauna Loa, Hawaii, match the composition of the iridium-clay layer much more closely than that of any known meteorite.

Winters of discontent

Today there is a competing theory. Every 60 to 70 million years the earth goes through a period of intense volcanic activity. The resulting "volcanic winters," although individually less catastrophic than those resulting from meteorites, have a cumulative effect that is equally drastic, and which may last more than a hundred thousand years.

However, some paleontologists remain unconvinced about both theories. In a recent poll, more than 10 percent maintained that even the mass extinctions themselves are an illusion. Say they: when a change in the world's dominant life-forms takes more than a hundred millennia to complete, no dramatic event is needed to explain it.

The scientific world has never been short of theories to explain the passing of the dinosaurs. But the search is still on, mostly for more facts to help us decide among them.

MAN OF MIRACLES

The amazing powers of a modern holy man

SAI BABA is an Indian guru blessed with extraordinary powers. He can produce gold rings and coins out of thin air, change rock into candy, and flowers into jewels. He heals the sick with the aid of *vibhuti* (sacred wood ash), which seems to appear from nowhere as he waves his hand. And, it is claimed, he has even brought the dead back to life.

Sai Baba has tens of thousands of followers around the world, many of whom claim to have witnessed his ability to work miracles. Several skeptical scientists and journalists have observed him at close range, but they have yet to find an explanation for his feats.

Although Sai Baba claims that his miracles are "tinsel" compared with his religious message, he performs them readily, often before huge audiences. Many witnesses claim that Sai Baba produces an object on demand: he asks people what they would like, then plucks it from the air. There are many accounts, too, of Sai Baba asking a number of people in a crowd to name their favorite fruit, then pointing to a single tree from which are hanging all the fruits that they have named.

Wonder cures

There are numerous testimonies to the acts of healing performed by Sai Baba, some involving surgery. One tells of the time that a man with cancer of the stomach was brought to him. Sai Baba put the man into a trance and brushed his forehead with *vibhuti;* he plucked a surgical knife from the air, removed the growth, and healed the wound instantly by closing the skin with his fingers.

Another case concerns a civil servant named Khare, of Dehra Dun, in northern India. In November 1971 Khare was told by eye specialists that he was going blind. Within three months he had lost his sight completely.

Khare's daughter was studying at the Sai Baba center at Whitefield, near Bangalore, and one day in May 1972 she talked to the holy man about her father's blindness. He told her not to worry and materialized some *vibhuti,* which he asked her to send to her father.

When Khare received the package, he was convinced that this was his cure. Daily, he rubbed a little sacred ash into his eyes; a week later his vision was back to normal. The doctors who had diagnosed permanent blindness only a short time before examined his eyes in amazement. He was cured.

But perhaps the most astonishing display of Sai Baba's powers took place in 1953, when a 60-year-old man named Radhakrishna visited the master to ask for relief from painful stomach ulcers. Sai Baba laughed and ignored him. In spite of the attentions of doctors, Radhakrishna went into a coma.

Three days later the body of Radhakrishna had turned blue and stiff; it was cold, shrunken, and starting to decompose. Then Sai Baba walked into

MEETING WITH A HOLY MAN *The Indian guru Sai Baba holds regular audiences with his band of followers. Many hand letters to him, telling of their troubles and asking for his help.*

the room and asked to be left alone. Minutes later relatives saw Radhakrishna walk out, flushed with life; an examination showed that his stomach ulcers had completely vanished.

Beyond belief

Australian journalist Howard Murphet set out to expose Sai Baba as a fraud; Murphet became convinced of the genuineness of his powers when, with a wave of his hand, the master produced a gold ring and presented it to him. Murphet has worn the ring, and been a believer, ever since.

One evening Sai Baba asked Murphet to tell him the year of his birth and then said that he would get him an American coin minted in that year. He circled his empty hand in front of Murphet and dropped a coin into the journalist's palm. "When the coin dropped from his hand to mine, I noted first that it was heavy and golden. On closer examination I found, to my delight, that it was a genuine minted American $10 coin, with the year of my birth stamped beneath a profile head of the Statue of Liberty."

London photographer David Bailey received much the same treatment when Sai Baba gave him a silver pendant bearing the holy man's portrait; it appeared out of thin air.

In the 50 years that Sai Baba has been demonstrating his apparently miraculous powers, no one has found any evidence of trickery. Investigators have examined the saffron robes that are the holy man's only form of clothing but have discovered no secret pockets, linings, or other hiding places.

A threat to science?

Sai Baba himself refuses to submit to rigorous scientific testing, insisting that he will use his powers only for religious purposes, such as inspiring faith or helping followers in need. "No one can understand my mystery," he says.

But it is possible to understand the anxiety of those who are attempting to unravel Sai Baba's remarkable accomplishments. As one experienced investigator put it: "If Sai Baba is indeed able to transform matter, then the whole basis of Western science is nonsense."

THE UNKNOWN LIFE OF JESUS

Where did Christ spend His early years?

THE GOSPELS tell us almost nothing about the early life of Jesus. In the 30 years between His birth and His baptism by John the Baptist, the only event recorded is His visit to Jerusalem with Mary and Joseph.

What did Jesus do during this time? Where did He go? Were at least some of these years spent away from Palestine?

There are some odd aspects regarding Christ's baptism by John. The two men were cousins; had they grown up together in Palestine, they should have met at least three times a year when their families gathered for the great Jewish festivals. However, according to the Gospel of Saint John, when Jesus arrived at "Bethabara beyond Jordan, where John was baptizing," John the Baptist said: "I knew Him not."

John seems not to have recognized Jesus, either as his own cousin or as the Messiah whose coming he had prophesied. Only when the Holy Ghost in the form of a dove descended upon Jesus did John realize who He was. "And I saw, and bare record that this is the Son of God."

Saint Luke's Gospel is no less mystifying about the relationship between John and Jesus. Very early in the ministry of Jesus, John was imprisoned, where rumors reached him that the people of Judea were hailing Jesus as a great prophet. John then sent messengers to ask Jesus, "Art thou He who should come?"—that is, the Messiah. It seems strange that John should not know of his cousin's mission in life, or even realize that He was his cousin. But if Jesus had been out of Palestine for some years, John's apparent ignorance of Jesus begins to make more sense.

A tax on strangers

Something curious also happened when Jesus arrived in Capernaum, His official home because Mary lived there. The tax collector asked Peter, Jesus' disciple, if his master was obliged to pay the tax. Since it was clear that Jesus was Jewish, the tax collector would have known that Jesus would pay taxes to the Temple. Referring to the Roman tax on strangers, the collector was asking if Jesus had been away from home so long that He was liable to this tax. If so, where had He been?

The answer to the mystery may lie partly in one legend: that Joseph of Arimathea, who took Jesus' body from the cross and placed it in his own tomb,

ATTENTIVE LISTENERS *According to one tradition, Christ spent part of His childhood in England with Joseph of Arimathea, a merchant whose trading contacts might well have taken him there in search of tin. Joseph is seen preaching to the Britons in this painting by 19th-century artist William Blake.*

was Christ's uncle. This may explain another belief, held by the tin miners of Cornwall in the far west of England, that Joseph was a tin merchant who took the young Jesus with him to Cornwall and taught Him the trade. When they extract the tin from its ore, Cornish tinners still shout: "Jesus was in the trade." Local miners also traditionally sing a song with the same refrain.

According to still another legend, Jesus and Joseph stayed for a time in the Somerset village of Priddy, only a few miles from Glastonbury, where Joseph is reputed to have returned after Christ's martyrdom. And there is some written evidence suggesting that as a young man, Christ lived for a while in Glastonbury.

A royal island

Saint Augustine, who journeyed to Britain in A.D. 597, wrote to Pope Gregory in Rome of "a certain royal island . . . surrounded by water" in "the western confines of Britain." This could describe Glastonbury, which at that time was surrounded by water. Augustine went on to report that there was also "a church constructed by no human art, but by the hands of Christ Himself."

Given the biblical hints that Jesus did spend some time away from Palestine, it seems plausible that the young, undeclared Christ might have gone away to seek solitude to meditate upon His destiny. Where better than the west of England, where He had been as a child and where His uncle would still have had contacts?

Another reason for His taking a journey to Glastonbury might be that the town was an important center of Celtic religion. The local priesthood might have been sympathetic to Jesus; although polytheistic, Druids believed in the existence and immortality of the human soul.

These legends concerning the unrecorded years of Christ's life have the ring of truth, if only because they are so consistent. If Jesus did not go to England during these years, where did He go? No comparable body of evidence exists to suggest that He might have gone elsewhere.

THE ENCHANTED CHILDREN

In search of the Pied Piper of Hamelin

IN 1284 THE SMALL TOWN of Hamelin, in Germany, was plagued with rats, to the desperation of its inhabitants and mayor. One day a mysterious piper appeared, dressed in a long, multicolored coat. He offered to get rid of the rats for a fee. The mayor and the townspeople gladly agreed to his suggestion.

The piper took out his pipe. No sooner did he begin to play than rats came scurrying out of the houses, enchanted by the magical sound of his music. The piper lured the rats out of the town and into the River Weser, where they all plunged into the water and drowned.

The job done, the piper went back to the town to receive his payment. But the townsfolk refused to pay him. Enraged, the piper exacted a grim revenge. He took up his pipe once more, but this time it was the children who came running out into the street, charmed by the notes. They danced away with the piper to nearby Koppelberg mountain, where an enormous cavern opened and swallowed them up; they were never seen again.

Fact or fiction?

The story of the Pied Piper of Hamelin, the well-known and much-loved children's tale, was immortalized by the poet Robert Browning. Any visitor to Hamelin (or Hameln, its correct German name) might be forgiven for believing the tale to be historical fact. Two 16th-century houses bear inscriptions commemorating the abduction of the children on June 26, 1284. Regular enactments of the story are held in the town, and on one street in particular, Bungenstrasse (believed to be the route taken by the children), no music is played for fear of rousing the piper's wrath once more. Until the 19th century, two crosses stood on the mountain to mark the spot where the children were last seen.

As far as written accounts go, however, there is some confusion. The earliest record of the events dates from 1450 and mentions only the disappearance of the children, 130 in all. It is not until the 16th century that chronicles for the first time identify the piper as a rat catcher.

In later, 17th-century accounts the crucial date becomes July 22, 1376. But although the difference between the date of the inscriptions, 1284, and the later date of 1376 may cast doubts on the story's reliability, the fact that the dates are recorded at all, and with such precision, suggests that there may be a grain of historical truth in the story.

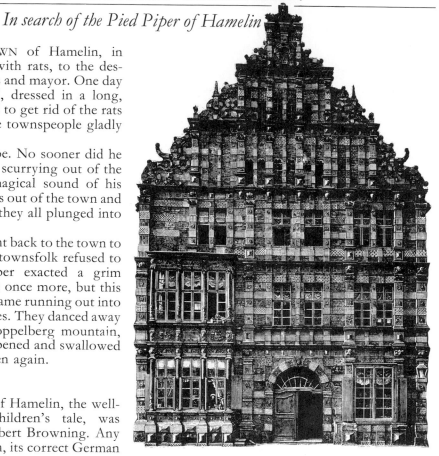

HOME OF A PIPER *The Rat-catcher's House in Hamelin, West Germany: one of two buildings in the town that bear plaques about the abduction of the children. Below: The piper as portrayed by Arthur Rackham in a 1930's edition of Robert Browning's poem, "The Pied Piper of Hamelin."*

The legend is certainly not the first, nor is it the only one, of its kind. Remarkably similar tales of pipers who spirit away children figure in folklore all over Europe and throughout the Middle East. But unlike most of the other folktales, the Hamelin story gives precise dates, contradictory though they may be.

Echoes of tragedy

Today many people believe that the earlier date of 1284 is in some way connected with the Children's Crusade. In 1212 the Crusade passed through Germany on its ill-fated attempt to recover the Holy Land from Muslim rulers, and almost certainly gathered recruits from Hamelin. Many children died on the lengthy and arduous journey, and none ever returned home.

Another theory connects the date with the death of large numbers of Hamelin's youth at the battle of Sedemunde, which resulted from a local feud in 1260. Either of these events from the 13th century may find an echo in the earliest form of the tale.

During the 14th century a far worse disaster was to befall the town of Hamelin. The Black Death—bubonic plague—raged through Europe from the mid-1340's to the late 1360's. It was carried by flea-infested rats, which then died of the disease. The fleas moved on to human hosts, who in turn died—an order of events similar to that in the tale.

Vague recollections of the Black Death might well account for the later, alternative date found in some of the written records.

Memories of another sickness may also be buried in the legend. The children in the story are described as dancing away to their death. This might well be a symbolic description of the pitiful bands of diseased suffering from Saint Vitus' dance who roved around the countryside in medieval times. Music played on a pipe was believed to calm the uncontrollable muscle spasms the unfortunate victims of the disease endured.

Truth and folklore

The most likely explanation, then, is that the tale of the Pied Piper is a strange amalgam of truth and myth. The original Pied Piper story must have taken on increased significance for the people of Hamelin as more and more of their children were lost to one cause after another.

In the 14th century the plague was often interpreted as a punishment from God upon a sinful people: this is reflected in the theme of grim poetic justice in the legend. This belief, together with the pattern of the symptoms of the Black Death, local history from the previous century, and other folktales about mysterious enchanters of animals, may have been fused in the imagination of past generations to create the story we know today.

A CUP THAT OVERFLOWETH

The mysterious history of the Holy Grail

AT THE LAST SUPPER of Jesus and the Twelve Apostles, Jesus broke the unleavened Passover bread and said, as He shared it among them: "This is my body which is given for you; this do in remembrance of me." Then, after the supper, as the Apostles passed around the cup of wine, He said: "This cup is the new testament in my blood, which is shed for you."

From these two sentences came the Christian tradition of Holy Communion, in which the bread represents the body of Jesus and the wine His blood. But the cup from which Jesus and His Apostles drank is the centerpiece of two different mysteries—unsolved for almost 2,000 years.

What happened to the cup?

The Gospels themselves make no other mention of the cup that was used at the Last Supper. But other early Christian writings say that it came into the

hands of Joseph of Arimathea, the wealthy Jew who may have been Jesus' uncle and who took the body for burial. Either at the time that Joseph was preparing the body for the tomb or while it was still on the cross, some of the blood of Jesus ran into the cup and it became a hallowed object—today called the Holy Grail.

When the body of Jesus disappeared from the tomb, the outraged Jewish elders accused Joseph of stealing it. They threw Joseph into prison and left him to starve. There Jesus appeared to Joseph in a vision and made him the official guardian of the Grail. For the remainder of his stay in prison, Joseph was miraculously kept alive by the appearance each day of a wafer in the cup, brought to his cell by a dove.

Finally released in A.D. 70, Joseph went into exile, eventually arriving in Britain where, it is said, he had once taken Jesus as a child. He set up the first Christian church in Glastonbury in Somerset and there—somewhere—many believe the Holy Grail is still hidden.

The quest begins

There are many other versions of the Grail legend, most of them far more complicated. In them the Grail is not necessarily a cup—it may be a stone, a series of visions, a dish, a womb, or even a symbol in alchemy, the fabled secret art of changing base metals into gold. All that is certain about the Grail in these legends is that it is hidden and that only the purest of men may find it.

This is the Grail that King Arthur's Knights of the Round Table set out to find, believing it to be preserved in the mysterious Castle of the Fisher King. Three of the knights succeeded: Sir Perceval, Sir Galahad, and Sir Bors. Only Sir Bors, the most ordinary of the knights, returned to tell the tale. So pure were the others, and so powerful the Grail, that they failed to return to everyday reality. The virgin knight Sir Galahad died in ecstasy at having found the Grail. Sir Perceval remained in the castle to become the new keeper of the Grail.

Guardians of the Grail

The origins of this legend lie partly in another version of the story of Joseph of Arimathea. According to it, Joseph went into exile with his brother-in-law Bron, who was dubbed the Rich Fisher after miraculously feeding a large gathering of people with a single fish. Bron's descendants, known as Fisher Kings, were the keepers of the Grail. Legend also has it that Sir Perceval was himself a descendant of Joseph's; that is why he stayed to guard the Grail.

It seems that these stories are poetic renderings of a search for a spiritual goal: the particular object that symbolizes the Grail is not important. And it is almost certain that the tales of King Arthur and the Knights of the Round Table are in fact retellings, in Christian form, of much older, pagan legends that may have originated, in part, in the East.

A holy bloodline

However, yet another Grail legend recounts how Mary Magdalene, who met Jesus wandering in the garden after His resurrection, brought the Grail to Marseilles. One modern theory actually suggests that Mary Magdalene's Grail was not an object either but the bloodline of Jesus Himself. According to this version, He had supposedly married Mary, and in due course their children founded the Merovingian dynasty of kings in Europe.

The idea is startling, but it is perhaps no less intriguing than the thought that the cup used at the Last Supper may lie buried, to this day, somewhere in the West Country of England.

ETERNAL QUEST *In Arthurian legend, probably the best-known interpretation of the Holy Grail, the Grail is depicted as the cup used by Christ at the Last Supper. Although opinions about the Grail's physical form have differed over the centuries, the Grail itself was always thought to have special mystical and magical significance. Its quest came to symbolize the spiritual goal of inner wholeness. In his painting "The Attainment," Victorian artist Edward Burne-Jones portrayed Galahad, Perceval, and Bors, three Arthurian knights, as they approached their long-sought objective.*

THY PRISON IS A HOLY PLACE

How a miracle saved a holy man from death

SADHU SUNDAR SINGH was sure that he was doomed to die. He was stranded naked at the bottom of a dry well, and the lid on top was locked shut. A blow from a club had almost broken his arm and it throbbed with pain. Worse, he found himself lying on a mass of putrefying corpses, previous victims of the slow death he now faced. All that he had done to deserve this was preach the gospel of Christ. In despair he used Christ's words: "Lord, why hast thou forsaken me?"

Then, on the third night of his appalling incarceration, he heard a grating sound from above. Someone was opening the lid of his prison. Sundar heard a key turn in the lock and the iron cover draw back. A voice spoke, telling him to look out for a rope. When it reached him, he put his foot in the loop in the end and was pulled to freedom.

Lying on the ground, his pain suddenly gone, Sundar could hear the well cover being replaced and locked. But when he turned to thank his rescuer, no one was to be seen. Sundar could only thank God for his unaccountable escape. He had yet to realize how miraculous it was.

A personal mission

Sundar was no stranger to signs and wonders. Born into a Sikh family in the Punjab in 1889, he was so opposed to Christianity by the age of 15 that he denounced the local missionaries and publicly burned a Bible in his native village. Three days afterward, Christ appeared to him in a vision. From then on, Sundar preached the Gospel as a Christian sadhu, a holy man dependent on the generosity of others. After some years in northern India, he took his message into neighboring Tibet.

For centuries Tibet had been a secret kingdom hidden high among the Himalayas. It was ruled by the Dalai Lama, a spiritual leader revered by his subjects as king, chief priest, and reincarnation of Buddha. Religious feeling in Tibet was strong. Foreigners were rarely welcome there, let alone anyone attempting to make religious conversions.

During a journey through this inhospitable land, sometime between 1912 and 1918, Sundar arrived at the city of Rasar. He so incensed the head lama there with his Christian preaching that he was condemned to death by starvation at the bottom of a dried-up well—the well from which he was so mysteriously rescued.

An angry rejection

As soon as he had recovered from his ordeal, Sundar again began to preach. Word spread that the "dead" man had returned, and he was arrested again. He was dragged before the head lama, who angrily rejected Sundar's story and declared that someone must have stolen the key to the well.

But the key was where it had always been, chained to the lama's own girdle. For a few moments the lama was speechless with amazement. He then ordered Sundar to leave Rasar, fearing that such a powerful god as Sundar's would bring some terrible disaster to the city.

Sundar went in peace, his faith strengthened by the knowledge that he, like Saint Peter centuries before, had been freed from prison by a miracle.

THE TWO FACES OF MARTIN GUERRE

A case of mistaken identity?

ON SEPTEMBER 16, 1560, in the small French village of Artigat in the foothills of the Pyrenees, an unusually large crowd gathered to witness the execution of a young peasant. He was neither a murderer nor a thief, but a man who had tried to pull off an audacious confidence trick—and had very nearly succeeded.

The affair had begun in the summer of 1556, when news reached Bertrande Guerre that her long-lost husband, Martin, was on his way home to Artigat. He had disappeared eight years earlier, after a visit to his native Spain, and his wife and family had not heard from him since.

Martin Guerre's return was celebrated in style. Everyone agreed that he looked a little different—stockier, with darker hair and a beard—but it might be expected that a man would change as he grew older. Only Martin's uncle, Pierre, voiced any doubts. He insisted that the man was an impostor, bent on robbing the family of its property.

It was Bertrande who settled the matter. Unsure at first, she quickly confirmed that the man was indeed Martin Guerre. She welcomed him home, reintroduced him to his son, and helped him to get reacquainted with their neighbors.

But the man was not her husband. He was an opportunist named Arnaud du Tilh.

A chance encounter

Arnaud first had the idea of impersonating Martin when two men he met on the road had mistaken him for the missing man. Arnaud gathered information about Martin, his family, and his property, and before long had created a detailed picture of Martin's past life.

A born actor, Arnaud had little difficulty in convincing the villagers that he was Martin. How did he fool Bertrande? How could a wife not know that the man she was living with was an impostor? Or did she know?

Perhaps Bertrande went along with the deception willingly. Her marriage to Martin had not been happy, and his disappearance had put her in a difficult position. Without a husband, yet neither single nor widowed, she was an outcast in her own community. When the handsome and charming Arnaud appeared, he may have seemed to offer her the chance she needed to start life anew. Whatever Bertrande's role, she and Arnaud lived as man and wife for three years.

But Martin's uncle would not let his suspicions lie and took steps to discover the true identity of the man calling himself Martin Guerre. Gradually he accumulated evidence and found witnesses who could positively identify the impostor as Arnaud du Tilh. Pierre pressed Bertrande to take legal action against him. Reluctantly she agreed, and Arnaud was brought to trial.

The trial went well for Arnaud. He seemed to know every detail of Martin's life, past and present. Where did he get the information? Was it from Bertrande? Then, just as it seemed he had persuaded the court that he was Martin Guerre, the real Martin Guerre suddenly appeared and the true story gradually unfolded.

After leaving Artigat, the real Martin had crossed the Pyrenees to Spain and joined the Spanish Army. His soldiering ended when he lost a leg in battle; he became a lay brother in a religious order. It is not known why, after an absence of many years, he decided to return to his old life. Neither is it certain whether or not he had heard about the imposture before his return, or only discovered it afterward. But it was a timely reappearance.

Instant recognition

The arrival of a second Martin did not settle the case immediately. When each man was asked to relate details of his past life, Arnaud's account was more accurate than that of the real Martin. But when Bertrande was brought into court, all doubts were removed. At the first sight of the newcomer she burst into tears and ran to embrace him. For the court this was proof enough of Arnaud's guilt, and he was sentenced to be hanged.

On the day of his execution, Arnaud made a full confession. But he refused to discuss Bertrande's part in the affair, maintaining to the end that she was innocent. Just how much Bertrande really knew remains a mystery.

FROM NOWHERE TO NOWHERE

Every year Louis Mathias, a shepherd, would take his sheep up into the Alps that rise near Nice, France. As the summer sun scorched the grass in the lowlands, the flock would find fresh pasture in the higher elevations until autumn. In 1976, however, Mathias happened upon an extraordinary sight in a tiny, remote valley in the mountains.

Upon hearing the old shepherd's report, local police commandant Henri Pelet had to investigate. After an hour's journey by jeep and an additional three hours on foot, what Pelet found were two huge parallel tracks, spaced six inches apart, in the snow. Each track was 7 inches wide and 10 inches deep, and they curved across the mountainside in an arc 70 yards long.

Only a heavy mechanical object could have made the tracks, it seemed; pebbles and rocks beneath them had been crushed almost to dust. Yet the remote valley was completely inaccessible to vehicles.

Had a patrolling French Army helicopter landed there? Not only did the army have no such report, but to touch down in such a spot would have been extremely risky.

It was also suggested that a flying saucer may have been responsible for the tracks. But no one had reported seeing any flying objects at all.

To this day, the authorities are still seeking an answer.

FLIGHT TO ETERNITY

The mysterious disappearance of an American hero

AT 1:45 P.M. on December 15, 1944, world-famous bandleader Glenn Miller, then director of the U.S. Air Force Band, boarded a small Norseman airplane at a Royal Air Force base near Bedford, England. By the personal order of Gen. Dwight D. Eisenhower, Major Miller was on his way to Paris to arrange a series of concerts for troops on leave.

Miller was apprehensive about the thick fog and near-freezing temperature. The Norseman had no deicing equipment and, in addition, would have to fly perilously close to the surface of the English Channel in order to avoid the fog.

"Where the hell are the parachutes?" demanded Miller as he climbed into the airplane. "What's the matter, Miller," mocked his companion, Col. Don Baesell. "Do you want to live forever?"

The door slammed shut, and the Norseman taxied down the runway and took off into the fog.

These were the last recorded moments of Miller's life. The Norseman never arrived.

On December 23 Miller was officially listed as "missing in flight." And for 40 years it was assumed that the airplane had gone down in the English Channel, its wing flaps frozen solid in the appalling conditions.

Then in 1984 ex-RAF navigator Fred Shaw came forward with an astonishing, hitherto unknown, version of that day's grim events.

Bombs away

On the December day that Miller vanished, Shaw was a member of a bomber crew taking part in a mission over Germany. At about 1:30 P.M. the squadron was unexpectedly recalled to base but told to jettison its 4,000-pound bomb load in a designated area of the Channel before landing.

As the bombardier dropped the bombs, Shaw saw a light Norseman aircraft flying almost directly below. He watched it dip into the waves as the bombs exploded near it just above the water.

Shaw told his story at a meeting of the South African Glenn Miller Appreciation Society in Johannesburg, where he now lives. Other members of the crew did not report the incident, he said, because the Norseman was just one of thousands of aircraft they had seen blown up or go down. Miller's death was not announced until days later, and at the time no one saw a connection between the two events.

It was not until Shaw saw the movie *The Glenn Miller Story* years later that he checked his logbook and realized that the Norseman may have been carrying the bandleader.

Shaw's story may finally have shattered the bizarre myths that grew up around Miller's disappearance. One theory held that Miller was a secret agent and had faked his own death; another that Baesell was a black-marketeer who killed both Miller and the pilot before escaping in the airplane; a third that Miller, hideously scarred, had survived and was living in secret in a sanatorium.

Although final proof must await discovery of the wreckage, the truth of Glenn Miller's story seems simple: British bombs may have accidentally destroyed one of America's heroes.

POSTHUMOUS FAME
Glenn Miller's reputation as the finest bandleader of his day has been enhanced by the tragedy of his death — a mystery that may now be solved.

AN AMAZING PUZZLE

The enigma of mazes

IN 1950 Canon Harry Cheales, parish priest of Wyck Rissington, a small village in the south of England, had a curious dream. In it, he was looking out of a window of the rectory while below him, in the garden, he could see people walking around a maze. A shadowy figure behind him was describing the scene.

The dream was so vivid that, on waking, the rector felt compelled to build a real-life version of the maze he had seen. The newly constructed maze was modeled on a set of religious carvings in the village church and the design was symbolic. The winding pathways represented the journey of life. The wrong turnings and culs-de-sac symbolized the sins that people commit before death, obstacles on the way to paradise and heaven.

Patterns and puzzles

Throughout history mazes, or labyrinths, have been found all over the world, both as real constructions and as symbolic representations in art. There is even evidence that mazelike patterns were used by the ancients. They are found on Sumerian seals, Babylonian tablets, Etruscan wine jars, Roman mosaic pavements, on a pillar at Pompeii, even on the magnificent carved entrance stone to one of the oldest buildings in the world, the 5,000-year-old Newgrange Tomb in Ireland.

But despite the frequency with which they have appeared, there is still remarkably little understanding of the real significance of mazes or why they were built. To some people they have always been places of amusement; to others, they are puzzles or mental teasers. And some people regard them as symbols with a hidden meaning.

ANCIENT INSCRIPTION *A Cretan labyrinth traced on the pillar of a 2,000-year-old house in Pompeii, Italy.*

The most famous labyrinth of ancient times is said to have been constructed at Knossos in Crete by the famed architect and sculptor Daedalus, under the orders of King Minos. According to legend, its innermost sanctum was the lair of the fearful Minotaur. A monstrous creature that was half man, half bull, the Minotaur devoured the seven young men and seven maidens whom the people of Athens were forced to send annually to Minos. Minos demanded this as compensation for the death of his son at the hands of the Athenians. Finally Theseus—with the help of Ariadne, the beautiful daughter of Minos—slew the Minotaur and escaped the winding passageways.

Despite the popularity of the legend, the actual form of the Cretan labyrinth is unknown. It may have been no more than a decorated pavement for ritual dances, or the legend may refer to a network of caverns today known as the Gortyna Caves; they are linked by winding tunnels near the Palace of Minos at Knossos.

Some experts believe that the Labyrinth never existed at all, that the word is derived from the Greek word *labrys,* meaning "double ax." Crete, and Knossos in particular, was well known for a bull cult that flourished in classical times. Double-headed axes were used to slaughter sacrificial bulls, and the Palace of Minos may simply have been called the Labyrinth because it was "the place of the double axes." So far, at least, the archeologist's spade has revealed at Knossos no trace of the kind of labyrinth described in the legend.

Rituals and games

In medieval times, mazes were drawn on the floors and walls of some of the great churches and cathedrals built in Europe. Some of these were known as the Chemin de Jerusalem. The idea seems to have been that people who were unable to make an actual pilgrimage to the Holy Land could make a symbolic one, either by tracing the paths of a maze on the church wall with a finger or, on their knees, shuffling uncomfortably along the pathway of a floor maze. Other mazes were thought to represent Christ's final journey from the house of Pontius Pilate to Calvary.

In Britain mazes specifically designed for pagan games were cut in the fields; probably hundreds of such turf mazes existed in ancient times. They had different local names, such as Mizmaze, the Shepherd's Race, or Julian's Bower, and the country

people played games such as the Game of Troy or Treading the Maze on them. Unfortunately, the rules have long been lost. Today there are only nine turf mazes left in Britain.

After the 14th century, hedge mazes were built in the gardens of grand homes to entertain visitors. Louis XIV of France built a spectacular one at Versailles; it was destroyed in 1775. The most famous hedge maze is probably the one laid out in 1690 at Hampton Court in London.

In less verdant areas of Europe, such as the coastline of Scandinavia, mazes have been constructed from the most abundant available material: stones, ranging in size from pebbles to boulders. Yet once again their purpose is in dispute. For example, at Visby on the island of Gotland off Sweden, a historian making inquiries in the 19th century was told that the local maze was used for

children's games, but other evidence suggests that they may have been ritual sites where sailors danced for luck before a voyage.

More recent times have seen a revival of maze building in places as diverse as Varmland in Sweden, the Château de Beloeil in Belgium, and Floors Castle in Scotland. In 1968 the sculptor Michael Ayrton constructed a 1,680-foot-long "Cretan labyrinth" at Arkville in New York State, using stone and 200,000 bricks.

New mazes and labyrinths will continue to be built. Whether they are symbols, places of ritual, or for entertainment, mazes are testaments to human ingenuity and to a love of puzzles as old as time.

FOOTSTEPS INTO THE UNKNOWN

ENVELOPE OF LIGHT

A phenomenon that may surround the human body

IN SOMERSET, ENGLAND, during World War I folk song collector Ruth L. Tongue befriended a young soldier, Dick Garland, who was recovering from wounds received in France. One night just before he returned to the western front, Garland sang several songs for her. Then he got up to go, and as he stood in the doorway, Ruth saw a black shadow around his head and shoulders.

Ruth was one of those rare individuals who claim they see the human aura, a glow of colored light said to surround the whole body. To her, the darkness around Garland was the shadow of death. Less than a week after his return to France, the young man was killed.

Psychic healer Edgar Cayce was another who claimed to be aware of people's auras. Based on the colors he saw, he said that he could accurately assess a person's physical and psychological state.

The meaning of color

This phenomenon is by no means new to mystics. Over the centuries a consensus has emerged, defining the meaning of each color in the aura.

Each color has its positive and negative aspects, and its exact significance depends on the state of the other colors in the aura.

A strong presence of red, for instance, indicates a willful personality; it may signify selfishness, physical strength, or powers of leadership. Green is the color of nature and healing, but may reveal a deceitful character. Orange is an indicator of physical health. A strong yellow presence reveals intellectual abilities. Blue refers to a person's religious or spiritual state: the deeper the blue, the more enlightened the individual. Black is the color of death, malice, or evil. And gray indicates a depressed or melancholy personality.

Scientific trials

Several investigators have claimed that the human aura is detectable by mechanical means. In 1911 Dr. Walter J. Kilner published an account of his researches entitled *The Human Atmosphere,* and each copy of his book included a lens containing a chemical dye. With this, Kilner said, it was possible to see the aura, in three separate layers, extending as

AURA OF LIGHT *Named for its inventor, Semyon Kirlian, in 1939, Kirlian photography claims to capture the aura many mystics and clairvoyants say surrounds all living things. Below is a geranium leaf photographed with a conventional camera. At left: The same leaf, photographed with Kirlian high-voltage techniques, has a "corona" around it.*

far as two feet from the human body; the condition of the aura depended upon the health of the body.

Few others found Kilner's lenses effective, however, and his research was greeted with derision by medical colleagues.

A similar fate met the work of a Russian inventor, Semyon Kirlian, when it reached the West in the 1970's. Kirlian believed that he had succeeded in photographing the aura by placing his subjects within high-voltage electrical fields. The remarkable effects of what became known as Kirlian photography are due entirely to physical factors, such as sweat, although they can be used in medical diagnosis.

Saints and holy men

In 1973 scientist Dr. Lyall Watson suggested that the aura seen by mystics and sensitives *is* a physical emanation, although it is visible only to people with eyes especially sensitive to low-frequency light. This idea may lend credence to the reports of auras and halos that, through the ages, people say they have seen surrounding saints and holy men.

For example, on returning from Mount Sinai with the Tablets of the Law, Moses glowed so brightly that he alarmed the people and had to cover himself with a veil. Among many medieval examples, the 14th-century Franciscan monk Blessed Thomas of Cori lit up an entire church with the radiance of his faith, while the cell of Saint Louis Bertran was regularly lit up as if by powerful lamps.

Such accounts suggest that the aura is a physical phenomenon; the effect of profound spirituality would appear to heighten the normally invisible aura in such a way that even people lacking special sensitivity see it. Paradoxically, therefore, it may be the most spiritual people who provide the best proof that the human aura is not simply an illusion.

IN POSSESSION OF THE FACTS

Dead men can tell tales

ONE JANUARY DAY in 1939 seventeen-year-old Maria Talarico was walking with her grandmother through her hometown of Catanzaro, in southern Italy. As the two passed a bridge, Maria suddenly stopped, stared at the riverbank, and collapsed. Only after being taken home did she recover consciousness—and then astonished her family by addressing her mother in a gruff male voice.

"You are not my mother," she said. "My mother lives in the wooden hut, and her name is Catarina Veraldi. I am Pepe."

Pepe Veraldi had drowned himself nearly three years previously, on February 13, 1936. His body had been found under the bridge where Maria had collapsed. Had his spirit taken over Maria's body?

Maria asked for a piece of paper and wrote a few words in Veraldi's handwriting. She then demanded wine and cigarettes, and began to play cards with the people gathered around her, calling them Toto, Rosario, Elio, and Damiano—names of the dead man's friends.

Matters took an even more surprising turn when Veraldi's mother arrived. Still speaking in Veraldi's voice, Maria declared: "My friends murdered me; they threw me into the river. Then, as I lay there, they beat me with a piece of iron and tried to make the whole thing look like suicide."

Maria then fled from the house, ran to the bridge, and threw herself off of it, shouting "Leave me alone! Why are you beating me?"

On the ground below, she lay in precisely the same position as had Veraldi when he had been found. The dead man's mother approached Maria and commanded that her son leave the girl's body. Maria opened her eyes, looked about, and stood up. She had returned to normal; Veraldi was gone.

Unexpected proof

No one knew what to make of the bizarre incident at first. The police report on Veraldi's death suggested that he might have died in the way the possessed girl had described. But the friends she had named could not, or would not, cast further light on the mystery. Besides, Toto had immigrated to South America; Elio was dead.

Then in 1951 Toto, otherwise known as Luigi Marchete, wrote to Veraldi's mother from Tucumán, Argentina; he confessed to the murder of her son. In the letter, Marchete told of the attention Veraldi had been giving to Lillina, Marchete's wife. Marchete had beaten Veraldi with an iron bar, with fatal results. After he and his three friends had tried to make the death look like suicide, Marchete had fled to Argentina. To ease his conscience, he was now leaving the fortune he had made to the victim's mother.

The letter confirmed Maria's extraordinary episode 12 years before. The spirit of Pepe Veraldi had, it seems, briefly taken possession of the body of Maria Talarico in order to reveal the true circumstances of his death.

JUDGMENT DAYS

Labor leader John Blackman of Eastbourne, England, had no intention of paying the alimony his wife had demanded. And those who tried to make him pay put their lives at risk.

Blackman's stubbornness first brought him into court in April 1922. He was sent to jail. Shortly afterward one of the magistrates—John Duke—died.

Blackman again failed to pay and was again sentenced. After the hearing, Major Molineux, one of the magistrates, fell seriously ill and soon died.

A few minutes after sentence was passed at Blackman's third appearance in court on the same charge, magistrate H. D. Farnell suffered a seizure and died without regaining consciousness.

Still refusing to pay, Blackman was again arraigned in October 1923, this time before Judge MacKarness in the Eastbourne County Court. The judge once again sent him to prison. Blackman finished his sentence in time to attend the judge's funeral.

Late in July 1924 Blackman received his fifth sentence. By September one of the magistrates present at that hearing, J. T. Helby, was dead.

Blackman's comment on the five deaths was this: "It may be an insignificant coincidence. I bear them no ill will."

A BURNING QUESTION

Can science explain the mystery of the fire walk?

ON APRIL 14, 1985, about a thousand people gathered at the California Institute of Technology sports field in Pasadena to see a demonstration of one of the most mysterious of human feats: walking on red-hot coals. By the end of the afternoon 125 of the audience had themselves walked through a pit of fire with a temperature that reached 1,400°F.

None had any special training or preparation for the event. None had been hypnotized, and none were in a state of religious or mystical ecstasy. They were just ordinary people.

Traditionally, matters have been rather different at fire walks. All over the world, from Japan to Sri Lanka, Spain to Bora Bora, fire walking has been a high point of intense religious ritual. The mystery has always been how the human body can withstand the high temperatures involved, how fire walkers emerge unscathed from the burning pit with no apparent sensation of pain.

Mind over matter?

The usual explanation has been that the powerful rituals preceding the fire walk and the unshakable religious beliefs of the participants have somehow created the conditions for mind to control matter. In this case the matter is human flesh, which the mind makes fireproof.

Citing this premise, a number of self-help groups in the United States and in Europe have proclaimed that they can train people to have total mental control of the body. The results, they claim, include the ability to defeat cancer without drugs, to cure impotence, defeat depression, or restore failing eyesight. Their proof that such miracles are possible? That people have been seen to gain such remarkable mental control that they can walk over coals unharmed.

Strangely enough, it was to disprove such claims that two University of California scientists, Dr. Bernard Leikind, a plasma physicist, and Dr. William McCarthy, a psychologist, had arranged the demonstration at the sports field in Pasadena. They said that anyone can fire walk, and that paranormal powers have nothing to do with it.

The energy question

Leikind believes that the secret of fire walking lies in the difference between the temperature of the hot coals and the amount of heat, or thermal energy, they contain. He explains this crucial difference by pointing out that if you put your hand into a hot oven, the air inside does not burn you. But a cake pan in the same oven will burn you at once. Both are at the same temperature, but they contain different amounts of thermal energy.

Leikind insists that the coals used in fire walks are more like the hot air in an oven than like the cake pan. They simply do not contain enough thermal energy to burn the soles of the feet in the short time it takes to walk the length of the pit. He points out, too, that fire walkers frequently perform with wet feet; the dampness acts as an extra insulation against burns.

Not everyone, however, is convinced by this explanation. Commentators have pointed out that, like the self-help groups and the priests at religious rituals, Leikind first persuaded his audience in California that walking on fire was easy. Although he used the language of science, whereas others have used psychological and emotional terms, he was still aiming to induce a "fireproof" mentality in his audience. Leikind may have succeeded in a way that he did not intend.

UNTOUCHED BY FIRE *A Balinese dancer performs a ritual fire walk while in a trance.*

THE MYSTICAL MICROSCOPE

Meditating on atomic physics

FROM 1895 TO 1933 English occultists C. W. Leadbeater and Annie Besant made a series of discoveries about the nature of atomic particles that physicists ignored for decades. The reason: Leadbeater and Besant had conducted their research not in a laboratory but by means of extrasensory perception. They put themselves into a trance and then selected the atom of a particular element to examine in the mind's eye.

As early as 1895 the two mystics published drawings of their vision of hydrogen atoms, the simplest that exist in nature. The pair saw the atom as a transparent, egg-shaped body that contained six smaller bodies in rotation. And inside each of the smaller bodies were three even smaller, heart-shaped particles. Leadbeater and Besant called them the "ultimate physical atoms," and said they were joined together by "lines of force."

At odds with scientists

At that time scientists believed that the hydrogen atom consisted of only two particles: a nucleus, consisting of a proton, and an electron in orbit around it. By the 1920's this theory had been modified. The electron was thought to be less a solid particle than an electrically charged sphere with extremely erratic behavior.

Yet this theoretical development did not help substantiate the claims of Besant and Leadbeater. They had described six distinct particles, not two.

Not until 1964, when two American physicists concluded that the atomic nucleus was composed of minute objects named quarks, did the description the two psychics had given 69 years earlier begin to make sense. But it would take more research in physics, and a dash of common sense, before the truth of their vision became apparent.

A true likeness

In the early 1980's, Dr. Stephen M. Phillips, a physicist at Cambridge University in England, realized that Leadbeater and Besant would not have "seen" a single, solitary hydrogen atom. Hydrogen atoms occur only in pairs, as a hydrogen molecule.

Phillips concluded that the transparent sphere that Leadbeater and Besant reported was the orbit of the two electrons in the hydrogen molecule. The six inner particles—linked, the psychics said, in two triangles—were the three quarks that make up the protons at the centers of the two atoms. The

GHOST CAR 42

May 5, 1963, began as a great day for auto racing fans in Japan. The country's first Grand Prix since the war was to be held at the ultramodern Suzuka circuit in Nagoya. Favored to win was Masao Asano, driving a white Austin-Healey. Its number: 42.

The choice of the number astonished the crowd, for 42 is one that most Japanese avoid if possible. The arabic numerals for 42 translate as *shi ni,* which is related to the Japanese word *shingu* ("to die"). But Asano dismissed worried comments as "old superstitions."

Toward the end of the first lap, Asano took the lead. Then, as he approached the final, tricky bend at more than 130 miles per hour, his Austin-Healey went out of control. Bouncing across the track, it ripped through crash barriers and hurtled into a ravine. By the time officials reached the wreck, Asano was dead.

A few weeks later the Japan Auto Federation, which controls all of the country's motor sports, banned the use of the number 42 on any vehicle racing in Japan.

A year later, some 150,000 fans arrived at the Suzuka circuit for Japan's second Grand Prix, a much larger event than the first. Two teams of spotters took up their positions in the control tower; they would check the running order of the cars every time each completed a circuit, and after the race they would compare notes for accuracy.

During the race, with the crowded track, the spotters had no time to think—only to call out the numbers on the cars as each flashed by. But when they compared notes after the race, they discovered that a car with the number 42 had passed by in no fewer than 8 of the 25 laps.

No one could describe the kind of car it had been, or its driver. Had Masao Asano returned to the course to run one final race in the sport he loved so much?

three "ultimate physical atoms" within them were subquarks; Phillips himself had recently helped to prove their existence.

The "lines of force" linking the "ultimate atoms" corresponded to the magnetic fields that bind subquarks together. Even the diagrams Leadbeater and Besant drew of the relations between their "ultimate atoms" were strikingly similar to the ones physicists use when representing the inner structure of quarks. The psychics' accounts of the atomic structure of many other elements more complex than hydrogen were similarly confirmed.

Phillips regards the findings of Leadbeater and Besant as a conclusive proof of extrasensory perception. As he points out, they could hardly have been making it up.

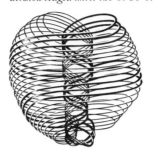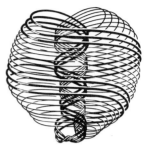

BEFORE THEIR TIME *In 1895 two English occultists employed extrasensory perception and drew (below) what they called "ultimate physical atoms." The two kinds of atom— positive and negative—consisted of currents of energy that formed spiral whorls. The discovery's full significance was not acknowledged until the 1980's.*

THE MOUTHS OF BABES

Children who lived before their time

IN 1955, WHEN SHE WAS about 18 months old, Sukla Gupta of the village of Kampa in West Bengal began to cradle her pillow and call it Minu. When asked who Minu was, Sukla would reply, "My daughter."

During the next three years the small child often spoke to her family about her husband and her daughter and the life that they had led together. She told them that she was a reincarnation of a woman named Mana, and that her husband, brothers-in-law Khetu and Karuna, and Minu were still living at Rathtala in Bhatpara, 11 miles away.

Sukla asked to be taken to Rathtala, but her family had never heard of this district. Sukla said that she could show them the way herself. Then her father discovered that Rathtala did exist and that someone named Khetu did live there. Investigation revealed that Khetu had had a sister-in-law named Mana; she had died some years before, leaving a small child, Minu. His curiosity aroused, Sukla's father arranged for the two families to meet.

When Sukla and her parents arrived in Rathtala in the summer of 1959, Sukla led the way to the house of her alleged father-in-law, where she identified all of the people she had mentioned over the years. It was especially striking that she addressed her brother-in-law as Karuna; everyone else called him Kutu. Even close neighbors did not know his true name.

Sukla recognized many of the objects in the house and picked out Mana's saris from a trunkful of clothes that had belonged to a number of other people. She showed extraordinary affection for her husband and for Minu.

Subsequent inquiries revealed no history of fraud in either family, nor any motive for fraud.

True or false?

The case of Sukla is one of hundreds in the files of Professor Ian Stevenson of the University of Virginia. For more than a quarter of a century Stevenson has been investigating cases in which children recall the homes, work, and families of individuals unknown to them in this life, and sometimes long dead. Stevenson suggests that these may be genuine instances of reincarnation.

However, two Dutch researchers, Titus and Esteban Rivers, have questioned many of Stevenson's cases. In particular, they point out that in many instances the alleged former incarnation belonged, or was known to, the family of the claimant, who may have simply remembered information stored subconsciously.

Of the hundreds of examples in Stevenson's files, only two, in addition to that of Sukla, pass the test of the dubious Dutchmen. These, they believe, may be instances of "real reincarnation memories."

Beautiful Kumkum

Born in 1955, Kumkum Verma had never been away from her village of Bahera, 25 miles from Darbhanga in what is today Bangladesh. When she was about 3½ years old, she began to talk about a previous life. She had lived in Urdu Bazar, a district of Darbhanga, and had married a blacksmith, from a lower caste than that of her present father, a doctor. Kumkum had had a son named Misri Lal, who had also become a blacksmith, and a grandson, Gouri Shankar. She said that her daughter-in-law had poisoned her during an altercation.

Often, while talking about her previous life, Kumkum would say, "Call me *sunnary*," which means "beautiful"—or so her family thought. Anxious to know the truth, in 1959 Dr. Verma discovered that Misri Lal really was a blacksmith in Urdu Bazar and had a son named Gouri Shankar. His mother's name had been Sundari, which he pronounced "Sunnary."

Misri Lal confirmed everything that Kumkum had said. Sundari had been born about 1900 and died in 1950. She married and had two sons, one of them Misri Lal. About five years after her husband's death she again married.

It was not a happy union, and Misri Lal became convinced that his stepfather had squandered his family's money. In 1950 he sued his stepfather and called his mother as a witness in the case. But before the trial date she suddenly died. These and a host of other details of Sundari's life that Kumkum described were also confirmed by independent investigators. Stevenson could discover no suspicious motive behind Kumkum's story and no previous connection between the families.

The girl who was a boy

Born in central Ceylon (Sri Lanka today) in 1956, Gnanatilleka Baddewithana confused her parents when she was a year old by saying that she had "another" mother and father. By the time she was two she had made it clear that these parents were from another existence.

Gnanatilleka gave details of their village, Talawakele, in a remote highland location only 16 miles away. She also named her two former brothers and several sisters. She herself, she said, had been a boy.

A local priest who heard of Gnanatilleka's claims identified the family that she had described. Fifteen months before Gnanatilleka had been born, one of their children had died, a boy named Tillekeratne. In 1961 arrangements were made for Gnanatilleka to go to Talawakele to meet the family.

She correctly recognized seven of Tillekeratne's family and two people from the village, whom she picked out unprompted in a crowd. She delightedly embraced her former mother and former teacher, whom she especially remembered for his gentleness. And Gnanatilleka showed the same warmth or hostility as had Tillekeratne toward individual members of the family.

There were other striking correspondences. Tillekeratne had been markedly effeminate; Gnanatilleka's parents think she is slightly masculine. Both children share the same favorite color, blue. Tillekeratne suffered a fall that contributed to his death; Gnanatilleka avoids heights and has a distinct fear of anything medical.

Once again Stevenson could find no motive for fraud and no evidence of contact between the families. And once again even the skeptics had to agree on the only plausible explanation: Gnanatilleka was telling the truth.

LIGHT FANTASTIC

Latest research into one UFO phenomenon

NO SOUND CAME from the flashing light in the sky. The speed and silence with which it flew—indeed, everything about it—convinced observers on the ground that it was yet another of the unidentified flying objects (UFO's) that had visited the area for years.

One of the watchers, Erling Strand, directed a laser beam at the light. Instantly, flashes on the UFO doubled in frequency. After a few moments Strand turned off the laser; just as rapidly, the light on the object resumed its previous pace.

Strand is leader of Project Hessdalen, an international venture instituted to study the luminous phenomena that have been seen regularly since December 1981 in the skies above the isolated valley of Hessdalen, in central Norway.

The UFO's take the form of simple balls of light of various colors. They appear from nowhere and travel silently up the valley. Sometimes they hover for a while before moving on, and always vanish as mysteriously as they arrive. Hundreds of lights have been reported in the valley.

Light work

Armed with equipment ranging from Geiger counters and seismographs to infrared viewers and lasers, teams of observers have braved the fierce northern cold to record the phenomena. Some 190 sightings were made during one five-week period and the observers have taken more than 100 photographs of the lights.

Investigators are certain that they are dealing with UFO's. The behavior of the Hessdalen lights rules out the likelihood that they are from aircraft, satellites, stars—or even from ground vehicles or distant farms. On some occasions the visual sightings have been confirmed by radar. Whatever creates the lights is definitely flying—and is unidentified by official sources.

But the most dramatic encounters with the Hessdalen UFO's have involved Strand's laser beam. With it, he has successfully induced a response from the lights on eight of nine occasions.

Strand's successes raise several questions. Are the lights intelligent? Or does an intelligence, alien or otherwise, control them? Could they be a natural phenomenon that has yet to be explained?

Leif Havik, a principal member of Project Hessdalen, is convinced that the lights are intelligent and that whatever controls them is aware of being observed. On at least five occasions the UFO's have vanished just as he was about to record their presence, as if avoiding observation.

Theories aside, the members of Project Hessdalen persist in collecting as much data as they can about the valley's flying lights. Most investigators of UFO sightings have only secondhand reports from witnesses whose reliability or honesty cannot always be guaranteed. The Hessdalen team is unusual, and important, in that direct contact with UFO's is being attempted. It would appear that sometimes the UFO's are answering back.

SKY LIGHTS *Since 1981, when the Hessdalen lights were first spotted in central Norway, scientists have been trying to discover the source of the brightly colored luminous shapes. Left: One of many UFO's that have been captured on film. Below: The range of equipment Project Hessdalen employs may one day provide the answer.*

SECRETARY TO THE SPIRITS

She takes dictation from the dead

IN A SMALL TERRACED HOUSE in the north of England a retired schoolteacher regularly performs an eerie and exhausting labor of love. Hour after hour Stella Horrocks sits in her chair with a notepad before her—waiting, she claims, for the spirits of dead writers to make contact.

Suddenly the pen she holds in her right hand begins to move. Soon it is sweeping across the paper as the words come tumbling out— sometimes at the rate of more than 200 a minute.

Stella Horrocks numbers many of the world's greatest literary figures among the authors she says have dictated new works to her. They include Virginia Woolf, Thomas Hardy, Charles Dickens, and Jane Austen. President John F. Kennedy, movie star David Niven, and Lord Louis Mountbatten are other well-known names whose latest writings Stella has apparently transcribed.

The output of this "secretary to the spirits" is astonishing: from her pen have come letters, speeches, diaries, memoirs, plays, and books, each in a different handwriting. So far Stella has failed to find a publisher that is willing to take any of the enormous quantity of writings she has amassed. She finds their attitude discouraging. "I am not in it for the money," she says. "I'd just like to see these works reach a wider public."

Personal touches

Stella says that she can recognize the individual characteristics of each of her authors. "Jane Austen has a much lighter touch than Charles Dickens, though he's full of life," she says. "And Noël Coward digs into the paper with his pen as if he's gardening. Another one is Thomas Hardy and he's entirely different: more of a businessman."

Keeping up with the writers when they are in full flood can be daunting. "They can go on writing for three hours at a stretch when it's a novel. When Dickens wrote about the Battle of Waterloo, I got through about 200 pages in a couple of days."

Others seem to dictate more slowly. Stella is particularly proud of a new work from Jane Austen, which started "coming through" one

DEATH IS NOT THE END? *Stella Horrocks takes dictation from one of the 300 spirits with whom she claims to be in contact. Among the entries in her unique diary, the one below, she says, is the work of Arthur Wellesley, Duke of Wellington, who defeated Napoleon at Waterloo.*

Easter Sunday at a rate of 2,000 words an hour and was completed six weeks later. She has a stockpile of plays by Noël Coward and a "new" collection of four war stories by W. Somerset Maugham.

Stella's technique for "tuning in" to dead authors is simple, she says. "You can't contact them, they have to contact you when they are ready. You have to keep your mind a complete blank to receive. I don't know what they are going to write before they start: they tell me each word as they go."

Stella is only one of a number of people who apparently have the ability to take dictation from the dead. What is the explanation for this remarkable phenomenon?

Practitioners of the art, known in psychic circles as "automatic writers," sincerely believe that they are in touch with the spirits of writers of the past who are anxious to give proof that life continues beyond the grave. Those who are skeptical have found no easy alternative explanations.

Some compare the writings produced by an author in his or her lifetime with the "spirit" output and point out that often the quality is inferior. Others invoke ideas of multiple personality, of subconscious memories, and ponder the complexities of the human psyche. Ultimately most have been able to do no more than watch in wonder as the pen sweeps across page after page after page.

TIME WARP

A strange encounter at Versailles

THE GARDENS at Versailles were in their full glory on August 10, 1901. It was a hot afternoon, the scent from the plants was heady, and the colors brilliant. Yet two Englishwomen, visiting the magnificent French palace for the first time, felt unaccountably depressed as they walked through the grounds.

Miss Anne Moberly, principal of St. Hugh's, a women's college of Oxford University, was spending a few days sightseeing in Paris. She was accompanied by Miss Eleanor Jourdain, who was soon to become vice-principal of the college.

While strolling through the palace gardens, the two women decided to find the Petit Trianon, the small, private château that had belonged to the ill-fated Queen Marie Antoinette. Deep in conversation, they soon noticed that they had lost their way.

"I began to feel as though I was walking in my sleep; the heavy dreaminess was oppressive," Miss Jourdain later wrote. Miss Moberly felt similarly strange, but each kept her feelings to herself.

A walk into the past

They were surprised to see very few people, given the time of year. They passed two men standing near a wheelbarrow, whom they took to be gardeners, despite their long coats and tricorn hats. The men directed them straight ahead. A small bandstand came into view beneath a canopy of trees. Nearby sat a man dressed in a cloak and large hat; he seemed a sinister character and made the women feel ill at ease. They moved on and were later given directions by another man whose appearance seemed strangely old-fashioned.

At last, through the trees, they caught sight of the Petit Trianon. Near the house, Miss Moberly noticed a woman sketching on the grass. The woman stared at her, much to Miss Moberly's irritation. Once the ladies were inside the château, their depression lifted and the arrival of a lively wedding party soon helped them to forget the strange atmosphere they had sensed earlier.

A haunting experience

A week later, while Miss Moberly was writing a letter about the visit to Versailles, she experienced the same oppressive sensation again. The feeling was so strong that she felt compelled to ask Miss Jourdain if she thought the Petit Trianon was haunted.

Miss Jourdain had to admit that she did. For the first time the women discussed their experiences and became convinced that something quite extraordinary had happened to them. For instance, they had walked up to the lady who was sketching alone in the garden and she had stared at them. But Miss Moberly was astonished to learn that Miss Jourdain had seen nothing but trees and grass. Intrigued, they decided to investigate.

On her return to England Miss Moberly discovered that in 1792 on August 10—the same date the two had visited Versailles—Marie Antoinette and her husband, Louis XVI, were imprisoned all day in a small room in Paris awaiting trial. Miss Moberly believed it likely that the humiliated and oppressed queen's thoughts might have returned to the last moments of happiness she knew—at her château in Versailles shortly before the Revolution began. Perhaps the queen's memory of the time was so vivid that, as Miss Moberly put it, "some impress of it was imparted to the place." Could this be an explanation for their strange experience?

When Miss Moberly and Miss Jourdain returned to Versailles two years later, they found, to their astonishment, that everything had changed. The grounds and buildings they remembered were no longer the same.

Puzzling discoveries

But old records and plans of the palace revealed that in 1789 the gardens were as the two women had first seen them. The clothes people had worn, which had struck them as slightly odd and dated for 1901, were the height of fashion in 1789. Miss Moberly's excitement increased when she discovered a portrait of Marie Antoinette: it was the exact image of the "sketching lady" she had seen near the château.

Over the years the two ladies dedicated their vacations to their research. All their findings confirmed their belief that they had seen Versailles as it was 112 years before. In 1911 they published their account in a book, *An Adventure*. The two women were so concerned about losing their professional credibility that they felt compelled to publish their account of the story under pseudonyms. It was only after Miss Jourdain's death in 1924 that their true identities were revealed. The book caused a sensation and was considered to be the best authenticated ghost story of its time.

A few critics, however, were reluctant to accept the women's findings. Some thought that they had been hallucinating. Others believed that the women had met and spoken to ordinary people, became confused about the layout of the gardens, and made their story fit their romantic notions.

There can be no doubt that the events of that summer afternoon were real enough to Miss Moberly and Miss Jourdain. But the nature of their experience—whether they stepped back in time, were caught up in the traces of a distraught queen's memory, or shared a particularly vivid hallucination—remains, to this day, a baffling mystery.

THE GARDEN IN THE STARS

A visit to paradise

FOR MONTHS, two-and-a-half-year-old Durdana Khan had been partly paralyzed, intermittently blind, and always in pain. One morning in the autumn of 1968, lying in her cot in the garden of her parents' home in the Himalayan foothills, she seemed to give up the struggle for life.

Her mother immediately sent for her husband, a doctor; he found no signs of life. Mrs. Khan carried Durdana into the house and Dr. Khan made a last attempt to revive his daughter, murmuring "Come back, my child, come back."

As a last resort, Mrs. Khan poured a few drops of a respiratory stimulant into Durdana's mouth, but they trickled uselessly down her cheek.

Suddenly, to the amazement of her parents, Durdana opened her eyes and announced that the medicine was bitter. After 15 minutes of clinical death, Durdana had come back to life.

Journey into the unknown

One day afterward, Mrs. Khan asked her daughter what had happened during that quarter hour. Through a series of questions and answers, Mrs. Khan gradually learned that Durdana had been to a garden in the stars, where apples, grapes, and pomegranates grew. There were four streams in the garden—white, brown, blue, and green. There were people there as well: "My grandfather, his mother, and another lady who looked like you. Grandpa said he was glad to see me, and his mother took me in her lap. . . . Then I heard Daddy calling me, 'Come back, my child, come back.'"

Durdana's grandfather said they would have to ask God if she could return to her father. So they went to God, who asked her if she wanted to go back. "I have to," she answered, "my daddy is calling me. 'All right,' said God, 'go.' And down, down, down I came from the stars."

God, said Durdana, had been "blue." Despite repeated questioning, this was all she would say.

Not long after her strange experience, Durdana underwent an operation in Karachi, Pakistan. While she was convalescing, she and her mother visited one of Dr. Khan's uncles. As Durdana wandered about the room, she suddenly became very excited and pointed at a photograph on a table.

"This is my grandfather's mother," she said. "I met her in the stars." Durdana had never seen her great-grandmother or her photograph before. Only two pictures existed, and both were in her great-uncle's house in Karachi, which Durdana was visiting for the first time in her life that day.

Later Durdana's family moved to London, and in the early 1980's Durdana appeared on British television with pictures she had painted of the garden she had visited in the stars.

The next day, one of Dr. Khan's patients, Rachel Goldsmith, telephoned him about the program. She had had a similar experience of death while in a German concentration camp. She too had been to a garden with four streams and had been to the spot illustrated in one of Durdana's paintings. When she and Durdana met and talked about what had happened to them, Mrs. Goldsmith could even describe details that Durdana remembered but had left out of the painting.

Vision of infinity

What is one to make of Durdana's experience? She herself admits that apples, pomegranates, and pears are mentioned in the Koran, as are four streams in paradise. But Durdana was not raised as a Muslim and had never attended a mosque.

Dr. Khan suggests that perhaps the reason God appeared to be blue and formless is that the closest we on earth come to a vision of God's infinity is the infinite blue of the sky. "On Mars the sky is red," adds Durdana. "So, to a Martian, maybe God would appear to be red."

Durdana's recognition of the picture of her great-grandmother, and Mrs. Goldsmith's recognition of the garden, suggest that more than imagination was at work in the quarter hour that Durdana was, for all intents and purposes, dead.

PAINTED VISION *When Durdana returned from her "visit to the stars," she described a garden she had seen with apples, grapes, and pomegranates, and four running streams—colored white, brown, blue, and green. Her impression of the white stream, painted in 1980, is above.*

GENTLE GHOSTS

The spiritual habits of the Beaulieu monks

MICHAEL SEDGWICK, who was research director of the Montagu Motor Museum at Beaulieu Abbey, England, had been working into the small hours one night before Christmas in 1959. His office was thick with tobacco smoke. Throwing open a window to clear the air, he heard the chanting of a Catholic mass.

"It came in uneven waves, as if from a faulty wireless," he said. "It was so beautiful that I tried to find it on my own wireless . . . and I couldn't."

That same evening, Bertha Day, the abbey's catering manager, also heard the singing. "I knew that Mrs. Mears, a local lady, had died," she said. Later both Sedgwick and Mrs. Day realized that they had heard the monks of Beaulieu Abbey singing a mass—their custom when one of the inhabitants of the nearby village had died. But no monks had lived in Beaulieu Abbey since 1538.

Founded by Cistercian monks in 1204, the abbey flourished until Henry VIII dissolved it. But the monks, it would seem, had really never left.

To local people the ghosts of Beaulieu are just another part of life in the village. One vicar, the Reverend Robert Frazer Powles, was on such good terms with the ghosts that he knew several by name; at Christmas he would hold services for them in the village church. A parishioner at one Sunday service remarked on how small the congregation had been that day. Replied the vicar: "It's bigger than you can see."

Not everyone has accepted the Beaulieu ghosts so readily. One member of a film crew working at the abbey heard someone following him down a flight of stairs. When the footsteps overtook him, he was terrified: whoever was there was invisible. Other people have been unnerved by noises at night that appear to come from the former graveyard of the monks. The sounds have been likened to those of a burial taking place.

The monks have also been seen as well as heard. They are always dressed in brown, the garb of the lay brothers of the abbey who, unlike the white-robed choir monks, did not take holy orders. Dame Margaret Rutherford, the English actress, once saw a brown-clad monk reading in the ruined cloister, as did a member of the abbey staff in 1965. During World War II, officers from a nearby antiaircraft unit saw a group of monks near the church. In 1979 a monk was seen pruning the vines in the newly revived abbey vineyard.

Lord Montagu, whose family has owned Beaulieu Abbey since 1673, claims that the ghosts "have never been anything but . . . friendly."

Seeing their beloved abbey still so well tended after so many centuries, perhaps the monks feel they have no reason to be anything else.

TELLING PHOTOGRAPH

A survival of the spirit?

RAYMOND LODGE became more famous after his death than he had ever been in life. In a best-selling book published in 1916, Sir Oliver Lodge, Raymond's father and one of Britain's most prominent scientists, claimed that his son was in regular communication with him from beyond the grave.

Raymond Lodge was Sir Oliver's youngest son. He enlisted in the British Army in September 1914, soon after the outbreak of World War I. A little more than a year later, the 25-year-old officer was dead, killed by a shell fragment in the frontline trenches in Belgium.

Yet within days Raymond, who had been close to his family and sent home many letters from the front, was apparently in touch with his grief-stricken parents. But this time his communications were through mediums: men and women who profess to be able to communicate with the dead.

Hoping to hear

Sir Oliver was an experienced researcher into paranormal phenomena and a former president of the British Society for Psychical Research. He needed no convincing that communication with the dead was possible. He and his wife, Lady Mary, began a series of sittings with mediums, hoping to receive a message from Raymond.

They seem to have had little trouble making contact with their son, who painted an extraordinary picture of the spirit world. He called it Summerland and said it was a place where the dead were allowed time to recover from the shock of death. The deceased were reunited with relatives who had died earlier. Raymond himself, the medium reported, had found a brother and sister waiting for him, and the first person to welcome him to his new existence had been his grandfather.

Raymond's surroundings seemed to be much like those on earth. He described how he lived in "a house built of bricks—and there are trees and flowers, and the ground is solid." There were libraries and rivers, and newcomers were allowed to wear earthly clothes, although most people were dressed in white robes. Even cigars and whiskey were available for those who craved them.

Intimate details

Sir Oliver approached the sittings in a scientific manner, taking careful notes and visiting mediums anonymously to prevent any charlatans among them from gathering information about him in advance. Gradually he accumulated the proof, he believed, that his son did continue to exist and was communicating with him.

In many instances Raymond the spirit seemed to display an impressive knowledge of details of his earthly life. Mediums told Sir Oliver, correctly, that Raymond had been nicknamed Pat by his brothers, and that he had been in the habit of calling his teammates Norman during hockey games. He also accurately described the drawing room of his home, which the medium had never visited. He even knew the name of the family's pet peacock and was able to describe a tent and a sand yacht that he and his brothers had built during their seaside holidays.

Sir Oliver admitted that many of these facts about Raymond could have been unconsciously transmitted to the mediums by living people through telepathy. One piece of evidence, however, could not be explained away so easily.

FROM THE GRAVE *A week after Raymond Lodge died in 1915, his spirit allegedly began to communicate with his family. On one occasion, the spirit was able to tell his mother of the existence of a photograph (above) that was unknown to her. (Raymond is in the front row, second from right.) Raymond also pointed out an error on his memorial plaque (right): he had died on a Tuesday, not a Wednesday.*

Remember RAYMOND LODGE, Sec. Lieutenant 2nd South Lancashire Regiment, beloved son of SIR OLIVER and LADY LODGE of this parish who gave his life for his Country. He was born Jan. 25 1889, and was killed in action in Flanders about noon on Wednesday Sept. 14 in the year of Our Lord 1915 aged 26 years.

Whoso bears the whole heaviness of the wronged world's weight
And puts it by,
It is well with him suffering, though he face man's fate
How should he die?
SWINBURNE.

On September 27, 1915, a medium told Lady Mary that Raymond was talking about a photograph in which he was one of a group. Lady Mary did not remember such a photograph and assumed that the medium had made a mistake. But two months later Lady Mary received a letter from the mother of one of Raymond's fellow officers. The woman wrote that Raymond had been photographed with members of his regiment a few months before his death, and asked if Lady Mary would like a copy of it.

Before the picture arrived, Sir Oliver asked a few questions about it at a séance. Through the medium, Raymond told him that the photograph had been taken against "a black background with lines at the back of them." Raymond also said that while they were posing "someone wanted to lean on him, but he was not sure if he was taken with someone leaning on him."

When the photograph arrived, Raymond was seen with a group of officers in front of a wooden building: the roof timbers formed vertical lines behind the group. Far more astonishing to Sir Oliver, however, was that the officer sitting behind Raymond appeared to be leaning on him. Why had Raymond been uncertain as to whether or not this had happened when the picture was taken? The group had been photographed three times; in one of the frames no one was leaning on Raymond.

Proof from the beyond?

Did Raymond communicate with his family from beyond the grave? Although the spirit Raymond did seem to have intimate knowledge of parts of his life, he was surprisingly vague about many important details. And skeptics point out that the incident of the photograph may have been no more than the result of a couple of lucky guesses on the part of the medium.

But Sir Oliver and his family had no doubts. And the story of Raymond is still quoted by spiritualists as irrefutable evidence that the human personality survives bodily death.

FORCEFUL PERSONALITIES

Extraordinary cases of irresistible attraction

WHEN FRANK MCKINSTRY of Joplin, Missouri, stepped out onto the street in the early morning, he knew that he would have to keep moving. If he stopped walking, his feet would become fixed to the ground; in effect, he would be rooted to the spot until he could persuade a passer-by to lift his feet and release the mysterious force that held him.

McKinstry is just one of a number of "human magnets" who have been studied by scientists since the mid-19th century. Also known as electric people, they seem to be able to store and discharge powerful electric currents, sometimes with bizarre and unpredictable results.

Anyone who touches such people may receive an electric shock. Sparks may fly from their fingertips, and some objects may become immovable or move apparently of their own accord.

Teenage magnet

One of the first cases scientists investigated was that of a 14-year-old French girl, Angélique Cottin, who worked as a glove maker in Normandy. For a period of 10 weeks in 1846, the wooden frames on which she worked would twist in her hands, her bed would rock, chairs would move away when she attempted to sit on them, and the slightest touch from her hand could send furniture spinning uncontrollably across her room.

Angélique was studied by an eminent member of the Academy of Sciences in Paris, but beyond likening her power to that of electromagnetism, he could offer no explanation for the phenomena.

Around 1890, scientists at the Maryland College of Pharmacy in Baltimore examined the curious ability of a student named Louis Hamburger. Pins and other metal objects would attach themselves to him, dangling from his open hands.

A striking case of human magnetism came to light in 1938 when the Universal Council for Psychic Research in New York City offered a $10,000 prize for demonstrable proof of psychic phenomena. Mrs. Antoine Timmer came forward to show how cutlery would stick to her hands so firmly that it could be removed only by a sharp tug.

The council dismissed the case. Although members made no allegations of fraud against Mrs. Timmer, they claimed that a competent magician could reproduce the effect using concealed thread.

In sickness and in health

Occasionally, extraordinary discharges of electricity are related to periods of illness. For example, in January 1837 brilliant sparks up to $1\frac{1}{2}$ inches long were emitted from the fingers of a woman in Orford, New Hampshire, who suffered from a variety of problems with her joints and muscles. The woman's electrification lasted six weeks. Her doctor attributed the cause to a dramatic aurora borealis in the sky during the same period.

In 1879, when 19-year-old Caroline Clare of London, Ontario, was recovering from a lengthy and baffling neurologic illness, she found that metal objects jumped into her hands as she reached for them. If she held on to any item, it would stick, and someone else would have to pull it off.

STRANGE FOREBODING

In the fall of 1955, English actor Alec Guinness happened to meet film idol James Dean in a restaurant in Los Angeles.

Dean took Guinness outside and proudly showed him his latest acquisition: a gleaming brand-new sports car, wrapped in cellophane and tied with ribbon. It had just been delivered, Dean explained excitedly.

Guinness looked at the car uneasily and urged Dean not to get inside it, but to return it to the supplier. Guinness then looked at his watch and said: "It is now 10 o'clock, Friday the 23rd of September, 1955. If you get in that car, you will be found dead in it by this time next week."

Dean laughed off the remark and Guinness apologized for what he had said, attributing it to tiredness and hunger. After a pleasant evening, the two actors parted; no further reference to the incident had been made.

The body of James Dean was discovered at 4 P.M. on Friday, September 30, exactly one week after his meeting with Alec Guinness. Dean had been killed while driving his new car.

In 1920 the chief physician of a state prison in New York reported on a number of inmates who carried strong charges of static electricity during an outbreak of food poisoning. Paper would stick to their hands, and they could deflect compass needles and make a metal tape sway by moving their hands over it. The phenomena ceased when the men recovered their health.

Nothing is known about the health of an Englishwoman, Mrs. Grace Charlesworth, who was tormented by electrical phenomena for two years in the 1960's. Objects in her home would give her electric shocks, she would vibrate in her bed, and sparks ran up the walls. An examination of the house where Mrs. Charlesworth had lived uneventfully for 40 years uncovered nothing that could account for the shocks; scientists could conclude only that they originated from Mrs. Charlesworth.

Among the more recent cases on record are those of people who have had strange effects on electrical equipment. In 1973 a woman in London had to appeal publicly for help; she claimed that radios, automatic ticket machines, and household appliances malfunctioned when she approached them.

Perhaps the most dramatic of contemporary cases is that of Jacqueline Priestman of Manchester, England. In 1983 she had an adverse effect on 30 vacuum cleaners, five irons, and two washing machines. Whenever she passed her television set or any electrical equipment, the appliance started to act up and often emitted sparks.

Continuing mysteries

Despite more than 100 years of investigation, to date physical science has failed to account for the bizarre phenomenon of electric people. One thing seems certain: more than ordinary electricity or magnetism is involved.

Some researchers have suggested that an undiscovered source of transmittable electromagnetic power within the human body may be responsible or that atmospheric conditions may play a part. But there is little evidence to support their theories— and electric people still defy explanation.

SHOCKING BEHAVIOR
Through the centuries many cases have been recorded of "electric people" — those who, because of electric currents discharged by their bodies, are able to move unwieldy objects with the slightest touch. One of the earliest cases to be investigated was that of a 14-year-old French girl, Angélique Cottin, who demonstrated her abilities at the Academy of Sciences in Paris.

UNLOCKING THE AFTERLIFE

Codes and ciphers may reveal life after death

FOR THOUSANDS OF YEARS mankind has cherished a belief that the individual identity survives after the death of the body, although evidence for this belief is as rare as the phoenix.

But today researchers in the United States and Britain have set up experiments that, if successful, would provide powerful evidence that physical death does not necessarily mean extinction.

Safety in numbers

Professor Ian Stevenson of the University of Virginia has devised a test with combination locks. Inspired by a report that an English medium had received a message from her dead husband giving her the correct sequence of numbers to unlock a case of documents, Stevenson asks participants in his project to buy a six-dial combination lock, set it, and send him the lock.

Volunteers are instructed neither to tell the combination to anyone nor to write it down. After death, they are to communicate the combination to a medium or to a member of their family. The odds against getting the number for such a lock correct by chance are a million to one.

Acts of friendship

In Britain, David Christie-Murray, a member of the Association for the Scientific Study of Anomalous Phenomena, asks pairs of acquaintances to make a pact to communicate with each other after death. Ideally, participants should not have too intimate a knowledge of the other's daily life. This, says Christie-Murray, is to prevent one from learning of the death of the other by the usual means.

The communication may take the form of a direct message conveyed psychically by one friend to the other, a message sent through a medium, or even an intuition or conviction by one friend that the other is dead. Christie-Murray keeps a register of everyone taking part in the scheme and will investigate any messages that are received.

Secret words

Dr. Arthur S. Berger, president of the Survival Research Foundation in Pembroke Pines, Florida, is offering a $1,000 reward to anyone able to identify either of two code words left with the foundation by British parapsychologist Robert H. Thouless before his death in 1984. Each word is a key that will decipher a sentence encoded by Thouless; both were, or are, known only to him.

Thouless said he would attempt to communicate the words to a medium after his death. So far the only information received from the "other side" is that his earthly life seems like a dream to him now, and that he cannot remember the code words.

Undeterred, some 200 people worldwide have volunteered to encode sentences and attempt posthumously to pass on the secret words that will decipher them. All have used the same coding system as Thouless.

If even one of these experiments succeeds, faith and science may find themselves in an extremely rare, perhaps very unique, accord.

WALKING TALL

Defying nature

THE 19TH-CENTURY Scottish medium Daniel Dunglass Home had extraordinary gifts that seemed to overrule laws of nature. Home could, for example, regularly defy gravity. In one famous séance Home moved from one room to another by floating through the windows, three stories above the ground. He also seemed immune to heat and could handle red-hot coals without any discomfort—he even rolled his face around in the fire as if it were a basin of water.

Perhaps most amazing of all, Home could change the size and shape of his body. Before the eyes of amazed onlookers, he could grow by as much as 12 inches. His chest would expand and his arms grow visibly longer; his ribs would pull upward away from the waist eight inches or more, with the flesh and muscles of his torso clearly stretching and moving.

The long and the short of it

Not only could Home expand, he could also contract, shrinking from his regular height of 5 feet 10 inches to little more than 5 feet. His face became distorted, with all the features growing much larger at first, then suddenly becoming smaller and deeply wrinkled before returning to normal size.

Two regular observers of these strange contortions were Home's friends Lord Adare and Lord Lindsay. Adare made a detailed study of the bizarre phenomena that surrounded Home and faithfully recorded what occurred during a series of séances between 1867 and 1869. There were 80 séances in all, during which Adare, Lindsay, and several others witnessed the medium's bodily elongation on 10 separate occasions.

Instructed by the spirits

The usual pattern was for Home to go into a trance and be taken over by a "spirit controller," who spoke through him. The spirits seemed to encourage the investigators and usually announced the kind of change that was about to take place, saying, for example, "Daniel will grow tall." This cued the investigators to move into action to ensure that they recorded every detail.

Home, in a trance, would be placed against the wall, with others stationed around him. One person would check his feet, sometimes stepping on them to make sure they remained firmly on the ground. Others would monitor Home's arms, waist, or face while someone stood by with a pencil to mark his growth on the wall.

Sometimes Home was made to stand in the middle of the room back to back with another man for comparison as he shrank or stretched. At other times Home, closely watched by the observers, would walk around, elongating and shortening three or four times, until the trance state ceased and the spirit voice said "Good-night" to let those present know that the evening had ended.

Truth or trickery?

At one of the séances, Home lay down on the floor between two other men; his head touched one man and his feet the other. As his body elongated, Home seemed to grow at both ends, pushing each of the men away from him. Using a tape measure, another observer was staggered to find that the men were now seven feet apart. Then Home began to levitate and, swaying from side to side in the air, slowly floated onto a nearby sofa.

Needless to say, there were many doubters who were only too ready to explain away these events—which they had not personally seen—as trickery or deception. But, incredible though Home's feats seemed, they were witnessed by literally hundreds of people, including eminent scientists, cynical newspapermen, and the crowned heads of Europe. What they saw convinced all of them.

Lord Adare, Home's almost constant companion for two years, never discovered any evidence of fraud or deceit. Although he could not provide an explanation for what the medium did, he never doubted that it was genuine.

A DEAD FRIEND VISITS

The distinguished Swiss psychologist Carl Gustav Jung was well known for his interest in the afterlife. Although he once stated that the immortality of the soul could never be proved, he believed that telepathy between this world and the next could take place. In his autobiography he writes of a very curious personal experience that seems to lend some support to his belief.

In bed one night Jung was thinking about the funeral he had attended the day before. Suddenly he had a vision: his dead friend was standing at the foot of his bed, looking down at him.

The friend went to the door and beckoned Jung to follow. In his imagination Jung obeyed, trailing him out of the house, into the street, and finally into his friend's house, where he was ushered into the library. His friend then climbed onto a stool and pointed out a specific book—the second of five volumes with a red leather binding—that sat on the second shelf from the top. At this point Jung's vision ended.

Consumed with great curiosity, Jung visited his friend's widow the next morning and asked to see the library, a room in which he had never been before. Once inside, everything was as he had "seen" it the previous night, including the stool by the bookcase. Stepping onto the stool so that he could read the titles of the books, Jung found the one his friend had pointed out. It was a translation of a novel by Emile Zola, *The Legacy of Death*.

Although this was just one of many similar occurrences during Jung's lifetime, he was reluctant to speak out about them publicly. As he once said: "I prefer not to communicate too many of my experiences. They would confront the scientific world with too many problems."

SURVIVORS OF HELL'S FIRE

The victims of a mysterious combustion

ON THE MORNING of July 19, 1980, a 31-year-old woman living in Toronto woke to find that severe second- and third-degree burns had developed on her thighs and abdomen. So extensive were they that it took six months of painful skin-graft operations to repair the wounds. Yet whatever created the burns had left no marks on the woman's nightclothes or bed linen.

This extraordinary story is from the files of Larry E. Arnold of Harrisburg, Pennsylvania. Arnold has devoted many years to investigating the bizarre and, so far, inexplicable phenomenon known as spontaneous human combustion (SHC).

When the impossible happens

Most medical scientists refuse to acknowledge that SHC exists. They insist that it is impossible for the human body to burst into flames; there must be another, more rational explanation, they claim. But Arnold and a few like-minded investigators have accumulated a fascinating amount of case material on the subject.

From evidence assembled to date, it is assumed that most victims of SHC burn to death, quickly, quietly, and very nearly completely. The police and scientists are left with few clues regarding the precise circumstances surrounding the demise. But there are a fortunate few, such as the woman in Toronto, who survive. Of these cases, one of the most mysterious is the story of Jack Angel.

Fire from within

Jack Angel, today in his seventies, made a comfortable living as a clothing salesman. On the night of November 12, 1974, he parked his trailer, which he had converted into a traveling showroom, at a Ramada Inn in Savannah, Georgia. He made up the bed, changed into his pajamas, and went to sleep.

Four days later, Angel woke up. He noticed that his right hand was black from the wrist to the fingertips. "It was just burned, blistered," he told Arnold. "And I had this big explosion in my chest. It left a hell of a hole. I was burned . . . on my ankle, and up and down my back, in spots."

Since Arnold felt no pain, he showered and dressed in the shirt and trousers he had taken off four days earlier. Neither his clothing nor his bedding bore any trace of scorching. Nursing his injured hand, Angel then walked across the parking lot to the motel. Minutes later he collapsed, unconscious, on the floor.

When he awoke, Angel was in a hospital, in shock and experiencing an "excruciating pain." The doctors who examined him were baffled. It was evident that whatever had burned his hand had been inside the tissue, and that the burning had continued up *inside* his forearm. Angel then called his wife and asked her to go to the trailer and search it thoroughly. She found no sign of a fire or scorching on the bedding or any of the many clothes hanging in the closet.

Angel's hand failed to respond to antibiotics and became infected. Rather than face months of surgery, he agreed to an amputation.

After he was discharged in mid-January 1975, Angel sued the manufacturers of the trailer for $3 million in damages, believing that the fire had been caused by a faulty design or equipment malfunction. During the next two and a half years a prestigious engineering and technical laboratory took the vehicle apart, but found no evidence whatsoever to support Angel's case.

On the eve of the court hearing, the suit had to be withdrawn, leaving Angel without compensation and none the wiser about what had happened.

An unknown force

Arnold believes that the force that burned Angel's arm bears the characteristics of many well-documented cases in which the whole body has been incinerated. The unfortunate victim is usually unaware of the pain or flames; the fire is strangely contained in the body, usually without scorching flammable objects close by; and the high temperatures required to carbonize living flesh are reached in a very short time—and then fade away just as quickly and as mysteriously.

A number of causes of spontaneous combustion have been suggested, ranging from ball lightning and fluctuations in the earth's magnetism to malfunctions in bodily processes and the accumulation of flammable gases within the body. But to date no one has been able to explain *how* any of them might operate. It is possible that several different unidentified forces may be at work, giving rise to the different forms of SHC that have been recorded.

Walking inferno

A more recent instance of SHC is that of a 19-year-old computer operator, Paul Hayes, who was walking along a quiet street near his home in London on the night of May 25, 1985. Suddenly he was surrounded by flames from the waist up. He thought he had been doused with gasoline and set on fire. The heat was agonizingly intense. Fearing for his eyes, Hayes covered them with his hands and attempted to run for help. He fell to the ground, doubled up in pain.

Inexplicably, the fire died out as quickly as it had started. Hayes staggered into the emergency room of a nearby hospital, where he received treatment for burns over most of his upper torso and head.

Like Jack Angel, Hayes is still mystified by the experience. In the absence of any hypothesis from medical scientists, both men suppose that they were victims of spontaneous human combustion. But they are still waiting for an explanation.

FIERY END *Spontaneous human combustion is not a recent phenomenon. In a contemporary illustration (at right) from* Bleak House *by Charles Dickens, William Guppy and Tony Weevle discover the smoking ashes that were once the evil Krook. Some people, however, have survived SHC. In 1974 Jack Angel (below) lost his right arm after a fire. Some believe that the fire started internally.*

THE WATSEKA WONDER

The double life of Lurancy Vennum

MARY LURANCY VENNUM was born in April 1864 in Milford, a small town near Watseka in eastern Illinois. She had an ordinary, unremarkable childhood until she was 13. Then, in July 1877, she told her family: "There were persons in my room last night, and they called 'Rancy! Rancy!' and I felt their breath on my face."

A few days later Lurancy had a seizure, followed by another. She announced that she could see heaven, angels, and people who were now dead but whom she had known. Her distressed family anxiously sought medical advice and were grateful when their friends Mr. and Mrs. Roff recommended Dr. E. W. Stevens of Janesville, Wisconsin.

A disturbing spirit

On January 3, 1878, Mr. Roff brought Stevens to the Vennums' home. Lurancy had become increasingly disturbed and seemed to be having a continual inner struggle. With great difficulty Stevens calmed the girl down. She then told him that a spirit called Mary Roff wanted to control her. In surprise Roff exclaimed: "That is my daughter Mary Roff. Why! She has been in heaven 12 years. Yes, let her come; we'll be glad to let her come."

Mary Roff had died in July 1865 at the age of 18, having suffered from fits throughout her life. It now seemed to Roff that his daughter had returned from the grave and taken over Lurancy's body. Indeed, Lurancy was giving every sign of *being* Mary Roff and was constantly pleading to be allowed to go home to her parents.

On February 11 "Mary Roff" moved to the Roff household. For three months she behaved exactly as if she were the dead daughter of the Roffs', immediately recognizing friends, relatives, clothes, and belongings. She also remembered scores of events from her past, many of which had occurred up to 25 years before. When the Vennums visited, "Mary Roff" behaved as if she hardly knew them.

On May 7 the personality of Lurancy reemerged. Sitting down, the girl closed her eyes, immediately opened them again, and asked: "Where am I? I was never here before." She pleaded to be taken home. But five minutes later the "Mary Roff" personality took control once more. Between May 7 and May 21 this temporary displacing of "Mary" by Lurancy occurred several times. Finally, "Mary" announced that it was time for Lurancy to return, and she said good-bye to her family and friends.

Lurancy was welcomed back into the bosom of her family, and she settled in happily. From time to time the "Mary" personality would emerge, but only briefly, and Lurancy was able to lead a normal life. The days of full possession seemed to be over.

The case of the Watseka Wonder, as the Lurancy Vennum affair became known, came to the attention of Dr. Richard Hodgson, a notoriously skeptical researcher into psychic phenomena. He studied it carefully in 1890 and concluded that there was no way that the strange case could be explained by any normal means. Either Mary Roff had returned from the dead to possess the body of Lurancy Vennum, or Lurancy had developed a secondary personality that used psychic powers to gather details about Mary Roff's past life. The truth may never be known. The case of the Watseka Wonder retains its mystery to the present day.

A TERRIFYING VISION

A wife's premonition is confirmed

IN 1611 THE ENGLISH POET John Donne was asked by his patron, Sir Robert Drury, to accompany him on a journey to Paris. The invitation threw Donne into a quandary. Sir Robert was one of the richest men in England, and no one turned him down lightly. Yet Donne's wife was pregnant and became distraught at the idea of being left behind. She pleaded with her husband to stay, and told him that she had had a premonition that disaster would befall her if he left her.

Sir Robert, however, would not tolerate a refusal; he insisted that Donne make the journey with him. To ease the separation he arranged for Mrs. Donne to stay in comfort at Drury House, his mansion in London.

Donne had been in Paris for just two days when he had a vision that seemed to confirm his wife's forebodings. According to Donne's biographer, Izaak Walton, after the two travelers had had dinner together, the poet lingered in the room by himself. Half an hour later Sir Robert returned and was astonished to see that his ashen-faced companion was obviously terrified.

"I have seen a dreadful vision since I saw you," Donne explained. "I have seen my dear wife pass twice by me through this room, with her hair . . . about her shoulders, and a dead child in her arms."

Sir Robert was skeptical. Was Donne sure he had not simply dropped off to sleep for a few minutes and dreamed the whole thing? Donne was adamant that he had been awake all the time.

Bad tidings

Donne was just as certain the next day, and Sir Robert, who now admitted to "a faint belief that the vision was true," agreed to send a servant back to London to find out if disaster had indeed struck.

The emissary returned 12 days later with bad news. He had "found and left Mrs. Donne very sad, and sick in her bed; and, that after a long and dangerous labor she had been deliver'd of a dead child." The stillbirth had occurred on "the same day and about the very hour that Mr. Donne affirmed he saw her pass by him."

Since it was reported by Walton, this remarkable story has often been quoted. But is it true?

Walton claims that it was told to him "by a Person of Honour," whom he does not name. Whoever it was, Walton was clearly convinced that the incident had taken place as reported. He asserts that his source was a close friend of Donne's who "knew more of the secrets of his soul then any person then living."

Later biographers, however, have had their doubts; the sequence of events given by Walton does not seem to tally with the facts they have established about Donne's life. It is possible that Walton may have embroidered the accounts of Donne's anxiety about his wife's health and conjured up a dramatic and touching vision, perhaps to enhance his subject's reputation for piety in the eyes of his readers.

Walton's account was published some 60 years after the vision is supposed to have occurred, and he makes it scrupulously clear that the story is secondhand. Almost four centuries later it is impossible to establish the truth of a tale that Walton dryly predicted "will beget some wonder."

GHOSTLY GUIDES OF GLASTONBURY

An archeologist receives help from the dead

ARCHEOLOGIST AND ARCHITECT Frederick Bligh Bond was delighted when, in 1907, he was given the job of excavating England's most important Christian site, the buried ruins of Glastonbury Abbey. But he was faced with a major problem: no one knew the exact location of the abbey before its destruction in 1539, during the English Reformation, and the budget could not possibly accommodate a full-scale dig.

To find anything of historical value, Bond had to guess the site correctly the first time—or his efforts would be wasted.

Against all odds, over the next 11 years Bond uncovered most of the foundations of the vast building. The accuracy of his work was uncanny. But he did have unusual help. He was told precisely where to dig by monks from the abbey itself. And they had been dead for nearly 400 years.

Questioning the spirits

Bond had long been fascinated by spiritualism. His friend Capt. John Allen Bartlett had produced several interesting "automatic scripts"—messages allegedly written by the dead through the hands of the living. In November 1907 Bond and Bartlett decided, not very seriously, to experiment with the method to see if it would help with the problem of the Glastonbury excavations. Their first question was simply: "Can you tell us anything about Glastonbury Abbey?"

Both men were amazed at the wealth of information that they then received. And, as they were to discover, it was startlingly accurate.

Instant results

The very first session produced the solution—in Latin—to one of Glastonbury's best-known mysteries: the location of the Edgar Chapel, a 15th-century addition to the abbey that had disappeared without a trace. The spirit of a monk called Johannes Bryant, who claimed he had been born in 1497 and died in 1533, gave the chapel's precise site, dimensions, and decor. Johannes also said that there was a door in the east wall of the chapel—a highly unusual feature.

Bond uncovered the Edgar chapel, and the doorway, in 1908. He found that it had "azure glass" in its windows—another unusual feature—just as

Johannes had said, and that its ceiling, too, matched the dead monk's description exactly.

Later sessions proved equally fruitful. Johannes said that "thin walls and poor foundations" characterized the later building in the abbey, which Bond in due course found to be true. Other monks referred to a crypt, which had collapsed; Bond unearthed the stairs to it and the double handrail the monks had described. The monks also provided details of the interior colors and of the altar screen in the abbey; Bond's excavations proved that these, too, were perfectly accurate.

A broken skull

Bond's most extraordinary find was a human skeleton with another, broken skull between its legs. The strange burial method puzzled Bond and, together with Bartlett, he asked the spirit monks if they could offer an explanation.

One replied that the skull belonged to Eawulf, an 11th-century Saxon earl, who had been killed by a Norman named Radulphus. By accident the two men had been buried in the same spot. Bond knew

historical records that mentioned Radulphus, the Norman treasurer at the abbey, but he had never heard of Eawulf. After exhaustive searches he found two ancient chronicles that referred to an Eanulf. In different ways each confirmed that Eanulf and the man the monk named Eawulf were one and the same.

Bond never completely believed that he and Bartlett had been in touch with spirits. He preferred to think that through his own subconscious he had tapped a kind of universal memory. But the fear of ridicule made him keep the reason for his phenomenal archeological success a closely guarded secret. Then, in 1918, Bond finally published the truth about how he had made his discoveries.

The results were catastrophic. Bond's career was ruined, his reputation destroyed. Within a few years he had been removed from his post at the abbey, while his architectural practice dwindled to nothing. The man who had proved beyond reasonable doubt that a source of knowledge could exist beyond reach of our normal senses remained an outcast from society the rest of his life.

THE HOUSE THE SPIRITS BUILT

A monument to immortality

FOR 38 YEARS Sarah Winchester went to sleep with the sound of hammering all around her. No lullaby could have soothed her more. Mrs. Winchester, a widow, was neither deaf nor, by most accounts, particularly eccentric. The constant noise was simply part of her life's special mission.

Mrs. Winchester found her strange vocation not long after her husband, William, died in 1881. At that time she inherited about $20 million, as well as an income of about $1,000 a day, from William's holdings in the Winchester Repeating Arms Co. But unconsoled by her wealth, grieving for her husband, and troubled by the death of their only child, Mrs. Winchester sought comfort from a spiritualist in Boston.

The spirits' revenge

The medium's message was straightforward but alarming. A considerable part of the Winchester fortune had come from sales of the Winchester '73 rifle, "the gun that won the West." The souls of the rifle's victims—and there were thousands of them—had revenged themselves by taking Mrs. Winchester's family from her. Her life would also be cursed, said the medium, unless she bought a

house, enlarged it, and continued building it for the rest of her life. As long as there was the sound of hammering, Mrs. Winchester would be untroubled by evil spirits.

In 1884 Mrs. Winchester bought an eight-room farmhouse in the Santa Clara Valley in California. There, until her death in 1922, she employed a crew of between 10 and 22 carpenters and dozens of other workmen to help her escape the terrible curse that had been placed on her name.

Work continued day and night, precisely as instructed. Each evening Mrs. Winchester would retire to her séance room to receive the next day's plans from the spirits; in the morning she would relay these to the chief carpenter. As the work progressed, it became apparent that the house was being constructed as much to keep good spirits in as to shut evil ones out.

Designed by ghosts for ghosts

This dual purpose helps to explain the myriad of oddities the house contains. Some doors can be opened from one side only; some open onto thin air. One reveals a closet no more than an inch deep. Facing this opening, what appears to be the door to a closet opens onto a 30-room suite. One set of stairs leads down to another set of stairs, which then leads back to the same story. Another stairway has 44 steps and turns seven corners—but rises a mere nine feet. Yet another ends at a ceiling.

To spare the spirits embarrassment due to the fact that they are not reflective, only two mirrors are in the house. And since spirits cast no shadow, the lighting of the rooms is arranged in such a way that humans cast none either.

Rooms for all

Unremitting labor for 38 years wrought a house that contains 160 rooms and covers six acres. Actually, some 750 rooms were built, but many were torn out and replaced as the spirits changed their plans. The Winchester house today remains prodigious nonetheless. It contains three elevators, six kitchens, 40 bedrooms, 467 doors, 10,000 windows, 47 fireplaces, 40 stairways, 52 skylights, six safes, and a shower.

Mrs. Winchester spent close to $5.5 million of what she called her blood money to lift a curse—and provided a feast for lovers of the bizarre and the extravagant.

MYSTERY HOUSE *Although it has undergone many changes since construction was started in 1884, the grand scale and architectural complexity still make Winchester House an outstanding sight. At the turn of the century, the building rose some seven stories at a time when the surrounding area was predominantly farmland. Staircases that lead to ceilings (above) are just one of the bizarre features introduced by Mrs. Winchester, the eccentric owner.*

FOOD, GLORIOUS FOOD

Saint John Bosco, who founded the Salesian order to care for destitute boys, has been called the greatest miracle worker of the 19th century.

His most famous miracle took place in 1860 at a Salesian house in Turin. The baker who supplied bread to the house had refused to send more until his bill was paid. For breakfast that day, there were only 15 small rolls to divide among 300 hungry boys.

When Bosco heard of the situation he directed that the rolls be put in a basket. He would hand them out himself.

Up stepped each boy, one by one, to take his roll. All 300 were given their breakfast, and 15 or 20 rolls still remained in the basket. So impressed was one young boy, who counted the rolls both before and after, that he vowed then and there to join the Salesian order.

This was by no means the only time that such a miracle had occurred for Bosco. In 1849, on the Sunday after All Souls' Day, he took some 600 boys to pray at the local cemetery, promising all of them a treat of hot chestnuts afterward. Bosco's mother was cooking the chestnuts, and she prepared only a few of the treats because she thought that only a few boys had gone. After their return from the cemetery, Bosco ignored the boys' cries of disappointment and proceeded to hand out large handfuls to everyone.

Members of Salesian houses throughout the world today always celebrate All Souls' Day with a feast of boiled chestnuts.

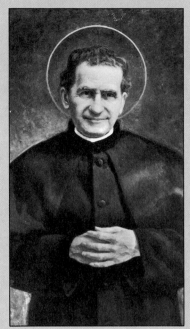

Saint John Bosco

DOUBLE VISION

Some strange encounters

IN 1771 A YOUNG MAN was riding along a path toward Drusenheim, Germany, when he was overtaken by a strange foreboding. Then something bizarre happened. Riding toward him on the same road was an identical replica of himself, except that the figure was wearing gray with a touch of gold—clothes the young man had never seen before. Then the vision suddenly disappeared. The rider shrugged off the incident.

But eight years later it was to have strange repercussions: the young man found himself on the same road, wearing exactly the same clothes he had seen in his vision.

The man in question was the German writer and poet Johann Wolfgang von Goethe. Many years later Goethe was still intrigued by the apparent encounter with his own double. When it happened he had found it comforting, for he had just said a sad farewell to the woman he loved, Frederika.

"However it may be with matters of this kind generally," he wrote in his autobiography, "this strange illusion in some measure calmed me at the moment of parting."

Soul meetings

Accounts of people meeting their own doubles have been recorded from earliest times, when the belief was widely held that the soul existed independently of the body and could depart from it. In the 16th and 17th centuries, witches were accused of sending their "fetches," or doubles, to carry out wicked deeds.

John Aubrey, the 17th-century author of *Brief Lives,* quotes several examples of the double as a harbinger of death. One is the story of astrologer Sir Richard Napier. After arriving at an inn one night, Napier was led upstairs to his room by the innkeeper. When Napier looked at the bed, he was astounded to see a dead man lying in it. Napier expressed his indignation, but the innkeeper replied that there was no dead man in the bed. Napier looked at the bed again; the body was his own. According to Aubrey's account, Napier died shortly afterward.

More recent witnesses of the phenomenon have taken a cooler view, unworried by omens of death. In 1929 a clergyman described waking from a nap in his chair one night.

"I saw an apparition, luminous, vaporous, wonderfully real of myself, looking interestedly and delightedly at myself. . . . After I and myself had looked at each other for the space of about five seconds, my ghostly self vanished."

Possible explanations

In searching for an explanation, researchers of psychic phenomena have turned to medical literature. It contains many descriptions, particularly by migraine sufferers, of people who have encountered their own doubles. In instances where no physical condition or disease can be singled out, psychiatrists have suggested that an unduly narcissistic personality may be involved, or that the witness's imagination has somehow been able to project his self-image onto the outside world.

In Goethe's case, the explanation may be even simpler. He had just said good-bye to Frederika. Perhaps his dramatist's eye was at work as he set off on his journey.

This may not be as illogical as it sounds: the author of *Faust* had a powerful imagination. In his account of the incident, Goethe refers to it as a dream, saying that he "saw not with the eyes of the body, but with those of the mind."

However, this does not explain how Goethe saw himself in the clothes he was to wear eight years later on a return visit. Beyond saying that his choice of clothing was "quite accidental," he does not provide enough details for anyone today to evaluate what remains a double mystery.

A Leap of the Imagination

Mysterious marsupials of North America

WAITRESS MARILYN HOLLENBACK reportedly laughed for 20 minutes when a customer in the diner announced that he had just hit a kangaroo with his pickup truck. Tulsa, Oklahoma, was an unlikely place to meet a kangaroo running wild.

Two Tulsa police officers also listened to the man's story. He had seen two of the creatures, he said, and on swerving to avoid one he had hit the other. The dead kangaroo was in his truck. Hollenback and the officers went to look, and there lay a three-and-a-half-foot-long kangaroo. Having satisfied his skeptical audience, the man climbed back into his truck and drove away.

On the hop

The incident took place on August 31, 1981. Later, patrolman Ed Compos commented ruefully that he wished he had taken a picture of the animal. This was by no means the only occasion that someone had seen a wild kangaroo in the United States, but it was the only time that anyone had actually managed to catch one.

Weighing as much as 220 pounds and measuring up to five feet in height, kangaroos can reach speeds of 25 miles per hour in bounds that cover more than 30 feet at a time. But wild kangaroos are believed to live only in Australia, Tasmania, New Guinea, and a few other islands.

However, sightings of kangaroos in the United States date back to at least 1899 and have been reported, mainly in the Midwest, on a regular basis ever since. On the first occasion, a Mrs. Glover in Richmond, Wisconsin, saw a kangaroo racing through a neighbor's yard. At the time, both a traveling circus and a tornado were visiting Richmond, and everyone assumed that the anomalous marsupial had escaped in the confusion of the storm. But Robert H. Gollmar, the son of the circus owner, denied that the show owned a kangaroo.

Another outbreak of wild kangaroos in Wisconsin took place between April 5 and May 21, 1978, this time in Waukesha County. Eight sightings were reported. On April 23 tracks were found after Lance Nero of Brookfield Township saw two kangaroos hopping cross-country near his house. The next day two young men from Menomonee Falls managed to photograph a kangaroo that they had spotted by the side of the highway. And in the last week of May two additional sightings were reported in Wisconsin.

Probably the most dramatic encounter with kangaroos in the United States occurred in 1974 in Illinois. On October 18 two Chicago patrolmen

CAMERA-SHY *A fleeting glimpse of an elusive kangaroo was captured on film in the high brush country near Waukesha, Wisconsin, in 1978. Various sightings of the mysterious marsupials have been reported across the United States.*

cornered a five-foot specimen in an alley on the city's North Side.

Fearful and panicked, the kangaroo growled defensively and used its powerful legs to kick the policemen aside. A split second later the creature leaped over a fence and disappeared from view.

One jump ahead

Later that day another sighting of a kangaroo was reported in the nearby suburb of Oak Park. Over the next five days kangaroos were seen in Chicago at least five more times. The following month the creatures reappeared in Chicago and were reported simultaneously in Plano, Illinois, 50 miles to the west. Then reports stopped; the animals had disappeared as mysteriously as they had arrived.

Various theories have been put forward in an attempt to explain the bizarre phenomenon, but to date no satisfactory answers have been found. Some commentators suggest that kangaroos in the United States are the shy descendants of animals that, on some unknown occasion in the past, escaped from a circus or zoo. One rational explanation is that they are native marsupials not yet officially discovered or classified; however, the only evolutionary ancestors come from South, not North, America.

Not surprisingly, some people believe that the mystery animals of North America are paranormal manifestations of some kind. But that might be jumping to conclusions.

PART

5

THE ENIGMA
OF SPACE

UNDER THE SUN

The solar influence on the earth

IT WAS IN 1611 that the telescope was first used, by Galileo, to look at the sun. Although philosophers had taught that the sun was unblemished and unchanging, Galileo's telescope revealed that the surface was covered with spots. In addition, the number of spots grew and then decreased within an average cycle of 11 years. The phenomenon remains true today as it has, perhaps, since the birth of the sun.

The maximum number of spots present during each cycle varies. For the period between 1640 and 1700, there were very few, although the 11-year cycle was still discernible. Intriguingly, this period coincided with what came to be called the latest phase of the Little Ice Age on earth—unprecedented cold years when the Thames River in England and the Zuider Zee in the Netherlands froze. Speculation about possible links between solar activity and earthly affairs has existed ever since.

Some of the suggested relationships are very dubious. Enthusiasts claim to have found the rhythm of the sunspots in everything from the occurrence of earthquakes to the fluctuations in stock-market prices, the number of admissions to mental institutions, suicide rates, and declarations of war. Other people even claim that the 11-year cycle can be found in the statistics describing the number of driving licenses that are issued annually.

Other research by an Italian professor, Giorgio Piccardi, suggests that the speed of chemical reactions in ordinary water also varies according to sunspot activity.

More controversially, a Japanese researcher, Dr. Maki Takata, claims that the time it takes laboratory samples of blood to clot varies with the sunspot cycle.

Strange but true

True, some events on earth are unquestionably linked with the sunspot cycle. When sunspots are at their maximum, the entire sun is more active. It is slightly brighter—by about 0.1 percent—than when sunspots are at a minimum. Also, the gigantic eruptions of hot gas from the surface of the sun—solar flares—are more numerous. When the electrically charged particles flung out by the flares enter the earth's magnetic field, they create magnetic "storms," and compasses become unreliable.

Unusually intense and widespread luminous displays, such as the aurora borealis, are also common during these periods of activity, and radio and telephone communications can be interrupted. Even changes in the rate at which the earth rotates can be related to sunspot activity

Scientific research also links variations in sunspot numbers with annual rainfall. Tree rings offer a reliable method of measuring past rainfall. A fresh ring forms in the trunk every year; its thickness depends on the amount of rain that fell during the growing season—and the formation of rings reflects the pattern of sunspot activity that has occurred during the entire life of the tree.

Sedimentary evidence

An equally impressive relationship is found in rocks in southern Australia that are 680 million years old. Each of the fine, reddish bands in the rocks is a record of the sediment that was laid down on a lake bed in one year; over the millennia, the sediment has been transformed into rock. That the bands regularly vary from thick to thin and back to thick again in a pattern closely resembling that of the sunspot cycle, confirms that the young sun behaved much as it does today.

Among suggested explanations for the link between the formation of sedimentary rocks and the activity of sunspots are that either the sun was warmer in the past, or that more heat reached the earth's surface because the atmosphere had little oxygen and no ozone layer to protect it. Extreme variations in the brightness of the sun over an 11-year cycle would lead to more dramatic changes in the spring thaw, and therefore in the quantities of silt that rivers and streams would transport down to the lake beds.

Whatever effects the sun has had on the earth in the past, it still seems plausible that the sun could affect a wide range of processes in living beings today. In the words of Dr. Takata, man might very well be "a living sundial."

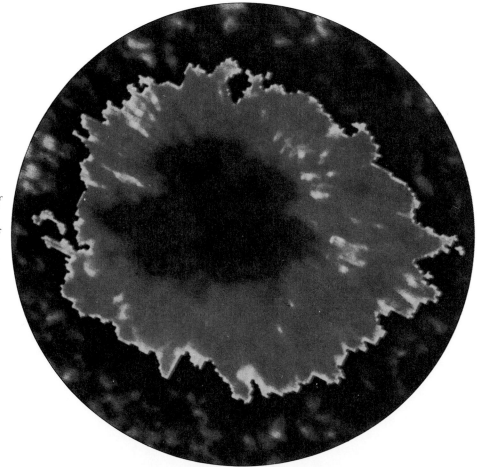

FACE OF THE SUN *Seen with the naked eye, the sun is a yellow ball, occasionally blemished with darker spots. The sunspots are created by intense magnetic forces that push up streams of gas from deep within the core. They appear darker because they are cooler. This photograph of a sunspot was taken from the space shuttle in July 1985. Its colorful appearance is due to computer enhancement, which reveals subtle variations in temperature that are not understood by astronomers as yet. This sunspot has a diameter of 10,000 miles, although spots as wide as 100,000 miles have been observed from earth.*

THE CHANGING BODY

Living in zero gravity

AFTER SOVIET COSMONAUTS Valery Ryumin and Vladimir Lyakhov had completed their record-breaking 175 days on board the *Salyut 6* space station in 1979, they seemed to be in poor shape. For four days they were unable to stand unaided, they sweated profusely, their hearts raced, and they suffered giddiness and nausea. Only after a six-week program of therapy and total rest were they pronounced fit again.

The cosmonauts were experiencing the adverse effects of prolonged exposure to zero gravity, or weightlessness. In space the heart becomes weaker because, without the resistance of gravity, it does not have to work as hard to pump blood. Internal organs in the abdominal cavity float slightly out of position. And the mechanisms responsible for balance and orientation are severely disrupted. For example, an astronaut climbing a ladder may have the sensation that he is descending, headfirst.

Worst of all, the skeleton deteriorates rapidly in the absence of gravity; the bones lose calcium, and become weaker and more brittle. After only seven days of weightlessness, eight-week-old rats on board the U.S. *Spacelab 3* in 1985 suffered a marked loss of bone mass and strength and a 40 percent deterioration in muscle power.

If the effects on the rats are a guide, young human beings are more at risk than their elders. Scientists believe that the effects on a developing fetus would be even more drastic.

Future generations of humans perfectly adapted to life in space would probably be short, round, and have brittle bones. They would be almost helpless if they ever returned to earth.

LIFE IN A DEEP FREEZE

Does Antarctica hold a clue to life on Mars?

SCIENTISTS SEEKING to determine whether life once existed on Mars believe that the perennially frozen lakes of Antarctica may provide the answer.

According to astrophysicist Dr. Christopher McKay and biologist Dr. Robert Wharton of the Ames Research Center at the University of California at Berkeley, the Antarctic lakes resemble some that existed on Mars in the distant past. Life has been found in Antarctica; could there once have been life on Mars?

Warmth for life

Recent research indicates that primitive life arose on Earth in the first 500 million years of its existence, when the environment was warm and wet. And indications are that Mars, too, was very warm and wet during its first 500 million years. Therefore, it is reasonable to suppose that microorganisms could have evolved on Mars just as they did on Earth.

While Earth's atmosphere stabilized and more complex organisms developed, for reasons not yet understood the atmosphere on Mars cooled off. This would have destroyed any early life-forms, but the research conducted by McKay and Wharton in the Antarctic suggests that fossil evidence of life on Mars could still be found locked up in lakes that gradually froze and dried up.

Although the Antarctic lakes are covered with a thick layer of ice, the temperature of the water beneath is comparatively warm all year round. Single-celled plants and microorganisms live there, descendants of primitive life-forms deposited by the wind when the lakes were formed hundreds of thousands of years ago.

McKay and Wharton believe that these conditions could have existed on Mars. Although there is little surface water on the planet today, it seems to have been more abundant in the past. Great canyons have been carved out, apparently by water action, and on their floors sedimentary layers mark the levels of successive lake beds.

The next step is to find a way of establishing how sediments are preserved in the Antarctic lakes and to identify the remains of dead microorganisms there. Then, say the scientists, they can use the same techniques to study similar sediments on Mars and discover if life could have existed.

The research team makes no claim to be searching for clues to life on Mars today; the aim is to discover if there ever *was* life. And if so, how did it end? If that question can be answered, it may further our understanding of the solar system.

WAVES FROM SPACE

In search of the elusive gravity waves

I N 1687 THE ENGLISH PHYSICIST Isaac Newton published his work formulating the laws of gravity. He described it as a universal force that all objects exert on others by reason of their mass. Gravity made the apple fall on Newton's head, and it kept the planets in their orbits around the sun.

Newton's laws became the cornerstone of the way scientists perceived the universe for more than two centuries. For Albert Einstein, however, they were not sufficient. Newton's theory explained how the *force* of gravity affected objects, but it did not explain what *gravity* was.

According to the complex mathematical logic of Einstein's general theory of relativity, gravity is a form of radiation emitted by accelerating bodies. Therefore, it should be detectable as waves moving through space at the speed of light, creating minute, fleeting deformations in a solid or liquid object as they pass.

However, despite the theoretical existence of such waves, none had ever been detected. In practice, only waves generated by massive bodies under extreme acceleration—such as double stars collapsing into each other, or matter rushing into a black hole—were thought to be strong enough to be observed. Gravity waves emitted during less violent circumstances were thought to be so weak that they were virtually nonexistent.

Detecting the undetectable

The search for gravity waves began in earnest in the early 1960's. American scientist Joseph Weber built two gravity wave antennas consisting of large cylinders of pure aluminum. To these he attached highly sensitive vibration detectors; he hoped they would register any gravity waves passing through the antennas. In 1969 Weber announced that he was recording one gravity wave daily. But other researchers were unable to confirm or duplicate his results. Nevertheless, the Weber method is still applied in the search for gravity waves today.

Modern gravity wave antennas are rods made either of aluminum or of the metal niobium. The rods are isolated from the slightest external shock and cooled to $-460°F$. At that temperature the aluminum atoms almost cease to vibrate. Within the cylinder, vibrations of less than the diameter of the nucleus of an atom can be registered.

In May 1986, results were compared from three gravity detectors—two in the United States and one in Europe. Although each recorded 60 to 70

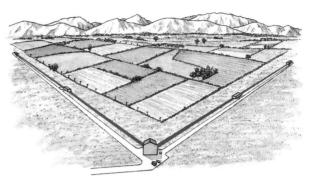

DETECTING GRAVITY *Using recent laser technology, a group of British scientists are planning to build a gravity wave detector in Scotland. The L-shaped detector will consist of two vacuum tubes, each nearly a mile long; rods of aluminum will be suspended inside. Laser beams trained on the rods will be able to detect the slightest movement—as little as 1/10,000 the size of an atomic nucleus—as the aluminum responds to any gravity waves passing through it.*

disturbances a day, none of the observations coincided exactly. The researchers' conclusion: no gravity waves had been detected after all.

Measuring the universe

However, scientists remain convinced that the search for gravity waves is not a wild-goose chase. Today plans are under way to construct a new generation of detectors that will use laser technology to achieve levels of accuracy many times greater than that of current equipment.

Plans exist to build two of the new instruments in the United States and one each in Germany and in Scotland. The designers predict that not only will the equipment record gravity waves for the first time but that it will continue to do so on a regular basis. Working in unison, the detectors will, in addition, act as a kind of gravity telescope, able to pinpoint black holes, neutron stars, binary star systems, and other sources of gravity waves.

One result of these observations will be that astronomers can calculate, to an accuracy of about 3 percent, the distance that waves have traveled from their source. Armed with this information, scientists will have a far more accurate idea of the true scale of the universe.

If everything goes as planned, gravity waves may at last cease to be objects of purely theoretical interest and prove to have practical application. But first, they must be found.

STAR GUIDES

The idea of using the stars to navigate on land is not new. Today, however, astronomers believe they may actually be able to use them to navigate through space. The main instruments in this venture will be tiny objects known as pulsars.

First discovered in 1967, pulsars are rapidly rotating condensed stars, formed from the core of dead stars. They were named pulsars because they emit radio waves, or pulses, in the form of light beams.

The pulse coming from each was analyzed and each was found to be unique—a kind of "cosmic signature" by which one can identify an individual pulsar. In addition, it was observed that the interval between the emission of pulses was actually increasing. In other words, the pulsars are gradually slowing down—at a rate of, on average, one-thousandth of a second every thousand years.

Many experts have suggested that these discoveries may be put to further use in the future exploration of space. They believe that the unique radio signature of pulsars could be programmed into the memory bank of the computers that control unmanned space probes and could serve as a navigational point on missions to other stars.

Pulsars could also help to position space telescopes and other equipment with pinpoint accuracy. And the regularity of their pulses and the fact that astronomers know exactly the rate at which each is slowing down could make them ideal as external checks on the precision of timing devices on board spacecraft.

Early explorers on earth used the sun and the stars to navigate and tell time. Perhaps pioneers to the stars will use pulsars in very much the same way.

MISSIONS TO VENUS

Probing the inferno of the hothouse planet

VENUS IS OUR NEAREST neighbor in space, and the planet closest in size to our own. But there the comparisons end. The Venus revealed by recent space probes in many ways resembles a medieval vision of hell. Its surface is roasted at temperatures of more than 900°F, the atmospheric pressure is more than 90 times greater than that of Earth, and the "air" is a thick smog of carbon dioxide and sulfuric acid.

A great deal of what is known about this most inhospitable of planets comes from the Venera spacecraft program of the U.S.S.R., started in the 1960's. In addition, the United States has surveyed the planet with Pioneer probes and with other unmanned vehicles.

The first Venera probes did not survive the journey through the Venusian atmosphere to the surface, although in 1967 *Venera 4* transmitted data for 94 minutes before burning up during its descent. In 1970 *Venera 7* landed on the surface and broadcast for 23 minutes before being destroyed, and in 1982 *Venera 13* landed and transmitted for 127 minutes. The data sent back included two color photographs of the flat, desolate terrain.

Two American Pioneer craft arrived at Venus in 1978. One was an orbiter that sent back radar observations of the surface of the planet and measurements of its upper atmosphere.

The second Pioneer was a "multiprobe," consisting of a "bus" with four smaller probes that transmitted data while falling through the atmosphere. One probe survived the impact of landing to transmit from the surface for 67 minutes.

These achievements may seem modest compared with those of the missions to the moon and to Mars. Yet building instruments to withstand the extreme conditions on and around Venus represents a remarkable feat of engineering, and one that has yielded some fascinating results.

Mapping Venus

The radar mapping of Venus by the orbiting Pioneer revealed surface details of areas as small as 60 miles. Because of the extreme temperatures, there is no surface water on Venus. The planet is very smooth, much of it covered by a flat rolling plain; only about 10 percent of the area consists of highlands. The largest upland region is Ishtar

Terra, about the same size as Australia. At Ishtar's eastern end are the Maxwell Montes, the highest mountains on Venus; they rise some seven miles above the surface, higher than Mount Everest.

But scientists are most interested in two other highland areas—Beta Regio and the Scorpion's Tail—which they suspect may contain active volcanoes. A sudden fiftyfold increase in the amount of sulfur dioxide in the atmosphere detected in 1978 is thought to have been the result of a massive volcanic eruption some 20 times more powerful than that of Mount St. Helens in 1980.

Much remains to be learned about what lies beneath the clouds of Venus, but conditions there make it extraordinarily difficult to uncover new information. However, in 1985 the U.S.S.R. adopted new tactics in its exploration of the planet.

Venus rotates on its axis very slowly; a Venusian day lasts 243 Earth days. But its atmosphere moves very quickly, as winds of up to 250 miles per hour circle the planet in just four Earth days.

The U.S.S.R. made good use of these winds. As the spacecraft *Vega 1* and *Vega 2* flew past Venus, balloons were dropped from the craft. For 46 hours they floated 33 miles above the surface of Venus.

Conditions are more tolerable at this height: the atmospheric pressure is about half that of Earth's at sea level, and the temperature is a comfortable 90°F, although the balloons still had to withstand the corrosive sulfuric acid of the planet's clouds.

The missions were successful. For the present it seems that floating experiments above the hellish surface conditions is probably the best strategy for getting a long look at Venus.

THE INCONSTANT SUN

Is the sun going out?

NEW EVIDENCE FROM the heart of the sun is forcing astronomers to question one of their fundamental beliefs: that the sun is a constant, stable body that has been shining steadily for most of the 5 billion years of its existence.

The challenge to this idea comes from the study of neutrinos, tiny particles produced in the heart of the sun. They occur as a by-product of the thermonuclear reaction that turns hydrogen into helium and releases the solar energy that sustains all of life on earth.

The ghost particle

The neutrino is an almost ghostlike particle. It has no electrical charge and no mass, or only a minute amount. Neutrinos stream through matter as if it did not exist: some 25 million pass through every square inch of the earth every second. Only a very few react with the other particles they meet.

Elusive as neutrinos are, scientists have designed equipment to detect them. Each detector is buried deep underground in order to screen out other particles and some forms of radiation that bombard the earth's surface.

The world's first detector was set up in the Homestake Mine at Lead, South Dakota. It consists of a tank the size of a swimming pool filled with perchloroethylene (commonly used as a dry-cleaning fluid). Very occasionally, a neutrino reacts with one of the chlorine atoms in the liquid and produces a radioactive form of argon gas. Every

CATCHING THE SUN *The world's first neutrino detector is located deep in an abandoned gold mine in Lead, South Dakota. Smaller than atoms, neutrinos may hold clues to the processes taking place deep within the sun.*

argon atom detected indicates a neutrino strike and provides evidence of the nuclear reactions that are taking place in the core of the sun.

WIMP's and changelings

The sun has a surface temperature of about 10,000°F, and from this astronomers can calculate the amount of energy being released at the core and therefore the number of neutrinos they might expect to catch in the underground tanks.

If their theories are correct, researchers should have detected around 25 neutrinos per month. But the Homestake instrument has detected an average of only eight. The experiment has been repeated many times, and the results are consistent: about two-thirds of the neutrinos that should be coming from the sun are missing.

Why this anomaly? Is the sun changing? Some astronomers have argued that the expected number of neutrinos is produced, but that two-thirds of them change into a different type of neutrino before they reach the detectors on earth. (There are three types of neutrino, but equipment exists to detect only one kind.) No one has yet come up with a convincing theory to explain why these neutrinos should become "changelings."

Another possibility is that the sun's core is 10 percent cooler than has been calculated from the surface temperature. This, suggest some scientists, could be because hitherto unknown weakly interacting massive particles (WIMP's) are busy in the heart of the sun, diffusing its heat, lowering the average temperature, and reducing the number of neutrinos produced. In those circumstances, the stability of the sun over the long term would not be affected; it would remain constant.

Cycles of activity

It could also be that the sun *is* changing. Its core might be cooling and the effects may not have yet reached the surface.

Even if this is so, it would not mean that the sun would simply continue cooling until it faded out. Instead, as the core cooled, it would shrink slightly, releasing gravitational energy that would heat up the core once again. This heat would eventually find its way to the surface, and the sun would expand slightly as the core again cooled.

If the sun is a varying, changeable body, it raises disconcerting possibilities. A drop of 2 percent in the sun's surface temperature would plunge the earth into a major ice age such as the one that ended 11,000 years ago. A corresponding rise in temperature could melt the polar ice caps. The traditional idea of a constant, stable sun—true or not—is much more comforting to live with.

CLOSE ENCOUNTER

A mission to discover the secrets of a comet

IN MARCH 1986 a small fleet of spacecraft intercepted Halley's comet as it plunged through the inner solar system, 100 million miles from earth. The boldest of the robot explorers was a probe called *Giotto*. It flew close to the comet's heart and received a battering that knocked out nearly half of the instruments it carried. But mankind's first close encounter with a comet was triumphantly successful.

Halley's comet requires 75 years to travel its elongated orbit. For most of the time it is in the outer reaches of the solar system—a cold, dark object invisible to earthbound astronomers. But when Halley approaches the inner planets, the warmth of the sun drives off a cloud of gas and dust thousands of miles wide. The pressure of sunlight and the solar wind—a stream of electrically charged particles constantly flowing out from the sun—sweep the gas and dust out into a great tail, millions of miles long.

Before the Halley missions, the precise nature of comets was a mystery. Astronomers knew that comets were made up of material left over after the formation of the planets and their satellites, but the exact composition of comets remained obscure. Several explanations had been proposed. Most favored was the "dirty snowball" theory suggested by the American astronomer Fred Whipple in the 1950's. Whipple believed that the nucleus of a comet, hidden within the gas and dust of its head, consisted of a compact mass of ice, dust, and rock.

A violent core

Two Japanese probes, *Sakigake* ("Forerunner") and *Suisei* ("Comet"), and two Soviet ones, *Vega 1* and *2*, were the first to investigate Halley. The information they provided about its motion was used to guide *Giotto* on its near-collision course. Passing 5,000 miles from the comet, the Soviets' two Vega craft were the first to spot the nucleus.

Their television cameras revealed a potato-shaped object nine miles long and five miles wide that rotated end over end once every 53 hours.

On the side facing the sun, bright jets of gas mingled with dust that rose from the surface as ice was heated by sunlight and turned into vapor. Fortunately this violent activity subsided before *Giotto* met the comet. Otherwise the probe would have encountered an even fiercer dust storm.

The *Giotto* satellite, built by a British company and launched by a French Ariane rocket, carried experiments designed by British, French, and German scientists. It encountered the comet at a speed of 40 miles per second. A large two-layer dust shield surmounting the probe doubled as a dust detector, recording the impact of the minute grains of dust that bombarded the spacecraft.

Hazard in space

As *Giotto* plunged toward the comet's nucleus on March 13, its camera sent a stream of pictures back to earth. But just 12 seconds before the closest approach, impact from a dust particle set the probe wobbling. Its pencil-thin radio beam, which had been accurately pointed at the earth, swung wildly.

For 30 tense minutes, as the probe passed the nucleus at a distance of only 400 miles, scientists and engineers at mission control in Darmstadt, West Germany, thought that *Giotto* had been destroyed. Then the probe's automatic stabilizing equipment finally locked the beam back onto earth, and the stream of data resumed.

OBSERVING HALLEY *Although not as bright as on previous visits, Halley's comet was visible from earth when it made its recent appearance in the winter of 1985–86. Taken through the Schmidt telescope in Great Britain, even this high-speed photograph makes the stars appear to be streaks of light. The tail streams out behind the core of the comet.*

Of the 14 instruments on board, six had been knocked out, including the camera. But the remaining equipment continued to function and provide data that will keep scientists busy for years.

Some of the most important questions about comets have already been answered. Whipple's dirty snowball theory has been confirmed: the icy part of the comet does consist of water mixed with frozen gases.

Most intriguing of all, the surface of the nucleus is coated with a layer of sooty material containing carbon. Probably no more than half an inch thick, it makes the nucleus one of the darkest bodies in the solar system. Since such materials can be produced by living matter, scientists conjecture that bacteria may live on comets and spread diseases to earth.

The working lives of the comet probes are not yet over. *Vega 1* and *2* are continuing their journey to take a close-up look at the asteroid Adonis, another little-changed relic of the early days of the solar system. And in 1992, after six years of orbiting the sun, *Giotto* will be directed toward a comet called Grigg-Skjellerup. The goal is to discover whether Halley's comet is unique or just like the thousands of comets that swarm around the sun.

INTERCEPTING HALLEY

THE APPEARANCE OF HALLEY'S COMET in 1986 was its first since the dawn of the modern space age. To ensure that the world could learn as much as possible about this infrequent visitor, scientists from many countries tried to make the best use of the latest available technology.

Launched by the European Space Agency, *Giotto* was the most ambitious of five spacecraft. After an eight-month journey, it reached the comet around midnight on March 13, 1986. Traveling in opposite directions around the sun, *Giotto* and Halley met only briefly; an intensive program of scientific observation had to be carried out in just a few hours.

Perhaps the most valuable of *Giotto*'s many instruments was its highly sensitive television camera. Controlled by three microprocessors, the camera could rotate through 180 degrees. This flexibility enabled it to search for the nucleus of the comet and automatically follow its course.

At right is one of the many photographs *Giotto* sent back to earth. Even though partially obscured by dust and the blaze of light from the sun, the dark mass that forms the comet's solid core could not escape the penetrating eye of the camera.

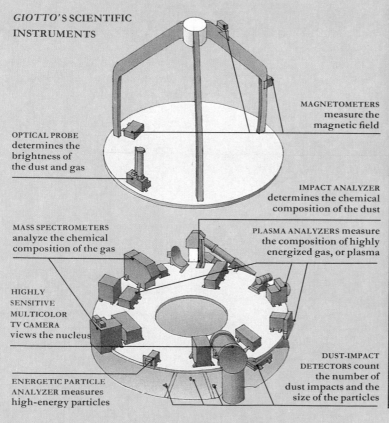

GIOTTO'S SCIENTIFIC INSTRUMENTS

MAGNETOMETERS measure the magnetic field

OPTICAL PROBE determines the brightness of the dust and gas

IMPACT ANALYZER determines the chemical composition of the dust

MASS SPECTROMETERS analyze the chemical composition of the gas

PLASMA ANALYZERS measure the composition of highly energized gas, or plasma

HIGHLY SENSITIVE MULTICOLOR TV CAMERA views the nucleus

DUST-IMPACT DETECTORS count the number of dust impacts and the size of the particles

ENERGETIC PARTICLE ANALYZER measures high-energy particles

THE SPACECRAFT *Nearly 10 feet high, and 6 feet 2 inches in diameter, Giotto weighed 2,116 pounds when launched. By the time it reached Halley, its weight had been reduced to 1,213 pounds because of spent fuel. Spinning at 15 revolutions per minute to maintain its stability, Giotto's radio antenna always pointed toward the earth. Its forward-facing dust shield was able to deflect particles that struck it at speeds as high as 42 miles per second.*

WHERE THERE'S HOPE...

The continuing quest for life on Mars

WHEN THE UNITED STATES landed two Viking space probes on the surface of Mars in July and September 1976, scientists hoped to end a century of speculation. The probes had one major task: to search for life.

While no one expected to find the bug-eyed monsters of science fiction, many scientists did believe that the planet had to support some form of life, if only of a primitive kind.

The Viking probes were equipped with nine-foot-long robot arms. These were to scoop up samples of the soil, which were tested for any signs of life in experiment chambers on board the spacecraft. The results of the tests were transmitted to scientists on Earth for analysis.

Samples of life?

The simplest test involved heating a sample of soil to see if the gases given off were typical of those found when organic material—containing carbon, as all living things do—is burned. But no organic substances whatever were indicated, even though some were expected to have been deposited at some time by meteorites or formed by nonbiological processes.

Scientists speculated that the reason for this was that Mars, unlike Earth, has no protective ozone layer. The Martian surface is bombarded by ultraviolet radiation from the sun, which destroys all living matter. Therefore, the top layer of soil has been rendered lifeless.

A more complex series of tests was designed to detect biological life.

LIFE ON MARS? *For years scientists have speculated that if life existed elsewhere in the solar system, it would be on Mars—a speculation that has been the source of endless inspiration for science fiction writers. At right: Hostile Martian beings invading Earth, as envisioned by an artist illustrating the H. G. Wells story* War of the Worlds. *In reality Mars is a cold, arid world where only microscopic life could survive. The goal of the Viking mission: to use biochemical tests to detect if such microbes exist.*

The first experiment involved dampening a sample of soil and then adding a rich "soup" of chemical nutrients. Scientists were astonished by the burst of oxygen given off when the soil was first moistened: it resembled the way that plants on Earth produce oxygen. Could it be that similar plant life existed on Mars?

But the effect persisted after the soil had been heated to temperatures that would have destroyed any living organism. And when the nutrients were added, the gases given off did not suggest the presence of any living thing. Scientists concluded that some unusual chemical factor in the Martian soil had been responsible for the oxygen burst.

In a second experiment, soil was placed in a chamber with a sample of Martian air, which consists almost entirely of carbon dioxide. Then radioactive carbon dioxide and carbon monoxide were added. If the soil gave off radioactive carbon gas, it could indicate that organisms in the soil were reacting with carbon from the atmosphere.

The first measurements showed radioactive carbon being emitted. But later experiments produced different results, and the researchers began to consider ways in which the initial reaction could have been created by inorganic processes.

The results of the third experiment were more exciting. Soil was covered with a solution of amino acids and carbohydrates that would be broken down if digested by any microorganism. Analysis of the gases given off indicated that some biological process *was* taking place. The process ceased when the soil was heated, and the level of gases decreased when the sample was stored on board the Viking lander—two indications that a living organism might be involved.

Yet close analysis revealed that the details of the reaction did not match the way that terrestrial organisms behave. The scientists were baffled.

Alone in the solar system?

Taking into account all the evidence from the Viking landers, and the way in which most of the results could be reproduced on Earth by non-biological means, a committee of the prestigious National Academy of Sciences was forced to conclude that the "Viking results have lowered the possibility of life on Mars."

Based on an additional 10 years' work on the Viking findings and other observations of Mars, Norman H. Horowitz, a principal researcher on the Viking missions, was ready to be categorical: "We have come to the end of the dream. We are alone in the solar system."

Most scientists agree. But there are dissenters. Gilbert Levin and Patricia A. Straat, who were responsible for the amino acid and carbohydrate experiment, believe that Martian life is still the most likely explanation of their results. The reasons: Martian life is likely to be different from that on Earth and thus difficult to detect. The nutrients provided may not have been suitable, or the concentrations too strong. Or, in digesting the nutrients, Martian organisms may have produced substances that the experiments were not designed to detect.

Or perhaps the probes landed in a part of Mars that was inhospitable to life. Or possibly Martian life exists deep underground, away from the harmful ultraviolet rays that fall on the planet's surface. Levin and Straat feel there are still too many unanswered questions to permit definite conclusions to be drawn.

The claims and counterclaims are not likely to be settled without further missions. And such missions are planned. Both the United States and the U.S.S.R. are scheduled to send unmanned probes to Mars in the 1990's. And there are persistent rumors that around the turn of the century the U.S.S.R. intends to launch a manned mission to Mars. Perhaps only then will the debate over the existence of life on Mars be settled.

THE CENTER OF THE GALAXY

Until recently, the center of the earth's galaxy, the Milky Way, was a mysterious region, hidden by great clouds of gas and dust. However, observations of X-rays, radio waves, and infrared radiation from the Milky Way have revealed some surprising facts about the galaxy of which our solar system is but a tiny part.

Analysis of infrared radiation recorded by satellite suggests that there is a tightly packed cluster of stars at the center of the galaxy, with huge clouds of dust spinning around at the center.

At the very heart, scientists have pinpointed a source of powerful emissions of radio waves, X-rays, and gamma rays. The total impression is one of intense activity that is quite unlike the stable picture of the Milky Way that astronomers had formed only 20 years ago.

Many astronomers believe that the explanation lies in a black hole at the center of our galaxy; it radiates energy as stars, cosmic dust, and gas are constantly being drawn into it. Since not even light can escape a black hole—its gravitational pull is too strong—no one has ever seen one. But we know that black holes exist by the behavior of stars and other matter in their vicinity.

Although the black hole theory may ultimately prove to be wrong, most astronomers think it is logical—until someone comes up with a better explanation.

THE MYSTERY OF ANTIMATTER

Mirror-image worlds in the depths of space?

ANTIMATTER MAY SOUND like something that was invented by a science fiction writer, but it does exist, although only for fleeting fractions of a second. Antimatter consists of antiparticles. They resemble such particles as electrons, neutrons, and protons—except that they have an opposite electric charge. Despite its short duration, antimatter poses some intriguing and important questions for physicists.

The story begins in the early 1900's, when scientists first started to explore the structure of atoms by smashing them at an extremely high speed. The atoms split into their component particles: the heavy protons and neutrons of the nucleus, and the smaller, lighter electrons that surround it.

Because electrons carry a unit of negative electric charge, theorists maintained that there had to be another particle—which they called a positron—with the same mass as the electron but an opposite electric charge. When they observed the positron in 1932, physicists saw that when an electron and positron met, they annihilated each other.

As atoms were made to collide at ever-higher speeds, more and more particles were discovered. Each seemed to have an equal and opposite antiparticle: antiprotons as well as protons, and antineutrons as well as neutrons. In the natural world, these particles sometimes form when a high-energy cosmic ray from the sun or another star strikes a particle of ordinary matter. But just as in the laboratory, any antiparticle created this way is short-lived; in the instant that the opposites encounter each other, both are destroyed.

Preponderance of matter

According to the logic of science, matter and antimatter should have been created in equal amounts in the early stages of the formation of the universe. But to date no one has been able to explain why our universe appears to consist almost exclusively of matter.

Some theorists speculate that the universe as a whole does in fact contain equal amounts of matter and antimatter, and that antimatter is concentrated in galaxies that are billions of miles away from those composed of ordinary matter. Antimatter stars and galaxies would produce light and other radiation in the same way that stars and galaxies in our universe do. Since the examination of radiation is, so far, the only method we have for studying distant galaxies, we are unable to determine whether or not they are made up of antimatter.

No one, however, has yet been able to theorize a process by which separate islands of antimatter and matter might have been created in the first place. Why did the two types not annihilate each other? Were forces at play in the early stages of the universe that prevented this?

One thing is certain. If there *are* antimatter worlds somewhere in space, close encounters of any kind are strictly prohibited.

GALILEO'S WORLDS

The moons of Jupiter

IN MARCH 1979 the *Voyager 1* unmanned spacecraft was approaching the great system of satellites surrounding Jupiter, the largest planet of the solar system. Scientists at NASA's Ames Research Center at the University of California at Berkeley had published the results of calculations they had made regarding conditions on Io, the innermost of Jupiter's four principal moons. Only days later they looked at the photographs that *Voyager* had sent back to earth and saw their predictions spectacularly fulfilled.

The scientists had calculated that because of the combined effects of Jupiter's gravity and that of Europa, the neighboring moon, Io would be stretched and squeezed continuously over millennia. The constant oscillations in the moon's shape would be violent enough to heat up its center and make Io a highly volcanic world.

But the cameras on board *Voyager 1* revealed that volcanic activity on Io was even greater than scientists had predicted; eight enormous volcanoes were erupting simultaneously. And the eruptions continued during the four months between the departure from Jupiter of *Voyager 1* and the arrival of its sister vehicle, *Voyager 2.* Umbrella-shaped plumes of gas arced 200 miles above Io's surface,

ERUPTING IO *In 1979, when* Voyager 1 *flew past Io, one of the moons of Jupiter, the spacecraft was able to observe volcanic activity on the surface at close range (right). Volcanoes on Io are far more violent than those on Earth, throwing out sulfurous gas and dust that moves as fast as 200 m.p.h. Because the gravity on Io is much less than on Earth, volcanic gases can rise more than 100 miles above the surface. Inset: A close-up look at an eruption.*

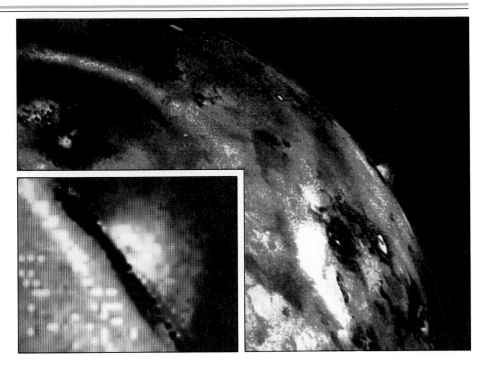

spraying huge areas with sulfurous compounds in shades of white, orange, and yellow.

This was just one of the probes' remarkable revelations about Jupiter's large moons, named the Galilean satellites, for the Italian scientist Galileo, who had observed them through the newly invented telescope in 1610. They must have developed in very different ways, for it was four extraordinarily diverse worlds that were recorded by the cameras of the Voyagers.

Io's neighbor Europa shows no trace of volcanic activity. By astronomical standards its light-colored, icy surface is as smooth as a billiard ball, the smoothest in the solar system. But it is crisscrossed by long, shallow cracks and low, curved ridges.

Scientists think the cracks were caused when Europa's interior heated up, just as Earth's has; but the origin of the ridges, no more than 1,000 feet high and unique to Europa, remains a mystery.

Ganymede, the third moon from Jupiter, is the largest satellite in the solar system. On its icy surface, large dark areas with numerous craters testify to the pounding that all planets and moons endured during the formation of the solar system nearly 5 billion years ago.

And between the dark areas, parallel ridges and valleys that have been formed from lighter material stretch for hundreds of miles. Scientists have yet to discover what happened on Ganymede to create the two different kinds of landscapes.

The fourth major moon, Callisto, is probably the most heavily cratered celestial object known. Its scarred face has survived almost unchanged from the early days of the solar system. Many of its craters are 60 miles across. At some remote time in the past, an enormous object hurtled into Callisto, shattering, melting, and vaporizing millions of tons of surface material and creating an enormous series of ripples named the Valhalla Basin. The ripples form no less than 15 rings; the outermost is nearly 2,000 miles in diameter.

Taking a second look

Eager to find out more about these distant worlds, astronomers have designed an investigation to be carried out by the next spacecraft to visit Jupiter. Appropriately named *Galileo,* the craft will go into orbit around the planet for about two years. It will monitor the volcanic eruptions on Io and should be able to provide the information scientists need to work out just what happened to create the landscapes of Ganymede and Callisto.

But it is perhaps the results of *Galileo*'s examination of Europa that the scientists will await most eagerly. Beneath the frozen ice covering the surface may lie oceans of water, warmed by the heat of radioactive rocks. And just as life formed in the oceans of Earth, life of some kind may have developed in the seas of Europa.

Although this is only speculation, one thing is certain: *Galileo* has exciting tasks to perform.

CHASING THE SUN

A supersonic celestial observation

WHEN THE MOON passes between the earth and the sun, it casts a huge shadow over the earth as it blocks out the sunlight. For those at the edge of the shadow (the penumbra) the eclipse is partial; the moon seems to take a bite out of the sun as it passes. But observers standing in the center of the shadow (the umbra) see a spectacular solar eclipse.

Unfamiliar and beautiful features become visible around the edge of the sun. The prominences—the reddish spikes that protrude from the sun beyond the dark edge of the moon—are columns of incandescent hydrogen; they extend thousands of miles above the sun's surface. The sun's halo, the pearly white corona, also becomes visible.

For less than eight minutes these wondrous aspects of the sun are revealed in an eerie twilight. Then the moon continues inexorably in its orbit around the earth, and the spectacle is over.

Suspending the eclipse

But on June 30, 1973, a group of astronomers was able to lengthen that eight minutes and take a longer look at the eclipse. They had the help of a newly built Anglo-French supersonic airliner, the Concorde, which at that time was not yet in commercial service.

The eclipse could be observed best along an arc across northern Africa. *Concorde 001* took off from Las Palmas in the Canary Islands, intercepted the moon's shadow over Mauritania, and then raced east at 1,260 miles per hour to keep pace with it.

Normally, the view for a Concorde passenger is restricted because the cabin windows are very small, but for this occasion special windows were installed in the top of the plane's fuselage. Measuring five inches in diameter and made of tough quartz glass and special plastics, the windows allowed instruments to be directed upward.

The narrowness of the view was amply compensated by its direction. The Concorde kept up with the moon's shadow as it raced across Mauritania, Mali, Algeria, Niger, and Chad. During this time, astronomers from the University of Paris photographed the eclipse through a telescope stabilized by gyroscopes. Other French scientists and a U.S. team from Los Alamos, New Mexico, used different techniques to study the corona.

British scientists examined the infrared light from the chromosphere, a relatively cool layer of hydrogen that shrouds the visible corona. They studied the convective movement of the gas, rising and falling as it is driven by the heat of the sun.

Such observations were made possible by the clarity of the view from the Concorde as it soared high above the haze of the lower atmosphere and above much of the ozone layer, which absorbs infrared light from the sun. Although nothing surprising was revealed, the scientists had a unique opportunity to study the phenomenon of a total eclipse, and to observe the sun while the moon hid its extremely harmful glare.

Concorde 001 kept up with the path of the eclipse for 74 minutes before breaking away to land at Fort-Lamy in Chad. The brief spell of celestial suspended animation had ended. It will be the year 2150—when the next suitable eclipse occurs—before a successor can equal the Concorde's feat.

IS ANYBODY OUT THERE?

The search for extraterrestrial intelligence

PEOPLE HAVE SPECULATED about the existence of extraterrestrial life for thousands of years. Today we know that within our solar system the earth is almost certainly unique in supporting intelligent life. But our solar system is only a tiny part of the universe: there are millions of stars in our galaxy, and around some may circle planets with life—even intelligent life.

No matter where we look in the universe, we find that everything is composed of the same chemical elements in much the same proportions. And stars, nebulae, star clusters, and galaxies are found throughout. The same chemical and physical processes operate. The "sameness" of the universe implies that life elsewhere could be similar to life on earth. The sheer size of the universe makes it likely that the same conditions that produced life on earth could be present elsewhere.

Scientists believe that in the depths of space millions of earth-type planets are revolving around sun-type stars at a distance that provides the right conditions for life. However, obtaining proof of the existence of such planets presents immense practical problems. Any planet would be visible only from the faint reflected light from its parent star—and this would be lost because of the glare from the star itself. The difficulty has been compared with trying to distinguish between a candle and a searchlight when the two are side by side and being observed from many miles away.

More hope lies in studying the infrared radiation that a planet would emit. In this case the comparison becomes more like looking for a flashlight instead of a candle next to the searchlight.

Detection in space

Because the earth's atmosphere filters out infrared radiation, any search for new planets has to take place in space. The Infrared Astronomy Satellite (IRAS), launched as a U.S.-British-Dutch venture in 1983, is undoubtedly the most important tool available. In orbit above the atmosphere of the earth, the satellite has detected thousands of new infrared sources and analyzed others in far greater detail than had previously been possible with earthbound equipment.

IRAS has sent back information that certain stars are emitting slightly higher levels of infrared radiation than had been expected. Astronomers believe that this excess is due to dust and gas clouds that surround the stars. Optical studies of one of the stars, Beta Pictoris, reveal faint wings, probably the side view of a disc-shaped dust cloud—the kind of cloud from which our planet was formed.

Wobbling stars

If bodies as large as planets are hidden within these dust clouds, their gravitational pull would make the stars appear to wobble across the sky over the years. Since a star is more massive than any planet, the effect would be very slight.

Many wobbling stars have been observed, but in most cases the effect is too great to be the result of planetary influence. Instead, the wobble seems to be caused by the pull of a small companion star. For those wobbling stars where the effect *may* be due to the pull of a planet, more evidence is needed.

The evidence could well be provided when NASA launches the space telescope in the 1990's. Free from the interference of the atmosphere of the earth, the telescope's optical equipment will be powerful enough to obtain images of unprecedented clarity and detail. If there is a planet circling Barnard's Star, six light-years away, the telescope should be able to detect it.

The next step, if such a planet is found, is for scientists to analyze its atmosphere by attaching a spectroscope to the telescope. The detection of

LISTENING FOR LIFE IN SPACE *NASA scientists have erected a series of radio antennas, such as the one at left in Goldstone, California. It is hoped that the antennas will detect radio signals sent out by any other civilizations in space.*

large amounts of oxygen would be evidence of plant life. Oxygen is a highly active element that would soon combine with other substances and disappear as an independent element unless it were continually being replaced by plant life. Careful study might reveal the traces of other gases, also the product of biological life.

The discovery of life-bearing planets would strengthen the probability that there is intelligent life elsewhere in the galaxy. How could we find positive evidence of its existence?

Broadcasting to the cosmos

For some 50 years, signals from radar and broadcasting systems on earth have been leaking into space. Any technologically advanced civilization may have noticed that there is a lot of energy being emitted on the wavelengths these systems use. Such a civilization would know that this amount of activity would not occur naturally and must be taken as evidence of deliberate, intelligently controlled radio traffic emanating from a planet bearing intelligent life.

Other intelligent species may be sending out radio signals, too. Astronomers in various parts of the world, attempting to discover such signals, have accumulated 120,000 hours of observations. So far they have found nothing—but they have covered only a tiny fraction of a myriad of possible frequencies and locations.

A program being established by NASA will eventually cover an area 10 million times larger than that investigated so far. Using specially designed equipment, it will focus on some 1,000 carefully chosen sun-type stars. The hope is to detect radio signals. The equipment will also scan the entire sky over a wide range of frequencies. Although each point will be observed for only a few seconds, the survey will increase the probability that all potential sites for intelligent life have been examined.

Whether or not the NASA program will find evidence of extraterrestrial life is unknown. But there is one certainty: if intelligent life is found elsewhere, the outlook of the human race will never again be the same.

THE RINGED PLANET

Until the two Voyager spacecraft flew by the broad sweep of Saturn's rings in 1980–81, scientists thought they understood them.

The Voyagers confirmed that the rings are not solid bodies, but consist of separate icy fragments. Some particles are tiny grains; others are as large as a house. However, the images sent back by the two spacecraft presented various new puzzles that have yet to be solved.

First, many of the photographs revealed more rings than had been previously observed. Each of the enormous main rings seemed to be made up of numerous smaller ringlets nestled one inside the other.

Astronomers thought they had found the reason for the ringlets when they analyzed photographs of the outermost, isolated F ring. Two satellites, too small to be

visible from earth, were near the ring. One was orbiting outside the ring; the other, just inside. Since the gravity of the satellites seemed to force the icy particles in the F ring to follow a narrow track, perhaps hundreds of unseen tiny moons were affecting the movements of all the ringlets? Yet none had been seen by the spacecraft. The enigma remains.

The first close-up pictures of the F ring further mystified scientists. The ring was not a smooth curve: it was irregular and had breaks at different points, giving it a braided appearance that was not in keeping with the orderly movements decreed by the known laws of gravity.

Many theories have been put forward to account for these anomalies. But it may be some time before Saturn yields all the secrets of its rings.

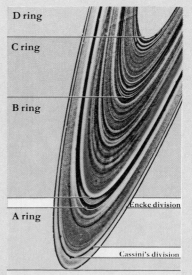

D ring
C ring
B ring
Encke division
A ring
Cassini's division
F ring

TOGETHER BUT SEPARATE
Probably no more than 400 feet thick, the rings of Saturn span more than 160,000 miles. Each ring differs from the others.

GALAXIES IN TURMOIL

Sources of power in the depths of space

IN RECENT YEARS astronomers have realized that some of the billions of galaxies scattered through space—a few in every hundred—are in violent turmoil at their cores. Huge quantities of light, heat radiation, radio waves, and X-rays pour out from the centers of these active galaxies.

One of the scenes of violent activity is a source of radio waves: Cygnus A. When the galaxy was first pinpointed in 1953, astronomers believed that its huge energy output was the result of the collision of two galaxies. But recent research indicates that Cygnus A, three times as wide as our own galaxy, with a thousand times more mass, is flanked by huge "lobes" of invisible matter that emit radio waves. These radio waves are a million times stronger than those emitted by our own galaxy.

What creates such activity in Cygnus A? Astronomers believe that two jets of electrically charged particles—two gigantic electric currents—are being fired out of the core of the galaxy in opposite directions. When the jets collide with intergalactic gas, they heat it up and create magnetic fields. The magnetic fields, in turn, force the particles into spiraling paths that emit radiation.

Power packs of the universe

What is responsible for the jets is a quasar. Through an optical telescope, quasars look like ordinary stars. But they pour out far more energy—actually more than many a galaxy, from an area no larger than the solar system. Quasar 3C 273, for example, is 20 times brighter than the galaxy in which it is embedded.

Some astronomers have suggested that a quasar is a young galaxy with a black hole at its center. Black holes are areas of intense gravitational strength in space that draw all surrounding matter into them; a black hole with the mass of the sun would be so dense it would be no larger than a baseball. As the massive gravitational pull draws matter into the black hole, intense amounts of energy are emitted. The jets consist of incandescent matter blown outward from the quasar and focused into beams by its magnetic field.

Another enormously powerful quasar lies in M87, a galaxy at the heart of the thickly populated Virgo cluster of galaxies. Astronomers believe that the stars of M87 are under the gravitational control of a black hole with the mass of 5 billion suns.

But there is another opinion. H. C. Arp of the Hale Observatories in Los Angeles claims to have detected "bridges of matter" that connect quasars with galaxies that are relatively close to earth.

If his theory is correct, quasars are nowhere near as distant as originally believed, and therefore are not as powerful. According to Arp and a growing number of supporters, quasars are large amounts of matter ejected from explosions at the heart of young, active galaxies.

Whatever quasars are, we could be seeing what happens when a galaxy is born. If, on the other hand, quasars *are* distant—the farthest may lie more than 15 billion light-years away—what we are observing today happened 15 billion years ago, which could offer important clues about the origin of the universe.

BIRTH OF THE MOON

Earth's companion in space

THE SIX MISSIONS to the moon between 1969 and 1972 did much to increase knowledge of its structure and its history. But the origin of the moon remains a mystery.

One theory suggests that the earth and moon were formed close together in space from smaller particles of gas and dust that swirled around a young sun. Analysis of lunar rock samples brought back by the Apollo astronauts reveals that, in some cases, they date back more than 4.6 billion years—as old as the earth itself. Both bodies may have been

formed at the same time. But if true, why then are earth and moon rocks of different composition? They contain the same elements and minerals, but in slightly different proportions. And why does the earth have a large molten iron core, while the moon has none at all, or only a very small one?

Descendant of earth

An alternative supposition is that the moon was originally part of the earth. While in a molten state, the young earth was spinning so fast that it bulged at the equator. The bulge grew larger and larger until the earth was shaped like a dumbbell; eventually part of it broke away to form the moon.

There are some problems with this theory. The earth would have had to be spinning implausibly fast for the moon to attain enough speed to escape the earth's gravity. And, if this had happened, the movements of the earth-moon system would be very different from those we observe today.

More dramatic is the idea that the moon was born in a different part of the solar system but for some reason was deflected into an orbit that brought it close to earth; eventually, it was captured by earth's gravity. This theory would explain the difference in the composition of the rocks. However, astronomers have difficulty explaining how the capture would have happened.

Worlds in collision

Of the rival theories, the one that many scientists consider the most likely is that the moon is a result of a planetary collision that took place during the early stages of the formation of the solar system.

Known as the giant impact theory, it suggests that a planet the size of Mars collided with the earth. Both the planet and the earth were still in a molten state; each had a core of dense rock with a layer of lighter rock on top. At the moment of impact, jets of molten rock were flung into space; in the course of time they coalesced to form the moon. Easily vaporized substances, including water, were driven out of the new moon by the fiery heat of its creation. The core of the colliding planet melted into the core of the earth.

At first, many astronomers resisted the giant impact theory because it depended on a highly improbable event. Some still refuse to accept it. But the advent of supercomputers has made it possible to work out what the composition of the moon should be if such an event had taken place. The facts fit the theory well.

Why are lunar rocks different from those of the earth? Because those on the moon contain a greater proportion of the colliding planet. The theory also explains why there is no water in lunar rock.

Further, the concept may provide a reason for why veins of heavy metals, such as gold and platinum, are found near the earth's surface. Had they been present in the earth from the beginning, they should have sunk deeper. But perhaps these precious metals arrived more recently—in the rogue body that sired the moon.

BEYOND THE FOURTH DIMENSION

Unraveling time and space

IN 1915, when Albert Einstein published a completely new explanation of gravity in his general theory of relativity, he presented the world with ideas that defied common sense.

According to Einstein, space and time are inextricably linked. Gravity, produced by curves in "space-time," can bend light, and one effect of traveling at the speed of light is that time slows down. Bizarre as they may seem, these conclusions have been confirmed through experiments.

One of Einstein's most revolutionary thoughts was that we live in a four-dimensional universe, consisting of the three spatial dimensions—length, breadth, and depth—plus time. Together they form a single entity, space-time. Today, however, some physicists are suggesting that we may in fact exist in 10 or 11 dimensions. But we cannot see them.

This speculation resulted from efforts to construct a single theory to explain the existence of the known forces in the universe: gravity; electromagnetism; the "strong" nuclear force, which holds the nuclei of atoms together; the "weak" nuclear force, which controls radioactivity; and a suspected "fifth force," which repels subatomic particles. The only way physicists could account for the coexistence of these different forces, however, was to postulate the existence of several extra dimensions.

Worlds within worlds

At first glance there seems to be no place for these extra dimensions to exist. But if we look closely at an object in the four dimensions of space-time, we get an idea of how other dimensions may be contained inside the world we know.

Consider the wing of an airplane. We can give an exact reference for the position of the wingtip in the four dimensions of space-time easily enough. For example, the time is 2:30 P.M. on Friday, May 13, 1994. The latitude is 36°N, the longitude is 113°W, and the wing is 29,000 feet above sea level.

Matters become more complicated, however, if we look through an electron microscope at the smooth, polished surface of that wing. It turns out not to be perfectly smooth at all, but to contain a variety of what appear to be towering peaks, huge rifts, and plunging valleys, littered with massive boulders and other debris.

To identify a point on one of the microscopic boulders at the wingtip, we have to provide two more figures in addition to those we already have: the "latitude" and "longitude" of the point we are seeking on the spherical surface of the boulder. Added to the four dimensions of space-time, this, say the theorists, gives us a total of six.

To the naked eye, however, the surface of the wing still seems to be two-dimensional. We know about the other dimensions of the boulder because of the electron microscope. Similarly, the additional dimensions of the universe have been detected thanks to our knowledge of subatomic particles and our ability to make mathematical calculations. But, for the theory to be mathematically sound, scientists need to postulate not just two but as many as six or seven extra dimensions in the universe. These additional dimensions exist on an unimaginably small scale. Even a subatomic particle can penetrate one of these dimensions only if it has extremely high energy—a level of energy that has not occurred since our universe was born.

Thus although we believe these extra dimensions existed at one time, we cannot verify them; they are inaccessible, wrapped up at the most fundamental level of matter. Physicists say that in the first few moments of the monumental explosion that created the universe, the necessary energy enabled particles to enter these dimensions. But as the universe cooled, and the energy of the initial explosion dissipated, matter continued to exist only in the four dimensions that we inhabit today. In effect, the other dimensions shrank.

While these dimensions may still exist in the universe, we, imprisoned within our four dimensions, can neither visualize them nor enter them.

BLAST FROM THE PAST

About 160,000 years ago, an enormous explosion lit the galaxy today known as the Large Magellanic Cloud. An aging star had ended its days as a supernova, dying in flames 100 million times brighter than the sun. But not until February 1987 did the light of that demise reach earth.

News of the explosion excited astronomers: it was the brightest supernova that anyone had been able to see from earth since 1604, and the Large Magellanic Cloud is the galaxy closest to the Milky Way. For the first time, astronomers were able to study a nearby supernova with modern, sophisticated instruments and test the accuracy of their theories about the birth and death of stars.

Scientists believe that the supernova will help them to determine whether the universe will collapse or will continue to expand forever. The event could give us advance knowledge of the future of the universe.

160,000 years old, this supernova was observed for the first time in 1987.

SHAKY DATA

You cannot check too often, and you cannot check too closely. This is a maxim most scientists take to heart. Astronomer Peter van de Kamp's work on wobbling stars pointedly illustrates the need for constant caution.

Beginning in the 1930's, Van de Kamp took many thousands of photographs of stars that are, relatively speaking, our near neighbors in space. Again and again he found that their tracks wavered in a regular manner, suggesting that an invisible companion, orbiting the visible star, was exerting a gravitational pull. Many of these companions were later discovered; they proved to be small, faint stars. But several could not be observed—they seemed so small that it was thought they had to be planets.

In 1968 one of Van de Kamp's students happened to compare the paths of nine of these wobbling stars to one another. He noticed that the unrelated stars seemed to be moving in suspiciously similar ways, a similarity too great to be coincidental.

After checking through the record books of the observatory, the student's doubts were confirmed. But it was not the stars that were wobbling; it was the telescope. He even noted that what was thought to be a jump in the usual positions of the nine stars coincided with an occasion when a major adjustment to the telescope had been made.

Van de Kamp accepted the student's evidence, rejected his previous work, and started over. He eventually published fresh claims of further discoveries of stellar companions, but checked his evidence more carefully.

His work on Barnard's Star, a faint red dwarf six light-years from Earth, led him to the conclusion that it does have two large planetary companions, one with about 70 percent the mass of Jupiter, the other with 50 percent. The launching of a powerful space telescope within the next decade should prove—or disprove—Van de Kamp's case.

RENDEZVOUS WITH A DISTANT GIANT

An encounter with Uranus

ALL THAT ASTRONOMERS can see of Uranus from Earth is the outer layer of the planet's dense atmosphere. Uranus is 32,000 miles in diameter—four times the size of Earth. But even under the scrutiny of the most powerful telescopes, it seems no more than a tiny blue-green disc. When the *Voyager 2* spacecraft swept past Uranus on January 24, 1986, it sent back the first detailed information about this distant world.

Unlike all the other planets in the solar system, Uranus orbits the sun lying on its side. Apparently something smashed into it billions of years ago and tipped it over. As a result, Uranus has two unique seasons: a resident living near one of the poles would experience daylight for 42 years followed by an equally long period of icy darkness.

Baffling anomaly

Information provided by *Voyager 2* shed little light on the reason for this oddity; in fact, it baffled scientists further. *Voyager 2* revealed that the planet's magnetic field is off-center and strongly tilted away from the axis of rotation. One magnetic pole is 75 degrees away from the geographic pole, while the other is 46 degrees distant—equivalent to the magnetic poles on Earth being in China and South America. Some scientists speculate that *Voyager 2* flew by Uranus during a period when the planet's magnetic field was flipping over and the magnetic poles were changing places.

Faint rings and new moons

Voyager sent back the first close-up pictures of the nine known rings around Uranus—discovered only in 1977—and revealed two more. Unlike the gloriously bright and broad rings of Saturn, those of Uranus are dark and thin. They consist of swarms of particles, probably made of rock and ice. But again, they differ from the rings of Saturn: they contain a proportion of frozen methane, which blackens when bombarded by cosmic rays.

Amazingly, the photographs from *Voyager* also revealed arcs, or "broken" rings. According to the laws of physics, the particles in these arcs should have spread around their orbits to create closed rings; why they have not remains a mystery.

Voyager 2 cameras also discovered that two "shepherd" moons flank the outer ring; their gravity holds the rings in place. But *Voyager* failed to reveal satellites for the other eight rings; possibly the moons were too small or too faint.

However, *Voyager* did find a further eight new moons beyond the rings and also gave astronomers a more detailed picture of the five moons that were already known. Like the material in the rings themselves, the five are all very dark.

Different worlds

The outer moon, Oberon, looked very much as expected. Its surface was dotted with craters of varying ages that meteors have created since the beginning of the solar system. One unexpected finding was a mountain 12 miles high, twice the size of Mount Everest.

Titania is the largest moon of Uranus; its diameter of 1,000 miles is roughly half that of Earth's moon. It has many comparatively young craters. But the oldest have been obliterated, probably as the surface melted (for unknown reasons); when it froze again, the surface swelled and cracked, much in the way that a water pipe bursts in freezing weather.

Umbriel, in contrast, appears to have only older craters. Scientists theorize that some unknown geological activity may have obliterated the more recent craters that must have been formed.

Ariel resembles Titania; the oldest craters on its young surface seem to have been wiped out by disturbances, such as lava flow.

The most violently active moon seems to have been tiny Miranda, only 300 miles across, one-seventh the diameter of the moon that circles Earth. Deeply ridged and furrowed, this miniature world reveals signs of old lava flows. And there are curious features, called chevrons and flapjacks, that appear to have been formed by the rising of oval-shaped plugs of rock.

Scientists have two possible explanations for the plugs. One is that Miranda once moved in a different orbit, closer to the other satellites, where it was heated by friction as their gravitational fields stretched and squeezed it. The other, that Miranda was smashed into several large chunks early in the formation of the solar system. As the orbiting fragments finally coalesced, lighter rocks rose over the denser rocks.

Astronomers have processed only a small amount of the information gathered about Uranus: much analysis has yet to be completed before the true outcome of *Voyager*'s exploration is known. As for *Voyager 2,* the spacecraft is headed deeper into space for a future rendezvous with Uranus's twin giant world, Neptune—more than a billion miles farther from the sun.

INSPECTING URANUS *On January 24, 1986,* Voyager 2 *passed within 50,000 miles of the cloud tops of Uranus, sending back the first detailed pictures of the planet's rings and moons. In this artist's impression, the bowl-shaped radio antenna of* Voyager 2 *is pointing toward earth. A platform with most of the scientific instruments is on the right-hand side, and the TV cameras are silhouetted against the planet.*

TO THE LIMITS OF THE SOLAR SYSTEM

The search for a 10th planet

BY 1996 FOUR AMERICAN SPACECRAFT will have broken out of the confines of the known solar system, 3,600 million miles from earth. Two Pioneer craft, launched in the early 1970's, and two Voyager craft, launched in 1977, have flown close by the giant outer planets and sent a wealth of data back to earth by radio.

In 1989 *Voyager 2* will encounter Neptune and then, like the other three craft, will travel beyond the orbit of the farthest known planet, Pluto. Their mission: to hunt for a world yet more distant, a planet astronomers have never seen but whose existence they have long suspected.

Predicting the planets

Such a planet could explain certain disturbances that have long puzzled scientists regarding the motions of known planets. Early in the 19th century astronomers found that Uranus, at the time the most distant known planet, was seemingly shifting its position in the heavens: it was sometimes behind, sometimes ahead of, its anticipated location. Astronomers believed that this anomaly was due to the gravitational pull of

another, unknown planet. An Englishman, John Adams, and a Frenchman, Urbain Leverrier, independently undertook the enormous calculations needed to work out its size and position. In due course a planet was found—in roughly the place they had predicted. It was named Neptune.

But astronomers soon realized that Neptune alone could not account for all the discrepancies in the orbit of Uranus, and the search for another planet began. It was not until 1930 that a new planet was found, by Clyde Tombaugh at Flagstaff Observatory in Arizona. It was christened Pluto.

Beyond the realm of Pluto

However, the mystery was still not solved. Pluto seemed to be tiny, and astronomers doubted its ability to create the irregularities in the orbit of

AN UNKNOWN PLANET? *Of the nine planets in the solar system, Pluto is the least well known. Deviations in the orbits of Pluto's two neighbors, Neptune and Uranus, were once attributed to the gravitational pull of Pluto, but today scientists realize that the planet is too small to exert such a force. Does another, 10th planet—yet undiscovered—lie beyond Pluto?*

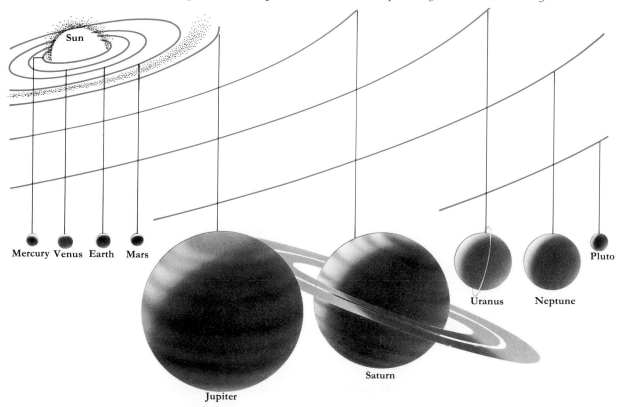

Sun   Mercury   Venus   Earth   Mars   Jupiter   Saturn   Uranus   Neptune   Pluto

Uranus—as well as newly discovered disturbances in Neptune's. Scientists' doubts were confirmed in 1978 when Pluto was found to have a satellite, later named Charon. The movement of Charon reveals that Pluto's mass is only a tiny fraction of Earth's; it is incapable of disturbing Uranus and Neptune.

So it was less the accuracy of scientific calculations than good fortune and the persistence of astronomers that led to the discovery of Pluto.

Most astronomers are convinced that yet another unknown planet must be responsible for the disorders in the paths of Uranus and Neptune. Indeed, there could be more than one. The sun's powerful gravitational field could hold planets in orbit to a distance 1,000 times greater than the distance of Pluto from the sun. Many planets may lurk out there; the distant sun illuminates most of them so faintly that telescopes on earth could never pick them out, even if astronomers knew in which direction to point them.

The search continues

Only the nearest of any undiscovered planets could produce noticeable deviations in the orbits of Uranus and Neptune. Even then they could do so only when they happened to be on the same side of the sun as the planets they were disturbing. Since such a planet would have an enormous orbit, taking at least 500 years to circle the sun, it could be centuries before one again indicated its presence.

Today the Pioneer and Voyager space probes offer new hope for finding a 10th planet—and perhaps others. Since they are headed into interstellar space in different directions, there is a chance that at least one of them will be in the same sector of the sky as an unknown planet. The tracking of the trajectories of the probes is so precise that if an unknown planet created a deviation of only a few miles, its presence would be revealed.

Were a planet to disturb the flight paths of one of the probes, astronomers would be able to determine not only the direction in which it lies, but also whether it is a large planet far from the sun or a small one closer in. A name for it has already been proposed: Persephone, the goddess whom Pluto kept prisoner in the underworld.

THE PLANETS OF THE SOLAR SYSTEM

The planets	Average distance from the sun in millions of miles	Average distance from Earth in millions of miles
Mercury	36	57
Venus	67	26
Earth	93	—
Mars	141.5	48.5
Jupiter	483	390
Saturn	886	793
Uranus	1,783	1,690
Neptune	2,793	2,700
Pluto	3,666	3,573

A NEW LIFE FORCE?

The mystery of cosmic rays

WHEN AUSTRIAN PHYSICIST Victor Hess ascended into the stratosphere in a balloon in 1912, he was hoping to throw light on a mystery that had been baffling his scientific colleagues for years.

In the laboratory, experimenters had found that an object that had been electrically charged would lose its charge, slowly but inexorably, no matter how well insulated it was from the ground. The reason? They believed that electrically charged particles in the air flowed into the object and neutralized the charge already present.

But what was generating such charged particles? Was it in the earth or somewhere outside it? Hess meant to find out. He could not possibly have guessed that his balloon flight was to mark the beginning of 20 years' work that would, in 1936, bring him the Nobel Prize in physics.

During the first 2,000 feet of his ascent, Hess's crude instruments showed that the number of charged particles in the air were decreasing—proof that some of them, at least, were being caused by something in the earth. (Today we know that it is the natural radioactivity of the earth's crust.)

But as he climbed higher, the number of particles increased again, indicating that at least some influence from the skies was involved. As Hess rose toward the outer atmosphere, he encountered an increasingly intense barrage of what he would later dub "cosmic rays."

Although the term cosmic rays is still used, it is in fact a misnomer. Rays are normally defined as the lines along which radiation travels. But cosmic rays have only a slight connection with radiation: they consist mostly of fragments of atoms, electrons, and atomic nuclei—with a few high-energy gamma rays—mixed together. Some cosmic-ray particles get to the ground, but most smash into atoms of the earth's atmosphere and produce some electrically charged particles that ultimately bombard the earth. Special instruments can detect both types of particles on earth.

Just one of the fast-moving cosmic-ray particles contains enough energy to lift the book you are holding one inch—a hundred million times more energy than the most powerful atom smashers now envisioned can give to a particle. Astrophysicists have long been investigating the source of cosmic-ray particles and what raises them to such speeds.

Unknown origins

In studying the origins of cosmic rays, one of the greatest problems scientists face is that the rays never journey in a straight line. Deflected by the magnetic fields between the stars, they follow twisted, spiraling paths, making it impossible to discover where they have come from.

Since it seems logical that the rays originate in regions of space where there is violent activity, it is to these that scientists have turned their attention. The likely source of cosmic rays, they believe, may perhaps be exploding stars, or supernovas, and fast-spinning pulsars; both may shed some fast-moving atomic fragments.

Studies of ancient rock and polar ice reveal the strength of cosmic rays that reached the earth's surface in the past. Samples up to 10 million years old show that the intensity has at times been 30 percent above the average of a particular period. The high levels probably occurred when supernovas exploded near the earth.

Cosmic mutations

The possible effects of cosmic rays have also intrigued scientists. It is known that radioactivity can cause mutations in the genetic material of living creatures. Given the similarity between cosmic rays and radioactivity, could cosmic rays—in combination with the radioactivity of the earth's surface—have had the same effects on life-forms? Scientists believe that this is a strong possibility.

Mutations are the raw material of evolution—and are often harmful. But occasionally they enhance the chances of survival for the organisms in which they occur. As beneficial mutations accumulate, the end result is the gradual modification of species and their transformation into different ones.

Increases in the intensity of cosmic radiation, while harming individual organisms, might have speeded up the rate of evolution. However remote the origin of cosmic rays, their continued effects on the earth may have been profound.

THE SCALE OF THE UNIVERSE

Measuring the cosmos

IN ORDER TO HAVE an accurate map of the universe, astronomers must use some scale of measurement. But units such as miles are far too small to be useful in measuring the vast distances of objects beyond our solar system.

Instead, astronomers use the light-year, the distance that a ray of light travels in one year. Since light moves at a speed of about 186,300 miles per second, a light-year is approximately 6 million million, or 6 trillion, miles.

The nearest star to the sun is Proxima Centauri, 4.25 light-years distant. The galaxy that contains our solar system has a diameter of about 100,000 light-years; beyond it lie other galaxies at distances of thousands of millions, or billions, of light-years away. The most distant of objects, the recently discovered quasars, are at the edge of the observable universe, 10 to 20 billion light-years away.

Although such vast distances seem impossible for the human mind to visualize in any meaningful way, they are essential for astronomers, who must find ways to calculate these figures accurately.

Close to home

To measure the distances to other planets in our solar system or to nearby stars, a simple method derived by the ancient Greeks is often used. Called the parallax method, it measures the position of a star from the earth and then takes another measurement at a later date after the earth has moved through space in its orbit around the sun.

The distance that the earth has traveled forms the baseline of a triangle, and the two readings of the star's position give the angles for the triangle's two other sides. Where the two sides meet is the location of the star; its distance from the earth can be calculated using simple geometry. The method is fairly precise for objects within a distance of some 8.6 light-years and somewhat accurate for objects as far away as 1,000 light-years.

The brightness factor

A different method for measuring the distance of a star from earth is to observe its brightness. A star may shine brightly because it is large and highly active, radiating great quantities of light; or it may be that a star is bright simply because it is a near neighbor. By differentiating between a star's actual and *apparent* brightness, its distance from earth can be accurately estimated by analysis of its light.

In the early years of this century it was noted that stars demonstrated characteristic patterns when astronomers split the light into its component wavelengths and created a spectrum of colors.

Today, by studying a star's spectrum through a spectroscope, astronomers can determine how hot or cold a star is. This in turn can help them discover whether what appears to be a small, faint star is in fact a distant, active giant. By comparing the light of one star with the light of another of similar activity that lies a known distance from earth, an expert can calculate how far away the star lies.

The redshift

Eighty years ago most astronomers believed that our galaxy constituted the whole of the universe, and that beyond it lay nothing but empty space. However, more powerful telescopes revealed that this picture was fallacious. The faint fuzzy patches that had been observed were recognized as entire galaxies, as large, and often larger, than our own.

The astronomer Edwin Hubble studied these galaxies in the 1920's, using the telescope at Mount Wilson, California, that is today part of the Hale Observatories. Hubble analyzed the spectra of the galaxies and discovered that the wavelengths of the component light were shifted toward the red end of the spectrum.

The so-called redshift indicates that the galaxies are traveling away from the earth. The change in wavelength is caused by the Doppler effect, the same phenomenon that makes the pitch of a car horn change as the car rushes past. The farther away a galaxy is, the greater the redshift. The more distant galaxies are moving faster and faster as the universe expands.

Astronomers have not agreed on the rate at which the universe is expanding. The most conservative estimate puts the figure at 10 miles per second per million light-years: a galaxy 500 million light-years away is receding at 5,000 miles a second. Others suggest a rate twice as fast.

If the first estimate is correct, then the most distant objects in the universe lie some 10 billion light-years from earth. Using the second figure, the scale of the universe doubles to an incredible 20 billion light-years.

Given such vast distances, it is no wonder that astronomers continue to seek methods that will provide a more accurate map of the universe.

DOWNED BY THE SUN

In 1979 the giant 77-ton space station *Skylab 1* was circling the earth at an altitude of 270 miles. During its first year in space, in 1973, three crews in succession had completed an immensely fruitful program of research, including detailed observations of the sun. Since that time, *Skylab* had been on its own.

Then its orbit began to decay as friction from the earth's atmosphere slowed it down bit by bit. But NASA scientists had plans to save the ailing *Skylab* and stop it from plunging back to earth. One of the first missions facing the space shuttle that was about to be launched was to attempt to boost *Skylab* into a higher orbit, where friction would be negligible.

But the sun played an unexpected part. A series of solar flares—massive outpourings of highly energetic particles from the sun's surface—disturbed the earth's magnetic field. As a result, the atmosphere swelled significantly, and friction for *Skylab* at its altitude increased; the space station slowed down dramatically. In July 1979, long before the first shuttle left its launchpad, *Skylab 1* crashed to earth.

The impending event had triggered an international alert along *Skylab*'s lengthy flight path, for the thousands of pieces of debris posed the possible threat of a major disaster. As it turned out, there was no loss of life; most of the debris fell into the sea and in unpopulated areas of Western Australia. The major loss was the millions of dollars' worth of hardware. So ended the 87-million-mile flight of the most sophisticated spacecraft of its time.

THE WORLD TOMORROW

NAVSTAR

The ultimate navigation system

GETTING LOST may be a thing of the past, thanks to an innovative navigation system being planned by the U.S. Department of Defense. Virtually anything or anyone, from missiles to mountaineers, needing a precise location on or above the earth will be able to benefit from the system, in all weather conditions and at any time of the day or night.

NAVSTAR, officially known as the global positioning system, will make use of a constellation of 18 navigation satellites orbiting the earth once every 12 hours at a height of 11,000 nautical miles and a speed of 5 miles per second. Only 6 of the satellites are currently in position, but the remaining 12 will be launched by the year 2000.

Precise fix

Existing navigation systems use fixed visible points, such as mountains or stars, from which to plot a position. But the NAVSTAR satellites will be continually moving and will send out a steady stream of radio signals. Each user of the system will be equipped with a receiver that will monitor the signals from two or more satellites. The receiver will then decode the signals and set out an exact map reference on a visual display unit. So accurate is NAVSTAR, users will be able to pinpoint their precise location and their altitude instantly.

Multiuse

The primary use of NAVSTAR will be military. There will be a detector to spot nuclear detonations, and a mechanism for steering advanced weapons, such as guided missiles, to specific targets. Tactical air strikes, recovery operations, and target bombing will all be helped by the precise information NAVSTAR can make available.

There will also be many commercial and industrial benefits. Energy savings will result from the availability of better navigation information to long-distance aircraft and ships; by taking shorter routes, they will save fuel. Someday motorists will also benefit from this navigation aid. In addition, NAVSTAR will be employed to help locate wrecks and hazardous wastes on the seabed. The system will be an invaluable asset of the 21st century.

NAVIGATION BY SATELLITE *By the year 2000, 18 special satellites will be in orbit around the earth, providing the most accurate navigation system to date. Users of the system, NAVSTAR, will be able to ascertain their position anywhere on or above the earth to within 10 yards, their speed to within a fraction of a mile an hour, and the time of day to within one-millionth of a second. Below: Close-up of a NAVSTAR satellite.*

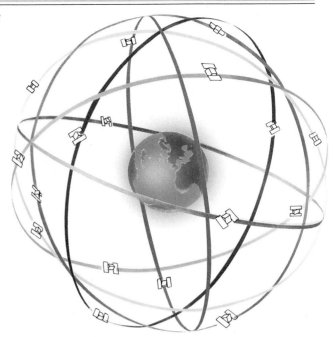

HAVING SECOND THOUGHTS

Sometimes, the less said, the better

"EVERYTHING THAT CAN be invented has been invented," wrote the director of the U.S. Patent Office to President William McKinley in 1899, and recommended that the president abolish the office. In 1958 the president of IBM, Thomas J. Watson, Jr., predicted: "There is a world market for about five computers." Experts do, it seems, have a talent for making bizarre errors in judgment about their own specialties.

The unimportant atom

After a series of brilliant experiments, in 1919 Ernest Rutherford succeeded in splitting the atom. In 1933 he wrote: "Anyone who looks for a source of power in the transformation of the atom is talking moonshine." The first atom bomb was detonated in New Mexico 12 years later, and in 1954 the world's first nuclear power plant was built at Obninsk, near Moscow in the U.S.S.R.

Pie in the sky

Professor Richard Woolley, Astronomer Royal, stoutly declared in 1957 that "the future of interplanetary travel is utter bilge." He was in good company. As early as 1920 *The New York Times* had pointed out that rocket pioneer Robert Goddard "only seems to lack the knowledge ladled out daily in high schools" because he believed that a spacecraft would operate in a vacuum.

As for flying to the moon, "the proposition appears to be basically impossible," observed Professor A. W. Bickerton in 1926. In 1936 J. P. Lockhart-Mummery clinched the argument: "The acceleration . . . from rockets . . . inevitably would damage the brain beyond repair." When *Apollo 11* landed on the moon in July 1969, the *Times* issued a posthumous apology to Goddard.

Horse sense

In 1875 the U.S. Congress denounced the gasoline-driven horseless carriage: "The development of this new power may displace the use of horses, which would wreck our agriculture."

Even interested parties could see no future in the internal-combustion engine. In 1896 the journal *Horseless Age* pronounced: "The vast majority of people would prefer a smooth-running, reliable steam-engine . . . to the evil-smelling, dangerous, wasteful, and at best uncertain and unreliable [gasoline] engine."

The Daimler-Benz automobile company might have disagreed. But in 1900 a spokesman reputedly announced that "there will probably be a mass market for no more than 1,000 motorcars in

Europe. There is, after all, a limit to the number of chauffeurs who could be found to drive them." By 1927 Henry Ford had sold 15 million Model T's.

Fuzzy reception

John Logie Baird encountered unexpected resistance when he tried to arouse interest in his new invention, which he called television. As he recalled in 1940: "They were convinced that the transmission of images—especially mentioning fog as an impediment—was impossible."

In 1936, after the world's first TV broadcasts in London, radio critic Rex Lambert wrote that "television won't matter in your lifetime or mine." As recently as 1948 radio pioneer Mary Somerville prophesied: "Television won't last. It's a flash in the pan." Newspaper editor C. P. Scott had the last word: "Television? No good will come of this device. The word is half Greek and half Latin."

Painfully wrong

Before the introduction of anesthetics, surgery was an agonizing experience for the patient and was limited mostly to amputations performed in haste. In 1839 the surgeon Alfred Velpeau concluded that "the abolition of pain in surgery is a chimera. It is absurd to go on seeking it today. Knife and pain are two words that . . . must forever be associated in the consciousness of the patient."

In 1847 James Young Simpson discovered the anesthetic properties of both ether and chloroform, opening the way to painless surgery.

Near misses

"No reader interest," was the judgment of the London publisher W. H. Allen on Frederick Forsyth's first novel, *The Day of the Jackal*. To date it has sold 8 million copies.

Frank Herbert's science fiction epic *Dune* was rejected by 13 publishers before the Chilton Book Company accepted it. Today sales top 10 million.

Once bitten

"Malaria has been licked," declared the World Health Organization (WHO) from its Geneva headquarters in May 1975. On the day of the announcement Dr. Thomas Lambo, deputy general of WHO, was rushed to the hospital. The diagnosis was malaria.

Dunces all

"He will never amount to anything," reported a Munich gymnasium (high school) about one of its pupils. His name: Albert Einstein.

Charles Darwin's father addressed his son this way: "You care for nothing but shooting, dogs, and rat catching, and you will be a disgrace to yourself and all your family."

Thomas Edison was labeled a "dunce" by his father and "addled" by his first teacher; one headmaster predicted that he "would never make a success of anything." Among Edison's inventions was the phonograph, which in 1915 he himself described as "not of any commercial value."

Long-winded

MGM rejected the novel *Gone With the Wind* with the observation: "No Civil War picture ever made a nickel." And a reader at 20th Century-Fox said: "To think they could hoodwink me with rot like that!" When producer David O. Selznick started to work on the film, the director refused Selznick's offer of a share in the profits, saying: "This picture is going to be one of the biggest white elephants of all time." Today the film is ranked as one of the highest grossing films ever made.

ONLY GOD AND ANGELS *Wrote Lord Kelvin, a leading scientist of his day, in 1894: "I have not the smallest molecule of faith in aerial navigation other than ballooning." He was not alone. "It is only given to God and angels to fly," said Bishop Milton Wright, father of Orville and Wilbur, just before they made man's first powered flight in Kitty Hawk in 1903.*

STORMY WEATHER

Battening down the hatches

ON JANUARY 22, 1986, television weather forecasters in the northeastern United States took telephone calls from a worried geophysicist at the Lamont-Doherty Geological Observatory of Columbia University. He told them there was a near certainty of floods or severe snowstorms in the next six days. The weathermen replied that the forecasts revealed nothing unusual and turned down the scientist's request that they mention his prediction as a footnote to theirs.

Three days later the storm broke, and it lasted more than 72 hours. Four inches of rain drenched the coastal region between Boston and Washington, D.C., and 40 inches of snow fell inland.

Fluke coincidence?

The man who had predicted the storm was Goesta Wollin. Since the early 1970's he has been convinced that the earth's magnetism affects climate.

In 1970 Wollin and a colleague, David Ericson, began to study climatic changes that have taken place since the last ice age, 11,000 years ago. By chance, the same week they finished plotting their temperature curves, an article published in *Science* outlined the changes in the earth's magnetic field over the identical span of time.

As Wollin studied the graph that accompanied the article, he thought it bore a tantalizing resemblance to his own. The next day, he suddenly saw the connection. The curves on his graph and those on the one in *Science* were mirror images of each other. Where one fell, the other rose, and vice versa. This meant that when the magnetic field was weak, the climate warmed up (the temperature curve rose). When magnetism increased, the climate cooled (the temperature curve fell).

But, as Wollin well knew, the history of science is filled with such fluke coincidences. He needed more evidence from different times and places.

Once again chance intervened. Wollin met William Ryan, a research student who had been studying magnetism in seabed sediments laid down in the Caribbean over the past 700,000 years. Ironically, Wollin and Ericson had based their climatic studies on samples from the same area.

Ryan had found evidence of five short-lived magnetic reversals, when the earth's north and south magnetic poles had changed places. After four months of intensive work, the three men could demonstrate that a strong long-term link did indeed exist between the earth's magnetic field and the climate—and not just in the Caribbean but in the Pacific and Mediterranean too.

However, the scientific response to Wollin's theory has been mixed. Climatologists have, on the whole, supported it, while geophysicists point out that Wollin has never been able to show exactly *how* magnetism and climate are linked.

Wollin suggests that the answer lies in the sun's magnetic field, which directly affects that of earth, or in changes in the solar winds that carry charged particles from the sun past the earth. But other scientists point out that although a weak magnetic field on earth would allow more radiation from space to penetrate to the ground, it would not be enough to account for the warming effect.

Wollin set out to provide more evidence. He reasoned that if long-term changes in the magnetic field can produce long-term changes in the climate, the same might be true over a shorter period. Wollin needed to analyze data on violent storms that had not been predicted. If such events could be linked to equally violent changes in the magnetic field, his theory would be greatly strengthened.

After looking through the records, Wollin found an unpredicted blizzard that had dropped a foot of snow on New York City on February 7, 1967. The magnetic record indicated that after a long period of calm there had been an abrupt dip in the field strength $2\frac{1}{2}$ days prior to the blizzard.

He also examined two other storms that had occurred in 1983. Neither had been anticipated. In both cases, dips had been recorded in the magnetic field precisely $2\frac{1}{2}$ days earlier. But Wollin still could not explain *how* the events were linked.

Forearmed is forewarned

Since all of Wollin's work to that point could be attacked as hindsight, it was time to make an accurate prediction based on his theory. He asked a friend, Al Travis, at the Fredericksburg Magnetic Observatory in Corbin, Virginia, to keep an eye on the recorders and alert him when they started to behave erratically. The call came on January 22, 1986, the date Wollin telephoned the forecasters.

At last the weathermen are beginning to admit that Wollin may have a point, and scientists are willing to investigate the phenomena he has so painstakingly unearthed. If the investigation bears fruit, then weather forecasters and the millions who rely on them may, for the first time, be able to anticipate and prepare for "freakish" storms.

SMART CARDS

A life in a pocket

THE PAST FEW YEARS have seen dramatic changes in the way information is stored, handled, and retrieved. Almost instantaneously, quantities of data can be made available through the smallest microcomputers. As the demand for more information has increased, new systems have evolved to store it.

One of the most versatile of storage systems is the pocket-size plastic card, similar to a credit card. The magnetic strip on each card contains an identification code number (in magnetic or optical form) that can be read by an electronic device and transmitted to a central computer.

Pocket books

Today these plastic cards are evolving into something more complex; with the addition of a microchip, the "smart" card can almost think.

For example, in making a purchase, the smart card is used instead of a credit card, checkbook, or cash. Fed into a reader device in a store, the card establishes its owner's identity and credit rating and then instructs a central bank computer to make all the financial arrangements necessary to complete the purchase. In the future the card could be used for virtually every sale and service.

Indelible data

The incorporation of a large memory bank also gives the card enormous potential. Optical data storage, similar to the system employed on compact discs, makes it possible for the plastic card to store hundreds of thousands of words or numbers. The information is transmitted onto the card with a laser; once there, it is permanent; it cannot be removed or altered. The card can be read on a visual display unit like a book.

Applications for the smart card are numerous. It has enough capacity to contain every word in a book the size of FACTS & FALLACIES or the complete record of a bank account or full details of a person's insurance coverage and medical history. With the latter information the card, once placed in a reader, would quickly give doctors everything they need to know about a patient in an emergency. Soon, smart cards may even be saving lives.

BEWITCHING THE CROPS

The next threat to Africa

WHEN THE RAINS returned to drought-stricken Africa in 1985, they brought with them fresh prospects for feeding millions of starving people. In countries all along the southern edge of the Sahara, subsistence farmers who had suffered years of hunger began to sow new crops. The arid landscape soon turned green. But as the world held its breath in hope, a new threat emerged from one of Africa's oldest enemies: the parasitic striga plant.

In the fields where cereal crops such as sorghum and millet are growing—the staple diet of millions of Africans—the striga is remorselessly strangling the next harvest. Like most parasitic plants, striga obtains life-sustaining water and nutrients at the expense of the host plant. Striga cannot support itself through its own rudimentary root system but lives off the roots of other plants, notably cereals, weakening them and causing disastrously reduced yields. In Sudan alone the cereal crop has been diminished by up to 70 percent.

The scale of the striga infiltration is enormous. Up to 50 striga plants can survive on one host. Worse, each plant can produce as many as 90,000 seeds, and each seed is capable of remaining dormant in the soil for up to 20 years, waiting for the right conditions in order to germinate.

Chemical stimulation

The process of germination is a further illustration of striga's tenacious ability to survive. Striga seeds do not respond to moisture alone. They require an additional stimulus to germinate: the chemicals exuded by the roots of host plants. Therefore, striga seedlings will not start to grow until there is a convenient host nearby.

Scientists struggling to halt the spread of striga are trying to turn these prerequisites for germination to their advantage. They have discovered that some plants that will not sustain striga produce the same chemicals as those that will. Cotton is one of them; when cotton is planted in infested fields, striga seeds germinate in the normal way but the seedlings soon become exhausted and die. Tests have shown that up to 90 percent of striga seeds can be destroyed this way. But valuable as this result is, starving people cannot eat cotton.

It has also been possible to provoke striga into what is known as suicide germination by the use of ethylene, a natural gas. In the United States, where striga became a minor problem in the mid-1950's (after being introduced into the country in a consignment of corn), ethylene helped to reduce the affected area by half. But the process of injecting the gas into the soil requires expensive machinery well beyond the means of African farmers. For them, the appearance of striga in a field is a sign that the crop has been bewitched—thus the parasite's common name, witchweed.

So while it has been demonstrated that modern technology can overcome striga, a way of applying these techniques to the needs of farmers in Africa is proving more difficult. Scientists believe the answer may lie in developing new strains of cereal able to resist or at least tolerate striga. But funds for research have been declining in recent years, a trend that can only bring further distress to people who are among the least able to help themselves.

ROOTS OF DEATH *What appears to be a field of flowers is instead a field of sorghum, heavily infested with the flowering striga plant. Unable to support itself, striga feeds off the roots of its host plant, as seen in microscopic detail in the inset. Striga so weakens its host that it can reduce the crop yield by as much as 70 percent. Difficult to eradicate, striga threatens many crops in its native Africa.*

TOMORROW'S VISION

Focusing on a coin 2,000 miles away

THE PAST 30 YEARS have witnessed enormous advances in astronomy. But as each discovery poses new questions, astronomers look forward to a new generation of telescopes that will help them derive some of the answers.

The most powerful conventional telescopes in the world are reflectors that use giant mirrors to capture light. But with the 200-inch telescope at the Hale Observatories in Los Angeles and the 236-inch reflector near Zelenchukskaya in the Caucasus Mountains of the U.S.S.R., the limits of building single mirrors free of the slightest aberration have been reached. Instead, designers are constructing telescopes that use a number of small mirrors aligned by a computer to act as one giant reflector.

The National New Technology Telescope on Mauna Kea, in Hawaii, is scheduled to become operational in the mid-1990's; it will be one of the first of the combined-mirror telescopes. With an effective diameter almost four times that of Hale's, it will be able to probe much farther into space. Similar telescopes are currently being developed in Europe and the U.S.S.R.

Getting the details

Seeing deeper into space is only one aim of the new generation of telescopes. Astronomers also want to look at previously observed stars in greater detail, which means improving the sharpness, or resolution, of the image the telescope obtains. A new technique known as optical interferometry holds great promise. It electronically combines the images obtained from two linked telescopes that are some distance apart. The light waves of both signals must coincide exactly to obtain an image; continual minute adjustments are made to each telescope with a computer-controlled feedback system.

The greater the distance between the two telescopes, the more difficult it is to coordinate the two images. The Very Large Telescope (VLT), a European project planned for the late 1990's, will use four reflectors nearly 500 feet apart. Its powerful mirrors will enable astronomers to see the surface detail of stars and easily detect the bending of light from distant galaxies or quasars.

Long-wave radio

The technique of radio interferometry has long been established in astronomy. Since a radio wave has a much longer wavelength than a light wave, it is easier to align the signals. But this longer

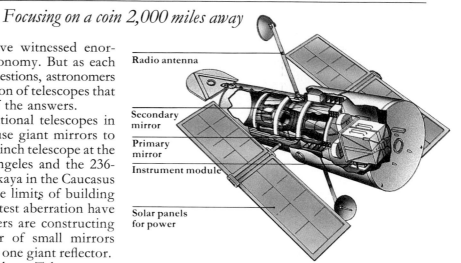

Radio antenna

Secondary mirror

Primary mirror

Instrument module

Solar panels for power

EYE IN SPACE *More than 40 feet long and weighing more than 11 tons, the Hubble Space Telescope may someday orbit 300 miles above the earth. The instrument is scheduled to be launched in the 1990's.*

wavelength also means that the radio telescopes must be much farther apart to achieve a fine resolution of the radio source.

The Very Long Baseline Array (VLBA) is a new radio telescope being developed in the United States today. Telescope units on the East and West coasts, in Puerto Rico, and in Hawaii will be linked together. The resolving power of the telescope will be equivalent to focusing on the edge of a coin from 2,000 miles away. The VLBA will study the behavior of such powerful radio sources as pulsars and quasars in heretofore unprecedented detail.

Astronomy in space

Because the earth's atmosphere absorbs most of the radiation that reaches it from space, ultraviolet light and X-rays in particular must be observed from high altitudes—or better still, from an orbit above the earth. Even the visible light from stars can be viewed with greater clarity and intensity by telescopes in space.

The most ambitious space astronomy project yet is the multimillion-dollar Hubble Space Telescope, due to be launched in the 1990's. The Hubble has a 94-inch reflector that will direct light onto extremely sensitive cameras and other apparatus. Although it is not particularly large by earth-based standards, the lack of atmosphere will enable the Hubble to see seven times farther into space and obtain a resolution five times greater than that of any telescope in existence today. The Hubble will also detect ultraviolet radiation, one of the least explored parts of the electromagnetic spectrum.

Scientists are proposing that large arrays of X-ray telescopes be put into orbit. In the past, X-rays have provided astronomers with evidence of violent objects, such as neutron stars, quasars, and superhot clouds of intergalactic gas. The extremely fine resolution of an orbiting X-ray telescope system could shed new light on some of the field's most fundamental phenomena.

Astronomy is poised at the beginning of a new era of research and understanding. Looking further ahead, a space station in orbit around the earth, or perhaps a base on the moon, seems to be the logical working environment for astronomers of the future. Proposals for a permanent space platform, to be constructed in orbit and equipped to study all cosmic radiations, exist. Advances made in the past 30 years may seem minuscule when compared with those that the next 30 years could bring.

TRAVELER'S TALE

A battle that revolutionized computer thinking

TO THE ENEMY COMMANDER, the 96 huge ships of the Eurisko battle fleet, slow and cumbersome and carrying only light arms, seemed an easy target. His own fleet consisted of only 20 small, highly maneuverable craft, but each boasted heavy guns and sophisticated laser weapons. The commander confidently gave the order to open fire.

Four salvos later, more than half of the Eurisko ships had been sunk, but their commander, Douglas B. Lenat, was preparing to accept the enemy's offer of surrender. Despite its huge losses, the lumbering Eurisko fleet had destroyed all but one of the opposition's highly vaunted high-tech ships. The battle had ended.

Helping itself to success

This confrontation of armed might took place on July 4, 1981, in San Mateo, California. The exercise was part of a futuristic war games tournament called Traveler. Lenat was a computer-science expert from Stanford University; Eurisko was his computer program. What made their joint victory so remarkable was that Eurisko itself had designed the battle fleet and developed its tactics.

Eurisko was a major innovation in the development of artificial intelligence. Before Lenat invented Eurisko, "intelligent" programs could rewrite sentences or create new culinary dishes—if supplied with massive amounts of information. But they were incapable of discovering facts or creating new ideas of their own.

Lenat envisioned a program that could not only solve problems from information at hand but also test and improve its answers and the techniques it used to work them out. Lenat wanted a program that could think for itself and discover entirely new information in the process.

The Traveler game demanded that each player calculate how to build a fleet of ships that would defeat all opponents. Lenat gave Eurisko enough details of its basic task to begin work, backed up by a huge memory bank of "heuristics"—rules about how to make discoveries, test concepts, and adapt them to form new ones.

Each time it designed a fleet, the program simulated a battle, examined the results, and adjusted its ships accordingly. Then it staged another battle and again made adjustments. Eurisko learned by experience. Lenat, its mentor, claimed to have created only 60 percent of the final program.

The solutions Eurisko devised were unorthodox. In the course of 10,000 simulated battles, it had discovered that a large fleet of heavily armored ships would outlast any small force of lightweight craft, no matter how elaborate their weapons or how fast they moved. The fleet that lasted the longest won the game. In case an enemy managed to sink all of Eurisko's ships, the program developed a fail-safe: a tiny, unarmed and agile "lifeboat" that was deemed unhittable.

Please stay away

Following Eurisko's victory in the 1981 Traveler tournament, the game's organizers changed the rules only a week before the 1982 event. Undaunted, Eurisko once again defeated the opposition. Politely, Lenat was requested not to participate the following year.

But he had proved that, with the right program, a computer, almost unaided, can make new discoveries. How had Lenat achieved this? He had simply explained to the program the principles that governed its operation and then let it "talk to itself"—a major step, perhaps, toward creating a machine that genuinely "thinks."

BUILDING A NEW LIFE

Creating green fields in space

ACCORDING TO the first chapter of Genesis, it took God less than a week to create the world. In Arizona, where miracles can sometimes take a little longer, a group of scientists plans to have its own version of the world ready to receive its first inhabitants in the near future.

When work on the privately funded $30 million steel and glass dome is completed, eight volunteers will be sealed inside hermetically for two years. They will be participating in a unique experiment—a prototype on earth of the intricate, self-sustaining environment that future generations might someday inhabit in space.

The people behind the venture have named it Biosphere 2; they consider the earth itself to be Biosphere 1. The two-acre structure on Sunspace Ranch, near Tucson, will contain miniature oceans, rain forests, grasslands, marshlands, deserts, a farm, laboratories, workshops, and living quarters.

Everything that is inside the airtight skin of Biosphere 2 will be recycled. Carbon dioxide exhaled by the volunteers and a variety of small mammals, birds, reptiles, and insects will sustain plants; the vegetation, in turn, will give off oxygen for the humans and the animals to breathe.

A stream of water will cascade from a wooded mountain onto a forest floor. From there it will cross a savanna plain, drop over a waterfall to feed a freshwater marsh, then flow into a saltwater marsh before reaching the man-made ocean. There it will

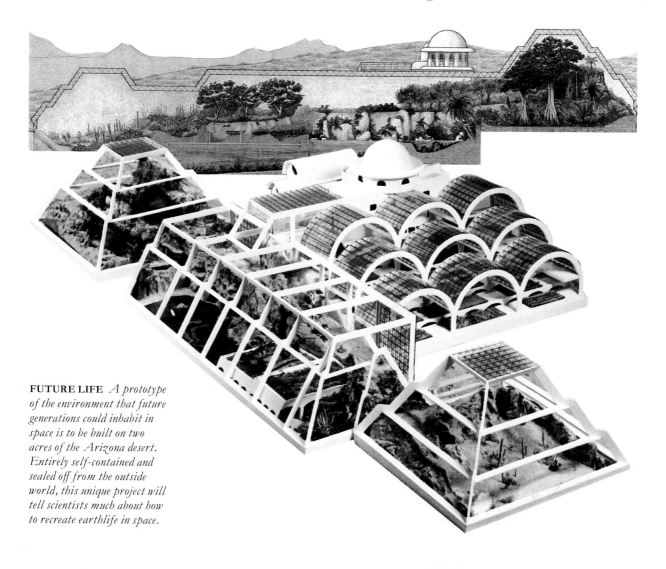

FUTURE LIFE *A prototype of the environment that future generations could inhabit in space is to be built on two acres of the Arizona desert. Entirely self-contained and sealed off from the outside world, this unique project will tell scientists much about how to recreate earthlife in space.*

return to the atmosphere through evaporation and fall as rain over the mountains to feed the stream, starting the cycle all over again.

Human and animal wastes will provide fertilizer for crops and feed algae, bacteria, and water plants that will in turn feed fish. Electricity will be generated by solar energy.

Biologists and botanists are particularly excited by the project; they believe that close study of the flora and fauna in this artificial environment will improve our understanding of the delicately balanced ecological systems of the earth. But the many applications of Biosphere 2 are not just earthbound; lessons learned from the project could have profound implications by paving the way for the creation of future colonies in space.

Life in space

For more than a decade Dr. Gerard K. O'Neill, professor of physics at Princeton University, has been urging the federal government to undertake a huge space colonization program with biospheres. O'Neill believes that future generations of space travelers will need more room than today's cramped spacecraft offer. His projected space city would be a self-sustaining community with as many as 10,000 people living in an idyllic subtropical environment similar to that of Biosphere 2.

The specifications for O'Neill's prototype space colony, known as Island One, are staggering. It would be cylindrical in shape, with a circumference of about one mile. The cylinder would rotate on an axis fast enough to create an earthlike gravity. Inside, people would work, grow their own food, enjoy leisure activities, and raise their children.

Materials for the construction of such a vast enterprise would be processed in space from minerals mined on the moon. The trick, says O'Neill, is to exploit the low gravity of the lunar surface for lifting objects weighing thousands of tons into space. And the first colony could become a manufacturing facility for other projects, such as space power plants; they would collect limitless supplies of solar energy and transmit it to earth.

O'Neill asserts that within 100 years, industrial activity could be moved away from the earth's fragile biosphere and thus help restore our planet to an unpolluted state for future generations to enjoy.

Not every scientist regards these ideas as practical, but O'Neill's optimism is today shared by America's National Commission on Space. In 1985 its members completed a two-year study. Recommendations included the colonization of the moon and Mars, and more research on the construction and maintenance of man-made biospheres. The report also suggests that colonies in space could become a reality early in the 21st century.

Members of the commission are not science fiction writers. In addition to Dr. O'Neill and other leading scientists, astronauts such as Neil Armstrong, the first man on the moon are included.

Hopes for future life in space could well hinge on the results of the Biosphere 2 experiment in the arid deserts of southern Arizona.

DRILL-LESS DENTISTRY

For anyone who dreads a visit to the dentist, help may be at hand. New techniques may soon reduce tooth decay and remove the need for extensive drilling and filling.

The main cause of tooth decay is the presence in the mouth of *Streptococcus mutans* — bacteria that convert sugars into acid. However, dental researcher Jeffrey D. Hillman, of the Forsyth Dental Center in Boston, has isolated forms of *S. mutans* that make only a small amount of acid.

Since these bacteria cannot compete with the "wild" varieties in the human mouth, Hillman and his colleagues are trying to find a variety of *S. mutans* that does establish itself readily.

To date they have come up with JH1005; not only does it colonize in the mouth but also produces a chemical that prevents the growth of related varieties of bacteria. Today the search continues for a strain of bacteria that combines low acid formation and the qualities of JH1005. If the scientists are successful, it may be possible to protect people against tooth decay for life.

Meanwhile, another new technique, Caridex, is being tried as a way to remove dental decay chemically. A harmless form of amino acid is applied to the area of decay and softens it by breaking down the chemical bonds. The loosened decay is then gently detached from the healthy part of the tooth and painlessly washed away. Although it may be necessary to drill a tooth in order to expose decay, tests indicate that dentists who employ the Caridex method will be able to reduce drilling time by some 80 percent.

INTELLIGENT BUILDINGS

Skyscrapers that care for themselves and their occupants

A NEW GENERATION of "smart" buildings is rising in our cities. No longer is an office or factory a mere shell of steel, concrete, and glass. Today many of the buildings in which we work can make decisions that enable them to look after themselves and their occupants.

These intelligent buildings are constructed rather like the people inside them: miles of control and communications cables act as a nervous system. A monitoring system with thermometers and smoke detectors corresponds to human senses, while a voice synthesizer and computerized telephone exchange act as a mouth. Just as our reflexes react to harm, an intelligent building can respond similarly and take corrective measures.

Should fire break out, the building's sensors alert a computer that immediately instructs the telephone exchange to call the fire department. The computer also tells the employees what to do, then activates doors to contain the fire but allow occupants to escape. The building can also take care of breakdowns—of an air conditioner, for example—by automatically telephoning the service engineers and conveying what has gone wrong.

Fine-tuning

But an intelligent building does more than just react to emergencies. The control and monitoring systems are active 24 hours a day checking lighting, heating, and ventilation; adjusting conditions to suit those working inside during the day; and turning off some of the systems at night.

Future supersmart buildings will have their own eyes and ears. Developments in sound and image processing will soon make it possible for buildings equipped with TV cameras and microphones to monitor all the people inside. The system will know where everyone is, will listen to them speaking, and be able to react to spoken instructions. Although privacy will be sacrificed, communication and security will be greatly improved. There will be other benefits as well: a highly intelligent hospital, for example, will give constant attention to every patient.

This may all seem like part of a futuristic vision of the 21st century, but many such buildings already exist today in cities and industrial parks throughout the world. Skyscrapers, office complexes, warehouses, and hospitals are being built to be intelligent. So too are homes: there are computers and robots capable of performing most domestic tasks, either automatically or to order.

For example, a prototype vacuum cleaner has been developed that can be programmed to remember the layout of individual rooms and how to clean them, and then complete the job unaided.

Microelectronics has already entered the home, improving the capabilities of individual appliances, such as washing machines. With the development of specialized microchips, it is already possible to let a computer control household appliances and lighting systems. And with versatile domestic robots also carrying out the computer's bidding, the days of manual housework may be ending.

THE GREENHOUSE EFFECT

Is the world heating up?

R ISING TEMPERATURES, melting ice caps, floods in Florida and the Netherlands, New York City underwater—these are just some of the problems that the world may face by the end of the next century.

A report from the U.S. Department of Energy indicates that the world is heating up and that within the next century temperatures may rise to levels that have not been reached for 100,000 years. The effects may be so far-reaching that some investigators are recommending that we take steps today to guard against them.

The reason for this global warming is a massive buildup of carbon dioxide. Carbon dioxide constitutes only a small part of the atmosphere, but it plays a crucial role in determining climate.

Insulation by atmosphere

As the earth is warmed by the sun, heat radiates back into space. Carbon dioxide prevents the heat from escaping completely and acts as an insulating screen, not unlike the glass panes of a greenhouse. It traps some of the heat and reflects it back down to earth—creating the so-called greenhouse effect.

Since the middle of the last century, however, the increased burning of fossil fuels such as coal and oil has caused more and more carbon dioxide to accumulate in the atmosphere. The result: less heat escapes back into space and temperatures grow warmer. The gradual destruction of the world's forests has aggravated the situation; if left intact, trees would have recycled the carbon dioxide into oxygen through photosynthesis.

In 1900, the first year for which reliable figures exist, the atmosphere contained about 300 parts of carbon dioxide per million (p.p.m.). By 1958 careful monitoring of the clean air at the top of Mauna Loa, Hawaii, revealed that the concentration had reached 316 p.p.m.; in 1985 the figure had risen to 345 p.p.m.

Scientists believe that this ratio could double by the end of the next century. Based on recently developed techniques, experts predict that with 600 p.p.m. of atmospheric carbon dioxide, the greenhouse effect could make global temperatures rise 3 to 10 degrees, making the world warmer than it has been at any time in the past 100,000 years.

Warming up

Fluctuations in the weather from year to year make it difficult to assess the impact of the carbon dioxide buildup, but 1980, 1981, and 1983 have been the warmest years on record to date. Climatologists believe that some effects are already being felt in certain parts of the world. Extreme weather patterns, such as the prolonged drought that began in Africa in the late 1960's, are no longer regarded today as random fluctuations; the odds against a 17-year-long African drought happening by chance are as high as 1 in 125,000.

Most scientists believe, too, that by the middle of the next century the increase in temperature may raise sea levels. Since ocean water itself would expand as it warmed, ice caps in the polar regions would start to melt. An increase in global water temperatures of only 2°F could raise the ocean level by 2 feet; melting ice caps could add as much as 230 feet more, creating extreme flooding and changing the face of the landscape the world over.

Low-lying cities, such as New York and New Orleans, would be the first to be affected. It has been estimated that if sea levels rose no more than 26 feet, senators of the future would travel from the Capitol by boat to visit the White House.

Speculative effects

Not all predictions are as alarming. Some scientists suggest that the greenhouse effect offers a few compensations. As the world heats up, the oceans

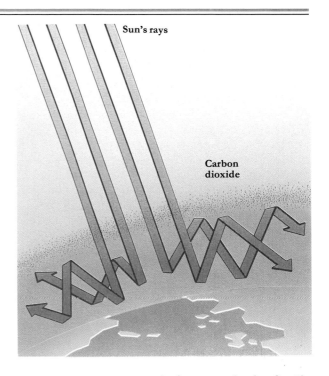

WARMING THE PLANET *As the amount of carbon dioxide in the atmosphere increases, it traps the infrared heat of the sun and prevents it from escaping. Some experts believe that this greenhouse effect is making temperatures on earth warmer.*

may evaporate more quickly, keeping the sea level constant as the ice melts and adding to the cloud cover above the earth; clouds help keep the heat of the sun from reaching the ground.

Warmer temperatures may also mean more pleasant living conditions for some of the world's population, and longer growing seasons in high-land areas and in countries farther from the equator. Even northern Canada and Siberia could become important producers of wheat.

Computer models also suggest that the Sahara in Africa and the desert areas of the southwestern United States would get more rain, and a region like Death Valley in California might become an important farming area. Changing temperatures would not necessarily cause a food shortage in the future.

The consequences of the greenhouse effect are still subject to speculation. And it is not the only factor likely to affect temperature.

Scientists predict that the next ice age, due in some 3,000 years, will put an end to the present spell of warm weather. Cooling effects from volcanic dust and changes in the output of energy from the sun are other considerations that make it difficult to predict temperature levels of the future with absolute certainty.

A CROP IN THE OCEAN

Energy from the sea

NEAR THE COASTLINE of California, hundreds of thousands of acres of crops sway gently in the ocean currents. The harvest, just getting under way, looks promising. It is expected to be a record one: 1,000 tons to the acre.

Incredible as this may seem, the farm is not some utopian dream; it is a reality. The crop being harvested is a remarkable seaweed, the giant kelp (*Macrocystis pyrifera*), the fastest-growing vegetable in the world.

Although kelp has long been enjoyed by the Japanese as a food, and is already used in the manufacture of such products as pharmaceuticals and fertilizers, its main value in the future may be as another source of energy. By the turn of the century, gas from processed kelp may be heating factories and homes, and yielding gasoline to fuel public transportation.

The reason that scientists are looking anew at what they call biomass—renewable organic energy resources, like wood—is obvious. Current supplies of energy depend on stocks of natural gas, crude oil, and coal, all of which are nonrenewable resources that will someday be depleted. As a form of biomass, kelp has become the focus of a great deal of scientific study.

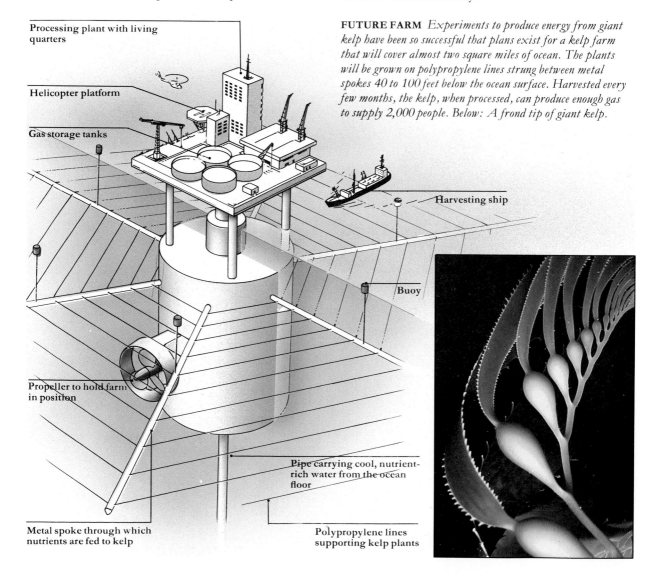

Processing plant with living quarters

Helicopter platform

Gas storage tanks

Harvesting ship

Buoy

Propeller to hold farm in position

Pipe carrying cool, nutrient-rich water from the ocean floor

Metal spoke through which nutrients are fed to kelp

Polypropylene lines supporting kelp plants

FUTURE FARM *Experiments to produce energy from giant kelp have been so successful that plans exist for a kelp farm that will cover almost two square miles of ocean. The plants will be grown on polypropylene lines strung between metal spokes 40 to 100 feet below the ocean surface. Harvested every few months, the kelp, when processed, can produce enough gas to supply 2,000 people. Below: A frond tip of giant kelp.*

Through a process of fermentation, vegetable matter can produce energy in the form of gases. But to be of practical economic use, the biomass must be available on a large scale. Most of the arable land in the world is needed to grow food, and there is little room for the production of organic fuels; the future development of this valuable resource will have to take place at sea.

The giant kelp fills the bill. It can grow as much as two feet a day; some specimens are 600 feet long. Scientists estimate that by spacing kelp plants 10 feet apart in an ocean farm no larger than two miles square, the resulting harvests could satisfy the energy needs of 2,000 people in perpetuity.

Testing the water

The technological challenges are complex and expensive, but efforts to put theories and ambitions into practice are gathering momentum. Most of the pioneering work is being carried out by the Gas Research Institute of America. The institute has been experimenting with a test farm moored five miles off the coast of California.

The farm itself looks much like a giant version of the rotating clothesline occasionally seen in some backyards. A central column and radiating spokes hold a weblike system of ropes together below the surface; buoys suspend the entire structure.

The seaweed plants have roots that attach themselves to the structure; they are fed with water pumped up from a depth of 1,500 feet. The cold water from the lower depths is richer in nutrients than the surface water. So far, scientists have been pleased with the results. The plants have been growing well, despite severe weather conditions, and have reproduced rapidly.

The massive floating farms that are envisioned will be equipped with docking facilities, helicopter landing pads, and accommodations for workers. Harvesting will take place at least three times yearly. The more the kelp is cut, the faster it grows. Once the seaweed has been harvested, it will be reduced to pulp and shipped to onshore processing plants for fermentation and the production of gas.

Since more than two-thirds of the earth's surface is covered by the sea, the area available for kelp production appears almost limitless. And the novel clothesline method of farming means that supplies of seaweed can be located in deep waters where nothing grows at present.

THE POWER OF LIGHT

Energy from the skies

THE SUN IS A MASSIVE FURNACE capable of sending more energy to earth in one hour than is consumed by human beings in a year. This alone demonstrates its potential as the supplier of most of the world's energy needs.

In the past 20 years, fluctuating oil prices and dwindling fossil fuels, combined with a growing mistrust of nuclear power plants, have resulted in increased attempts to develop a solar-power industry. But until recently, unpredictable weather and long hours of darkness have been insurmountable obstacles to the establishment of ground-based systems that can satisfy the demands of modern industry. Today, however, some scientists believe they have found the solution—in the advancing technology of space travel.

Power bases

The innovative technology in question consists of many solar-power satellites (SPS), which scientists believe will be able to intercept the sun's rays and convert them into usable energy. Placed in an orbit 22,300 miles above the earth, the satellites would be bathed in sunlight 99 percent of the time. The only blackouts would be for a few brief and predictable periods during solar eclipses.

Sunlight would be collected by vast banks of solar cells similar to those that already power weather and communications satellites. Aluminum frames housing the cells would be larger than anything seen on earth—about 12 miles by 3 miles, an area approaching the size of Manhattan Island.

The satellites would be positioned permanently in orbit over a fixed spot on the earth. The energy gathered would be converted into electricity and then beamed to earth as microwaves—invisible radio waves of a very high frequency. Microwaves would come streaming down from space even at night or on cloudy days.

In a scheme envisaged by American scientist Dr. Peter Glaser, the inventor of SPS, the beams would be focused onto receiving dishes known as rectennas, each covering an area of 50 square miles. There the microwaves would be converted back into electricity and fed into power grids. Dr. Glaser calculates that in the future one such satellite could supply as much electricity as do five medium-size nuclear-power plants today.

The technological hurdles are daunting. But Dr. Glaser argues that the space program has already demonstrated that the required scientific and engineering know-how exists.

The workhorses of the system would be a new generation of reusable space freighters; they would carry a cargo 20 times greater than the space shuttle's 30-ton payload. First, the spaceships would carry materials to staging bases in orbits close to earth, where preliminary assembly of the satellites would take place. The spaceships would then place the partially built satellites into their orbits, ready for final assembly. When completed, the satellites would weigh as much as 100,000 tons.

Astronomical prices

Although any estimate of the cost is speculative, some projections are mind-boggling. Dr. Glaser's concept of 110 solar-power satellites in orbit around the earth—the number he judges would be needed to supply the electrical needs of the United States—was estimated at $836 billion in 1977. Critics say that it would be a brave president who would commit taxpayers to a venture that is bound to be risky. Detractors also point out that environmental problems still need to be overcome. Microwaves can interfere with radio communications, and there is a possibility that earthbound beams might pose a health risk.

Dr. Glaser concedes that further studies are needed. Nonetheless, the U.S. National Commission on Space has been sufficiently intrigued by his proposals to recommend further research. The commission also points out that the U.S.S.R. has announced that it will build the first solar-power satellite to supply energy to earth in the 1990's.

As the requirements of a power-hungry world increase, the need for such satellites increases. There may come a time when the sun, worshiped by ancient pagan civilizations as the giver of all life, will once again be honored as the main provider of many of the world's basic needs.

CURES WITHIN OURSELVES

On the track of new wonder drugs

THE BIGGEST HELPER that doctors have in curing illness in the human body is—the human body. It has amazing powers to fight disease or injury. Sometimes it needs a little help in the form of drugs, but today it seems that even the most powerful drugs of the future will come from the body itself—and they will be derived from proteins.

Among their many components, proteins contain enzymes—themselves a type of protein—which help speed up chemical reactions in the body; antibodies, which help fight infection; and most hormones, which act as chemical messengers. Of approximately 25,000 proteins in the human body, scientists have been able to identify fewer than 2 percent. But of that 2 percent, a group known as peptides, or peptide hormones, has far-reaching medical significance.

Links in the chain

Proteins are formed from amino acids, which are made up chiefly of carbon, hydrogen, nitrogen, and oxygen. As far as we now know, some 20 amino acids form the proteins common to all living things. Amino acids are joined together by peptide bonds. The peptides are the links in the chain.

Many peptides are secreted by glands: by the thalamus, hypothalamus, and pituitary in the brain; and by the pancreas, which is located near the stomach. It is not known exactly what peptides do nor how they can be so specific in their operation.

One theory holds that they work on the jigsaw principle: each peptide is made in such a way that it will fit only into one particular receptor, a protein or a hormone, for example. It "searches" for the right receptor. Once the connection has been made, it starts a series of chemical reactions, activating enzymes that in turn send "messages" to the cells to produce specialized proteins according to the needs of the body.

Some peptide drugs have been in use for many years. Among them are insulin, used in treating diabetes; somatotrophin, the growth hormone; and oxytocin, which starts milk production in mothers. Peptide drugs have already been approved for use with some forms of dwarfism, infertility, and the premature onset of puberty. Other peptides being tested may be used for treatment of cancer, depression, insomnia, and acquired immune deficiency syndrome (AIDS).

In due course scientists hope to have peptide drugs for conditions that at present are impossible to treat, such as Alzheimer's disease. Future research will explore drugs for birth control and as replacements for antibiotics.

Improving on nature

Until recently it was not possible to extract sufficient quantities of human peptides to use as drugs. But in the 1970's chemists perfected a way to build up artificial peptides by bonding the first amino acid of a peptide chain to tiny resin beads. Unwanted amino acids were washed away, and a second amino acid was then bonded onto the first. This was repeated until the entire chain was created. The whole process, if computerized, can safely make drugs in the required commercial quantities in a matter of days.

Not only can chemists reproduce a natural peptide, they can also vary the sequence of the amino acids in order to make small but important changes. In this way they can give the artificial peptide certain characteristics, such as long-lasting action, that the natural version does not have.

Finally, because the new drugs are so powerful, the doses can be much smaller. And since they work the same way as the body's own peptides, they cause fewer undesirable side effects.

LONG-LIVED SEEDS

Nature has a way of preserving its own—for as long as 10,000 years. That is how long the seeds of an arctic lupine remained buried in frozen silt in the icy wastes of the Yukon, Canada, before they were dug out and germinated in 1966.

While this is an exceptional case, the seeds of the American lotus are known to be able to sprout after 1,000 years, and many common or garden seeds can be germinated successfully after 20 years or perhaps more.

Today scientists are able to match nature and preserve seeds artificially for hundreds of years. In refrigerated rooms around the world seeds are being stored for the 21st century—and beyond.

Preserving the future

One of the most successful seed banks in the world is managed by Britain's Royal Botanic Gardens. At Wakehurst Place, a 400-year-old mansion hidden deep in the English countryside, scientists have stored the seeds of more than 2,000 different species of garden plants and wildflowers.

FUTURE LIFE *Seed banks, such as this one at Wakehurst Place in Britain, store seeds for use by future generations. Deep-frozen, the seeds can be kept for up to a century.*

The seeds come from more than 50 countries and form one of the most comprehensive collections in the world.

The seeds are first dried, then frozen and kept on ice at $-36°F$ in three freezer rooms. Tests indicate that most seeds can be stored for up to 25 years and some for more than a century. Moreover, research suggests that essential seeds such as barley and other grains may have a storage life of many thousands of years.

The seed bank represents a considerable investment in the future. Many of the seeds are of rare or threatened species and are being saved from possible extinction. Others have no known use at the moment but in future years may prove to be valuable, possibly providing new sources of drugs, food, or fuel. As such they could benefit the economies of many developing countries.

Much of the work is still in the experimental stage, but scientists are hopeful that a wide range of wild and cultivated species will soon be preserved in seed banks. Establishing such institutions as Wakehurst Place will do much to ensure the survival of the planet's plants for future generations.

RINGWORLD

URNING OUT IN SPACE is an artificial ring 1 million miles wide and 584 million miles in circumference. Countless billions of people live on its inner surface, warmed by the sun at its center. This is the stunning concept at the heart of *Ringworld,* Larry Niven's award-winning science fiction novel. Awesome though it might seem, Niven's artificial world is no fictional fancy. It was inspired by a serious scientific proposal.

In the 1960's Freeman J. Dyson, professor of astronomy at Princeton University, suggested that an extraterrestrial society, under pressure from an expanding population and diminishing resources, might dismantle one of the uninhabited planets of its solar system and build from its debris a series of artificial worlds completely surrounding its sun. In our own solar system, suggested Dyson, a planet the size of Jupiter could serve as a source from which to carve out other worlds for human habitation.

The possibilities of this elaborate proposal for the human race were soon explored by other scientists. The actual mechanics were tackled by Professor Theodore Taylor, formerly of Princeton. He dreamed up the idea of a Santa Claus machine.

A cross between a garbage collector and a factory, the machine, remotely controlled, would travel through space scooping up rocks, gases, and liquids from the asteroid belt or from a dismantled Jupiter. After analysis it would then break these down into their constituent elements. With nuclear fusion, even the basic hydrogen that constitutes most of Jupiter could be converted into other elements and manufactured into whatever programmers requested. This could include artificial planets — or the apparatus required to build a single ringworld around the sun.

LIFE IN SPACE *Ringworld would orbit the sun at the same distance — 93 million miles — as earth, ensuring the same climatic conditions as on earth. A million miles wide and some 3,000 feet deep, ringworld would have a circumference as large as the earth's entire orbit. Making this huge mass rotate would create a gravitational field. But unlike on earth, where people live on the outer surface, residents of ringworld would inhabit the inside surface, facing the sun (below right). To create night and day, a stationary ring of squares would cast shadows as ringworld rotated in its orbit, blocking out sunlight for 12 hours at a time.*

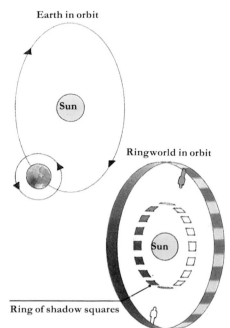

Earth in orbit

Sun

Ringworld in orbit

Sun

Ring of shadow squares

THE SUPERCOLLIDER

The ultimate atom smasher

PHYSICISTS in the United States plan to build a vast machine large enough to encircle Washington, D.C. Its purpose: to examine elementary particles, the smallest entities known. Called the superconducting supercollider, the machine promises to help scientists understand more about the origins and makeup of the universe.

Physicists developed the first atom-smashing machine, known as a particle accelerator, in the 1930's in order to study cosmic rays—the high-energy particles that strike the earth's atmosphere from space. Studies had revealed the fleeting existence of many particles more elementary than the three known components of the atom: electrons, neutrons, and protons. But since any new particles could be investigated only under very controlled laboratory conditions, there was need for a particle accelerator.

Holding power

The accelerators that were subsequently developed enabled physicists to discover a number of new particles that hold the atomic nucleus together. The accelerators also produced a wealth of evidence that clarified the four fundamental forces of nature: gravity, electromagnetism, and the strong and weak nuclear forces.

But the same experiments had also raised many questions as to how these forces are linked—questions that existing accelerators have not been able to answer. In addition, scientists know that many particles have yet to be studied. To foster the continuation of this innovative work, plans for a new particle accelerator—the superconducting supercollider—are today on the drawing board.

A modern accelerator is shaped like a doughnut. Inside, magnets propel beams of hydrogen protons millions of times around the ring. As the protons collide, they produce a debris of short-lived particles that scientists want to study.

Conceived in 1982, the supercollider was nicknamed the Desertron, because it was first thought that only the desert states would be large enough to accommodate it. The power that the new machine will require is so great that the ring of magnets guiding the particles during acceleration will be 52 miles in circumference.

Collision course

The accelerator will consist of two concentric rings. Two beams of protons will be propelled by more than 10,000 superconducting magnets. First the protons will be set into motion by preliminary accelerators. When they are traveling fast enough, one beam will be fired into the main accelerator in a clockwise direction, and one counterclockwise. Special magnets in the circuit will then force the protons going in opposite directions to collide. Detectors will measure the energy released and the paths of particles produced by the collisions.

This colossal project was approved by President Ronald Reagan in 1987 and is expected to cost $6 billion. Few, if any, immediate economic or industrial benefits are anticipated. But if the project succeeds, it will revolutionize our understanding of the basic forms of matter in the universe.

SELF-DRIVE WITH A DIFFERENCE

The car that knows where it goes

COMPUTERS in automobiles are nothing new. Many models currently in production incorporate computer systems that control the fuel injection and also warn the driver if the gas is running low or the engine is too hot. In Japan some models have a computer-controlled sensor on the hood that starts the windshield wipers if it is raining, and a photosensitive device that switches on the headlights when it gets dark.

But such devices will soon be overshadowed. Computers will soon take full control of the automobile to help a driver arrive at his destination quickly and safely.

All over the world, major car and computer manufacturers are working on in-automobile navigation systems. These systems may become a standard feature on all models by the year 2000.

Electronic front-seat driver

The system uses a map on a compact disc (CD). Each disc will have enough capacity to include the road networks of an entire state or a small country.

When the disc is inserted into the computer, a map is displayed in color on a monitor. The driver indicates the departure point and destination simply by touching the map at the desired positions.

The computer then plots a route and exactly which roads and turns to take. This information is relayed to the driver through a sound synthesizer that "talks" to the driver en route. Sensors attached to the wheels, in combination with an electronic compass, enable the computer to work out the automobile's exact position throughout the journey. The computer also checks distances and the different directions of travel against the map and makes corrections as necessary. If the driver takes a wrong turn, the computer "talks" the driver back to the correct route.

The computer will also be able to work out the quickest route for a journey and estimate the time of arrival, based on the car's average speed. In the not too distant future, information about traffic situations will be broadcast through a loudspeaker and also relayed in the form of digital signals. These signals will alert the computer navigator to upcoming obstructions, such as traffic jams or road construction, and other possible delays. The computer will also be able to advise the driver as to which alternate route to take.

Fendering for itself

The use of computer-navigation systems will not be limited solely to lengthy journeys. A new automobile sonar system being developed in Japan will warn the driver of any obstacles while his car is in reverse gear. As the driver backs into a parking spot, sonars mounted in the rear fender will measure the distance between the automobile and any obstruction, such as a wall. Should the car get too close, the sonar will transmit a warning sound through the right-hand speaker of the car's stereo system. Additional sonars will advise drivers of objects ahead that constitute a possible danger, and may also be able to apply the brakes or turn the wheels to avoid an accident.

To today's driver, such computerized help may seem very strange. But the industry is only a few steps away from producing robot automobiles that will drive themselves. The driver may soon be relegated to the backseat—a passenger in his or her own automobile. Driving in the 21st century may be equivalent to riding in a driverless taxi.

BACKSEAT DRIVER *Drivers will someday be able to navigate their automobiles with the help of a computerized map. Stored on a compact disc, the map will be displayed on a video screen. When the driver enters his departure and destination points on the computer, it works out the best route to take and a synthesized voice talks the driver through the journey.*

AROUND THE WORLD IN 80 MINUTES

Hypersonic travel on the new Orient Express

"WELCOME ABOARD flight OE001 from New York to Tokyo. Our flight time will be 45 minutes, and we will be cruising at an altitude of 100 miles."

An announcement like this might be greeting airplane passengers in the year 2000 if plans for a new type of airplane get off the drawing board. Dubbed the Orient Express of the 21st century by President Ronald Reagan, the spaceplane will combine features of both the supersonic Concorde and the space shuttle. It will be capable of flying around the world in a little more than an hour.

Future flight

Separate plans for such a spaceplane have been drawn up by both NASA in the United States and British Aerospace in Britain, and the plans have much in common. The spaceplane will fly at hypersonic speeds of up to 25 times the speed of sound, compared with twice the speed of sound achieved by the Concorde, currently the fastest passenger airliner.

The Orient Express will take off and land on an airport runway like an ordinary aircraft, yet it will cruise high above the atmosphere like a spacecraft. Sleek and dartlike in shape, the spaceplane will climb to the outer edge of the earth's atmosphere in about 10 minutes, reaching a speed twice as fast as the Concorde. It will then accelerate into space until it is traveling more than 10 times as fast as the supersonic airliner. At this speed, the spaceplane will cruise through space until it nears its destination. It will then reenter the atmosphere and land like a conventional airplane.

Preliminary research into the hypersonic spaceplane suggests that the project is feasible and that a prototype could be flying by the turn of the century. It is hoped that the spaceplane will not only speed passengers around the globe but also deliver satellites into space and service space stations orbiting around the earth.

Scramjet power

The spaceplane is seen by its designers as a successor to the ill-fated space shuttle. It should operate at less than a fifth of the cost of the shuttle, without using the solid-fuel rocket boosters responsible for the *Challenger* disaster in 1986. To achieve this goal, the spaceplane will need a revolutionary kind of engine.

Plans call for the engines of the spaceplane to make use of the air through which it climbs toward space; it will not need to carry as much fuel as present-day space launchers. The spaceplane will be powered by revolutionary supersonic-combustion ramjets called scramjets. The engines rely on the motion of the spaceplane to suck in oxygen from the atmosphere. The oxygen is then combined with liquid hydrogen fuel to push the spaceplane, at more than five times the speed of sound, to an altitude of 15 miles. At this height conventional liquid-fuel rocket engines will take over to push the spaceplane out into space, replacing the oxygen drawn from the atmosphere with liquid oxygen.

If the project is realized, Jules Verne's fictional circumnavigation of the world will soon be possible in 80 minutes, not 80 days.

FUTURE FLIGHT *Designed to take off and land like a present-day airplane, yet travel through space like a rocket, the spaceplane will fly at about 25 times the speed of sound. The first plane—which could be operational by the late 1990's—will be able to circumnavigate the world in slightly over 1 hour.*

MIRRORS OF SOUND

Messages in the sky

IN THE PAST, shooting stars, or meteors, have awed observers and served as inspiration for poets. But if scientists have their way, these marvels of the sky may soon play a more practical role—as carriers of radio messages.

Meteors are formed from pieces of matter that have been wandering in space for millions of years. Some of the particles plunge into the earth's atmosphere. The resulting friction heats them to incandescence, and after leaving a trail of light in the night sky, the largest fall to earth as meteorites.

In addition to the visible trail of cosmic dust, the meteorite also leaves behind a stream of ionized air. It is the electrically charged atoms of air, scientists believe, that may be used as pathways for sending voice messages.

The most important investigation into the subject has been carried out by research scientists in Waltham, Massachusetts. In recent experiments, they have transmitted a spoken message from one point on earth to another by bouncing FM radio signals off of ionized meteor trails.

Until today, the main problem in putting the system to practical use has been that meteor trails last only a few seconds. But the researchers believe they have found a solution. Once the voice has been converted into digital signals, the scientists have developed a way to compress them so that they can be transmitted in a few hundredths of a second. Since some half-dozen meteor trails are formed every second, they may well provide mirrors in the sky from which radio signals can be bounced to distant receivers over the earth's horizon.

Although renowned for their fleeting and irregular appearance, meteors may soon be playing a prominent role in keeping the world in touch.

SHOCK WARNING

The race to predict earthquakes

A YEAR SELDOM PASSES that an earthquake does not strike somewhere in the world, leaving death and destruction in its wake. Casualties can number in the thousands, and the damage to property is sometimes in the millions of dollars. Those living in an earthquake zone realize that it is only a matter of time; sooner or later it will be their turn to experience one.

Scientists know where future earthquakes are likely to occur: usually at those points on the earth's surface where the crustal plates meet. The west coasts of North and South America, parts of the Mediterranean, and the Pacific coast of Asia are the world's earthquake hot spots. Earthquakes often shake the same place twice—or three or four times. For example, the Portuguese capital, Lisbon, has been struck in 1344, 1531, and 1755. The last earthquake almost completely destroyed the city; the next one is overdue.

San Francisco is another city anticipating the worst. The last earthquake, in 1906, claimed well over 700 lives and started a fire that swept through the city. The next quake may be even more severe. The U.S. Geological Survey estimates 3,000 deaths —even 11,000, depending on the time of day. And it could happen soon, which is one of the reasons the race is on to discover a method of predicting earthquakes with much greater accuracy so that measures can be taken to minimize danger.

Taking the earth's pulse

San Francisco lies close to the San Andreas fault, one of the strongest areas of seismological activity on the earth and an area that has been more closely observed than any other in the United States. Small tremors that occur almost every day are plotted by scientists trying to identify a pattern of activity.

One team is using laser technology to detect the smallest movements. A laser beam is reflected off mirrors on either side of the fault; small changes in the direction of its reflection indicate that the earth under the laser itself has moved a tiny fraction of an inch. The seismographic equipment that picks up tremors is so sensitive that nearby traffic can create serious problems; the vibration of automobiles has to be screened out in order to record the earth's own movements.

Success . . . and then disaster

On February 4, 1975, in the province of Liaoning in northeastern China, authorities predicted an earthquake and ordered the evacuation of major cities in the earthquake zone. More than a million people poured into the open areas in and around these urban sites. That same afternoon a severe tremor hit the city of Haicheng, and 90 percent of its buildings were damaged or destroyed. The decision to evacuate had saved the lives of an estimated 10,000 people.

The accuracy of the prediction was totally unprecedented. Chinese scientists had based it on their observations of geological activity but had taken into account other, less technical phenomena. They had heeded reports of unusual animal activity—chickens roosting high in trees, fish leaping in rivers, and snakes leaving their burrows.

The accuracy of the Haicheng prediction was impressive, but a little more than a year later, the unpredictability of earthquakes reasserted itself. On July 28, 1976, as Chinese scientists were meeting to discuss signs of an impending earthquake in the city of Tangshan, some 120 miles east

of Peking, disaster struck. A massive shock hit the city, leaving nearly a quarter of a million dead, the worst toll recorded in modern times.

A pattern

Both natural and technological observations have failed to predict earthquakes reliably. But recently scientists have uncovered a surprising fact.

From the records, it appears that earthquakes occurring in the same place happen with remarkable regularity. The small community of Parkfield, located between San Francisco and Los Angeles, has experienced an earthquake almost every 22 years. The next one is due before 1993—and seismologists have moved in to study the phenomenon at first hand. The area is under detailed scrutiny by sensitive seismographs and the laser measuring system. If the earthquake hits, it will help confirm that the regularity theory offers a scientific basis for earthquake prediction.

THE WORLD'S LAST WILDERNESS

Antarctica's uncertain future

OF THE SEVEN CONTINENTS, Antarctica is the coldest, highest, driest, and windiest. With an area of some 5.5 million square miles—half as big again as the United States—it represents one-tenth of the land surface of the world. As much as 98 percent of Antarctica is covered by ice, much of it a mile and a half thick, and the continent is surrounded by seas filled with pack ice and icebergs for most of the year.

Yet far from being a desolate wasteland, it is suspected that Antarctica might be a treasure trove of precious metals, minerals, and food. Hundreds of scientists, geologists, and technicians from some 20 countries are permanently based at 44 different sites around the continent. The United States government alone has an Antarctic research budget well in excess of $100 million a year. All the latest techniques of drilling, seismology, and radar are being used to uncover the wealth that is believed to lie beneath the blanket of ice.

A giant jigsaw

Current scientific interest stems from the belief that 200 million years ago Antarctica formed the center of the vast supercontinent geologists call Gondwanaland. Then, as the seafloor began to move, South America, Africa, Australia, and the Indian subcontinent gradually broke away until, 28

million years ago, Antarctica was surrounded by water and floating packs of ice.

Antarctic researchers believe that they may be able to predict the location of mineral resources by reassembling the jigsaw and examining the relationship of Antarctica with continents where mineral and oil deposits are known to exist.

The Dufek Massif within Antarctica's Pensacola Mountains once lay adjacent to the mineral-rich Bushveld Complex in South Africa. Therefore, some geologists consider it likely that the Dufek Massif might also contain deposits of gold, platinum, chromium, manganese, and nickel. The Antarctic Peninsula is believed to be rich in copper and lead. The reason: it was formerly joined to the Andes of South America, where both minerals have already been found.

Enderby Land and Wilkes Land are known to hold large deposits of iron ore; they are geologically comparable to the Adelaide area in Australia, a major source of ore in the world.

There is no need to speculate about the presence of coal in Antarctica. Seams of coal many feet deep are visible on some of the mountains, and the Transantarctic Range rises above what is thought to be the largest coalfield in the world. Other minerals discovered to date include various micas, graphite, and some gemstones.

At present the feasibility of extracting any of these deposits is questionable. The remoteness of the region makes access and transportation difficult and expensive. The cost of drilling programs, too, is prohibitive. Apart from its daunting thickness, the ice sheet is moving constantly—as much as $1\frac{1}{4}$ miles a year near the coast (although as little as an inch a year inland). Thus, a hole drilled on the coast one month may not exist by the next.

The promise

Scientists think that Antarctica's continental shelves hold the most promise. In 1973 the U.S. drilling ship *Glomar Challenger* found quantities of ethane and methane gases, provoking speculation that the southern polar seas contain vast oil fields. The results of seismological surveys of rocks beneath the seabed are encouraging. And although no oil has yet been found, some U.S. experts have predicted a reservoir of 45 billion barrels, almost twice the known reserves in the entire United States.

However, the cost of extracting oil is unlikely to make commercial sense in the present economic climate. The waters over the continental shelves are extremely deep, requiring an extensive investment in oil rigs and drilling vessels—which would face the constant threat of being crushed by icebergs.

But there is one Antarctic resource that is being exploited to such an extent that it has been suggested as a source of food for the famine-struck Third World. Krill, a shrimplike creature, is an essential element in the food chain in Antarctica. Its numbers increased considerably following the slaughter that drove some species of whales and seals to the point of extinction in the 19th century. Today fishing fleets catch more than half a million tons of krill annually, and this is only a fraction of the total that is believed to be available.

The threats

However, because of the potentially devastating effect it might have on the environment, not everyone is in favor of the commercial exploitation of Antarctica. The Antarctica Treaty, which went into effect in 1961 and today represents the interests of 32 nations, has made some provision for the protection of the region and its native wildlife.

But many conservationists fear that it is inadequate, especially if workable mineral deposits are discovered. One treaty signatory, New Zealand, has proposed that the continent be declared a world park, where mineral development and human habitation would be prohibited. This may turn out to be the only certain way to preserve the area that is the last untouched region in the world.

NEIGHBORLY WEALTH *Two hundred million years ago, Antarctica was part of the supercontinent of Gondwanaland, surrounded by present-day South America, Africa, Australia, and the subcontinent of India. Gradually parts of the supercontinent drifted, creating the continents that exist today. Mineral deposits in areas of the continents that once bordered Antarctica have led scientists to predict that Antarctica may also be a rich source of minerals, oil, and natural gas.*

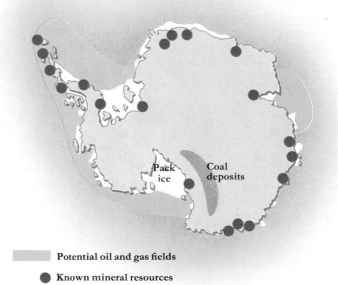

Potential oil and gas fields

Known mineral resources

HIDDEN RESOURCES *Antarctica is known to possess some mineral deposits. For example, coal is visible in mountains that tower over the continent, and other minerals have been found. But additional deposits may lie hidden beneath the ice cap, averaging $1\frac{1}{2}$ miles thick, that covers much of Antarctica.*

INDEX

Page numbers in **bold type** refer to illustrations and captions.

Picture Credits and Acknowledgments

b = bottom, l = left, r = right, t = top

Reproduced by Gracious Permission of Her Majesty the Queen: **119**. Amoco Services, Inc./Bob Lynn: **134**. Ancient Art and Architecture Collection, London: **172**. Anglo-Australian Observatory/Stephen Lee: **409**. Ardea, London: **12**(t) (John Mason); **63** (Ron & Valerie Taylor); **74** (Wardene Weisser). Peter Arnold, Inc.: **42**(b) (Ray Pfortner). Russell Ash: **211**; **216**. Associated Press: **81**; **227**; **253**. The Australian Information Service, London: **39**. BBC Hulton Picture Library: **38**(b). John Beckett: **37**; **370**. Beinecke Rare Book and Manuscript Library, Yale University: **341**; **342**. Benediktinerkloster, Einsiedeln: **292**. By courtesy of Birmingham Museums and Art Gallery: **110**(t); **356**. Bodleian Library, Oxford: **278** (Ms. Bodl. 264 pt.1 f.22); **298** (Ms. Eng. Misc. D1226 f.iir). Nicholas Booth: **395** (Brookhaven National Laboratory); **403** (NASA). Janet & Colin Bord: **300**(t); **360**. The Bridgeman Art Library: **38**(t) (Lindley Library); **331**(r); **353** (Sir Geoffrey Keynes Collection, Cambridge). British Library/Controller of Her Majesty's Stationery Office: **144**; **145**; **146**; **151**; **160**. By courtesy of the British Museum (Natural History): **12**(b); **16**. British Rail Research Division: **147**. Buffalo & Erie County Historical Society: **308**(b). Camera Press: **174**. J. Allan Cash Photolibrary: **126**. Martin Charles: **132**; **133**. Jean-Loup Charmet: **89**(t); **203**(l); **275**; **285**. Photographs by courtesy of Christie's: **327**. Bruce Coleman Limited: **41**(t) (J. T. Wright); **53**, **55** (Jeff Foott); **60** (G. B. Frith); **70** (Frans Lanting); **71** (Jan Taylor); **76** (Jane Burton); **428**. Corning Glass Works/Ayres A. Stephens: **116**. John Crook/Dean & Chapter of Winchester: **129**. John H. Cutten Associates: **363**. Edwin A. Dawes Collection: **313**. Eric Ellington: **19**. Robert Estall: **103**; **335**; **361**. E. T. Archive: **221**(r); **300**(b). Mary Evans Picture Library: **79** (Harry Price Collection); **108**; **137**; **139**; **161**; **187**; **214**; **237**; **244**; **274**; **297**; **307**; **319**; **331**(l); **333**; **354**(t); **354**(b) (courtesy Mrs. Barbara Edwards); **369** (Project Hessdalen); **377**. John Fasal: **228**. Vivien Fifield: **155**. Fortean Picture Library: **45**(t); **388** (courtesy Loren Coleman). John R. Freeman & Co. Ltd.: **165**. Michael Freeman: **48**; **49**; **101**; **115**. Glasgow University/Io Research Ltd.: **393** (Wyn Davies). Susan Griggs Agency: **2** (Adam Woolfitt); **112** (John Bulmer); **218**(t) (Nathan Benn); **271** (Kal Muller). Sonia Halliday: **41**(b) (J. Taylor); **110**(b). Robert Harding Picture Library: **45**(b); **365**. Phil & Loretta Hermann: **47**. John Hillelson Agency: **235**(t) (Begin-Tiziou/Sygma). Michael Holford: **154**; **248**. Michael Holmes: **224**; **225**. Illustrated London News: **261**. Imperial War Museum: **243**. Independence National Historical Park Collection: **276**. Jet Propulsion Laboratory: **405**. Dr. David E. H. Jones: **330**. KangaROOS U.S.A., Inc.: **180**(t). Dr A. G. Khan: **373**. King Features Syndicate, Inc./Yaffa Character Licensing: **264**. Kobal Collection: **283**; **359**. Koninklijk Museum voor Schone Kunsten: **305**(l). Kunsthistorisches Museum, Vienna: **305**(r). Frank Lane Picture Library: **21** (Silvestris); **77** (J. V. Spalding). R. Michael Laurs/N.O.A.A., Southwest Fisheries Center: **183**. Courtesy of the London Transport Museum: **195**. By permission of the Master & Fellows, Magdalen College, Cambridge: **279**. Mansell Collection: **198**; **203**(r); **337**. Arxiu Mas: **130**; **131**. The Mawson Institute for Antarctic Research, University of Adelaide: **322**; **323**. Metropolitan Museum of Art, New York: **197**. Metropolitan Police Office, London: **142**. Museum für Volkerkunde, Vienna: **267**. The Byron Collection, Museum of the City of New York: **209**. The Museum of London: **232**. NAAS/Peter Sanders: **351**. Natural History Photographic Agency: **33**; **59** (Biophoto Associates). Reprinted by permission from *Nature*, February 1984 (cover), © Macmillan Journals Ltd.: **67**. Charlie Nye/The Eugene (Oregon) *Register-Guard*: **345**. O.S.F. Picture Library: **93** (Animals Animals/E. R. Degginger); **263**. Courtesy ParaScience International; © 1982 by Larry E. Arnold, all rights reserved: **381**(b). Peabody Museum of Natural History, Yale University: **23**. People's Palace Museum, Glasgow/Andrew Brown: **153**. Pepsi Cola International: **252**. Philips Consumer Electronics: **435**. The Photo Source: **89**(b); **220**; **221**(l); **308**(t). Photri: **180**(b). Picker International: **184**. Popperfoto: **51**; **127**; **238**; **255**; **273**; **324**; **386**; **418**. Rex Features: **34**; **231**, **233** (SIPA). R.I.B.A./G. Butler: **120**. Maurice Rickards Collection: **150**; **258**. David Robinson: **316**. Ann Ronan Picture Library: **96**; **157**; **191**. Royal Botanic Gardens, Kew: **431**. Royal Observatory, Edinburgh: **397**. San Diego Historical Society: **188**. Scala, Florence: **86**. Reproduced by permission of the Trustees of the Science Museum: **256**. Science Photo Library: **18** (Peter Ryan/Scripps); **411** (Julian Baum). Smithsonian Institution: **248** (photo no. 30, 574). Society of Antiquaries of London: **98**. Space Biospheres Ventures: **424**. Spectrum Colour Library: **120**(t). Frank Spooner Pictures: **125** (Gamma); **169**(r) (Gamma/Novosti); **212**, **213** (Gamma); **281**, **291** (Gamma/Gaywood). G. R. Stewart, Quain Professor of Botany, University College London: **421**. Syndication International: **104**. The Taft Museum/Gift of Mr. & Mrs. Charles Phelps Taft: **247**. Topkapi Saray Museum: **334**. TRH Pictures: **167**; **391** (USAF/DOD); **398** (Max Planck Institute). University of California, San Diego: **179**. UPI/Bettmann: **42**; **123**; **218**(b); **226**; **235**(b). U.S. Marine Corps: **240**. Western Americana Picture Library: **287**. Winchester Mystery House, San Jose, California: **385**. Windsor Castle, Royal Library © 1986 Her Majesty the Queen: **288**(b). Woods Hole Oceanographic Institution: **176**. Jerry Wooldridge Photography: **15**(b). ZEFA: **109**; **169**(l).

Major illustrations by Brian Delf and Nicholas Hall.

Illustrations by Marion Appleton, David Ashby, Ray Brown, Brian Delf, Eugene Fleury, Stephen Gardner, Nicholas Hall, Janos Marffy, Peter Morter, Fraser Newman, John Woodcock.

Index compiled by Hilary Bird.

Dorling Kindersley would like to thank Loren Coleman, Robert Dunham, John Fasal, Jane Havell, Nigel Henbest, Jonathan Hilton, Dr A. G. Khan, Keith Lye, James McCarter, Geoffrey Prescott, and Michael Spira for their help with the text; and Alan Blackwood, Rebecca Collings, Hilary Evans, John Gaisford, Edward Horton, Adam Kean, Ann Lloyd, Margaret Mulvihill, Andy Oppenheimer, Stephen Paul, Bob Rickard, Malcolm Ross-Macdonald, Bob Sloan, Frank Smyth, and Judy Urquhart for their contributions. Dorling Kindersley would also like to thank Vida Adamoli, Graeme Kent, Enid Lake, Sarah Lumley-Smith, Neil MacDonald, Paul Sieveking, and Chris Thody for their research assistance; and Arthur Brown, Mark Kebell, Patrizio Semproni, and Jane Warring for their help with the design of the book.

Typesetting by Vantage Photosetting Co. Ltd., Eastleigh and London.
Reproduction by Reprocolor, Milan.

Reader's Digest Fund for the Blind is publisher of the Large-Type Edition of *Reader's Digest*. For subscription information about this magazine, please contact Reader's Digest Fund for the Blind, Inc., Dept. 250, Pleasantville, N.Y. 10570.